PRINCIPLES OF
MICROECONOMICS

THIRD CANADIAN EDITION

N. GREGORY MANKIW
HARVARD UNIVERSITY

RONALD D. KNEEBONE
UNIVERSITY OF CALGARY

KENNETH J. McKENZIE
UNIVERSITY OF CALGARY

NICHOLAS ROWE
CARLETON UNIVERSITY

THOMSON

NELSON

Australia   Canada   Mexico   Singapore   Spain   United Kingdom   United States

THOMSON

NELSON

Principles of Microeconomics
Third Canadian Edition

by N. Gregory Mankiw, Ronald D. Kneebone, Kenneth J. McKenzie, and Nicholas Rowe

Associate Vice-President, Editorial Director:
Evelyn Veitch

Senior Acquisitions Editor:
Anthony Rezek

Executive Marketing Manager:
Don Thompson

Senior Developmental Editor:
Katherine Goodes

Photo Researcher:
Cindy Howard

Permissions Coordinator:
Cindy Howard

Senior Production Editor:
Natalia Denesiuk

Copy Editor:
June Trusty

Proofreader:
Cy Strom

Indexer:
Jin Tan

Senior Production Coordinator:
Kathrine Pummell

Creative Director:
Angela Cluer

Interior Design:
Mike Stratton

Cover Design:
Peter Papayanakis

Cover Images:
People: www.firstlight.ca
City: Peter Gridley/Taxi/Getty Images

Senior Compositor:
Zenaida Diores

Printer:
Quebecor World

Library and Archives Canada Cataloguing in Publication Data

Principles of microeconomics / N. Gregory Mankiw ... [et al.]. — 3rd Canadian ed.

Includes bibliographical references and index.
ISBN 0-17-641603-X

1. Microeconomics—Textbooks.
I. Mankiw, N. Gregory

HB172.P744 2006   338.5
C2004-906232-8

To Catherine, Nicholas, and Peter,
my other contributions to the next generation

To our parents
and
Cindy,
Kathleen and Janetta,
Muriel and Julia
Thanks for your support and patience

PREFACE

During my 20-year career as a student, the course that excited me most was the two-semester sequence on the principles of economics that I took during freshman year in college. It is no exaggeration to say that it changed my life.

I had grown up in a family that often discussed politics over the dinner table. The pros and cons of various solutions to society's problems generated fervent debate. But in school, I had been drawn to the sciences. Whereas politics seemed vague, rambling, and subjective, science was analytic, systematic, and objective. While political debate continued without end, science made progress.

My freshman course on the principles of economics opened my eyes to a new way of thinking. Economics combines the virtues of politics and science. It is, truly, a social science. Its subject matter is society—how people choose to lead their lives and how they interact with one another. But it approaches the subject with the dispassion of a science. By bringing the methods of science to the questions of politics, economics tries to make progress on the challenges that all societies face.

I was drawn to write this book in the hope that I could convey some of the excitement of economics that I felt as a student in my first economics course. Economics is a subject in which a little knowledge goes a long way. (The same cannot be said, for instance, of the study of physics or the Japanese language.) Economists have a unique way of viewing the world, much of which can be taught in one or two semesters. My goal in this book is to transmit this way of thinking to the widest possible audience and to convince readers that it illuminates much about the world around them.

I believe that everyone should study the fundamental ideas that economics has to offer. One purpose of general education is to inform people about the world and thereby make them better citizens. The study of economics, as much as any discipline, serves this goal. Writing an economics textbook is, therefore, a great honour and a great responsibility. It is one way that economists can help promote better government and a more prosperous future. As the great economist Paul Samuelson put it, " I don't care who writes a nation's laws, or crafts its advanced treaties, if I can write its economics textbooks."

It is tempting for a professional economist writing a textbook to take the economist's point of view and to emphasize those topics that fascinate him and other economists. I have done my best to avoid that temptation. I have tried to put myself in the position of someone seeing economics for the first time. My goal is to emphasize the material that *students* should and do find interesting about the study of the economy.

One result is that this book is briefer than many books used to introduce students to economics. As a student, I was (and unfortunately still am) a slow reader. I groaned whenever a professor gave the class a 1000-page tome to read. Of course, my reaction was not unique. The Greek poet Callimachus put it succinctly: "Big book, big bore." Callimachus made that observation in 250 B.C., so he was probably not referring to an economics textbook, but today his sentiment is echoed around the world every semester when students first see their economics assignments. My goal in this book is to avoid that reaction by skipping the bells, whistles, and extraneous details that distract students from the key lessons.

Another result of this student orientation is that more of this book is devoted to applications and policies—and less to formal economic theory—than is the case with many other books written for the principles course. Throughout, I have tried to return to applications and policy questions as often as possible. Most chapters include case studies illustrating how the principles of economics are applied. In addition, "In the News" features (most of which are new to this edition) offer excerpts from newspaper articles showing how economic ideas shed light on current issues facing society. After students finish their first course in economics, they should think about news stories from a new perspective and with greater insight.

I am delighted that versions of this book are (or will soon be) available in many of the world's languages. Currently scheduled translations include Chinese (in both standard and simple characters), Czech, French, Georgian, German, Greek, Indonesian, Italian, Japanese, Korean, Portuguese, Romanian, Russian, and Spanish. In addition, adaptations of this book for Canadian and Australian students are also available. Instructors who would like more information about these books should contact Thomson Nelson.

Special thanks go to Karen Dynan, Douglas Elmendorf, and Dean Croushore, who drafted many of the problems and applications presented at the end of each chapter. Yvonne Zinfon, my assistant at Harvard, as usual went beyond the call of duty as this edition was being prepared. I am also grateful to Fuad Faridi, a Harvard undergraduate, for assisting me in the final stages of this project.

The team of editors who worked on this book improved it tremendously. Jane Tufts, developmental editor, provided truly spectacular editing—as she always does. Peter Adams, senior economics acquisitions editor, did a splendid job of overseeing the many people involved in such a large project. Sarah Dorger, developmental editor, assembled an excellent team to write the supplements while managing thousands of related details. Dan Plofchan, production editor, along with the staff at Thistle Hill Publishing Services and GAC Indianapolis, had the patience and dedication necessary to turn my manuscript into this book. Off-Center Concept House professionally executed the production of the print supplements. Mike Stratton, senior designer, gave this book its clean, friendly look. Michele Gitlin, copy editor, refined my prose, and Alexandra Nickerson, indexer, prepared a careful and thorough index. Janet Hennies, senior marketing manager, worked long hours getting the word out to the potential users of this book, even as she gave birth to a future reader of it. Tom Gay, formerly of Harcourt, was instrumental in early stages of planning. Jeff Gilbreath worked as developmental editor until his untimely death; we will miss him. The rest of the South-Western team was also consistently professional, enthusiastic, and dedicated: Jon Schneider, Jenny Fruechtenicht, Terron Sanders, Carrie Hochstrasser, Vicky True, Peggy Buskey, Pam Wallace, and Sandee Milewski.

I must also thank my "in-house" editor—Deborah Mankiw. As the first reader of almost everything I write, she continued to offer just the right mix of criticism and encouragement.

Finally, I am grateful to my children, Catherine, Nicholas, and Peter. Their unpredictable visits to my study offered welcome relief from long spans of writing and rewriting. Although now they are only ten, eight, and four years old, someday they will grow up and study the principles of economics. I hope this book provides its readers some of the education and enlightenment that I wish for my own children.

N. Gregory Mankiw
October 2002

As soon as we got our hands on the first U.S. edition of *Principles of Microeconomics*, it was clear to us that "this one is different." If other first-year economics textbooks are encyclopedias, Gregory Mankiw's was, and still is, a handbook.

Between the three of us, we have many years of experience teaching first-year economics. Like many instructors, we found it harder and harder to teach with each new edition of the thick, standard texts. It was simply impossible to cover all of the material. Of course, we could have skipped sections, features, or whole chapters, but then, apart from the sheer hassle of telling students which bits to read and not to read, and worries about the consistencies and completeness of the remaining material, we ran the risk of leaving students with the philosophy that what matters is only what's on the exam.

We do not believe that the writers of these other books set out with the intention of cramming so much material into them. It is a difficult task to put together the perfect textbook—one that all instructors would approve of and that all students would enjoy using. Therefore, to please all potential users, most of the books end up covering a wide range of topics. And so the books grow and grow.

Professor Mankiw made a fresh start in the first U.S. edition. He included all the important topics and presented them in order of importance. And in the third U.S. edition, he has resisted the temptation to add more and more material. We have, in adapting the text for Canadian students, taken a minimalist approach: "If it isn't broken, don't fix it!" While the book is easily recognizable as Mankiw's, we have made changes that increase its relevance to Canadian students. Some of these changes reflect important differences between the Canadian and U.S. economies. For example, the Canadian economy is much smaller and more open than the U.S. economy, and this fact is explicitly recognized in this edition. Other changes reflect important institutional differences between the two countries, including the structure of the tax system and the nature of competition policy. Finally, the Canadian edition focuses on issues and includes examples that are more familiar and relevant to a Canadian audience.

We would not have agreed to participate in the Canadian edition if we were not extremely impressed with the U.S. edition. Professor Mankiw has done an outstanding job of identifying the key concepts and principles that every first-year student should learn.

It was truly a pleasure to work with such a well-thought-out and well-written book. We have enjoyed teaching from the first and second Canadian editions and we look forward to using the third Canadian edition. We hope you do, too.

HOW THE BOOK IS ORGANIZED

To write a brief and student-friendly book, Mankiw considered new ways to organize familiar material. What follows is a whirlwind tour of this text. The tour, we hope, will give you a sense of how the pieces fit together.

Introductory Material

Chapter 1, "Ten Principles of Economics," introduces students to the economist's view of the world. It previews some of the big ideas that recur throughout economics, such as opportunity costs, marginal decision making, the role of incentives, the gain from trade, and the efficiency of market allocations. The ten principles are referred to throughout the book and an icon in the margin calls attention to these key, interconnected principles.

Chapter 2, "Thinking Like an Economist," examines how economists approach their field of study, discussing the role of assumptions in developing a theory and introducing the concepts of an economic model. It also discusses the role of economists in making policy. The appendix to this chapter offers a brief refresher course on how graphs are used and how they can be abused.

Chapter 3, "Interdependence and the Gains from Trade," presents the theory of comparative advantage. This theory explains why individuals trade with their neighbours, as well as why nations trade with other nations. Much of economics is about how market forces coordinate many individual production and consumption decisions. As a starting point for this analysis, students see in this chapter why specialization, interdependence, and trade can benefit everyone.

The Fundamental Tools of Supply and Demand

The next three chapters introduce the basic tools of supply and demand. Chapter 4, "The Market Forces of Supply and Demand," develops the supply curve, the demand curve, and the notion of market equilibrium. Chapter 5, "Elasticity and Its Application," introduces the concept of elasticity and uses it to analyze events in three different markets. Chapter 6, "Supply, Demand, and Government Policies," uses these tools to examine price controls, such as rent-control and minimum-wage laws, and tax incidence.

Chapter 7, "Consumers, Producers, and the Efficiency of Markets," extends the analysis of supply and demand using the concepts of consumer surplus and producer surplus. It begins by developing the link between consumers' willingness to pay and the demand curve, and the link between producers' costs of production and the supply curve. It then shows that the market equilibrium maximizes the sum of the producer and consumer surplus. Thus, students learn early about the efficiency of market allocations.

The next two chapters apply the concepts of producer and consumer surplus to questions of policy. Chapter 8, "Application: The Costs of Taxation," shows why taxation results in deadweight losses and what determines the size of those losses. Chapter 9, "Application: International Trade," considers who wins and who loses from international trade and presents the debate over protectionist trade policies.

More Microeconomics

Having examined why market allocations are often desirable, the book then considers how the government can sometimes improve on them. Chapter 10, "Externalities," explains how external effects such as pollution can render market outcomes inefficient and discusses the possible public and private solutions to those inefficiencies. Chapter 11, "Public Goods and Common Resources," considers the problems that arise when goods, such as national defence, have no market price. Chapter 12, "The Design of the Tax System," describes how the government raises the revenue necessary to pay for public goods. It presents some institutional background about the Canadian tax system and then discusses how the goals of efficiency and equity come into play when designing a tax system.

The next five chapters examine firm behaviour and industrial organization. Chapter 13, "The Costs of Production," discusses what to include in a firm's costs and introduces cost curves. Chapter 14, "Firms in Competitive Markets," analyzes the behaviour of price-taking firms and derives the market supply curve. Chapter 15, "Monopoly," discusses the behaviour of a firm that is the sole seller in its market, the inefficiency of monopoly pricing, the possible policy responses, and the attempts by monopolies to price-discriminate. Chapter 16, "Oligopoly," covers markets in which there are only a few sellers, using the prisoners' dilemma as the model for examining strategic interaction. Chapter 17, "Monopolistic Competition," looks at behaviour in a market in which many sellers offer similar but differentiated products. It also discusses the debate over the effects of advertising.

The next three chapters present issues related to labour markets. Chapter 18, "The Markets for the Factors of Production," emphasizes the link between factor prices and marginal productivity. Chapter 19, "Earnings and Discrimination," discusses the determinants of equilibrium wages, including compensating differentials, human capital, and discrimination. Chapter 20, "Income Inequality and Poverty," examines the degree of inequality in Canadian society, alternative views about the government's role in changing the distribution of income, and various policies aimed at helping society's poorest members.

The final two chapters present optional material. Chapter 21, "The Theory of Consumer Choice," analyzes individual decision making using budget constraints and indifference curves. Chapter 22, "Frontiers of Microeconomics," introduces the topics of asymmetric information, political economy, and behavioural economics. Some instructors may skip all or some of this material. Instructors who do cover these topics may choose to assign these chapters earlier than they are presented in this text, and they have been written to give that flexibility.

WALK-THROUGH

The purpose of this text is to help students learn the fundamental lessons of economics and to show how such lessons can be applied to the world in which they live. Toward that end, various learning tools recur throughout the book.

Chapter Openers   Well-designed chapter openers act as previews that summarize the major concepts to be learned in each chapter.

Case Studies   Economic theory is useful and interesting only if it can be applied to understanding actual events and policies. Updated or replaced with more current Canadian examples, this book therefore contains numerous case studies that apply the theory that has just been developed.

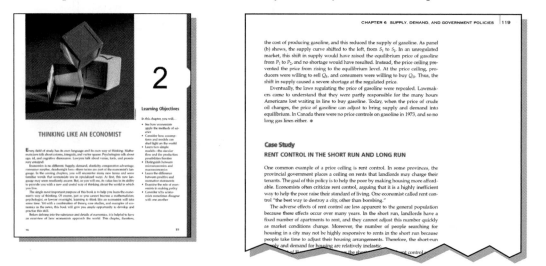

Figures and Tables   Colourful and eye-catching visuals are used to make important economic points and to clarify Canadian and other key economic concepts. These have also proved to be valuable and memorable teaching aids.

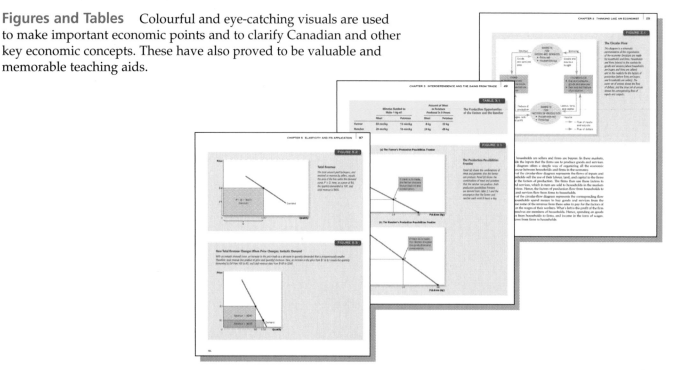

Updated Canadian "In the News" Features

One benefit that students gain from studying economics is a new perspective and greater understanding about news from Canada and around the world. To highlight this benefit, there are excerpts from many Canadian news articles, some of which are opinion columns written by prominent economists. These articles show how basic economic theory can be applied.

"FYI" Features

These features provide additional material "for your information." Some of them offer a glimpse into the history of economic thought. Others clarify technical issues. Still others discuss supplementary topics that instructors might choose either to discuss or skip in their lectures.

Key Concept Definitions

When key concepts are introduced in the chapter, they are presented in **bold** typeface. In addition, their definitions are placed in the margin. This treatment should aid students in learning and reviewing the material.

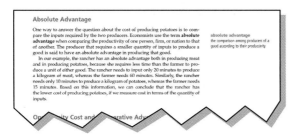

Interconnectedness of the Ten Principles of Economics

Whenever any of the ten principles of economics are discussed in the text, an icon appears in the margin. This draws the student's attention to an important discussion of one of the ten principles.

Quick Quizzes After each major section, students are offered a "quick quiz" to check their comprehension of what they have just learned. If students cannot readily answer these quizzes, they should stop and reread the material before continuing.

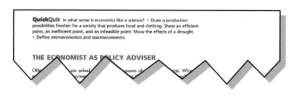

Chapter Summaries Each chapter ends with a brief summary that reminds students of the most important lessons that they have just learned. Later in their study, it offers an efficient way to review for exams.

List of Key Concepts A list of key concepts at the end of each chapter offers students a way to test their understanding of the new terms that have been introduced. Page references are included so that students can review the terms they do not understand.

Questions for Review At the end of each chapter are questions for review that cover the chapter's primary lessons. Students can use these questions to check their comprehension and to prepare for exams.

Problems and Applications Each chapter also contains a variety of problems and applications that ask students to apply the material they have learned. Some instructors may use these questions for homework assignments. Others may use them as a starting point for classroom discussion.

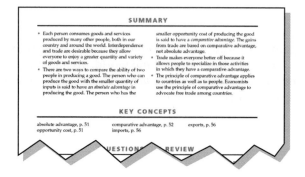

Internet Resources To end each chapter, some Internet resources are listed for students who like to search the Internet for further information on the chapter's topics.

NEW IN THIS THIRD CANADIAN EDITION

New Chapter   A new chapter has been written for this edition. Chapter 22, "Frontiers of Microeconomics," is an enticing introduction to the cutting-edge subject areas of asymmetric information, the political economy, and behavioural economics.

Updated Canadian "In the News" Features   One benefit that students gain from studying economics is a new perspective and greater understanding about news from around the world. To highlight this benefit, excerpts from many newspaper articles are included, some of which are opinion columns written by prominent economists. These articles, together with brief introductions, show how basic economic theory can be applied. Many of these features are new to this edition.

Chapter 4   The sections on supply and demand in Chapter 4, "The Market Forces of Supply and Demand," have been reorganized and revised extensively to make especially clear the distinction between a change in quantity supplied or quantity demanded and a change in supply or demand.

Chapter 10   The first section of Chapter 10, "Externalities," has been rewritten for simplification. The authors now refer to the discussion only with the terms *positive externalities* and *negative externalities*. The production/consumption distinction has been rewritten for a more efficient presentation.

Internet Resources   The Internet is a vital study tool for students, so Internet resources have been added to the end-of-chapter material. Students will be able to delve deeper into a topic and gain a more thorough understanding of the intricacies of economics.

Current Canadian Information   Tables, charts, graphs, and figures have been updated to reflect the most current Canadian information available at the time of publication. Several "In the News" and "Case Study" features have been updated or replaced with more current Canadian examples.

SUPPLEMENTS

For the Instructor

Instructor's Manual with Solutions and Classroom Activities for Microeconomics and Macroeconomics   For lecture preparation, the Instructor's Manual offers a detailed outline for each chapter of the text that provides learning objectives, identifies stumbling blocks that students may face, offers helpful teaching tips, and provides suggested in-classroom activities for a more cooperative learning experience. The Instructor's Manual also includes solutions to the quick quizzes, Questions for Review, and Problems and Applications found in the text.

Instructor's Resource CD-ROM for Microeconomics and Macroeconomics   Included on the CD-ROM are the key supplements designed to aid instructors: Instructor's Manual with Solutions and Classroom Activities, PowerPoint Lecture slides, PowerPoint slides of exhibits only, Computerized Test Bank, and a printable Test Bank for ease of use.

Test Bank   This updated and revised Test Bank consists of more than 200 questions per chapter. Every question has been checked to ensure the accuracy and clarity of the answers and painstakingly revised to address the text's revisions. Included are multiple-choice, true/false, and short-answer questions that assess students' critical thinking skills. Easy, medium, and difficult questions outline the process that students must use to arrive at their answers: recall, application, and integration. Questions are organized by text section to help instructors pick and choose their selections.

Computerized Test Bank   The ExamView Computerized Testing software contains all the questions in the printable Test Bank. This program is an easy-to-use test-creation software application that is compatible with Microsoft Windows. Instructors can add or edit questions, instructions, and answers, and can select questions by previewing them on the screen, selecting them randomly, or selecting them by number. Instructors can also create and administer quizzes online, whether over the Internet, a local area network (LAN), or a wide area network (WAN).

Microsoft® PowerPoint® Lecture and Exhibit Slides   Available on the CD and downloadable from the Mankiw website (http://www.mankiw3e. nelson.com) are two versions of the PowerPoint presentation. Instructors can save valuable time as they prepare for class using this comprehensive lecture presentation. This supplement covers all the essential topics presented in each chapter of the book. Graphs, tables, lists, and concepts are developed sequentially, much as one might develop them on a chalkboard. Additional examples and applications are used to reinforce major lessons. A separate exhibit presentation provides instructors with all the tables and graphs from the main text.

The "Ten Principles" Video Set   This video series illustrates the ten principles of economics as introduced in Chapter 1. Instructors can show these videos as an interesting and visually appealing introduction to topics discussed through the textbook.

CBC Videos   Instructors can bring the real world into the classroom by using the CBC videotape for Mankiw, *Principles of Microeconomics*, Third Canadian Edition. This video contains one video segment for each of the seven parts in the text, and provides current stories of economic interest.

Favourite Ways to Learn Economics   U.S. authors David Anderson, Centre College, and Jim Chasey, Homewood Flossmoor High School, use experiments to bring economic education to life. This is a U.S.-based lab manual for the classroom and for individual study that contains experiments and problem sets that reinforce key economic concepts (for both students and instructors).

Economic Viewpoints   The shape, pace, and spirit of the global economy has been greatly impacted by the events that occurred on September 11, 2001. A new collection of essays is offered that provides a variety of perspectives on the economic effects of these events. Each essay in this U.S. supplement is written by a U.S. economics textbook author, all of whom are highly regarded for both their academic and professional achievements. This unique collaboration results in one of the most cutting-edge resources available to help facilitate discussion of the impact of September 11 in the context of economic courses.

For the Student

Study Guide   This study guide was prepared to enhance student success. Each chapter of the study guide includes learning objectives, a description of the chapter's context and purpose, a chapter review, key terms and definitions, advanced critical thinking questions, and helpful hints for understanding difficult concepts. Students can develop their understanding by doing the practice problems and short-answer questions, and then assess their mastery of the key concepts with the self-test, which includes true/false and multiple-choice questions. Solutions to all problems are included in the study guide.

Microsoft® PowerPoint® Lecture Notes   A printable booklet available as a download from the Mankiw website (http://www.mankiw3e.nelson.com), this supplement contains the lecture presentation in the PowerPoint slides, with space next to each slide for taking notes during class. This allows students to focus on classroom activities by providing them with the confident knowledge that they have an excellent set of chapter notes for future reference.

Mankiw Website   Valuable resources for students can be found on the Internet at the Mankiw textbook support site: http://www.mankiw3e.nelson.com. Students will find more true/false, multiple-choice, and short-answer questions; links to economics-related Internet sites; PowerPoint slides for their review; and much more.

JORDI CABRÉ

N. Gregory Mankiw is Professor of Economics at Harvard University. As a student, he studied economics at Princeton University and MIT. As a teacher, he has taught macroeconomics, microeconomics, statistics, and principles of economics. He even spent one summer long ago as a sailing instructor on Long Beach Island.

Professor Mankiw is a prolific writer and a regular participant in academic and policy debates. His work has been published in scholarly journals such as the *American Economic Review, Journal of Political Economy*, and *Quarterly Journal of Economics*, and in more popular forums such as *The New York Times, The Financial Times, The Wall Street Journal*, and *Fortune*. He is also author of the best-selling intermediate-level textbook *Macroeconomics* (Worth Publishing). In addition to his teaching, research, and writing, Professor Mankiw is a research associate of the National Bureau of Economic Research, an adviser to the Federal Reserve Bank of Boston and the Congressional Budget Office, and a member of the Educational Testing Service (ETS) test development committee for the advanced placement exam in economics.

Ronald D. Kneebone is Professor of Economics at the University of Calgary. He received his Ph.D. from McMaster University. Professor Kneebone has taught courses in public finance and in macroeconomics from principles through to the Ph.D. level, and he is a two-time winner of the Faculty of Social Sciences Distinguished Teacher Award at the University of Calgary. His research interests are primarily in the areas of public sector finances and fiscal federalism. He shares with Ken McKenzie the Douglas Purvis Memorial Prize for the best published work in Canadian public policy in 1999.

Kenneth J. McKenzie is Professor of Economics at the University of Calgary. He received his Ph.D. from Queen's University. Specializing in public economics with an emphasis on taxation and political economy, Professor McKenzie has published extensively in these areas. He is the winner of the 1996 Harry Johnson Prize (with University of Calgary colleague Herb Emery) for the best article in the *Canadian Journal of Economics*, the 1999 Douglas Purvis Memorial Prize (with Ron Kneebone) for a published work relating to Canadian public policy, and the 2000 Faculty of Social Sciences Distinguished Researcher Award at the University of Calgary. Professor McKenzie has taught microeconomics and public economics from the principles to the graduate level, and has received several departmental teaching awards.

Nicholas Rowe is Associate Professor of Economics and Associate Dean of the Faculty of Public Affairs and Management at Carleton University. He received his Ph.D. from the University of Western Ontario. Professor Rowe has 25 years' experience in teaching economics at various levels, in Canada, Cuba, and Australia. His research interests are in the area of monetary policy, more specifically, inflation targeting by central banks. He is a member of C.D. Howe Institute's Monetary Policy Council, a panel of 12 top Canadian monetary economists that provides an independent recommendation for the Bank of Canada's monetary policy.

ACKNOWLEDGMENTS

In revising this third Canadian edition, we had the benefit of input from many talented people and wish to thank the following economics professors who read and commented on portions of the manuscript:

Aurelia Best, *Centennial College*

Bogdan Buduru, *Concordia University*

Byron Eastman, *Laurentian University*

Peter McCabe, *McMaster University*

Ugurhan G. Berkok, *Queen's University*

David Gray, *University of Ottawa*

Ather H. Akbari, *St. Mary's University*

Ibrahim Hayani, *Seneca College*

Michael Hare, *University of Toronto*

The success of the first two Canadian editions of this textbook was due in part to the many reviewers who helped us shape the manuscripts. We continue to be grateful for their comments:

Maurice Tugwell, *Acadia University*

Kevin Clinton, *Bank of Canada*

Keith Baxter, *Bishop's University*

Herb Emery, *University of Calgary*

Nancy Churchman, *Carleton University*

Stephen Rakocsy, *Humber College*

Chris McDonnell, *Malaspina University-College*

Costas Nicolau, *University of Manitoba*

Martin Looley, *McMaster University*

Ernie Jacobson, *Northern Alberta Institute of Technology*

Robin Neill, *University of Prince Edward Island and Carleton University*

Pierre Fortin, *University of Quebec at Montreal*

Gregor Smith, *Queen's University*

Special thanks go to Bill Scarth of McMaster University, who offered invaluable advice regarding the structure and emphasis of the Canadian editions. Dr. Scarth is an award-winning teacher and author, and to ignore his advice would have been perilous indeed. His extensive comments were instrumental in helping us formulate our approach to the Canadian editions.

We would also like to thank our colleagues at the University of Calgary and Carleton University who provided invaluable informal input and useful examples and applications. We, of course, bear full responsibility for any misinterpretations or errors.

Canadianizing this book has been a team effort from the very start. We would like to acknowledge the editorial, production, and marketing teams at Thomson Nelson for their professionalism, advice, and encouragement throughout the process. Deserving special attention are senior acquisitions editor Anthony Rezek and senior developmental editor Katherine Goodes for helping to ensure the timely completion of our work.

Finally, we are grateful to our families for their indulgence and encouragement throughout the research and writing process. Their patience and understanding are greatly appreciated.

Ronald D. Kneebone

Kenneth J. McKenzie

Nicholas Rowe

November 2004

BRIEF CONTENTS

TABLE OF CONTENTS

PART 1
INTRODUCTION   1

© JIM STEINHART

PART 2
SUPPLY AND DEMAND I:
HOW MARKETS WORK   63

© DON CARSTENS/TAXI

PART 3
SUPPLY AND DEMAND II: MARKETS AND WELFARE   137

© GEOFFREY CLIFFORD/IMAGE BANK

PART 4
THE ECONOMICS OF
THE PUBLIC SECTOR 201

PART 5
FIRM BEHAVIOUR AND
THE ORGANIZATION OF INDUSTRY 269

© CHRIS BAKER/STONE

PART 6
THE ECONOMICS
OF LABOUR MARKETS 399

PART 7
TOPICS FOR FURTHER STUDY 463

1

INTRODUCTION

© PHOTODISC

TEN PRINCIPLES OF ECONOMICS

Learning Objectives

In this chapter, you will …

- Learn that economics is about the allocation of scarce resources
- Examine some of the tradeoffs that people face
- Learn the meaning of *opportunity cost*
- See how to use marginal reasoning when making decisions
- Discuss how incentives affect people's behaviour
- Consider why trade among people or nations can be good for everyone
- Discuss why markets are a good, but not perfect, way to allocate resources
- Learn what determines some trends in the overall economy

The word *economy* comes from the Greek word for "one who manages a household." At first, this origin might seem peculiar. But, in fact, households and economies have much in common.

A household faces many decisions. It must decide which members of the household do which tasks and what each member gets in return: Who cooks dinner? Who does the laundry? Who gets the extra dessert at dinner? Who gets to choose what TV show to watch? In short, the household must allocate its scarce resources among its various members, taking into account each member's abilities, efforts, and desires.

Like a household, a society faces many decisions. A society must decide what jobs will be done and who will do them. It needs some people to grow food, other people to make clothing, and still others to design computer software. Once society has allocated people (as well as land, buildings, and machines) to various jobs, it must also allocate the output of goods and services that they produce. It must decide who will eat caviar and who will eat potatoes. It must decide who will drive a Ferrari and who will take the bus.

scarcity
the limited nature
of society's resources

economics
the study of how society
manages its scarce resources

The management of society's resources (e.g., people, land, buildings, machinery) is important because resources are scarce. **Scarcity** means that society has limited resources and therefore cannot produce all the goods and services people wish to have. Just as a household cannot give every member everything he or she wants, a society cannot give every individual the highest standard of living to which he or she might aspire.

Economics is the study of how society manages its scarce resources. In most societies, resources are allocated not by a single central planner but through the combined actions of millions of households and firms. Economists therefore study how people make decisions: how much they work, what they buy, how much they save, and how they invest their savings. Economists also study how people interact with one another. For instance, they examine how the multitude of buyers and sellers of a good together determine the price at which the good is sold and the quantity that is sold. Finally, economists analyze forces and trends that affect the economy as a whole, including the growth in average income, the fraction of the population that cannot find work, and the rate at which prices are rising.

Although the study of economics has many facets, the field is unified by several central ideas. In the rest of this chapter, we look at ten principles of economics. Don't worry if you don't understand them all at first, or if you don't find them completely convincing. In the coming chapters we will explore these ideas more fully. The ten principles are introduced here just to give you an overview of what economics is all about. You can think of this chapter as a "preview of coming attractions."

HOW PEOPLE MAKE DECISIONS

There is no mystery to what an "economy" is. Whether we are talking about the economy of Vancouver, of Canada, or of the whole world, an economy is just a group of people interacting with one another as they go about their lives. Because the behaviour of an economy reflects the behaviour of the individuals who make up the economy, we start our study of economics with four principles of individual decision making.

Principle #1: People Face Tradeoffs

The first lesson about making decisions is summarized in the adage "There is no such thing as a free lunch." To get one thing that we like, we usually have to give up another thing that we like. Making decisions requires trading off one goal against another.

Consider a student who must decide how to allocate her most valuable resource—her time. She can spend all of her time studying economics; she can spend all of her time studying psychology; or she can divide her time between the two fields. For every hour she studies one subject, she gives up an hour she could have used studying the other. And for every hour she spends studying, she gives up an hour that she could have spent napping, bike riding, watching TV, or working at her part-time job for some extra spending money.

Or consider parents deciding how to spend their family income. They can buy food, clothing, or a family vacation. Or they can save some of the family income for retirement or the children's college or university education. When they choose to spend an extra dollar on one of these goods, they have one less dollar to spend on some other good.

When people are grouped into societies, they face different kinds of tradeoffs. The classic tradeoff is between "guns and butter." The more we spend on national defence (guns) to protect our shores from foreign aggressors, the less we can spend on consumer goods (butter) to raise our standard of living at home. Also important in modern society is the tradeoff between a clean environment and a high level of income. Laws that require firms to reduce pollution raise the cost of producing goods and services. Because of the higher costs, these firms end up earning smaller profits, paying lower wages, charging higher prices, or some combination of these three. Thus, while pollution regulations give us the benefit of a cleaner environment and the improved health that comes with it, they have the cost of reducing the incomes of the firms' owners, workers, and customers.

Another tradeoff society faces is between efficiency and equity. **Efficiency** means that society is getting the most it can from its scarce resources. **Equity** means that the benefits of those resources are distributed fairly among society's members. In other words, efficiency refers to the size of the economic pie, and equity refers to how the pie is divided. Often, when government policies are being designed, these two goals conflict.

efficiency
the property of society getting the most it can from its scarce resources

equity
the property of distributing economic prosperity fairly among the members of society

Consider, for instance, policies aimed at achieving a more equal distribution of economic well-being. Some of these policies, such as the welfare system or employment insurance, try to help those members of society who are most in need. Others, such as the individual income tax, ask the financially successful to contribute more than others to support the government. Although these policies have the benefit of achieving greater equity, they have a cost in terms of reduced efficiency. When the government redistributes income from the rich to the poor, it reduces the reward for working hard; as a result, people work less and produce fewer goods and services. In other words, when the government tries to cut the economic pie into more equal slices, the pie gets smaller.

Recognizing that people face tradeoffs does not by itself tell us what decisions they will or should make. A student should not abandon the study of psychology just because doing so would increase the time available for the study of economics. Society should not stop protecting the environment just because environmental regulations reduce our material standard of living. The poor should not be ignored just because helping them distorts work incentives. Nonetheless, acknowledging life's tradeoffs is important because people are likely to make good decisions only if they understand the options that they have available.

Principle #2: The Cost of Something Is What You Give Up to Get It

Because people face tradeoffs, making decisions requires comparing the costs and benefits of alternative courses of action. In many cases, however, the cost of some action is not as obvious as it might first appear.

Consider, for example, the decision whether to go to college or university. The benefit is intellectual enrichment and a lifetime of better job opportunities. But what is the cost? To answer this question, you might be tempted to add up the money you spend on tuition, books, room, and board. Yet this total does not truly represent what you give up to spend a year in college or university.

The first problem with this answer is that it includes some things that are not really costs of going to college or university. Even if you quit school, you would need a place to sleep and food to eat. Room and board are costs of going to college or university only to the extent that they are more expensive there than elsewhere. Indeed, the cost of room and board at your school might be less than the rent and food expenses that you would pay living on your own. In this case, the savings on room and board are a benefit of going to college or university.

The second problem with this calculation of costs is that it ignores the largest cost of going to college or university—your time. When you spend a year listening to lectures, reading textbooks, and writing papers, you cannot spend that time working at a job. For most students, the wages given up to attend school are the largest single cost of their education.

opportunity cost
whatever must be given up to obtain some item

The **opportunity cost** of an item is what you give up to get that item. When making any decision, such as whether to attend college or university, decision makers should be aware of the opportunity costs that accompany each possible action. In fact, they usually are. College- or university-age athletes who can earn millions if they drop out of school and play professional sports are well aware that their opportunity cost of a postsecondary education is very high. It is not surprising that they often decide that the benefit is not worth the cost.

Principle #3: Rational People Think at the Margin

Decisions in life are rarely black and white but usually involve shades of gray. At dinnertime, the decision you face is not between fasting or eating like a pig, but whether to take that extra spoonful of mashed potatoes. When exams roll around, your decision is not between blowing them off or studying 24 hours a day, but whether to spend an extra hour reviewing your notes instead of watching TV. Economists use the term **marginal changes** to describe small incremental adjustments to an existing plan of action. Keep in mind that "margin" means "edge," so marginal changes are adjustments around the edges of what you are doing.

marginal changes
small incremental adjustments to a plan of action

In many situations, people make the best decisions by thinking at the margin. Suppose, for instance, that you asked a friend for advice about how many years to stay in school. If he were to compare for you the lifestyle of a person with a Ph.D. to that of an elementary-school dropout, you might complain that this comparison is not helpful in making your decision. You have some education already and most likely are deciding whether to spend an extra year or two in school. To make this decision, you need to know the additional benefits that an extra year in school would offer (higher wages throughout life and the sheer joy of learning) and the additional costs that you would incur (tuition and the forgone wages while you're in school). By comparing these *marginal benefits* and *marginal costs*, you can evaluate whether the extra year is worthwhile.

As another example, consider an airline deciding how much to charge passengers who fly standby. Suppose that flying a 200-seat plane across the country costs the airline $100 000. In this case, the average cost of each seat is $100 000/200, which is $500. One might be tempted to conclude that the airline should never sell a ticket for less than $500. In fact, however, the airline can raise its profits by thinking at the margin. Imagine that a plane is about to take off with ten empty seats, and a standby passenger is waiting at the gate willing to pay $300 for a seat. Should the airline sell it to him? Of course it should. If the plane has empty seats, the cost of adding one more passenger is minuscule. Although the *average* cost of flying a passenger is $500, the *marginal* cost is merely the cost of the bag of peanuts and can of soda that the extra passenger will consume. As long as the standby passenger pays more than the marginal cost, selling him a ticket is profitable.

As these examples show, individuals and firms can make better decisions by thinking at the margin. A rational decision maker takes an action if and only if the marginal benefit of the action exceeds the marginal cost.

Principle #4: People Respond to Incentives

Because people make decisions by comparing costs and benefits, their behaviour may change when the costs or benefits change. That is, people respond to incentives. When the price of an apple rises, for instance, people decide to eat more pears and fewer apples, because the cost of buying an apple is higher. At the same time, apple orchards decide to hire more workers and harvest more apples, because the benefit of selling an apple is also higher. As we will see, the effect of price on the behaviour of buyers and sellers in a market—in this case, the market for apples—is crucial for understanding how the economy works.

Public policymakers should never forget about incentives, because many policies change the costs or benefits that people face and, therefore, alter behaviour. A tax on gasoline, for instance, encourages people to drive smaller, more fuel-efficient cars. It also encourages people to take public transportation rather than drive, and to live closer to where they work. If the tax were large enough, people would start driving electric cars.

When policymakers fail to consider how their policies affect incentives, they often end up with results they did not intend. For example, consider public policy regarding auto safety. Today all cars have seat belts, but that was not true 50 years ago. In the 1960s, Ralph Nader's book *Unsafe at Any Speed* generated much public concern over auto safety. Parliament responded with laws requiring seat belts as standard equipment on new cars.

How does a seat belt law affect auto safety? The direct effect is obvious: When a person wears a seat belt, the probability of surviving a major auto accident rises. But that's not the end of the story, because the law also affects behaviour by altering incentives. The relevant behavior here is the speed and care with which drivers operate their cars. Driving slowly and carefully is costly because it uses the driver's time and energy. When deciding how safely to drive, rational people compare the marginal benefit from safer driving to the marginal cost. They drive more slowly and carefully when the benefit of increased safety is high. It is no surprise, for instance, that people drive more slowly and carefully when roads are icy than when roads are clear.

Consider how a seat belt law alters a driver's cost–benefit calculation. Seat belts make accidents less costly because they reduce the likelihood of injury or death. In other words, seat belts reduce the benefits to slow and careful driving. People respond to seat belts as they would to an improvement in road conditions—by faster and less careful driving. The end result of a seat belt law, therefore, is a larger number of accidents. The decline in safe driving has a clear, adverse impact on pedestrians, who are more likely to find themselves in an accident but (unlike the drivers) don't have the benefit of added protection.

Mick Jagger understood opportunity cost and incentives. In 1961, he became a scholarship student at the London School of Economics. In 1963, he abandoned a promising career as an economist, worked full-time on his music, and eventually earned millions of dollars with the Rolling Stones.

At first, this discussion of incentives and seat belts might seem like idle speculation. Yet, in a 1975 study, economist Sam Peltzman showed that the auto-safety laws have had many of these effects. According to Peltzman's evidence, these laws produce both fewer deaths per accident and more accidents. The net result is little change in the number of driver deaths and an increase in the number of pedestrian deaths.

Peltzman's analysis of auto safety is an example of the general principle that people respond to incentives. Many incentives that economists study are more straightforward than those of the auto-safety laws. No one is surprised that people drive smaller cars in Europe, where gasoline taxes are high, than in the United States, where gasoline taxes are low. Yet, as the seat belt example shows, policies can have effects that are not obvious in advance. When analyzing any policy, we must consider not only the direct effects but also the indirect effects that work through incentives. If the policy changes incentives, it will cause people to alter their behaviour.

QuickQuiz List and briefly explain the four principles of individual decision making.

HOW PEOPLE INTERACT

The first four principles discussed how individuals make decisions. As we go about our lives, many of our decisions affect not only ourselves but other people as well. The next three principles concern how people interact with one another.

Principle #5: Trade Can Make Everyone Better Off

You have probably heard on the news that the Americans are our competitors in the world economy. In some ways this is true, for Canadian and U.S. firms do produce many of the same goods. Nortel and Lucent compete for the same customers in the market for telecommunications. Inniskillin and Gallo compete for the same customers in the market for wine.

Yet it is easy to be misled when thinking about competition among countries. Trade between Canada and the United States is not like a sports contest, where one side wins and the other side loses. In fact, the opposite is true: Trade between two countries can make each country better off.

To see why, consider how trade affects your family. When a member of your family looks for a job, he or she competes against members of other families who are looking for jobs. Families also compete against one another when they go shopping, because each family wants to buy the best goods at the lowest prices. So, in a sense, each family in the economy is competing with all other families.

Despite this competition, your family would not be better off isolating itself from all other families. If it did, your family would need to grow its own food, make its own clothes, and build its own home. Clearly, your family gains much from its ability to trade with others. Trade allows each person to specialize in the activities he or she does best, whether it is farming, sewing, or home building. By trading with others, people can buy a greater variety of goods and services at lower cost.

Countries as well as families benefit from the ability to trade with one another. Trade allows countries to specialize in what they do best and to enjoy a greater variety of goods and services. The Americans, as well as the French and the Egyptians and the Brazilians, are as much our partners in the world economy as they are our competitors.

Principle #6: Markets Are Usually a Good Way to Organize Economic Activity

The collapse of communism in the Soviet Union and Eastern Europe in the 1980s may be the most important change in the world during the past half-century. Communist countries worked on the premise that central planners in the government were in the best position to guide economic activity. These planners decided what goods and services were produced, how much was produced, and who produced and consumed these goods and services. The theory behind central planning was that only the government could organize economic activity in a way that promoted economic well-being for the country as a whole.

Today, most countries that once had centrally planned economies have abandoned this system and are trying to develop market economies. In a **market economy,** the decisions of a central planner are replaced by the decisions of millions of firms and households. Firms decide whom to hire and what to make. Households decide which firms to work for and what to buy with their incomes. These firms and households interact in the marketplace, where prices and self-interest guide their decisions.

market economy
an economy that allocates resources through the decentralized decisions of many firms and households as they interact in markets for goods and services

At first glance, the success of market economies is puzzling. After all, in a market economy, no one is looking out for the economic well-being of society as a whole. Free markets contain many buyers and sellers of numerous goods and services, and all of them are interested primarily in their own well-being. Yet, despite decentralized decision making and self-interested decision makers, market economies have proven remarkably successful in organizing economic activity in a way that promotes overall economic well-being.

In his 1776 book *An Inquiry into the Nature and Causes of the Wealth of Nations,* economist Adam Smith made the most famous observation in all of economics: Households and firms interacting in markets act as if they are guided by an "invisible hand" that leads them to desirable market outcomes. One of our goals in this book is to understand how this invisible hand works its magic. As you study economics, you will learn that prices are the instrument with which the invisible hand directs economic activity. Prices reflect both the value of a good to society and the cost to society of making the good. Because households and firms look at prices when deciding what to buy and sell, they unknowingly take into account the social benefits and costs of their actions. As a result, prices guide these individual decision makers to reach outcomes that, in many cases, maximize the welfare of society as a whole.

There is an important corollary to the skill of the invisible hand in guiding economic activity: When the government prevents prices from adjusting naturally to supply and demand, it impedes the invisible hand's ability to coordinate the millions of households and firms that make up the economy. This corollary explains why taxes adversely affect the allocation of resources: Taxes distort prices and thus the decisions of households and firms. It also explains the even greater harm caused by policies that directly control prices, such as rent control. And it explains the failure of communism. In communist countries, prices were not determined in the marketplace but were dictated by central planners. These planners lacked the information that is reflected in prices when prices are free to respond to market forces. Central planners failed because they tried to run the economy with one hand tied behind their backs—the invisible hand of the marketplace.

IN THE NEWS

PRICES CONVEY INFORMATION

In most markets, people buy and sell goods like eggs, oil, or computers. The following newspaper article describes markets in some very peculiar goods. The goods being bought and sold in these markets are futures contracts. A futures contract in the weather, for example, might be a promise to pay $100 if there is a frost in Niagara in May. (Niagara fruit growers might be very interested in buying that futures contract for insurance.) If the market price of that futures contract is $20, it suggests that traders believe there is a 20 percent chance of frost in Niagara in May.

Why Markets Come Up with the Right Answers

By Jason Chow

Washington balked this week in its controversial plan to offer traders a chance to buy futures contracts on, among other things, the odds of an overthrow of the King of Jordan. But while the Pentagon's futures market failed for political reasons, the rationale behind using market efficiency to predict events in public affairs has been proven to be successful. Investors can already bet on the outcome of the chase for Al Qaeda leader Osama bin Laden and bid on the winner of the 2004 U.S. presidential elections.

Earlier this week, it was revealed the Pentagon was designing a market that would have allowed traders to place bets on terrorist attacks and political events in

the Middle East. The Pentagon was hoping its Policy Analysis Market (PAM)—the name of the ill-fated idea that was canned on Tuesday, only a day after the project was leaked to the public by two Democratic senators—would help the U.S. government intelligence agency predict events in the troubled region.

Though it was a public relations nightmare, fraught with objections of using public money to fund such an exchange and fears that terrorists might take large positions on the outcome of an attack and carry them out themselves, economists say, the idea in itself was a gem—both in its predictive abilities and in its broad appeal.

"It's bad publicity," said economist Robert Shiller at Yale University in New Haven, CT, and author of *Irrational Exu-*

berance. "But this idea could have worked, and it likely would have revealed information, just the same way as if you put up a US$15-million bounty for the heads of Uday and Qusai Hussein [sons of Iraqi leader Saddam Hussein]."

Alternative markets have been sprouting for some time to receptive audiences with strong reputations for being accurate.

The pioneering alternative futures exchange was the Iowa Electronic Markets, started in 1988, which allowed individuals to bet on the outcome of U.S. presidential elections. Research has shown that the IEM, even with its relatively small population of traders, has been a more effective forecaster than general opinion polls.

There are other similar exchanges. Dublin-based TradeSports.com has been the most active leader in the trading of futures contracts on political and cultural events. There, you can buy and sell contracts based on when you think Saddam Hussein will be captured and on whether you think basketball star Kobe Bryant will be found guilty on sexual charges. TradeSports attracted attention earlier this year when its futures contract on the date of the invasion into Iraq was on target.

The Athletic Stock Exchange allows individuals to ride the fortunes of sports stars while Hollywood Stock Exchange allows online traders to bet on the box-office success of upcoming releases. For example, the release of *S.W.A.T.*, starring Colin Farrell, is being primed as a bust, trading down US$5.67.

Why are markets so effective at predicting the future? Simply, markets can act as essentially virtual meeting places, where people get together to pay and profit for their opinions, economists argue, and the distilled collective thinking of several trumps the forecasting abilities of the individual.

Take the jar of jellybeans experiment: Ask a hundred people how many beans they think are in the jar. It's highly unlikely any one of the responses would have the exact number, but if you take the mean of all their answers you'll probably be close to the mark.

Markets are the same, economists say. Several participants are forced to answer an identical question—i.e., Will current U.S. president George Bush win a re-election in 2004?—and have to pay for that privilege.

Stanford University professors Eric Zitzewitz and Justin Wolfers, who have been researching TradeSports and the Saddam futures, says the markets reflect more wisdom than any single individual can possibly have, and therefore are more effective at assessing probabilities.

"The market is one of the best aggregators of information," said John Delaney, chief executive of TradeSports.com. "In essence, I'm asking people for their opinions, but asking them to back it up with real money. They have to put their money where their mouths are."

There's also a psychological element, says Mr. Shiller at Yale, who also runs a private research firm that is currently looking into the creation of markets for house prices and other macroeconomic indicators. The market appeals to those who like to gamble, he says, while at the same time, forces people to think harder about their opinions.

"There's a gambling instinct and it's human nature," he said. "When people are asked their opinions for a survey, they'll say whatever first comes to mind. But if they have money on the line, they'll likely think twice. It's more honest. They'll say what they really believe in."

Of course, not all market predictions are on the money, even those made on alternative markets. Earlier this week TradeSports offered a futures contract on whether John Poindexter, head of the Pentagon's Defence Advanced Research Projects Agency and leader of the PAM initiative, would be able to keep his job after all the controversy surrounding the proposed market.

Traders on TradeSports were pricing in a 65% chance of him still being on the Pentagon payroll at the end of August. Mr. Poindexter was fired on Thursday.

Source: *National Post*, August 2, 2003. Material reprinted with the express permission of "The National Post Company," a CanWest Partnership.

Principle #7: Governments Can Sometimes Improve Market Outcomes

If the invisible hand of the market is so great, why do we need government? One answer is that the invisible hand needs government to protect it. Markets work only if property rights are enforced. A farmer won't grow food if he expects his crop to be stolen, and a restaurant won't serve meals unless it is assured that customers will pay before they leave. We all rely on government-provided police and courts to enforce our rights over the things we produce.

Yet there is another answer to why we need government: Although markets are usually a good way to organize economic activity, this rule has some important exceptions. There are two broad reasons for a government to intervene in the economy—to promote efficiency and to promote equity. That is, most policies aim either to enlarge the economic pie or to change how the pie is divided.

FYI

ADAM SMITH AND THE INVISIBLE HAND

It may be only a coincidence that Adam Smith's great book *The Wealth of Nations* was published in 1776, the exact year American revolutionaries signed the Declaration of Independence. But the two documents do share a point of view that was prevalent at the time—that individuals are usually best left to their own devices, without the heavy hand of government guiding their actions. This political philosophy provides the intellectual basis for the market economy, and for free society more generally.

Why do decentralized market economies work so well? Is it because people can be counted on to treat one another with love and kindness? Not at all. Here is Adam Smith's description of how people interact in a market economy:

Adam Smith

Man has almost constant occasion for the help of his brethren, and it is vain for him to expect it from their benevolence only. He will be more likely to prevail if he can interest their self-love in his favor, and show them that it is for their own advantage to do for him what he requires of them. . . . It is not from the benevolence of the butcher, the brewer, or the baker that we expect our dinner, but from their regard to their own interest. . . .

Every individual . . . neither intends to promote the public interest, nor knows how much he is promoting it. . . . He intends only his own gain, and he is in this, as in many other cases, led by an invisible hand to promote an end which was no part of his intention. Nor is it always the worse for the society that it was no part of it. By pursuing his own interest he frequently promotes that of the society more effectually than when he really intends to promote it.

Smith is saying that participants in the economy are motivated by self-interest and that the "invisible hand" of the marketplace guides this self-interest into promoting general economic well-being.

Many of Smith's insights remain at the centre of modern economics. Our analysis in the coming chapters will allow us to express Smith's conclusions more precisely and to analyze fully the strengths and weaknesses of the market's invisible hand.

market failure
a situation in which a market left on its own fails to allocate resources efficiently

externality
the impact of one person's actions on the well-being of a bystander

market power
the ability of a single economic actor (or small group of actors) to have a substantial influence on market prices

Although the invisible hand usually leads markets to allocate resources efficiently, that is not always the case. Economists use the term **market failure** to refer to a situation in which the market on its own fails to produce an efficient allocation of resources. One possible cause of market failure is an **externality,** which is the impact of one person's actions on the well-being of a bystander. For instance, the classic example of an external cost is pollution. Another possible cause of market failure is **market power,** which refers to the ability of a single person (or small group) to unduly influence market prices. For example, if everyone in town needs water but there is only one well, the owner of the well is not subject to the rigorous competition with which the invisible hand normally keeps self-interest in check. In the presence of externalities or market power, well-designed public policy can enhance economic efficiency.

The invisible hand may also fail to ensure that economic prosperity is distributed equitably. A market economy rewards people according to their ability to produce things that other people are willing to pay for. The world's best basketball player earns more than the world's best chess player simply because people are willing to pay more to watch basketball than chess. The invisible hand does not ensure that everyone has sufficient food, decent clothing, and adequate health care. Many public policies, such as the income tax and welfare systems, aim to achieve a more equitable distribution of economic well-being.

To say that the government *can* improve on market outcomes at times does not mean that it always *will*. Public policy is made not by angels but by a political process that is far from perfect. Sometimes policies are designed simply to reward the politically powerful. Sometimes they are made by well-intentioned leaders who are not fully informed. One goal of the study of economics is to help you judge when a government policy is justifiable to promote efficiency or equity, and when it is not.

QuickQuiz   List and briefly explain the three principles concerning economic interactions.

HOW THE ECONOMY AS A WHOLE WORKS

We started by discussing how individuals make decisions and then looked at how people interact with one another. All these decisions and interactions together make up "the economy." The last three principles concern the workings of the economy as a whole.

Principle #8: A Country's Standard of Living Depends on Its Ability to Produce Goods and Services

The differences in living standards around the world are staggering. In 2001 the average Canadian had an income of about $40 700. In the same year, the average Mexican earned $12 550, and the average Nigerian earned $1300. Not surprisingly, this large variation in average income is reflected in various measures of the quality of life. Citizens of high-income countries have more TV sets, more cars, better nutrition, better health care, and longer life expectancy than citizens of low-income countries.

Changes in living standards over time are also large. In Canada, incomes have historically grown about 2 percent per year (after adjusting for changes in the cost of living). At this rate, average income doubles every 35 years. Over the past century, average income has risen about eightfold.

What explains these large differences in living standards among countries and over time? The answer is surprisingly simple. Almost all variation in living standards is attributable to differences in countries' **productivity**—that is, the amount of goods and services produced from each hour of a worker's time. In nations where workers can produce a large quantity of goods and services per unit of time, most people enjoy a high standard of living; in nations where workers are less productive, most people must endure a more meagre existence. Similarly, the growth rate of a nation's productivity determines the growth rate of its average income.

productivity
the quantity of goods and services produced from each hour of a worker's time

The fundamental relationship between productivity and living standards is simple, but its implications are far-reaching. If productivity is the primary determinant of living standards, other explanations must be of secondary importance. For example, it might be tempting to credit labour unions or minimum-wage laws for the rise in living standards of Canadian workers over the past century. Yet the real hero of Canadian workers is their rising productivity. As another example, some commentators have claimed that increased competition from Japan and other countries explained the slow growth in Canadian incomes during the 1970s and 1980s. Yet the real villain was not competition from abroad but flagging productivity growth in Canada.

The relationship between productivity and living standards also has profound implications for public policy. When thinking about how any policy will affect living standards, the key question is how it will affect our ability to produce goods and services. To boost living standards, policymakers need to raise productivity by ensuring that workers are well educated, have the tools needed to produce goods and services, and have access to the best available technology.

Principle #9: Prices Rise When the Government Prints Too Much Money

inflation
an increase in the overall level of prices in the economy

In Germany in January 1921, a daily newspaper cost 0.30 marks. Less than two years later, in November 1922, the same newspaper cost 70 000 000 marks. All other prices in the economy rose by similar amounts. This episode is one of history's most spectacular examples of **inflation,** an increase in the overall level of prices in the economy.

Although Canada has never experienced inflation even close to that in Germany in the 1920s, inflation has at times been an economic problem. During the 1970s, for instance, average inflation was 8 percent per year and the overall level of prices more than doubled. By contrast, inflation in the 1990s was about 2 percent per year; at this rate it would take 35 years for prices to double. Because high inflation imposes various costs on society, keeping inflation at a low level is a goal of economic policymakers around the world.

What causes inflation? In almost all cases of large or persistent inflation, the culprit turns out to be the same—growth in the quantity of money. When a government creates large quantities of the nation's money, the value of the money falls. In Germany in the early 1920s, when prices were on average tripling every month, the quantity of money was also tripling every month. Although less dramatic, the economic history of Canada points to a similar conclusion: The high inflation of the 1970s was associated with rapid growth in the quantity of money, and the low inflation of the 1990s was associated with slow growth in the quantity of money.

Principle #10: Society Faces a Short-Run Tradeoff between Inflation and Unemployment

Phillips curve
a curve that shows the short-run tradeoff between inflation and unemployment

When the government increases the amount of money in the economy, one result is inflation. Another result, at least in the short run, is a lower level of unemployment. The curve that illustrates this short-run tradeoff between inflation and unemployment is called the **Phillips curve,** after the economist who first examined this relationship.

The Phillips curve remains a controversial topic among economists, but most economists today accept the idea that society faces a short-run tradeoff between inflation and unemployment. This simply means that, over a period of a year or two, many economic policies push inflation and unemployment in opposite directions. Policymakers face this tradeoff regardless of whether inflation and unemployment both start out at high levels (as they were in the early 1980s), at low levels (as they were in the late 1990s), or someplace in between.

The tradeoff between inflation and unemployment is only temporary, but it can last for several years. The Phillips curve is, therefore, crucial for understanding many developments in the economy. In particular, it is important for understanding the **business cycle**—the irregular and largely unpredictable fluctuations in economic activity, as measured by the number of people employed or the production of goods and services.

business cycle
fluctuations in economic activity, such as employment and production

Policymakers can exploit the short-run tradeoff between inflation and unemployment using various policy instruments. By changing the amount that the government spends, the amount it taxes, and the amount of money it prints, policymakers can influence the combination of inflation and unemployment that the economy experiences. Because these instruments of monetary and fiscal policy are potentially so powerful, how policymakers should use these instruments to control the economy, if at all, is a subject of continuing debate.

QuickQuiz   List and briefly explain the three principles that describe how the economy as a whole works.

HOW TO READ THIS BOOK

Economics is fun, but it can also be hard to learn. Our aim in writing this text is to make it as fun and easy as possible. But you, the student, also have a role to play. Experience shows that if you are actively involved as you study this book, you will enjoy a better outcome, both on your exams and in the years that follow. Here are a few tips about how best to read this book.

1. *Summarize, don't highlight.* Running a yellow marker over the text is too passive an activity to keep your mind engaged. Instead, when you come to the end of a section, take a minute and summarize what you just learned in your own words, writing your summary in the wide margins we've provided. When you've finished the chapter, compare your summary with the one at the end of the chapter. Did you pick up the main points?

2. *Test yourself.* Throughout the book, Quick Quizzes offer instant feedback to find out if you've learned what you are supposed to. Take the opportunity. Write your answer in the book's margin. The quizzes are meant to test your basic comprehension. If you aren't sure your answer is right, you probably need to review the section.

3. *Practise, practise, practise.* At the end of each chapter, Questions for Review test your understanding, and Problems and Applications ask you to apply and extend the material. Perhaps your instructor will assign some of these exercises as homework. If so, do them. If not, do them anyway. The more you use your new knowledge, the more solid it becomes.

4. *Study in groups.* After you've read the book and worked the problems on your own, get together with classmates to discuss the material. You will learn from each other—an example of the gains from trade.

5. *Don't forget the real world.* In the midst of all the numbers, graphs, and strange new words, it is easy to lose sight of what economics is all about. The Case Studies and In the News boxes sprinkled throughout this book should help remind you. Don't skip them. They show how the theory is tied to events happening in all of our lives. If your study is successful, you won't be able to read a newspaper again without thinking about supply, demand, and the wonderful world of economics.

TABLE 1.1

Ten Principles of Economics

How People Make Decisions	#1:	People face tradeoffs
	#2:	The cost of something is what you give up to get it
	#3:	Rational people think at the margin
	#4:	People respond to incentives
How People Interact	#5:	Trade can make everyone better off
	#6:	Markets are usually a good way to organize economic activity
	#7:	Governments can sometimes improve market outcomes
How the Economy as a Whole Works	#8:	A country's standard of living depends on its ability to produce goods and services
	#9:	Prices rise when the government prints too much money
	#10:	Society faces a short-run tradeoff between inflation and unemployment

CONCLUSION

You now have a taste of what economics is all about. In the coming chapters we will develop many specific insights about people, markets, and economies. Mastering these insights will take some effort, but it is not an overwhelming task. The field of economics is based on a few basic ideas that can be applied in many different situations.

Throughout this book we will refer back to the ten principles of economics highlighted in this chapter and summarized in Table 1.1. Whenever we do so, an icon will be displayed in the margin, as it is now. But even when that icon is absent, you should keep these principles in mind. Even the most sophisticated economic analysis is built using the ten principles introduced here.

SUMMARY

- The fundamental lessons about individual decision making are that people face tradeoffs among alternative goals, that the cost of any action is measured in terms of forgone opportunities, that rational people make decisions by comparing marginal costs and marginal benefits, and that people change their behaviour in response to the incentives they face.

- The fundamental lessons about interactions among people are that trade can be mutually beneficial, that markets are usually a good way

of coordinating trade among people, and that the government can potentially improve market outcomes if there is some market failure or if the market outcome is inequitable.

- The fundamental lessons about the economy as a whole are that productivity is the ultimate source of living standards, that money growth is the ultimate source of inflation, and that society faces a short-run tradeoff between inflation and unemployment.

KEY CONCEPTS

scarcity, p. 4
economics, p. 4
efficiency, p. 5
equity, p. 5
opportunity cost, p. 6

marginal changes, p. 6
market economy, p. 9
market failure, p. 12
externality, p. 12
market power, p. 12

productivity, p. 13
inflation, p. 14
Phillips curve, p. 14
business cycle, p. 15

QUESTIONS FOR REVIEW

1. Give three examples of important tradeoffs that you face in your life.

2. What is the opportunity cost of seeing a movie?

3. Water is necessary for life. Is the marginal benefit of a glass of water large or small?

4. Why should policymakers think about incentives?

5. Why isn't trade among countries like a game, with some winners and some losers?

6. What does the "invisible hand" of the marketplace do?

7. Explain the two main causes of market failure and give an example of each.

8. Why is productivity important?

9. What is inflation, and what causes it?

10. How are inflation and unemployment related in the short run?

PROBLEMS AND APPLICATIONS

1. Describe some of the tradeoffs faced by each of the following.
   a. a family deciding whether to buy a new car
   b. a member of Parliament deciding how much to spend on national parks
   c. a company president deciding whether to open a new factory
   d. a professor deciding how much to prepare for class

2. You are trying to decide whether to take a vacation. Most of the costs of the vacation (airfare, hotel, forgone wages) are measured in dollars, but the benefits of the vacation are psychological. How can you compare the benefits to the costs?

3. You were planning to spend Saturday working at your part-time job, but a friend asks you to go skiing. What is the true cost of going skiing? Now suppose that you had been planning to spend the day studying at the library. What is the cost of going skiing in this case? Explain.

4. You win $100 in a hockey pool. You have a choice between spending the money now or putting it away for a year in a bank account that pays 5 percent interest. What is the opportunity cost of spending the $100 now?

5. The company that you manage has invested $5 million in developing a new product, but the development is not quite finished. At a recent meeting, your salespeople report that the introduction of competing products has reduced the expected sales of your new product to $3 million. If it would cost $1 million to finish development and make the product, should you go ahead and do so? What is the most that you should pay to complete development?

6. Three managers of the Magic Potion Company are discussing a possible increase in production. Each suggests a way to make this decision.

HARRY: We should examine whether our company's productivity— litres of potion per worker— would rise or fall.

RON: We should examine whether our average cost—cost per worker— would rise or fall.

HERMIONE: We should examine whether the extra revenue from selling the additional potion would be greater or smaller than the extra costs.

Who do you think is right? Why?

7. The welfare system provides income for people who are very poor, with low incomes and few assets. If a recipient of welfare payments decides to work and earn some money, the amount he or she receives in welfare payments is reduced.
   a. How does the existence of the welfare system affect people's incentive to save money for the future?
   b. How does the reduction in welfare payments associated with higher earnings affect welfare recipients' incentive to work?

8. In 1997 the Government of Ontario reformed the welfare system. The reform reduced the amount of welfare payments to a person with no income, but also allowed welfare recipients to keep a larger part of their welfare payments if they did earn some income.
   a. How does this reform affect the incentive to work?
   b. How might this reform represent a tradeoff between equity and efficiency?

9. Your roommate is a better cook than you are, but you can clean more quickly than your roommate can. If your roommate did all of the cooking and you did all of the cleaning, would your chores take you more or less time than if you divided each task evenly? Give a similar example of how specialization and trade can make two countries both better off.

10. Suppose Canada adopted central planning for its economy, and you became the chief planner. Among the millions of decisions that you need to make for next year are how many compact discs to produce, what artists to record, and who should receive the discs.
    a. To make these decisions intelligently, what information would you need about the compact disc industry? What information would you need about each of the people in Canada?
    b. How would your decisions about CDs affect some of your other decisions, such as how many CD players to make or cassette tapes to produce? How might some of your other decisions about the economy change your views about CDs?

11. Explain whether each of the following government activities is motivated by a concern about equity or a concern about efficiency. In the case of efficiency, discuss the type of market failure involved.
    a. regulating cable TV prices
    b. providing some poor people with free prescription drugs
    c. prohibiting smoking in public places
    d. preventing mergers between major banks
    e. imposing higher personal income tax rates on people with higher incomes
    f. instituting laws against driving while intoxicated

12. Discuss each of the following statements from the standpoints of equity and efficiency.
    a. "Everyone in society should be guaranteed the best health care possible."
    b. "When workers are laid off, they should be able to collect unemployment benefits until they find a new job."

13. In what ways is your standard of living different from that of your parents or grandparents when they were your age? Why have these changes occurred?

14. Suppose Canadians decide to save more of their incomes. If banks lend this extra saving to businesses, which use the funds to build new factories, how might this lead to faster growth in productivity? Who do you suppose benefits from the higher productivity? Is society getting a free lunch?

15. Imagine that you are a policymaker trying to decide whether to reduce the rate of inflation.

To make an intelligent decision, what would you need to know about inflation, unemployment, and the tradeoff between them?

16. Look at a newspaper or at the website http://www.economist.com to find three stories about the economy that have been in the news lately. For each story, identify one (or more) of the ten principles of economics discussed in this chapter that is relevant, and explain how it is relevant. Also, for each story, look through this book's table of contents and try to find a chapter that might shed light on the news event.

INTERNET RESOURCES

- Canadian economic and financial statistics can be found online through the University of British Columbia Library at http://data.library.ubc.ca/datalib/gen/analysis.html.

- Study original research and analysis of changes to the Canadian economy at the Industry Canada website: http://strategis.ic.gc.ca/sc_ecnmy/engdoc/homepage.html?categories=e_eco.

- The *Occupational Outlook Handbook* at http://www.bls.gov/oco describes the role of an economist, the future outlook of the position, and the training required. Although this is a U.S. site, much information relevant to Canadian economists is provided.

http://   For more study tools, please visit http://www.mankiw3e.nelson.com.

© PHOTODISC

THINKING LIKE AN ECONOMIST

Every field of study has its own language and its own way of thinking. Mathematicians talk about axioms, integrals, and vector spaces. Psychologists talk about ego, id, and cognitive dissonance. Lawyers talk about venue, torts, and promissory estoppel.

Economics is no different. Supply, demand, elasticity, comparative advantage, consumer surplus, deadweight loss—these terms are part of the economist's language. In the coming chapters, you will encounter many new terms and some familiar words that economists use in specialized ways. At first, this new language may seem needlessly arcane. But, as you will see, its value lies in its ability to provide you with a new and useful way of thinking about the world in which you live.

The single most important purpose of this book is to help you learn the economist's way of thinking. Of course, just as you cannot become a mathematician, psychologist, or lawyer overnight, learning to think like an economist will take some time. Yet with a combination of theory, case studies, and examples of economics in the news, this book will give you ample opportunity to develop and practise this skill.

Before delving into the substance and details of economics, it is helpful to have an overview of how economists approach the world. This chapter, therefore,

Learning Objectives

In this chapter, you will …

- See how economists apply the methods of science
- Consider how assumptions and models can shed light on the world
- Learn two simple models—the circular flow and the production possibilities frontier
- Distinguish between microeconomics and macroeconomics
- Learn the difference between positive and normative statements
- Examine the role of economists in making policy
- Consider why economists sometimes disagree with one another

discusses the field's methodology. What is distinctive about how economists confront a question? What does it mean to think like an economist?

THE ECONOMIST AS SCIENTIST

Economists try to address their subject with a scientist's objectivity. They approach the study of the economy in much the same way as a physicist approaches the study of matter and a biologist approaches the study of life: They devise theories, collect data, and then analyze these data in an attempt to verify or refute their theories.

To beginners, it can seem odd to claim that economics is a science. After all, economists do not work with test tubes or telescopes. The essence of science, however, is the *scientific method*—the dispassionate development and testing of theories about how the world works. This method of inquiry is as applicable to studying a nation's economy as it is to studying the earth's gravity or a species' evolution. As Albert Einstein once put it, "The whole of science is nothing more than the refinement of everyday thinking."

Although Einstein's comment is as true for social sciences such as economics as it is for natural sciences such as physics, most people are not accustomed to looking at society through the eyes of a scientist. Let's therefore discuss some of the ways in which economists apply the logic of science to examine how an economy works.

The Scientific Method: Observation, Theory, and More Observation

Isaac Newton, the famous seventeenth-century scientist and mathematician, allegedly became intrigued one day when he saw an apple fall from an apple tree. This observation motivated Newton to develop a theory of gravity that applies not only to an apple falling to the earth but to any two objects in the universe. Subsequent testing of Newton's theory has shown that it works well in many circumstances (although, as Einstein would later emphasize, not in all circumstances). Because Newton's theory has been so successful at explaining observation, it is still taught today in undergraduate physics courses around the world.

This interplay between theory and observation also occurs in the field of economics. An economist might live in a country experiencing rapid increases in prices and be moved by this observation to develop a theory of inflation. The theory might assert that high inflation arises when the government prints too much money. (As you may recall, this was one of the ten principles of economics in Chapter 1.) To test this theory, the economist could collect and analyze data on prices and money from many different countries. If growth in the quantity of money were not at all related to the rate at which prices are rising, the economist would start to doubt the validity of his theory of inflation. If money growth and inflation were strongly correlated in international data, as in fact they are, the economist would become more confident in his theory.

Although economists use theory and observation like other scientists, they do face an obstacle that makes their task especially challenging: Experiments are often difficult in economics. Physicists studying gravity can drop many objects in their laboratories to generate data to test their theories. By contrast, economists studying inflation are not allowed to manipulate a nation's monetary policy simply to generate useful data. Economists, like astronomers and evolutionary biologists, usually have to make do with whatever data the world happens to give them.

To find a substitute for laboratory experiments, economists pay close attention to the natural experiments offered by history. When a war in the Middle East interrupts the flow of crude oil, for instance, oil prices skyrocket around the world. For consumers of oil and oil products, such an event depresses living standards. For economic policymakers, it poses a difficult choice about how best to respond. But for economic scientists, it provides an opportunity to study the effects of a key natural resource on the world's economies, and this opportunity persists long after the wartime increase in oil prices is over. Throughout this book, therefore, we consider many historical episodes. These episodes are valuable to study because they give us insight into the economy of the past and, more important, because they allow us to illustrate and evaluate economic theories of the present.

The Role of Assumptions

If you ask a physicist how long it would take for a marble to fall from the top of a ten-storey building, she will answer the question by assuming that the marble falls in a vacuum. Of course, this assumption is false. In fact, the building is surrounded by air, which exerts friction on the falling marble and slows it down. Yet the physicist will correctly point out that friction on the marble is so small that its effect is negligible. Assuming that the marble falls in a vacuum greatly simplifies the problem without substantially affecting the answer.

Economists make assumptions for the same reason: Assumptions can simplify the complex world and make it easier to understand. To study the effects of international trade, for example, we may assume that the world consists of only two countries and that each country produces only two goods. Of course, the real world consists of dozens of countries, each of which produces thousands of different types of goods. But by assuming two countries and two goods, we can focus our thinking. Once we understand international trade in an imaginary world with two countries and two goods, we are in a better position to understand international trade in the more complex world in which we live.

The art in scientific thinking—whether in physics, biology, or economics—is deciding which assumptions to make. Suppose, for instance, that we were dropping a beach ball rather than a marble from the top of the building. Our physicist would realize that the assumption of no friction is far less accurate in this case: Friction exerts a greater force on a beach ball than on a marble because a beach ball is much larger. The assumption that gravity works in a vacuum is reasonable for studying a falling marble but not for studying a falling beach ball.

Similarly, economists use different assumptions to answer different questions. Suppose that we want to study what happens to the economy when the government changes the number of dollars in circulation. An important piece of this analysis, it turns out, is how prices respond. Many prices in the economy change infrequently; the newsstand prices of magazines, for instance, are changed only every few years. Knowing this fact may lead us to make different assumptions when studying the effects of the policy change over different time horizons. For studying the short-run effects of the policy, we may assume that prices do not change much. We may even make the extreme and artificial assumption that all prices are completely fixed. For studying the long-run effects of the policy, however, we may assume that all prices are completely flexible. Just as a physicist uses different assumptions when studying falling marbles and falling beach balls, economists use different assumptions when studying the short-run and long-run effects of a change in the quantity of money.

Economic Models

High-school biology teachers teach basic anatomy with plastic replicas of the human body. These models have all the major organs—the heart, the liver, the kidneys, and so on. The models allow teachers to show their students in a simple way how the important parts of the body fit together. Of course, these plastic models are not actual human bodies, and no one would mistake the model for a real person. These models are stylized, and they omit many details. Yet despite this lack of realism—indeed, because of this lack of realism—studying these models is useful for learning how the human body works.

Economists also use models to learn about the world, but instead of being made of plastic, they are most often composed of diagrams and equations. Like a biology teacher's plastic model, economic models omit many details to allow us to see what is truly important. Just as the biology teacher's model does not include all of the body's muscles and capillaries, an economist's model does not include every feature of the economy.

As we use models to examine various economic issues throughout this book, you will see that all the models are built with assumptions. Just as a physicist begins the analysis of a falling marble by assuming away the existence of friction, economists assume away many of the details of the economy that are irrelevant for studying the question at hand. All models—in physics, biology, or economics—simplify reality in order to improve our understanding of it.

Our First Model: The Circular-Flow Diagram

The economy consists of millions of people engaged in many activities—buying, selling, working, hiring, manufacturing, and so on. To understand how the economy works, we must find some way to simplify our thinking about all these activities. In other words, we need a model that explains, in general terms, how the economy is organized and how participants in the economy interact with one another.

circular-flow diagram
a visual model of the economy that shows how dollars flow through markets among households and firms

Figure 2.1 presents a visual model of the economy, called a **circular-flow diagram.** In this model, the economy is simplified to include only two types of decision makers—households and firms. Firms produce goods and services using inputs, such as labour, land (natural resources), and capital (buildings and machines). These inputs are called the *factors of production.* Households own the factors of production and consume all the goods and services that the firms produce.

Households and firms interact in two types of markets. In the *markets for goods and services,* households are buyers and firms are sellers. In particular, households buy the output of goods and services that firms produce. In the *markets for the*

FIGURE 2.1

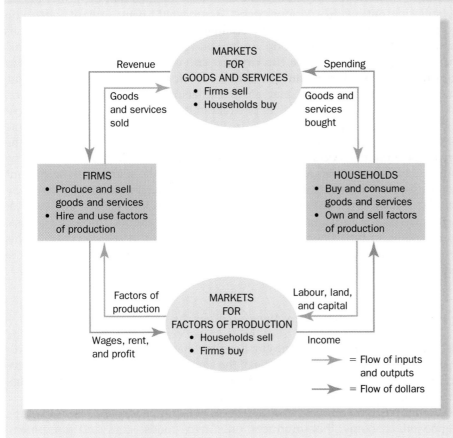

The Circular Flow

This diagram is a schematic representation of the organization of the economy. Decisions are made by households and firms. Households and firms interact in the markets for goods and services (where households are buyers and firms are sellers) and in the markets for the factors of production (where firms are buyers and households are sellers). The outer set of arrows shows the flow of dollars, and the inner set of arrows shows the corresponding flow of inputs and outputs.

factors of production, households are sellers and firms are buyers. In these markets, households provide the inputs that the firms use to produce goods and services. The circular-flow diagram offers a simple way of organizing all the economic transactions that occur between households and firms in the economy.

The inner loop of the circular-flow diagram represents the flows of inputs and outputs. The households sell the use of their labour, land, and capital to the firms in the markets for the factors of production. The firms then use these factors to produce goods and services, which in turn are sold to households in the markets for goods and services. Hence, the factors of production flow from households to firms, and goods and services flow from firms to households.

The outer loop of the circular-flow diagram represents the corresponding flow of dollars. The households spend money to buy goods and services from the firms. The firms use some of the revenue from these sales to pay for the factors of production, such as the wages of their workers. What's left is the profit of the firm owners, who themselves are members of households. Hence, spending on goods and services flows from households to firms, and income in the form of wages, rent, and profit flows from firms to households.

Let's take a tour of the circular flow by following a dollar coin as it makes its way from person to person through the economy. Imagine that the dollar begins at a household, sitting in, say, your pocket. If you want to buy a cup of coffee, you take the dollar to one of the economy's markets for goods and services, such as your local Tim Hortons coffee shop. There you spend it on your favourite drink. When the dollar moves into the Tim Hortons cash register, it becomes revenue for the firm. The dollar doesn't stay at Tim Hortons for long, however, because the firm uses it to buy inputs in the markets for the factors of production. For instance, Tim Hortons might use the dollar to pay rent to its landlord for the space it occupies or to pay the wages of its workers. In either case, the dollar enters the income of some household and, once again, is back in someone's pocket. At that point, the story of the economy's circular flow starts once again.

The circular-flow diagram in Figure 2.1 is one simple model of the economy. It dispenses with details that, for some purposes, are significant. A more complex and realistic circular-flow model would include, for instance, the roles of government and international trade. Yet these details are not crucial for a basic understanding of how the economy is organized. Because of its simplicity, this circular-flow diagram is useful to keep in mind when thinking about how the pieces of the economy fit together.

Our Second Model: The Production Possibilities Frontier

Most economic models, unlike the circular-flow diagram, are built using the tools of mathematics. Here we consider one of the simplest such models, called the production possibilities frontier, and see how this model illustrates some basic economic ideas.

Although real economies produce thousands of goods and services, let's imagine an economy that produces only two goods—cars and computers. Together the car industry and the computer industry use all of the economy's resources, or factors of production. The **production possibilities frontier** is a graph that shows the various combinations of output—in this case, cars and computers—that the economy can possibly produce given the available factors of production and the available production technology that firms can use to turn these factors into output.

Figure 2.2 is an example of a production possibilities frontier. In this economy, if all resources were used in the car industry, the economy would produce 1000 cars per year and no computers. If all resources were used in the computer industry, the economy would produce 3000 computers per year and no cars. The two end points of the production possibilities frontier represent these extreme possibilities. If the economy were to divide its resources between the two industries, it could produce 700 cars and 2000 computers, shown in the figure by point A. By contrast, the outcome at point D is not possible because resources are scarce: The economy does not have enough of the factors of production to support that level of output. In other words, the economy can produce at any point on or inside the production possibilities frontier, but it cannot produce at points outside the frontier.

An outcome is said to be *efficient* if the economy is getting all it can from the scarce resources it has available. Points on (rather than inside) the production possibilities frontier represent efficient levels of production. When the economy is producing at such a point, say point A, there is no way to produce more of one

production possibilities frontier
a graph that shows the combinations of output that the economy can possibly produce given the available factors of production and the available production technology

FIGURE 2.2

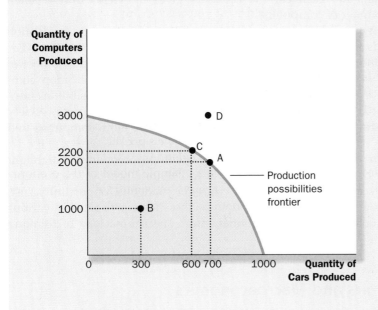

**The Production
Possibilities Frontier**

*The production possibilities frontier shows the
combinations of output—in this case, cars and
computers—that the economy can possibly produce. The
economy can produce any combination on or inside the
frontier. Points outside the frontier are not feasible given
the economy's resources.*

good without producing less of the other. Point B represents an *inefficient* outcome.
For some reason, perhaps widespread unemployment, the economy is producing
less than it could from the resources it has available: It is producing only 300 cars
and 1000 computers. If the source of the inefficiency were eliminated, the
economy could move from point B to point A, increasing production of both cars
(to 700) and computers (to 2000).

One of the ten principles of economics discussed in Chapter 1 is that people
face tradeoffs. The production possibilities frontier shows one tradeoff that society
faces. Once we have reached the efficient points on the frontier, the only way of
getting more of one good is to get less of the other. When the economy moves from
point A to point C, for instance, society produces more computers, but at the
expense of producing fewer cars.

Another of the ten principles of economics is that the cost of something is what
you give up to get it. This is called the *opportunity cost*. The production possibilities frontier shows the opportunity cost of one good as measured in terms of the
other good. When society reallocates some of the factors of production from the
car industry to the computer industry, moving the economy from point A to point
C, it gives up 100 cars to get 200 additional computers. In other words, when the
economy is at point A, the opportunity cost of 200 computers is 100 cars.

Notice that the production possibilities frontier in Figure 2.2 is bowed outward.
This means that the opportunity cost of cars in terms of computers depends on
how much of each good the economy is producing. When the economy is using
most of its resources to make cars, the production possibilities frontier is quite
steep. Because even workers and machines best suited to making computers are
being used to make cars, the economy gets a substantial increase in the number of
computers for each car it gives up. By contrast, when the economy is using most
of its resources to make computers, the production possibilities frontier is quite

flat. In this case, the resources best suited to making computers are already in the computer industry, and each car the economy gives up yields only a small increase in the number of computers.

The production possibilities frontier shows the tradeoff between the production of different goods at a given time, but the tradeoff can change over time. For example, if a technological advance in the computer industry raises the number of computers that a worker can produce per week, the economy can make more computers for any given number of cars. As a result, the production possibilities frontier shifts outward, as in Figure 2.3. Because of this economic growth, society might move production from point A to point E, enjoying more computers and more cars.

The production possibilities frontier simplifies a complex economy to highlight and clarify some basic ideas. We have used it to illustrate some of the concepts mentioned briefly in Chapter 1: scarcity, efficiency, tradeoffs, opportunity cost, and economic growth. As you study economics, these ideas will recur in various forms. The production possibilities frontier offers one simple way of thinking about them.

Microeconomics and Macroeconomics

Many subjects are studied on various levels. Consider biology, for example. Molecular biologists study the chemical compounds that make up living things. Cellular biologists study cells, which are made up of many chemical compounds and, at the same time, are themselves the building blocks of living organisms. Evolutionary biologists study the many varieties of animals and plants and how species change gradually over the centuries.

Economics is also studied on various levels. We can study the decisions of individual households and firms. Or we can study the interaction of households and firms in markets for specific goods and services. Or we can study the operation of the economy as a whole, which is just the sum of the activities of all these decision makers in all these markets.

microeconomics
the study of how households and firms make decisions and how they interact in markets

macroeconomics
the study of economy-wide phenomena, including inflation, unemployment, and economic growth

The field of economics is traditionally divided into two broad subfields. **Microeconomics** is the study of how households and firms make decisions and how they interact in specific markets. **Macroeconomics** is the study of economy-wide phenomena. A microeconomist might study the effects of rent control on housing in Toronto, the impact of foreign competition on the Canadian auto industry, or the effects of compulsory school attendance on workers' earnings. A macroeconomist might study the effects of borrowing by the federal government, the changes over time in the economy's rate of unemployment, or alternative policies to raise growth in national living standards.

Microeconomics and macroeconomics are closely intertwined. Because changes in the overall economy arise from the decisions of millions of individuals, it is impossible to understand macroeconomic developments without considering the associated microeconomic decisions. For example, a macroeconomist might study the effect of a cut in the federal income tax on the overall production of goods and services. To analyze this issue, he or she must consider how the tax cut affects the decisions of households about how much to spend on goods and services.

Despite the inherent link between microeconomics and macroeconomics, the two fields are distinct. In economics, as in biology, it may seem natural to begin

FIGURE 2.3

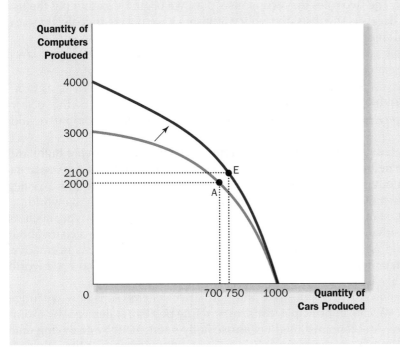

A Shift in the Production Possibilities Frontier

An economic advance in the computer industry shifts the production possibilities frontier outward, increasing the number of cars and computers the economy can produce.

with the smallest unit and build up. Yet doing so is neither necessary nor always the best way to proceed. Evolutionary biology is, in a sense, built upon molecular biology, since species are made up of molecules. Yet molecular biology and evolutionary biology are separate fields, each with its own questions and its own methods. Similarly, because microeconomics and macroeconomics address different questions, they sometimes take quite different approaches and are often taught in separate courses.

QuickQuiz   In what sense is economics like a science? • Draw a production possibilities frontier for a society that produces food and clothing. Show an efficient point, an inefficient point, and an infeasible point. Show the effects of a drought. • Define *microeconomics* and *macroeconomics.*

THE ECONOMIST AS POLICY ADVISER

Often economists are asked to explain the causes of economic events. Why, for example, is unemployment higher for teenagers than for older workers? Sometimes economists are asked to recommend policies to improve economic outcomes. What, for instance, should the government do to improve the economic well-being of teenagers? When economists are trying to explain the world, they are scientists. When they are trying to help improve it, they are policy advisers.

Positive versus Normative Analysis

To help clarify the two roles that economists play, we begin by examining the use of language. Because scientists and policy advisers have different goals, they use language in different ways.

For example, suppose that two people are discussing minimum-wage laws. Here are two statements you might hear:

POLLY: Minimum-wage laws cause unemployment.

NORMA: The government should raise the minimum wage.

Ignoring for now whether you agree with these statements, notice that Polly and Norma differ in what they are trying to do. Polly is speaking like a scientist: She is making a claim about how the world works. Norma is speaking like a policy adviser: She is making a claim about how she would like to change the world.

In general, statements about the world are of two types. One type, such as Polly's, is positive. **Positive statements** are descriptive. They make a claim about how the world *is*. A second type of statement, such as Norma's, is normative. **Normative statements** are prescriptive. They make a claim about how the world *ought to be*.

A key difference between positive and normative statements is how we judge their validity. We can, in principle, confirm or refute positive statements by examining evidence. An economist might evaluate Polly's statement by analyzing data on changes in minimum wages and changes in unemployment over time. By contrast, evaluating normative statements involves values as well as facts. Norma's statement cannot be judged using data alone. Deciding what is good or bad policy is not merely a matter of science. It also involves our views on ethics, religion, and political philosophy.

Of course, positive and normative statements may be related. Our positive views about how the world works affect our normative views about what policies are desirable. Polly's claim that the minimum-wage laws cause unemployment, if true, might lead us to reject Norma's conclusion that the government should raise the minimum wage. Yet our normative conclusions cannot come from positive analysis alone; they involve value judgments as well.

As you study economics, keep in mind the distinction between positive and normative statements. Much of economics just tries to explain how the economy works. Yet often the goal of economics is to improve how the economy works. When you hear economists making normative statements, you know they have crossed the line from scientist to policy adviser.

Economists in Ottawa

U.S. President Harry Truman once said that he wanted to find a one-armed economist. When he asked his economists for advice, they always answered, "On the one hand, . . . On the other hand, ..."

Truman was right in realizing that economists' advice is not always straightforward. This tendency is rooted in one of the ten principles of economics in Chapter 1: People face tradeoffs. Economists are aware that tradeoffs are involved in most policy decisions. A policy might increase efficiency at the cost of equity. It

positive statements
claims that attempt to describe the world as it is

normative statements
claims that attempt to prescribe how the world should be

might help future generations but hurt current generations. An economist who says that all policy decisions are easy is an economist not to be trusted.

The Government of Canada, like other governments, relies on the advice of economists. Economists at Finance Canada help design tax policy. Economists at Industry Canada help design and enforce Canada's antimonopoly laws. Economists at the departments of Foreign Affairs Canada and International Trade Canada help negotiate trade agreements with other countries. Economists at Human Resources and Skills Development Canada analyze data on workers and on those looking for work to help formulate labour-market policies. Economists at Environment Canada help design environmental regulations. The Canadian International Development Agency employs economists, both on staff and as consultants, to give advice on overseas development projects. Statistics Canada employs economists to collect the data analyzed by other economists and then give policy advice. The Bank of Canada, the quasi-independent institution that sets Canada's monetary policy, employs more than 200 economists to analyze financial markets and macroeconomic developments.

Economists outside the government also give policy advice. The C.D. Howe Institute, the Fraser Institute, the Institute for Research on Public Policy, the Canadian Centre for Policy Alternatives, and other independent organizations publish reports by economists that analyze current issues such as poverty, unemployment, and the deficit. These reports try to influence public opinion and give advice on government policies. The Internet Resources section just before the appendix to this chapter provides the URLs for the websites of these organizations.

The influence of economists on policy goes beyond their role as advisers: Their research and writings often affect policy indirectly. Economist John Maynard Keynes offered this observation:

> The ideas of economists and political philosophers, both when they are right and when they are wrong, are more powerful than is commonly understood. Indeed, the world is ruled by little else. Practical men, who believe themselves to be quite exempt from intellectual influences, are usually the slaves of some defunct economist. Madmen in authority, who hear voices in the air, are distilling their frenzy from some academic scribbler of a few years back.

Although these words were written in 1935, they remain true today. Indeed, the "academic scribbler" now influencing public policy is often Keynes himself.

QuickQuiz Give an example of a positive statement and an example of a normative statement. • Name three parts of government that regularly rely on advice from economists.

WHY ECONOMISTS DISAGREE

"If all economists were laid end to end, they would not reach a conclusion." This quip by George Bernard Shaw is revealing. Economists as a group are often criticized for giving conflicting advice to policymakers.

Why do economists so often appear to give conflicting advice to policymakers?

There are two basic reasons:

- Economists may disagree about the validity of alternative positive theories about how the world works.
- Economists may have different values and, therefore, different normative views about what policy should try to accomplish.

Let's discuss each of these reasons.

Differences in Scientific Judgments

Several centuries ago, astronomers debated whether the earth or the sun was at the centre of the solar system. More recently, meteorologists have debated whether the earth is experiencing global warming and, if so, why. Science is a search for understanding about the world around us. It is not surprising that as the search continues, scientists can disagree about the direction in which truth lies.

Economists often disagree for the same reason. Economics is a young science, and there is still much to be learned. Economists sometimes disagree because they have different hunches about the validity of alternative theories or about the size of important parameters.

For example, economists disagree about whether the government should levy taxes based on a household's income or its consumption (spending). Advocates of a switch from the current income tax to a consumption tax believe that the change would encourage households to save more, because income that is saved would not be taxed. Higher saving, in turn, would lead to more rapid growth in productivity and living standards. Advocates of the current income tax system believe that household saving would not respond much to a change in the tax laws. These two groups of economists hold different normative views about the tax system because they have different positive views about the responsiveness of saving to tax incentives.

Differences in Values

Suppose that Peter and Paul both take the same amount of water from the town well. To pay for maintaining the well, the town taxes its residents. Peter has income of $50 000 and is taxed $5000, or 10 percent of his income. Paul has income of $10 000 and is taxed $2000, or 20 percent of his income.

Is this policy fair? If not, who pays too much and who pays too little? Does it matter whether Paul's low income is due to a medical disability or to his decision to pursue a career in acting? Does it matter whether Peter's high income is due to a large inheritance or to his willingness to work long hours at a dreary job?

These are difficult questions on which people are likely to disagree. If the town hired two experts to study how the town should tax its residents to pay for the well, we would not be surprised if they offered conflicting advice.

This simple example shows why economists sometimes disagree about public policy. As we learned earlier in our discussion of normative and positive analysis, policies cannot be judged on scientific grounds alone. Economists give conflicting advice sometimes because they have different values. Perfecting the science of economics will not tell us whether it is Peter or Paul who pays too much.

Perception versus Reality

Because of differences in scientific judgments and differences in values, some disagreement among economists is inevitable. Yet one should not overstate the amount of disagreement. In many cases, economists do offer a united view.

Table 2.1 (p. 34) contains ten propositions about economic policy. In a survey of economists in business, government, and academia, these propositions were endorsed by an overwhelming majority of respondents. Most of these propositions would fail to command a similar consensus among the general public.

The first proposition in the table is about rent control. For reasons we will discuss later, almost all economists believe that rent control adversely affects the availability and quality of housing and is a very costly way of helping the most needy members of society. Nonetheless, some provincial governments choose to ignore the advice of economists and place ceilings on the rents that landlords may charge their tenants.

The second proposition in the table concerns tariffs and import quotas, two policies that restrict trade among nations. For reasons we will discuss more fully in later chapters, almost all economists oppose such barriers to free trade. Nonetheless, over the years, Parliament has often chosen to restrict the import of certain goods.

Why do policies such as rent control and trade barriers persist if the experts are united in their opposition? The reason may be that economists have not yet convinced the general public that these policies are undesirable. One purpose of this book is to make you understand the economist's view of these and other subjects and, perhaps, to persuade you that it is the right one.

QuickQuiz Why might economic advisers to the prime minister disagree about a question of policy?

LET'S GET GOING

The first two chapters of this book have introduced you to the ideas and methods of economics. We are now ready to get to work. In the next chapter we start learning in more detail the principles of economic behaviour and economic policy.

As you proceed through this book, you will be asked to draw on many of your intellectual skills. You might find it helpful to keep in mind some advice from the great economist John Maynard Keynes:

> The study of economics does not seem to require any specialized gifts of an unusually high order. Is it not . . . a very easy subject compared with the higher branches of philosophy or pure science? An easy subject, at which very few excel! The paradox finds its explanation, perhaps, in that the master-economist must possess a rare *combination* of gifts. He must be mathematician, historian, statesman, philosopher—in some degree. He must understand symbols and speak in words. He must contemplate the particular in terms of the general, and touch abstract and concrete in the same flight of thought. He must study the present in the light of the past for the purposes of the future. No part of

TABLE 2.1

Ten Propositions about Which Most Economists Agree

Source: Richard M. Alston, J.R. Kearl, and Michael B. Vaughn, "Is There Consensus among Economists in the 1990s?" *American Economic Review* (May 1992): 203–209. Reprinted by permission.

Proposition (and percentage of economists who agree)

1. A ceiling on rents reduces the quantity and quality of housing available. (93%)
2. Tariffs and import quotas usually reduce general economic welfare. (93%)
3. Flexible and floating exchange rates offer an effective international monetary arrangement. (90%)
4. Fiscal policy (e.g., tax cut and/or government expenditure increase) has a significant stimulative impact on a less than fully employed economy. (90%)
5. If the federal budget is to be balanced, it should be done over the business cycle rather than yearly. (85%)
6. Cash payments increase the welfare of recipients to a greater degree than do transfers-in-kind of equal cash value. (84%)
7. A large federal budget deficit has an adverse effect on the economy. (83%)
8. A minimum wage increases unemployment among young and unskilled workers. (79%)
9. The government should restructure the welfare system along the lines of a "negative income tax." (79%)
10. Effluent taxes and marketable pollution permits represent a better approach to pollution control than imposition of pollution ceilings. (78%)

man's nature or his institutions must lie entirely outside his regard. He must be purposeful and disinterested in a simultaneous mood; as aloof and incorruptible as an artist, yet sometimes as near the earth as a politician.

It is a tall order. But with practice, you will become more and more accustomed to thinking like an economist.

SUMMARY

- Economists try to address their subject with a scientist's objectivity. Like all scientists, they make appropriate assumptions and build simplified models in order to understand the world around them. Two simple economic models are the circular-flow diagram and the production possibilities frontier.

- The field of economics is divided into two subfields: microeconomics and macroeconomics. Microeconomists study decision making by households and firms and the interaction among households and firms in the marketplace. Macroeconomists study the forces and trends that affect the economy as a whole.

- A positive statement is an assertion about how the world *is*. A normative statement is an assertion about how the world *ought to be*. When economists make normative statements, they are acting more as policy advisers than scientists.

- Economists who advise policymakers offer conflicting advice either because of differences in scientific judgments or because of differences in values. At other times, economists are united in the advice they offer, but policymakers may choose to ignore it.

KEY CONCEPTS

circular-flow diagram, p. 24
production possibilities frontier,
    p. 26

microeconomics, p. 28
macroeconomics, p. 28
positive statements, p. 30

normative statements, p. 30

QUESTIONS FOR REVIEW

1. How is economics like a science?

2. Why do economists make assumptions?

3. Should an economic model describe reality exactly?

4. Draw and explain a production possibilities frontier for an economy that produces milk and cookies. What happens to this frontier if disease kills half of the economy's cow population?

5. Use a production possibilities frontier to describe the idea of "efficiency."

6. What are the two subfields into which economics is divided? Explain what each subfield studies.

7. What is the difference between a positive and a normative statement? Give an example of each.

8. What is the Bank of Canada?

9. Why do economists sometimes offer conflicting advice to policymakers?

PROBLEMS AND APPLICATIONS

1. Describe some unusual language used in one of the other fields that you are studying. Why are these special terms useful?

2. One common assumption in economics is that the products of different firms in the same industry are indistinguishable. For each of the following industries, discuss whether this is a reasonable assumption.
   a. steel
   b. novels
   c. wheat
   d. fast food

3. Draw a circular-flow diagram. Identify the parts of the model that correspond to the flow of goods and services and the flow of dollars for each of the following activities.
   a. Sam pays a storekeeper $1 for a litre of milk.
   b. Sally earns $7 per hour working at a fast-food restaurant.
   c. Serena spends $10 to see a movie.
   d. Stuart earns $10 000 from his 10 percent ownership of Acme Industrial.

4. Imagine a society that produces military goods and consumer goods, which we'll call "guns" and "butter."

a. Draw a production possibilities frontier for guns and butter. Explain why it most likely has a bowed-out shape.

b. Show a point that is impossible for the economy to achieve. Show a point that is feasible but inefficient.

c. Imagine that the society has two political parties, called the Hawks (who want a strong military) and the Doves (who want a smaller military). Show a point on your production possibilities frontier that the Hawks might choose and a point the Doves might choose.

d. Imagine that an aggressive neighbouring country reduces the size of its military. As a result, both the Hawks and the Doves reduce their desired production of guns by the same amount. Which party would get the bigger "peace dividend," measured by the increase in butter production? Explain.

5. The first principle of economics discussed in Chapter 1 is that people face tradeoffs. Use a production possibilities frontier to illustrate

society's tradeoff between a clean environment and the quantity of industrial output. What do you suppose determines the shape and position of the frontier? Show what happens to the frontier if engineers develop an automobile engine with almost no emissions.

6. Classify the following topics as relating to microeconomics or macroeconomics.
   a. a family's decision about how much income to save
   b. the effect of government regulations on auto emissions
   c. the impact of higher national saving on economic growth
   d. a firm's decision about how many workers to hire
   e. the relationship between the inflation rate and changes in the quantity of money

7. Classify each of the following statements as positive or normative. Explain.
   a. Society faces a short-run tradeoff between inflation and unemployment.
   b. A reduction in the rate of growth of money will reduce the rate of inflation.
   c. The Bank of Canada should reduce the rate of growth of money.
   d. Society ought to require welfare recipients to look for jobs.
   e. Lower tax rates encourage more work and more saving.

8. Classify each of the statements in Table 2.1 as positive, normative, or ambiguous. Explain.

9. If you were prime minister, would you be more interested in your economic advisers' positive views or their normative views? Why?

10. The C.D. Howe Institute, the Fraser Institute, the Institute for Research on Public Policy, and the Canadian Centre for Policy Alternatives regularly publish reports containing economic commentary and policy recommendations. Find a recent publication from one of these organizations at your library (or on its website; see the Internet Resources section at the end of this Problems and Applications section) and read about an issue that interests you. Summarize the discussion of this issue and the author's proposed policy.

11. Who is the current governor of the Bank of Canada? Who is the current minister of Finance Canada? Who are the current ministers of Foreign Affairs Canada and International Trade Canada? Are they economists? Does it matter?

12. Would you expect economists to disagree less about public policy as time goes on? Why or why not? Can their differences be completely eliminated? Why or why not?

13. Look up one of the websites listed in the Internet Resources section on p. 37. What recent economic trends or issues are addressed there?

INTERNET RESOURCES

Here are the websites of some of the organizations that hire economists and influence economic policy.

Bank of Canada	http://www.bankofcanada.ca
Canadian Centre for Policy Alternatives	http://www.policyalternatives.ca
C.D. Howe Institute	http://www.cdhowe.org
Environment Canada	http://www.ec.gc.ca
Finance Canada	http://www.fin.gc.ca
Foreign Affairs Canada	http://www.fac-aec.gc.ca
Fraser Institute	http://www.fraserinstitute.ca
Human Resources and Skills Development Canada	http://www.hrsdc.gc.ca
Industry Canada	http://www.ic.gc.ca
Institute for Research on Public Policy	http://www.irpp.org
International Trade Canada	http://www.itcan-cican.gc.ca
Social Development Canada	http://www.sdc.gc.ca
Statistics Canada	http://www.statcan.ca

http://   For more study tools, please visit http://www.mankiw3e.nelson.com.

APPENDIX
Graphing: A Brief Review

Many of the concepts that economists study can be expressed with numbers—the price of bananas, the quantity of bananas sold, the cost of growing bananas, and so on. Often these economic variables are related to one another; for example, when the price of bananas rises, people buy fewer bananas. One way of expressing the relationships among variables is with graphs.

Graphs serve two purposes. First, when developing economic theories, graphs offer a way to visually express ideas that might be less clear if described with equations or words. Second, when analyzing economic data, graphs provide a way of finding how variables are in fact related in the world. Whether we are working with theory or with data, graphs provide a lens through which a recognizable forest emerges from a multitude of trees.

Numerical information can be expressed graphically in many ways, just as a thought can be expressed in words in many ways. A good writer chooses words that will make an argument clear, a description pleasing, or a scene dramatic. An effective economist chooses the type of graph that best suits the purpose.

In this appendix we discuss how economists use graphs to study the mathematical relationships among variables. We also discuss some of the pitfalls that can arise in the use of graphical methods.

Graphs of a Single Variable

Three common types of graphs are shown in Figure 2A.1. The *pie chart* in panel (a) shows how total income in Canada is divided among the sources of income, including wages and salaries, corporation profits, and so on. A slice of the pie represents each source's share of the total. The *bar graph* in panel (b) compares income for three countries. The height of each bar represents the average income in each country. The *time-series graph* in panel (c) traces the Canadian unemployment rate over time. The height of the line shows the unemployment rate in each month. You have probably seen similar graphs in newspapers and magazines.

Graphs of Two Variables: The Coordinate System

Although the three graphs in Figure 2A.1 are useful in showing how a variable changes over time or across individuals, such graphs are limited in how much they can tell us. These graphs display information only on a single variable. Economists are often concerned with the relationships between variables. Thus, they need to be able to display two variables on a single graph. The *coordinate system* makes this possible.

Suppose you want to examine the relationship between study time and grade point average. For each student in your class, you could record a pair of numbers: hours per week spent studying and grade point average. These numbers could then be placed in parentheses as an *ordered pair* and appear as a single point on the graph. Albert E., for instance, is represented by the ordered pair (25 hours/week,

Types of Graphs

The pie chart in panel (a) shows how Canadian 2002 national income is derived from various sources. The bar graph in panel (b) compares the average income in three countries. The time-series graph in panel (c) shows the unemployment rate in Canada from January 2000 to August 2003.

Sources: Panel (a): Statistics Canada, http://statcan.ca/Daily/English/030829/d030829a.htm; Panel (b): World Bank; Panel (c): Statistics Canada, "Latest Release from the Labour Force Survey," September 5, 2003, www.statcan.ca/english/Subjects/Labour/LFS/lfs-en.htm.

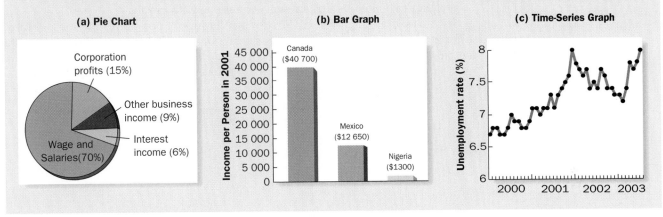

3.5 GPA), while his "what-me-worry?" classmate Alfred E. is represented by the ordered pair (5 hours/week, 2.0 GPA).

We can graph these ordered pairs on a two-dimensional grid. The first number in each ordered pair, called the *x-coordinate,* tells us the horizontal location of the point. The second number, called the *y-coordinate,* tells us the vertical location of the point. The point with both an *x*-coordinate and a *y*-coordinate of zero is known as the *origin.* The two coordinates in the ordered pair tell us where the point is located in relation to the origin: *x* units to the right of the origin and *y* units above it.

Figure 2A.2 (p. 40) graphs grade point average against study time for Albert E., Alfred E., and their classmates. This type of graph is called a *scatterplot* because it plots scattered points. Looking at this graph, we immediately notice that points farther to the right (indicating more study time) also tend to be higher (indicating a better grade point average). Because study time and grade point average typically move in the same direction, we say that these two variables have a *positive correlation.* By contrast, if we were to graph party time and grades, we would likely find that higher party time is associated with lower grades; because these variables typically move in opposite directions, we would call this a *negative correlation.* In either case, the coordinate system makes the correlation between the two variables easy to see.

Curves in the Coordinate System

Students who study more do tend to get higher grades, but other factors also influence a student's grade. Previous preparation is an important factor, for

FIGURE 2A.2

Using the Coordinate System

Grade point average is measured on the vertical axis and study time on the horizontal axis. Albert E., Alfred E., and their classmates are represented by various points. We can see from the graph that students who study more tend to get higher grades.

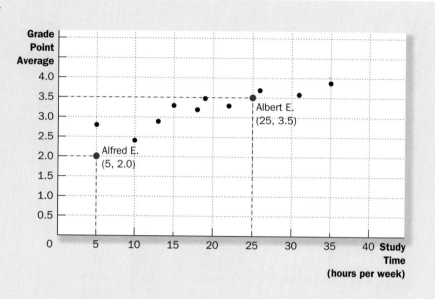

instance, as are talent, attention from teachers, and even eating a good breakfast. A scatterplot like Figure 2A.2 does not attempt to isolate the effect that study has on grades from the effects of other variables. Often, however, economists prefer looking at how one variable affects another holding everything else constant.

To see how this is done, let's consider one of the most important graphs in economics—the *demand curve*. The demand curve traces the effect of a good's price on the quantity of the good consumers want to buy. Before showing a demand curve, however, consider Table 2A.1, which shows how the number of novels that Emma buys depends on her income and on the price of novels. When novels are cheap, Emma buys them in large quantities. As they become more expensive, she borrows books from the library instead of buying them or chooses to go to the movies instead of reading. Similarly, at any given price, Emma buys more novels when she has a higher income. That is, when her income increases, she spends part of the additional income on novels and part on other goods.

We now have three variables—the price of novels, income, and the number of novels purchased—which is more than we can represent in two dimensions. To put the information from Table 2A.1 in graphical form, we need to hold one of the three variables constant and trace the relationship between the other two. Because the demand curve represents the relationship between price and quantity demanded, we hold Emma's income constant and show how the number of novels she buys varies with the price of novels.

Suppose that Emma's income is $30 000 per year. If we place the number of novels Emma purchases on the *x*-axis and the price of novels on the *y*-axis, we can graphically represent the middle column of Table 2A.1. When the points that represent these entries from the table—5 novels, $10; 9 novels, $9; and so on—are connected, they form a line. This line, pictured in Figure 2A.3, is known as Emma's demand curve for novels; it tells us how many novels Emma purchases at any

	Income		
Price	$20 000	$30 000	$40 000
$10	2 novels	5 novels	8 novels
9	6	9	12
8	10	13	16
7	14	17	20
6	18	21	24
5	22	25	28
	Demand curve, D_3	Demand curve, D_1	Demand curve, D_2

Novels Purchased by Emma

This table shows the number of novels Emma buys at various incomes and prices. For any given level of income, the data on price and quantity demanded can be graphed to produce Emma's demand curve for novels, as shown in Figures 2A.3 and 2A.4.

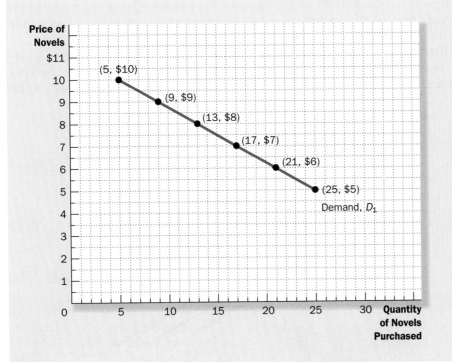

Demand Curve

The line D_1 shows how Emma's purchases of novels depend on the price of novels when her income is held constant. Because the price and the quantity demanded are negatively related, the demand curve slopes downward.

given price. The demand curve is downward sloping, indicating that a higher price reduces the quantity of novels demanded. Because the quantity of novels demanded and the price move in opposite directions, we say that the two variables are *negatively related.* (Conversely, when two variables move in the same direction, the curve relating them is upward sloping, and we say the variables are *positively related.*)

Now suppose that Emma's income rises to $40 000 per year. At any given price, Emma will purchase more novels than she did at her previous level of income. Just as earlier we drew Emma's demand curve for novels using the entries from the middle column of Table 2A.1, we now draw a new demand curve using the entries from the right-hand column of the table. This new demand curve (curve D_2) is pictured alongside the old one (curve D_1) in Figure 2A.4; the new curve is a similar line drawn farther to the right. We therefore say that Emma's demand curve for novels *shifts* to the right when her income increases. Likewise, if Emma's income were to fall to $20 000 per year, she would buy fewer novels at any given price and her demand curve would shift to the left (to curve D_3).

In economics, it is important to distinguish between *movements along a curve* and *shifts of a curve*. As we can see from Figure 2A.3, if Emma earns $30 000 per year and novels cost $8 apiece, she will purchase 13 novels per year. If the price of novels falls to $7, Emma will increase her purchases of novels to 17 per year. The demand curve, however, stays fixed in the same place. Emma still buys the same number of novels *at each price,* but as the price falls she moves along her demand curve from left to right. By contrast, if the price of novels remains fixed at $8 but her income rises to $40 000, Emma increases her purchases of novels from 13 to 16 per year. Because Emma buys more novels *at each price,* her demand curve shifts out, as shown in Figure 2A.4.

There is a simple way to tell when it is necessary to shift a curve. When a variable that is not named on either axis changes, the curve shifts. Income is on neither the *x*-axis nor the *y*-axis of the graph, so when Emma's income changes, her

---

FIGURE 2A.4

Shifting Demand Curves

The location of Emma's demand curve for novels depends on how much income she earns. The more she earns, the more novels she will purchase at any given price, and the farther to the right her demand curve will lie. Curve D_1 represents Emma's original demand curve when her income is $30 000 per year. If her income rises to $40 000 per year, her demand curve shifts to D_2. If her income falls to $20 000 per year, her demand curve shifts to D_3.

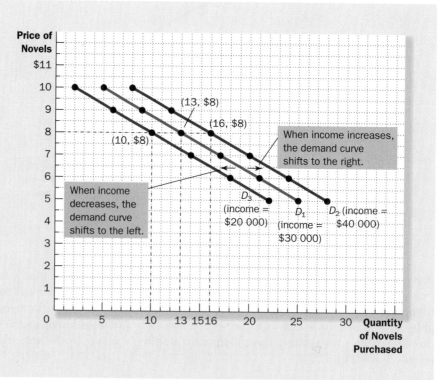

demand curve must shift. Any change that affects Emma's purchasing habits besides a change in the price of novels will result in a shift in her demand curve. If, for instance, the public library closes and Emma must buy all the books she wants to read, she will demand more novels at each price, and her demand curve will shift to the right. Or, if the price of movies falls and Emma spends more time at the movies and less time reading, she will demand fewer novels at each price, and her demand curve will shift to the left. By contrast, when a variable on an axis of the graph changes, the curve does not shift. We read the change as a movement along the curve.

Slope

One question we might want to ask about Emma is how much her purchasing habits respond to price. Look at the demand curve pictured in Figure 2A.5. If this curve is very steep, Emma purchases nearly the same number of novels regardless of whether they are cheap or expensive. If this curve is much flatter, Emma purchases many fewer novels when the price rises. To answer questions about how much one variable responds to changes in another variable, we can use the concept of *slope*.

The slope of a line is the ratio of the vertical distance covered to the horizontal distance covered as we move along the line. This definition is usually written out in mathematical symbols as follows:

$$\text{slope} = \frac{\Delta y}{\Delta x}$$

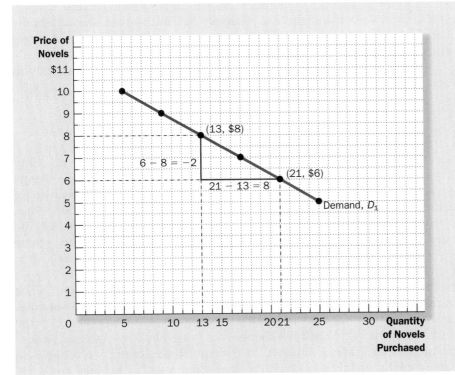

Calculating the Slope of a Line

To calculate the slope of the demand curve, we can look at the changes in the x- and y-coordinates as we move from the point (21 novels, $6) to the point (13 novels, $8). The slope of the line is the ratio of the change in the y-coordinate (−2) to the change in the x-coordinate (+8), which equals −1/4.

where the Greek letter Δ (delta) stands for the change in a variable. In other words, the slope of a line is equal to the "rise" (change in y) divided by the "run" (change in x). The slope will be a small positive number for a fairly flat upward-sloping line, a large positive number for a steep upward-sloping line, and a negative number for a downward-sloping line. A horizontal line has a slope of zero because in this case the y-variable never changes; a vertical line is said to have an infinite slope because the y-variable can take any value without the x-variable changing at all.

What is the slope of Emma's demand curve for novels? First of all, because the curve slopes down, we know the slope will be negative. To calculate a numerical value for the slope, we must choose two points on the line. With Emma's income at $30 000, she will purchase 21 novels at a price of $6 or 13 novels at a price of $8. When we apply the slope formula, we are concerned with the change between these two points; in other words, we are concerned with the difference between them, which lets us know that we will have to subtract one set of values from the other, as follows:

$$\text{slope} = \frac{\Delta y}{\Delta x} = \frac{\text{first } y\text{-coordinate} - \text{second } y\text{-coordinate}}{\text{first } x\text{-coordinate} - \text{second } x\text{-coordinate}} = \frac{6 - 8}{21 - 13} = \frac{-2}{8} = \frac{-1}{4}$$

Figure 2A.5 shows graphically how this calculation works. Try computing the slope of Emma's demand curve using two different points. You should get exactly the same result, $-1/4$. One of the properties of a straight line is that it has the same slope everywhere. This is not true of other types of curves, which are steeper in some places than in others.

The slope of Emma's demand curve tells us something about how responsive her purchases are to changes in the price. A small slope (a number close to zero) means that Emma's demand curve is relatively flat; in this case, she adjusts the number of novels she buys substantially in response to a price change. A larger slope (a number farther from zero) means that Emma's demand curve is relatively steep; in this case, she adjusts the number of novels she buys only slightly in response to a price change.

Cause and Effect

Economists often use graphs to advance an argument about how the economy works. In other words, they use graphs to argue about how one set of events *causes* another set of events. With a graph like the demand curve, there is no doubt about cause and effect. Because we are varying price and holding all other variables constant, we know that changes in the price of novels cause changes in the quantity Emma demands. Remember, however, that our demand curve came from a hypothetical example. When graphing data from the real world, it is often more difficult to establish how one variable affects another.

The first problem is that it is difficult to hold everything else constant when measuring how one variable affects another. If we are not able to hold variables constant, we might decide that one variable on our graph is causing changes in the other variable, when actually those changes are caused by a third *omitted variable* not pictured on the graph. Even if we have identified the correct two variables to look at, we might run into a second problem—*reverse causality*. In other words, we might decide that A causes B when in fact B causes A. The omitted-variable and reverse-causality traps require us to proceed with caution when using graphs to draw conclusions about causes and effects.

Omitted Variables   To see how omitting a variable can lead to a deceptive graph, let's consider an example. Imagine that the government, spurred by public concern about the large number of deaths from cancer, commissions an exhaustive study from Big Brother Statistical Services, Inc. Big Brother examines many of the items found in people's homes to see which of them are associated with the risk of cancer. Big Brother reports a strong relationship between two variables: the number of cigarette lighters that a household owns and the probability that someone in the household will develop cancer. Figure 2A.6 shows this relationship.

What should we make of this result? Big Brother advises a quick policy response. It recommends that the government discourage the ownership of cigarette lighters by taxing their sale. It also recommends that the government require warning labels: "Big Brother has determined that this lighter is dangerous to your health."

In judging the validity of Big Brother's analysis, one question is paramount: Has Big Brother held constant every relevant variable except the one under consideration? If the answer is no, the results are suspect. An easy explanation for Figure 2A.6 is that people who own more cigarette lighters are more likely to smoke cigarettes and that cigarettes, not lighters, cause cancer. If Figure 2A.6 does not hold constant the amount of smoking, it does not tell us the true effect of owning a cigarette lighter.

This story illustrates an important principle: When you see a graph being used to support an argument about cause and effect, it is important to ask whether the movements of an omitted variable could explain the results you see.

Reverse Causality   Economists can also make mistakes about causality by misreading its direction. To see how this is possible, suppose the Association of Canadian Anarchists commissions a study of crime in Canada and arrives at Figure 2A.7 (p. 46), which plots the number of violent crimes per thousand people in major cities against the number of police officers per thousand people. The

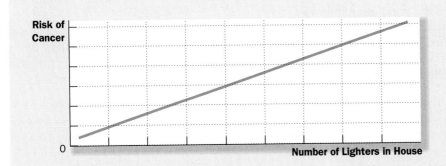

FIGURE 2A.6

Graph with an Omitted Variable

The upward-sloping curve shows that members of households with more cigarette lighters are more likely to develop cancer. Yet we should not conclude that ownership of lighters causes cancer, because the graph does not take into account the number of cigarettes smoked.

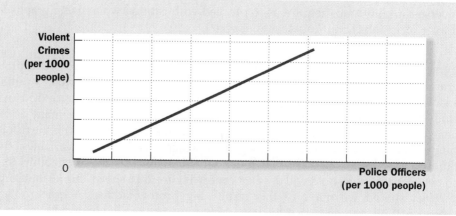

FIGURE 2A.7

Graph Suggesting Reverse Causality

The upward-sloping curve shows that cities with a higher concentration of police are more dangerous. Yet the graph does not tell us whether police cause crime or crime-plagued cities hire more police.

anarchists note the curve's upward slope and argue that because police increase rather than decrease the amount of urban violence, law enforcement should be abolished.

If we could run a controlled experiment, we would avoid the danger of reverse causality. To run an experiment, we would set the number of police officers in different cities randomly and then examine the correlation between police and crime. Figure 2A.7, however, is not based on such an experiment. We simply observe that more dangerous cities have more police officers. The explanation for this may be that more dangerous cities hire more police. In other words, rather than police causing crime, crime may cause police. Nothing in the graph itself allows us to establish the direction of causality.

It might seem that an easy way to determine the direction of causality is to examine which variable moves first. If we see crime increase and then the police force expand, we reach one conclusion. If we see the police force expand and then crime increase, we reach the other. Yet there is also a flaw with this approach: Often people change their behaviour not in response to a change in their present conditions but in response to a change in their *expectations* of future conditions. A city that expects a major crime wave in the future, for instance, might well hire more police now. This problem is even easier to see in the case of babies and minivans. Couples often buy a minivan in anticipation of the birth of a child. The minivan comes before the baby, but we wouldn't want to conclude that the sale of minivans causes the population to grow!

There is no complete set of rules that says when it is appropriate to draw causal conclusions from graphs. Yet just keeping in mind that cigarette lighters don't cause cancer (omitted variable) and minivans don't cause larger families (reverse causality) will keep you from falling for many faulty economic arguments.

© PHOTODISC

3

Learning Objectives

In this chapter, you will ...

- Consider how everyone can benefit when people trade with one another
- Learn the meaning of *absolute advantage* and *comparative advantage*
- See how comparative advantage explains the gains from trade
- Apply the theory of comparative advantage to everyday life and national policy

INTERDEPENDENCE AND THE GAINS FROM TRADE

Consider your typical day. You wake up in the morning, and you pour yourself juice from oranges grown in Florida and coffee from beans grown in Brazil. Over breakfast, you watch a news program broadcast from Toronto on your television made in Japan. You get dressed in clothes made of cotton grown in Georgia and sewn in factories in Thailand. You drive to class in a car made of parts manufactured in more than a dozen countries around the world. Then you open up your economics textbook written by authors living in Massachusetts, Alberta, and Quebec, published by a company located in Ontario, and printed on paper made from trees grown in New Brunswick.

Every day you rely on many people from around the world, most of whom you do not know, to provide you with the goods and services that you enjoy. Such interdependence is possible because people trade with one another. Those people who provide you with goods and services are not acting out of generosity or concern for your welfare. Nor is some government agency directing them to make what you want and to give it to you. Instead, people provide you and other consumers with the goods and services they produce because they get something in return.

In subsequent chapters we will examine how our economy coordinates the activities of millions of people with varying tastes and abilities. As a starting point for this analysis, here we consider the reasons for economic interdependence. One of the ten principles of economics highlighted in Chapter 1 is that trade can make everyone better off. This principle explains why people trade with their neighbours and why nations trade with other nations. In this chapter we examine this principle more closely. What exactly do people gain when they trade with one another? Why do people choose to become interdependent?

A PARABLE FOR THE MODERN ECONOMY

To understand why people choose to depend on others for goods and services and how this choice improves their lives, let's look at a simple economy. Imagine that there are two goods in the world—meat and potatoes. And there are two people in the world—a cattle rancher and a potato farmer—each of whom would like to eat both meat and potatoes.

The gains from trade are most obvious if the rancher can produce only meat and the farmer can produce only potatoes. In one scenario, the rancher and the farmer could choose to have nothing to do with each other. But after several months of eating beef roasted, boiled, broiled, and grilled, the rancher might decide that self-sufficiency is not all it's cracked up to be. The farmer, who has been eating potatoes mashed, fried, baked, and scalloped, would likely agree. It is easy to see that trade would allow them to enjoy greater variety: Each could then have a steak with a baked potato.

Although this scenario illustrates most simply how everyone can benefit from trade, the gains would be similar if the rancher and the farmer were each capable of producing the other good, but only at great cost. Suppose, for example, that the potato farmer is able to raise cattle and produce meat, but that he is not very good at it. Similarly, suppose that the cattle rancher is able to grow potatoes, but that her land is not very well suited for it. In this case, it would be easy to show that the farmer and the rancher can each benefit by specializing in what he or she does best and then trading with the other.

The gains from trade are less obvious, however, when one person is better at producing *every* good. For example, suppose that the rancher is better at raising cattle *and* better at growing potatoes than the farmer. In this case, should the rancher or farmer choose to remain self-sufficient? Or is there still reason for them to trade with each other? To answer this question, we need to look more closely at the factors that affect such a decision.

Production Possibilities

Suppose that the farmer and the rancher each work 8 hours a day and can devote this time to growing potatoes, raising cattle, or a combination of the two. Table 3.1 shows the amount of time each person requires to produce 1 kg of each good. The farmer can produce a kilogram of potatoes in 15 minutes and a kilogram of meat in 60 minutes. The rancher, who is more productive in both activities, can produce a kilogram of potatoes in 10 minutes and a kilogram of meat in 20 minutes. The last columns in Table 3.1 show the amounts of meat or potatoes the farmer and rancher can produce if they work an 8-hour day, producing only that good.

Panel (a) of Figure 3.1 illustrates the amounts of meat and potatoes that the farmer can produce. If the farmer devotes all 8 hours of his time to potatoes, he

TABLE 3.1

	Minutes Needed to Make 1 kg of:		Amount of Meat or Potatoes Produced in 8 Hours	
	Meat	Potatoes	Meat	Potatoes
Farmer	60 min/kg	15 min/kg	8 kg	32 kg
Rancher	20 min/kg	10 min/kg	24 kg	48 kg

The Production Opportunities of the Farmer and the Rancher

FIGURE 3.1

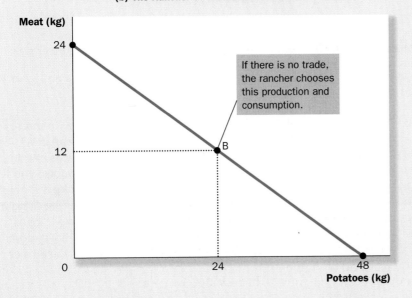

(a) The Farmer's Production Possibilities Frontier

Meat (kg)

If there is no trade, the farmer chooses this production and consumption.

8

4 · · · · · · · A

0 · · · · · · · 16 · · · · · · · 32 · · · Potatoes (kg)

(b) The Rancher's Production Possibilities Frontier

Meat (kg)

24

If there is no trade, the rancher chooses this production and consumption.

12 · · · · · · · B

0 · · · · · · · 24 · · · · · · · 48

Potatoes (kg)

The Production Possibilities Frontier

Panel (a) shows the combinations of meat and potatoes that the farmer can produce. Panel (b) shows the combinations of meat and potatoes that the rancher can produce. Both production possibilities frontiers are derived from Table 3.1 and the assumption that the farmer and rancher each work 8 hours a day.

produces 32 kg of potatoes (measured on the horizontal axis) and no meat. If he devotes all his time to meat, he produces 8 kg of meat (measured on the vertical axis) and no potatoes. If the farmer divides his time equally between the two activities, spending 4 hours on each, he produces 16 kg of potatoes and 4 kg of meat. The figure shows these three possible outcomes and all others in between.

This graph is the farmer's production possibilities frontier. As we discussed in Chapter 2, a production possibilities frontier shows the various mixes of output that an economy can produce. It illustrates one of the ten principles of economics in Chapter 1: People face tradeoffs. Here the farmer faces a tradeoff between producing meat and producing potatoes. You may recall that the production possibilities frontier in Chapter 2 was drawn bowed out; in that case, the tradeoff between the two goods depended on the amounts being produced. Here, however, the farmer's technology for producing meat and potatoes (as summarized in Table 3.1) allows him to switch between one good and the other at a constant rate. In this case, the production possibilities frontier is a straight line.

Panel (b) of Figure 3.1 shows the production possibilities frontier for the rancher. If the rancher devotes all 8 hours of her time to potatoes, she produces 48 kg of potatoes and no meat. If she devotes all her time to meat, she produces 24 kg of meat and no potatoes. If the rancher divides her time equally, spending 4 hours on each activity, she produces 24 kg of potatoes and 12 kg of meat. Once again, the production possibilities frontier shows all the possible outcomes.

If the farmer and rancher choose to be self-sufficient, rather than trade with each other, then each consumes exactly what he or she produces. In this case, the production possibilities frontier is also the consumption possibilities frontier. That is, without trade, Figure 3.1 shows the possible combinations of meat and potatoes that the farmer and rancher can each consume.

Although these production possibilities frontiers are useful in showing the tradeoffs that the farmer and rancher face, they do not tell us what the farmer and rancher will actually choose to do. To determine their choices, we need to know the tastes of the farmer and the rancher. Let's suppose they choose the combinations identified by points A and B in Figure 3.1: The farmer produces and consumes 16 kg of potatoes and 4 kg of meat, while the rancher produces and consumes 24 kg of potatoes and 12 kg of meat.

Specialization and Trade

After several years of eating combination B, the rancher gets an idea and goes to talk to the farmer:

RANCHER: Farmer, my friend, have I got a deal for you! I know how to improve life for both of us. I think you should stop producing meat altogether and devote all your time to growing potatoes. According to my calculations, if you work 8 hours a day growing potatoes, you'll produce 32 kg of potatoes. If you give me 15 of those 32 kg, I'll give you 5 kg of meat in return. In the end, you'll get to eat 17 kg of potatoes and 5 kg of meat, instead of the 16 kg of potatoes and 4 kg of meat you now get. If you go along with my plan, you'll have more of *both* foods. [To illustrate her point, the rancher shows the farmer panel (a) of Figure 3.2.]

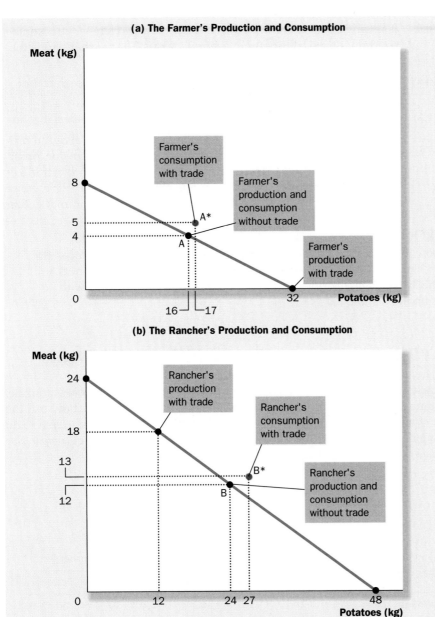

FIGURE 3.2

(a) The Farmer's Production and Consumption

Meat (kg)

Farmer's consumption with trade

Farmer's production and consumption without trade

Farmer's production with trade

A*

A

8

5
4

0   16   17   32   Potatoes (kg)

(b) The Rancher's Production and Consumption

Meat (kg)

Rancher's production with trade

Rancher's consumption with trade

Rancher's production and consumption without trade

B*

B

24

18

13
12

0   12   24 27   48   Potatoes (kg)

How Trade Expands the Set of Consumption Opportunities

The proposed trade between the farmer and the rancher offers each of them a combination of meat and potatoes that would be impossible in the absence of trade. In panel (a), the farmer gets to consume at point A* rather than point A. In panel (b), the rancher gets to consume at point B* rather than point B. Trade allows each to consume more meat and more potatoes.

FARMER: *(sounding skeptical)* That seems like a good deal for me. But I don't understand why you are offering it. If the deal is so good for me, it can't be good for you too.

RANCHER: Oh, but it is! Suppose I spend 6 hours a day raising cattle and 2 hours growing potatoes. Then I can produce 18 kg of meat and 12 kg of potatoes. After I give you 5 kg of my meat in exchange for 15 kg of your potatoes, I'll end up with 13 kg of meat and 27 kg of potatoes. So I'll also consume more of both foods than I do now. [She points out panel (b) of Figure 3.2.]

FARMER: I don't know. . . . This sounds too good to be true.

RANCHER: It's really not as complicated as it seems at first. Here—I've summarized my proposal for you in a simple table. [The rancher hands the farmer a copy of Table 3.2.]

FARMER: *(after pausing to study the table)* These calculations seem correct, but I'm puzzled. How can this deal make us both better off?

RANCHER: We can both benefit because trade allows each of us to specialize in doing what we do best. You will spend more time growing potatoes and less time raising cattle. I will spend more time raising cattle and less time growing potatoes. As a result of specialization and trade, each of us can consume more meat and more potatoes without working any more hours.

QuickQuiz Draw an example of a production possibilities frontier for Robinson Crusoe, a shipwrecked sailor who spends his time gathering coconuts and catching fish. Does this frontier limit Crusoe's consumption of coconuts and fish if he lives by himself? Does he face the same limits if he can trade with natives on the island?

THE PRINCIPLE OF COMPARATIVE ADVANTAGE

The rancher's explanation of the gains from trade, though correct, poses a puzzle: If the rancher is better at both raising cattle and growing potatoes, how can the farmer ever specialize in doing what he does best? The farmer doesn't seem to do anything best. To solve this puzzle, we need to look at the principle of *comparative advantage*.

TABLE 3.2

The Gains from Trade: A Summary

	Farmer		Rancher	
	Meat	Potatoes	Meat	Potatoes
Without Trade:				
Production and Consumption	4 kg	16 kg	12 kg	24 kg
With Trade:				
Production	0 kg	32 kg	18 kg	12 kg
Trade	Gets 5 kg	Gives 15 kg	Gives 5 kg	Gets 15 kg
Consumption	5 kg	17 kg	13 kg	27 kg
Gains from Trade:				
Increase in Consumption	+1 kg	+1 kg	+1 kg	+3 kg

As a first step in developing this principle, consider the following question: In our example, who can produce potatoes at lower cost—the farmer or the rancher? There are two possible answers, and in these two answers lie the solution to our puzzle and the key to understanding the gains from trade.

Absolute Advantage

One way to answer the question about the cost of producing potatoes is to compare the inputs required by the two producers. Economists use the term **absolute advantage** when comparing the productivity of one person, firm, or nation to that of another. The producer that requires a smaller quantity of inputs to produce a good is said to have an absolute advantage in producing that good.

In our example, the rancher has an absolute advantage both in producing meat and in producing potatoes, because she requires less time than the farmer to produce a unit of either good. The rancher needs to input only 20 minutes to produce a kilogram of meat, whereas the farmer needs 60 minutes. Similarly, the rancher needs only 10 minutes to produce a kilogram of potatoes, whereas the farmer needs 15 minutes. Based on this information, we can conclude that the rancher has the lower cost of producing potatoes, if we measure cost in terms of the quantity of inputs.

absolute advantage
the comparison among producers of a good according to their productivity

Opportunity Cost and Comparative Advantage

There is another way to look at the cost of producing potatoes. Rather than comparing inputs required, we can compare the opportunity costs. Recall from Chapter 1 that the **opportunity cost** of some item is what we give up to get that item. In our example, we assumed that the farmer and the rancher each spend 8 hours a day working. Time spent producing potatoes, therefore, takes away from time available for producing meat. As the rancher and farmer reallocate time between producing the two goods, they move along their production possibility frontiers; they give up units of one good to produce units of the other. The opportunity cost measures the tradeoff between the two goods that each producer faces.

Let's first consider the rancher's opportunity cost. According to Table 3.1, producing 1 kg of potatoes takes her 10 minutes of work. When the rancher spends that 10 minutes producing potatoes, she spends 10 minutes less producing meat. Because the rancher needs 20 minutes to produce 1 kg of meat, 10 minutes of work would yield 0.5 kg of meat. Hence, the rancher's opportunity cost of producing 1 kg of potatoes is 0.5 kg of meat.

Now consider the farmer's opportunity cost. Producing 1 kg of potatoes takes him 15 minutes. Because he needs 60 minutes to produce 1 kg of meat, 15 minutes of work would yield 0.25 kg of meat. Hence, the farmer's opportunity cost of 1 kg of potatoes is 0.25 kg of meat.

Table 3.3 (p. 54) shows the opportunity costs of meat and potatoes for the two producers. Notice that the opportunity cost of meat is the inverse of the opportunity cost of potatoes. Because 1 kg of potatoes costs the rancher 0.5 kg of meat, 1 kg of meat costs the rancher 2 kg of potatoes. Similarly, because 1 kg of potatoes costs the farmer 0.25 kg of meat, 1 kg of meat costs the farmer 4 kg of potatoes.

opportunity cost
whatever must be given up to obtain some item

TABLE 3.3		Opportunity Cost of:	
The Opportunity Cost of Meat and Potatoes		1 kg of Meat	1 kg of Potatoes
	Farmer	4 kg potatoes	0.25 kg meat
	Rancher	2 kg potatoes	0.50 kg meat

comparative advantage
the comparison among producers of a good according to their opportunity cost

Economists use the term **comparative advantage** when describing the opportunity cost of two producers. The producer who gives up less of other goods to produce good X has the smaller opportunity cost of producing good X and is said to have a comparative advantage in producing it. In our example, the farmer has a lower opportunity cost of producing potatoes than does the rancher: A kilogram of potatoes costs the farmer only 0.25 kg of meat, while it costs the rancher 0.50 kg of meat. Conversely, the rancher has a lower opportunity cost of producing meat than does the farmer: A kilogram of meat costs the rancher 2 kg of potatoes, while it costs the farmer 4 kg of potatoes. Thus, the farmer has a comparative advantage in growing potatoes, and the rancher has a comparative advantage in producing meat.

Although it is possible for one person to have an absolute advantage in both goods (as the rancher does in our example), it is impossible for one person to have a comparative advantage in both goods. Because the opportunity cost of one good is the inverse of the opportunity cost of the other, if a person's opportunity cost of one good is relatively high, his opportunity cost of the other good must be relatively low. Comparative advantage reflects the relative opportunity cost. Unless two people have exactly the same opportunity cost, one person will have a comparative advantage in one good, and the other person will have a comparative advantage in the other good.

Comparative Advantage and Trade

The rancher has an absolute advantage over the farmer in both meat and potatoes, and will therefore be able to enjoy a higher standard of living than the farmer. Her greater productivity will make the rancher richer than the farmer, but both the rancher and the farmer could improve their standards of living through trade.

Differences in opportunity cost and comparative advantage create the gains from trade. When each person specializes in producing the good for which he or she has a comparative advantage, total production in the economy rises, and this increase in the size of the economic pie can be used to make everyone better off. In other words, as long as two people have different opportunity costs, each can benefit from trade by obtaining a good at a price that is lower than his or her opportunity cost of that good.

Consider the proposed deal from the viewpoint of the farmer. The farmer gets 5 kg of meat in exchange for 15 kg of potatoes. In other words, the farmer buys each kilogram of meat for a price of 3 kg of potatoes. This price of meat is lower than his opportunity cost for 1 kg of meat, which is 4 kg of potatoes. Thus, the farmer benefits from the deal because he gets to buy meat at a good price.

FYI

THE LEGACY OF ADAM SMITH AND DAVID RICARDO

Economists have long understood the principle of comparative advantage. Here is how the great economist Adam Smith put the argument:

It is a maxim of every prudent master of a family, never to attempt to make at home what it will cost him more to make than to buy. The tailor does not attempt to make his own shoes, but buys them of the shoemaker. The shoemaker does not attempt to make his own clothes but employs a tailor. The farmer attempts to make neither the one nor the other, but employs those different artificers. All of them find it for their interest to employ their whole industry in a way in which they have some advantage over their neighbors, and to purchase with a part of its produce, or what is the same thing, with the price of part of it, whatever else they have occasion for.

This quotation is from Smith's 1776 book *An Inquiry into the Nature and Causes of the Wealth of Nations,* which was a landmark in the analysis of trade and economic interdependence.

Smith's book inspired David Ricardo, a millionaire stockbroker, to become an economist. In his 1817 book *Principles of Political Economy and Taxation,* Ricardo developed the principle of comparative advantage as we know it today. His defence of free trade was not a mere academic exercise. Ricardo put his economic beliefs to work as a member of the British Parliament, where he opposed the Corn Laws, which restricted the import of grain.

The conclusions of Adam Smith and David Ricardo on the gains from trade have held up well over time. Although economists often disagree on questions of policy, they are united in their support of free trade. Moreover, the central argument for free trade has not changed much in the past two centuries. Even though the field of economics has broadened its scope and refined its theories since the time of Smith and Ricardo, economists' opposition to trade restrictions is still based largely on the principle of comparative advantage.

David Ricardo

Now consider the deal from the rancher's viewpoint. The rancher buys 15 kg of potatoes for a price of 5 kg of meat. That is, the price of potatoes is one-third of a kilogram of meat. This price of potatoes is lower than her opportunity cost of 1 kg of potatoes, which is 0.5 kg of meat. The rancher benefits because she can buy potatoes at a good price.

These benefits arise because each person concentrates on the activity for which he or she has the lower opportunity cost: The farmer spends more time growing potatoes, and the rancher spends more time producing meat. As a result, the total production of potatoes and the total production of meat both rise. In our example, potato production rises from 40 to 44 kg, and meat production rises from 16 to 18 kg. The farmer and rancher share the benefits of this increased production. The moral of the story of the farmer and the rancher should now be clear: *Trade can benefit everyone in society because it allows people to specialize in activities in which they have a comparative advantage.*

QuickQuiz Robinson Crusoe can gather 10 coconuts or catch 1 fish per hour. His friend Friday can gather 30 coconuts or catch 2 fish per hour. What is Crusoe's opportunity cost of catching one fish? What is Friday's? Who has an absolute advantage in catching fish? Who has a comparative advantage in catching fish?

APPLICATIONS OF COMPARATIVE ADVANTAGE

The principle of comparative advantage explains interdependence and the gains from trade. Because interdependence is so prevalent in the modern world, the principle of comparative advantage has many applications. Here are two examples, one fanciful and one of great practical importance.

Should Mike Weir Mow His Own Lawn?

Mike Weir spends a lot of time walking around on grass. One of the most talented golfers in the PGA today, he can hit a drive and sink a putt in a way that most casual golfers only dream of doing. Most likely, he is talented at other activities

IN THE NEWS

DOES CANADA HAVE FREE TRADE?

Canada has removed many trade restrictions over the years, especially with our NAFTA partners, the United States and Mexico. But as economics professor William Watson explains in this article, many trade restrictions still remain.

Why Does a Tiger Need Tariffs?

By William Watson

The WTO [World Trade Organization] issued its biennial report on Canadian trade policies last week. Generally speaking, we got a good review. Our trade regime is "amongst the world's most transparent and liberal." The Canadian economy "is generally free from significant policy-induced distortions." We are a shining example of "the benefits for improved living standards of pro-competitive policies that support production based on comparative advantage"—comparative advantage

being the economist's term for specializing in what you do best and buying from other countries what you don't do so well.

As was to be expected, the good news was trumpeted by the folks at the Department of Foreign Affairs and International Trade in their unfailingly self-congratulatory free e-mail service. (One of the more entertaining pastimes for Canadian international trade economists is to try to anticipate what positive spin official e-mail will put on news of another Canadian loss before the WTO dispute settlement panels. Had the DFAIT communications officers been at Pearl Harbor, their communique would

have read: "Warm, sunny Sunday, once smoke cleared.")

In fact, the WTO isn't entirely approving. We still have "barriers to imports in a few ... important sectors" and "a number of activities remain subject to interventions, notably in agriculture, textiles and clothing, steel, telecommunications, audiovisual, air and maritime transport, and insurance."

That's just from the executive summary. When you get into the 150 or so pages of detail you're impressed by the number of trade restrictions we still have in place. Take tariffs—in particular, our most-favoured-nation (MFN) tariffs, those paid by all our trading partners too. For example, let's imagine that Weir can mow his lawn faster than anyone else. But just because he *can* mow his lawn fast, does this mean he *should*?

To answer this question, we can use the concepts of opportunity cost and comparative advantage. Let's say that Weir can mow his lawn in 2 hours. In that same 2 hours, he could film a television commercial for Bell Canada and earn $10 000. By contrast, Forrest Gump, the boy next door, can mow Weir's lawn in 4 hours. In that same 4 hours, he could work at McDonald's and earn $20.

In this example, Weir's opportunity cost of mowing the lawn is $10 000 and Forrest's opportunity cost is $20. Weir has an absolute advantage in mowing lawns because he can do the work in less time. Yet Forrest has a comparative advantage in mowing lawns because he has the lower opportunity cost.

The gains from trade in this example are tremendous. Rather than mowing his own lawn, Weir should make the commercial and hire Forrest to mow the lawn.

except the countries we have free trade deals with, who generally don't pay any tariffs, and North Korea and Libya, our very own little axis of evil, who pay the punitive "general" tariff rate.

Half of the items (or "lines," referring to lines of text in our official tariff schedules) covered by our MFN trade are now completely tariff-free. But on the other half, our average tariff was 13.1% in 2002, down from 13.4% in 2000. And on 657 tariff lines, our tariffs exceed 15%. On boats, for example, we charge 25%. We also charge high tariffs on the iron fittings for coffins, of all things, and on pruning shears. Our average tariff on agricultural products is 21.7%, on dairy products a whopping 237.3%. Our tariff on chocolate ice cream is over 200%. What kind of country taxes chocolate ice cream?

Indeed, what kind of country relies on protective tariffs at all? Not us, surely. We're the Northern Tiger, our economy burning bright. We top the world growth charts. We beat the United States at job growth. Our books are balanced, our dollar is rising. Our exports grow and grow. We are Tiger, hear us roar.

But if all that is true, why are we still protecting the dark, backward corners of our world-beating economy?

To be fair, most of our trade is tariff-free. At latest count we have free-trade deals with the United States, Mexico, Chile, Israel, the Palestinian Authority (yes, we do), Costa Rica and 20 Caribbean countries, and we're currently negotiating separate deals with at least five more countries, plus the entire Western hemisphere (minus Cuba) in the Free Trade Area of the Americas initiative.

But that only strengthens the argument for ditching our tariffs entirely. We have survived free trade both with the world's economic colossus and with Mexico, a poor country that was supposed to swallow up our economy with a giant sucking sound. And we haven't just survived. We've thrived—to the point where serious people in Ottawa (there are some) are thinking of ourselves as real economic tigers. Well, real economic tigers don't need tariffs. They give up the sectors they're weak in and focus on their strengths. Maybe if we drop the ice cream tariff to zero we won't have an ice cream industry any more. But we'll still have ice cream. In fact, we'll have even more of it, because we'll be richer focusing on what we do best and trading for all the rest.

Another good argument for putting all our tariffs to zero—right away, unilaterally—is to solve an increasingly complex "rules of origin" problem. At the moment, all our free trade deals include byzantine rules for deciding where a product comes from. Why? Because where it comes from determines what tariff it faces. But if we put all our tariffs to zero, that problem disappears. No matter where you're from (except Libya and North Korea), you'd pay the same tariff. I don't actually know how many of our customs agents spend all their time administering rules of origin, but it must be lots. They could all be moved to more useful work.

This idea is not as strange as it sounds. The United States has announced a goal of zero tariffs in manufacturing by 2015. Unless it gets badly sidetracked, that's where the world is heading.

A tiger, fearless beast, should want to lead the way.

Source: *National Post*, March 19, 2003, p. FP19. Material reprinted with the express permission of "The National Post Company," a CanWest Partnership.

As long as Weir pays Forrest more than $20 and less than $10 000, both of them are better off.

Should Canada Trade with Other Countries?

Just as individuals can benefit from specialization and trade with one another, as the farmer and rancher did, so can populations of people in different countries. Many of the goods that Canadians enjoy are produced abroad, and many of the goods produced in Canada are sold abroad. Goods produced abroad and sold domestically are called **imports**. Goods produced domestically and sold abroad are called **exports**.

To see how countries can benefit from trade, suppose there are two countries, Canada and Japan, and two goods, food and cars. Imagine that the two countries produce cars equally well: A Canadian worker and a Japanese worker can each produce 1 car per month. By contrast, because Canada has more and better land, it is better at producing food: A Canadian worker can produce 2 tonnes of food per month, whereas a Japanese worker can produce only 1 tonne of food per month.

The principle of comparative advantage states that each good should be produced by the country that has the smaller opportunity cost of producing that good. Because the opportunity cost of a car is 2 tonnes of food in Canada but only 1 tonne of food in Japan, Japan has a comparative advantage in producing cars. Japan should produce more cars than it wants for its own use and export some of them to Canada. Similarly, because the opportunity cost of a tonne of food is 1 car in Japan but only 1/2 car in Canada, Canada has a comparative advantage in producing food. Canada should produce more food than it wants to consume and export some of it to Japan. Through specialization and trade, both countries can have more food and more cars.

In reality, of course, the issues involved in trade among nations are more complex than this example suggests, as we will see in Chapter 9. Most important among these issues is that each country has many citizens with different interests. International trade can make some individuals worse off, even as it makes the country as a whole better off. When Canada exports food and imports cars, the impact on a Canadian farmer is not the same as the impact on a Canadian autoworker. Yet, contrary to the opinions sometimes voiced by politicians and political commentators, international trade is not like war, in which some countries win and others lose. Trade allows all countries to achieve greater prosperity.

QuickQuiz Suppose that the world's fastest typist happens to be trained in brain surgery. Should he do his own typing or hire a secretary? Explain.

imports
goods produced abroad and sold domestically

exports
goods produced domestically and sold abroad

CONCLUSION

The principle of comparative advantage shows that trade can make everyone better off. You should now understand more fully the benefits of living in an interdependent economy. But having seen why interdependence is desirable, you might naturally ask how it is possible. How do free societies coordinate the diverse activities of all the people involved in their economies? What ensures that goods and services will get from those who should be producing them to those who should be consuming them?

In a world with only two people, such as the rancher and the farmer, the answer is simple: These two people can directly bargain and allocate resources between themselves. In the real world with billions of people, the answer is less obvious. We take up this issue in the next chapter, where we see that free societies allocate resources through the market forces of supply and demand.

SUMMARY

- Each person consumes goods and services produced by many other people, both in our country and around the world. Interdependence and trade are desirable because they allow everyone to enjoy a greater quantity and variety of goods and services.

- There are two ways to compare the ability of two people in producing a good. The person who can produce the good with the smaller quantity of inputs is said to have an *absolute advantage* in producing the good. The person who has the

smaller opportunity cost of producing the good is said to have a *comparative advantage.* The gains from trade are based on comparative advantage, not absolute advantage.

- Trade makes everyone better off because it allows people to specialize in those activities in which they have a comparative advantage.

- The principle of comparative advantage applies to countries as well as to people. Economists use the principle of comparative advantage to advocate free trade among countries.

KEY CONCEPTS

absolute advantage, p. 53
opportunity cost, p. 53

comparative advantage, p. 54
imports, p. 58

exports, p. 58

QUESTIONS FOR REVIEW

1. Explain how absolute advantage and comparative advantage differ.

2. Give an example in which one person has an absolute advantage in doing something but another person has a comparative advantage.

3. Is absolute advantage or comparative advantage more important for trade? Explain your

reasoning using the example in your answer to question 2.

4. Will a nation tend to export or import goods for which it has a comparative advantage? Explain.

5. Why do economists oppose policies that restrict trade among nations?

PROBLEMS AND APPLICATIONS

1. Consider the farmer and the rancher from our example in this chapter. Explain why the farmer's opportunity cost of producing

1 kg of meat is 4 kg of potatoes. Explain why the rancher's opportunity cost of producing 1 kg of meat is 2 kg of potatoes.

2. Maria can read 20 pages of economics in an hour. She can also read 50 pages of sociology in an hour. She spends 5 hours per day studying.
   a. Draw Maria's production possibilities frontier for reading economics and sociology.
   b. What is Maria's opportunity cost of reading 100 pages of sociology?

3. Canadian and Japanese workers can each produce 4 cars per year. A Canadian worker can produce 10 tonnes of grain per year, whereas a Japanese worker can produce 5 tonnes of grain per year. To keep things simple, assume that each country has 100 million workers.
   a. For this situation, construct a table analogous to Table 3.1.
   b. Graph the production possibilities frontier of the Canadian and Japanese economies.
   c. For Canada, what is the opportunity cost of a car? Of grain? For Japan, what is the opportunity cost of a car? Of grain? Put this information in a table analogous to Table 3.3.
   d. Which country has an absolute advantage in producing cars? In producing grain?
   e. Which country has a comparative advantage in producing cars? In producing grain?
   f. Without trade, half of each country's workers produce cars and half produce grain. What quantities of cars and grain does each country produce?
   g. Starting from a position without trade, give an example in which trade makes each country better off.

4. Pat and Kris are roommates. They spend most of their time studying (of course), but they leave some time for their favourite activities: making pizza and brewing root beer. Pat takes 4 hours to brew 5 L of root beer and 2 hours to make a pizza. Kris takes 6 hours to brew 5 L of root beer and 4 hours to make a pizza.
   a. What is each roommate's opportunity cost of making a pizza? Who has the absolute advantage in making pizza? Who has the comparative advantage in making pizza?
   b. If Pat and Kris trade foods with each other, who will trade away pizza in exchange for root beer?

   c. The price of pizza can be expressed in terms of litres of root beer. What is the highest price at which pizza can be traded that would make both roommates better off? What is the lowest price? Explain.

5. Suppose that there are 10 million workers in Canada, and that each of these workers can produce either 2 cars or 30 tonnes of wheat in a year.
   a. What is the opportunity cost of producing a car in Canada? What is the opportunity cost of producing a tonne of wheat in Canada? Explain the relationship between the opportunity costs of the two goods.
   b. Draw Canada's production possibilities frontier. If Canada chooses to consume 10 million cars, how much wheat can it consume without trade? Label this point on the production possibilities frontier.
   c. Now suppose that the United States offers to buy 10 million cars from Canada in exchange for 20 tonnes of wheat per car. If Canada continues to consume 10 million cars, how much wheat does this deal allow Canada to consume? Label this point on your diagram. Should Canada accept the deal?

6. Consider a professor who is writing a book. The professor can both write the chapters and gather the needed data faster than anyone else at his university. Still, he pays a student to collect data at the library. Is this sensible? Explain.

7. England and Scotland both produce scones and sweaters. Suppose that an English worker can produce 50 scones per hour or 1 sweater per hour. Suppose that a Scottish worker can produce 40 scones per hour or 2 sweaters per hour.
   a. Which country has the absolute advantage in the production of each good? Which country has the comparative advantage?
   b. If England and Scotland decide to trade, which commodity will Scotland trade to England? Explain.
   c. If a Scottish worker could produce only 1 sweater per hour, would Scotland still gain

from trade? Would England still gain from trade? Explain.

8. The following table describes the production possibilities of two cities.

	Red Sweaters per Worker per Hour	Blue Sweaters per Worker per Hour
Montreal	3	3
Toronto	2	1

a. Without trade, what is the price of blue sweaters (in terms of red sweaters) in Montreal? What is the price in Toronto?
b. Which city has an absolute advantage in the production of each colour sweater? Which city has a comparative advantage in the production of each colour sweater?
c. If the cities trade with each other, which colour sweater will each export?
d. What is the range of prices at which trade can occur?

9. Suppose that all goods can be produced with fewer worker hours in Germany than in France.
a. In what sense is the cost of all goods lower in Germany than in France?
b. In what sense is the cost of some goods lower in France?
c. If Germany and France traded with each other, would both countries be better off as a result? Explain in the context of your answers to parts (a) and (b).

10. Are the following statements true or false? Explain in each case.
a. "Two countries can achieve gains from trade even if one of the countries has an absolute advantage in the production of all goods."
b. "Certain very talented people have a comparative advantage in everything they do."
c. "If a certain trade is good for one person, it can't be good for the other one."

INTERNET RESOURCES

- To learn more about economist Adam Smith, follow the many links available at http://cepa.newschool.edu/het/profiles/smith.htm.

- You can read Adam Smith's classic book *The Wealth of Nations* (and many other classic texts) at the Liberty Fund's online library at http://oll.libertyfund.org.

- To read more about David Ricardo and his ideas, go to http://cepa.newschool.edu/het/profiles/ricardo.htm.

- If the principle of comparative advantage is such a simple idea that can be taught in first-year college and university textbooks, why do so many educated people reject the argument that there are gains from trade? MIT professor of economics Paul Krugman tries to answer that question in his essay "Ricardo's Difficult Idea": http://web.mit.edu/krugman/www/ricardo.htm.

http://   For more study tools, please visit http://www.mankiw3e.nelson.com.

2

SUPPLY AND DEMAND I: HOW MARKETS WORK

THE MARKET FORCES
OF SUPPLY AND DEMAND

When a cold snap hits Florida, the price of orange juice rises in supermarkets throughout Canada. When the weather turns warm in Quebec every summer, the price of hotel rooms in the Caribbean plummets. When a war breaks out in the Middle East, the price of gasoline in Canada rises, and the price of a used SUV falls. What do these events have in common? They all show the workings of supply and demand.

Supply and *demand* are the two words that economists use most often—and for good reason. Supply and demand are the forces that make market economies work. They determine the quantity of each good produced and the price at which it is sold. If you want to know how any event or policy will affect the economy, you must think first about how it will affect supply and demand.

This chapter introduces the theory of supply and demand. It considers how buyers and sellers behave and how they interact with one another. It shows how supply and demand determine prices in a market economy and how prices, in turn, allocate the economy's scarce resources.

4

Learning Objectives

In this chapter, you will …

- Learn the nature of a competitive market
- Examine what determines the demand for a good in a competitive market
- Examine what determines the supply of a good in a competitive market
- See how supply and demand together set the price of a good and the quantity sold
- Consider the key role of prices in allocating scarce resources in market economies

MARKETS AND COMPETITION

market
a group of buyers and sellers
of a particular good or service

The terms *supply* and *demand* refer to the behaviour of people as they interact with one another in markets. A **market** is a group of buyers and sellers of a particular good or service. The buyers as a group determine the demand for the product, and the sellers as a group determine the supply of the product. Before discussing how buyers and sellers behave, let's first consider more fully what we mean by a "market" and the various types of markets we observe in the economy.

Competitive Markets

Markets take many forms. Sometimes markets are highly organized, such as the markets for many agricultural commodities. In these markets, buyers and sellers meet at a specific time and place, where an auctioneer helps set prices and arrange sales.

More often, markets are less organized. For example, consider the market for ice cream in a particular town. Buyers of ice cream do not meet together at any one time. The sellers of ice cream are in different locations and offer somewhat different products. There is no auctioneer calling out the price of ice cream. Each seller posts a price for an ice-cream cone, and each buyer decides how much ice cream to buy at each store.

Even though it is not organized, the group of ice-cream buyers and ice-cream sellers forms a market. Each buyer knows that there are several sellers from which to choose, and each seller is aware that his product is similar to that offered by other sellers. The price of ice cream and the quantity of ice cream sold are not determined by any single buyer or seller. Rather, price and quantity are determined by all buyers and sellers as they interact in the marketplace.

competitive market
a market in which there are many
buyers and many sellers so that
each has a negligible impact on
the market price

The market for ice cream, like most markets in the economy, is highly competitive. A **competitive market** is a market in which there are many buyers and many sellers so that each has a negligible impact on the market price. Each seller of ice cream has limited control over the price because other sellers are offering similar products. A seller has little reason to charge less than the going price, and if he or she charges more, buyers will make their purchases elsewhere. Similarly, no single buyer of ice cream can influence the price of ice cream because each buyer purchases only a small amount.

In this chapter we examine how buyers and sellers interact in competitive markets. We see how the forces of supply and demand determine both the quantity of the good sold and its price.

Competition: Perfect and Otherwise

We assume in this chapter that markets are *perfectly competitive*. Perfectly competitive markets are defined by two primary characteristics: (1) the goods being offered for sale are all the same, and (2) the buyers and sellers are so numerous that no single buyer or seller can influence the market price. Because buyers and sellers in perfectly competitive markets must accept the price the market determines, they are said to be *price takers*.

There are some markets in which the assumption of perfect competition applies almost perfectly. In the wheat market, for example, there are thousands of farmers who sell wheat and millions of consumers who use wheat and wheat products. Because no single buyer or seller can influence the price of wheat, each takes the price as given.

Not all goods and services, however, are sold in perfectly competitive markets. Some markets have only one seller, and this seller sets the price. Such a seller is called a *monopoly*. Your local cable television company, for instance, may be a monopoly. Residents of your town probably have only one cable company from which to buy this service.

Some markets fall between the extremes of perfect competition and monopoly. One such market, called an *oligopoly*, has a few sellers that do not always compete aggressively. Airline routes are an example. If a route between two cities is serviced by only two or three carriers, the carriers may avoid rigorous competition so they can keep prices high. Another type of market is *monopolistically competitive*; it contains many sellers but each offers a slightly different product. Because the products are not exactly the same, each seller has some ability to set the price for its own product. An example is the market for magazines. Magazines compete with one another for readers and anyone can enter the market by starting a new one, but each magazine offers different articles and can set its own price.

Despite the diversity of market types we find in the world, we begin by studying perfect competition. Perfectly competitive markets are the easiest to analyze. Moreover, because some degree of competition is present in most markets, many of the lessons that we learn by studying supply and demand under perfect competition apply in more complicated markets as well.

QuickQuiz   What is a market? • What are the characteristics of a competitive market?

DEMAND

We begin our study of markets by examining the behaviour of buyers. To focus our thinking, let's keep in mind a particular good—ice cream.

The Demand Curve: The Relationship between Price and Quantity Demanded

The **quantity demanded** of any good is the amount of the good that buyers are willing to purchase. As we will see, many things determine the quantity demanded of any good, but when analyzing how markets work, one determinant plays a central role—the price of the good. If the price of ice cream rose to $20 per scoop, you would buy less ice cream. You might buy frozen yogurt instead. If the price of ice cream fell to $0.20 per scoop, you would buy more. Because the quantity demanded falls as the price rises and rises as the price falls, we say that the quantity demanded is *negatively related* to the price. This relationship between price and quantity demanded is true for most goods in the economy and, in fact,

quantity demanded
the amount of a good that buyers are willing to purchase

law of demand
the claim that, other things equal, the quantity demanded of a good falls when the price of the good rises

demand schedule
a table that shows the relationship between the price of a good and the quantity demanded

demand curve
a graph of the relationship between the price of a good and the quantity demanded

is so pervasive that economists call it the **law of demand:** Other things equal, when the price of a good rises, the quantity demanded of the good falls, and when the price falls, the quantity demanded rises.

The table in Figure 4.1 shows how many ice-cream cones Catherine buys each month at different prices of ice cream. If ice cream is free, Catherine eats 12 cones. At $0.50 per cone, Catherine buys 10 cones. As the price rises further, she buys fewer and fewer cones. When the price reaches $3.00, Catherine doesn't buy any ice cream at all. This table is a **demand schedule,** a table that shows the relationship between the price of a good and the quantity demanded, holding constant everything else that influences how much consumers of the good want to buy.

The graph in Figure 4.1 uses the numbers from the table to illustrate the law of demand. By convention, the price of ice cream is on the vertical axis, and the quantity of ice cream demanded is on the horizontal axis. The downward-sloping line relating price and quantity demanded is called the **demand curve.**

Market Demand versus Individual Demand

The demand curve in Figure 4.1 shows an individual's demand for a product. To analyze how markets work, we need to determine the *market demand*, which is the sum of all the individual demands for a particular good or service.

FIGURE 4.1

Catherine's Demand Schedule and Demand Curve

The demand schedule shows the quantity demanded at each price. The demand curve, which graphs the demand schedule, shows how the quantity demanded of the good changes as its price varies. Because a lower price increases the quantity demanded, the demand curve slopes downward.

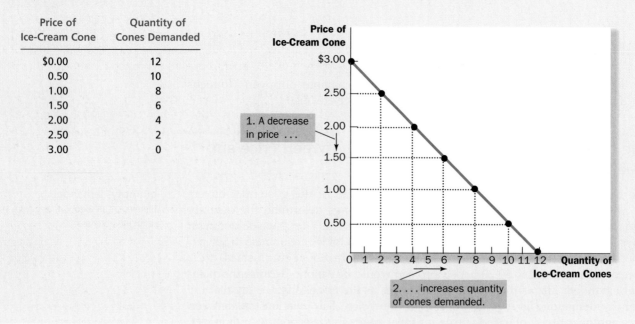

Price of Ice-Cream Cone	Quantity of Cones Demanded
$0.00	12
0.50	10
1.00	8
1.50	6
2.00	4
2.50	2
3.00	0

1. A decrease in price . . .

2. . . . increases quantity of cones demanded.

The table in Figure 4.2 shows the demand schedules for ice cream of two individuals—Catherine and Nicholas. At any price, Catherine's demand schedule tells us how much ice cream she buys, and Nicholas's demand schedule tells us how much ice cream he buys. The market demand at each price is the sum of the two individual demands.

The graph in Figure 4.2 shows the demand curves that correspond to these demand schedules. Notice that we sum the individual demand curves *horizontally* to obtain the market demand curve. That is, to find the total quantity demanded at any price, we add the individual quantities found on the horizontal axis of the individual demand curves. Because we are interested in analyzing how markets work, we will work most often with the market demand curve. The market demand curve shows how the total quantity demanded of a good varies as the price of the good varies, while all the other factors that affect how much consumers want to buy are held constant.

Shifts in the Demand Curve

The demand curve for ice cream shows how much ice cream people buy at any given price, holding constant the many other factors beyond price that influence

FIGURE 4.2

Market Demand as the Sum of Individual Demands

The quantity demanded in a market is the sum of the quantities demanded by all the buyers at each price. Thus, the market demand curve is found by adding horizontally the individual demand curves. At a price of $2, Catherine demands 4 ice-cream cones, and Nicholas demands 3 ice-cream cones. The quantity demanded in the market at this price is 7 cones.

Price of Ice-Cream Cone	Catherine		Nicholas		Market
$0.00	12	+	7	=	19
0.50	10		6		16
1.00	8		5		13
1.50	6		4		10
2.00	4		3		7
2.50	2		2		4
3.00	0		1		1

consumers' buying decisions. As a result, this demand curve need not be stable over time. If something happens to alter the quantity demanded at any given price, the demand curve shifts. For example, suppose nutritionists discovered that people who regularly eat ice cream live longer, healthier lives. The discovery would raise the demand for ice cream. At any given price, buyers would now want to purchase a larger quantity of ice cream, and the demand curve for ice cream would shift.

Figure 4.3 illustrates shifts in demand. Any change that increases the quantity demanded at every price, such as our imaginary discovery by nutritionists, shifts the demand curve to the right and is called *an increase in demand.* Any change that reduces the quantity demanded at every price shifts the demand curve to the left and is called *a decrease in demand.*

There are many variables that can shift the demand curve. Here are the most important:

Income   What would happen to your demand for ice cream if you lost your job one summer? Most likely, it would fall. A lower income means that you have less to spend in total, so you would have to spend less on some—and probably most—goods. If the demand for a good falls when income falls, the good is called a **normal good.**

Not all goods are normal goods. If the demand for a good rises when income falls, the good is called an **inferior good.** An example of an inferior good might be bus rides. As your income falls, you are less likely to buy a car or take a cab, and more likely to ride the bus.

Prices of Related Goods   Suppose that the price of frozen yogurt falls. The law of demand says that you will buy more frozen yogurt. At the same time, you will probably buy less ice cream. Because ice cream and frozen yogurt are both cold, sweet, creamy desserts, they satisfy similar desires. When a fall in the

normal good
a good for which, other things equal, an increase in income leads to an increase in demand

inferior good
a good for which, other things equal, an increase in income leads to a decrease in demand

---

FIGURE 4.3

Shifts in the Demand Curve

Any change that raises the quantity that buyers wish to purchase at a given price shifts the demand curve to the right. Any change that lowers the quantity that buyers wish to purchase at a given price shifts the demand curve to the left.

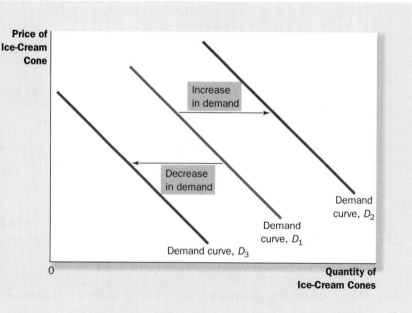

price of one good reduces the demand for another good, the two goods are called **substitutes.** Substitutes are often pairs of goods that are used in place of each other, such as hot dogs and hamburgers, sweaters and sweatshirts, and movie tickets and video rentals.

Now suppose that the price of hot fudge falls. According to the law of demand, you will buy more hot fudge. Yet, in this case, you will buy more ice cream as well, because ice cream and hot fudge are often used together. When a fall in the price of one good raises the demand for another good, the two goods are called **complements.** Complements are often pairs of goods that are used together, such as gasoline and automobiles, computers and software, and peanut butter and jelly.

substitutes
two goods for which an increase in the price of one leads to an increase in the demand for the other

Tastes The most obvious determinant of your demand is your tastes. If you like ice cream, you buy more of it. Economists normally do not try to explain people's tastes because tastes are based on historical and psychological forces that are beyond the realm of economics. Economists do, however, examine what happens when tastes change.

complements
two goods for which an increase in the price of one leads to a decrease in the demand for the other

Expectations Your expectations about the future may affect your demand for a good or service today. For example, if you expect to earn a higher income next month, you may be more willing to spend some of your current savings buying ice cream. As another example, if you expect the price of ice cream to fall tomorrow, you may be less willing to buy an ice-cream cone at today's price.

Number of Buyers Because market demand is derived from individual demands, it depends on all those factors that determine the demand of individual buyers, including buyers' incomes, tastes, expectations, and the prices of related goods. In addition, it depends on the number of buyers. If Peter, another consumer of ice cream, were to join Catherine and Nicholas, the quantity demanded in the market would be higher at every price and the demand curve would shift to the right.

Summary The demand curve shows what happens to the quantity demanded of a good when its price varies, holding constant all the other variables that influence buyers. When one of these other variables changes, the demand curve shifts. Table 4.1 lists all the variables that influence how much consumers choose to buy of a good.

TABLE 4.1

Variables That Influence Buyers

This table lists the variables that affect how much consumers choose to buy of any good. Notice the special role that the price of the good plays: A change in the good's price represents a movement along the demand curve, whereas a change in one of the other variables shifts the demand curve.

Variable	A Change in This Variable . . .
Price	Represents a movement along the demand curve
Income	Shifts the demand curve
Prices of related goods	Shifts the demand curve
Tastes	Shifts the demand curve
Expectations	Shifts the demand curve
Number of buyers	Shifts the demand curve

Case Study

TWO WAYS TO REDUCE THE QUANTITY OF SMOKING DEMANDED

Public policymakers often want to reduce the amount that people smoke. There are two ways that policy can attempt to achieve this goal.

One way to reduce smoking is to shift the demand curve for cigarettes and other tobacco products. Public service announcements, mandatory health warnings on cigarette packages, and the prohibition of cigarette advertising on television are all policies aimed at reducing the quantity of cigarettes demanded at any given price. If successful, these policies shift the demand curve for cigarettes to the left, as in panel (a) of Figure 4.4.

Alternatively, policymakers can try to raise the price of cigarettes. If the government taxes the manufacture of cigarettes, for example, cigarette companies pass much of this tax on to consumers in the form of higher prices. A higher price encourages smokers to reduce the numbers of cigarettes they smoke. In this case,

FIGURE 4.4

Shifts in the Demand Curve versus Movements along the Demand Curve

If warnings on cigarette packages convince smokers to smoke less, the demand curve for cigarettes shifts to the left. In panel (a), the demand curve shifts from D_1 to D_2. At a price of $2 per pack, the quantity demanded falls from 20 to 10 cigarettes per day, as reflected by the shift from point A to point B. By contrast, if a tax raises the price of cigarettes, the demand curve does not shift. Instead, we observe a movement to a different point on the demand curve. In panel (b), when the price rises from $2 to $4, the quantity demanded falls from 20 to 12 cigarettes per day, as reflected by the movement from point A to point C.

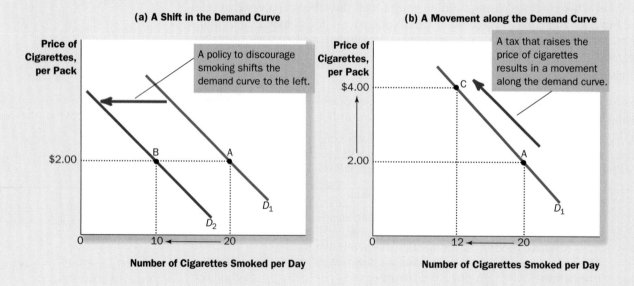

the reduced amount of smoking does not represent a shift in the demand curve. Instead, it represents a movement along the same demand curve to a point with a higher price and lower quantity, as in panel (b) of Figure 4.4.

How much does the amount of smoking respond to changes in the price of cigarettes? Economists have attempted to answer this question by studying what happens when the tax on cigarettes changes. They have found that a 10 percent increase in the price causes a 4 percent reduction in the quantity demanded. Teenagers are found to be especially sensitive to the price of cigarettes: A 10 percent increase in the price causes a 12 percent drop in teenage smoking.

A related question is how the price of cigarettes affects the demand for illicit drugs, such as marijuana. Opponents of cigarette taxes often argue that tobacco and marijuana are substitutes, so that high cigarette prices encourage marijuana use. By contrast, many experts on substance abuse view tobacco as a "gateway drug" leading the young to experiment with other harmful substances. Most studies of the data are consistent with this view: They find that lower cigarette prices are associated with greater use of marijuana. In other words, tobacco and marijuana appear to be complements rather than substitutes. ●

QuickQuiz Make up an example of a demand schedule for pizza, and graph the implied demand curve. • Give an example of something that would shift this demand curve. • Would a change in the price of pizza shift this demand curve?

© ROYALTY FREE/CORBIS/MAGMA

What is the best way to stop this?

SUPPLY

We now turn to the other side of the market and examine the behaviour of sellers. Once again, to focus our thinking, let's consider the market for ice cream.

The Supply Curve: The Relationship between Price and Quantity Supplied

The **quantity supplied** of any good or service is the amount that sellers are willing to sell. There are many determinants of quantity supplied, but once again price plays a special role in our analysis. When the price of ice cream is high, selling ice cream is profitable, and so the quantity supplied is large. Sellers of ice cream work long hours, buy many ice-cream machines, and hire many workers. By contrast, when the price of ice cream is low, the business is less profitable, and so sellers produce less ice cream. At a low price, some sellers may even choose to shut down, and their quantity supplied falls to zero. Because the quantity supplied rises as the price rises and falls as the price falls, we say that the quantity supplied is *positively related* to the price of the good. This relationship between price and quantity supplied is called the **law of supply:** Other things equal, when the price of a good rises, the quantity supplied of the good also rises, and when the price falls, the quantity supplied falls as well.

quantity supplied
the amount of a good that sellers are willing to sell

law of supply
the claim that, other things equal, the quantity supplied of a good rises when the price of the good rises

The table in Figure 4.5 shows the quantity supplied by Ben, an ice-cream seller, at various prices of ice cream. At a price below $1.00, Ben does not supply any ice cream at all. As the price rises, he supplies a greater and greater quantity. This is the **supply schedule,** a table that shows the relationship between the price of a good and the quantity supplied, holding constant everything else that influences how much producers of the good want to sell.

The graph in Figure 4.5 uses the numbers from the table to illustrate the law of supply. The curve relating price and quantity supplied is called the **supply curve.** The supply curve slopes upward because, other things equal, a higher price means a greater quantity supplied.

supply schedule
a table that shows the relationship between the price of a good and the quantity supplied

supply curve
a graph of the relationship between the price of a good and the quantity supplied

Market Supply versus Individual Supply

Just as market demand is the sum of the demands of all buyers, market supply is the sum of the supplies of all sellers. The table in Figure 4.6 shows the supply schedules for two ice-cream producers—Ben and Jerry. At any price, Ben's supply schedule tells us the quantity of ice cream Ben supplies, and Jerry's supply schedule tells us the quantity of ice cream Jerry supplies. The market supply is the sum of the two individual supplies.

FIGURE 4.5

Ben's Supply Schedule and Supply Curve

The supply schedule shows the quantity supplied at each price. This supply curve, which graphs the supply schedule, shows how the quantity supplied of the good changes as its price varies. Because a higher price increases the quantity supplied, the supply curve slopes upward.

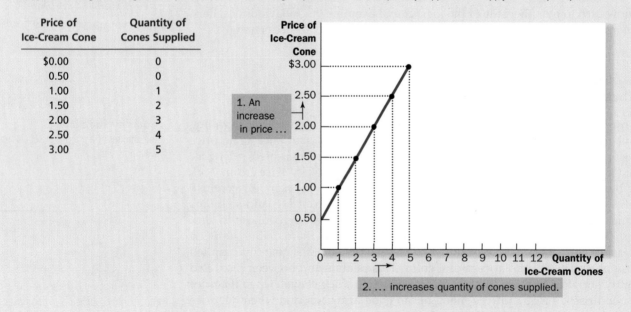

Price of Ice-Cream Cone	Quantity of Cones Supplied
$0.00	0
0.50	0
1.00	1
1.50	2
2.00	3
2.50	4
3.00	5

1. An increase in price ...

2. ... increases quantity of cones supplied.

FIGURE 4.6

Market Supply as the Sum of Individual Supplies

The quantity supplied in a market is the sum of the quantities supplied by all the sellers at each price. Thus, the market supply curve is found by adding horizontally the individual supply curves. At a price of $2, Ben supplies 3 ice-cream cones, and Jerry supplies 4 ice-cream cones. The quantity supplied in the market at this price is 7 cones.

Price of Ice-Cream Cone	Ben		Jerry		Market
$0.00	0	+	0	=	0
0.50	0		0		0
1.00	1		0		1
1.50	2		2		4
2.00	3		4		7
2.50	4		6		10
3.00	5		8		13

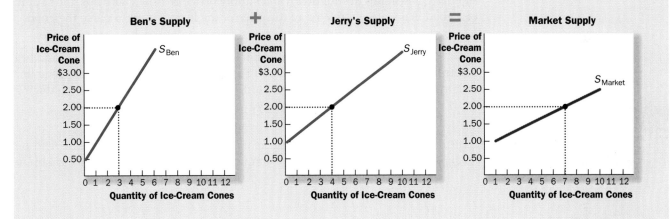

The graph in Figure 4.6 shows the supply curves that correspond to the supply schedules. As with demand curves, we sum the individual supply curves *horizontally* to obtain the market supply curve. That is, to find the total quantity supplied at any price, we add the individual quantities found on the horizontal axis of the individual supply curves. The market supply curve shows how the total quantity supplied varies as the price of the good varies.

Shifts in the Supply Curve

The supply curve for ice cream shows how much ice cream producers offer for sale at any given price, holding constant all the other factors beyond price that influence producers' decisions about how much to sell. This relationship can change over time, which is represented by a shift in the supply curve. For example, suppose the price of sugar falls. Because sugar is an input into producing ice cream, the fall in the price of sugar makes selling ice cream more profitable. This raises the supply of ice cream: At any given price, sellers are now willing to produce a larger quantity. Thus, the supply curve for ice cream shifts to the right.

Figure 4.7 illustrates shifts in supply. Any change that raises quantity supplied at every price, such as a fall in the price of sugar, shifts the supply curve to the right and is called *an increase in supply.* Similarly, any change that reduces the quantity supplied at every price shifts the supply curve to the left and is called *a decrease in supply.*

There are many variables that can shift the supply curve. Here are some of the most important:

Input Prices   To produce their output of ice cream, sellers use various inputs: cream, sugar, flavouring, ice-cream machines, the buildings in which the ice cream is made, and the labour of workers to mix the ingredients and operate the machines. When the price of one or more of these inputs rises, producing ice cream is less profitable, and firms supply less ice cream. If input prices rise substantially, a firm might shut down and supply no ice cream at all. Thus, the supply of a good is negatively related to the price of the inputs used to make the good.

Technology   The technology for turning the inputs into ice cream is yet another determinant of supply. The invention of the mechanized ice-cream machine, for example, reduced the amount of labour necessary to make ice cream. By reducing firms' costs, the advance in technology raised the supply of ice cream.

Expectations   The amount of ice cream a firm supplies today may depend on its expectations of the future. For example, if it expects the price of ice cream to

FIGURE 4.7

Shifts in the Supply Curve

Any change that raises the quantity that sellers wish to produce at a given price shifts the supply curve to the right. Any change that lowers the quantity that sellers wish to produce at a given price shifts the supply curve to the left.

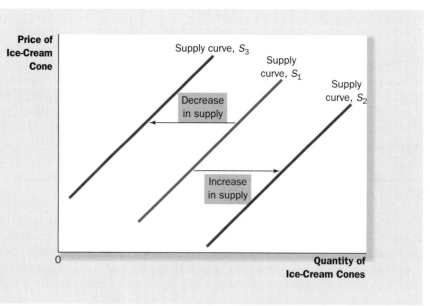

rise in the future, it will put some of its current production into storage and supply less to the market today.

Number of Sellers   Market supply depends on all those factors that influence the supply of individual sellers, such as the prices of inputs used to produce the good, the available technology, and expectations. In addition, the supply in a market depends on the number of sellers. If Ben or Jerry were to retire from the ice-cream business, the supply in the market would fall.

Summary   The supply curve shows what happens to the quantity supplied of a good when its price varies, holding constant all the other variables that influence sellers. When one of these other variables changes, the supply curve shifts. Table 4.2 lists all the variables that influence how much producers choose to sell of a good.

QuickQuiz   Make up an example of a supply schedule for pizza, and graph the implied supply curve. • Give an example of something that would shift this supply curve. • Would a change in the price of pizza shift this supply curve?

SUPPLY AND DEMAND TOGETHER

Having analyzed supply and demand separately, we now combine them to see how they determine the quantity of a good sold in a market and its price.

Equilibrium

Figure 4.8 (p. 78) shows the market supply curve and market demand curve together. Notice that there is one point at which the supply and demand curves intersect. This point is called the market's **equilibrium.** The price at this intersection is called the **equilibrium price,** and the quantity is called the **equilibrium**

equilibrium
a situation in which the price has reached the level where quantity supplied equals quantity demanded

equilibrium price
the price that balances quantity supplied and quantity demanded

equilibrium quantity
the quantity supplied and the quantity demanded at the equilibrium price

---

TABLE 4.2

Variables That Influence Sellers

This table lists the variables that affect how much producers choose to sell of any good. Notice the special role that the price of the good plays: A change in the good's price represents a movement along the supply curve, whereas a change in one of the other variables shifts the supply curve.

Variable	A Change in This Variable . . .
Price	Represents a movement along the supply curve
Input prices	Shifts the supply curve
Technology	Shifts the supply curve
Expectations	Shifts the supply curve
Number of sellers	Shifts the supply curve

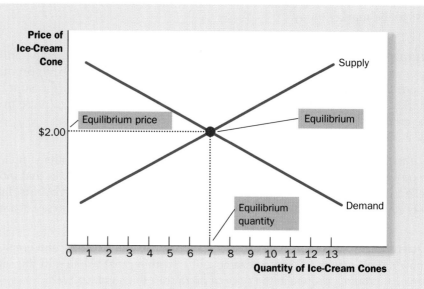

FIGURE 4.8

The Equilibrium of Supply and Demand

The equilibrium is found where the supply and demand curves intersect. At the equilibrium price, the quantity supplied equals the quantity demanded. Here the equilibrium price is $2: At this price, 7 ice-cream cones are supplied, and 7 ice-cream cones are demanded.

quantity. Here the equilibrium price is $2.00 per cone, and the equilibrium quantity is 7 ice-cream cones.

The dictionary defines the word *equilibrium* as a situation in which various forces are in balance—and this also describes a market's equilibrium. *At the equilibrium price, the quantity of the good that buyers are willing to buy exactly balances the quantity that sellers are willing to sell.* The equilibrium price is sometimes called the *market-clearing price* because, at this price, everyone in the market has been satisfied: Buyers can buy all they want to buy, and sellers can sell all they want to sell.

The actions of buyers and sellers naturally move markets toward the equilibrium of supply and demand. To see why, consider what happens when the market price is not equal to the equilibrium price.

Suppose first that the market price is above the equilibrium price, as in panel (a) of Figure 4.9. At a price of $2.50 per cone, the quantity of the good supplied (10 cones) exceeds the quantity demanded (4 cones). There is a **surplus** of the good: Suppliers are unable to sell all they want at the going price. A surplus is sometimes called a situation of *excess supply*. When there is a surplus in the ice-cream market, sellers of ice cream find their freezers increasingly full of ice cream they would like to sell but cannot. They respond to the surplus by cutting their prices. Falling prices, in turn, increase the quantity demanded and decrease the quantity supplied. Prices continue to fall until the market reaches the equilibrium.

Suppose now that the market price is below the equilibrium price, as in panel (b) of Figure 4.9. In this case, the price is $1.50 per cone, and the quantity of the good demanded exceeds the quantity supplied. There is a **shortage** of the good: Demanders are unable to buy all they want at the going price. A shortage is sometimes called a situation of *excess demand*. When a shortage occurs in the ice-cream market, buyers have to wait in long lines for a chance to buy one of the few cones that are available. With too many buyers chasing too few goods, sellers can

surplus
a situation in which quantity supplied is greater than quantity demanded

shortage
a situation in which quantity demanded is greater than quantity supplied

FIGURE 4.9

Markets Not in Equilibrium

In panel (a), there is a surplus. Because the market price of $2.50 is above the equilibrium price, the quantity supplied (10 cones) exceeds the quantity demanded (4 cones). Suppliers try to increase sales by cutting the price of a cone, and this moves the price toward its equilibrium level. In panel (b), there is a shortage. Because the market price of $1.50 is below the equilibrium price, the quantity demanded (10 cones) exceeds the quantity supplied (4 cones). With too many buyers chasing too few goods, suppliers can take advantage of the shortage by raising the price. Hence, in both cases, the price adjustment moves the market toward the equilibrium of supply and demand.

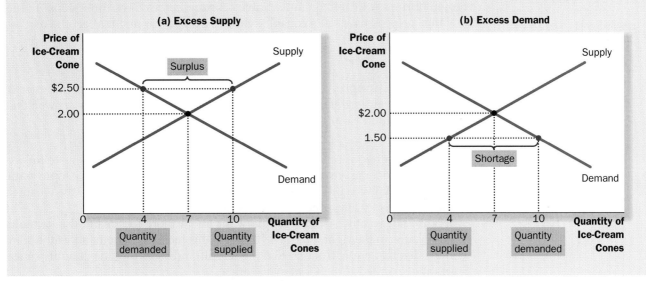

respond to the shortage by raising their prices without losing sales. As the price rises, quantity demanded falls, quantity supplied rises, and the market once again moves toward the equilibrium.

Thus, the activities of the many buyers and sellers automatically push the market price toward the equilibrium price. Once the market reaches its equilibrium, all buyers and sellers are satisfied, and there is no upward or downward pressure on the price. How quickly equilibrium is reached varies from market to market, depending on how quickly prices adjust. In most free markets, surpluses and shortages are only temporary because prices eventually move toward their equilibrium levels. Indeed, this phenomenon is so pervasive that it is called the **law of supply and demand:** The price of any good adjusts to bring the quantity supplied and quantity demanded for that good into balance.

law of supply and demand
the claim that the price of any good adjusts to bring the quantity supplied and the quantity demanded for that good into balance

Three Steps to Analyzing Changes in Equilibrium

So far we have seen how supply and demand together determine a market's equilibrium, which in turn determines the price of the good and the quantity of the good that buyers buy and sellers sell. Of course, the equilibrium price and quantity depend on the position of the supply and demand curves. When some event shifts one of these curves, the equilibrium in the market changes. The analysis of such a change is called *comparative statics* because it involves comparing two unchanging situations—an initial equilibrium and a new equilibrium.

When analyzing how some event affects a market, we proceed in three steps. First, we decide whether the event shifts the supply curve, the demand curve, or in some cases, both curves. Second, we decide whether the curve shifts to the right or to the left. Third, we use the supply-and-demand diagram to compare the initial equilibrium and the new equilibrium, which shows how the shift affects the equilibrium price and quantity. Table 4.3 summarizes these three steps. To see how this recipe is used, let's consider various events that might affect the market for ice cream.

Example: A Change in Demand

Suppose that one summer the weather is very hot. How does this event affect the market for ice cream? To answer this question, let's follow our three steps.

1. The hot weather affects the demand curve by changing people's taste for ice cream. That is, the weather changes the amount of ice cream that people want to buy at any given price. The supply curve is unchanged because the weather does not directly affect the firms that sell ice cream.
2. Because hot weather makes people want to eat more ice cream, the demand curve shifts to the right. Figure 4.10 shows this increase in demand as the shift in the demand curve from D_1 to D_2. This shift indicates that the quantity of ice cream demanded is higher at every price.
3. As Figure 4.10 shows, the increase in demand raises the equilibrium price from \$2.00 to \$2.50 and the equilibrium quantity from 7 to 10 cones. In other words, the hot weather increases the price of ice cream and the quantity of ice cream sold.

Shifts in Curves versus Movements along Curves

Notice that when hot weather drives up the price of ice cream, the quantity of ice cream that firms supply rises, even though the supply curve remains the same. In this case, economists say there has been an increase in "quantity supplied" but no change in "supply."

TABLE 4.3

A Three-Step Program for Analyzing Changes in Equilibrium

1. Decide whether the event shifts the supply or demand curve (or perhaps both).
2. Decide in which direction the curve shifts.
3. Use the supply-and-demand diagram to see how the shift changes the equilibrium price and quantity.

FIGURE 4.10

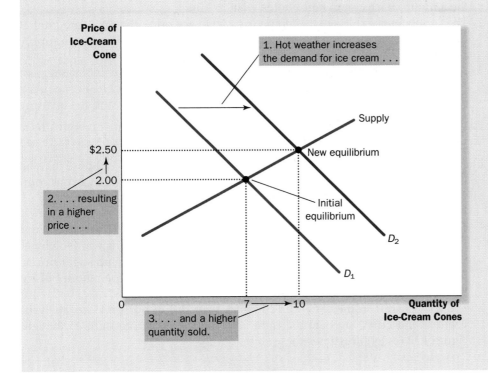

How an Increase in Demand Affects the Equilibrium

An event that raises quantity demanded at any given price shifts the demand curve to the right. The equilibrium price and the equilibrium quantity both rise. Here, an abnormally hot summer causes buyers to demand more ice cream. The demand curve shifts from D_1 to D_2, which causes the equilibrium price to rise from $2.00 to $2.50 and the equilibrium quantity to rise from 7 to 10 cones.

"Supply" refers to the position of the supply curve, whereas the "quantity supplied" refers to the amount suppliers wish to sell. In this example, supply does not change, because the weather does not alter firms' desire to sell at any given price. Instead, the hot weather alters consumers' desire to buy at any given price and thereby shifts the demand curve. The increase in demand causes the equilibrium price to rise. When the price rises, the quantity supplied rises. This increase in quantity supplied is represented by the movement along the supply curve.

To summarize, a shift *in* the supply curve is called a "change in supply," and a shift *in* the demand curve is called a "change in demand." A movement *along* a fixed supply curve is called a "change in the quantity supplied," and a movement *along* a fixed demand curve is called a "change in the quantity demanded."

Example: A Change in Supply   Suppose that, during another summer, a hurricane destroys part of the sugar cane crop and drives up the price of sugar. How does this event affect the market for ice cream? Once again, to answer this question, we follow our three steps.

1. The change in the price of sugar, an input into making ice cream, affects the supply curve. By raising the costs of production, it reduces the amount of ice cream that firms want to produce and sell at any given price. The demand

curve does not change, because the higher cost of inputs does not directly affect the amount of ice cream households wish to buy.

2. The supply curve shifts to the left because, at every price, the total amount that firms are willing to sell is reduced. Figure 4.11 illustrates this decrease in supply as a shift in the supply curve from S_1 to S_2.

3. As Figure 4.11 shows, the shift in the supply curve raises the equilibrium price from $2.00 to $2.50 and lowers the equilibrium quantity from 7 to 4 cones. As a result of the sugar price increase, the price of ice cream rises, and the quantity of ice cream sold falls.

Example: A Change in Both Supply and Demand   Now suppose that the heat wave and the hurricane occur during the same summer. To analyze this combination of events, we again follow our three steps.

1. We determine that both curves must shift. The hot weather affects the demand curve because it alters the amount of ice cream that households want to buy at any given price. At the same time, when the hurricane drives up sugar prices, it alters the supply curve for ice cream because it changes the amount of ice cream that firms want to sell at any given price.

2. The curves shift in the same directions as they did in our previous analysis: The demand curve shifts to the right, and the supply curve shifts to the left. Figure 4.12 (p. 84) illustrates these shifts.

FIGURE 4.11

How a Decrease in Supply Affects the Equilibrium

An event that reduces quantity supplied at any given price shifts the supply curve to the left. The equilibrium price rises, and the equilibrium quantity falls. Here, an increase in the price of sugar (an input) causes sellers to supply less ice cream. The supply curve shifts from S_1 to S_2, which causes the equilibrium price of ice cream to rise from $2.00 to $2.50 and the equilibrium quantity to fall from 7 to 4 cones.

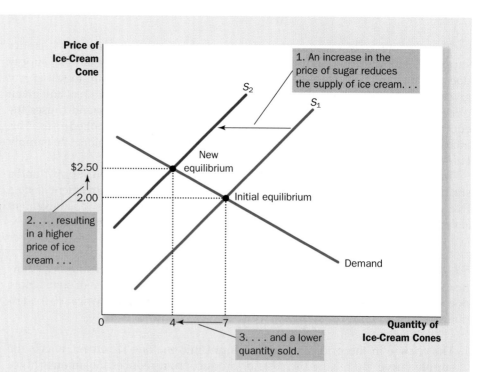

IN THE NEWS

SUPPLY, DEMAND, AND THE PRICE OF LUMBER

This article discusses the impact of forest fires, construction booms, and trade restrictions on the demand, the supply, and the price of Canadian lumber. Notice that expectations of future demand and supply, and hence expectations of the future price of lumber, play an important role.

Lumber Prices Seen Declining

By Peter Kennedy

VANCOUVER – Lumber prices are slipping as fears of supply shortages continue to ease in the wake of damp weather and cooling temperatures in fire-ravaged British Columbia.

Yesterday, the price of lumber for September delivery slipped to $350 (U.S.) for 1,000 board feet from a 2003 high of $366.70 reached last week.

Lumber traders said prices could soon fall below $300 as the market turns its attention from forest fires in B.C. and the northwestern United States to a supply glut that was fuelled in part by U.S. duties on Canadian softwood lumber.

"It's hard to be bullish when prices have been trading near 370," said Graham Dallimore, senior vice-president with Global Futures Corp., a Vancouver-based commodities trader. Analysts say an exceptionally strong residential construction season in the United States has contributed to the rise in futures prices from $285.50 in early July.

But market speculation that prices will continue to retreat are based not only on the waning threat of forest fires but also on the fact that the North American construction season begins to wind down in September.

Prices are expected to come under pressure as the fires die down and the industry gets back to normal business in B.C. and other key forestry regions such as Washington and Oregon.

"There is an expectation that logging [in the B.C. interior] will resume in the coming weeks," Mr. Dallimore said.

Industry officials say forest fires in the interior of B.C. burned through 240,000 hectares, an area that is roughly the equivalent of the annual timber harvest across the entire province.

That in turn led to the closing of nine sawmills in the B.C. interior due to a lack of available logs.

The companies that own those operations include Gorman Bros., Weyerhaeuser Co., Louisiana-Pacific Corp., Tembec Inc. and Slocan Forest Products Ltd. Fire also destroyed ... Tolko Industries Ltd.'s sawmill at Louis Creek, B.C.

"If weather permits, my sense is that in many cases it will take about a week or so for many of them to get enough logs to start up again," said Peter Affleck, vice-president of forestry at the Council of Forest Industries in Kelowna, B.C.

However, Mr. Dallimore said any decline from existing price levels may be gradual because inventories remain relatively low, and the construction sector still needs lumber. He is not alone in taking that view.

"Prices will stay quite high for at least another month and then ease off in the fourth quarter," said Patricia Mohr, vice-president of economics at Bank of Nova Scotia in Toronto.

Some people believe the cash price of western SPF [spruce–pine–fir] two-by-four construction lumber—which traded at $370 for 1,000 board feet yesterday—will go as low as $270, Ms. Mohr said.

However, prices may be supported in the near term by fears of how much damage the fires have done to logs, especially in B.C., she said.

Industry officials say it is still too early to determine how much of the damaged wood will turn out to be salvageable. "The actual harvesting of the charred wood is not going to be pleasant," Mr. Affleck said. "The job will be dirty, black and difficult."

Source: *The Globe and Mail,* September 12, 2003.

FIGURE 4.12

A Shift in Both Supply and Demand

Here we observe a simultaneous increase in demand and decrease in supply. Two outcomes are possible. In panel (a), the equilibrium price rises from P_1 to P_2, and the equilibrium quantity rises from Q_1 to Q_2. In panel (b), the equilibrium price again rises from P_1 to P_2, but the equilibrium quantity falls from Q_1 to Q_2.

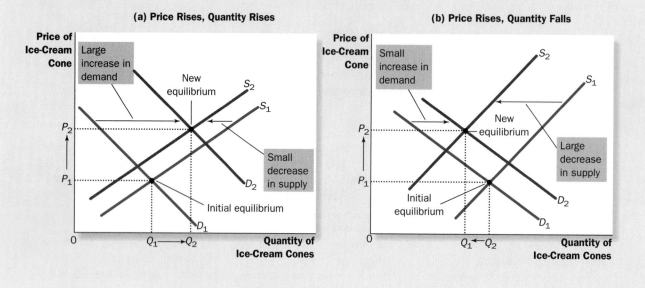

3. As Figure 4.12 shows, there are two possible outcomes that might result, depending on the relative size of the demand and supply shifts. In both cases, the equilibrium price rises. In panel (a), where demand increases substantially while supply falls just a little, the equilibrium quantity also rises. By contrast, in panel (b), where supply falls substantially while demand rises just a little, the equilibrium quantity falls. Thus, these events certainly raise the price of ice cream, but their impact on the amount of ice cream sold is ambiguous (that is, it could go either way).

Summary We have just seen three examples of how to use supply and demand curves to analyze a change in equilibrium. Whenever an event shifts the supply curve, the demand curve, or perhaps both curves, you can use these tools to predict how the event will alter the amount sold in equilibrium and the price at which the good is sold. Table 4.4 shows the predicted outcome for any combination of shifts in the two curves. To make sure you understand how to use the tools of supply and demand, pick a few entries in this table and make sure you can explain to yourself why the table contains the prediction it does.

TABLE 4.4

What Happens to Price and Quantity When Supply or Demand Shifts?

As a quick quiz, make sure you can explain each of the entries in this table using a supply-and-demand diagram.

	No Change in Supply	An Increase in Supply	A Decrease in Supply
No Change in Demand	P same Q same	P down Q up	P up Q down
An Increase in Demand	P up Q up	P ambiguous Q up	P up Q ambiguous
A Decrease in Demand	P down Q down	P down Q ambiguous	P ambiguous Q down

QuickQuiz   Analyze what happens to the market for pizza if the price of tomatoes rises. • Analyze what happens to the market for pizza if the price of hamburgers falls.

CONCLUSION: HOW PRICES ALLOCATE RESOURCES

This chapter has analyzed supply and demand in a single market. Although our discussion has centred around the market for ice cream, the lessons learned here apply in most other markets as well. Whenever you go to a store to buy something, you are contributing to the demand for that item. Whenever you look for a job, you are contributing to the supply of labour services. Because supply and demand are such pervasive economic phenomena, the model of supply and demand is a powerful tool for analysis. We will be using this model repeatedly in the following chapters.

One of the ten principles of economics discussed in Chapter 1 is that markets are usually a good way to organize economic activity. Although it is still too early to judge whether market outcomes are good or bad, in this chapter we have begun to see how markets work. In any economic system, scarce resources have to be allocated among competing uses. Market economies harness the forces of supply and demand to serve that end. Supply and demand together determine the prices of the economy's many different goods and services; prices in turn are the signals that guide the allocation of resources.

For example, consider the allocation of beachfront land. Because the amount of this land is limited, not everyone can enjoy the luxury of living by the beach. Who gets this resource? The answer is: whoever is willing to pay the price. The price of beachfront land adjusts until the quantity of land demanded exactly balances the quantity supplied. Thus, in market economies, prices are the mechanism for rationing scarce resources.

Similarly, prices determine who produces each good and how much is produced. For instance, consider farming. Because we need food to survive, it is crucial that some people work on farms. What determines who is a farmer and who is not? In a free society, there is no government planning agency making this decision and ensuring an adequate supply of food. Instead, the allocation of workers to farms is based on the job decisions of millions of workers. This decentralized system works well because these decisions depend on prices. The prices of food and the wages of farmworkers (the price of their labour) adjust to ensure that enough people choose to be farmers.

If a person had never seen a market economy in action, the whole idea might seem preposterous. Economies are large groups of people engaged in many interdependent activities. What prevents decentralized decision making from degenerating into chaos? What coordinates the actions of the millions of people with their varying abilities and desires? What ensures that what needs to be done does in fact get done? The answer, in a word, is *prices*. If market economies are guided by an invisible hand, as Adam Smith famously suggested, then the price system is the baton that the invisible hand uses to conduct the economic orchestra.

SUMMARY

- Economists use the model of supply and demand to analyze competitive markets. In a competitive market, there are many buyers and sellers, each of whom has little or no influence on the market price.

- The demand curve shows how the quantity of a good demanded depends on the price. According to the law of demand, as the price of a good falls, the quantity demanded rises. Therefore, the demand curve slopes downward.

- In addition to price, other determinants of how much consumers want to buy include income, the prices of substitutes and complements, tastes, expectations, and the number of buyers. If one of these factors changes, the demand curve shifts.

- The supply curve shows how the quantity of a good supplied depends on the price. According to the law of supply, as the price of a good rises, the quantity supplied rises. Therefore, the supply curve slopes upward.

- In addition to price, other determinants of how much producers want to sell include input prices, technology, expectations, and the number of sellers. If one of these factors changes, the supply curve shifts.

- The intersection of the supply and demand curves determines the market equilibrium. At the equilibrium price, the quantity demanded equals the quantity supplied.

- The behaviour of buyers and sellers naturally drives markets toward their equilibrium. When the market price is above the equilibrium price, there is a surplus of the good, which causes the market price to fall. When the market price is below the equilibrium price, there is a shortage, which causes the market price to rise.

- To analyze how any event influences a market, we use the supply-and-demand diagram to examine how the event affects the equilibrium price and quantity. To do this we follow three steps. First, we decide whether the event shifts the supply curve or the demand curve (or both). Second, we decide which direction the curve shifts. Third, we compare the new equilibrium with the initial equilibrium.

- In market economies, prices are the signals that guide economic decisions and thereby allocate scarce resources. For every good in the economy, the price ensures that supply and demand are in balance. The equilibrium price then determines how much of the good buyers choose to purchase and how much sellers choose to produce.

KEY CONCEPTS

market, p. 66
competitive market, p. 66
quantity demanded, p. 67
law of demand, p. 68
demand schedule, p. 68
demand curve, p. 68
normal good, p. 70

inferior good, p. 70
substitutes, p. 71
complements, p. 71
quantity supplied, p. 73
law of supply, p. 73
supply schedule, p. 74
supply curve, p. 74

equilibrium, p. 77
equilibrium price, p. 77
equilibrium quantity, p. 77
surplus, p. 78
shortage, p. 78
law of supply and demand, p. 79

QUESTIONS FOR REVIEW

1. What is a competitive market? Briefly describe the types of markets other than perfectly competitive markets.

2. What determines the quantity of a good that buyers demand?

3. What are the demand schedule and the demand curve, and how are they related? Why does the demand curve slope downward?

4. Does a change in consumers' tastes lead to a movement along the demand curve or a shift in the demand curve? Does a change in price lead to a movement along the demand curve or a shift in the demand curve?

5. Popeye's income declines and, as a result, he buys more spinach. Is spinach an inferior or a normal good? What happens to Popeye's demand curve for spinach?

6. What determines the quantity of a good that sellers supply?

7. What are the supply schedule and the supply curve, and how are they related? Why does the supply curve slope upward?

8. Does a change in producers' technology lead to a movement along the supply curve or a shift in the supply curve? Does a change in price lead to a movement along the supply curve or a shift in the supply curve?

9. Define the equilibrium of a market. Describe the forces that move a market toward its equilibrium.

10. Beer and pizza are complements because they are often enjoyed together. When the price of beer rises, what happens to the supply, demand, quantity supplied, quantity demanded, and the price in the market for pizza?

11. Describe the role of prices in market economies.

PROBLEMS AND APPLICATIONS

1. Explain each of the following statements using supply-and-demand diagrams.
   a. When a cold snap hits Florida, the price of orange juice rises in supermarkets throughout Canada.
   b. When the weather turns warm in Quebec every summer, the prices of hotel rooms in Caribbean resorts plummet.
   c. When a war breaks out in the Middle East, the price of gasoline rises, while the price of a used SUV falls.

2. "An increase in the demand for notebooks raises the quantity of notebooks demanded, but not the quantity supplied." Is this statement true or false? Explain.

3. Consider the market for minivans. For each of the events listed here, identify which of the determinants of demand or supply are affected. Also indicate whether demand or supply is increased or decreased. Then show the effect on the price and quantity of minivans.
   a. People decide to have more children.

  b. A strike by steelworkers raises steel prices.

  c. Engineers develop new automated machinery for the production of minivans.

  d. The price of SUVs rises.

  e. A stock market crash lowers people's wealth.

4. During the 1990s, technological advances reduced the cost of computer chips. How do you think this affected the market for computers? For computer software? For typewriters?

5. Using supply-and-demand diagrams, show the effect of the following events on the market for sweatshirts.

  a. A hurricane in South Carolina damages the cotton crop.

  b. The price of leather jackets falls.

  c. All colleges require morning calisthenics in appropriate attire.

  d. New knitting machines are invented.

6. Suppose that in the year 2005 the number of births is temporarily high. How does this baby boom affect the price of baby-sitting services in 2010 and 2020? (Hint: 5-year-olds need baby-sitters, whereas 15-year-olds can be baby-sitters.)

7. Ketchup is a complement (as well as a condiment) for hot dogs. If the price of hot dogs rises, what happens to the market for ketchup? For tomatoes? For tomato juice? For orange juice?

8. The case study presented in the chapter discussed cigarette taxes as a way to reduce smoking. Now think about the markets for other tobacco products such as cigars and chewing tobacco.

  a. Are these goods substitutes or complements for cigarettes?

  b. Using a supply-and-demand diagram, show what happens in the markets for cigars and chewing tobacco if the tax on cigarettes is increased.

  c. If policymakers wanted to reduce total tobacco consumption, what policies could they combine with the cigarette tax?

9. The market for pizza has the following demand and supply schedules:

Price	Quantity Demanded	Quantity Supplied
$4	135	26
5	104	53
6	81	81
7	68	98
8	53	110
9	39	121

Graph the demand and supply curves. What is the equilibrium price and quantity in this market? If the actual price in this market were *above* the equilibrium price, what would drive the market toward the equilibrium? If the actual price in this market were *below* the equilibrium price, what would drive the market toward the equilibrium?

10. Because bagels and cream cheese are often eaten together, they are complements.

  a. We observe that both the equilibrium price of cream cheese and the equilibrium quantity of bagels have risen. What could be responsible for this pattern—a fall in the price of flour or a fall in the price of milk? Illustrate and explain your answer.

  b. Suppose instead that the equilibrium price of cream cheese has risen but the equilibrium quantity of bagels has fallen. What could be responsible for this pattern—a rise in the price of flour or a rise in the price of milk? Illustrate and explain your answer.

11. Suppose that the price of basketball tickets at your school is determined by market forces. Currently, the demand and supply schedules are as follows:

Price	Quantity Demanded	Quantity Supplied
$4	10 000	8000
8	8 000	8000
12	6 000	8000
16	4 000	8000
20	2 000	8000

  a. Draw the demand and supply curves. What is unusual about this supply curve? Why might this be true?

  b. What are the equilibrium price and quantity of tickets?

c. Your school plans to increase total enrollment next year by 5000 students. The additional students will have the following demand schedule:

Price	Quantity Demanded
$4	4000
8	3000
12	2000
16	1000
20	0

Now add the old demand schedule and the demand schedule for the new students to calculate the new demand schedule for the entire school. What will be the new equilibrium price and quantity?

12. An article in *The New York Times* described a successful marketing campaign by the French champagne industry. The article noted that "many executives felt giddy about the stratospheric champagne prices. But they also feared that such sharp price increases would cause demand to decline, which would then cause prices to plunge." What mistake are the executives making in their analysis of the situation? Illustrate your answer with a graph.

13. Market research has revealed the following information about the market for chocolate bars: The demand schedule can be represented by the equation $Q^D = 1600 - 300P$, where Q^D is the quantity demanded and P is the price. The supply schedule can be represented by the equation $Q^S = 1400 + 700P$, where Q^S is the quantity supplied. Calculate the equilibrium price and quantity in the market for chocolate bars.

14. What do we mean by a perfectly competitive market? Do you think that the example of ice cream used in this chapter fits this description? Is there another type of market that better characterizes the market for ice cream?

INTERNET RESOURCES

Economist Alfred Marshall published his *Principles of Economics* in 1890. You can read the entire book online at http://www.econlib.org/library/Marshall/marP.html. Although Marshall's book is over 100 years old, you can still recognize it as an introductory textbook—as the great-great-grandfather of this textbook. Just like modern economists, Marshall thought about demand and supply as schedules or curves, as a relationship between price and quantity. You will find what Marshall has to say about demand and supply in Book V of his *Principles of Economics.*

http://   For more study tools, please visit http://www.mankiw3e.nelson.com.

© JIM STEINHART

5

Learning Objectives

In this chapter, you will ...

- Learn the meaning of the elasticity of demand
- Examine what determines the elasticity of demand
- Learn the meaning of the elasticity of supply
- Examine what determines the elasticity of supply
- Apply the concept of elasticity in two very different markets

ELASTICITY AND ITS APPLICATION

Imagine yourself as a Saskatchewan wheat farmer. Because you earn all your income from selling wheat, you devote much effort to making your land as productive as it can be. You monitor weather and soil conditions, check your fields for pests and disease, and study the latest advances in farm technology. You know that the more wheat you grow, the more you will have to sell after the harvest, and the higher your income and your standard of living will be.

One day the University of Saskatchewan announces a major discovery. Researchers in its Plant Sciences department have devised a new hybrid of wheat that raises the amount farmers can produce from each hectare of land by 20 percent. How should you react to this news? Should you use the new hybrid? Does this discovery make you better off or worse off than you were before? In this chapter we will see that these questions can have surprising answers. The surprise will come from applying the most basic tools of economics—supply and demand—to the market for wheat.

The previous chapter introduced supply and demand. In any competitive market, such as the market for wheat, the upward-sloping supply curve represents the behaviour of sellers, and the downward-sloping demand curve represents the behaviour of buyers. The price of the good adjusts to bring the quantity supplied and quantity demanded of the good into balance. To apply this basic analysis to understand the impact of the plant scientists' discovery, we must first develop one more tool: the concept of *elasticity*. Elasticity, a measure of how much buyers and sellers respond to changes in market conditions, allows us to analyze supply and demand with greater precision. When studying how some event or policy affects a market, we can discuss not only the direction of the effects but their magnitude as well.

THE ELASTICITY OF DEMAND

When we introduced demand in Chapter 4, we noted that consumers usually buy more of a good when its price is lower, when their incomes are higher, when the prices of substitutes for the good are higher, or when the prices of complements of the good are lower. Our discussion of demand was qualitative, not quantitative. That is, we discussed the direction in which quantity demanded moves, but not the size of the change. To measure how much consumers respond to changes in these variables, economists use the concept of **elasticity.**

elasticity
a measure of the responsiveness of quantity demanded or quantity supplied to one of its determinants

The Price Elasticity of Demand and Its Determinants

The law of demand states that a fall in the price of a good raises the quantity demanded. The **price elasticity of demand** measures how much the quantity demanded responds to a change in price. Demand for a good is said to be *elastic* if the quantity demanded responds substantially to changes in the price. Demand is said to be *inelastic* if the quantity demanded responds only slightly to changes in the price.

price elasticity of demand
a measure of how much the quantity demanded of a good responds to a change in the price of that good, computed as the percentage change in quantity demanded divided by the percentage change in price

The price elasticity of demand for any good measures how willing consumers are to move away from the good as its price rises. Thus, the elasticity reflects the many economic, social, and psychological forces that shape consumer tastes. Based on experience, however, we can state some general rules about what determines the price elasticity of demand.

Availability of Close Substitutes   Goods with close substitutes tend to have more elastic demand because it is easier for consumers to switch from that good to others. For example, butter and margarine are easily substitutable. A small increase in the price of butter, assuming the price of margarine is held fixed, causes the quantity of butter sold to fall by a large amount. By contrast, because eggs are a food without a close substitute, the demand for eggs is less elastic than the demand for butter.

Necessities versus Luxuries   Necessities tend to have inelastic demands, whereas luxuries have elastic demands. When the price of a visit to the dentist rises, people will not dramatically alter the number of times they go to the dentist, although they might go somewhat less often. By contrast, when the price of sailboats rises, the quantity of sailboats demanded falls substantially. The reason is that most people view dentist visits as a necessity and sailboats as a luxury. Of course, whether a good is a necessity or a luxury depends not on the intrinsic properties of the good but on the preferences of the buyer. For an avid sailor with little concern about his teeth, sailboats might be a necessity with inelastic demand and dentist visits a luxury with elastic demand.

Definition of the Market   The elasticity of demand in any market depends on how we draw the boundaries of the market. Narrowly defined markets tend to have more elastic demand than broadly defined markets, because it is easier to find close substitutes for narrowly defined goods. For example, food, a broad category, has a fairly inelastic demand because there are no good substitutes for food. Ice cream, a more narrow category, has a more elastic demand because it is easy to substitute other desserts for ice cream. Vanilla ice cream, a very narrow category, has a very elastic demand because other flavours of ice cream are almost perfect substitutes for vanilla.

Time Horizon   Goods tend to have more elastic demand over longer time horizons. When the price of gasoline rises, the quantity of gasoline demanded falls only slightly in the first few months. Over time, however, people buy more fuel-efficient cars, switch to public transportation, and move closer to where they work. Within several years, the quantity of gasoline demanded falls substantially.

Computing the Price Elasticity of Demand

Now that we have discussed the price elasticity of demand in general terms, let's be more precise about how it is measured. Economists compute the price elasticity of demand as the percentage change in the quantity demanded divided by the percentage change in the price. That is,

$$\text{Price elasticity of demand} = \frac{\text{Percentage change in quantity demanded}}{\text{Percentage change in price}}$$

For example, suppose that a 10 percent increase in the price of an ice-cream cone causes the amount of ice cream you buy to fall by 20 percent. We calculate your elasticity of demand as

$$\text{Price elasticity of demand} = \frac{20 \text{ percent}}{10 \text{ percent}} = 2$$

In this example, the elasticity is 2, reflecting that the change in the quantity demanded is proportionately twice as large as the change in the price.

Because the quantity demanded of a good is negatively related to its price, the percentage change in quantity will always have the opposite sign as the percentage change in price. In this example, the percentage change in price is a *positive* 10 percent (reflecting an increase), and the percentage change in quantity demanded is a *negative* 20 percent (reflecting a decrease). For this reason, price elasticities of demand are sometimes reported as negative numbers. In this book we follow the common practice of dropping the minus sign and reporting all price elasticities as positive numbers. (Mathematicians call this the *absolute value*.) With this convention, a larger price elasticity implies a greater responsiveness of quantity demanded to price.

The Midpoint Method: A Better Way to Calculate Percentage Changes and Elasticities

If you try calculating the price elasticity of demand between two points on a demand curve, you will quickly notice an annoying problem: The elasticity from point A to point B seems different from the elasticity from point B to point A. For example, consider these numbers:

Point A: Price = $4 Quantity = 120

Point B: Price = $6 Quantity = 80

Going from point A to point B, the price rises by 50 percent, and the quantity falls by 33 percent, indicating that the price elasticity of demand is 33/50, or 0.66. By contrast, going from point B to point A, the price falls by 33 percent, and the quantity rises by 50 percent, indicating that the price elasticity of demand is 50/33, or 1.5.

One way to avoid this problem is to use the *midpoint method* for calculating elasticities. The standard way to compute a percentage change is to divide the change by the initial level. By contrast, the midpoint method computes a percentage change by dividing the change by the midpoint (or average) of the initial and final levels. For instance, $5 is the midpoint of $4 and $6. Therefore, according to the midpoint method, a change from $4 to $6 is considered a 40 percent rise, because $(6 - 4)/5 \times 100 = 40$. Similarly, a change from $6 to $4 is considered a 40 percent fall.

Because the midpoint method gives the same answer regardless of the direction of change, it is often used when calculating the price elasticity of demand between two points. In our example, the midpoint between point A and point B is

Midpoint: Price = $5 Quantity = 100

According to the midpoint method, when going from point A to point B, the price rises by 40 percent and the quantity falls by 40 percent. Similarly, when going from point B to point A, the price falls by 40 percent and the quantity rises by 40 percent. In both directions, the price elasticity of demand equals 1.

We can express the midpoint method with the following formula for the price elasticity of demand between two points, denoted (Q_1, P_1) and (Q_2, P_2):

$$\text{Price elasticity of demand} = \frac{(Q_2 - Q_1)/[(Q_2 + Q_1)/2]}{(P_2 - P_1)/[(P_2 + P_1)/2]}$$

The numerator is the percentage change in quantity computed using the midpoint method, and the denominator is the percentage change in price computed using the midpoint method. If you ever need to calculate elasticities, you should use this formula.

In this book, however, we rarely perform such calculations. For most of our purposes, what elasticity represents—the responsiveness of quantity demanded to price—is more important than how it is calculated.

The Variety of Demand Curves

Economists classify demand curves according to their elasticity. Demand is *elastic* when the elasticity is greater than 1, so that quantity moves proportionately more than the price. Demand is *inelastic* when the elasticity is less than 1, so that quantity moves proportionately less than the price. If the elasticity is exactly 1, so that quantity moves the same amount proportionately as price, demand is said to have *unit elasticity.*

Because the price elasticity of demand measures how much quantity demanded responds to changes in the price, it is closely related to the slope of the demand curve. The following rule of thumb is a useful guide: The flatter the demand curve that passes through a given point, the greater the price elasticity of demand. The steeper the demand curve that passes through a given point, the smaller the price elasticity of demand.

Figure 5.1 (p. 96) shows five cases. In the extreme case of a zero elasticity shown in panel (a), demand is *perfectly inelastic,* and the demand curve is vertical. In this case, regardless of the price, the quantity demanded stays the same. As the elasticity rises, the demand curve gets flatter and flatter, as shown in panels (b), (c), and (d). At the opposite extreme shown in panel (e), demand is *perfectly elastic.* This occurs as the price elasticity of demand approaches infinity and the demand curve becomes horizontal, reflecting the fact that very small changes in the price lead to huge changes in the quantity demanded.

Finally, if you have trouble keeping straight the terms *elastic* and *inelastic,* here's a memory trick for you: I̲nelastic curves, such as in panel (a) of Figure 5.1, look like the letter *I.* E̲lastic curves, as in panel (e), look like the letter *E.* This is not a deep insight, but it might help on your next exam.

Total Revenue and the Price Elasticity of Demand

When studying changes in supply or demand in a market, one variable we often want to study is **total revenue,** the amount paid by buyers and received by sellers of the good. In any market, total revenue is $P \times Q$, the price of the good times the quantity of the good sold. We can show total revenue graphically, as in Figure 5.2 (p. 97). The height of the box under the demand curve is P, and the width is Q. The area of this box, $P \times Q$, equals the total revenue in this market. In Figure 5.2, where $P = \$4$ and $Q = 100$, total revenue is $\$4 \times 100$, or $\$400$.

How does total revenue change as one moves along the demand curve? The answer depends on the price elasticity of demand. If demand is inelastic, as in Figure 5.3 (p. 97), then an increase in the price causes an increase in total revenue. Here an increase in price from $\$1$ to $\$3$ causes the quantity demanded to fall only from 100 to 80, and so total revenue rises from $\$100$ to $\$240$. An increase in price raises $P \times Q$ because the fall in Q is proportionately smaller than the rise in P.

total revenue
the amount paid by buyers and received by sellers of a good, computed as the price of the good times the quantity sold

FIGURE 5.1

The Price Elasticity of Demand

The price elasticity of demand determines whether the demand curve is steep or flat. Note that all percentage changes are calculated using the midpoint method.

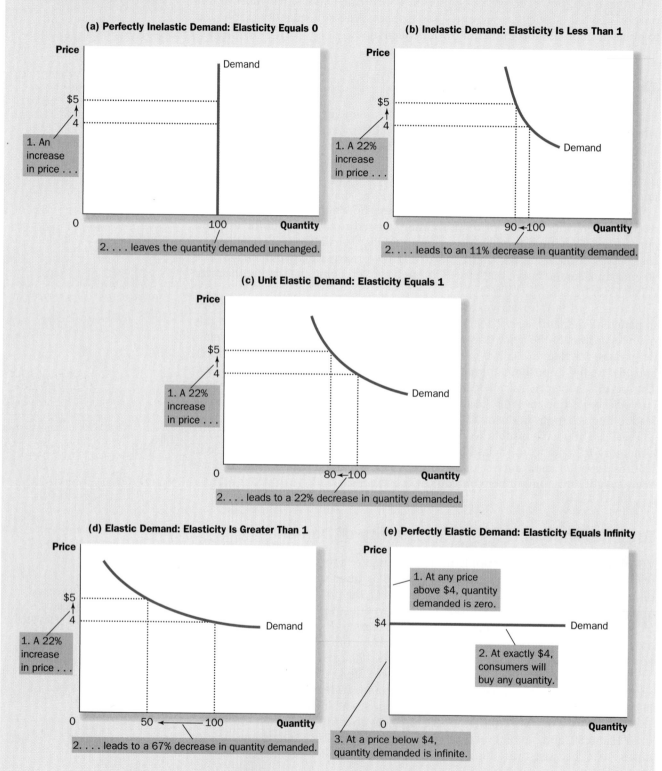

(a) Perfectly Inelastic Demand: Elasticity Equals 0

Price

$5
4

Demand

1. An increase in price . . .

0   100   Quantity

2. . . . leaves the quantity demanded unchanged.

(b) Inelastic Demand: Elasticity Is Less Than 1

Price

$5
4

Demand

1. A 22% increase in price . . .

0   90 ← 100   Quantity

2. . . . leads to an 11% decrease in quantity demanded.

(c) Unit Elastic Demand: Elasticity Equals 1

Price

$5
4

Demand

1. A 22% increase in price . . .

0   80 ← 100   Quantity

2. . . . leads to a 22% decrease in quantity demanded.

(d) Elastic Demand: Elasticity Is Greater Than 1

Price

$5
4

Demand

1. A 22% increase in price . . .

0   50 ← 100   Quantity

2. . . . leads to a 67% decrease in quantity demanded.

(e) Perfectly Elastic Demand: Elasticity Equals Infinity

Price

1. At any price above $4, quantity demanded is zero.

$4   Demand

2. At exactly $4, consumers will buy any quantity.

0   Quantity

3. At a price below $4, quantity demanded is infinite.

FIGURE 5.2

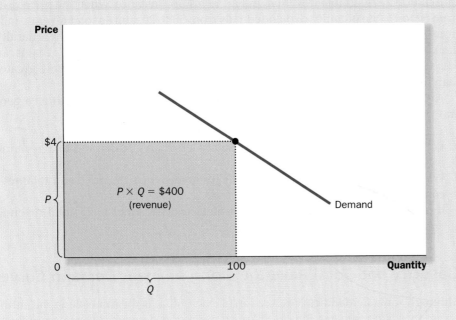

Total Revenue

The total amount paid by buyers, and received as revenue by sellers, equals the area of the box under the demand curve, $P \times Q$. Here, at a price of $4, the quantity demanded is 100, and total revenue is $400.

FIGURE 5.3

How Total Revenue Changes When Price Changes: Inelastic Demand

With an inelastic demand curve, an increase in the price leads to a decrease in quantity demanded that is proportionately smaller. Therefore, total revenue (the product of price and quantity) increases. Here, an increase in the price from $1 to $3 causes the quantity demanded to fall from 100 to 80, and total revenue rises from $100 to $240.

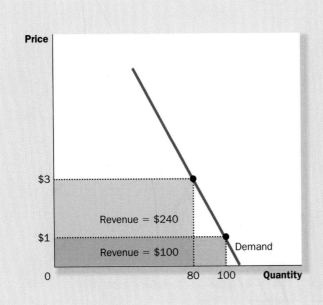

We obtain the opposite result if demand is elastic: An increase in the price causes a decrease in total revenue. In Figure 5.4, for instance, when the price rises from $4 to $5, the quantity demanded falls from 50 to 20, and so total revenue falls from $200 to $100. Because demand is elastic, the reduction in the quantity demanded is so great that it more than offsets the increase in the price. That is, an increase in price reduces $P \times Q$ because the fall in Q is proportionately greater than the rise in P.

Although the examples in these two figures are extreme, they illustrate a general rule:

- When demand is inelastic (a price elasticity less than 1), price and total revenue move in the same direction.
- When demand is elastic (a price elasticity greater than 1), price and total revenue move in opposite directions.
- If demand is unit elastic (a price elasticity exactly equal to 1), total revenue remains constant when the price changes.

Elasticity and Total Revenue along a Linear Demand Curve

Although some demand curves have an elasticity that is the same along the entire curve, that is not always the case. An example of a demand curve along which elasticity changes is a straight line, as shown in Figure 5.5. A linear demand curve has a constant slope. Recall that slope is defined as "rise over run," which here is the ratio of the change in price ("rise") to the change in quantity ("run"). This par-

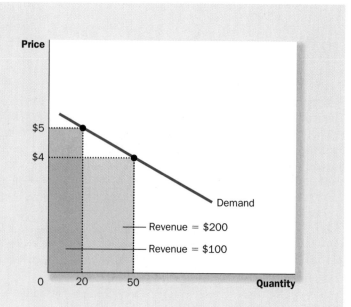

FIGURE 5.4

How Total Revenue Changes When Price Changes: Elastic Demand

With an elastic demand curve, an increase in the price leads to a decrease in quantity demanded that is proportionately larger. Therefore, total revenue (the product of price and quantity) decreases. Here, an increase in the price from $4 to $5 causes the quantity demanded to fall from 50 to 20, so total revenue falls from $200 to $100.

FIGURE 5.5

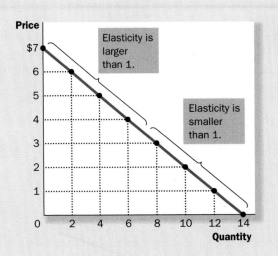

Elasticity of a Linear Demand Curve

The slope of a linear demand curve is constant, but its elasticity is not. The demand schedule in the table was used to calculate the price elasticity of demand by the midpoint method. At points with a low price and high quantity, the demand curve is inelastic. At points with a high price and low quantity, the demand curve is elastic.

Price	Quantity	Total Revenue (Price × Quantity)	Percent Change in Price	Percent Change in Quantity	Elasticity	Description
$7	0	$ 0				
			15	200	13.0	Elastic
6	2	12				
			18	67	3.7	Elastic
5	4	20				
			22	40	1.8	Elastic
4	6	24				
			29	29	1.0	Unit elastic
3	8	24				
			40	22	0.6	Inelastic
2	10	20				
			67	18	0.3	Inelastic
1	12	12				
			200	15	0.1	Inelastic
0	14	0				

ticular demand curve's slope is constant, because each $1 increase in price causes the same 2-unit decrease in the quantity demanded.

Even though the slope of a linear demand curve is constant, the elasticity is not. The reason is that the slope is the ratio of *changes* in the two variables, whereas the elasticity is the ratio of *percentage changes* in the two variables. You can see this by looking at the table in Figure 5.5, which shows the demand schedule for the linear demand curve in the graph. The table uses the midpoint method to calculate the price elasticity of demand. At points with a low price and high quantity, the demand curve is inelastic. At points with a high price and low quantity, the demand curve is elastic.

The table also presents total revenue at each point on the demand curve. These numbers illustrate the relationship between total revenue and elasticity. When the price is $1, for instance, demand is inelastic, and a price increase to $2 raises total revenue. When the price is $5, demand is elastic, and a price increase to $6 reduces total revenue. Between $3 and $4, demand is exactly unit elastic, and total revenue is the same at these two prices.

IN THE NEWS

THE ELASTICITY OF DEMAND FOR CDs

Faced with competition from file-sharing, some companies are reducing the prices of CDs. Try to calculate the price elasticity of demand for CDs from the numbers given in this article, or from surveying your friends. From your calculations, do you think that the cut in price will cause revenues from CD sales to increase?

CD Savings Coming: Price Could Drop $7—Consumers Expected to Start Buying Again

By Bernard Perusse

Lowering prices on compact discs? It's a wacky idea, but it just might work.

Universal Music Canada's announcement Wednesday that it will lower its suggested list price to $14.98 on most of its CDs—including new releases by huge sellers like Eminem and Shania Twain—was met with enthusiasm by consumers yesterday. The new policy, which echoes a similar initiative by Universal's U.S. division, takes effect Oct. 1.

Since retailers generally sell for less than the suggested price, consumers could end up saving about $7 per disc. New releases now sell for $18 to $20 in most stores.

Jim Savary, an adviser to the Consumers' Association of Canada, said the move was long overdue. "The cost of manufacturing CDs is only a fraction of the list price, even though there are royalties and [other expenses]. It has seemed to me for some time that the recording companies have misinterpreted what economists call the elasticity of demand: the assumption they're making is that the consumer is willing to pay pretty much any price to get a hot-off-the-press new release," Savary said. "In fact, as we know from the popularity of file-swapping, which can't be driven out, apparently, the consumers are reluctant to pay those prices—not so much because they can't afford them, but because they resent the fact that, as they see it, there's been a lot of price-gouging going on. Lowering the price by that much will probably cause a flood of consumers to return to buying CDs," he said.

If the price of admission were higher, how much shorter would this line become?

Case Study

PRICING ADMISSION TO A MUSEUM

You are curator of a major art museum. Your director of finance tells you that the museum is running short of funds and suggests that you consider changing the price of admission to increase total revenue. What do you do? Do you raise the price of admission, or do you lower it?

The answer depends on the elasticity of demand. If the demand for visits to the museum is inelastic, then an increase in the price of admission would increase total revenue. But if the demand is elastic, then an increase in price would cause the number of visitors to fall by so much that total revenue would decrease. In this

If it plays out that way, it won't be a moment too soon for the Canadian recording industry, which has lost more than $250 million in retail sales over the past three years. Tyson Parker, manager of national media and artist relations at Universal Canada, acknowledged that business was down as a result of illegal file-sharing and legally downloadable services like iTunes, but he said those weren't the only factors in Universal's decision to slash its prices.

"There are variables that have caused [dollar loss]. File-sharing certainly is one of them. The stretching of the entertainment dollar into different media has also played a large role in this," Parker said, citing DVD sales and Sony's PlayStation games as key competitors for the consumer coin. Sure enough, statistics from the Canadian Recording Industry Association show that DVD sales have gone the opposite way: in June, they were up 91 per cent over last year.

"What we have done is pay close attention to the pulse of our industry and got inside the hearts and minds of the record-buying community and listened to what they had to say," Parker said. "The large majority of people had concerns about the pricing. We have listened." According to Parker, Universal estimates that incremental sales could go up by 20 to 30 per cent, thereby blunting the anticipated loss on the company's profit margin.

Humphrey Kadaner, president of HMV North America, said he was firmly on board with Universal's move. He expressed hope that a reduced wholesale price to retailers would make things easier on HMV's own margin.

"We're pleased to be the end destination for the consumer and offer better volume for money. Given the challenge and the significant decline in the music business, this initiative can only help to re-energize the industry," Kadaner said.

Other labels closed ranks yesterday and kept a terse silence on whether they would adopt similar initiatives. Sony and Warner Bros. refused to comment, while EMI did not return phone calls.

"My guess is, over time, they're going to follow suit," Savary said. "If the demand of consumers for CDs is price-sensitive, they're all going to be better off. They will win back consumers who had simply been making other arrangements."

If the other major players get on board, they might make new friends in consumers like Argiris Argirou, who was browsing through the heavy-metal section at HMV on Ste-Catherine St. W. yesterday. Argirou said he buys 10 to 20 discs a month but would not hesitate to buy twice as many if the prices were halved. Natasha Watson, doing some serious buying in the rock section, also said she would end up buying more discs if the costs go down. "[When you buy a disc], you get the songs you want, plus some other songs you might not have heard," she said. Both consumers said they weren't regular users of file-sharing services.

Parker said the Universal policy will apply to both new releases and archive material, excluding classical music discs and multiple-disc sets. Apart from Twain and Eminem, the label's roster includes Sheryl Crow, Diana Krall and Sam Roberts. Its back catalogue includes James Brown, Jimi Hendrix, the Who and the entire Motown catalogue.

Source: *The Montreal Gazette*, September 5, 2003, p. D1/BREAK.

case, you should cut the price. The number of visitors would rise by so much that total revenue would increase.

To estimate the price elasticity of demand, you would need to turn to your statisticians. They might use historical data to study how museum attendance varied from year to year as the admission price changed. Or they might use data on attendance at the various museums around the country to see how the admission price affects attendance. In studying either of these sets of data, the statisticians would need to take account of other factors that affect attendance—weather, population, size of collection, and so forth—to isolate the effect of price. In the end, such data analysis would provide an estimate of the price elasticity of demand, which you could use in deciding how to respond to your financial problem. ●

Other Demand Elasticities

In addition to the price elasticity of demand, economists also use other elasticities to describe the behaviour of buyers in a market.

income elasticity of demand
a measure of how much the quantity demanded of a good responds to a change in consumers' income, computed as the percentage change in quantity demanded divided by the percentage change in income

The Income Elasticity of Demand   The **income elasticity of demand** measures how the quantity demanded changes as consumer income changes. It is calculated as the percentage change in quantity demanded divided by the percentage change in income. That is,

$$\text{Income elasticity of demand} = \frac{\text{Percentage change in quantity demanded}}{\text{Percentage change in income}}$$

As we discussed in Chapter 4, most goods are *normal goods:* Higher income raises quantity demanded. Because quantity demanded and income move in the same direction, normal goods have positive income elasticities. A few goods, such as bus rides, are *inferior goods:* Higher income lowers the quantity demanded. Because quantity demanded and income move in opposite directions, inferior goods have negative income elasticities.

Even among normal goods, income elasticities vary substantially in size. Necessities, such as food and clothing, tend to have small income elasticities because consumers, regardless of how low their incomes, choose to buy some of these goods. Luxuries, such as caviar and diamonds, tend to have large income elasticities because consumers feel that they can do without these goods altogether if their income is too low.

cross-price elasticity of demand
a measure of how much the quantity demanded of one good responds to a change in the price of another good, computed as the percentage change in quantity demanded of the first good divided by the percentage change in the price of the second good

The Cross-Price Elasticity of Demand   The **cross-price elasticity of demand** measures how the quantity demanded of one good changes as the price of another good changes. It is calculated as the percentage change in quantity demanded of good 1 divided by the percentage change in the price of good 2. That is,

$$\text{Cross-price elasticity of demand} = \frac{\text{Percentage change in quantity demanded of good 1}}{\text{Percentage change in the price of good 2}}$$

Whether the cross-price elasticity is a positive or negative number depends on whether the two goods are substitutes or complements. As we discussed in Chapter 4, substitutes are goods that are typically used in place of one another, such as hamburgers and hot dogs. An increase in hot dog prices induces people to grill hamburgers instead. Because the price of hot dogs and the quantity of hamburgers demanded move in the same direction, the cross-price elasticity is positive. Conversely, complements are goods that are typically used together, such as computers and software. In this case, the cross-price elasticity is negative, indicating that an increase in the price of computers reduces the quantity of software demanded.

QuickQuiz Define the price elasticity of demand. • Explain the relationship between total revenue and the price elasticity of demand.

THE ELASTICITY OF SUPPLY

When we introduced supply in Chapter 4, we noted that producers of a good offer to sell more of it when the price of the good rises, when their input prices fall, or when their technology improves. To turn from qualitative to quantitative statements about quantity supplied, we once again use the concept of elasticity.

The Price Elasticity of Supply and Its Determinants

The law of supply states that higher prices raise the quantity supplied. The **price elasticity of supply** measures how much the quantity supplied responds to changes in the price. Supply of a good is said to be *elastic* if the quantity supplied responds substantially to changes in the price. Supply is said to be *inelastic* if the quantity supplied responds only slightly to changes in the price.

> **price elasticity of supply**
> a measure of how much the quantity supplied of a good responds to a change in the price of that good, computed as the percentage change in quantity supplied divided by the percentage change in price

The price elasticity of supply depends on the flexibility of sellers to change the amount of the good they produce. For example, beachfront land has an inelastic supply because it is almost impossible to produce more of it. By contrast, manufactured goods, such as books, cars, and televisions, have elastic supplies because the firms that produce them can run their factories longer in response to a higher price.

In most markets, a key determinant of the price elasticity of supply is the time period being considered. Supply is usually more elastic in the long run than in the short run. Over short periods of time, firms cannot easily change the size of their factories to make more or less of a good. Thus, in the short run, the quantity supplied is not very responsive to the price. By contrast, over longer periods, firms can build new factories or close old ones. In addition, new firms can enter a market, and old firms can shut down. Thus, in the long run, the quantity supplied can respond substantially to price changes.

Computing the Price Elasticity of Supply

Now that we have some idea about what the price elasticity of supply is, let's be more precise. Economists compute the price elasticity of supply as the percentage change in the quantity supplied divided by the percentage change in the price. That is,

$$\text{Price elasticity of supply} = \frac{\text{Percentage change in quantity supplied}}{\text{Percentage change in price}}$$

For example, suppose that an increase in the price of milk from $2.85 to $3.15 per litre raises the amount that dairy farmers produce from 9000 to 11 000 L per month. Using the midpoint method, we calculate the percentage change in price as

$$\text{Percentage change in price} = (3.15 - 2.85)/3.00 \times 100 = 10 \text{ percent}$$

Similarly, we calculate the percentage change in quantity supplied as

$$\text{Percentage change in quantity supplied} = (11\,000 - 9000)/10\,000 \times 100 = 20 \text{ percent}$$

In this case, the price elasticity of supply is

$$\text{Price elasticity of supply} = \frac{20 \text{ percent}}{10 \text{ percent}} = 2.0$$

In this example, the elasticity of 2 reflects the fact that the quantity supplied moves proportionately twice as much as the price.

The Variety of Supply Curves

Because the price elasticity of supply measures the responsiveness of quantity supplied to the price, it is reflected in the appearance of the supply curve. Figure 5.6 shows five cases. In the extreme case of a zero elasticity, as shown in panel (a), supply is *perfectly inelastic* and the supply curve is vertical. In this case, the quantity supplied is the same regardless of the price. As the elasticity rises, the supply curve gets flatter, which shows that the quantity supplied responds more to changes in the price. At the opposite extreme shown in panel (e), supply is *perfectly elastic*. This occurs as the price elasticity of supply approaches infinity and the supply curve becomes horizontal, meaning that very small changes in the price lead to very large changes in the quantity supplied.

In some markets, the elasticity of supply is not constant but varies over the supply curve. Figure 5.7 (p. 106) shows a typical case for an industry in which firms have factories with a limited capacity for production. For low levels of quantity supplied, the elasticity of supply is high, indicating that firms respond substantially to changes in the price. In this region, firms have capacity for production that is not being used, such as plants and equipment sitting idle for all or part of the day. Small increases in price make it profitable for firms to begin using this idle capacity. As the quantity supplied rises, firms begin to reach capacity. Once capacity is fully used, increasing production further requires the construction of new plants. To induce firms to incur this extra expense, the price must rise substantially, so supply becomes less elastic.

Figure 5.7 presents a numerical example of this phenomenon. When the price rises from $3 to $4 (a 29 percent increase, according to the midpoint method), the quantity supplied rises from 100 to 200 (a 67 percent increase). Because quantity supplied moves proportionately more than the price, the supply curve has elasticity greater than 1. By contrast, when the price rises from $12 to $15 (a 22 percent increase), the quantity supplied rises from 500 to 525 (a 5 percent increase). In this case, quantity supplied moves proportionately less than the price, so the elasticity is less than 1.

QuickQuiz Define the price elasticity of supply. • Explain why the price elasticity of supply might be different in the long run than in the short run.

TWO APPLICATIONS OF SUPPLY, DEMAND, AND ELASTICITY

Can good news for farming be bad news for farmers? Why did the Organization of Petroleum Exporting Countries (OPEC) fail to keep the price of oil high?

FIGURE 5.6

The Price Elasticity of Supply

The price elasticity of supply determines whether the supply curve is steep or flat. Note that all percentage changes are calculated using the midpoint method.

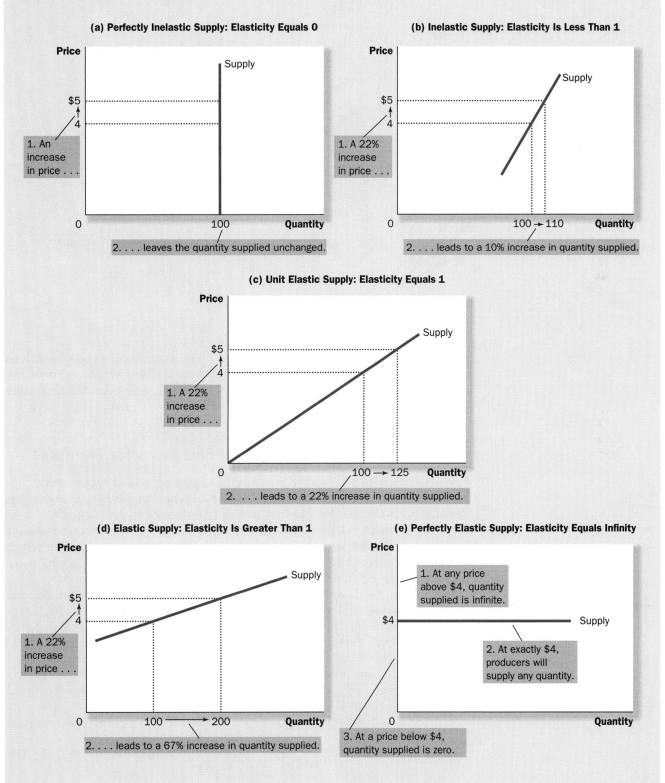

(a) Perfectly Inelastic Supply: Elasticity Equals 0

Price

$5
4

1. An increase in price . . .

Supply

0   100   Quantity

2. . . . leaves the quantity supplied unchanged.

(b) Inelastic Supply: Elasticity Is Less Than 1

Price

$5
4

1. A 22% increase in price . . .

Supply

0   100 → 110   Quantity

2. . . . leads to a 10% increase in quantity supplied.

(c) Unit Elastic Supply: Elasticity Equals 1

Price

$5
4

1. A 22% increase in price . . .

Supply

0   100 → 125   Quantity

2. . . . leads to a 22% increase in quantity supplied.

(d) Elastic Supply: Elasticity Is Greater Than 1

Price

$5
4

1. A 22% increase in price . . .

Supply

0   100 ——→ 200   Quantity

2. . . . leads to a 67% increase in quantity supplied.

(e) Perfectly Elastic Supply: Elasticity Equals Infinity

Price

1. At any price above $4, quantity supplied is infinite.

$4   Supply

2. At exactly $4, producers will supply any quantity.

0   Quantity

3. At a price below $4, quantity supplied is zero.

FIGURE 5.7

How the Price Elasticity of Supply Can Vary

Because firms often have a maximum capacity for production, the elasticity of supply may be very high at low levels of quantity supplied and very low at high levels of quantity supplied. Here, an increase in price from $3 to $4 increases the quantity supplied from 100 to 200. Because the increase in quantity supplied of 67 percent (computed using the midpoint method) is larger than the increase in price of 29 percent, the supply curve is elastic in this range. By contrast, when the price rises from $12 to $15, the quantity supplied rises only from 500 to 525. Because the increase in quantity supplied of 5 percent is smaller than the increase in price of 22 percent, the supply curve is inelastic in this range.

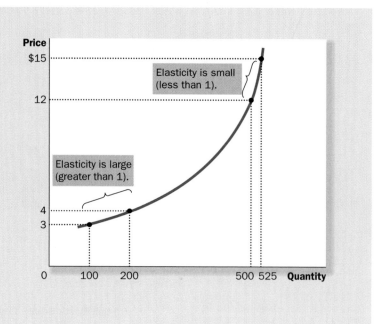

At first, these questions might seem to have little in common. Yet both questions are about markets, and all markets are subject to the forces of supply and demand. Here we apply the versatile tools of supply, demand, and elasticity to answer these seemingly complex questions.

Can Good News for Farming Be Bad News for Farmers?

Let's now return to the question posed at the beginning of this chapter: What happens to wheat farmers and the market for wheat when university plant scientists discover a new wheat hybrid that is more productive than existing varieties? Recall from Chapter 4 that we answer such questions in three steps. First, we examine whether the supply or demand curve shifts. Second, we consider which direction the curve shifts. Third, we use the supply-and-demand diagram to see how the market equilibrium changes.

In this case, the discovery of the new hybrid affects the supply curve. Because the hybrid increases the amount of wheat that can be produced on each hectare of land, farmers are now willing to supply more wheat at any given price. In other words, the supply curve shifts to the right. The demand curve remains the same because consumers' desire to buy wheat products at any given price is not affected by the introduction of a new hybrid. Figure 5.8 shows an example of such a change. When the supply curve shifts from S_1 to S_2, the quantity of wheat sold increases from 100 to 110, and the price of wheat falls from $3 to $2.

But does this discovery make farmers better off? As a first cut at answering this question, consider what happens to the total revenue received by farmers. Farmers' total revenue is $P \times Q$, the price of the wheat times the quantity sold. The

FIGURE 5.8

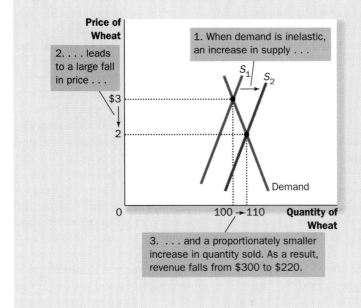

Price of Wheat

2. . . . leads to a large fall in price . . .

1. When demand is inelastic, an increase in supply . . .

S_1 S_2

$3

2

Demand

0   100 → 110   **Quantity of Wheat**

3. . . . and a proportionately smaller increase in quantity sold. As a result, revenue falls from $300 to $220.

An Increase in Supply in the Market for Wheat

When an advance in farm technology increases the supply of wheat from S_1 to S_2, the price of wheat falls. Because the demand for wheat is inelastic, the increase in the quantity sold from 100 to 110 is proportionately smaller than the decrease in the price from $3 to $2. As a result, farmers' total revenue falls from $300 ($3 × 100) to $220 ($2 × 110).

discovery affects farmers in two conflicting ways. The hybrid allows farmers to produce more wheat (Q rises), but now each tonne of wheat sells for less (P falls).

Whether total revenue rises or falls depends on the elasticity of demand. In practice, the demand for basic foodstuffs such as wheat is usually inelastic, for these items are relatively inexpensive and have few good substitutes. When the demand curve is inelastic, as it is in Figure 5.8, a decrease in price causes total revenue to fall. You can see this in the figure: The price of wheat falls substantially, whereas the quantity of wheat sold rises only slightly. Total revenue falls from $300 to $220. Thus, the discovery of the new hybrid lowers the total revenue that farmers receive for the sale of their crops.

If farmers are made worse off by the discovery of this new hybrid, why do they adopt it? The answer to this question goes to the heart of how competitive markets work. Because each farmer is a small part of the market for wheat, he or she takes the price of wheat as given. For any given price of wheat, it is better to use the new hybrid in order to produce and sell more wheat. Yet when all farmers do this, the supply of wheat rises, the price falls, and farmers are worse off.

Although this example may at first seem only hypothetical, in fact it helps to explain a major change in the Canadian economy over the past century. Two hundred years ago, most Canadians lived on farms. Knowledge about farm methods was sufficiently primitive that most of us had to be farmers to produce enough food. Yet, over time, advances in farm technology increased the amount of food that each farmer could produce. This increase in food supply, together with inelastic food demand, caused farm revenues to fall, which in turn encouraged people to leave farming.

A few numbers show the magnitude of this historic change. Two hundred years ago, about 75 percent of the Canadian labour force worked in agriculture and produced enough food to feed their own families and the families of the other

25 percent of the labour force. One hundred years ago, about 50 percent of the Canadian labour force worked on farms and each agricultural worker produced enough to feed his or her own family and one other family. As recently as 50 years ago, about 25 percent of the Canadian labour force worked on farms. In 2003, however, only 3 percent of employed Canadians were employed in agriculture, which means that each agricultural worker produced enough food to feed 33 workers and their families (and to export food as well). Since Canadians today eat at least as well as they did in the past, this decrease in the proportion of Canadians working in agriculture represents a tremendous increase in farm productivity.

This analysis of the market for farm products also helps to explain a seeming paradox of public policy: Certain farm programs try to help farmers by restricting the amount of milk and eggs that farmers are allowed to produce. Why do these programs do this? Their purpose is to reduce the supply of milk and eggs and thereby raise prices. Because demand is inelastic, farmers as a group receive greater total revenue if they supply a smaller amount of milk and eggs to the market. No single farmer would choose to restrict supply on his or her own, since each takes the market price as given. But if all farmers do so together, each of them can be better off.

When analyzing the effects of farm technology or farm policy, it is important to keep in mind that what is good for farmers is not necessarily good for society as a whole. Improvement in farm technology can be bad for farmers who become increasingly unnecessary, but it is surely good for consumers who pay less for food. Similarly, a policy aimed at reducing the supply of farm products may raise the incomes of farmers, but it does so at the expense of consumers.

Why Did OPEC Fail to Keep the Price of Oil High?

Many of the most disruptive events for the world's economies over the past several decades have originated in the world market for oil. In the 1970s members of OPEC decided to raise the world price of oil in order to increase their incomes. These countries accomplished this goal by jointly reducing the amount of oil they supplied. From 1973 to 1974, the price of oil (adjusted for overall inflation) rose more than 50 percent. Then, a few years later, OPEC did the same thing again. The price of oil rose 14 percent in 1979, followed by 34 percent in 1980, and another 34 percent in 1981.

Yet OPEC found it difficult to maintain a high price. From 1982 to 1985, the price of oil steadily declined at about 10 percent per year. Dissatisfaction and disarray soon prevailed among the OPEC countries. In 1986 cooperation among OPEC members completely broke down, and the price of oil plunged 45 percent. In 1990 the price of oil (adjusted for overall inflation) was back to where it began in 1970, and it stayed at that low level throughout most of the 1990s.

This episode shows how supply and demand can behave differently in the short run and in the long run. In the short run, both the supply and demand for oil are relatively inelastic. Supply is inelastic because the quantity of known oil reserves and the capacity for oil extraction cannot be changed quickly. Demand is inelastic because buying habits do not respond immediately to changes in price. Many drivers with old gas-guzzling cars, for instance, will just pay the higher price. Thus, as panel (a) of Figure 5.9 shows, the short-run supply-and-demand

FIGURE 5.9

A Reduction in Supply in the World Market for Oil

When the supply of oil falls, the response depends on the time horizon. In the short run, supply and demand are relatively inelastic, as in panel (a). Thus, when the supply curve shifts from S_1 to S_2, the price rises substantially. By contrast, in the long run, supply and demand are relatively elastic, as in panel (b). In this case, the same size shift in the supply curve (S_1 to S_2) causes a smaller increase in the price.

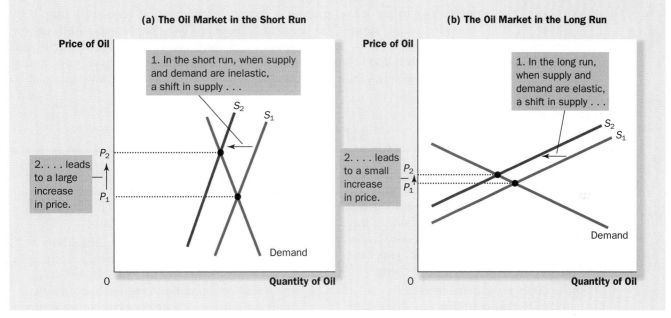

curves are steep. When the supply of oil shifts from S_1 to S_2, the price increase from P_1 to P_2 is large.

The situation is very different in the long run. Over long periods of time, producers of oil outside of OPEC respond to high prices by increasing oil exploration and by building new extraction capacity. Consumers respond with greater conservation, for instance by replacing old inefficient cars with newer efficient ones. Thus, as panel (b) of Figure 5.9 shows, the long-run supply and demand curves are more elastic. In the long run, the shift in the supply curve from S_1 to S_2 causes a much smaller increase in the price.

This analysis shows why OPEC succeeded in maintaining a high price of oil only in the short run. When OPEC countries agreed to reduce their production of oil, they shifted the supply curve to the left. Even though each OPEC member sold less oil, the price rose by so much in the short run that OPEC incomes rose. By contrast, in the long run when supply and demand are more elastic, the same reduction in supply, measured by the horizontal shift in the supply curve, caused a smaller increase in the price. Thus, OPEC's coordinated reduction in supply proved less profitable in the long run.

OPEC still exists today, and it has from time to time succeeded at reducing supply and raising prices. But the price of oil (adjusted for overall inflation) has never returned to the peak reached in 1981. The cartel now seems to understand that raising prices is easier in the short run than in the long run.

QuickQuiz   How might a drought that destroys half of all farm crops be good for farmers? If such a drought is good for farmers, why don't farmers destroy their own crops in the absence of a drought?

CONCLUSION

According to an old quip, even a parrot can become an economist simply by learning to say "supply and demand." These last two chapters should have convinced you that there is much truth in this statement. The tools of supply and demand allow you to analyze many of the most important events and policies that shape the economy. You are now well on your way to becoming an economist.

SUMMARY

- The price elasticity of demand measures how much the quantity demanded responds to changes in the price. Demand tends to be more elastic if close substitutes are available, if the good is a luxury rather than a necessity, if the market is narrowly defined, or if buyers have substantial time to react to a price change.

- The price elasticity of demand is calculated as the percentage change in quantity demanded divided by the percentage change in price. If the elasticity is less than 1, so that quantity demanded moves proportionately less than the price, demand is said to be inelastic. If the elasticity is greater than 1, so that quantity demanded moves proportionately more than the price, demand is said to be elastic.

- Total revenue, the total amount paid for a good, equals the price of the good times the quantity sold. For inelastic demand curves, total revenue rises as price rises. For elastic demand curves, total revenue falls as price rises.

- The income elasticity of demand measures how much the quantity demanded responds to changes in consumers' income. The cross-price elasticity of demand measures how much the quantity demanded of one good responds to changes in the price of another good.

- The price elasticity of supply measures how much the quantity supplied responds to changes in the price. This elasticity often depends on the time horizon under consideration. In most markets, supply is more elastic in the long run than in the short run.

- The price elasticity of supply is calculated as the percentage change in quantity supplied divided by the percentage change in price. If the elasticity is less than 1, so that quantity supplied moves proportionately less than the price, supply is said to be inelastic. If the elasticity is greater than 1, so that quantity supplied moves proportionately more than the price, supply is said to be elastic.

- The tools of supply and demand can be applied in many different kinds of markets. This chapter uses them to analyze the market for wheat and the market for oil.

KEY CONCEPTS

QUESTIONS FOR REVIEW

1. Define the price elasticity of demand and the income elasticity of demand.

2. List and explain some of the determinants of the price elasticity of demand.

3. If the elasticity is greater than 1, is demand elastic or inelastic? If the elasticity equals 0, is demand perfectly elastic or perfectly inelastic?

4. On a supply-and-demand diagram, show equilibrium price, equilibrium quantity, and the total revenue received by producers.

5. If demand is elastic, how will an increase in price change total revenue? Explain.

6. What do we call a good whose income elasticity is less than 0?

7. How is the price elasticity of supply calculated? Explain what this measures.

8. What is the price elasticity of supply of Picasso paintings?

9. Is the price elasticity of supply usually larger in the short run or in the long run? Why?

10. In the 1970s, OPEC caused a dramatic increase in the price of oil. What prevented it from maintaining this high price through the 1980s?

PROBLEMS AND APPLICATIONS

1. For each of the following pairs of goods, which good would you expect to have more elastic demand and why?
   a. required textbooks or mystery novels
   b. Beethoven recordings or classical music recordings in general
   c. heating oil during the next six months or heating oil during the next five years
   d. root beer or water

2. Suppose that business travellers and vacationers have the following demand for airline tickets from Toronto to Montreal:

Price	Quantity Demanded (business travellers)	Quantity Demanded (vacationers)
$150	2100	1000
200	2000	800
250	1900	600
300	1800	400

   a. As the price of tickets rises from $200 to $250, what is the price elasticity of demand for (i) business travellers and (ii) vacationers? (Use the midpoint method in your calculations.)
   b. Why might vacationers have a different elasticity than business travellers?

3. Suppose that your demand schedule for compact discs is as follows:

Price	Quantity Demanded (income = $10 000)	Quantity Demanded (income = $12 000)
$ 8	40	50
10	32	45
12	24	30
14	16	20
16	8	12

   a. Use the midpoint method to calculate your price elasticity of demand as the price of compact discs increases from $8 to $10 if (i) your income is $10 000, and (ii) your income is $12 000.
   b. Calculate your income elasticity of demand as your income increases from $10 000 to $12 000 if (i) the price is $12, and (ii) the price is $16.

4. Emily has decided always to spend one-third of her income on clothing.
   a. What is her income elasticity of clothing demand?
   b. What is her price elasticity of clothing demand?
   c. If Emily's tastes change and she decides to spend only one-fourth of her income

on clothing, how does her demand curve change? What are her income elasticity and price elasticity now?

5. *The Globe and Mail* (December 16, 1997) reported that milk consumption declined following price increases: "Since the early 1980s, the price of milk in Canada has increased 22 per cent. As prices rose, the demand for milk fell off. Total [consumption] of milk on a per capita basis dropped . . . to 2.62 hectolitres in 1995 from 2.92 hectolitres in 1986."
   a. Use these data to estimate the price elasticity of demand for milk.
   b. According to your estimate, what happens to milk producers' revenue when the price of milk rises?
   c. Why might your estimate of the elasticity be unreliable? (Hint: Notice that *The Globe and Mail* is careless about the distinction between demand and quantity demanded.)

6. Two drivers—Tom and Jerry—each drive up to a gas station. Before looking at the price, each places an order. Tom says, "I'd like 40 litres of gas." Jerry says, "I'd like $40 worth of gas." What is each driver's price elasticity of demand?

7. Economists have observed that spending on restaurant meals declines more during economic downturns than does spending on food to be eaten at home. How might the concept of elasticity help to explain this phenomenon?

8. Consider public policy aimed at smoking.
   a. Studies indicate that the price elasticity of demand for cigarettes is about 0.4. If a pack of cigarettes currently costs $8 and the government wants to reduce smoking by 20 percent, by how much should it increase the price?
   b. If the government permanently increases the price of cigarettes, will the policy have a greater effect on smoking one year from now or five years from now?
   c. Studies also find that teenagers have a higher price elasticity than do adults. Why might this be true?

9. Would you expect the price elasticity of *demand* to be larger in the market for all ice cream or in the market for vanilla ice cream? Would you expect the price elasticity of *supply* to be larger in the market for all ice cream or in the market for vanilla ice cream? Be sure to explain your answers.

10. Pharmaceutical drugs have an inelastic demand, and computers have an elastic demand. Suppose that technological advance doubles the supply of both products (that is, the quantity supplied at each price is twice what it was).
    a. What happens to the equilibrium price and quantity in each market?
    b. Which product experiences a greater change in price?
    c. Which product experiences a greater change in quantity?
    d. What happens to total consumer spending on each product?

11. Beachfront resorts have an inelastic supply, and automobiles have an elastic supply. Suppose that a rise in population doubles the demand for both products (that is, the quantity demanded at each price is twice what it was).
    a. What happens to the equilibrium price and quantity in each market?
    b. Which product experiences a greater change in price?
    c. Which product experiences a greater change in quantity?
    d. What happens to total consumer spending on each product?

12. Several years ago, flooding along the Red River in Manitoba destroyed thousands of hectares of wheat.
    a. Farmers whose crops were destroyed by the floods were much worse off, but farmers whose crops were not destroyed benefited from the floods. Why?
    b. What information would you need about the market for wheat to assess whether farmers as a group were hurt or helped by the floods?

13. Explain why the following might be true: A drought around the world raises the total revenue that farmers receive from the sale of grain, but a drought only in Alberta reduces the total revenue that Alberta farmers receive.

14. Because better weather makes farmland more productive, farmland in regions with good weather conditions is more expensive than farmland in regions with bad weather conditions. Over time, however, as advances in technology have made all farmland more productive, the price of farmland (adjusted for overall inflation) has fallen. Use the concept of elasticity to explain why productivity and farmland prices are positively related across space but negatively related over time.

INTERNET RESOURCES

- How large or small are the elasticities of demand for various types of food? You can see some estimates in the tables at the end of the paper entitled "Income and Price Elasticities of Demand for Foods Consumed in the Home," which can be accessed at http://statistics.defra.gov.uk/esg/publications/nfs/2000/Section6.pdf. See if you can explain why some foods have a more elastic demand than others.

- Some estimates of the elasticity of demand for various types of transportation are available in tables in the paper that can be accessed at http://www.worldbank.org/transport/publicat/inu-70.pdf ("A Survey of Recent Estimates of Price Elasticities of Demand for Transport"). See if you can explain why some types of transportation have a more elastic demand than others.

http://   For more study tools, please visit http://www.mankiw3e.nelson.com.

© JIM STEINHART

SUPPLY, DEMAND, AND GOVERNMENT POLICIES

Economists have two roles. As scientists, they develop and test theories to explain the world around them. As policy advisers, they use their theories to help change the world for the better. The focus of the preceding two chapters has been scientific. We have seen how supply and demand determine the price of a good and the quantity of the good sold. We have also seen how various events shift supply and demand and thereby change the equilibrium price and quantity.

This chapter offers our first look at policy. Here we analyze various types of government policy using only the tools of supply and demand. As you will see, the analysis yields some surprising insights. Policies often have effects that their architects did not intend or anticipate.

We begin by considering policies that directly control prices. For example, rent-control laws dictate a maximum rent that landlords may charge tenants. Minimum-wage laws dictate the lowest wage that firms may pay workers. Price controls are usually enacted when policymakers believe that the market price of a good or service is unfair to buyers or sellers. Yet, as we will see, these policies can generate inequities of their own.

6

Learning Objectives

In this chapter, you will …

- Examine the effects of government policies that place a ceiling on prices
- Examine the effects of government policies that put a floor under prices
- Consider how a tax on a good affects the price of the good and the quantity sold
- Learn that taxes levied on buyers and taxes levied on sellers are equivalent
- See how the burden of a tax is split between buyers and sellers

After our discussion of price controls, we will consider the impact of taxes. Policymakers use taxes both to influence market outcomes and to raise revenue for public purposes. Although the prevalence of taxes in our economy is obvious, their effects are not. For example, when the government levies a tax on the amount that firms pay their workers, do the firms or the workers bear the burden of the tax? The answer is not at all clear—until we apply the powerful tools of supply and demand.

CONTROLS ON PRICES

To see how price controls affect market outcomes, let's look once again at the market for ice cream. As we saw in Chapter 4, if ice cream is sold in a competitive market free of government regulation, the price of ice cream adjusts to balance supply and demand: At the equilibrium price, the quantity of ice cream that buyers want to buy exactly equals the quantity that sellers want to sell. To be concrete, suppose the equilibrium price is $3 per cone.

Not everyone may be happy with the outcome of this free-market process. Let's say the Canadian Association of Ice-Cream Eaters complains that the $3 price is too high for everyone to enjoy a cone a day (their recommended diet). Meanwhile, the Canadian Organization of Ice-Cream Makers complains that the $3 price—the result of "cutthroat competition"—is too low and is depressing the incomes of its members. Each of these groups lobbies the government to pass laws that alter the market outcome by directly controlling the price of an ice-cream cone.

Of course, because buyers of any good always want a lower price while sellers want a higher price, the interests of the two groups conflict. If the Ice-Cream Eaters are successful in their lobbying, the government imposes a legal maximum on the price at which ice cream can be sold. Because the price is not allowed to rise above this level, the legislated maximum is called a **price ceiling.** By contrast, if the Ice-Cream Makers are successful, the government imposes a legal minimum on the price. Because the price cannot fall below this level, the legislated minimum is called a **price floor.** Let us consider the effects of these policies in turn.

price ceiling
a legal maximum on the price at which a good can be sold

price floor
a legal minimum on the price at which a good can be sold

How Price Ceilings Affect Market Outcomes

When the government, moved by the complaints and campaign contributions of the Ice-Cream Eaters, imposes a price ceiling on the market for ice cream, two outcomes are possible. In panel (a) of Figure 6.1, the government imposes a price ceiling of $4 per cone. In this case, because the price that balances supply and demand ($3) is below the ceiling, the price ceiling is *not binding*. Market forces naturally move the economy to the equilibrium, and the price ceiling has no effect on the price or the quantity sold.

Panel (b) of Figure 6.1 shows the other, more interesting, possibility. In this case, the government imposes a price ceiling of $2 per cone. Because the equilibrium price of $3 is above the price ceiling, the ceiling is a *binding constraint* on the market. The forces of supply and demand tend to move the price toward the equilibrium price, but when the market price hits the ceiling, it can rise no further. Thus, the market price equals the price ceiling. At this price, the quantity of ice cream demanded (125 cones in the figure) exceeds the quantity supplied

FIGURE 6.1

A Market with a Price Ceiling

In panel (a), the government imposes a price ceiling of $4. Because the price ceiling is above the equilibrium price of $3, the price ceiling has no effect, and the market can reach the equilibrium of supply and demand. In this equilibrium, quantity supplied and quantity demanded both equal 100 cones. In panel (b), the government imposes a price ceiling of $2. Because the price ceiling is below the equilibrium price of $3, the market price equals $2. At this price, 125 cones are demanded and only 75 are supplied, so there is a shortage of 50 cones.

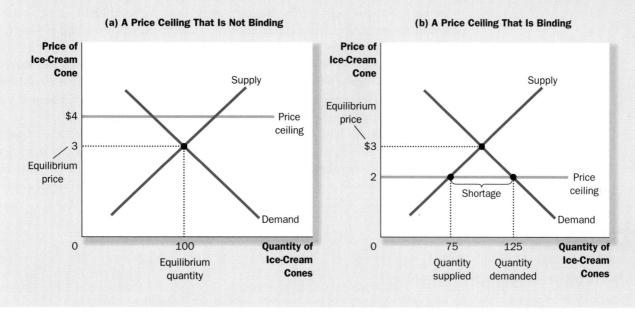

(75 cones). There is a shortage of ice cream, so some people who want to buy ice cream at the going price are unable to.

When a shortage of ice cream develops because of this price ceiling, some mechanism for rationing ice cream will naturally develop. The mechanism could be long lines: Buyers who are willing to arrive early and wait in line get a cone, while those unwilling to wait do not. Alternatively, sellers could ration ice cream according to their own personal biases, selling it only to friends, relatives, or members of their own racial or ethnic group. Notice that even though the price ceiling was motivated by a desire to help buyers of ice cream, not all buyers benefit from the policy. Some buyers do get to pay a lower price, although they may have to wait in line to do so, but other buyers cannot get any ice cream at all.

This example in the market for ice cream shows a general result: *When the government imposes a binding price ceiling on a competitive market, a shortage of the good arises, and sellers must ration the scarce goods among the large number of potential buyers.* The rationing mechanisms that develop under price ceilings are rarely desirable. Long lines are inefficient, because they waste buyers' time. Discrimination according to seller bias is both inefficient (because the good does not necessarily go to the buyer who values it most highly) and potentially unfair. By contrast, the rationing mechanism in a free, competitive market is both efficient and impersonal. When the market for ice cream reaches its equilibrium, anyone who wants to pay the market price can get a cone. Free markets ration goods with prices.

Case Study

LINES AT THE GAS PUMP

As we discussed in the preceding chapter, in 1973 the Organization of Petroleum Exporting Countries (OPEC) raised the price of crude oil in world oil markets. Because crude oil is the major input used to make gasoline, the higher oil prices reduced the supply of gasoline. In Canada the price of gas increased, but there were very few shortages. In the United States, it was very different. Long lines at gas stations became commonplace, and American motorists often had to wait for hours to buy only a few litres of gas.

What was responsible for the long gas lines? Most people blame OPEC. Surely, if OPEC had not raised the price of crude oil, the shortage of gasoline would not have occurred. Yet economists blame U.S. government regulations that limited the price that oil companies could charge for gasoline.

Figure 6.2 shows what happened. As shown in panel (a), before OPEC raised the price of crude oil, the equilibrium price of gasoline, P_1, was below the price ceiling. The price regulation, therefore, had no effect. When the price of crude oil rose, however, the situation changed. The increase in the price of crude oil raised

FIGURE 6.2

The Market for Gasoline with a Price Ceiling

Panel (a) shows the gasoline market when the price ceiling is not binding because the equilibrium price, P_1, is below the ceiling. Panel (b) shows the gasoline market after an increase in the price of crude oil (an input into making gasoline) shifts the supply curve to the left from S_1 to S_2. In an unregulated market, the price would have risen from P_1 to P_2. The price ceiling, however, prevents this from happening. At the binding price ceiling, consumers are willing to buy Q_D, but producers of gasoline are willing to sell only Q_S. The difference between quantity demanded and quantity supplied, $Q_D - Q_S$, measures the gasoline shortage.

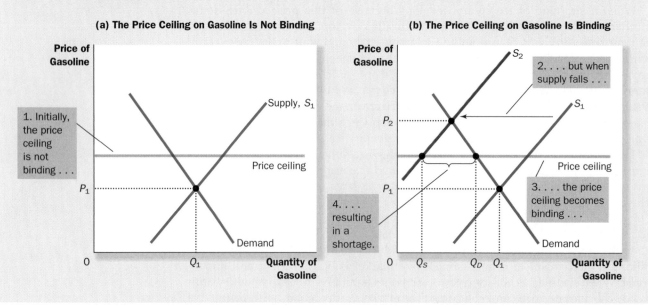

the cost of producing gasoline, and this reduced the supply of gasoline. As panel (b) shows, the supply curve shifted to the left, from S_1 to S_2. In an unregulated market, this shift in supply would have raised the equilibrium price of gasoline from P_1 to P_2, and no shortage would have resulted. Instead, the price ceiling prevented the price from rising to the equilibrium level. At the price ceiling, producers were willing to sell Q_S, and consumers were willing to buy Q_D. Thus, the shift in supply caused a severe shortage at the regulated price.

Eventually, the laws regulating the price of gasoline were repealed. Lawmakers came to understand that they were partly responsible for the many hours Americans lost waiting in line to buy gasoline. Today, when the price of crude oil changes, the price of gasoline can adjust to bring supply and demand into equilibrium. In Canada there were no price controls on gasoline in 1973, and so no long gas lines either. ●

Case Study
RENT CONTROL IN THE SHORT RUN AND LONG RUN

One common example of a price ceiling is rent control. In some provinces, the provincial government places a ceiling on rents that landlords may charge their tenants. The goal of this policy is to help the poor by making housing more affordable. Economists often criticize rent control, arguing that it is a highly inefficient way to help the poor raise their standard of living. One economist called rent control "the best way to destroy a city, other than bombing."

The adverse effects of rent control are less apparent to the general population because these effects occur over many years. In the short run, landlords have a fixed number of apartments to rent, and they cannot adjust this number quickly as market conditions change. Moreover, the number of people searching for housing in a city may not be highly responsive to rents in the short run because people take time to adjust their housing arrangements. Therefore, the short-run supply and demand for housing are relatively inelastic.

Panel (a) of Figure 6.3 (p. 120) shows the short-run effects of rent control on the housing market. As with any binding price ceiling, rent control causes a shortage. Yet because supply and demand are inelastic in the short run, the initial shortage caused by rent control is small. The primary effect in the short run is to reduce rents.

The long-run story is very different because the buyers and sellers of rental housing respond more to market conditions as time passes. On the supply side, landlords respond to low rents by not building new apartments and by failing to maintain existing ones. On the demand side, low rents encourage people to find their own apartments (rather than living with their parents or sharing apartments with roommates) and induce more people to move into a city. Therefore, both supply and demand are more elastic in the long run.

Panel (b) of Figure 6.3 illustrates the housing market in the long run. When rent control depresses rents below the equilibrium level, the quantity of apartments

FIGURE 6.3

Rent Control in the Short Run and in the Long Run

Panel (a) shows the short-run effects of rent control: Because the supply and demand for apartments are relatively inelastic, the price ceiling imposed by a rent-control law causes only a small shortage of housing. Panel (b) shows the long-run effects of rent control: Because the supply and demand for apartments are more elastic, rent control causes a large shortage.

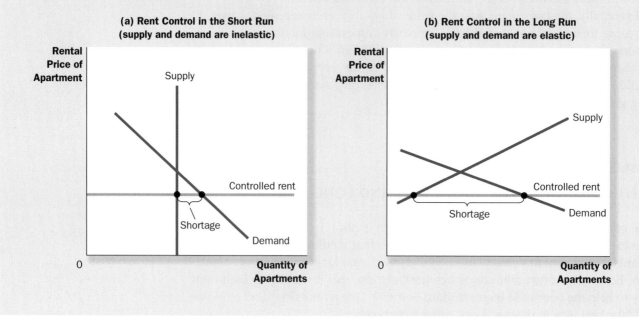

supplied falls substantially, and the quantity of apartments demanded rises substantially. The result is a large shortage of housing.

In provinces with rent control, landlords use various mechanisms to ration housing. Some landlords keep long waiting lists. Others give a preference to tenants without children. Still others discriminate on the basis of race. Sometimes, apartments are allocated to those willing to offer under-the-table payments to building superintendents. In essence, these bribes bring the total price of an apartment (including the bribe) closer to the equilibrium price.

To understand fully the effects of rent control, we have to remember one of the ten principles of economics from Chapter 1: People respond to incentives. In free markets, landlords try to keep their buildings clean and safe because desirable apartments command higher prices. By contrast, when rent control creates shortages and waiting lists, landlords lose their incentive to respond to tenants' concerns. Why should a landlord spend his money to maintain and improve his property when people are waiting to get in as it is? In the end, tenants get lower rents, but they also get lower-quality housing.

Policymakers often react to the effects of rent control by imposing additional regulations. For example, there are laws that make racial discrimination in housing illegal and require landlords to provide minimally adequate living conditions.

IN THE NEWS

DOES A DROUGHT NEED TO CAUSE A WATER SHORTAGE?

During the summer of 1999, the east coast of the United States experienced unusually little rain and a shortage of water. The following article suggests a way that the shortage could have been averted.

Trickle-Down Economics

By Terry L. Anderson and Clay J. Landry

Water shortages are being blamed on the drought in the East, but that's giving Mother Nature a bum rap. Certainly the drought is the immediate cause, but the real culprit is regulations that don't allow markets and prices to equalize demand and supply.

The similarity between water and gasoline is instructive. The energy crisis of the 1970s, too, was blamed on nature's stingy supply of oil, but in fact it was the actions of the Organization of Petroleum Exporting Countries, combined with price controls, that was the main cause of the shortages. . . .

Once again, regulators are responding to shortages—in this case of water—with controls and regulations rather than allowing the market to work. Cities are restricting water usage; some have even gone so far as to prohibit restaurants from serving water except if the customer asks for a glass. But although cities initially saw declines in water use, some are starting to report increases in consumption. This has prompted some police departments to collect lists of residents suspected of wasting water.

There's a better answer than sending out the cops. Market forces could ensure plentiful water availability even in drought years. Contrary to popular belief, the supply of water is no more fixed than the supply of oil. Like all resources, water supplies change in response to economic growth and to the price. In developing countries, despite population growth, the percentage of people with access to safe drinking water has increased to 74 percent in 1994 from 44 percent in 1980. Rising incomes have given those countries the wherewithal to supply potable water.

Supplies also increase when current users have an incentive to conserve their surplus in the marketplace. California's drought-emergency water bank illustrates this. The bank allows farmers to lease water from other users during dry spells. In 1991, the first year the bank was tried, when the price was $125 per acre-foot (326,000 gallons), supply exceeded demand by two to one. That is, many more people wanted to sell their water than wanted to buy.

Data from every corner of the world show that when cities raise the price of water by 10 percent, water use goes down by as much as 12 percent. When the price of agricultural water goes up

10 percent, usage goes down by 20 percent. . . .

Unfortunately, Eastern water users do not pay realistic prices for water. According to the American Water Works Association, only 2 percent of municipal water suppliers adjust prices seasonally. . . .

Even more egregious, Eastern water laws bar people from buying and selling water. Just as tradable pollution permits established under the Clean Air Act have encouraged polluters to find efficient ways to reduce emissions, tradable water rights can encourage conservation and increase supplies. It is mainly a matter of following the lead of Western water courts that have quantified water rights and Western legislatures that have allowed trades.

By making water a commodity and unleashing market forces, policymakers can ensure plentiful water supplies for all. New policies won't make droughts disappear, but they will ease the pain they impose by priming the invisible pump of water markets.

These laws, however, are difficult and costly to enforce. By contrast, when rent control is eliminated and a market for housing is regulated by the forces of competition, such laws are less necessary. In a free market, the price of housing adjusts to eliminate the shortages that give rise to undesirable landlord behaviour. ●

How Price Floors Affect Market Outcomes

To examine the effects of another kind of government price control, let's return to the market for ice cream. Imagine now that the government is persuaded by the pleas of the Canadian Organization of Ice-Cream Makers. In this case, the government might institute a price floor. Price floors, like price ceilings, are an attempt by the government to maintain prices at other than equilibrium levels. Whereas a price ceiling places a legal maximum on prices, a price floor places a legal minimum.

When the government imposes a price floor on the ice-cream market, two outcomes are possible. If the government imposes a price floor of $2 per cone when the equilibrium price is $3, we obtain the outcome in panel (a) of Figure 6.4. In this case, because the equilibrium price is above the floor, the price floor is not binding. Market forces naturally move the economy to the equilibrium, and the price floor has no effect.

Panel (b) of Figure 6.4 shows what happens when the government imposes a price floor of $4 per cone. In this case, because the equilibrium price of $3 is below

---

FIGURE 6.4

A Market with a Price Floor

In panel (a), the government imposes a price floor of $2. Because this is below the equilibrium price of $3, the price floor has no effect. The market price adjusts to balance supply and demand. At the equilibrium, quantity supplied and quantity demanded both equal 100 cones. In panel (b), the government imposes a price floor of $4, which is above the equilibrium price of $3. Therefore, the market price equals $4. Because 120 cones are supplied at this price and only 80 are demanded, there is a surplus of 40 cones.

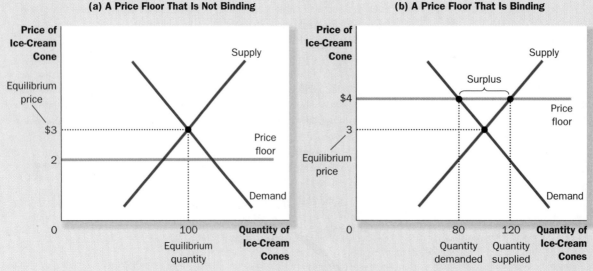

the floor, the price floor is a binding constraint on the market. The forces of supply and demand tend to move the price toward the equilibrium price, but when the market price hits the floor, it can fall no further. The market price equals the price floor. At this floor, the quantity of ice cream supplied (120 cones) exceeds the quantity demanded (80 cones). Some people who want to sell ice cream at the going price are unable to. *Thus, a binding price floor causes a surplus.*

Just as price ceilings and shortages can lead to undesirable rationing mechanisms, so can price floors and surpluses. In the case of a price floor, some sellers are unable to sell all they want at the market price. The sellers who appeal to the personal biases of the buyers, perhaps due to racial or familial ties, are better able to sell their goods than those who do not. By contrast, in a free market, the price serves as the rationing mechanism, and sellers can sell all they want at the equilibrium price.

Case Study
THE MINIMUM WAGE

An important example of a price floor is the minimum wage. Minimum-wage laws dictate the lowest price for labour that any employer may pay. Minimum-wage rates differ by province, as shown in Table 6.1. In 2003, minimum wages ranged from a low of $5.90 per hour in Alberta to a high of $8.50 in Nunavut. Lower rates may apply for inexperienced workers and for restaurant and bar staff who can earn tips to supplement their wages.

To examine the effects of a minimum wage, we must consider the market for labour. Panel (a) of Figure 6.5 (p. 124) shows the labour market which, like all markets, is subject to the forces of supply and demand. Workers determine the supply

TABLE 6.1

Jurisdiction	Hourly Rate*	Effective Date
Nunavut	$8.50	March 3, 2003
Northwest Territories	8.25	December 28, 2003
British Columbia	8.00	November 1, 2001
Quebec	7.30	February 1, 2003
Yukon	7.20	October 1, 1998
Ontario	7.15	February 1, 2004
Manitoba	6.75	April 1, 2003
Saskatchewan	6.65	November 1, 2002
Prince Edward Island	6.50	January 1, 2004
Nova Scotia	6.25	October 1, 2003
New Brunswick	6.20	January 1, 2004
Newfoundland and Labrador	6.00	November 1, 2002
Alberta	5.90	October 1, 1999

Current Minimum-Wage Levels across Canada

Source: Saskatchewan Labour, *Current Minimum Wage Levels Across Canada*. Retrieved February 5, 2004, from the Saskatchewan Labour website: http://www.labour.gov.sk.ca/minwage.htm.

*These are the general minimum-wage rates in each jurisdiction—some have different rates based on regional and occupational considerations, and some have lower rates for students, inexperienced workers, and/or employees receiving gratuities.

FIGURE 6.5

How the Minimum Wage Affects the Labour Market

Panel (a) shows a labour market in which the wage adjusts to balance labour supply and labour demand. Panel (b) shows the impact of a binding minimum wage. Because the minimum wage is a price floor, it causes a surplus: The quantity of labour supplied exceeds the quantity demanded. The result is unemployment.

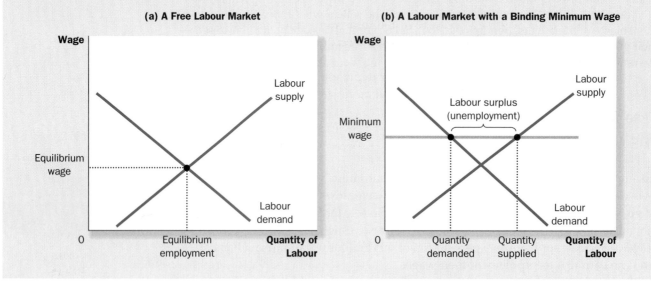

of labour, and firms determine the demand. If the government doesn't intervene, the wage normally adjusts to balance labour supply and labour demand.

Panel (b) of Figure 6.5 shows the labour market with a minimum wage. If the minimum wage is above the equilibrium level, as it is here, the quantity of labour supplied exceeds the quantity demanded. The result is unemployment. Thus, the minimum wage raises the incomes of those workers who have jobs, but it lowers the incomes of those workers who cannot find jobs.

To fully understand the minimum wage, keep in mind that the economy contains not a single labour market, but many labour markets for different types of workers. The impact of the minimum wage depends on the skill and experience of the worker. Workers with high skills and much experience are not affected, because their equilibrium wages are well above the minimum. For these workers, the minimum wage is not binding.

The minimum wage has its greatest impact on the market for teenage labour. The equilibrium wages of teenagers are low because teenagers are among the least skilled and least experienced members of the labour force. In addition, teenagers are often willing to accept a lower wage in exchange for on-the-job training. (Some teenagers are willing to work as "interns" for no pay at all. Because internships pay nothing, however, the minimum wage does not apply to them. If it did, these jobs might not exist.) As a result, the minimum wage is more often binding for teenagers than for other members of the labour force.

Many economists have studied how minimum-wage laws affect the teenage labour market. These researchers compare the changes in the minimum wage over time with the changes in teenage employment. Although there is some debate about how much the minimum wage affects employment, the typical study finds that a 10 percent increase in the minimum wage depresses teenage employment between 1 and 3 percent. In interpreting this estimate, note that a 10 percent increase in the minimum wage does not raise the average wage of teenagers by 10 percent. A change in the law does not directly affect those teenagers who are already paid well above the minimum, and enforcement of minimum-wage laws is not perfect. Thus, the estimated drop in employment of 1 to 3 percent is significant.

In addition to altering the quantity of labour demanded, the minimum wage also alters the quantity supplied. Because the minimum wage raises the wage that teenagers can earn, it increases the number of teenagers who choose to look for jobs. Studies have found that a higher minimum wage influences which teenagers are employed. When the minimum wage rises, some teenagers who are still attending school choose to drop out and take jobs. These new dropouts displace other teenagers who had already dropped out of school and who now become unemployed.

The minimum wage is a frequent topic of political debate. Advocates of the minimum wage view the policy as one way to raise the income of the working poor. They correctly point out that workers who earn the minimum wage can afford only a meagre standard of living. For example, at a minimum wage of $7.00 per hour, two adults working 40 hours a week for every week of the year at minimum-wage jobs had a total annual income of only $29 120, while the average income in 2001 for a two-earner family was over $80 000. Many advocates of the minimum wage admit that it has some adverse effects, including unemployment, but they believe that these effects are small and that, all things considered, a higher minimum wage makes the poor better off.

Opponents of the minimum wage contend that it is not the best way to combat poverty. They note that a high minimum wage causes unemployment, encourages teenagers to drop out of school, and prevents some unskilled workers from getting the on-the-job training they need. Moreover, opponents of the minimum wage point out that the minimum wage is a poorly targeted policy. Not all minimum-wage workers are heads of households trying to help their families escape poverty. In fact, fewer than a third of minimum-wage earners are in families with incomes below the poverty line. Many are teenagers from middle-class homes working at part-time jobs for extra spending money. ●

Evaluating Price Controls

One of the ten principles of economics discussed in Chapter 1 is that markets are usually a good way to organize economic activity. This principle explains why economists usually oppose price ceilings and price floors. To economists, prices are not the outcome of some haphazard process. Prices, they contend, are the result of the millions of business and consumer decisions that lie behind the supply and demand curves. Prices have the crucial job of balancing supply and demand and, thereby, coordinating economic activity. When policymakers set prices by legal decree, they obscure the signals that normally guide the allocation of society's resources.

Another of the ten principles of economics is that governments can sometimes improve market outcomes. Indeed, policymakers are led to control prices because they view the market's outcome as unfair. Price controls are often aimed at helping the poor. For instance, rent-control laws try to make housing affordable for everyone, and minimum-wage laws try to help people escape poverty.

Yet price controls often hurt those they are trying to help. Rent control may keep rents low, but it also discourages landlords from maintaining their buildings and makes housing hard to find. Minimum-wage laws may raise the incomes of some workers, but they also cause other workers to be unemployed.

Helping those in need can be accomplished in ways other than controlling prices. For instance, the government can make housing more affordable by paying a fraction of the rent for poor families. Unlike rent control, such rent subsidies do not reduce the quantity of housing supplied and, therefore, do not lead to housing shortages. Similarly, wage subsidies raise the living standards of the working poor without discouraging firms from hiring them.

Although these alternative policies are often better than price controls, they are not perfect. Rent and wage subsidies cost the government money and, therefore, require higher taxes. As we see in the next section, taxation has costs of its own.

QuickQuiz Define *price ceiling* and *price floor*, and give an example of each. Which leads to a shortage? Which leads to a surplus? Why?

TAXES

All governments—from the federal government in Ottawa to the local governments in small towns—use taxes to raise revenue for public projects, such as roads, schools, and national defence. Because taxes are such an important policy instrument, and because they affect our lives in many ways, the study of taxes is a topic to which we return several times throughout this book. In this section we begin our study of how taxes affect the economy.

To set the stage for our analysis, imagine that a local government decides to hold an annual ice-cream celebration—with a parade, fireworks, and speeches by town officials. To raise revenue to pay for the event, it decides to place a $0.50 tax on the sale of ice-cream cones. When the plan is announced, our two lobbying groups swing into action. The Canadian Organization of Ice-Cream Makers claims that its members are struggling to survive in a competitive market, and it argues that *buyers* of ice cream should have to pay the tax. The Canadian Association of Ice-Cream Eaters claims that consumers of ice cream are having trouble making ends meet, and it argues that *sellers* of ice cream should pay the tax. The town mayor, hoping to reach a compromise, suggests that half the tax be paid by the buyers and half be paid by the sellers.

To analyze these proposals, we need to address a simple but subtle question: When the government levies a tax on a good, who bears the burden of the tax? The people buying the good? The people selling the good? Or, if buyers and sellers share the tax burden, what determines how the burden is divided? Can the government simply legislate the division of the burden, as the mayor is suggesting, or is the division determined by more fundamental forces in the economy? Economists use the term **tax incidence** to refer to the distribution of a tax burden. As we will see, some surprising lessons about tax incidence arise just by applying the tools of supply and demand.

tax incidence
the manner in which the burden of a tax is shared among participants in a market

How Taxes on Buyers Affect Market Outcomes

We first consider a tax levied on buyers of a good. Suppose, for instance, that our local government passes a law requiring buyers of ice-cream cones to send $0.50 to the government for each ice-cream cone they buy. How does this law affect the buyers and sellers of ice cream? To answer this question, we can follow the three steps in Chapter 4 for analyzing supply and demand: (1) We decide whether the law affects the supply curve or demand curve. (2) We decide which way the curve shifts. (3) We examine how the shift affects the equilibrium.

Step One The initial impact of the tax is on the demand for ice cream. The supply curve is not affected because, for any given price of ice cream, sellers have the same incentive to provide ice cream to the market. By contrast, buyers now have to pay a tax to the government (as well as the price to the sellers) whenever they buy ice cream. Thus, the tax shifts the demand curve for ice cream.

Step Two The direction of the shift is easy to determine. Because the tax on buyers makes buying ice cream less attractive, buyers demand a smaller quantity of ice cream at every price. As a result, the demand curve shifts to the left (or, equivalently, downward), as shown in Figure 6.6 (p. 128).

We can, in this case, be precise about how much the curve shifts. Because of the $0.50 tax levied on buyers, the effective price to buyers is now $0.50 higher than the market price (whatever the market price happens to be). For example, if the market price of a cone happened to be $2.00, the effective price to buyers would be $2.50. Because buyers look at their total cost including the tax, they demand a quantity of ice cream as if the market price were $0.50 higher than it actually is. In other words, to induce buyers to demand any given quantity, the market price must now be $0.50 lower to make up for the effect of the tax. Thus, the tax shifts the demand curve *downward* from D_1 to D_2 by exactly the size of the tax ($0.50).

Step Three Having determined how the demand curve shifts, we can now see the effect of the tax by comparing the initial equilibrium and the new equilibrium. You can see in the figure that the equilibrium price of ice cream falls from $3.00 to $2.80 and the equilibrium quantity falls from 100 to 90 cones. Because sellers sell less and buyers buy less in the new equilibrium, the tax on ice cream reduces the size of the ice-cream market.

FIGURE 6.6

A Tax on Buyers

When a tax of $0.50 is levied on buyers, the demand curve shifts down by $0.50 from D₁ to D₂. The equilibrium quantity falls from 100 to 90 cones. The price that sellers receive falls from $3.00 to $2.80. The price that buyers pay (including the tax) rises from $3.00 to $3.30. Even though the tax is levied on buyers, buyers and sellers share the burden of the tax.

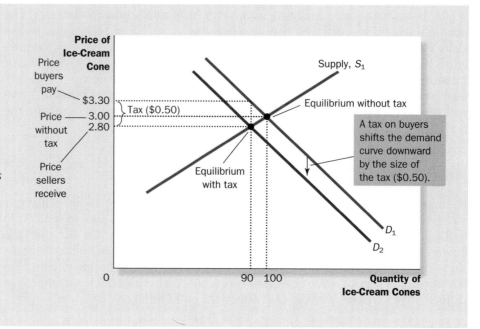

Implications We can now return to the question of tax incidence: Who pays the tax? Although buyers send the entire tax to the government, buyers and sellers share the burden. Because the market price falls from $3.00 to $2.80 when the tax is introduced, sellers receive $0.20 less for each ice-cream cone than they did without the tax. Thus, the tax makes sellers worse off. Buyers pay sellers a lower price ($2.80), but the effective price including the tax rises from $3.00 before the tax to $3.30 with the tax ($2.80 + $0.50 = $3.30). Thus, the tax also makes buyers worse off.

To sum up, the analysis yields two lessons:

- Taxes discourage market activity. When a good is taxed, the quantity of the good sold is smaller in the new equilibrium.
- Buyers and sellers share the burden of taxes. In the new equilibrium, buyers pay more for the good, and sellers receive less.

How Taxes on Sellers Affect Market Outcomes

Now consider a tax levied on sellers of a good. Suppose the local government passes a law requiring sellers of ice-cream cones to send $0.50 to the government for each cone they sell. What are the effects of this law? Again, we apply our three steps.

Step One In this case, the immediate impact of the tax is on the sellers of ice cream. Because the tax is not levied on buyers, the quantity of ice cream demanded at any given price is the same; thus, the demand curve does not change. By contrast, the tax on sellers makes the ice-cream business less profitable at any given price, so it shifts the supply curve.

Step Two Because the tax on sellers raises the cost of producing and selling ice cream, it reduces the quantity supplied at every price. The supply curve shifts to the left (or, equivalently, upward).

Once again, we can be precise about the magnitude of the shift. For any market price of ice cream, the effective price to sellers—the amount they get to keep after paying the tax—is $0.50 lower. For example, if the market price of a cone happened to be $2.00, the effective price received by sellers would be $1.50. Whatever the market price, sellers will supply a quantity of ice cream as if the price were $0.50 lower than it is. Put differently, to induce sellers to supply any given quantity, the market price must now be $0.50 higher to compensate for the effect of the tax. Thus, as shown in Figure 6.7, the supply curve shifts *upward* from S_1 to S_2 by exactly the size of the tax ($0.50).

Step Three Having determined how the supply curve shifts, we can now compare the initial and the new equilibrium. The figure shows that the equilibrium price of ice cream rises from $3.00 to $3.30, and the equilibrium quantity falls from 100 to 90 cones. Once again, the tax reduces the size of the ice-cream market. And once again, buyers and sellers share the burden of the tax. Because the market price rises, buyers pay $0.30 more for each cone than they did before the tax was enacted. Sellers receive a higher price than they did without the tax, but the effective price (after paying the tax) falls from $3.00 to $2.80.

Implications If you compare Figures 6.6 and 6.7, you will notice a surprising conclusion: *Taxes on buyers and taxes on sellers are equivalent.* In both cases, the tax places a wedge between the price that buyers pay and the price that sellers

FIGURE 6.7

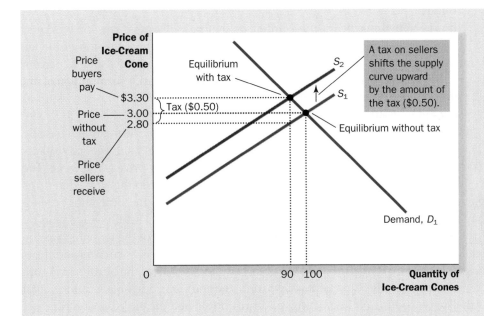

A Tax on Sellers

When a tax of $0.50 is levied on sellers, the supply curve shifts up by $0.50 from S_1 to S_2. The equilibrium quantity falls from 100 to 90 cones. The price that buyers pay rises from $3.00 to $3.30. The price that sellers receive (after paying the tax) falls from $3.00 to $2.80. Even though the tax is levied on sellers, buyers and sellers share the burden of the tax.

receive. The wedge between the buyers' price and the sellers' price is the same, regardless of whether the tax is levied on buyers or sellers. In either case, the wedge shifts the relative position of the supply and demand curves. In the new equilibrium, buyers and sellers share the burden of the tax. The only difference between taxes on buyers and taxes on sellers is who sends the money to the government.

The equivalence of these two taxes is easy to understand if we imagine that the government collects the $0.50 ice-cream tax in a bowl on the counter of each ice-cream store. When the government levies the tax on buyers, the buyer is required to place $0.50 in the bowl every time a cone is bought. When the government levies the tax on sellers, the seller is required to place $0.50 in the bowl after the sale of each cone. Whether the $0.50 goes directly from the buyer's pocket into the bowl, or indirectly from the buyer's pocket into the seller's hand and then into the bowl, does not matter. Once the market reaches its new equilibrium, buyers and sellers share the burden, regardless of how the tax is levied.

Case Study

CAN PARLIAMENT DISTRIBUTE THE BURDEN OF A PAYROLL TAX?

If you have ever received a paycheque, you probably noticed that taxes were deducted from the amount you earned. One of these taxes is called Employment Insurance (EI). The federal government uses the revenue from the EI tax to pay for benefits to unemployed workers, as well as for training programs and other policies. EI is an example of a payroll tax, which is a tax on the wages that firms pay their workers. In 2003, the total EI tax for the typical worker was about 5 percent of earnings.

Who do you think bears the burden of this payroll tax—firms or workers? When Parliament passed this legislation, it tried to mandate a division of the tax burden. According to the law, 58 percent of the tax is paid by firms, and 42 percent is paid by workers. That is, 58 percent of the tax is paid out of firm revenue, and 42 percent is deducted from workers' paycheques. The amount that shows up as a deduction on your pay stub is the worker contribution.

Our analysis of tax incidence, however, shows that lawmakers cannot so easily dictate the distribution of a tax burden. To illustrate, we can analyze a payroll tax as merely a tax on a good, where the good is labour and the price is the wage. The key feature of the payroll tax is that it places a wedge between the wage that firms pay and the wage that workers receive. Figure 6.8 shows the outcome. When a payroll tax is enacted, the wage received by workers falls, and the wage paid by firms rises. In the end, workers and firms share the burden of the tax, much as the legislation requires. Yet this division of the tax burden between workers and firms has nothing to do with the legislated division: The division of the burden in Figure 6.8 is not necessarily 58 percent–42 percent, and the same outcome would prevail if the law levied the entire tax on workers or if it levied the entire tax on firms.

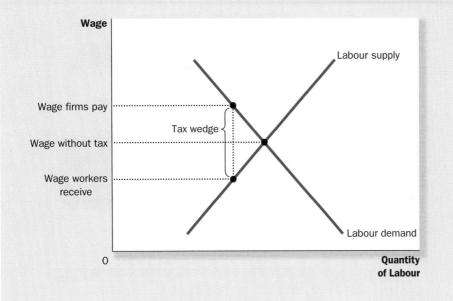

A Payroll Tax

A payroll tax places a wedge between the wage that workers receive and the wage that firms pay. Comparing wages with and without the tax, you can see that workers and firms share the tax burden. This division of the tax burden between workers and firms does not depend on whether the government levies the tax on workers, levies the tax on firms, or divides the tax equally between the two groups.

This example shows that the most basic lesson of tax incidence is often overlooked in public debate. Lawmakers can decide whether a tax comes from the buyer's pocket or from the seller's, but they cannot legislate the true burden of a tax. Rather, tax incidence depends on the forces of supply and demand. ●

Elasticity and Tax Incidence

When a good is taxed, buyers and sellers of the good share the burden of the tax. But how exactly is the tax burden divided? Only rarely will it be shared equally. To see how the burden is divided, consider the impact of taxation in the two markets in Figure 6.9 (p. 132). In both cases, the figure shows the initial demand curve, the initial supply curve, and a tax that drives a wedge between the amount paid by buyers and the amount received by sellers. (Not drawn in either panel of the figure is the new supply or demand curve. Which curve shifts depends on whether the tax is levied on buyers or sellers. As we have seen, this is irrelevant for the incidence of the tax.) The difference in the two panels is the relative elasticity of supply and demand.

Panel (a) of Figure 6.9 shows a tax in a market with very elastic supply and relatively inelastic demand. That is, sellers are very responsive to changes in the price of the good (so the supply curve is relatively flat), whereas buyers are not very responsive (so the demand curve is relatively steep). When a tax is imposed on a market with these elasticities, the price received by sellers does not fall much, so sellers bear only a small burden. By contrast, the price paid by buyers rises substantially, indicating that buyers bear most of the burden of the tax.

Panel (b) of Figure 6.9 shows a tax in a market with relatively inelastic supply and very elastic demand. In this case, sellers are not very responsive to changes in the price (so the supply curve is steeper), while buyers are very responsive (so the

FIGURE 6.9

How the Burden of a Tax Is Divided

In panel (a), the supply curve is elastic, and the demand curve is inelastic. In this case, the price received by sellers falls only slightly, while the price paid by buyers rises substantially. Thus, buyers bear most of the burden of the tax. In panel (b), the supply curve is inelastic, and the demand curve is elastic. In this case, the price received by sellers falls substantially, while the price paid by buyers rises only slightly. Thus, sellers bear most of the burden of the tax.

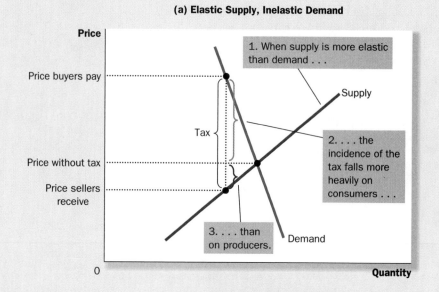

(a) Elastic Supply, Inelastic Demand

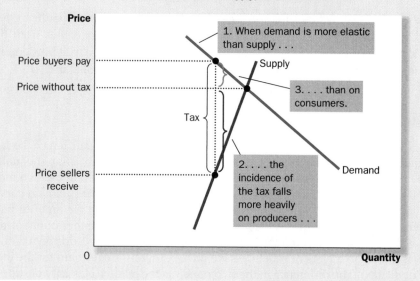

(b) Inelastic Supply, Elastic Demand

demand curve is flatter). The figure shows that when a tax is imposed, the price paid by buyers does not rise much, while the price received by sellers falls substantially. Thus, sellers bear most of the burden of the tax.

The two panels of Figure 6.9 show a general lesson about how the burden of a tax is divided: *A tax burden falls more heavily on the side of the market that is less elastic.* Why is this true? In essence, the elasticity measures the willingness of buyers or sellers to leave the market when conditions become unfavourable. A small elasticity of demand means that buyers do not have good alternatives to consuming this particular good. A small elasticity of supply means that sellers do not have good alternatives to producing this particular good. When the good is taxed, the side of the market with fewer good alternatives cannot easily leave the market and must, therefore, bear more of the burden of the tax.

We can apply this logic to the payroll tax discussed in the previous case study. Most labour economists believe that the supply of labour is much less elastic than the demand. This means that workers, rather than firms, bear most of the burden of the payroll tax. In other words, the distribution of the tax burden is not at all close to the 58–42 split that lawmakers intended.

QuickQuiz In a supply-and-demand diagram, show how a tax on car buyers of $1000 per car affects the quantity of cars sold and the price of cars. In another diagram, show how a tax on car sellers of $1000 per car affects the quantity of cars sold and the price of cars. In both of your diagrams, show the change in the price paid by car buyers and the change in price received by car sellers.

CONCLUSION

The economy is governed by two kinds of laws: the laws of supply and demand and the laws enacted by governments. In this chapter we have begun to see how these laws interact. Price controls and taxes are common in various markets in the economy, and their effects are frequently debated in the press and among policy-makers. Even a little bit of economic knowledge can go a long way toward understanding and evaluating these policies.

In subsequent chapters we will analyze many government policies in greater detail. We will examine the effects of taxation more fully, and we will consider a broader range of policies than we considered here. Yet the basic lessons of this chapter will not change: When analyzing government policies, supply and demand are the first and most useful tools of analysis.

SUMMARY

- A price ceiling is a legal maximum on the price of a good or service. An example is rent control. If the price ceiling is below the equilibrium price, the quantity demanded exceeds the quantity supplied. Because of the resulting shortage, sellers must in some way ration the good or service among buyers.

- A price floor is a legal minimum on the price of a good or service. An example is the minimum wage. If the price floor is above the equilibrium price, the quantity supplied exceeds the quantity demanded. Because of the resulting surplus, buyers' demands for the good or service must in some way be rationed among sellers.

- When the government levies a tax on a good, the equilibrium quantity of the good falls. That is, a tax on a market shrinks the size of the market.

- A tax on a good places a wedge between the price paid by buyers and the price received by sellers. When the market moves to the new equilibrium, buyers pay more for the good and sellers receive less for it. In this sense, buyers and sellers share the tax burden. The incidence of a tax (that is, the division of the tax burden) does not depend on whether the tax is levied on buyers or sellers.

- The incidence of a tax depends on the price elasticities of supply and demand. The burden tends to fall on the side of the market that is less elastic because that side of the market can respond less easily to the tax by changing the quantity bought or sold.

KEY CONCEPTS

price ceiling, p. 116   price floor, p. 116   tax incidence, p. 127

QUESTIONS FOR REVIEW

1. Give an example of a price ceiling and an example of a price floor.

2. Which causes a shortage of a good—a price ceiling or a price floor? Which causes a surplus?

3. What mechanisms allocate resources when the price of a good is not allowed to bring supply and demand into equilibrium?

4. Explain why economists usually oppose controls on prices.

5. What is the difference between a tax paid by buyers and a tax paid by sellers?

6. How does a tax on a good affect the price paid by buyers, the price received by sellers, and the quantity sold?

7. What determines how the burden of a tax is divided between buyers and sellers? Why?

PROBLEMS AND APPLICATIONS

1. Lovers of classical music persuade Parliament to impose a price ceiling of $40 per concert ticket. Does this policy get more or fewer people to attend classical music concerts?

2. The government has decided that the free-market price of cheese is too low.

   a. Suppose the government imposes a binding price floor in the cheese market. Use a supply-and-demand diagram to show the effect of this policy on the price of cheese and the quantity of cheese sold. Is there a shortage or surplus of cheese?

   b. Farmers complain that the price floor has reduced their total revenue. Is this possible? Explain.

   c. In response to farmers' complaints, the government agrees to purchase all of the surplus cheese at the price floor. Compared to the basic price floor, who benefits from this new policy? Who loses?

3. A recent study found that the demand and supply schedules for Frisbees are as follows:

Price per Frisbee	Quantity Demanded	Quantity Supplied
$11	1 million	15 million
10	2	12
9	4	9
8	6	6
7	8	3
6	10	1

   a. What are the equilibrium price and quantity of Frisbees?

   b. Frisbee manufacturers persuade the government that Frisbee production improves scientists' understanding of aerodynamics and thus is important for national security. A concerned Parliament votes to impose a price floor $2 above the equilibrium price. What is the new market price? How many Frisbees are sold?

   c. Irate students march on Ottawa and demand a reduction in the price of Frisbees. An even more concerned Parliament votes to repeal the price floor and impose a price ceiling $1 below the former price floor. What is the new market price? How many Frisbees are sold?

4. Suppose the provincial government requires beer drinkers to pay a $2 tax on each case of beer purchased.

    a. Draw a supply-and-demand diagram of the market for beer without the tax. Show the price paid by consumers, the price received by producers, and the quantity of beer sold. What is the difference between the price paid by consumers and the price received by producers?

    b. Now draw a supply-and-demand diagram for the beer market with the tax. Show the price paid by consumers, the price received by producers, and the quantity of beer sold. What is the difference between the price paid by consumers and the price received by producers? Has the quantity of beer sold increased or decreased?

5. An MP wants to raise tax revenue and make workers better off. A staff member proposes raising the payroll tax paid by firms and using part of the extra revenue to reduce the payroll tax paid by workers. Would this accomplish the MP's goal?

6. If the government places a $500 tax on luxury cars, will the price paid by consumers rise by more than $500, less than $500, or exactly $500? Explain.

7. Parliament decides that Canada should reduce air pollution by reducing its use of gasoline. It imposes a $0.50 tax for each litre of gasoline sold.

    a. Should it impose this tax on producers or consumers? Explain carefully, using a supply-and-demand diagram.

    b. If the demand for gasoline were more elastic, would this tax be more effective or less effective in reducing the quantity of gasoline consumed? Explain with both words and a diagram.

    c. Are consumers of gasoline helped or hurt by this tax? Why?

    d. Are workers in the oil industry helped or hurt by this tax? Why?

8. A case study in this chapter discusses the minimum-wage law.

    a. Suppose the minimum wage is above the equilibrium wage in the market for unskilled labour. Using a supply-and-demand diagram of the market for unskilled labour, show the market wage, the number of workers who are employed, and the number of workers who are unemployed. Also show the total wage payments to unskilled workers.

    b. Now suppose the provincial government proposes an increase in the minimum wage. What effect would this increase have on employment? Does the change in employment depend on the elasticity of demand, the elasticity of supply, both elasticities, or neither?

    c. What effect would this increase in the minimum wage have on unemployment? Does the change in unemployment depend on the elasticity of demand, the elasticity of supply, both elasticities, or neither?

    d. If the demand for unskilled labour were inelastic, would the proposed increase in the minimum wage raise or lower total wage payments to unskilled workers? Would your answer change if the demand for unskilled labour were elastic?

9. Consider the following policies, each of which is aimed at reducing violent crime by reducing the use of guns. Illustrate each of these proposed policies in a supply-and-demand diagram of the gun market.

    a. a tax on gun buyers

    b. a tax on gun sellers

    c. a price floor on guns

    d. a tax on ammunition

10. The Canadian government administers two programs that affect the market for cigarettes. Media campaigns and labelling requirements are aimed at making the public aware of the

dangers of cigarette smoking. At the same time, Agriculture and Agri-Food Canada imposes production quotas on tobacco farmers, which raise the price of tobacco above the equilibrium price.

a. How do these two programs affect cigarette consumption? Use a graph of the cigarette market in your answer.

b. What is the combined effect of these two programs on the price of cigarettes?

c. Cigarettes are also heavily taxed. What effect does this tax have on cigarette consumption?

11. A subsidy is the opposite of a tax. With a $0.50 tax on the buyers of ice-cream cones, the government collects $0.50 for each cone purchased; with a $0.50 subsidy for the buyers of ice-cream cones, the government pays buyers $0.50 for each cone purchased.

a. Show the effect of a $0.50 per cone subsidy on the demand curve for ice-cream cones, the effective price paid by consumers, the effective price received by sellers, and the quantity of cones sold.

b. Do consumers gain or lose from this policy? Do producers gain or lose? Does the government gain or lose?

INTERNET RESOURCES

- For an argument against rent control, read the article by economist Walter Block at http://www.econlib.org/library/Enc/RentControl.html. Economists like Walter Block usually argue that rent controls are wrong because they have bad consequences for landlords and tenants alike.

  For a very different argument against rent controls, read philosopher Michael Berliner's article at http://www.aynrand.org/objectivism/rent_control.html.

  For an argument in favour of rent controls, read the article on the Ontario Tenants site at http://www.geocities.com/torontotenants/rentcontrols.html.

- The Canadian Centre for Policy Alternatives argues in favour of raising the minimum wage on its website: http://www.policyalternatives.ca/bc/bcminwageqf.html.

  The Fraser Institute argues against raising the minimum wage on its website:

  http://oldfraser.lexi.net/media/media_releases/1999/19990209.html.

http://   For more study tools, please visit http://www.mankiw3e.nelson.com.

3

SUPPLY AND DEMAND II: MARKETS AND WELFARE

© DON CARSTENS/TAXI

7

In this chapter, you will …

- Examine the link between buyers' willingness to pay for a good and the demand curve
- Learn how to define and measure consumer surplus
- Examine the link between sellers' cost of producing a good and the supply curve
- Learn how to define and measure producer surplus
- See that the equilibrium of supply and demand maximizes total surplus in a market

消費者   生者.

CONSUMERS, PRODUCERS, AND THE EFFICIENCY OF MARKETS

When consumers go to grocery stores to buy their turkeys for a holiday dinner, they may be disappointed that the price of turkey is as high as it is. At the same time, when farmers bring to market the turkeys they have raised, they wish the price of turkey were even higher. These views are not surprising: Buyers always want to pay less, and sellers always want to be paid more. But is there a "right price" for turkey from the standpoint of society as a whole?

In previous chapters we saw how, in market economies, the forces of supply and demand determine the prices of goods and services and the quantities sold. So far, however, we have described the way markets allocate scarce resources without directly addressing the question of whether these market allocations are desirable. In other words, our analysis has been *positive* (what is) rather than *normative* (what should be). We know that the price of turkey adjusts to ensure that the quantity of turkey supplied equals the quantity of turkey demanded. But, at this equilibrium, is the quantity of turkey produced and consumed too small, too large, or just right?

welfare economics
the study of how the allocation of resources affects economic well-being

In this chapter we take up the topic of **welfare economics,** the study of how the allocation of resources affects economic well-being. We begin by examining the benefits that buyers and sellers receive from taking part in a market. We then examine how society can make these benefits as large as possible. This analysis leads to a profound conclusion: The equilibrium of supply and demand in a market maximizes the total benefits received by buyers and sellers.

As you may recall from Chapter 1, one of the ten principles of economics is that markets are usually a good way to organize economic activity. The study of welfare economics explains this principle more fully. It also answers our question about the right price of turkey: The price that balances the supply and demand for turkey is, in a particular sense, the best one because it maximizes the total welfare of turkey consumers and turkey producers.

CONSUMER SURPLUS

We begin our study of welfare economics by looking at the benefits buyers receive from participating in a market.

Willingness to Pay

Imagine that you own a mint-condition recording of Elvis Presley's first album. Because you are not an Elvis Presley fan, you decide to sell it. One way to do so is to hold an auction.

Four Elvis fans show up for your auction: John, Paul, George, and Ringo. Each of them would like to own the album, but there is a limit to the amount that each is willing to pay for it. Table 7.1 shows the maximum price that each of the four possible buyers would pay. Each buyer's maximum is called his **willingness to pay,** and it measures how much that buyer values the good. Each buyer would be eager to buy the album at a price less than his willingness to pay, would refuse to buy the album at a price more than his willingness to pay, and would be indifferent about buying the album at a price exactly equal to his willingness to pay.

To sell your album, you begin the bidding at a low price, say $10. Because all four buyers are willing to pay much more, the price rises quickly. The bidding stops when John bids $80 (or slightly more). At this point, Paul, George, and Ringo

willingness to pay
the maximum amount that a buyer will pay for a good

TABLE 7.1

Four Possible Buyers' Willingness to Pay

Buyer	Willingness to Pay
John	$100
Paul	80
George	70
Ringo	50

have dropped out of the bidding, because they are unwilling to bid any more than $80. John pays you $80 and gets the album. Note that the album has gone to the buyer who values the album most highly.

What benefit does John receive from buying the Elvis Presley album? In a sense, John has found a real bargain: He is willing to pay $100 for the album but pays only $80 for it. We say that John receives *consumer surplus* of $20. **Consumer surplus** is the amount a buyer is willing to pay for a good minus the amount the buyer actually pays for it.

Consumer surplus measures the benefit to buyers of participating in a market. In this example, John receives a $20 benefit from participating in the auction because he pays only $80 for a good he values at $100. Paul, George, and Ringo get no consumer surplus from participating in the auction, because they left without the album and without paying anything.

Now consider a somewhat different example. Suppose that you had two identical Elvis Presley albums to sell. Again, you auction them off to the four possible buyers. To keep things simple, we assume that both albums are to be sold for the same price and that no buyer is interested in buying more than one album. Therefore, the price rises until two buyers are left.

In this case, the bidding stops when John and Paul bid $70 (or slightly higher). At this price, John and Paul are each happy to buy an album, and George and Ringo are not willing to bid any higher. John and Paul each receive consumer surplus equal to his willingness to pay minus the price. John's consumer surplus is $30, and Paul's is $10. John's consumer surplus is higher now than it was previously, because he gets the same album but pays less for it. The total consumer surplus in the market is $40.

Using the Demand Curve to Measure Consumer Surplus

Consumer surplus is closely related to the demand curve for a product. To see how they are related, let's continue our example and consider the demand curve for this rare Elvis Presley album.

We begin by using the willingness to pay of the four possible buyers to find the demand schedule for the album. The table in Figure 7.1 (p. 142) shows the demand schedule that corresponds to Table 7.1. If the price is above $100, the quantity demanded in the market is 0, because no buyer is willing to pay that much. If the price is between $80 and $100, the quantity demanded is 1, because only John is willing to pay such a high price. If the price is between $70 and $80, the quantity demanded is 2, because both John and Paul are willing to pay the price. We can continue this analysis for other prices as well. In this way, the demand schedule is derived from the willingness to pay of the four possible buyers.

The graph in Figure 7.1 shows the demand curve that corresponds to this demand schedule. Note the relationship between the height of the demand curve and the buyers' willingness to pay. At any quantity, the price given by the demand curve shows the willingness to pay of the *marginal buyer*, the buyer who would leave the market first if the price were any higher. At a quantity of 4 albums, for instance, the demand curve has a height of $50, the price that Ringo (the marginal buyer) is willing to pay for an album. At a quantity of 3 albums, the demand curve has a height of $70, the price that George (who is now the marginal buyer) is willing to pay.

consumer surplus
a buyer's willingness to pay minus the amount the buyer actually pays

FIGURE 7.1

The Demand Schedule and the Demand Curve

The table shows the demand schedule for the buyers in Table 7.1. The graph shows the corresponding demand curve. Note that the height of the demand curve reflects buyers' willingness to pay.

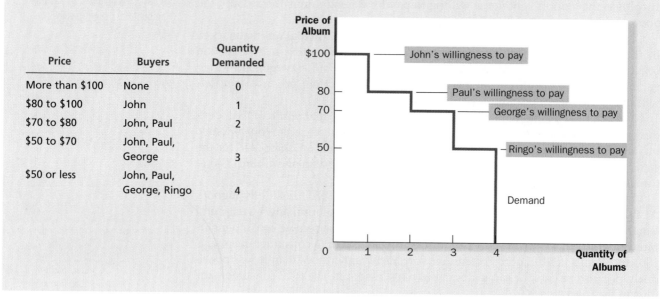

Price	Buyers	Quantity Demanded
More than $100	None	0
$80 to $100	John	1
$70 to $80	John, Paul	2
$50 to $70	John, Paul, George	3
$50 or less	John, Paul, George, Ringo	4

Because the demand curve reflects buyers' willingness to pay, we can also use it to measure consumer surplus. Figure 7.2 uses the demand curve to compute consumer surplus in our example. In panel (a), the price is $80 (or slightly above), and the quantity demanded is 1. Note that the area above the price and below the demand curve equals $20. This amount is exactly the consumer surplus we computed earlier when only 1 album is sold.

Panel (b) of Figure 7.2 shows consumer surplus when the price is $70 (or slightly above). In this case, the area above the price and below the demand curve equals the total area of the two rectangles: John's consumer surplus at this price is $30 and Paul's is $10. This area equals a total of $40. Once again, this amount is the consumer surplus we computed earlier.

The lesson from this example holds for all demand curves: *The area below the demand curve and above the price measures the consumer surplus in a market.* The reason is that the height of the demand curve measures the value buyers place on the good, as measured by their willingness to pay for it. The difference between this willingness to pay and the market price is each buyer's consumer surplus. Thus, the total area below the demand curve and above the price is the sum of the consumer surplus of all buyers in the market for a good or service.

How a Lower Price Raises Consumer Surplus

Because buyers always want to pay less for the goods they buy, a lower price makes buyers of a good better off. But how much does buyers' well-being rise in

FIGURE 7.2

Measuring Consumer Surplus with the Demand Curve

In panel (a), the price of the good is $80, and the consumer surplus is $20. In panel (b), the price of the good is $70, and the consumer surplus is $40.

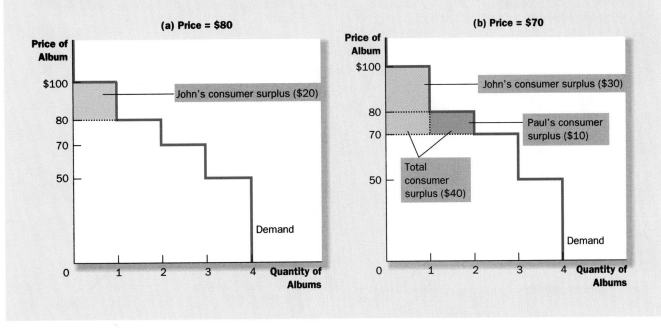

response to a lower price? We can use the concept of consumer surplus to answer this question precisely.

Figure 7.3 (p. 144) shows a typical downward-sloping demand curve. Although this demand curve appears somewhat different in shape from the steplike demand curves in our previous two figures, the ideas we have just developed apply nonetheless: Consumer surplus is the area above the price and below the demand curve. In panel (a), consumer surplus at a price of P_1 is the area of triangle ABC.

Now suppose that the price falls from P_1 to P_2, as shown in panel (b). The consumer surplus now equals area ADF. The increase in consumer surplus attributable to the lower price is the area BCFD.

This increase in consumer surplus is composed of two parts. First, those buyers who were already buying Q_1 of the good at the higher price P_1 are better off because they now pay less. The increase in consumer surplus of existing buyers is the reduction in the amount they pay; it equals the area of the rectangle BCED. Second, some new buyers enter the market because they are now willing to buy the good at the lower price. As a result, the quantity demanded in the market increases from Q_1 to Q_2. The consumer surplus these newcomers receive is the area of the triangle CEF.

What Does Consumer Surplus Measure?

Our goal in developing the concept of consumer surplus is to make normative judgments about the desirability of market outcomes. Now that you have seen

FIGURE 7.3

How the Price Affects Consumer Surplus

In panel (a), the price is P_1, the quantity demanded is Q_1, and consumer surplus equals the area of the triangle ABC. When the price falls from P_1 to P_2, as in panel (b), the quantity demanded rises from Q_1 to Q_2, and the consumer surplus rises to the area of the triangle ADF. The increase in consumer surplus (area BCFD) occurs in part because existing consumers now pay less (area BCED) and in part because new consumers enter the market at the lower price (area CEF).

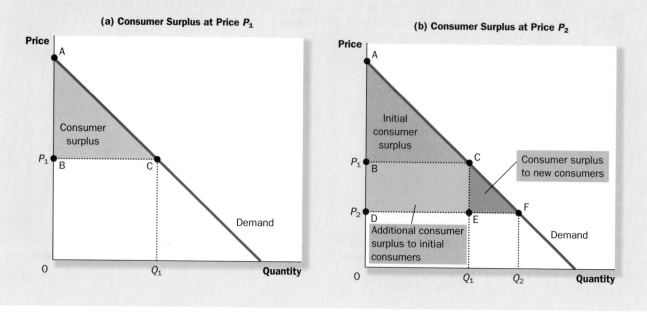

(a) Consumer Surplus at Price P_1

(b) Consumer Surplus at Price P_2

what consumer surplus is, let's consider whether it is a good measure of economic well-being.

Imagine that you are a policymaker trying to design a good economic system. Would you care about the amount of consumer surplus? Consumer surplus, the amount that buyers are willing to pay for a good minus the amount they actually pay for it, measures the benefit that buyers receive from a good *as the buyers themselves perceive it.* Thus, consumer surplus is a good measure of economic well-being if policymakers want to respect the preferences of buyers.

In some circumstances, policymakers might choose not to care about consumer surplus because they do not respect the preferences that drive buyer behaviour. For example, drug addicts are willing to pay a high price for heroin. Yet we would not say that addicts get a large benefit from being able to buy heroin at a low price (even though addicts might say they do). From the standpoint of society, willingness to pay in this instance is not a good measure of the buyers' benefit, and consumer surplus is not a good measure of economic well-being, because addicts are not looking after their own best interests.

In most markets, however, consumer surplus does reflect economic well-being. Economists normally presume that buyers are rational when they make decisions and that their preferences should be respected. In this case, consumers are the best judges of how much benefit they receive from the goods they buy.

QuickQuiz Draw a demand curve for turkey. In your diagram, show a price of turkey and the consumer surplus that results from that price. Explain in words what this consumer surplus measures.

PRODUCER SURPLUS

We now turn to the other side of the market and consider the benefits sellers receive from participating in a market. As you will see, our analysis of sellers' welfare is similar to our analysis of buyers' welfare.

Cost and the Willingness to Sell

Imagine now that you are a homeowner, and you need to get your house painted. You turn to four sellers of painting services: Mary, Frida, Georgia, and Grandma. Each painter is willing to do the work for you if the price is right. You decide to take bids from the four painters and auction off the job to the painter who will do the work for the lowest price.

Each painter is willing to take the job if the price she would receive exceeds her cost of doing the work. Here the term **cost** should be interpreted as the painters' opportunity cost: It includes the painters' out-of-pocket expenses (for paint, brushes, and so on) as well as the value that the painters place on their own time. Table 7.2 shows each painter's cost. Because a painter's cost is the lowest price she would accept for her work, cost is a measure of her willingness to sell her services. Each painter would be eager to sell her services at a price greater than her cost, would refuse to sell her services at a price less than her cost, and would be indifferent about selling her services at a price exactly equal to her cost.

cost
the value of everything a seller must give up to produce a good

When you take bids from the painters, the price might start off high, but it quickly falls as the painters compete for the job. Once Grandma has bid $600 (or slightly less), she is the sole remaining bidder. Grandma is happy to do the job for this price, because her cost is only $500. Mary, Frida, and Georgia are unwilling to do the job for less than $600. Note that the job goes to the painter who can do the work at the lowest cost.

What benefit does Grandma receive from getting the job? Because she is willing to do the work for $500 but gets $600 for doing it, we say that she receives *producer*

TABLE 7.2

The Costs of Four Possible Sellers

Seller	Cost
Mary	$900
Frida	800
Georgia	600
Grandma	500

producer surplus
the amount a seller is paid for a good minus the seller's cost

surplus of $100. **Producer surplus** is the amount a seller is paid minus the cost of production. Producer surplus measures the benefit to sellers of participating in a market.

Now consider a somewhat different example. Suppose that you have two identical houses that need painting. Again, you auction off the jobs to the four painters. To keep things simple, let's assume that no painter is able to paint both houses and that you will pay the same amount to paint each house. Therefore, the price falls until two painters are left.

In this case, the bidding stops when Georgia and Grandma each offer to do the job for a price of $800 (or slightly less). At this price, Georgia and Grandma are willing to do the work, and Mary and Frida are not willing to bid a lower price. At a price of $800, Grandma receives producer surplus of $300, and Georgia receives producer surplus of $200. The total producer surplus in the market is $500.

Using the Supply Curve to Measure Producer Surplus

Just as consumer surplus is closely related to the demand curve, producer surplus is closely related to the supply curve. To see how, let's continue our example.

We begin by using the costs of the four painters to find the supply schedule for painting services. The table in Figure 7.4 shows the supply schedule that corresponds to the costs in Table 7.2. If the price is below $500, none of the four painters is willing to do the job, so the quantity supplied is zero. If the price is between $500 and $600, only Grandma is willing to do the job, so the quantity supplied

FIGURE 7.4

The Supply Schedule and the Supply Curve

The table shows the supply schedule for the sellers in Table 7.2. The graph shows the corresponding supply curve. Note that the height of the supply curve reflects sellers' costs.

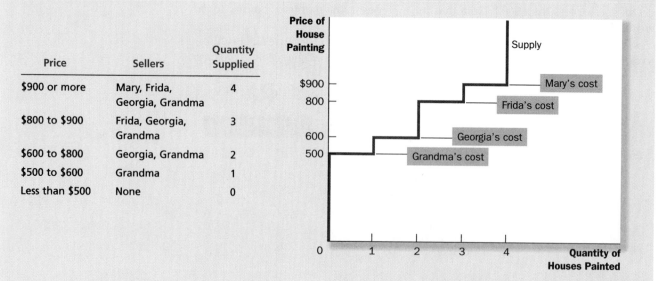

Price	Sellers	Quantity Supplied
$900 or more	Mary, Frida, Georgia, Grandma	4
$800 to $900	Frida, Georgia, Grandma	3
$600 to $800	Georgia, Grandma	2
$500 to $600	Grandma	1
Less than $500	None	0

is 1. If the price is between $600 and $800, Grandma and Georgia are willing to do the job, so the quantity supplied is 2, and so on. Thus, the supply schedule is derived from the costs of the four painters.

The graph in Figure 7.4 shows the supply curve that corresponds to this supply schedule. Note that the height of the supply curve is related to the sellers' costs. At any quantity, the price given by the supply curve shows the cost of the *marginal seller*, the seller who would leave the market first if the price were any lower. At a quantity of 4 houses, for instance, the supply curve has a height of $900, the cost that Mary (the marginal seller) incurs to provide her painting services. At a quantity of 3 houses, the supply curve has a height of $800, the cost that Frida (who is now the marginal seller) incurs.

Because the supply curve reflects sellers' costs, we can use it to measure producer surplus. Figure 7.5 uses the supply curve to compute producer surplus in our example. In panel (a), we assume that the price is $600. In this case, the quantity supplied is 1. Note that the area below the price and above the supply curve equals $100. This amount is exactly the producer surplus we computed earlier for Grandma.

Panel (b) of Figure 7.5 shows producer surplus at a price of $800. In this case, the area below the price and above the supply curve equals the total area of the two rectangles. This area equals $500, the producer surplus we computed earlier for Georgia and Grandma when two houses needed painting.

FIGURE 7.5

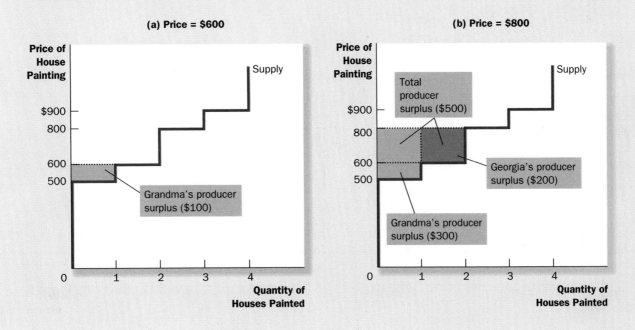

Measuring Producer Surplus with the Supply Curve

In panel (a), the price of the good is $600, and the producer surplus is $100. In panel (b), the price of the good is $800, and the producer surplus is $500.

The lesson from this example applies to all supply curves: *The area below the price and above the supply curve measures the producer surplus in a market.* The logic is straightforward: The height of the supply curve measures sellers' costs, and the difference between the price and the cost of production is each seller's producer surplus. Thus, the total area is the sum of the producer surplus of all sellers.

How a Higher Price Raises Producer Surplus

You will not be surprised to hear that sellers always want to receive a higher price for the goods they sell. But how much does sellers' well-being rise in response to a higher price? The concept of producer surplus offers a precise answer to this question.

Figure 7.6 shows a typical upward-sloping supply curve. Even though this supply curve differs in shape from the steplike supply curves in the previous figure, we measure producer surplus in the same way: Producer surplus is the area below the price and above the supply curve. In panel (a), the price is P_1, and producer surplus is the area of triangle ABC.

FIGURE 7.6

How the Price Affects Producer Surplus

In panel (a), the price is P_1, the quantity demanded is Q_1, and producer surplus equals the area of the triangle ABC. When the price rises from P_1 to P_2, as in panel (b), the quantity supplied rises from Q_1 to Q_2, and the producer surplus rises to the area of the triangle ADF. The increase in producer surplus (area BCFD) occurs in part because existing producers now receive more (area BCED) and in part because new producers enter the market at the higher price (area CEF).

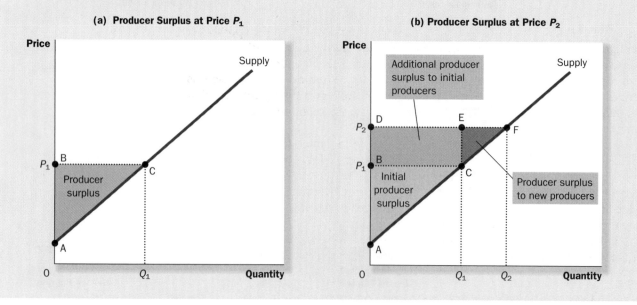

Panel (b) shows what happens when the price rises from P_1 to P_2. Producer surplus now equals area ADF. This increase in producer surplus has two parts. First, those sellers who were already selling Q_1 of the good at the lower price P_1 are better off because they now get more for what they sell. The increase in producer surplus for existing sellers equals the area of the rectangle BCED. Second, some new sellers enter the market because they are now willing to produce the good at the higher price, resulting in an increase in the quantity supplied from Q_1 to Q_2. The producer surplus of these newcomers is the area of the triangle CEF.

As this analysis shows, we use producer surplus to measure the well-being of sellers in much the same way as we use consumer surplus to measure the well-being of buyers. Because these two measures of economic welfare are so similar, it is natural to use them together. And, indeed, that is exactly what we do in the next section.

QuickQuiz Draw a supply curve for turkey. In your diagram, show a price of turkey and the producer surplus that results from that price. Explain in words what this producer surplus measures.

MARKET EFFICIENCY

Consumer surplus and producer surplus are the basic tools that economists use to study the welfare of buyers and sellers in a market. These tools can help us address a fundamental economic question: Is the allocation of resources determined by free markets in any way desirable?

The Benevolent Social Planner

To evaluate market outcomes, we introduce into our analysis a new, hypothetical character, called the benevolent social planner. The benevolent social planner is an all-knowing, all-powerful, well-intentioned dictator. This planner wants to maximize the economic well-being of everyone in society. What do you suppose this planner should do? Should he just leave buyers and sellers at the equilibrium that they reach naturally on their own? Or can he increase economic well-being by altering the market outcome in some way?

To answer this question, the benevolent social planner must first decide how to measure the economic well-being of a society. One possible measure is the sum of consumer and producer surplus, which we call *total surplus*. Consumer surplus is the benefit that buyers receive from participating in a market, and producer surplus is the benefit that sellers receive. It is therefore natural to use total surplus as a measure of society's economic well-being.

To better understand this measure of economic well-being, recall how we measure consumer and producer surplus. We define consumer surplus as

Consumer surplus = Value to buyers − Amount paid by buyers

Similarly, we define producer surplus as

$$\text{Producer surplus} = \text{Amount received by sellers} - \text{Cost to sellers}$$

When we add consumer and producer surplus together, we obtain

$$\text{Total surplus} = \text{Value to buyers} - \text{Amount paid by buyers}$$
$$+ \text{Amount received by sellers} - \text{Cost to sellers}$$

The amount paid by buyers equals the amount received by sellers, so the middle two terms in this expression cancel each other. As a result, we can write total surplus as

$$\text{Total surplus} = \text{Value to buyers} - \text{Cost to sellers}$$

Total surplus in a market is the total value to buyers of the goods, as measured by their willingness to pay, minus the total cost to sellers of providing those goods.

 If an allocation of resources maximizes total surplus, we say that the allocation exhibits **efficiency.** If an allocation is not efficient, then some of the gains from trade among buyers and sellers are not being realized. For example, an allocation is inefficient if a good is not being produced by the sellers with lowest cost. In this case, moving production from a high-cost producer to a low-cost producer will lower the total cost to sellers and raise total surplus. Similarly, an allocation is inefficient if a good is not being consumed by the buyers who value it most highly. In this case, moving consumption of the good from a buyer with a low valuation to a buyer with a high valuation will raise total surplus.

 In addition to efficiency, the social planner might also care about **equity**—the fairness of the distribution of well-being among the various buyers and sellers. In essence, the gains from trade in a market are like a pie to be distributed among the market participants. The question of efficiency is whether the pie is as big as possible. The question of equity is whether the pie is divided fairly. Evaluating the equity of a market outcome is more difficult than evaluating the efficiency. Whereas efficiency is an objective goal that can be judged on strictly positive grounds, equity involves normative judgments that go beyond economics and enter into the realm of political philosophy.

 In this chapter we concentrate on efficiency as the social planner's goal. Keep in mind, however, that real policymakers often care about equity as well. That is, they care about both the size of the economic pie and how the pie gets sliced and distributed among members of society.

efficiency
the property of a resource allocation of maximizing the total surplus received by all members of society

equity
the fairness of the distribution of well-being among the members of society

Evaluating the Market Equilibrium

Figure 7.7 shows consumer and producer surplus when a market reaches the equilibrium of supply and demand. Recall that consumer surplus equals the area above the price and under the demand curve, and producer surplus equals the

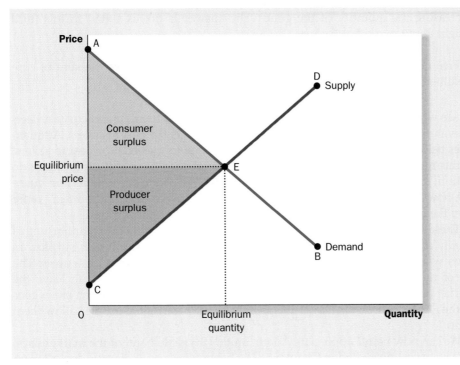

FIGURE 7.7

Consumer and Producer Surplus in the Market Equilibrium

Total surplus—the sum of consumer and producer surplus—is the area between the supply and demand curves up to the equilibrium quantity.

area below the price and above the supply curve. Thus, the total area between the supply and demand curves up to the point of equilibrium represents the total surplus in this market.

Is this equilibrium allocation of resources efficient? Does it maximize total surplus? To answer these questions, keep in mind that when a market is in equilibrium, the price determines which buyers and sellers participate in the market. Those buyers who value the good more than the price (represented by the segment AE on the demand curve) choose to buy the good; those buyers who value it less than the price (represented by the segment EB) do not. Similarly, those sellers whose costs are less than the price (represented by the segment CE on the supply curve) choose to produce and sell the good; those sellers whose costs are greater than the price (represented by the segment ED) do not.

These observations lead to two insights about market outcomes:

1. Free markets allocate the supply of goods to the buyers who value them most highly, as measured by their willingness to pay.
2. Free markets allocate the demand for goods to the sellers who can produce them at least cost.

Thus, given the quantity produced and sold in a market equilibrium, the social planner cannot increase economic well-being by changing the allocation of consumption among buyers or the allocation of production among sellers.

But can the social planner raise total economic well-being by increasing or decreasing the quantity of the good? The answer is no, as stated in this third insight about market outcomes:

3. Free markets produce the quantity of goods that maximizes the sum of consumer and producer surplus.

To see why this is true, consider Figure 7.8. Recall that the demand curve reflects the value to buyers and that the supply curve reflects the cost to sellers. At quantities below the equilibrium level, the value to buyers exceeds the cost to sellers. In this region, increasing the quantity raises total surplus, and it continues to do so until the quantity reaches the equilibrium level. Beyond the equilibrium quantity, however, the value to buyers is less than the cost to sellers. Producing more than the equilibrium quantity would, therefore, lower total surplus.

These three insights about market outcomes tell us that the equilibrium of supply and demand maximizes the sum of consumer and producer surplus. In other words, the equilibrium outcome is an efficient allocation of resources. The job of the benevolent social planner is, therefore, very easy: He can leave the market outcome just as he finds it. This policy of leaving well enough alone goes by the French expression *laissez-faire*, which literally translated means "allow them to do."

We can now better appreciate Adam Smith's invisible hand of the marketplace, which we first discussed in Chapter 1. The benevolent social planner doesn't need to alter the market outcome because the invisible hand has already guided buyers and sellers to an allocation of the economy's resources that maximizes total

FIGURE 7.8

The Efficiency of the Equilibrium Quantity

At quantities less than the equilibrium quantity, the value to buyers exceeds the cost to sellers. At quantities greater than the equilibrium quantity, the cost to sellers exceeds the value to buyers. Therefore, the market equilibrium maximizes the sum of producer and consumer surplus.

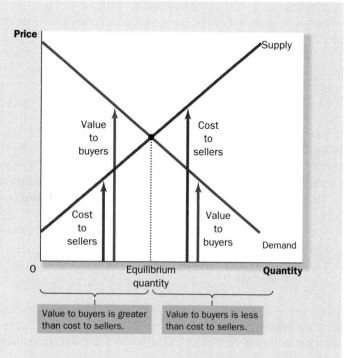

surplus. This conclusion explains why economists often advocate free markets as the best way to organize economic activity.

Case Study

SHOULD THERE BE A MARKET IN ORGANS?

On April 12, 2001, the front page of *The Boston Globe* ran the headline "How a Mother's Love Helped Save Two Lives." The newspaper told the story of Susan Stephens, a woman whose son needed a kidney transplant. When the doctor learned that the mother's kidney was not compatible, he proposed a novel solution: If Stephens donated one of her kidneys to a stranger, her son would move to the top of the kidney waiting list. The mother accepted the deal, and soon two patients had the transplant they were waiting for.

The ingenuity of the doctor's proposal and the nobility of the mother's act cannot be doubted. But the story raises many intriguing questions. If the mother could trade a kidney for a kidney, would the hospital allow her to trade a kidney for an expensive, experimental cancer treatment that she could not afford otherwise? Should she be allowed to exchange her kidney for free tuition for her son at the hospital's medical school? Should she be able to sell her kidney so she can use the cash to trade in her old Chevy for a new Lexus?

As a matter of public policy, people are not allowed to sell their organs. In essence, in the market for organs, the government has imposed a price ceiling of zero. The result, as with any binding price ceiling, is a shortage of the good. The deal in the Stephens case did not fall under this prohibition because no cash changed hands.

Some economists believe that there would be large benefits to allowing a free market in organs. People are born with two kidneys, but they usually need only one. Meanwhile, a few people suffer from illnesses that leave them without any working kidney. Despite the obvious gains from trade, the current situation is dire: In Canada in 2002, 3000 people were waiting for a kidney transplant, but only 1000 transplants were performed and 237 people died while waiting for a transplant. If those needing a kidney were allowed to buy one from those who have two, the price would rise to balance supply and demand. Sellers would be better off with the extra cash in their pockets. Buyers would be better off with the organ they need to save their lives. The shortage of kidneys would disappear.

Such a market would lead to an efficient allocation of resources, but critics of this plan worry about fairness. A market for organs, they argue, would benefit the rich at the expense of the poor, because organs would then be allocated to those most willing and able to pay. But you can also question the fairness of the current system. Now, most of us walk around with an extra organ that we don't really need, while some people are dying to get one. Is that fair? ●

QuickQUIZ Draw the supply and demand for turkey. In the equilibrium, show producer and consumer surplus. Explain why producing more turkey would lower total surplus.

IN THE NEWS

HOW PILGRIMS EMBRACED THE MARKET

Most people think of Americans as being committed to a market economy, and would be surprised to learn that it didn't start out that way.

Thanksgiving Pays Homage to the Invisible Hand

By Caroline Baum

It is the tradition of this column every year at this time to tell the story of Thanksgiving, not just the Pilgrims' first bountiful harvest but the system that made it possible. For source material, I am grateful to the accounts of William Bradford, the first governor of the Plymouth Bay Colony (Bradford's History "Of Plimoth Plantation.")

Most Americans think of Thanksgiving as a time to gather with friends and family and celebrate with a huge feast. If children know anything about the origins of the national holiday, declared each year by presidential proclamation, it's that the Pilgrims were grateful for a good harvest in their new land and set aside this day to give thanks.

What they don't know is that things weren't always so good for the Pilgrims, who came to the new world from England (via Holland) to escape religious persecution. Their first winters after they landed at Plymouth Rock in 1620 and established the Plymouth Bay colony were harsh. The weather was lousy and crop yields were poor. Half the Pilgrims died or returned to England.

Private Property

Those who remained went hungry. Despite their deep religious convictions, the colonists took to stealing from one another. In the spring of 1623, following three grueling winters and widespread famine, Governor Bradford and the others "began to think how they might raise as much as they could, and obtain a better crop than they had done, that they might not still thus

CONCLUSION: MARKET EFFICIENCY AND MARKET FAILURE

This chapter introduced the basic tools of welfare economics—consumer and producer surplus—and used them to evaluate the efficiency of free markets. We showed that the forces of supply and demand allocate resources efficiently. That is, even though each buyer and seller in a market is concerned only about his or her own welfare, they are together led by an invisible hand to an equilibrium that maximizes the total benefits to buyers and sellers.

A word of warning is in order. To conclude that markets are efficient, we made several assumptions about how markets work. When these assumptions do not hold, our conclusion that the market equilibrium is efficient may no longer be true. As we close this chapter, let's consider briefly two of the most important of these assumptions.

First, our analysis assumed that markets are perfectly competitive. In the world, however, competition is sometimes far from perfect. In some markets, a languish in misery," Bradford relates in his history.

One of the traditions the Pilgrims brought with them from England was something called "farming in common." The colonists pooled the fruits of their labor, and the harvest was rationed among them.

The idea that "the taking away of property, and bringing them into common community was found to breed too much confusion and discontent, and retard much employment that would have been to their benefit and comfort."

Young and able men resented working hard for other men and their wives, without any compensation.

So after three winters of starvation, Bradford instituted a new policy when it came time to plant in the spring of 1623. He set aside a plot of land for each family, allowing each to "plant for his own particular, and in that regard trust to them selves."

Miracle of the Market

For the colonists, the results were nothing short of miraculous. The women went willingly into the field, carrying their young children with them. Those who previously claimed to be too ill or weak to work were eager to till their own soil.

Bradford writes of the new plan: "This had very good success; for it made all hands very industrious, so as much more corn was planted than other wise would have been by any means ye Govr or any other could use, and saved him a great deal of trouble, and gave far better content."

Yet it was no miracle. Without knowing it, Bradford and the Pilgrims discovered what Eastern Europe learned—the hard way—more than 350 years later: socialism doesn't work. Deprived of property rights and lacking economic incentives to work, produce and save, human beings behave in a predictable manner.

It was that way in 1620, and it's that way now.

Allowing the Pilgrims to farm their own plot of land and reap the benefits produced a bountiful harvest in the fall of 1623. They set aside "a day of thanksgiving" to thank God for their good fortune.

Invisible Hand

From that day forth, "Any general want or famine hath not been amongst them since to this day," Bradford writes in an entry from 1647, the last year covered by his History.

Pretty soon, the colonists had more than enough food for their own needs and started to trade their excess corn for other commodities, such as furs.

After three winters of famine, the Pilgrims viewed their times of plenty as a stroke of good fortune when they were merely responding to market signals. Even before there was an official market, the invisible hand was at work.

Thanksgiving is a time to give thanks for our system of government, which allows the invisible hand to guide and protect us.

Source: *Bloomberg News.* (Retrieved November 21, 2001, at the *Bloomberg.com* website: http://www.bloomberg.com.) Reprinted with permission.

single buyer or seller (or a small group of them) may be able to control market prices. This ability to influence prices is called *market power*. Market power can cause markets to be inefficient because it keeps the price and quantity away from the equilibrium of supply and demand.

Second, our analysis assumed that the outcome in a market matters only to the buyers and sellers in that market. Yet, in the world, the decisions of buyers and sellers sometimes affect people who are not participants in the market at all. Pollution is the classic example of a market outcome that affects people not in the market. Such side effects, called *externalities*, cause welfare in a market to depend on more than just the value to the buyers and the cost to the sellers. Because buyers and sellers do not take these side effects into account when deciding how much to consume and produce, the equilibrium in a market can be inefficient from the standpoint of society as a whole.

Market power and externalities are examples of a general phenomenon called *market failure*—the inability of some unregulated markets to allocate resources efficiently. When markets fail, public policy can potentially remedy the problem and increase economic efficiency. Microeconomists devote much effort to studying when market failure is likely and what sorts of policies are best at correcting market failures. As you continue your study of economics, you will see that the tools of welfare economics developed here are readily adapted to that endeavour.

Despite the possibility of market failure, the invisible hand of the marketplace is extraordinarily important. In many markets, the assumptions we made in this chapter work well, and the conclusion of market efficiency applies directly. Moreover, our analysis of welfare economics and market efficiency can be used to shed light on the effects of various government policies. In the next two chapters we apply the tools we have just developed to study two important policy issues—the welfare effects of taxation and of international trade.

SUMMARY

- Consumer surplus equals buyers' willingness to pay for a good minus the amount they actually pay for it, and it measures the benefit that buyers receive from participating in a market. Consumer surplus can be computed by finding the area below the demand curve and above the price.

- Producer surplus equals the amount that sellers receive for their goods minus their costs of production, and it measures the benefit that sellers receive from participating in a market. Producer surplus can be computed by finding the area below the price and above the supply curve.

- An allocation of resources that maximizes the sum of consumer and producer surplus is said to be efficient. Policymakers are often concerned with the efficiency, as well as the equity, of economic outcomes.

- The equilibrium of supply and demand maximizes the sum of consumer and producer surplus. That is, the invisible hand of the marketplace leads buyers and sellers to allocate resources efficiently.

- Markets do not allocate resources efficiently in the presence of market failures such as market power or externalities.

KEY CONCEPTS

welfare economics, p. 140
willingness to pay, p. 140
consumer surplus, p. 141

cost, p. 143
producer surplus, p. 144
efficiency, p. 148

equity, p. 148

QUESTIONS FOR REVIEW

1. Explain how buyers' willingness to pay, consumer surplus, and the demand curve are related.

2. Explain how sellers' costs, producer surplus, and the supply curve are related.

3. In a supply-and-demand diagram, show producer and consumer surplus in the market equilibrium.

4. What is efficiency? Is it the only goal of economic policymakers?

5. What does the invisible hand do?

6. Name two types of market failure. Explain why each may cause market outcomes to be inefficient.

PROBLEMS AND APPLICATIONS

1. A drought in Nova Scotia reduces the apple harvest. What happens to consumer surplus in the market for apples? What happens to consumer surplus in the market for apple juice? Illustrate your answers with diagrams.

2. Suppose the demand for French bread rises. What happens to producer surplus in the market for French bread? What happens to producer surplus in the market for flour? Illustrate your answer with diagrams.

3. It is a hot day, and Bert is thirsty. Here is the value he places on a bottle of water:

Value of first bottle	$7
Value of second bottle	5
Value of third bottle	3
Value of fourth bottle	1

    a. From this information, derive Bert's demand schedule. Graph his demand curve for bottled water.
    b. If the price of a bottle of water is $4, how many bottles does Bert buy? How much consumer surplus does Bert get from his purchases? Show Bert's consumer surplus in your graph.
    c. If the price falls to $2, how does quantity demanded change? How does Bert's consumer surplus change? Show these changes in your graph.

4. Ernie owns a water pump. Because pumping large amounts of water is harder than pumping small amounts, the cost of producing a bottle of water rises as he pumps more. Here is the cost he incurs to produce each bottle of water:

Cost of first bottle	$1
Cost of second bottle	3
Cost of third bottle	5
Cost of fourth bottle	7

    a. From this information, derive Ernie's supply schedule. Graph his supply curve for bottled water.
    b. If the price of a bottle of water is $4, how many bottles does Ernie produce and sell? How much producer surplus does Ernie get from these sales? Show Ernie's producer surplus in your graph.

    c. If the price rises to $6, how does quantity supplied change? How does Ernie's producer surplus change? Show these changes in your graph.

5. Consider a market in which Bert from problem 3 is the buyer and Ernie from problem 4 is the seller.
    a. Use Ernie's supply schedule and Bert's demand schedule to find the quantity supplied and quantity demanded at prices of $2, $4, and $6. Which of these prices brings supply and demand into equilibrium?
    b. What are consumer surplus, producer surplus, and total surplus in this equilibrium?
    c. If Ernie produced and Bert consumed one fewer bottle of water, what would happen to total surplus?
    d. If Ernie produced and Bert consumed one additional bottle of water, what would happen to total surplus?

6. The cost of producing stereo systems has fallen over the past several decades. Let's consider some implications of this fact.
    a. Use a supply-and-demand diagram to show the effect of falling production costs on the price and quantity of stereos sold.
    b. In your diagram, show what happens to consumer surplus and producer surplus.
    c. Suppose the supply of stereos is very elastic. Who benefits most from falling production costs—consumers or producers of stereos?

7. Four consumers are willing to pay the following amounts for haircuts:

    Jerry: $7   Oprah: $2   Ricki: $8   Montel: $5

    Four haircutting businesses have the following costs:

    Firm A: $3   Firm B: $6   Firm C: $4   Firm D: $2

    Each firm has the capacity to produce only one haircut. For efficiency, how many haircuts should be given? Which businesses should cut hair, and which consumers should have their hair cut? How large is the maximum possible total surplus?

8. Suppose a technological advance reduces the cost of making computers.
   a. Use a supply-and-demand diagram to show what happens to price, quantity, consumer surplus, and producer surplus in the market for computers.
   b. Computers and adding machines are substitutes. Use a supply-and-demand diagram to show what happens to price, quantity, consumer surplus, and producer surplus in the market for adding machines. Should adding machine producers be happy or sad about the technological advance in computers?
   c. Computers and software are complements. Use a supply-and-demand diagram to show what happens to price, quantity, consumer surplus, and producer surplus in the market for software. Should software producers be happy or sad about the technological advance in computers?
   d. Does this analysis help explain why software producer Bill Gates is one of the world's richest men?

9. Consider how health insurance affects the quantity of health care services performed. Suppose that the typical medical procedure has a cost of $100, yet a person with health insurance pays nothing when she chooses to have an additional procedure performed. Her provincial health insurance pays the full $100. (The province will recoup the $100 through higher premiums or taxes for everybody, but the share paid by this individual is small.)
   a. Draw the demand curve in the market for medical care. (In your diagram, the horizontal axis should represent the number of medical procedures.) Show the quantity of procedures demanded if each procedure has a price of $100.
   b. On your diagram, show the quantity of procedures demanded if consumers pay nothing per procedure. If the cost of each procedure to society is truly $100, and if individuals have health insurance as just described, will the number of procedures performed maximize total surplus? Explain.
   c. Economists often blame the health insurance system for excessive use of medical care. Given your analysis, why might the use of care be viewed as "excessive"?
   d. What sort of policies might prevent this excessive use?

10. Many parts of California experienced a severe drought in the late 1980s and early 1990s.
    a. Use a diagram of the water market to show the effects of the drought on the equilibrium price and quantity of water.
    b. Many communities did not allow the price of water to change, however. What is the effect of this policy on the water market? Show on your diagram any surplus or shortage that arises.
    c. A 1991 op-ed piece in The Wall Street Journal stated that "all Los Angeles residents are required to cut their water usage by 10 percent as of March 1 and another 5 percent starting May 1, based on their 1986 consumption levels." The author criticized this policy on both efficiency and equity grounds, saying "not only does such a policy reward families who 'wasted' more water back in 1986, it does little to encourage consumers who could make more drastic reductions, [and] . . . punishes consumers who cannot so readily reduce their water use." In what way is the Los Angeles system for allocating water inefficient? In what way does the system seem unfair?
    d. Suppose instead that Los Angeles allowed the price of water to increase until the quantity demanded equalled the quantity supplied. Would the resulting allocation of water be more efficient? In your view, would it be more or less fair than the proportionate reductions in water use mentioned in the newspaper article? What could be done to make the market solution more fair?

INTERNET RESOURCES

One of the ten principles of economics listed in Chapter 1 is "Markets are usually a good way to organize economic activity." In this chapter we have seen how a competitive market can maximize total surplus. But could a benevolent social planner, who knew producers' costs and consumers' willingness to pay, do just as well as the market?

Until the collapse of the centrally planned economies of Russia and Eastern Europe in the 1980s and 1990s, the efficiency of markets versus central planning was a very real question. A farsighted 1945 essay by Austrian economist Friedrich Hayek, arguing that real-world central planners could never gather and use all the information that markets gather and use, can be accessed at http://www.econlib.org/library/Essays/hykKnw1.html.

http:// For more study tools, please visit http://www.mankiw3e.nelson.com.

© DON CARSTENS/TAXI

8

Learning Objectives

In this chapter, you will …

- Examine how taxes reduce consumer and producer surplus
- Learn the meaning and causes of the deadweight loss of a tax
- Consider why some taxes have larger deadweight losses than others
- Examine how tax revenue and deadweight loss vary with the size of a tax

APPLICATION: THE COSTS OF TAXATION

Taxes are often a source of heated political debate. In 1993, Jean Chrétien became prime minister of Canada, in part because voters believed he would scrap the Goods and Services Tax (GST) introduced by Brian Mulroney's government. In the 2000 federal election, a key issue was the Canadian Alliance plan to cut federal income taxes. When oil prices and gasoline prices spiked in the summer of 2000, truckers and other motorists demanded a reduction in gasoline taxes. In 2003, Jean Charest replaced Bernard Landry as premier of Quebec on a promise to cut provincial income taxes. Municipal elections are often fought on the issue of whether to raise or lower property taxes.

We began our study of taxes in Chapter 6. There we saw how a tax on a good affects its price and the quantity sold and how the forces of supply and demand divide the burden of a tax between buyers and sellers. In this chapter we extend this analysis and look at how taxes affect welfare, the economic well-being of participants in a market.

The effects of taxes on welfare might at first seem obvious. The government enacts taxes to raise revenue, and that revenue must come out of someone's pocket. As we saw in Chapter 6, both buyers and sellers are worse off when a good is taxed: A tax raises the price buyers pay and lowers the price sellers receive. Yet to understand fully how taxes affect economic well-being, we must compare the reduced welfare of buyers and sellers to the amount of revenue the government raises. The tools of consumer and producer surplus allow us to make this comparison. The analysis will show that the costs of taxes to buyers and sellers exceeds the revenue raised by the government.

THE DEADWEIGHT LOSS OF TAXATION

We begin by recalling one of the surprising lessons from Chapter 6: It does not matter whether a tax on a good is levied on buyers or sellers of the good. When a tax is levied on buyers, the demand curve shifts downward by the size of the tax; when it is levied on sellers, the supply curve shifts upward by that amount. In either case, when the tax is enacted, the price paid by buyers rises, and the price received by sellers falls. In the end, buyers and sellers share the burden of the tax, regardless of how it is levied.

Figure 8.1 shows these effects. To simplify our discussion, this figure does not show a shift in either the supply or demand curve, although one curve must shift. Which curve shifts depends on whether the tax is levied on sellers (the supply curve shifts) or buyers (the demand curve shifts). In this chapter, we can simplify the graphs by not bothering to show the shift. The key result for our purposes here is that the tax places a wedge between the price buyers pay and the price sellers receive. Because of this tax wedge, the quantity sold falls below the level that would be sold without a tax. In other words, a tax on a good causes the size of the market for the good to shrink. These results should be familiar from Chapter 6.

FIGURE 8.1

The Effects of a Tax

A tax on a good places a wedge between the price that buyers pay and the price that sellers receive. The quantity of the good sold falls.

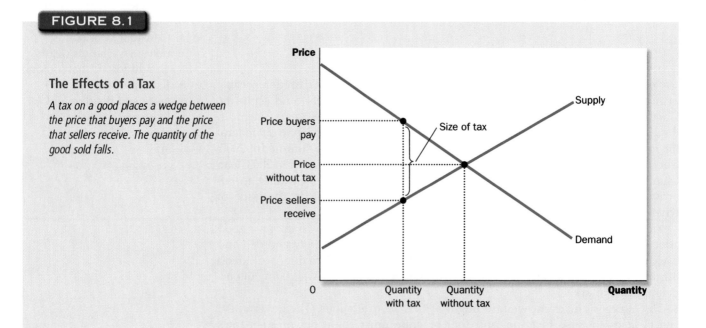

How a Tax Affects Market Participants

Now let's use the tools of welfare economics to measure the gains and losses from a tax on a good. To do this, we must take into account how the tax affects buyers, sellers, and the government. The benefit received by buyers in a market is measured by consumer surplus—the amount buyers are willing to pay for the good minus the amount they actually pay for it. The benefit received by sellers in a market is measured by producer surplus—the amount sellers receive for the good minus their costs. These are precisely the measures of economic welfare we used in Chapter 7.

What about the third interested party, the government? If T is the size of the tax and Q is the quantity of the good sold, then the government gets total tax revenue of $T \times Q$. It can use this tax revenue to provide services, such as roads, police, and public education, or to help the needy. Therefore, to analyze how taxes affect economic well-being, we use tax revenue to measure the government's benefit from the tax. Keep in mind, however, that this benefit actually accrues not to government but to those on whom the revenue is spent.

Figure 8.2 shows that the government's tax revenue is represented by the rectangle between the supply and demand curves. The height of this rectangle is the size of the tax, T, and the width of the rectangle is the quantity of the good sold, Q. Because a rectangle's area is its height times its width, this rectangle's area is $T \times Q$, which equals the tax revenue.

Welfare without a Tax   To see how a tax affects welfare, we begin by considering welfare before the government has imposed a tax. Figure 8.3 (p. 164) shows the supply-and-demand diagram and marks the key areas with the letters A through F.

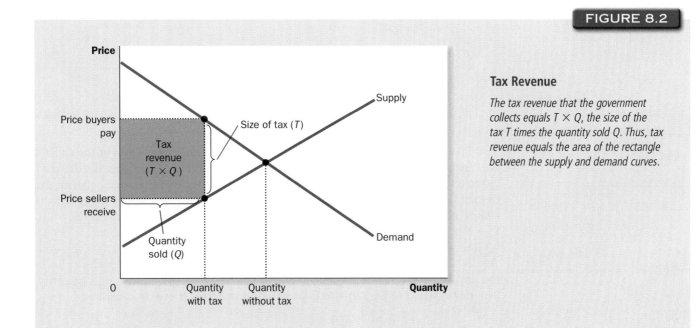

Tax Revenue

The tax revenue that the government collects equals T × Q, the size of the tax T times the quantity sold Q. Thus, tax revenue equals the area of the rectangle between the supply and demand curves.

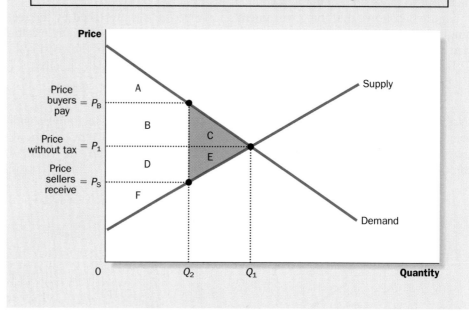

FIGURE 8.3

How a Tax Affects Welfare

A tax on a good reduces consumer surplus (by the area B + C) and producer surplus (by the area D + E). Because the fall in producer and consumer surplus exceeds tax revenue (area B + D), the tax is said to impose a deadweight loss (area C + E).

	Without Tax	With Tax	Change
Consumer Surplus	A + B + C	A	−(B + C)
Producer Surplus	D + E + F	F	−(D + E)
Tax Revenue	None	B + D	+(B + D)
Total Surplus	A + B + C + D + E + F	A + B + D + F	−(C + E)

The area C + E shows the fall in total surplus and is the deadweight loss of the tax.

Without a tax, the price and quantity are found at the intersection of the supply and demand curves. The price is P_1, and the quantity sold is Q_1. Because the demand curve reflects buyers' willingness to pay, consumer surplus is the area between the demand curve and the price, A + B + C. Similarly, because the supply curve reflects sellers' costs, producer surplus is the area between the supply curve and the price, D + E + F. In this case, because there is no tax, tax revenue equals zero.

Total surplus—the sum of consumer and producer surplus—equals the area A + B + C + D + E + F. In other words, as we saw in Chapter 7, total surplus is the area between the supply and demand curves up to the equilibrium quantity. The first column of the table in Figure 8.3 summarizes these conclusions.

Welfare with a Tax Now consider welfare after the tax is enacted. The price paid by buyers rises from P_1 to P_B, so consumer surplus now equals only area A (the area below the demand curve and above the buyer's price). The price received by sellers falls from P_1 to P_S, so producer surplus now equals only area F (the area above the supply curve and below the seller's price). The quantity sold falls from Q_1 to Q_2, and the government collects tax revenue equal to the area B + D.

To compute total surplus with the tax, we add consumer surplus, producer surplus, and tax revenue. Thus, we find that total surplus is area A + B + D + F. The second column of the table provides a summary.

Changes in Welfare   We can now see the effects of the tax by comparing welfare before and after the tax is enacted. The last column in the table in Figure 8.3 shows the changes. The tax causes consumer surplus to fall by the area B + C and producer surplus to fall by the area D + E. Tax revenue rises by the area B + D. Not surprisingly, the tax makes buyers and sellers worse off and the government better off.

The change in total welfare includes the change in consumer surplus (which is negative), the change in producer surplus (which is also negative), and the change in tax revenue (which is positive). When we add these three pieces together, we find that total surplus in the market falls by the area C + E. Thus, *the losses to buyers and sellers from a tax exceed the revenue raised by the government.* The fall in total surplus that results when a tax (or some other policy) distorts a market outcome is called the **deadweight loss.** The area C + E measures the size of the deadweight loss.

To understand why taxes impose deadweight losses, recall one of the ten principles of economics in Chapter 1: People respond to incentives. In Chapter 7 we saw that markets normally allocate scarce resources efficiently. That is, the equilibrium of supply and demand maximizes the total surplus of buyers and sellers in a market. When a tax raises the price to buyers and lowers the price to sellers, however, it gives buyers an incentive to consume less and sellers an incentive to produce less than they otherwise would. As buyers and sellers respond to these incentives, the size of the market shrinks below its optimum. Thus, because taxes distort incentives, they cause markets to allocate resources inefficiently.

deadweight loss
the fall in total surplus that results from a market distortion, such as a tax

Deadweight Losses and the Gains from Trade

To gain some intuition for why taxes result in deadweight losses, consider an example. Imagine that Joe cleans Jane's house each week for $100. The opportunity cost of Joe's time is $80, and the value of a clean house to Jane is $120. Thus, Joe and Jane each receive a $20 benefit from their deal. The total surplus of $40 measures the gains from trade in this particular transaction.

Now suppose that the government levies a $50 tax on the providers of cleaning services. There is now no price that Jane can pay Joe that will leave both of them better off after paying the tax. The most Jane would be willing to pay is $120, but then Joe would be left with only $70 after paying the tax, which is less than his $80 opportunity cost. Conversely, for Joe to receive his opportunity cost of $80, Jane would need to pay $130, which is above the $120 value she places on a clean house. As a result, Jane and Joe cancel their arrangement. Joe goes without the income, and Jane lives in a dirtier house.

The tax has made Joe and Jane worse off by a total of $40, because they have lost this amount of surplus. At the same time, the government collects no revenue from Joe and Jane because they decide to cancel their arrangement. The $40 is pure deadweight loss: It is a loss to buyers and sellers in a market not offset by an increase in government revenue. From this example, we can see the ultimate source of deadweight losses: *Taxes cause deadweight losses because they prevent buyers and sellers from realizing some of the gains from trade.*

The area of the triangle between the supply and demand curves (area C + E in Figure 8.3) measures these losses. This loss can be seen most easily in Figure 8.4 by recalling that the demand curve reflects the value of the good to consumers and that the supply curve reflects the costs of producers. When the tax raises the price to buyers to P_B and lowers the price to sellers to P_S, the marginal buyers and sellers leave the market, so the quantity sold falls from Q_1 to Q_2. Yet, as the figure shows, the value of the good to these buyers still exceeds the cost to these sellers. As in our example with Joe and Jane, the gains from trade—the difference between buyers' value and sellers' cost—is less than the tax. Thus, these trades do not get made once the tax is imposed. The deadweight loss is the surplus lost because the tax discourages these mutually advantageous trades.

QuickQuiz Draw the supply and demand curve for cookies. If the government imposes a tax on cookies, show what happens to the quantity sold, the price paid by buyers, and the price paid by sellers. In your diagram, show the deadweight loss from the tax. Explain the meaning of the deadweight loss.

THE DETERMINANTS OF THE DEADWEIGHT LOSS

What determines whether the deadweight loss from a tax is large or small? The answer is the price elasticities of supply and demand, which measure how much the quantity supplied and quantity demanded respond to changes in the price.

FIGURE 8.4

The Deadweight Loss

When the government imposes a tax on a good, the quantity sold falls from Q_1 to Q_2. As a result, some of the potential gains from trade among buyers and sellers do not get realized. These lost gains from trade create the deadweight loss.

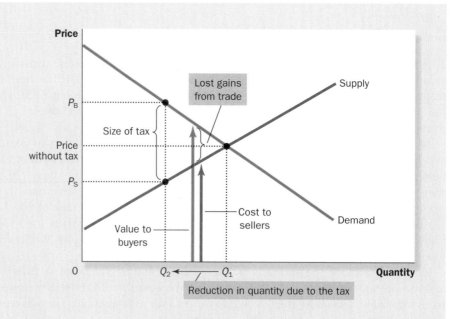

Let's consider first how the elasticity of supply affects the size of the deadweight loss. In the top two panels of Figure 8.5, the demand curve and the size of the tax are the same. The only difference in these figures is the elasticity of the supply curve. In panel (a), the supply curve is relatively inelastic: Quantity supplied

FIGURE 8.5

Tax Distortions and Elasticities

In panels (a) and (b), the demand curve and the size of the tax are the same, but the price elasticity of supply is different. Notice that the more elastic the supply curve, the larger the deadweight loss of the tax. In panels (c) and (d), the supply curve and the size of the tax are the same, but the price elasticity of demand is different. Notice that the more elastic the demand curve, the larger the deadweight loss of the tax.

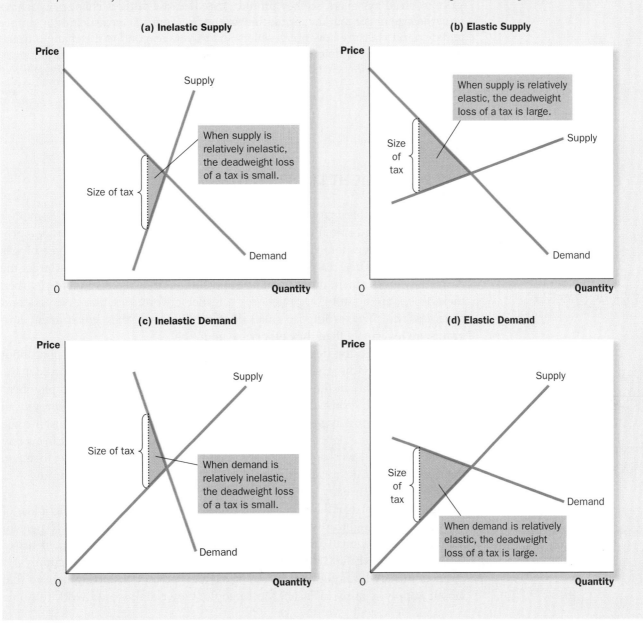

(a) Inelastic Supply

Price

Supply

When supply is relatively inelastic, the deadweight loss of a tax is small.

Size of tax

Demand

0   Quantity

(b) Elastic Supply

Price

When supply is relatively elastic, the deadweight loss of a tax is large.

Size of tax

Supply

Demand

0   Quantity

(c) Inelastic Demand

Price

Supply

Size of tax

When demand is relatively inelastic, the deadweight loss of a tax is small.

Demand

0   Quantity

(d) Elastic Demand

Price

Supply

Size of tax

Demand

When demand is relatively elastic, the deadweight loss of a tax is large.

0   Quantity

responds only slightly to changes in the price. In panel (b), the supply curve is relatively elastic: Quantity supplied responds substantially to changes in the price. Notice that the deadweight loss, the area of the triangle between the supply and demand curves, is larger when the supply curve is more elastic.

Similarly, the bottom two panels of Figure 8.5 show how the elasticity of demand affects the size of the deadweight loss. Here the supply curve and the size of the tax are held constant. In panel (c) the demand curve is relatively inelastic, and the deadweight loss is small. In panel (d) the demand curve is more elastic, and the deadweight loss from the tax is larger.

The lesson from this figure is easy to explain. A tax has a deadweight loss because it induces buyers and sellers to change their behaviour. The tax raises the price paid by buyers, so they consume less. At the same time, the tax lowers the price received by sellers, so they produce less. Because of these changes in behaviour, the size of the market shrinks below the optimum. The elasticities of supply and demand measure how much sellers and buyers respond to the changes in the price and, therefore, determine how much the tax distorts the market outcome. Hence, *the greater the elasticities of supply and demand, the greater the deadweight loss of a tax.*

Case Study

THE DEADWEIGHT LOSS DEBATE

Supply, demand, elasticity, deadweight loss—all this economic theory is enough to make your head spin. But believe it or not, these ideas go to the heart of a profound political question: How big should the government be? The debate hinges on these concepts because the larger the deadweight loss of taxation, the larger the cost of any government program. If taxation entails large deadweight losses, then these losses are a strong argument for a leaner government that does less and taxes less. But if taxes impose small deadweight losses, then government programs are less costly than they otherwise might be.

So how big are the deadweight losses of taxation? This is a question about which economists disagree. To see the nature of the disagreement, consider the most important tax in the Canadian economy—the tax on labour. Employment Insurance contributions are a tax on labour. Both the federal and provincial income taxes are, to a large extent, labour taxes, because the source of most income is labour earnings. A labour tax places a wedge between the wage that firms pay and the wage that workers receive. If we add all forms of labour taxes together, the marginal tax rate on labour income—the tax on the last dollar of earnings—is over 50 percent for many workers.

Although the size of the labour tax is easy to determine, the deadweight loss of this tax is less straightforward. Economists disagree about whether this 50 percent labour tax has a small or a large deadweight loss. This disagreement arises because economists hold different views about the elasticity of labour supply.

Economists who argue that labour taxes are not very distorting believe that labour supply is fairly inelastic. Most people, they claim, would work full-time regardless of the wage. If so, the labour supply curve is almost vertical, and a tax on labour has a small deadweight loss.

Economists who argue that labour taxes are highly distorting believe that labour supply is more elastic. They admit that some groups of workers may supply their labour inelastically but claim that many other groups respond more to incentives. Here are some examples:

- Many workers can adjust the number of hours they work—for instance, by working overtime or by choosing jobs with longer or shorter hours. The higher the wage, the more hours they choose to work.
- Some families have second earners—often married women with children—with some discretion over whether to do unpaid work at home or paid work in the marketplace. When deciding whether to take a job, these second earners compare the benefits of being at home (including savings on the cost of child care) with the wages they could earn.
- Many of the elderly can choose when to retire, and their decisions are partly based on the wage. Once they are retired, the wage determines their incentive to work part-time.
- Some people consider engaging in illegal economic activity, such as the drug trade, or working at jobs that pay "under the table" to evade taxes. Economists call this the *underground economy*. In deciding whether to work in the underground economy or at a legitimate job, these potential criminals compare what they can earn by breaking the law with the wage they can earn legally.

In each of these cases, the quantity of labour supplied responds to the wage (the price of labour). Thus, the decisions of these workers are distorted when their labor earnings are taxed. Labour taxes encourage workers to work fewer hours, second earners to stay at home, the elderly to retire early, and the unscrupulous to enter the underground economy.

These two views of labour taxation persist to this day. Indeed, whenever you see two political candidates debating whether the government should provide more services or reduce the tax burden, keep in mind that part of the disagreement may rest on different views about the elasticity of labour supply and the deadweight loss of taxation. ●

QuickQuiz The demand for beer is more elastic than the demand for milk. Would a tax on beer or a tax on milk have larger deadweight loss? Why?

DEADWEIGHT LOSS AND TAX REVENUE AS TAXES VARY

Taxes rarely stay the same for long periods of time. Policymakers in local, provincial, and federal governments are always considering raising one tax or lowering

HENRY GEORGE AND THE LAND TAX

Is there an ideal tax? Henry George, the nineteenth-century American economist and social philosopher, thought so. In his 1879 book *Progress and Poverty,* George argued that the government should raise all its revenue from a tax on land. This "single tax" was, he claimed, both equitable and efficient. George's ideas won him a large political following, and in 1886 he lost a close race for mayor of New York City (although he finished well ahead of Republican candidate Theodore Roosevelt).

George's proposal to tax land was motivated largely by a concern over the distribution of economic well-being. He deplored the "shocking contrast between monstrous wealth and debasing want" and thought landowners benefited more than they should from the rapid growth in the overall economy.

George's arguments for the land tax can be understood using the tools of modern economics. Consider first supply and demand in the market for renting land. As immigration causes the population to rise and technological progress causes incomes to grow, the demand for land rises over time. Yet because the amount of land is fixed, the supply is perfectly inelastic. Rapid increases in demand together with inelastic supply lead to large increases in the equilibrium rents on land, so that economic growth makes rich landowners even richer.

Henry George

Now consider the incidence of a tax on land. As we first saw in Chapter 6, the burden of a tax falls more heavily on the side of the market that is less elastic. A tax on land takes this principle to an extreme. Because the elasticity of supply is zero, the landowners bear the entire burden of the tax.

Consider next the question of efficiency. As we just discussed, the deadweight loss of a tax depends on the elasticities of supply and demand. Again, a tax on land is an extreme case. Because supply is perfectly inelastic, a tax on land does not alter the market allocation. There is no deadweight loss, and the government's tax revenue exactly equals the loss of the landowners.

Although taxing land may look attractive in theory, it is not as straightforward in practice as it may appear. For a tax on land not to distort economic incentives, it must be a tax on raw land. Yet the value of land often comes from improvements, such as clearing trees, providing sewers, and building roads. Unlike the supply of raw land, the supply of improvements has an elasticity greater than zero. If a land tax were imposed on improvements, it would distort incentives. Landowners would respond by devoting fewer resources to improving their land.

Today, few economists support George's proposal for a single tax on land. Not only is taxing improvements a potential problem, but the tax would not raise enough revenue to pay for the much larger government we have today. Yet many of George's arguments remain valid. Here is the assessment of the eminent economist Milton Friedman a century after George's book:

"In my opinion, the least bad tax is the property tax on the unimproved value of land, the Henry George argument of many, many years ago."

another. Here we consider what happens to the deadweight loss and tax revenue when the size of a tax changes.

Figure 8.6 shows the effects of a small, medium, and large tax, holding constant the market's supply and demand curves. The deadweight loss—the reduction in total surplus that results when the tax reduces the size of a market below the optimum—equals the area of the triangle between the supply and demand curves. For the small tax in panel (a), the area of the deadweight loss triangle is quite small. But as the size of a tax rises in panels (b) and (c), the deadweight loss grows larger and larger.

Indeed, the deadweight loss of a tax rises even more rapidly than the size of the tax. The reason is that the deadweight loss is an area of a triangle, and an area of a triangle depends on the *square* of its size. If we double the size of a tax, for instance, the base and height of the triangle double, so the deadweight loss rises

FIGURE 8.6

Deadweight Loss and Tax Revenue from Three Taxes of Different Size

The deadweight loss is the reduction in total surplus due to the tax. Tax revenue is the amount of the tax times the amount of the good sold. In panel (a), a small tax has a small deadweight loss and raises a small amount of revenue. In panel (b), a somewhat larger tax has a larger deadweight loss and raises a larger amount of revenue. In panel (c), a very large tax has a very large deadweight loss, but because it has reduced the size of the market so much, the tax raises only a small amount of revenue.

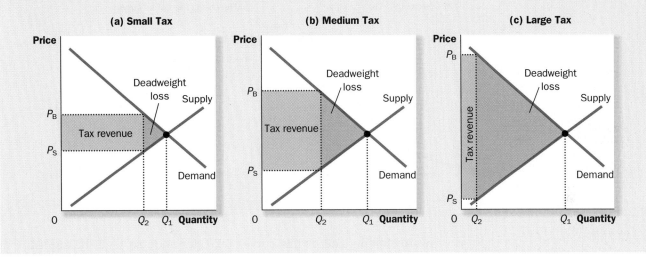

by a factor of 4. If we triple the size of a tax, the base and height triple, so the deadweight loss rises by a factor of 9.

The government's tax revenue is the size of the tax times the amount of the good sold. As Figure 8.6 shows, tax revenue equals the area of the rectangle between the supply and demand curves. For the small tax in panel (a), tax revenue is small. As the size of a tax rises from panel (a) to panel (b), tax revenue grows. But as the size of the tax rises further from panel (b) to panel (c), tax revenue falls because the higher tax drastically reduces the size of the market. For a very large tax, no revenue would be raised, because people would stop buying and selling the good altogether.

Figure 8.7 (p. 172) summarizes these results. In panel (a) we see that as the size of a tax increases, its deadweight loss quickly gets larger. By contrast, panel (b) shows that tax revenue first rises with the size of the tax, but then, as the tax gets larger, the market shrinks so much that tax revenue starts to fall.

Case Study

THE LAFFER CURVE AND SUPPLY-SIDE ECONOMICS

One day in 1974, economist Arthur Laffer sat in a Washington restaurant with some prominent journalists and politicians. He took out a napkin and drew a figure on it to show how tax rates affect tax revenue. It looked much like panel (b) of our Figure 8.7. Laffer then suggested that the United States was on the

FIGURE 8.7

How Deadweight Loss and Tax Revenue Vary with the Size of a Tax

Panel (a) shows that as the size of a tax grows larger, the deadweight loss grows larger. Panel (b) shows that tax revenue first rises, then falls. This relationship is sometimes called the Laffer curve.

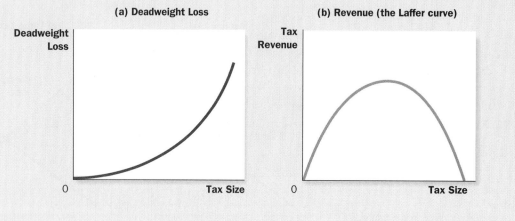

downward-sloping side of this curve. Tax rates were so high, he argued, that reducing them would actually raise tax revenue.

Most economists were skeptical of Laffer's suggestion. The idea that a cut in tax rates could raise tax revenue was correct as a matter of economic theory, but there was more doubt about whether it would do so in practice. There was little evidence for Laffer's view that U.S. tax rates had in fact reached such extreme levels.

Nonetheless, the *Laffer curve* (as it became known) captured the imagination of Ronald Reagan. David Stockman, budget director in the first Reagan administration, offers the following story:

> [Reagan] had once been on the Laffer curve himself. "I came into the Big Money making pictures during World War II," he would always say. At that time the wartime income surtax hit 90 percent. "You could only make four pictures and then you were in the top bracket," he would continue. "So we all quit working after four pictures and went off to the country." High tax rates caused less work. Low tax rates caused more. His experience proved it.

When Reagan ran for president in 1980, he made cutting taxes part of his platform. Reagan argued that taxes were so high that they were discouraging hard work. He argued that lower taxes would give people the proper incentive to work, which would raise economic well-being and perhaps even tax revenue. Because the cut in tax rates was intended to encourage people to increase the quantity of labour they supplied, the views of Laffer and Reagan became known as *supply-side economics.*

Subsequent history failed to confirm Laffer's conjecture that lower tax rates would raise tax revenue. When Reagan cut taxes after he was elected, the result was less tax revenue, not more. Revenue from personal income taxes (per person, adjusted for inflation) fell by 9 percent from 1980 to 1984, even though average income (per person, adjusted for inflation) grew by 4 percent over this period. The tax cut, together with policymakers' unwillingness to restrain spending, began a long period during which the government spent more than it collected in taxes. Throughout Reagan's two terms in office, and for many years thereafter, the government ran large budget deficits.

Yet Laffer's argument is not completely without merit. Although an overall cut in tax rates normally reduces revenue, some taxpayers at some times may be on the wrong side of the Laffer curve. In the 1980s, tax revenue collected from the richest Americans, who face the highest tax rates, did rise when their taxes were cut. The idea that cutting taxes can raise revenue may be correct if applied to those taxpayers facing the highest tax rates. In addition, Laffer's argument may be more plausible when applied to countries where tax rates are much higher than in the United States. In Sweden in the early 1980s, for instance, the typical worker faced a marginal tax rate of about 80 percent. Such a high tax rate provides a substantial disincentive to work. Studies have suggested that Sweden would indeed have raised more tax revenue if it had lowered its tax rates. And when the Republic of Ireland cut the tax rate on corporate profits in the 1990s, investment by foreign corporations increased so much that tax revenue increased.

In Canada, tax rates on labour income are higher than they are in the United States, but not as high as they are in Sweden. Canadian tax rates are probably not so high that cutting tax rates would raise tax revenues.

Provincial governments have much less ability to increase tax revenue by raising tax rates than does the federal government. A provincial government that raised income tax rates would find some of its residents migrating to other provinces in search of lower taxes. Because people can migrate more easily between provinces than they can migrate between countries, the supply of labour is more elastic in a single province than it is for Canada as a whole. The supply of labour would be even more elastic between different municipalities. Perhaps this explains why municipalities rely on property taxes rather than trying to tax labour income.

Policymakers disagree about these issues in part because they disagree about the size of the relevant elasticities. The more elastic that supply and demand are in any market, the more taxes in that market distort behaviour, and the more likely it is that a tax cut will raise tax revenue. There is no debate, however, about the general lesson: How much revenue the government gains or loses from a tax change cannot be computed just by looking at tax rates. It also depends on how the tax change affects people's behaviour. ●

QuickQuiz   If the government doubles the tax on gasoline, can you be sure that revenue from the gasoline tax will rise? Can you be sure that the deadweight loss from the gasoline tax will rise? Explain.

CONCLUSION

Taxes, Oliver Wendell Holmes once said, are the price we pay for a civilized society. Indeed, our society cannot exist without some form of taxes. We all expect the government to provide us certain services, such as roads, parks, police, and national defence. These public services require tax revenue.

This chapter has shed some light on how high the price of civilized society can be. One of the ten principles of economics discussed in Chapter 1 is that markets are usually a good way to organize economic activity. When the government imposes taxes on buyers or sellers of a good, however, society loses some of the benefits of market efficiency. Taxes are costly to market participants not only because taxes transfer resources from those participants to the government, but also because they alter incentives and distort market outcomes.

SUMMARY

- A tax on a good reduces the welfare of buyers and sellers of the good, and the reduction in consumer and producer surplus usually exceeds the revenue raised by the government. The fall in total surplus—the sum of consumer surplus, producer surplus, and tax revenue—is called the deadweight loss of the tax.

- Taxes have deadweight losses because they cause buyers to consume less and sellers to produce less, and this change in behaviour shrinks the size of the market below the level that maximizes total surplus. Because the elasticities of supply and demand measure how much market participants respond to market conditions, larger elasticities imply larger deadweight losses.

- As a tax grows larger, it distorts incentives more, and its deadweight loss grows larger. Tax revenue first rises with the size of a tax. Eventually, however, a larger tax reduces tax revenue because it reduces the size of the market.

KEY CONCEPTS

deadweight loss, p. 165

QUESTIONS FOR REVIEW

1. What happens to consumer and producer surplus when the sale of a good is taxed? How does the change in consumer and producer surplus compare to the tax revenue? Explain.

2. Draw a supply-and-demand diagram with a tax on the sale of the good. Show the deadweight loss. Show the tax revenue.

3. How do the elasticities of supply and demand affect the deadweight loss of a tax? Why do they have this effect?

4. Why do experts disagree about whether labour taxes have small or large deadweight losses?

5. What happens to the deadweight loss and tax revenue when a tax is increased?

PROBLEMS AND APPLICATIONS

1. The market for pizza is characterized by a downward-sloping demand curve and an upward-sloping supply curve.

a. Draw the competitive market equilibrium. Label the price, quantity, consumer surplus, and producer surplus. Is there any deadweight loss? Explain.

b. Suppose that the government forces each pizzeria to pay a $1 tax on each pizza sold. Illustrate the effect of this tax on the pizza market, being sure to label the consumer surplus, producer surplus, government revenue, and deadweight loss. How does each area compare to the pre-tax case?

c. If the tax were removed, pizza eaters and sellers would be better off, but the government would lose tax revenue. Suppose that consumers and producers voluntarily transferred some of their gains to the government. Could all parties (including the government) be better off than they were with a tax? Explain using the labelled areas in your graph.

2. Evaluate the following two statements. Do you agree? Why or why not?
   a. "If the government taxes land, wealthy landowners will pass the tax on to their poorer renters."
   b. "If the government taxes apartment buildings, wealthy landlords will pass the tax on to their poorer renters."

3. Evaluate the following two statements. Do you agree? Why or why not?
   a. "A tax that has no deadweight loss cannot raise any revenue for the government."
   b. "A tax that raises no revenue for the government cannot have any deadweight loss."

4. Consider the market for rubber bands.
   a. If this market has very elastic supply and very inelastic demand, how would the burden of a tax on rubber bands be shared between consumers and producers? Use the tools of consumer surplus and producer surplus in your answer.
   b. If this market has very inelastic supply and very elastic demand, how would the burden of a tax on rubber bands be shared between consumers and producers? Contrast your answer with your answer to part (a).

5. Suppose that the government imposes a tax on heating oil.
   a. Would the deadweight loss from this tax likely be greater in the first year after it is imposed or in the fifth year? Explain.

b. Would the revenue collected from this tax likely be greater in the first year after it is imposed or in the fifth year? Explain.

6. After economics class one day, your friend suggests that taxing food would be a good way to raise revenue because the demand for food is quite inelastic. In what sense is taxing food a "good" way to raise revenue? In what sense is it not a "good" way to raise revenue?

7. U.S. Senator Daniel Patrick Moynihan once introduced a bill that would levy a 10 000 percent tax on certain hollow-tipped bullets.
   a. Do you expect that this tax would raise much revenue? Why or why not?
   b. Even if the tax would raise no revenue, what might be Senator Moynihan's reason for proposing it?

8. The government places a tax on the purchase of socks.
   a. Illustrate the effect of this tax on equilibrium price and quantity in the sock market. Identify the following areas both before and after the imposition of the tax: total spending by consumers, total revenue for producers, and government tax revenue.
   b. Does the price received by producers rise or fall? Can you tell whether total receipts for producers rise or fall? Explain.
   c. Does the price paid by consumers rise or fall? Can you tell whether total spending by consumers rises or falls? Explain carefully. (Hint: Think about elasticity.) If total consumer spending falls, does consumer surplus rise? Explain.

9. Suppose the government currently raises $100 million through a $0.01 tax on widgets, and another $100 million through a $0.10 tax on gadgets. If the government doubled the tax rate on widgets and eliminated the tax on gadgets, would it raise more money than today, less money, or the same amount of money? Explain.

10. Suppose the Canadian government decides that it needs to raise an additional $100 million in tax revenues. One Cabinet minister argues for a tax on all soft drinks. A second Cabinet minister argues for a tax on cola only, since this would give consumers a choice of paying the tax (by drinking cola) or avoiding it (by switching to another soft drink).

a. Which market has the more elastic supply and demand curves: the market for cola, or the market for all soft drinks?

b. To raise the same $100 million in revenue, which would require a higher rate: a tax on cola, or a tax on all soft drinks?

c. Which would cause a larger deadweight loss: a tax on cola, or a tax on all soft drinks?

d. Which would be the better tax? Explain.

11. Some years ago the British government imposed a "poll tax" that required each person to pay a flat amount to the government independent of his or her income or wealth. What is the effect of such a tax on economic efficiency? What is the effect on economic equity? Do you think this was a popular tax?

12. This chapter analyzed the welfare effects of a tax on a good. Consider now the opposite policy. Suppose that the government *subsidizes* a good: For each unit of the good sold, the government pays $2 to the buyer. How does the subsidy affect consumer surplus, producer surplus, tax revenue, and total surplus? Does a subsidy lead to a deadweight loss? Explain.

13. (This problem uses some high-school algebra and is challenging.) Suppose that a market is described by the following supply and demand equations:

$$Q^S = 2P$$
$$Q^D = 300 - P$$

a. Solve for the equilibrium price and the equilibrium quantity.

b. Suppose that a tax of T is placed on buyers, so the new demand equation is

$$Q^D = 300 - (P + T).$$

Solve for the new equilibrium. What happens to the price received by sellers, the price paid by buyers, and the quantity sold?

c. Tax revenue is $T \times Q$. Use your answer to part (b) to solve for tax revenue as a function of T. Graph this relationship for T between 0 and 300.

d. The deadweight loss of a tax is the area of the triangle between the supply and demand curves. Recalling that the area of a triangle is $1/2 \times$ base $\times$ height, solve for deadweight loss as a function of T. Graph this relationship for T between 0 and 300. (Hint: Looking sideways, the base of the deadweight loss triangle is T, and the height is the difference between the quantity sold with the tax and the quantity sold without the tax.)

e. The government now levies a tax on this good of $200 per unit. Is this a good policy? Why or why not? Can you propose a better policy?

INTERNET RESOURCES

In Canada, taxes are collected by the Canada Customs and Revenue Agency, but Finance Canada decides tax policy. Visit the Finance Canada website at http://www.fin.gc.ca/access/taxe.html to learn about the latest changes in tax policy. Finance Canada also provides some useful links to more information about taxes in Canada and around the world at http://www.fin.gc.ca/LINKS/taxe.html.

http://   For more study tools, please visit http://www.mankiw3e.nelson.com.

© DON CARSTENS/TAXI

APPLICATION: INTERNATIONAL TRADE

9

Learning Objectives

In this chapter, you will …

- Consider what determines whether a country imports or exports a good
- Examine who wins and who loses from international trade
- Learn that the gains to winners from international trade exceed the losses to losers
- Analyze the welfare effects of tariffs and import quotas
- Examine the arguments people use to advocate trade restrictions

If you check the labels on the clothes you are now wearing, you will probably find that some of your clothes were made in another country. A century ago the textiles and clothing industry was a major part of the Canadian economy, but that is no longer the case. Faced with foreign competitors that could produce quality goods at low cost, many Canadian firms found it increasingly difficult to produce and sell textiles and clothing at a profit. As a result, they laid off their workers and shut down their factories. Today, much of the textiles and clothing that Canadians consume is imported from abroad.

The story of the textiles industry raises important questions for economic policy: How does international trade affect economic well-being? Who gains and who loses from free trade among countries, and how do the gains compare to the losses?

Chapter 3 introduced the study of international trade by applying the principle of comparative advantage. According to this principle, all countries can benefit from trading with one another because trade allows each country to specialize in doing what it does best. But the analysis in Chapter 3 was incomplete. It did not explain how the international marketplace achieves these gains from trade or how the gains are distributed among various economic actors.

We now return to the study of international trade and take up these questions. Over the past several chapters, we have developed many tools for analyzing how markets work: supply, demand, equilibrium, consumer surplus, producer surplus, and so on. With these tools we can learn more about the effects of international trade on economic well-being.

THE DETERMINANTS OF TRADE

Consider the market for steel. The steel market is well suited to examining the gains and losses from international trade: Steel is made in many countries around the world, and there is much world trade in steel. Moreover, the steel market is one in which policymakers often consider (and sometimes implement) trade restrictions to protect domestic steel producers from foreign competitors. We examine here the steel market in the imaginary country of Isoland.

The Equilibrium without Trade

As our story begins, the Isolandian steel market is isolated from the rest of the world. By government decree, no one in Isoland is allowed to import or export steel, and the penalty for violating the decree is so large that no one dares try.

Because there is no international trade, the market for steel in Isoland consists solely of Isolandian buyers and sellers. As Figure 9.1 shows, the domestic price adjusts to balance the quantity supplied by domestic sellers and the quantity

FIGURE 9.1

The Equilibrium without International Trade

When an economy cannot trade in world markets, the price adjusts to balance domestic supply and demand. This figure shows consumer and producer surplus in an equilibrium without international trade for the steel market in the imaginary country of Isoland.

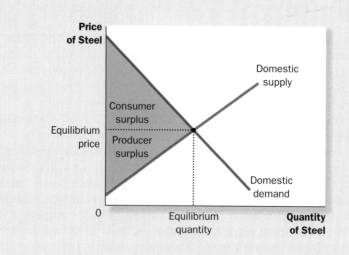

demanded by domestic buyers. The figure shows the consumer and producer surplus in the equilibrium without trade. The sum of consumer and producer surplus measures the total benefits that buyers and sellers receive from the steel market.

Now suppose that, in an election upset, Isoland elects a new president. The president campaigned on a platform of "change" and promised the voters bold new ideas. Her first act is to assemble a team of economists to evaluate Isolandian trade policy. She asks them to report back on three questions:

1. If the government allowed Isolandians to import and export steel, what would happen to the price of steel and the quantity of steel sold in the domestic steel market?
2. Who would gain from free trade in steel and who would lose, and would the gains exceed the losses?
3. Should a tariff (a tax on steel imports) or an import quota (a limit on steel imports) be part of the new trade policy?

After reviewing supply and demand in their favourite textbook (this one, of course), the Isolandian economics team begins its analysis.

The World Price and Comparative Advantage

The first issue our economists take up is whether Isoland is likely to become a steel importer or a steel exporter. In other words, if free trade were allowed, would Isolandians end up buying or selling steel in world markets?

To answer this question, the economists compare the current Isolandian price of steel to the price of steel in other countries. We call the price prevailing in world markets the **world price.** If the world price of steel is higher than the domestic price, then Isoland would become an exporter of steel once trade is permitted. Isolandian steel producers would be eager to receive the higher prices available abroad and would start selling their steel to buyers in other countries. Conversely, if the world price of steel is lower than the domestic price, then Isoland would become an importer of steel. Because foreign sellers offer a better price, Isolandian steel consumers would quickly start buying steel from other countries.

In essence, comparing the world price and the domestic price before trade indicates whether Isoland has a comparative advantage in producing steel. The domestic price reflects the opportunity cost of steel: It tells us how much an Isolandian must give up to get one unit of steel. If the domestic price is low, the cost of producing steel in Isoland is low, suggesting that Isoland has a comparative advantage in producing steel relative to the rest of the world. If the domestic price is high, then the cost of producing steel in Isoland is high, suggesting that foreign countries have a comparative advantage in producing steel.

As we saw in Chapter 3, trade among nations is ultimately based on comparative advantage. That is, trade is beneficial because it allows each nation to specialize in doing what it does best. By comparing the world price and the domestic price before trade, we can determine whether Isoland is better or worse at producing steel than the rest of the world.

world price
the price of a good that prevails in the world market for that good

QuickQuiz The country Autarka does not allow international trade. In Autarka, you can buy a wool suit for 3 ounces of gold. Meanwhile, in neighbouring countries, you can buy the same suit for 2 ounces of gold. If Autarka were to allow free trade, would it import or export suits?

THE WINNERS AND LOSERS FROM TRADE

To analyze the welfare effects of free trade, the Isolandian economists begin with the assumption that Isoland is a small economy compared to the rest of the world, so its actions have a negligible effect on world markets. The small-economy assumption has a specific implication for analyzing the steel market: If Isoland is a small economy, then the change in Isoland's trade policy will not affect the world price of steel. The Isolandians are said to be *price takers* in the world economy. That is, they take the world price of steel as given. They can sell steel at this price and be exporters or buy steel at this price and be importers.

The small-economy assumption is not necessary to analyze the gains and losses from international trade. But the Isolandian economists know from experience that this assumption greatly simplifies the analysis. They also know that the basic lessons do not change in the more complicated case of a large economy.

The Gains and Losses of an Exporting Country

Figure 9.2 shows the Isolandian steel market when the domestic equilibrium price before trade is below the world price. Once free trade is allowed, the domestic price rises to equal the world price. No seller of steel would accept less than the world price, and no buyer would pay more than the world price.

With the domestic price now equal to the world price, the domestic quantity supplied differs from the domestic quantity demanded. The supply curve shows the quantity of steel supplied by Isolandian sellers. The demand curve shows the

FIGURE 9.2

International Trade in an Exporting Country

Once trade is allowed, the domestic price rises to equal the world price. The supply curve shows the quantity of steel produced domestically, and the demand curve shows the quantity consumed domestically. Exports from Isoland equal the difference between the domestic quantity supplied and the domestic quantity demanded at the world price.

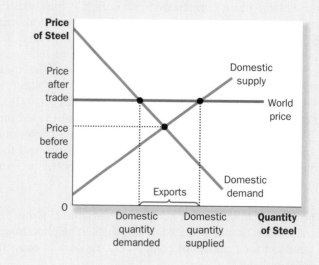

quantity of steel demanded by Isolandian buyers. Because the domestic quantity supplied is greater than the domestic quantity demanded, Isoland sells steel to other countries. Thus, Isoland becomes a steel exporter.

Although domestic quantity supplied and domestic quantity demanded differ, the steel market is still in equilibrium because there is now another participant in the market: the rest of the world. One can view the horizontal line at the world price as representing the demand for steel from the rest of the world. This demand curve is perfectly elastic because Isoland, as a small economy, can sell as much steel as it wants at the world price.

Now consider the gains and losses from opening up trade. Clearly, not everyone benefits. Trade forces the domestic price to rise to the world price. Domestic producers of steel are better off because they can now sell steel at a higher price, but domestic consumers of steel are worse off because they have to buy steel at a higher price.

To measure these gains and losses, we look at the changes in consumer and producer surplus, which are shown in the graph and table in Figure 9.3. Before trade is allowed, the price of steel adjusts to balance domestic supply and domestic demand. Consumer surplus, the area between the demand curve and the

FIGURE 9.3

How Free Trade Affects Welfare in an Exporting Country

When the domestic price rises to equal the world price, sellers are better off (producer surplus rises from C to B + C + D), and buyers are worse off (consumer surplus falls from A + B to A). Total surplus rises by an amount equal to area D, indicating that trade raises the economic well-being of the country as a whole.

	Before Trade	After Trade	Change
Consumer Surplus	A + B	A	−B
Producer Surplus	C	B + C + D	+(B + D)
Total Surplus	A + B + C	A + B + C + D	+D

The area D shows the increase in total surplus and represents the gains from trade.

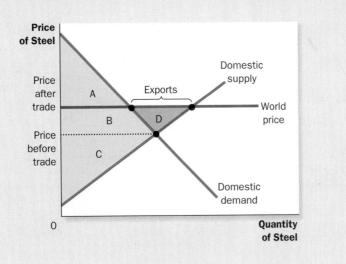

before-trade price, is area A + B. Producer surplus, the area between the supply curve and the before-trade price, is area C. Total surplus before trade, the sum of consumer and producer surplus, is area A + B + C.

After trade is allowed, the domestic price rises to the world price. Consumer surplus is area A (the area between the demand curve and the world price). Producer surplus is area B + C + D (the area between the supply curve and the world price). Thus, total surplus with trade is area A + B + C + D.

These welfare calculations show who wins and who loses from trade in an exporting country. Sellers benefit because producer surplus increases by the area B + D. Buyers are worse off because consumer surplus decreases by the area B. Because the gains of sellers exceed the losses of buyers by the area D, total surplus in Isoland increases.

This analysis of an exporting country yields two conclusions:

1. When a country allows trade and becomes an exporter of a good, domestic producers of the good are better off, and domestic consumers of the good are worse off.
2. Trade raises the economic well-being of a nation in the sense that the gains of the winners exceed the losses of the losers.

The Gains and Losses of an Importing Country

Now suppose that the domestic price before trade is above the world price. Once again, after free trade is allowed, the domestic price must equal the world price. As Figure 9.4 shows, the domestic quantity supplied is less than the domestic

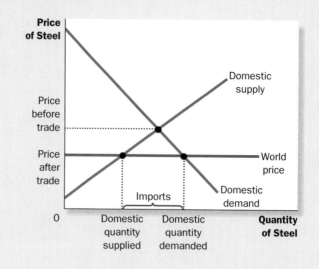

FIGURE 9.4

International Trade in an Importing Country

Once trade is allowed, the domestic price falls to equal the world price. The supply curve shows the amount produced domestically, and the demand curve shows the amount consumed domestically. Imports equal the difference between the domestic quantity demanded and the domestic quantity supplied at the world price.

quantity demanded. The difference between the domestic quantity demanded and the domestic quantity supplied is bought from other countries, and Isoland becomes a steel importer.

In this case, the horizontal line at the world price represents the supply of the rest of the world. This supply curve is perfectly elastic because Isoland is a small economy and, therefore, can buy as much steel as it wants at the world price.

Now consider the gains and losses from trade. Once again, not everyone benefits. When trade forces the domestic price to fall, domestic consumers are better off (they can now buy steel at a lower price), and domestic producers are worse off (they now have to sell steel at a lower price). Changes in consumer and producer surplus measure the size of the gains and losses, as shown in the graph and table in Figure 9.5. Before trade, consumer surplus is area A, producer surplus is area B + C, and total surplus is area A + B + C. After trade is allowed, consumer surplus is area A + B + D, producer surplus is area C, and total surplus is area A + B + C + D.

These welfare calculations show who wins and who loses from trade in an importing country. Buyers benefit because consumer surplus increases by the

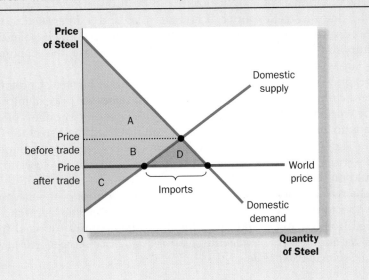

FIGURE 9.5

How Free Trade Affects Welfare in an Importing Country

When the domestic price falls to equal the world price, buyers are better off (consumer surplus rises from A to A + B + D), and sellers are worse off (producer surplus falls from B + C to C). Total surplus rises by an amount equal to area D, indicating that trade raises the economic well-being of the country as a whole.

	Before Trade	After Trade	Change
Consumer Surplus	A	A + B + D	+(B + D)
Producer Surplus	B + C	C	−B
Total Surplus	A + B + C	A + B + C + D	+D

The area D shows the increase in total surplus and represents the gains from trade.

area B + D. Sellers are worse off because producer surplus falls by the area B. The gains of buyers exceed the losses of sellers, and total surplus increases by the area D.

This analysis of an importing country yields two conclusions parallel to those for an exporting country:

1. When a country allows trade and becomes an importer of a good, domestic consumers of the good are better off, and domestic producers of the good are worse off.
2. Trade raises the economic well-being of a nation in the sense that the gains of the winners exceed the losses of the losers.

Having completed our analysis of trade, we can better understand one of the ten principles of economics in Chapter 1: Trade can make everyone better off. If Isoland opens up its steel market to international trade, that change will create winners and losers, regardless of whether Isoland ends up exporting or importing steel. In either case, however, the gains of the winners exceed the losses of the losers, so the winners could compensate the losers and still be better off. In this sense, trade *can* make everyone better off. But *will* trade make everyone better off? Probably not. In practice, compensation for the losers from international trade is rare. Without such compensation, opening up to international trade is a policy that expands the size of the economic pie, while perhaps leaving some participants in the economy with a smaller slice.

We can now see why the debate over trade policy is so often contentious. Whenever a policy creates winners and losers, the stage is set for a political battle. Nations sometimes fail to enjoy the gains from trade simply because the losers from free trade have more political clout than the winners. The losers lobby for trade restrictions, such as tariffs and import quotas.

The Effects of a Tariff

tariff
a tax on goods produced abroad and sold domestically

The Isolandian economists next consider the effects of a **tariff**—a tax on imported goods. The economists quickly realize that a tariff on steel will have no effect if Isoland becomes a steel exporter. If no one in Isoland is interested in importing steel, a tax on steel imports is irrelevant. The tariff matters only if Isoland becomes a steel importer. Concentrating their attention on this case, the economists compare welfare with and without the tariff.

The graph in Figure 9.6 shows the Isolandian market for steel. Under free trade, the domestic price equals the world price. A tariff raises the price of imported steel above the world price by the amount of the tariff. Domestic suppliers of steel, who compete with suppliers of imported steel, can now sell their steel for the world price plus the amount of the tariff. Thus, the price of steel—both imported and domestic—rises by the amount of the tariff and is, therefore, closer to the price that would prevail without trade.

The change in price affects the behaviour of domestic buyers and sellers. Because the tariff raises the price of steel, it reduces the domestic quantity demanded from Q_1^D to Q_2^D and raises the domestic quantity supplied from Q_1^S to Q_2^S. *Thus, the tariff reduces the quantity of imports and moves the domestic market closer to its equilibrium without trade.*

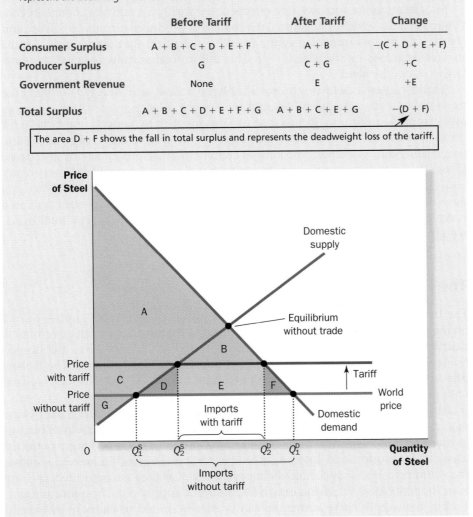

FIGURE 9.6

The Effects of a Tariff

A tariff reduces the quantity of imports and moves a market closer to the equilibrium that would exist without trade. Total surplus falls by an amount equal to area D + F. *These two triangles represent the deadweight loss from the tariff.*

	Before Tariff	After Tariff	Change
Consumer Surplus	A + B + C + D + E + F	A + B	−(C + D + E + F)
Producer Surplus	G	C + G	+C
Government Revenue	None	E	+E
Total Surplus	A + B + C + D + E + F + G	A + B + C + E + G	−(D + F)

The area D + F shows the fall in total surplus and represents the deadweight loss of the tariff.

Now consider the gains and losses from the tariff. Because the tariff raises the domestic price, domestic sellers are better off and domestic buyers are worse off. In addition, the government raises revenue. To measure these gains and losses, we look at the changes in consumer surplus, producer surplus, and government revenue. These changes are summarized in the table in Figure 9.6.

Before the tariff, the domestic price equals the world price. Consumer surplus, the area between the demand curve and the world price, is area A + B + C + D + E + F. Producer surplus, the area between the supply curve and the world price, is area G.

Government revenue equals zero. Total surplus—the sum of consumer surplus, producer surplus, and government revenue—is area A + B + C + D + E + F + G.

Once the government imposes a tariff, the domestic price exceeds the world price by the amount of the tariff. Consumer surplus is now area A + B. Producer surplus is area C + G. Government revenue, which is the quantity of after-tariff imports times the size of the tariff, is area E. Thus, total surplus with the tariff is area A + B + C + E + G.

To determine the total welfare effects of the tariff, we add the change in consumer surplus (which is negative), the change in producer surplus (positive), and the change in government revenue (positive). We find that total surplus in the market decreases by the area D + F. This fall in total surplus is called the *deadweight loss* of the tariff.

A tariff causes a deadweight loss simply because a tariff is a type of tax. Like most taxes, it distorts incentives and pushes the allocation of scarce resources away from the optimum. In this case, we can identify two effects. First, the tariff on steel raises the price of steel that domestic producers can charge above the world price and, as a result, encourages them to increase production of steel (from Q_1^S to Q_2^S). Second, the tariff raises the price that domestic steel buyers have to pay and, therefore, encourages them to reduce consumption of steel (from Q_1^D to Q_2^D). Area D represents the deadweight loss from the overproduction of steel, and area F represents the deadweight loss from the underconsumption. The total deadweight loss of the tariff is the sum of these two triangles.

The Effects of an Import Quota

import quota
a limit on the quantity of a good that can be produced abroad and sold domestically

The Isolandian economists next consider the effects of an **import quota**—a limit on the quantity of imports. In particular, imagine that the Isolandian government distributes a limited number of import licences. Each licence gives the licence holder the right to import 1 tonne of steel into Isoland from abroad. The Isolandian economists want to compare welfare under a policy of free trade and welfare with the addition of this import quota.

The graph and table in Figure 9.7 show how an import quota affects the Isolandian market for steel. Because the import quota prevents Isolandians from buying as much steel as they want from abroad, the supply of steel is no longer perfectly elastic at the world price. Instead, as long as the price of steel in Isoland is above the world price, the licence holders import as much as they are permitted, and the total supply of steel in Isoland equals the domestic supply plus the quota amount. That is, the supply curve above the world price is shifted to the right by exactly the amount of the quota. (The supply curve below the world price does not shift because, in this case, importing is not profitable for the licence holders.)

The price of steel in Isoland adjusts to balance supply (domestic plus imported) and demand. As the figure shows, the quota causes the price of steel to rise above the world price. The domestic quantity demanded falls from Q_1^D to Q_2^D, and the domestic quantity supplied rises from Q_1^S to Q_2^S. Not surprisingly, the import quota reduces steel imports.

Now consider the gains and losses from the quota. Because the quota raises the domestic price above the world price, domestic sellers are better off, and domestic buyers are worse off. In addition, the licence holders are better off because they make a profit from buying at the world price and selling at the higher domestic

FIGURE 9.7

The Effects of an Import Quota

An import quota, like a tariff, reduces the quantity of imports and moves a market closer to the equilibrium that would exist without trade. Total surplus falls by an amount equal to area D + F. These two triangles represent the deadweight loss from the quota. In addition, the import quota transfers E' + E" to whoever holds the import licences.

	Before Quota	After Quota	Change
Consumer Surplus	A + B + C + D + E' + E" + F	A + B	−(C + D + E' + E" + F)
Producer Surplus	G	C + G	+C
Licence-Holder Surplus	None	E' + E"	+(E' + E")
Total Surplus	A + B + C + D + E' + E" + F + G	A + B + C + E' + E" + G	−(D + F)

The area D + F shows the fall in total surplus and represents the deadweight loss of the quota.

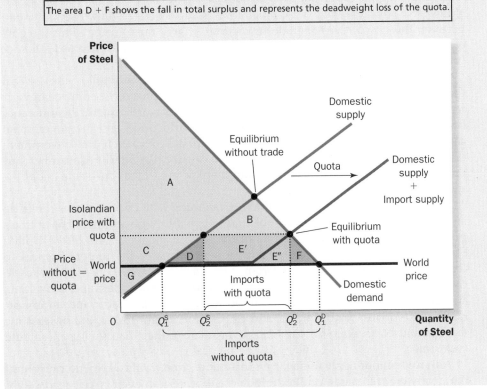

price. To measure these gains and losses, we look at the changes in consumer surplus, producer surplus, and licence-holder surplus.

Before the government imposes the quota, the domestic price equals the world price. Consumer surplus, the area between the demand curve and the world price, is area A + B + C + D + E' + E" + F. Producer surplus, the area between the supply curve and the world price, is area G. The surplus of licence holders equals zero because there are no licences. Total surplus, the sum of consumer, producer, and licence-holder surplus, is area A + B + C + D + E' + E" + F + G.

After the government imposes the import quota and issues the licences, the domestic price exceeds the world price. Domestic consumers get surplus equal to area A + B, and domestic producers get surplus equal to area C + G. The licence holders make a profit on each unit imported equal to the difference between the Isolandian price of steel and the world price. Their surplus equals this price differential times the quantity of imports. Thus, it equals the area of the rectangle E' + E''. Total surplus with the quota is the area A + B + C + E' + E'' + G.

To see how total welfare changes with the imposition of the quota, we add the change in consumer surplus (which is negative), the change in producer surplus (positive), and the change in licence-holder surplus (positive). We find that total surplus in the market decreases by the area D + F. This area represents the deadweight loss of the import quota.

This analysis should seem somewhat familiar. Indeed, if you compare the analysis of import quotas in Figure 9.7 with the analysis of tariffs in Figure 9.6, you will see that they are essentially identical. *Both tariffs and import quotas raise the domestic price of the good, reduce the welfare of domestic consumers, increase the welfare of domestic producers, and cause deadweight losses.* There is only one difference between these two types of trade restriction: A tariff raises revenue for the government (area E in Figure 9.6), whereas an import quota creates surplus for licence holders (area E' + E'' in Figure 9.7).

Tariffs and import quotas can be made to look even more similar. Suppose that the government tries to capture the licence-holder surplus for itself by charging a fee for the licences. A licence to sell 1 tonne of steel is worth exactly the difference between the Isolandian price of steel and the world price, and the government can set the licence fee as high as this price differential. If the government does this, the licence fee for imports works exactly like a tariff: Consumer surplus, producer surplus, and government revenue are exactly the same under the two policies.

In practice, however, countries that restrict trade with import quotas rarely do so by selling the import licences. For example, the U.S. government has at times pressured Japan to "voluntarily" limit the sale of Japanese cars in the United States. In this case, the Japanese government allocates the import licences to Japanese firms, and the surplus from these licences (area E' + E'') accrues to those firms. This kind of import quota is, from the standpoint of U.S. welfare, strictly worse than a U.S. tariff on imported cars. Both a tariff and an import quota raise prices, restrict trade, and cause deadweight losses, but at least the tariff produces revenue for the U.S. government rather than for Japanese auto companies.

Although in our analysis so far import quotas and tariffs appear to cause similar deadweight losses, a quota can potentially cause an even larger deadweight loss, depending on the mechanism used to allocate the import licences. Suppose that when Isoland imposes a quota, everyone understands that the licences will go to those who spend the most resources lobbying the Isolandian government. In this case, there is an implicit licence fee—the cost of lobbying. The revenues from this fee, however, rather than being collected by the government, are spent on lobbying expenses. The deadweight losses from this type of quota include not only the losses from overproduction (area D) and underconsumption (area F) but also whatever part of the licence-holder surplus (area E' + E'') is wasted on the cost of lobbying.

The Lessons for Trade Policy

The team of Isolandian economists can now write to the new president:

Dear Madam President,

You asked us three questions about opening up trade. After much hard work, we have the answers.

Question: If the government allowed Isolandians to import and export steel, what would happen to the price of steel and the quantity of steel sold in the domestic steel market?

Answer: Once trade is allowed, the Isolandian price of steel would be driven to equal the price prevailing around the world.

If the world price is now higher than the Isolandian price, our price would rise. The higher price would reduce the amount of steel Isolandians consume and raise the amount of steel that Isolandians produce. Isoland would, therefore, become a steel exporter. This occurs because, in this case, Isoland would have a comparative advantage in producing steel.

Conversely, if the world price is now lower than the Isolandian price, our price would fall. The lower price would raise the amount of steel that Isolandians consume and lower the amount of steel that Isolandians produce. Isoland would, therefore, become a steel importer. This occurs because, in this case, other countries would have a comparative advantage in producing steel.

Question: Who would gain from free trade in steel and who would lose, and would the gains exceed the losses?

Answer: The answer depends on whether the price rises or falls when trade is allowed. If the price rises, producers of steel gain, and consumers of steel lose. If the price falls, consumers gain, and producers lose. In both cases, the gains are larger than the losses. Thus, free trade raises the total welfare of Isolandians.

Question: Should a tariff or an import quota be part of the new trade policy?

Answer: A tariff, like most taxes, has deadweight losses: The revenue raised would be smaller than the losses to the buyers and sellers. In this case, the deadweight losses occur because the tariff would move the economy closer to our current no-trade equilibrium. An import quota works much like a tariff and would cause similar deadweight losses. The best policy, from the standpoint of economic efficiency, would be to allow trade without a tariff or an import quota.

We hope you find these answers helpful as you decide on your new policy.

Your faithful servants,
Isolandian economics team

QuickQuiz Draw the supply and demand curve for wool suits in the country of Autarka. When trade is allowed, the price of a suit falls from 3 to 2 ounces of gold. In your diagram, what is the change in consumer surplus, the change in producer surplus, and the change in total surplus? How would a tariff on suit imports alter these effects?

THE ARGUMENTS FOR RESTRICTING TRADE

The letter from the economics team persuades the new president of Isoland to consider opening up trade in steel. She notes that the domestic price is now high compared to the world price. Free trade would, therefore, cause the price of steel to fall and hurt domestic steel producers. Before implementing the new policy, she asks Isolandian steel companies to comment on the economists' advice.

Not surprisingly, the steel companies are opposed to free trade in steel. They believe that the government should protect the domestic steel industry from foreign competition. Let's consider some of the arguments they might give to support their position and how the economics team would respond.

The Jobs Argument

Opponents of free trade often argue that trade with other countries destroys domestic jobs. In our example, free trade in steel would cause the price of steel to fall, reducing the quantity of steel produced in Isoland and thus reducing employment in the Isolandian steel industry. Some Isolandian steelworkers would lose their jobs.

FYI

OTHER BENEFITS OF INTERNATIONAL TRADE

Our conclusions so far have been based on the standard analysis of international trade. As we have seen, there are winners and losers when a nation opens itself up to trade, but the gains to the winners exceed the losses of the losers. Yet the case for free trade can be made even stronger. There are several other economic benefits of trade beyond those emphasized in the standard analysis.

Here, in a nutshell, are some of these other benefits:

- *Increased variety of goods:* Goods produced in different countries are not exactly the same. British beer, for instance, is not the same as Canadian beer. Free trade gives consumers in all countries greater variety from which to choose.
- *Lower costs through economies of scale:* Some goods can be produced at low cost only if they are produced in large quantities—a phenomenon called *economies of scale*. A firm in a small country cannot take full advantage of economies of scale if it can sell only in a small domestic market. Free trade gives firms access to larger world markets and allows them to realize economies of scale more fully.
- *Increased competition:* A company shielded from foreign competitors is more likely to have market power, which in turn gives it the ability to raise prices above competitive levels. This is a type of market failure. Opening up trade fosters competition and gives the invisible hand a better chance to work its magic.
- *Enhanced flow of ideas:* The transfer of technological advances around the world is often thought to be linked to international trade in the goods that embody those advances. The best way for a poor, agricultural nation to learn about the computer revolution, for instance, is to buy some computers from abroad, rather than trying to make them domestically.

Thus, free international trade increases variety for consumers, allows firms to take advantage of economies of scale, makes markets more competitive, and facilitates the spread of technology. If the Isolandian economists thought these effects were important, their advice to their president would be even more forceful.

Yet free trade creates jobs at the same time that it destroys them. When Isolandians buy steel from other countries, those countries obtain the resources to buy other goods from Isoland. Isolandian workers would move from the steel industry to those industries in which Isoland has a comparative advantage. Although the transition may impose hardship on some workers in the short run, it allows Isolandians as a whole to enjoy a higher standard of living.

Opponents of trade are often skeptical that trade creates jobs. They might respond that *everything* can be produced more cheaply abroad. Under free trade, they might argue, Isolandians could not be profitably employed in any industry. As Chapter 3 explains, however, the gains from trade are based on comparative advantage, not absolute advantage. Even if one country is better than another country at producing everything, each country can still gain from trading with the other. Workers in each country will eventually find jobs in the industry in which that country has a comparative advantage.

To see how this happens, suppose that Isolandian prices are higher than world prices for every good. Isolandians then import everything and export nothing, which is exactly what the opponents of free trade fear would happen. But then everybody wants to sell their Isolandian dollars to buy foreign currency to buy imported goods. As a result, the exchange rate of the Isoland dollar falls, which in turn raises world prices as measured in Isoland dollars. With higher world prices, some Isolandian industries become exporters and hire the workers who lost their jobs in the other industries.

Alternatively, if the exchange rate is held fixed, the unemployment caused by the flood of imports reduces wages and costs in Isoland. As a result, some Isolandian industries become competitive exporters and hire the unemployed workers. Thus, either the exchange rate or wages adjust to ensure that some Isoland industries (those with a comparative advantage) are able to compete and export at world prices.

The National-Security Argument

When an industry is threatened with competition from other countries, opponents of free trade often argue that the industry is vital for national security. In our example, Isolandian steel companies might point out that steel is used to make guns and tanks. Free trade would allow Isoland to become dependent on foreign countries to supply steel. If a war later broke out, Isoland might be unable to produce enough steel and weapons to defend itself.

Economists acknowledge that protecting key industries may be appropriate when there are legitimate concerns over national security. Yet they fear that this argument may be used too quickly by producers eager to gain at consumers' expense. Certainly, it is tempting for those in an industry to exaggerate their role in national defence to obtain protection from foreign competition.

The Infant-Industry Argument

New industries sometimes argue for temporary trade restrictions to help them get started. After a period of protection, the argument goes, these industries will mature and be able to compete with foreign competitors. Similarly, older industries sometimes argue that they need temporary protection to help them adjust to new conditions. Canada's "National Policy," started by Sir John A. Macdonald in 1878, could be seen as an attempt to protect the infant Canadian manufacturing sector from foreign (especially U.S.) competition. This protection from foreign competition lasted for 110 years, until the Canada–U.S. Free Trade Agreement of 1989.

Economists are often skeptical about such claims. The primary reason is that the infant-industry argument is difficult to implement in practice. To apply protection successfully, the government would need to decide which industries will eventually be profitable and decide whether the benefits of establishing these industries exceed the costs to consumers of protection. Yet "picking winners" is extraordinarily difficult. It is made even more difficult by the political process, which often awards protection to those industries that are politically powerful. And once a powerful industry is protected from foreign competition, the "temporary" policy is hard to remove.

In addition, many economists are skeptical about the infant-industry argument even in principle. Suppose, for instance, that the Isolandian steel industry is young and unable to compete profitably against foreign rivals. Yet there is reason to believe that the industry can be profitable in the long run. In this case, the owners of the firms should be willing to incur temporary losses to obtain the eventual profits. Protection is not necessary for an industry to grow. Firms in various industries—such as many Internet firms today—incur temporary losses in the hope of growing and becoming profitable in the future. And many of them succeed, even without protection from foreign competition.

The Unfair-Competition Argument

A common argument is that free trade is desirable only if all countries play by the same rules. If firms in different countries are subject to different laws and regulations, then it is unfair (the argument goes) to expect the firms to compete in the international marketplace. For instance, suppose that the government of Neighbourland subsidizes its steel industry by giving steel companies large tax breaks. The Isolandian steel industry might argue that it should be protected from this foreign competition because Neighbourland is not competing fairly.

Would it, in fact, hurt Isoland to buy steel from another country at a subsidized price? Certainly, Isolandian steel producers would suffer, but Isolandian steel consumers would benefit from the low price. Moreover, the case for free trade is no different: The gains of the consumers from buying at the low price would exceed the losses of the producers. Neighbourland's subsidy to its steel industry may be a bad policy, but it is the taxpayers of Neighbourland who bear the burden. Isoland can benefit from the opportunity to buy steel at a subsidized price.

The Protection-as-a-Bargaining-Chip Argument

Another argument for trade restrictions concerns the strategy of bargaining. Many policymakers claim to support free trade but, at the same time, argue that trade restrictions can be useful when we bargain with our trading partners. They claim that the threat of a trade restriction can help remove a trade restriction already imposed by a foreign government. For example, Isoland might threaten to impose a tariff on steel unless Neighbourland removes its tariff on wheat. If Neighbourland responds to this threat by removing its tariff, the result can be freer trade.

IN THE NEWS

TRADE POLICY IN JAPAN

Japan has a large population, little agricultural land, and high food prices. Free trade in food could lower prices and benefit Japanese consumers, but the government's policy prevents this.

Japan Tariff Hike on Beef Imports Takes Effect, Angering Farmers Overseas

TOKYO (AP)—Japan hiked its tariff on imported refrigerated beef on Friday despite protests from trading partners.

Japan raised the tariff to 50 per cent from 38.5 per cent by invoking an emergency provision in international trade agreements. But trading partners have questioned the validity of the provision in current circumstances.

Agriculture minister Yoshiyuki Kamei defended the move Friday, saying the emergency measure lasting through March 2004 would allow Japanese farmers to recover from a recent surge in beef imports.

"Producers need to adapt, and in the mid- to long term, this will benefit consumers," he told reporters.

The move fanned objections in beef-exporting countries like Australia, where cattle farmers staged a steak barbecue protest outside the Japanese embassy in

Canberra. Cattle Council president Keith Adams said the new tariff will cost Australian farmers at least $52 million US a year in lost exports.

"We want to send a clear and unequivocal message that we are not happy with this," Adams said, adding that higher beef prices were also bad for Japanese consumers.

Australian Prime Minister John Howard failed to convince Japan to abandon the plan during talks earlier this month in Tokyo.

Japan, citing World Trade Organization guidelines, says it is allowed to raise tariffs on imported beef if imports during a given quarter show a year-on-year increase of 17 per cent or more. Imports for the April–June quarter rose 34 per cent, according to Japan's finance ministry.

U.S. Agriculture Secretary Ann Veneman called the tariff increase "both unnecessary and unwarranted" earlier this week.

The United States argued Japan is not justified in raising tariffs because

beef imports only rebounded to the level they were at before the detection of mad cow disease in Japan in late 2001 triggered an abnormal plunge in beef imports last year. Japanese beef imports have increased as mad cow fears have gradually subsided.

The new rate applies only to refrigerated beef imports. Frozen beef will not be affected.

Australia and the United States were the two largest exporters of refrigerated beef to Japan in 2002, with 59 per cent and 38 per cent shares of the market, respectively, according to Meat and Livestock Australia Ltd., a company owned by Australian meat producers.

Canadian beef has been banned from key export markets such as the United States and Japan since a single case of mad cow disease was discovered in Alberta on May 20.

Source: Canadian Press NewsWire, August 1, 2003.

The problem with this bargaining strategy is that the threat may not work. If it doesn't work, the country has a difficult choice. It can carry out its threat and implement the trade restriction, which would reduce its own economic welfare. Or it can back down from its threat, which would cause it to lose prestige in international affairs. Faced with this choice, the country would probably wish that it had never made the threat in the first place.

IN THE NEWS

GLOBALIZATION

The movement toward free world trade—sometimes called globalization—*has some vocal opponents, but as this article discusses, they are not always well informed.*

Hearts and Heads

By Paul Krugman

There is an old European saying: anyone who is not a socialist before he is 30 has no heart, anyone who is still a socialist after he is 30 has no head. Suitably updated, this applies perfectly to the movement against globalization—the movement that made its big splash in Seattle back in 1999 and is doing its best to disrupt the Summit of the Americas in Quebec City this weekend.

The facts of globalization are not always pretty. If you buy a product made in a third-world country, it was produced by workers who are paid incredibly little by Western standards and probably work under awful conditions. Anyone who is not bothered by those facts, at least some of the time, has no heart.

But that doesn't mean the demonstrators are right. On the contrary: anyone who thinks that the answer to world poverty is simple outrage against global trade has no head—or chooses not to use it. The anti-globalization movement already has a remarkable track record of hurting the very people and causes it claims to champion. . . .

Could anything be worse than having children work in sweatshops? Alas, yes. In 1993, child workers in Bangladesh were found to be producing clothing for Wal-Mart, and Senator Tom Harkin proposed legislation banning imports from countries employing underage workers. The direct result was that Bangladeshi textile factories stopped employing

Case Study

TRADE AGREEMENTS AND THE WORLD TRADE ORGANIZATION

A country can take one of two approaches to achieving free trade. It can take a *unilateral* approach and remove its trade restrictions on its own. This is the approach that Great Britain took in the nineteenth century and that Chile and South Korea have taken in recent years. Alternatively, a country can take a *multilateral* approach and reduce its trade restrictions while other countries do the same. In other words, it can bargain with its trading partners in an attempt to reduce trade restrictions around the world.

One important example of the multilateral approach is the North American Free Trade Agreement (NAFTA), which in 1994 lowered trade barriers among the United States, Mexico, and Canada. Another is the General Agreement on Tariffs and Trade (GATT), which is a continuing series of negotiations among many of the world's countries with the goal of promoting free trade. Canada helped to found GATT after World War II in response to the high tariffs imposed during the Great Depression of the 1930s. Many economists believe that the high tariffs contributed children. But did the children go back to school? Did they return to happy homes? Not according to Oxfam, which found that the displaced child workers ended up in even worse jobs, or on the streets—and that a significant number were forced into prostitution.

The point is that third-world countries aren't poor because their export workers earn low wages; it's the other way around. Because the countries are poor, even what look to us like bad jobs at bad wages are almost always much better than the alternatives: millions of Mexicans are migrating to the north of the country to take the low-wage export jobs that outrage opponents of NAFTA. And those jobs wouldn't exist if the wages were much higher: the same factors that make poor countries poor— low productivity, bad infrastructure, general social disorganization—mean that such countries can compete on world markets only if they pay wages much lower than those paid in the West.

Of course, opponents of globalization have heard this argument, and they have answers. At a conference last week, I heard paeans to the superiority of traditional rural lifestyles over modern, urban life—a claim that not only flies in the face of the clear fact that many peasants flee to urban jobs as soon as they can, but that (it seems to me) has a disagreeable element of cultural condescension, especially given the overwhelming preponderance of white faces in the crowds of demonstrators. (Would you want to live in a pre-industrial village?) I also heard claims that rural poverty in the third world is mainly the fault of multinational corporations— which is just plain wrong, but is a convenient belief if you want to think of globalization as an unmitigated evil.

The most sophisticated answer was that the movement doesn't want to stop exports—it just wants better working conditions and higher wages.

But it's not a serious position. Third-world countries desperately need their export industries—they cannot retreat to an imaginary rural Arcadia. They can't have those export industries unless they are allowed to sell goods produced under conditions that Westerners find appalling, by workers who receive very low wages. And that's a fact the anti-globalization activists refuse to accept.

So who are the bad guys? The activists are getting the images they wanted from Quebec City: leaders sitting inside their fortified enclosure, with thousands of police protecting them from the outraged masses outside. But images can deceive. Many of the people inside that chain-link fence are sincerely trying to help the world's poor. And the people outside the fence, whatever their intentions, are doing their best to make the poor even poorer.

Source: Originally published in *The New York Times*, April 22, 2001, OP-ED WK/ p. 17. © 2001 by The New York Times Co. Reprinted by permission.

to the economic hardship during that period. GATT has successfully reduced the average tariff among member countries from about 40 percent after World War II to about 5 percent today.

The rules established under GATT are now enforced by an international institution called the World Trade Organization (WTO). The WTO was established in 1995 and has its headquarters in Geneva, Switzerland. As of April 2004, 147 countries have joined the organization, accounting for 97 percent of world trade. The functions of the WTO are to administer trade agreements, provide a forum for negotiations, and handle disputes that arise among member countries.

What are the pros and cons of the multilateral approach to free trade? One advantage is that the multilateral approach has the potential to result in freer trade than a unilateral approach because it can reduce trade restrictions abroad as well as at home. If international negotiations fail, however, the result could be more restricted trade than under a unilateral approach.

In addition, the multilateral approach may have a political advantage. In most markets, producers are fewer and better organized than consumers—and thus wield greater political influence. Reducing the Isolandian tariff on steel, for example, may be politically difficult if considered by itself. The steel companies would oppose free trade, and the users of steel who would benefit are so numerous that organizing their support would be difficult. Yet suppose that Neighbourland promises to reduce its tariff on wheat at the same time that Isoland reduces its tariff on steel. In this case, the Isolandian wheat farmers, who are also politically powerful, would back the agreement. Thus, the multilateral approach to free trade can sometimes win political support when a unilateral reduction cannot. ●

QuickQuiz The textile industry of Autarka advocates a ban on the import of wool suits. Describe five arguments its lobbyists might make. Give a response to each of these arguments.

CONCLUSION

Economists and the general public often disagree about free trade. In 1988, for example, Canada faced the question of whether to sign the Canada–U.S. Free Trade Agreement, which reduced trade restrictions between Canada and the United States. Opinion polls showed the general public in Canada to be about evenly split on the issue. Prime Minister Brian Mulroney campaigned for the Free Trade Agreement and won re-election, but with a minority of the popular vote. Opponents viewed free trade as a threat to job security and the Canadian standard of living. By contrast, economists overwhelmingly supported the agreement. They viewed free trade as a way of allocating production efficiently and raising living standards in both countries.

Economists see the benefits of trade between countries in the same way that they see the benefits of trade between provinces, or between cities, or between people. Individuals would have a much lower standard of living if they had to produce all their own food, clothing, and housing. So would a city. So would a province. The United States has always had unrestricted trade among the states, and the country as a whole has benefited from the specialization that trade allows in such a large market. With a few exceptions, Canada too has free trade among the provinces: Ontario builds cars, Alberta pumps oil, British Columbia saws lumber, and so on. The world could similarly benefit from free trade among countries.

To better understand economists' view of trade, let's continue our parable. Suppose that the country of Isoland ignores the advice of its economics team and decides not to allow free trade in steel. The country remains in the equilibrium without international trade.

Then, one day, some Isolandian inventor discovers a new way to make steel at very low cost. The process is quite mysterious, however, and the inventor insists on keeping it a secret. What is odd is that the inventor doesn't need any workers or iron ore to make steel. The only input he requires is wheat.

The inventor is hailed as a genius. Because steel is used in so many products, the invention lowers the cost of many goods and allows all Isolandians to enjoy a higher standard of living. Workers who had previously produced steel do suffer when their factories close, but eventually they find work in other industries. Some become farmers and grow the wheat that the inventor turns into steel. Others enter new industries that emerge as a result of higher Isolandian living standards. Everyone understands that the displacement of these workers is an inevitable part of progress.

After several years, a newspaper reporter decides to investigate this mysterious new steel process. She sneaks into the inventor's factory and learns that the inventor is a fraud. The inventor has not been making steel at all. Instead, he has been smuggling wheat abroad in exchange for steel from other countries. The only thing that the inventor had discovered was the gains from international trade.

When the truth is revealed, the government shuts down the inventor's operation. The price of steel rises, and workers return to jobs in steel factories. Living standards in Isoland fall back to their former levels. The inventor is jailed and held up to public ridicule. After all, he was no inventor. He was just an economist.

SUMMARY

- The effects of free trade can be determined by comparing the domestic price without trade to the world price. A low domestic price indicates that the country has a comparative advantage in producing the good and that the country will become an exporter. A high domestic price indicates that the rest of the world has a comparative advantage in producing the good and that the country will become an importer.

- When a country allows trade and becomes an exporter of a good, producers of the good are better off, and consumers of the good are worse off. When a country allows trade and becomes an importer of a good, consumers are better off, and producers are worse off. In both cases, the gains from trade exceed the losses.

- A tariff—a tax on imports—moves a market closer to the equilibrium that would exist

without trade and, therefore, reduces the gains from trade. Although domestic producers are better off and the government raises revenue, the losses to consumers exceed these gains.

- An import quota—a limit on imports—has effects that are similar to those of a tariff. Under a quota, however, the holders of the import licences receive the revenue that the government would collect with a tariff.

- There are various arguments for restricting trade: protecting jobs, defending national security, helping infant industries, preventing unfair competition, and responding to foreign trade restrictions. Although some of these arguments have some merit in some cases, economists believe that free trade is usually the better policy.

KEY CONCEPTS

world price, p. 179   tariff, p. 184   import quota, p. 186

QUESTIONS FOR REVIEW

1. What does the domestic price that prevails without international trade tell us about a nation's comparative advantage?

2. When does a country become an exporter of a good? An importer?

3. Draw the supply-and-demand diagram for an importing country. What is consumer surplus and producer surplus before trade is allowed? What is consumer surplus and producer surplus with free trade? What is the change in total surplus?

4. Describe what a tariff is, and describe its economic effects.

5. What is an import quota? Compare its economic effects with those of a tariff.

6. List five arguments often given to support trade restrictions. How do economists respond to these arguments?

7. What is the difference between the unilateral and multilateral approaches to achieving free trade? Give an example of each.

PROBLEMS AND APPLICATIONS

1. Canada represents a small part of the world apple market.
   a. Draw a diagram depicting the equilibrium in the Canadian apple market without international trade. Identify the equilibrium price, equilibrium quantity, consumer surplus, and producer surplus.
   b. Suppose that the world apple price is below the Canadian price before trade, and that the Canadian apple market is now opened to trade. Identify the new equilibrium price, quantity consumed, quantity produced domestically, and quantity imported. Also show the change in the surplus of domestic consumers and producers. Has domestic total surplus increased or decreased?

2. The world price of wine is below the price that would prevail in Canada in the absence of trade.
   a. Assuming that Canadian imports of wine are a small part of total world wine production, draw a graph for the Canadian market for wine under free trade. Identify consumer surplus, producer surplus, and total surplus in an appropriate table.
   b. Now suppose that an unusual shift of the Gulf Stream leads to an unseasonably cold summer in Europe, destroying much of the grape harvest there. What effect does this shock have on the world price of wine? Using your graph and table from part (a), show the effect on consumer surplus, producer surplus, and total surplus in Canada. Who are the winners and losers? Is Canada as a whole better or worse off?

3. The world price of cotton is below the no-trade price in country A and above the no-trade price in country B. Using supply-and-demand diagrams and welfare tables such as those in the chapter, show the gains from trade in each country. Compare your results for the two countries.

4. Suppose that Parliament imposes a tariff on imported clothes to protect the Canadian clothing industry from foreign competition. Assuming that Canada is a price taker in the world clothing market, show on a diagram: the change in the quantity of imports, the loss to Canadian consumers, the gain to Canadian manufacturers, government revenue, and the deadweight loss associated with the tariff. The loss to consumers can be decomposed into three pieces: a transfer to domestic producers, a transfer to the government, and a deadweight loss. Use your diagram to identify these three pieces.

5. Most Canadian dairy farmers oppose free trade, and most Canadian lumber producers support it. For simplicity, assume that Canada is a small country in the markets for both milk and lumber, and that without free trade, Canada would not trade these goods internationally. (Both of these assumptions are false, but they do not affect the qualitative responses to the following questions.)
   a. Based on who opposes and who supports free trade, do you think the world milk price is above or below the Canadian no-trade milk price? Do you think the world lumber price is above or below the Canadian no-trade lumber price? Now analyze the

welfare consequences of free trade for both markets.

b. Considering both markets together, would free trade make Canadian producers as a group better off or worse off? Would it make Canadian consumers as a group better off or worse off? Does it make Canada as a whole better off or worse off?

6. Imagine that winemakers in British Columbia petitioned the provincial government to tax wines imported from Ontario. They argue that this tax would both raise tax revenue for the provincial government and raise employment in the B.C. wine industry. Do you agree with these claims? Is it a good policy?

7. U.S. Senator Ernest Hollings once wrote that "consumers *do not* benefit from lower-priced imports. Glance through some mail-order catalogs and you'll see that consumers pay exactly the same price for clothing whether it is U.S.-made or imported." Comment.

8. Write a brief essay advocating or criticizing each of the following policy positions.
   a. The government should not allow imports if foreign firms are selling below their costs of production (a phenomenon called "dumping").
   b. The government should temporarily stop the import of goods for which the domestic industry is new and struggling to survive.
   c. The government should not allow imports from countries with weaker environmental regulations than ours.

9. Suppose that a technological advance in Japan lowers the world price of televisions.
   a. Assume that Canada is an importer of televisions and there are no trade restrictions. How does the technological advance affect the welfare of Canadian consumers and Canadian producers? What happens to total surplus in Canada?
   b. Now suppose that Canada has a quota on television imports. How does the Japanese technological advance affect the welfare of Canadian consumers, Canadian producers, and the holders of import licences?

10. When the government of Tradeland decides to impose an import quota on foreign cars, three proposals are suggested: (1) Sell the import licences in an auction. (2) Distribute the licences randomly in a lottery. (3) Let people wait in line and distribute the licences on a first-come, first-served basis. Compare the effects of these policies. Which policy do you think has the largest deadweight losses? Which policy has the smallest deadweight losses? Why? (Hint: The government's other ways of raising tax revenue all cause deadweight losses themselves.)

11. Canada and other rich countries are participants in the Multi-Fibre Arrangement (MFA), which restricts imports of clothing from developing countries in order to protect the clothing industries of participating countries from competition from low-wage countries.
    a. Illustrate the effect of import quotas on the Canadian market for clothes. Label the relevant prices and quantities under free trade and under the quota.
    b. Analyze the effect of the quota using the tools of welfare analysis.
    c. Critics of the MFA say that it has deprived numerous developing countries of export markets for their clothing industries. Illustrate the effect of the MFA quotas on the market for clothes in developing countries. Label the relevant prices and quantities under free trade and under the quota.
    d. Analyze the effect of the quota on developing countries using the tools of welfare analysis.
    e. Our usual welfare analysis includes only the gains and losses of Canadian producers and consumers. What role do you think the gains and losses to people in other countries should play in our economic policymaking?

12. (This question is challenging.) Consider a small country that exports steel. Suppose that a "pro-trade" government decides to subsidize the export of steel by paying a certain amount for each tonne sold abroad. How does this export subsidy affect the domestic price of steel, the quantity of steel produced, the quantity of steel consumed, and the quantity of steel exported? How does it affect consumer surplus, producer surplus, government revenue, and

total surplus? (Hint: The analysis of an export subsidy is similar to the analysis of a tariff.)

13. What trade disputes or trade agreements have been in the news lately? In this case, who do you think are the winners and losers from free trade? Which group has more political clout?

Note: Places to look for this information include the websites of the World Trade Organization (http://www.wto.org) and International Trade Canada (http://www.itcan-cican.gc.ca).

INTERNET RESOURCES

The government department in charge of Canada's international trade policy is International Trade Canada (ITCan), which was formerly part of the Department of Foreign Affairs and International Trade. Visit the ITCan website (http://www.itcan-cican.gc.ca) to see the latest trade news and a wide variety of other information. On the site's main page, click on "Trade and Economic Policy" to learn about Canada's trade agreements under the North American Free Trade Agreement (NAFTA), the Canada–Asia Pacific Economic Cooperation (Canada–APEC) forum, and the World Trade Organization (WTO).

Access to the complete text of the NAFTA agreement is provided on the NAFTA Secretariat website (http://www.nafta-sec-alena.org/DefaultSite/home/index_e.aspx).

You can learn about APEC at http://www.apec.org; click on "About APEC."

Visit the WTO's website (http://www.wto.org) to find out about the agenda and progress (or lack of progress) in the latest round of WTO trade talks.

http://   For more study tools, please visit http://www.mankiw3e.nelson.com.

4

THE ECONOMICS OF THE PUBLIC SECTOR

© GEOFFREY CLIFFORD/IMAGE BANK

EXTERNALITIES

Learning Objectives

In the chapter, you will …

- Learn the nature of an externality
- See why externalities can make market outcomes inefficient
- Examine how people can sometimes solve the problem of externalities on their own
- Consider why private solutions to externalities sometimes do not work
- Examine the various government policies aimed at solving the problem of externalities

Firms that make and sell paper also create, as a byproduct of the manufacturing process, a chemical called dioxin. Scientists believe that once dioxin enters the environment, it raises the population's risk of cancer, birth defects, and other health problems.

Is the production and release of dioxin a problem for society? In Chapters 4 through 9 we examined how markets allocate scarce resources with the forces of supply and demand, and we saw that the equilibrium of supply and demand is typically an efficient allocation of resources. To use Adam Smith's famous metaphor, the "invisible hand" of the marketplace leads self-interested buyers and sellers in a market to maximize the total benefit that society derives from that market. This insight is the basis for one of the ten principles of economics in Chapter 1: Markets are usually a good way to organize economic activity. Should we conclude, therefore, that the invisible hand prevents firms in the paper market from emitting too much dioxin?

Markets do many things well, but they do not do everything well. In this chapter we begin our study of another of the ten principles of economics: Governments can sometimes improve market outcomes. We examine why markets sometimes fail to

externality
the uncompensated impact of one person's actions on the well-being of a bystander

allocate resources efficiently, how government policies can potentially improve the market's allocation, and what kinds of policies are likely to work best.

The market failures examined in this chapter fall under a general category called *externalities*. An **externality** arises when a person engages in an activity that influences the well-being of a bystander and yet neither pays nor receives any compensation for that effect. If the impact on the bystander is adverse, it is called a *negative externality*; if it is beneficial, it is called a *positive externality*. In the presence of externalities, society's interest in a market outcome extends beyond the well-being of buyers and sellers who participate in the market; it also includes the well-being of bystanders who are affected indirectly. Because buyers and sellers neglect the external effects of their actions when deciding how much to demand or supply, the market equilibrium is not efficient when there are externalities. That is, the equilibrium fails to maximize the total benefit to society as a whole. The release of dioxin into the environment, for instance, is a negative externality. Self-interested paper firms will not consider the full cost of the pollution they create and, therefore, will emit too much pollution unless the government prevents or discourages them from doing so.

Externalities come in many varieties, as do the policy responses that try to deal with the market failure. Here are some examples:

- The exhaust from automobiles is a negative externality because it creates smog that other people have to breathe. As a result of this externality, drivers tend to pollute too much. The federal government attempts to solve this problem by setting emission standards for cars. It also taxes gasoline to reduce the amount that people drive.
- Restored historic buildings convey a positive externality because people who walk or ride by them can enjoy their beauty and the sense of history that these buildings provide. Building owners do not get the full benefit of restoration and, therefore, tend to discard older buildings too quickly. Many local governments respond to this problem by regulating the destruction of historic buildings and by providing tax breaks to owners who restore them.
- Barking dogs create a negative externality because neighbours are disturbed by the noise. Dog owners do not bear the full cost of the noise and, therefore, tend to take too few precautions to prevent their dogs from barking. Local governments address this problem by making it illegal to "disturb the peace."
- Research into new technologies provides a positive externality because it creates knowledge that other people can use. Because inventors cannot capture the full benefits of their inventions, they tend to devote too few resources to research. The federal government addresses this problem partially through the patent system, which gives inventors exclusive rights to their inventions for a period of time.

In each of these cases, some decision maker fails to take account of the external effects of his or her behaviour. The government responds by trying to influence this behaviour to protect the interests of bystanders.

EXTERNALITIES AND MARKET INEFFICIENCY

In this section we use the tools from Chapter 7 to examine how externalities affect economic well-being. The analysis shows precisely why externalities cause markets to allocate resources inefficiently. Later in the chapter we examine various ways in which private actors and public policymakers may remedy this type of market failure.

Welfare Economics: A Recap

We begin by recalling the key lessons of welfare economics from Chapter 7. To make our analysis concrete, we will consider a specific market—the market for aluminum. Figure 10.1 shows the supply and demand curves in the market for aluminum.

As you should recall from Chapter 7, the supply and demand curves contain important information about costs and benefits. The demand curve for aluminum reflects the value of aluminum to consumers, as measured by the prices they are willing to pay. At any given quantity, the height of the demand curve shows the willingness to pay of the marginal buyer. In other words, it shows the value to the consumer of the last unit of aluminum bought. Similarly, the supply curve reflects the costs of producing aluminum. At any given quantity, the height of the supply curve shows the cost of the marginal seller. In other words, it shows the cost to the producer of the last unit of aluminum sold.

In the absence of government intervention, the price adjusts to balance the supply and demand for aluminum. The quantity produced and consumed in the market equilibrium, shown as Q_{MARKET} in Figure 10.1, is efficient in the sense that it maximizes the sum of producer and consumer surplus. That is, the market allocates resources in a way that maximizes the total value to the consumers who buy and use aluminum minus the total costs to the producers who make and sell aluminum.

FIGURE 10.1

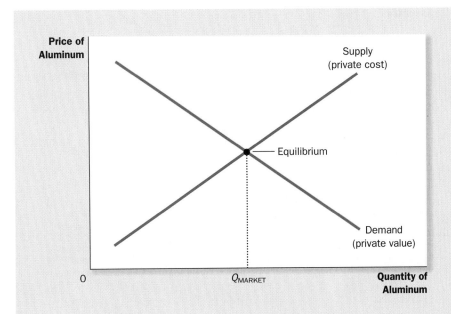

The Market for Aluminum

The demand curve reflects the value to buyers, and the supply curve reflects the costs of sellers. The equilibrium quantity, Q_{MARKET}, maximizes the total value to buyers minus the total costs of sellers. In the absence of externalities, therefore, the market equilibrium is efficient.

Negative Externalities

Now let's suppose that aluminum factories emit pollution: For each unit of aluminum produced, a certain amount of smoke enters the atmosphere. Because this smoke creates a health risk for those who breathe the air, it is a negative externality. How does this externality affect the efficiency of the market outcome?

Because of the externality, the cost to *society* of producing aluminum is larger than the cost to the aluminum producers. For each unit of aluminum produced, the *social cost* includes the private costs of the aluminum producers plus the costs to those bystanders affected adversely by the pollution. Figure 10.2 shows the social cost of producing aluminum. The social-cost curve is above the supply curve because it takes into account the external costs imposed on society by aluminum producers. The difference between these two curves reflects the cost of the pollution emitted.

What quantity of aluminum should be produced? To answer this question, we once again consider what a benevolent social planner would do. The planner wants to maximize the total surplus derived from the market—the value to consumers of aluminum minus the cost of producing aluminum. The planner understands, however, that the cost of producing aluminum includes the external costs of the pollution.

The planner would choose the level of aluminum production at which the demand curve crosses the social-cost curve. This intersection determines the optimal amount of aluminum from the standpoint of society as a whole. Below this level of production, the value of the aluminum to consumers (as measured by the height of the demand curve) exceeds the social cost of producing it (as measured by the height of the social-cost curve). The planner does not produce more than this level because the social cost of producing additional aluminum exceeds the value to consumers.

FIGURE 10.2

Pollution and the Social Optimum

In the presence of a negative externality, such as pollution, the social cost of the good exceeds the private cost. The optimal quantity, $Q_{OPTIMUM}$, is therefore smaller than the equilibrium quantity, Q_{MARKET}.

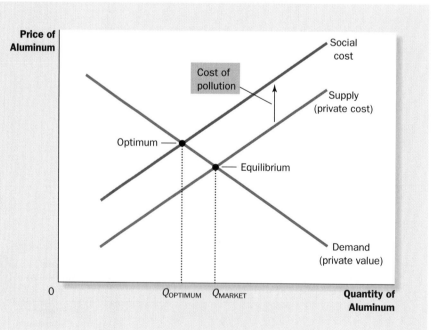

Note that the equilibrium quantity of aluminum, Q_{MARKET}, is larger than the socially optimal quantity, $Q_{OPTIMUM}$. The reason for this inefficiency is that the market equilibrium reflects only the private costs of production. In the market equilibrium, the marginal consumer values aluminum at less than the social cost of producing it. That is, at Q_{MARKET} the demand curve lies below the social-cost curve. Thus, reducing aluminum production and consumption below the market equilibrium level raises total economic well-being.

We can measure the value of this increase in economic well-being using the concept of *deadweight loss* introduced in Chapters 8 and 9. In those chapters the deadweight loss was the reduction in total surplus that resulted from the imposition of a tax or tariff. The same approach can be used to measure the reduction in total surplus associated with the inefficient allocation of resources due to the presence of an externality.

Figure 10.3 shows how we use the concepts of consumer and producer surplus to determine the deadweight loss of the externality caused by the aluminum factory emitting pollution. To simplify the diagram, the producer's supply curve, which measures the private cost of producing aluminum, is not shown. However, the equilibrium quantity of aluminum determined by the intersection of the producer's supply curve with the demand curve, Q_{MARKET}, is shown.

At the equilibrium level of aluminum production, Q_{MARKET}, and the corresponding market price, P_{MARKET}, consumer surplus is measured in the usual way as the area between the demand curve and the equilibrium price, A + B + C + D. The measure of producer surplus is slightly more complicated but follows the same logic used in Chapters 8 and 9. We showed in Chapter 7 that in the absence of a market failure, producer surplus is simply the amount received by sellers less the cost to those sellers. In the presence of an externality, the basic idea is the same. However, rather than using the private cost to sellers of producing aluminum, as

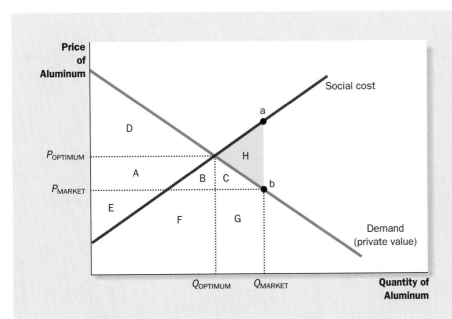

FIGURE 10.3

Deadweight Loss of a Negative Externality

A negative externality means that the social-cost curve lies above the demand curve at the market equilibrium quantity, Q_{MARKET}. Compared with the social optimum, $Q_{OPTIMUM}$, consumer surplus at the market equilibrium is higher by area A + B + C, and producer surplus measured using the social-cost curve is lower by A + B + C + H. The net effect is a reduction in total surplus, shown by deadweight loss triangle H.

measured by the height of the supply or private-cost curve, we use the *social cost of producing aluminum*, as measured by the height of the social-cost curve.

The social-cost curve includes both the private costs of the aluminum producers and the external costs imposed on bystanders affected by the pollution. In Figure 10.3, the cost to society of producing the quantity of aluminum sold is the area between the social-cost curve and the market quantity, Q_{MARKET}, area F + G + B + C + H. The amount received by the sellers is simply the quantity of aluminum sold, Q_{MARKET}, times the market price of aluminum, P_{MARKET}, which is given by area E + F + G. So, producer surplus measured using the social cost of producing aluminum is the amount received by sellers less the social cost to society, or (E + F + G) – (F + G + B + C + H), which simplifies to E – (B + C + H).

Total surplus at the market equilibrium level of aluminum production then consists of consumer surplus (A + B + C + D) plus producer surplus (E – (B + C + H)). The first column of Table 10.1 summarizes these conclusions.

Now consider economic welfare measured at the socially optimal level of aluminum production, $Q_{OPTIMUM}$. The price of aluminum that would generate this socially optimal level of production is $P_{OPTIMUM}$. We will discuss below ways in which this price might be achieved. For now, let's say that the social planner simply imposes this price on the market. At this price, consumers will demand $Q_{OPTIMUM}$ units of aluminum, and consumer surplus is reduced to D. Producer surplus measured using the social-cost curve is the amount received by sellers at price $P_{OPTIMUM}$, the area of rectangle A + E + F + B, less the social cost of producing $Q_{OPTIMUM}$ units of aluminum, area F + B. This gives a producer surplus of A + E. These conclusions are summarized in the second column of Table 10.1.

We can now see the change in economic welfare associated with moving from the market equilibrium level of aluminum production, Q_{MARKET}, to the socially optimal level of aluminum production, $Q_{OPTIMUM}$. The third column of Table 10.1 shows the changes. Moving from Q_{MARKET} to $Q_{OPTIMUM}$ causes consumer surplus to fall by area A + B + C, and producer surplus to rise by area A + B + C + H. In the case of a negative externality in production, the increase in producer surplus of moving from Q_{MARKET} to $Q_{OPTIMUM}$, measured using the social-cost curve, exceeds the reduction in consumer surplus by the area of triangle H in Figure 10.3. Triangle H is the deadweight loss to society, or reduction in total surplus, caused by the externality (pollution) associated with producing aluminum.

TABLE 10.1

Deadweight Loss of a Negative Production Externality

This table refers to the areas marked in Figure 10.3 to show how a negative externality generates a deadweight loss in the economy.

	At Q_{MARKET}	At $Q_{OPTIMUM}$	Change
Consumer surplus	A + B + C + D	D	–(A + B + C)
Producer surplus	E – (B + C + H)	A + E	A + B + C + H
Total surplus	D + A + E – H	D + A + E	H

Another way of understanding the nature of the market failure arising from an externality and determining the deadweight loss triangle is to consider the difference between the social-cost curve and the demand curve for aluminum at the equilibrium level of production, Q_{MARKET}. In Chapter 7 we saw that the height of the demand curve at a given level of demand measures the value that buyers place on the last unit of the good demanded, as measured by their willingness to pay for it. We also saw that the height of the private supply curve at a particular level of production measures the cost to the seller of producing the last unit of the good produced.

The height of the social-cost curve in the presence of a negative production externality incorporates the seller's private costs of production plus the costs imposed on others due to the negative externality. At Q_{MARKET}, the social-cost curve lies above the demand curve. This means that at Q_{MARKET} the social cost of the last unit of aluminum produced exceeds the value placed on that unit by buyers. Total surplus would therefore be higher if this unit of aluminum was not produced at all. In fact, the social cost of production exceeds the value placed on aluminum by the buyers for all units of aluminum produced in excess of $Q_{OPTIMUM}$. The loss in total surplus of producing Q_{MARKET} units of aluminum rather than $Q_{OPTIMUM}$ units is equal to the area of the triangle formed by the social-cost curve and the demand curve between $Q_{OPTIMUM}$ and Q_{MARKET}. This is the deadweight loss associated with the negative production externality.

How might a social planner achieve the socially optimal level of aluminum production and eliminate the deadweight loss associated with the externality? One way would be to tax aluminum producers for each tonne of aluminum sold. The tax would shift the supply curve for aluminum up by the size of the tax. If the tax accurately reflects the social cost of pollution, the new supply curve coincides with the social-cost curve.

Such a tax is said to **internalize the externality** because it gives buyers and sellers in the market the incentive to take account of the external effects of their actions. Taxes that internalize negative externalities are called **Pigovian taxes,** after economist Arthur Pigou (1877–1959), an early advocate of their use. In Figure 10.3, the Pigovian tax is the difference between the actual social marginal cost and the private marginal cost of producing the socially optimal amount of aluminum, $Q_{OPTIMUM}$. Since the cost curves are assumed to be linear in Figure 10.3, this is equal to the distance ab, which is the distance between the social and the private cost of producing an additional unit of aluminum measured at Q_{MARKET} instead.

In the presence of a Pigovian tax, aluminum producers take into account the full social costs of pollution, rather than just their private costs, when deciding how much aluminum to supply. This is because the tax now makes them pay for the external costs in addition to their private costs.

The market equilibrium outcome in the presence of a Pigovian tax is the same as the socially optimal and surplus-maximizing outcome. We saw in Chapter 8 that when taxes are imposed in a market that is otherwise free of market failure, these taxes can result in a deadweight loss on society. Here we see that when taxes are imposed in a market that already suffers from a deadweight loss due to market failure, they can actually improve social welfare (as well as raise revenue for the government). Later in this chapter we consider other ways in which policymakers can deal with externalities.

internalize the externality
alter incentives so that people take account of the external effects of their actions

Pigovian taxes
taxes enacted to correct the effects of negative externalities

Positive Externalities

Although some activities impose costs on third parties, others yield benefits. For example, consider education. Education yields positive externalities because a more educated population leads to better government, which benefits everyone. Notice that the productivity benefit of education is not necessarily an externality: The consumer of education reaps most of the benefit in the form of higher wages. But if some of the productivity benefits of education spill over and benefit other people, then this effect would count as a positive externality as well.

The analysis of positive externalities is similar to the analysis of negative externalities. As Figure 10.4 shows, the demand curve does not reflect the value to society of the good. Because the social value is greater than the private value, the social-value curve lies above the demand curve. The optimal quantity is found where the social-value curve and the supply curve (which represents costs) intersect. Hence, the socially optimal quantity is greater than the quantity determined by the private market.

Once again, the government can correct the market failure by inducing market participants to internalize the externality. The appropriate response in the case of positive externalities is exactly the opposite to the case of negative externalities. To move the market equilibrium closer to the social optimum, a positive externality requires a subsidy. In fact, that is exactly the policy the government follows: Education is heavily subsidized through public schools and government scholarships.

To summarize: *Negative externalities lead markets to produce a larger quantity than is socially desirable. Positive externalities lead markets to produce a smaller quantity than is socially desirable. To remedy the problem, the government can internalize the externality by taxing goods that have negative externalities and subsidizing goods that have positive externalities.*

FIGURE 10.4

Education and the Social Optimum

In the presence of a positive externality, the social value of the good exceeds the private value. The optimal quantity, $Q_{OPTIMUM}$, is therefore larger than the equilibrium quantity, Q_{MARKET}.

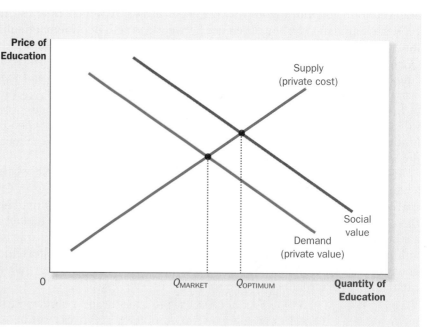

Case Study

TECHNOLOGY SPILLOVERS AND INDUSTRIAL POLICY

Consider the market for industrial robots. Robots are at the frontier of a rapidly changing technology. Whenever a firm builds a robot, there is some chance that the firm will discover a new and better design. This new design will benefit not only this firm but society as a whole because the design will enter society's pool of technological knowledge. This type of positive externality is called a *technology spillover.*

In this case, the government can internalize the externality by subsidizing the production of robots. If the government paid firms a subsidy for each robot produced, the supply curve would shift down by the amount of the subsidy, and this shift would increase the equilibrium quantity of robots. To ensure that the market equilibrium equals the social optimum, the subsidy should equal the value of the technology spillover.

How large are technology spillovers, and what do they imply for public policy? This is an important question, because technological progress is the key to why living standards rise over time. Yet it is also a difficult question on which economists often disagree.

Some economists believe that technology spillovers are pervasive and that the government should encourage those industries that yield the largest spillovers. For instance, these economists argue that if making computer chips yields greater spillovers than making potato chips, then the government should use the tax laws to encourage the production of more computer chips relative to potato chips. Government intervention in the economy that aims to promote technology-enhancing industries is sometimes called *industrial policy.*

Other economists are skeptical about industrial policy. Even if technology spillovers are common, the success of an industrial policy requires that the government be able to measure the size of the spillovers from different markets. This measurement problem is difficult at best. Moreover, without precise measurements, the political system may end up subsidizing those industries with the most political clout, rather than those that yield the largest positive externalities.

Another way to deal with technology spillovers is patent protection. The patent laws protect inventors by giving them exclusive rights to their inventions for a period of time. When a firm makes a technological breakthrough, it can patent the idea and capture much of the economic benefit for itself. The patent is said to internalize the externality by giving the firm a *property right* over its invention. If other firms want to use the new technology, they would have to obtain permission from the inventing firm and pay it some royalty. Thus, the patent system gives firms a greater incentive to engage in research and other activities that advance technology. ●

QuickQuiz Give an example of a negative externality and a positive externality.
• Explain why market outcomes are inefficient in the presence of externalities.

PRIVATE SOLUTIONS TO EXTERNALITIES

We have discussed why externalities lead markets to allocate resources inefficiently, but have mentioned only briefly how this inefficiency can be remedied. In practice, both private actors and public policymakers respond to externalities in various ways. All of the remedies share the goal of moving the allocation of resources closer to the social optimum. In this section we examine private solutions.

The Types of Private Solutions

Although externalities tend to cause markets to be inefficient, government action is not always needed to solve the problem. In some circumstances, people can develop private solutions.

Sometimes, the problem of externalities is solved with moral codes and social sanctions. Consider, for instance, why most people do not litter. Although there are laws against littering, these laws are not vigorously enforced. Most people do not litter just because it is the wrong thing to do. The Golden Rule taught to most children says, "Do unto others as you would have them do unto you." This moral injunction tells us to take account of how our actions affect other people. In economic terms, it tells us to internalize externalities.

Another private solution to externalities is charities, many of which are established to deal with externalities. For example, Greenpeace, whose goal is to protect the environment, is a nonprofit organization funded with private donations. As another example, colleges and universities receive gifts from alumni, corporations, and foundations in part because education has positive externalities for society.

The private market can often solve the problem of externalities by relying on the self-interest of the relevant parties. Sometimes the solution takes the form of integrating different types of business. For example, consider an apple grower and a beekeeper who are located next to each other. Each business confers a positive externality on the other: By pollinating the flowers on the trees, the bees help the orchard produce apples. At the same time, the bees use the nectar they get from the apple trees to produce honey. Nonetheless, when the apple grower is deciding how many trees to plant and the beekeeper is deciding how many bees to keep, they neglect the positive externality. As a result, the apple grower plants too few trees and the beekeeper keeps too few bees. These externalities could be internalized if the beekeeper bought the apple orchard or if the apple grower bought the beehives: Both activities would then take place within the same firm, and this single firm could choose the optimal number of trees and bees. Internalizing externalities is one reason that some firms are involved in different types of business.

Another way for the private market to deal with external effects is for the interested parties to enter into a contract. In the foregoing example, a contract between the apple grower and the beekeeper can solve the problem of too few trees and too few bees. The contract can specify the number of trees, the number of bees, and perhaps a payment from one party to the other. By setting the right number of trees and bees, the contract can solve the inefficiency that normally arises from these externalities and make both parties better off.

The Coase Theorem

How effective is the private market in dealing with externalities? A famous result, called the **Coase theorem** after economist Ronald Coase, suggests that it can be very effective in some circumstances. According to the Coase theorem, if private parties can bargain without cost over the allocation of resources, then the private market will always solve the problem of externalities and allocate resources efficiently.

To see how the Coase theorem works, consider an example. Suppose that Dick owns a dog named Spot. Spot barks and disturbs Jane, Dick's neighbour. Dick gets a benefit from owning the dog, but the dog confers a negative externality on Jane. Should Dick be forced to send Spot to the pound, or should Jane have to suffer sleepless nights because of Spot's barking?

Consider first what outcome is socially efficient. A social planner, considering the two alternatives, would compare the benefit that Dick gets from the dog to the cost that Jane bears from the barking. If the benefit exceeds the cost, it is efficient for Dick to keep the dog and for Jane to live with the barking. Yet if the cost exceeds the benefit, then Dick should get rid of the dog.

According to the Coase theorem, the private market will reach the efficient outcome on its own. How? Jane can simply offer to pay Dick to get rid of the dog. Dick will accept the deal if the amount of money Jane offers is greater than the benefit of keeping the dog.

By bargaining over the price, Dick and Jane can always reach the efficient outcome. For instance, suppose that Dick gets a $500 benefit from the dog and Jane bears an $800 cost from the barking. In this case, Jane can offer Dick $600 to get rid of the dog, and Dick will gladly accept. Both parties are better off than they were before, and the efficient outcome is reached.

It is possible, of course, that Jane would not be willing to offer any price that Dick would accept. For instance, suppose that Dick gets a $1000 benefit from the dog and Jane bears an $800 cost from the barking. In this case, Dick would turn down any offer below $1000, while Jane would not offer any amount above $800. Therefore, Dick ends up keeping the dog. Given these costs and benefits, however, this outcome is efficient.

So far, we have assumed that Dick has the legal right to keep a barking dog. In other words, we have assumed that Dick can keep Spot unless Jane pays him enough to induce him to give up the dog voluntarily. How different would the outcome be, on the other hand, if Jane had the legal right to peace and quiet?

According to the Coase theorem, the initial distribution of rights does not matter for the market's ability to reach the efficient outcome. For instance, suppose that Jane can legally compel Dick to get rid of the dog. Although having this right works to Jane's advantage, it probably will not change the outcome. In this case, Dick can offer to pay Jane to allow him to keep the dog. If the benefit of the dog to Dick exceeds the cost of the barking to Jane, then Dick and Jane will strike a bargain in which Dick keeps the dog.

Although Dick and Jane can reach the efficient outcome regardless of how rights are initially distributed, the distribution of rights is not irrelevant: It determines the distribution of economic well-being. Whether Dick has the right to a barking dog or Jane the right to peace and quiet determines who pays whom in the final bargain. But, in either case, the two parties can bargain with each other

Coase theorem
the proposition that if private parties can bargain without cost over the allocation of resources, they can solve the problem of externalities on their own

and solve the externality problem. Dick will end up keeping the dog only if the benefit exceeds the cost.

To sum up: *The Coase theorem says that private economic actors can solve the problem of externalities among themselves. Whatever the initial distribution of rights, the interested parties can always reach a bargain in which everyone is better off and the outcome is efficient.*

Why Private Solutions Do Not Always Work

Despite the appealing logic of the Coase theorem, private actors on their own often fail to resolve the problems caused by externalities. The Coase theorem applies only when the interested parties have no trouble reaching and enforcing an agreement. In the world, however, bargaining does not always work, even when a mutually beneficial agreement is possible.

transaction costs
the costs that parties incur in the process of agreeing and following through on a bargain

Sometimes the interested parties fail to solve an externality problem because of **transaction costs,** the costs that parties incur in the process of agreeing to and following through on a bargain. In our example, imagine that Dick and Jane speak different languages so that, to reach an agreement, they will need to hire a translator. If the benefit of solving the barking problem is less than the cost of the translator, Dick and Jane might choose to leave the problem unsolved. In more realistic examples, the transaction costs are the expenses not of translators but of the lawyers required to draft and enforce contracts.

At other times, bargaining simply breaks down. The recurrence of wars and labour strikes shows that reaching agreement can be difficult and that failing to reach agreement can be costly. The problem is often that each party tries to hold out for a better deal. For example, suppose that Dick gets a $500 benefit from the dog, and Jane bears an $800 cost from the barking. Although it is efficient for Jane to pay Dick to get rid of the dog, there are many prices that could lead to this outcome. Dick might demand $750, and Jane might offer only $550. As they haggle over the price, the inefficient outcome with the barking dog persists.

Reaching an efficient bargain is especially difficult when the number of interested parties is large because coordinating everyone is costly. For example, consider a factory that pollutes the water of a nearby lake. The pollution confers a negative externality on the local fishermen. According to the Coase theorem, if the pollution is inefficient, then the factory and the fishermen could reach a bargain in which the fishermen pay the factory not to pollute. If there are many fishermen, however, trying to coordinate them all to bargain with the factory may be almost impossible.

When private bargaining does not work, the government can sometimes play a role. The government is an institution designed for collective action. In this example, the government can act on behalf of the fishermen, even when it is impractical for the fishermen to act for themselves. In the next section, we examine how the government can try to remedy the problem of externalities.

QuickQuiz Give an example of a private solution to an externality. • What is the Coase theorem? • Why are private economic actors sometimes unable to solve the problems caused by an externality?

PUBLIC POLICIES TOWARD EXTERNALITIES

When an externality causes a market to reach an inefficient allocation of resources, the government can respond in one of two ways. *Command-and-control policies* regulate behaviour directly. *Market-based policies* provide incentives so that private decision makers will choose to solve the problem on their own.

Regulation

The government can remedy an externality by making certain behaviours either required or forbidden. For example, it is a crime to dump poisonous chemicals into the water supply. In this case, the external costs to society far exceed the benefits to the polluter. The government therefore institutes a command-and-control policy that prohibits this act altogether.

In most cases of pollution, however, the situation is not this simple. Despite the stated goals of some environmentalists, it would be impossible to prohibit all polluting activity. For example, virtually all forms of transportation—even the horse—produce some undesirable polluting byproducts. But it would not be sensible for the government to ban all transportation. Thus, instead of trying to eradicate pollution altogether, society has to weigh the costs and benefits to decide the kinds and quantities of pollution it will allow. In Canada, environmental policy is shared among all three levels of government—federal, provincial, and municipal. At the federal level, Environment Canada is the department responsible for developing and enforcing regulations aimed at protecting the environment.

Environmental regulations can take many forms. Sometimes Environment Canada dictates a maximum level of pollution that a factory may emit. Other times Environment Canada requires that firms adopt a particular technology to reduce emissions. In all cases, to design good rules, the government regulators need to know the details about specific industries and about the alternative technologies that those industries could adopt. This information is often difficult for government regulators to obtain.

Pigovian Taxes and Subsidies

Instead of regulating behaviour in response to an externality, the government can use market-based policies to align private incentives with social efficiency. For instance, as we saw earlier, the government can internalize the externality by imposing Pigovian taxes on activities that have negative externalities and subsidizing activities that have positive externalities.

Economists usually prefer Pigovian taxes over regulations as a way to deal with pollution because such taxes can reduce pollution at a lower cost to society. To see why, let us consider an example.

Suppose that two factories—a paper mill and a steel mill—are each dumping 500 tonnes of glop into a river each year. Environment Canada decides that it wants to reduce the amount of pollution. It considers two solutions:

1. Regulation: Environment Canada could tell each factory to reduce its pollution to 300 tonnes of glop per year.

2. Pigovian tax: Environment Canada could levy a tax on each factory of $50 000 for each tonne of glop it emits.

The regulation would dictate a level of pollution, whereas the tax would give factory owners an economic incentive to reduce pollution. Which solution do you think is better?

Most economists would prefer the tax. They would first point out that a tax is just as effective as a regulation in reducing the overall level of pollution. Environment Canada can achieve whatever level of pollution it wants by setting the tax at the appropriate level. The higher the tax, the larger the reduction in pollution. Indeed, if the tax is high enough, the factories will close down altogether, reducing pollution to zero.

The reason why economists would prefer the tax is that it reduces pollution more efficiently. The regulation requires each factory to reduce pollution by the same amount, but an equal reduction is not necessarily the least expensive way to clean up the water. It is possible that the paper mill can reduce pollution at lower cost than the steel mill. If so, the paper mill would respond to the tax by reducing pollution substantially to avoid the tax, whereas the steel mill would respond by reducing pollution less and paying the tax.

In essence, the Pigovian tax places a price on the right to pollute. Just as markets allocate goods to those buyers who value them most highly, a Pigovian tax allocates pollution to those factories that face the highest cost of reducing it. Whatever the level of pollution Environment Canada chooses, it can achieve this goal at the lowest total cost using a tax.

Economists also argue that Pigovian taxes are better for the environment. Under the command-and-control policy of regulation, the factories have no reason to reduce emission further once they have reached the target of 300 tonnes of glop. By contrast, the tax gives the factories an incentive to develop cleaner technologies, because a cleaner technology would reduce the amount of tax the factory has to pay.

Pigovian taxes are unlike most other taxes. As we discussed in Chapter 8, most taxes distort incentives and move the allocation of resources away from the social optimum. The reduction in economic well-being—that is, in consumer and producer surplus—exceeds the amount of revenue the government raises, resulting in a deadweight loss. By contrast, when externalities are present, society also cares about the well-being of the bystanders who are affected. Pigovian taxes correct incentives for the presence of externalities and thereby move the allocation of resources closer to the social optimum. Thus, while Pigovian taxes raise revenue for the government, they also enhance economic efficiency.

Case Study

WHY IS GASOLINE TAXED SO HEAVILY?

In many countries, gasoline is among the most heavily taxed goods in the economy. In Canada, for instance, half of what drivers pay for gasoline goes to the gas tax. In many European countries, the tax is even larger, and the price of gasoline is three or four times the Canadian price.

"If the gas tax were any larger, I'd take the bus."

Why is this tax so common? One possible answer is that the gas tax is a Pigovian tax aimed at correcting three negative externalities associated with driving:

1. *Congestion:* If you have ever been stuck in bumper-to-bumper traffic, you have probably wished that there were fewer cars on the road. A gasoline tax keeps congestion down by encouraging people to take public transportation, carpool more often, and live closer to work.
2. *Accidents:* Whenever a person buys a large car or a sport utility vehicle, he makes himself safer, but he puts his neighbours at risk. A person driving a typical car is much more likely to die if hit by a sport utility vehicle than if hit by another car. The gas tax is an indirect way of making people pay when their large, gas-guzzling vehicles impose risk on others, which in turn makes them take account of this risk when choosing what vehicle to purchase.
3. *Pollution:* The burning of fossil fuels such as gasoline is widely believed to be the cause of global warming. Experts disagree about how dangerous this threat is, but there is no doubt that the gas tax reduces the risk by reducing the use of gasoline.

So the gas tax, rather than causing deadweight losses like most taxes, could actually make the economy work better. It means less traffic congestion, safer roads, and a cleaner environment. Having said this, there is little evidence that the taxes actually levied on gasoline in Canada reflect concerns related to the negative externalities associated with driving. More likely, these taxes are imposed simply to raise revenue for the government. ●

Tradable Pollution Permits

Returning to our example of the paper mill and the steel mill, let us suppose that, despite the advice of its economists, Environment Canada adopts the regulation and requires each factory to reduce its pollution to 300 tonnes of glop per year. Then one day, after the regulation is in place and both mills have complied, the two firms go to Environment Canada with a proposal. The steel mill wants to increase its emission of glop by 100 tonnes. The paper mill has agreed to reduce its emission by the same amount if the steel mill pays it $5 million. Should Environment Canada allow the two factories to make this deal?

From the standpoint of economic efficiency, allowing the deal is good policy. The deal must make the owners of the two factories better off, because they are voluntarily agreeing to it. Moreover, the deal does not have any external effects because the total amount of pollution remains the same. Thus, social welfare is enhanced by allowing the paper mill to sell its right to pollute to the steel mill.

The same logic applies to any voluntary transfer of the right to pollute from one firm to another. If Environment Canada allows firms to make these deals, it will, in essence, have created a new scarce resource: pollution permits. A market to trade these permits will eventually develop, and that market will be governed by the forces of supply and demand. The invisible hand will ensure that this new market efficiently allocates the right to pollute. The firms that can reduce pollution only at high cost will be willing to pay the most for the pollution permits. The firms that can reduce pollution at low cost will prefer to sell whatever permits they have.

One advantage of allowing a market for pollution permits is that the initial allocation of pollution permits among firms does not matter from the standpoint of economic efficiency. The logic behind this conclusion is similar to that behind the Coase theorem. Those firms that can reduce pollution most easily would be willing to sell whatever permits they get, and those firms that can reduce pollution only at high cost would be willing to buy whatever permits they need. As long as there is a free market for the pollution rights, the final allocation will be efficient whatever the initial allocation.

Although reducing pollution using pollution permits may seem quite different from using Pigovian taxes, in fact the two policies have much in common. In both cases, firms pay for their pollution. With Pigovian taxes, polluting firms must pay a tax to the government. With pollution permits, polluting firms must pay to buy the permit. (Even firms that already own permits must pay to pollute: The opportunity cost of polluting is what they could have received by selling their permits on the open market.) Both Pigovian taxes and pollution permits internalize the externality of pollution by making it costly for firms to pollute.

The similarity of the two policies can be seen by considering the market for pollution. Both panels in Figure 10.5 show the demand curve for the right to pollute.

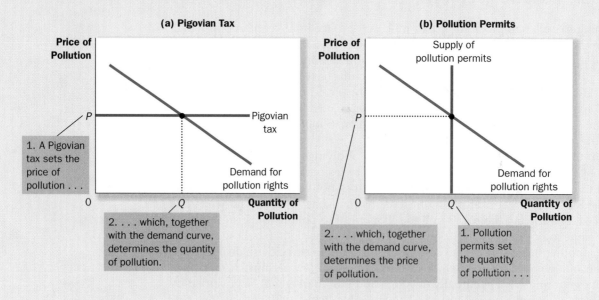

FIGURE 10.5

The Equivalence of Pigovian Taxes and Pollution Permits

In panel (a), Environment Canada sets a price on pollution by levying a Pigovian tax, and the demand curve determines the quantity of pollution. In panel (b), Environment Canada limits the quantity of pollution by limiting the number of pollution permits, and the demand curve determines the price of pollution. The price and quantity of pollution are the same in the two cases.

This curve shows that the lower the price of polluting, the more firms will choose to pollute. In panel (a), Environment Canada uses a Pigovian tax to set a price for pollution. In this case, the supply curve for pollution rights is perfectly elastic (because firms can pollute as much as they want by paying the tax), and the position of the demand curve determines the quantity of pollution. In panel (b), Environment Canada sets a quantity of pollution by issuing pollution permits. In this case, the supply curve for pollution rights is perfectly inelastic (because the quantity of pollution is fixed by the number of permits), and the position of the demand curve determines the price of pollution. Hence, for any given demand curve for pollution, Environment Canada can achieve any point on the demand curve either by setting a price with a Pigovian tax or by setting a quantity with pollution permits.

In some circumstances, however, selling pollution permits may be better than levying a Pigovian tax. Suppose Environment Canada wants no more than 600 tonnes of glop to be dumped into the river. But, because Environment Canada does not know the demand curve for pollution, it is not sure what size tax would achieve that goal. In this case, it can simply auction off 600 pollution permits. The auction price would yield the appropriate size of the Pigovian tax.

The idea of the government auctioning off the right to pollute may at first sound like a figment of some economist's imagination. And, in fact, that is how the idea began. But increasingly pollution permits, like Pigovian taxes, are now widely viewed as a cost-effective way to keep the environment clean.

Objections to the Economic Analysis of Pollution

Many environmentalists object to the use of pollution permits and other market-based solutions to pollution on the grounds that it is simply not right to allow someone to pollute for a fee. Clean air and clean water, they argue, are fundamental human rights that should not be debased by considering them in economic terms. How can you put a price on clean air and clean water? The environment is so important, they claim, that we should protect it as much as possible, regardless of the cost.

Economists have little sympathy with this type of argument. To economists, good environmental policy begins by acknowledging the first of the ten principles of economics in Chapter 1: People face tradeoffs. Certainly, clean air and clean water have value. But their value must be compared to their opportunity cost— that is, to what one must give up to obtain them. Eliminating all pollution is impossible. Trying to eliminate all pollution would reverse many of the technological advances that allow us to enjoy a high standard of living. Few people would be willing to accept poor nutrition, inadequate medical care, or shoddy housing to make the environment as clean as possible.

Economists argue that some environmental activists hurt their own cause by not thinking in economic terms. A clean environment is a good like other goods. Like all normal goods, it has a positive income elasticity: Rich countries can afford a cleaner environment than poor ones and, therefore, usually have more rigorous environmental protection. In addition, like most other goods, clean air and water obey the law of demand: The lower the price of environmental protection, the more the public will want. The economic approach of using pollution permits and Pigovian taxes reduces the cost of environmental protection and should, therefore, increase the public's demand for a clean environment.

IN THE NEWS

IMPLEMENTING KYOTO

In December of 2002 Canada ratified the Kyoto Protocol, which commits the country to reducing greenhouse gas emissions to 6 percent below 1990 levels by 2012. Ratification of the protocol has been controversial. The following article argues that whether you agree with it or not, we need to think carefully about how the protocol is implemented.

Kyoto's Empty Black Box

By William Watson

Suspend disbelief for a moment. Suppose the Kyoto Protocol on the environment is a good thing and that adhering to it would bring net benefits for Canada and the world. Even if you buy all that, the problem remains of how best to implement it. That's the problem Peter Kennedy, an economist at the University of Victoria, takes on in a paper in a recent issue of the *Canadian Journal of Economics*. He concludes that the wrong decision could impose billions of dollars in unnecessary costs.

Professor Kennedy distinguishes between "technological abatement" and "behavioural abatement." Technological abatement occurs when we figure out how to reduce the environmental damage per unit of benefit delivered: If someone develops a more efficient boiler, we can use less fuel and therefore create fewer emissions per gallon of hot water used. By contrast, behavioural abatement means taking fewer showers, shorter showers or cooler showers. It's tempting to think of technological abatement as good abatement, since we don't have to change our lifestyle, and behavioural abatement as bad, since we do have to change, but of course that depends on how much each costs.

The Kyoto agreement requires that we hit our declared targets by 2112. But since we're currently 36% above them, common sense suggests we should consider taking what has come to be known as "early action." In fact, Mr. Kennedy argues, common sense may be wrong. It all depends what kind of early action you have in mind. Is it doing research and development that will help prepare future technological abatement? Modifying capital equipment by making investments now, using existing technology? Or encouraging behavioural adjustment today, thus trimming output and emissions right away?

When you take the trade-offs among the three types of action into account,

QuickQuiz A glue factory and a steel mill emit smoke containing a chemical that is harmful if inhaled in large amounts. Describe three ways the town government might respond to this externality. What are the pros and cons of each of your solutions?

CONCLUSION

The invisible hand is powerful but not omnipotent. A market's equilibrium maximizes the sum of producer and consumer surplus. When the buyers and sellers in the market are the only interested parties, this outcome is efficient from the

the best "early action" may not involve early reductions in emissions. You may well get a bigger payoff from R&D that makes later technological abatement possible. Not cutting emissions as soon as possible may seem disloyal to the spirit of Kyoto. On the other hand, Canada produces just 3% of the world's greenhouse gases, so our getting half a decade ahead in the reduction game isn't going to have much effect on global warming especially if it jeopardizes later progress.

What kinds of policies would lead to the most efficient combination of R&D and immediate action? Market-oriented economists will be glad to hear that Mr. Kennedy's calculations suggest a system of tradable emissions permits will do the job nicely. Make companies buy permits for the emissions they produce and that creates a financial incentive for them to find ways of reducing their emissions, a job which, since they understand their operations better than anyone else does, they'll do much better than some central planner who tries to do it for them. And even if they don't have to start buying permits until 2008, they'll start planning now. Businesses, especially big ones, are always looking ahead.

The increasingly popular alternative of an early cap-and-trade program, which would set pre-Kyoto targets and let companies, countries and individuals trade permits back and forth, could easily put too high a premium on early emissions reductions, to the detriment of early R&D. Moreover, Mr. Kennedy writes, as is always the case with such programs, "calculating the right cap with any precision in practice requires more knowledge about marginal abatement costs than the regulator can hope to have."

For its part, the much-touted "credit for early action" would similarly tilt the incentives too much in the direction of early rather than later reductions. In fact, like any subsidy program, it might even cause companies to increase their emissions in the short term, so as to maximize the credit they get for then reducing them.

Where a standard permit-trading program breaks down is when there are immediate environmental benefits from early emissions reductions. As mentioned, because Canada is a bit player, any global warming benefits would be negligible. But if there are collateral benefits in terms of particulate reductions

and so on, traditional emissions taxes could encourage those before the Kyoto permit scheme kicked in.

Mr. Kennedy calculates that the cost of getting the incentive structures wrong could be as high as $5 billion. What he does not do, unfortunately, is calculate "the optimal early action strategy for the Canadian economy." His reason? Environment ministers take note: "There are not enough data available to conduct such an exercise."

Nor does he say whether even a carefully designed Kyoto permit system would be a good thing or a bad thing for Canada, or the world. In determining the right amount of emissions, the goal is to set the limit where the market price of permits will be just equal to the environmental damage done by the extra unit of emissions. That's easy enough to say or write. In principle, the calculations can be done. In practice, they are horrifically complicated.

Source: *National Post*, April 3, 2002, p. FP19. Material reprinted with the express permission of "The National Post Company," a CanWest Partnership.

standpoint of society as a whole. But when there are external effects, such as pollution, evaluating a market outcome requires taking into account the well-being of third parties as well. In this case, the invisible hand of the marketplace may fail to allocate resources efficiently.

In some cases, people can solve the problem of externalities on their own. The Coase theorem suggests that the interested parties can bargain among themselves and agree on an efficient solution. Sometimes, however, an efficient outcome cannot be reached, perhaps because the large number of interested parties makes bargaining difficult.

When people cannot solve the problem of externalities privately, the government often steps in. Yet, even now, society should not abandon market forces entirely. Rather, the government can address the problem by requiring decision makers to bear the full costs of their actions. Pigovian taxes on emissions and pollution permits, for instance, are designed to internalize the externality of pollution. More and more, they are the policy of choice for those interested in protecting the environment. Market forces, properly redirected, are often the best remedy for market failure.

SUMMARY

- When a transaction between a buyer and seller directly affects a third party, the effect is called an externality. Negative externalities, such as pollution, cause the socially optimal quantity in a market to be less than the equilibrium quantity. Positive externalities, such as technology spillovers, cause the socially optimal quantity to be greater than the equilibrium quantity.

- Those affected by externalities can sometimes solve the problem privately. For instance, when one business confers an externality on another business, the two businesses can internalize the externality by merging. Alternatively, the interested parties can solve the problem by negotiating a contract. According to the Coase theorem, if people can bargain without cost, then

they can always reach an agreement in which resources are allocated efficiently. In many cases, however, reaching a bargain among the many interested parties is difficult, so the Coase theorem does not apply.

- When private parties cannot adequately deal with external effects, such as pollution, the government often steps in. Sometimes the government prevents socially inefficient activity by regulating behaviour. Other times it internalizes an externality using Pigovian taxes. Another public policy is to issue permits. For instance, the government could protect the environment by issuing a limited number of pollution permits. The end result of this policy is largely the same as imposing Pigovian taxes on polluters.

KEY CONCEPTS

externality, p. 204
internalize the externality,
   p. 209

Pigovian taxes, p. 209
Coase theorem, p. 213

transaction costs, p. 214

QUESTIONS FOR REVIEW

1. Give an example of a negative externality and an example of a positive externality.

2. Use a supply-and-demand diagram to explain the effect of a negative externality in production.

3. In what way does the patent system help society solve an externality problem?

4. List some of the ways that the problems caused by externalities can be solved without government intervention.

5. Imagine that you are a nonsmoker sharing a room with a smoker. According to the Coase theorem, what determines whether your roommate smokes in the room? Is this outcome efficient? How do you and your roommate reach this solution?

6. What are Pigovian taxes? Why do economists prefer them over regulations as a way to protect the environment from pollution?

PROBLEMS AND APPLICATIONS

1. There are two ways to protect your car from theft. The Club makes it difficult for a car thief to take your car. LoJack makes it easier for the police to catch a car thief. Which of these types of protection conveys a negative externality on other car owners? Which conveys a positive externality? Do you think there are any policy implications of your analysis?

2. Do you agree with the following statements? Why or why not?
   a. "The benefits of Pigovian taxes as a way to reduce pollution have to be weighed against the deadweight losses that these taxes cause."
   b. "When deciding whether to levy a Pigovian tax on consumers or producers, the government should be careful to levy the tax on the side of the market generating the externality."

3. Consider the market for fire extinguishers.
   a. Why might fire extinguishers exhibit positive externalities?
   b. Draw a graph of the market for fire extinguishers, labelling the demand curve, the social-value curve, the supply curve, and the social-cost curve.
   c. Indicate the market equilibrium level of output and the efficient level of output. Give an intuitive explanation for why these quantities differ.
   d. If the external benefit is $10 per extinguisher, describe a government policy that would result in the efficient outcome.

4. Contributions to charitable organizations are deductible under the federal income tax. In what way does this government policy encourage private solutions to externalities?

5. Ringo loves playing rock-and-roll music at high volume. Luciano loves opera and hates rock-and-roll. Unfortunately, they are next-door neighbours in an apartment building with paper-thin walls.
   a. What is the externality here?

   b. What command-and-control policy might the landlord impose? Could such a policy lead to an inefficient outcome?
   c. Suppose the landlord lets the tenants do whatever they want. According to the Coase theorem, how might Ringo and Luciano reach an efficient outcome on their own? What might prevent them from reaching an efficient outcome?

6. It is rumoured that the Swiss government subsidizes cattle farming, and that the subsidy is larger in areas with more tourist attractions. Can you think of a reason why this policy might be efficient?

7. Greater consumption of alcohol leads to more motor vehicle accidents and, thus, imposes costs on people who do not drink and drive.
   a. Illustrate the market for alcohol, labelling the demand curve, the social-value curve, the supply curve, the social-cost curve, the market equilibrium level of output, and the efficient level of output.
   b. On your graph, shade the area corresponding to the deadweight loss of the market equilibrium. (Hint: The deadweight loss occurs because some units of alcohol are consumed for which the social cost exceeds the social value.) Explain.

8. Many observers believe that the levels of pollution in our economy are too high.
   a. If society wishes to reduce overall pollution by a certain amount, why is it efficient to have different amounts of reduction at different firms?
   b. Command-and-control approaches often rely on uniform reductions among firms. Why are these approaches generally unable to target the firms that should undertake larger reductions?
   c. Economists argue that appropriate Pigovian taxes or tradable pollution rights will result in efficient pollution reduction. How do these approaches target the firms that should undertake larger reductions?

9. The Pristine River has two polluting firms on its banks. Acme Industrial and Creative Chemicals each dump 100 tonnes of glop into the river each year. The cost of reducing glop emissions per tonne equals $10 for Acme and $100 for Creative. The local government wants to reduce overall pollution from 200 tonnes to 50 tonnes.
   a. If the government knew the cost of reduction for each firm, what reductions would it impose to reach its overall goal? What would be the cost to each firm and the total cost to the firms together?
   b. In a more typical situation, the government would not know the cost of pollution reduction at each firm. If the government decided to reach its overall goal by imposing uniform reductions on the firms, calculate the reduction made by each firm, the cost to each firm, and the total cost to the firms together.
   c. Compare the total cost of pollution reduction in parts (a) and (b). If the government does not know the cost of reduction for each firm, is there still some way for it to reduce pollution to 50 tonnes at the total cost you calculated in part (a)? Explain.

10. "A fine is a tax for doing something wrong. A tax is a fine for doing something right." Discuss.

11. Figure 10.5 shows that for any given demand curve for the right to pollute, the government can achieve the same outcome either by setting a price with a Pigovian tax or by setting a quantity with pollution permits. Suppose there is a sharp improvement in the technology for controlling pollution.
   a. Using graphs similar to those in Figure 10.5, illustrate the effect of this development on the demand for pollution rights.
   b. What is the effect on the price and quantity of pollution under each regulatory system? Explain.

12. Suppose that the government decides to issue tradable permits for a certain form of pollution.

   a. Does it matter for economic efficiency whether the government distributes or auctions the permits? Does it matter in any other ways?
   b. If the government chooses to distribute the permits, does the allocation of permits among firms matter for efficiency? Does it matter in any other ways?

13. The primary cause of global warming is carbon dioxide, which enters the atmosphere in varying amounts from different countries but is distributed equally around the globe within a year. In 1997, as part of an international environmental agreement reached in Kyoto, Japan, Canada made a "commitment" to reduce carbon dioxide and other greenhouse gases to 6 percent below 1990 levels by 2012. In December of 2002 the federal government formally ratified the Kyoto Protocol. Some people have criticized this type of international agreement. They argue that emissions should be reduced in countries where the costs are lowest, and that the countries that bear the cost of these reductions should be compensated by the rest of the world.
   a. Why is international cooperation necessary to reach an efficient outcome?
   b. Is it possible to devise a compensation scheme such that all countries would be better off than under a system of uniform emission reductions? Explain.

14. Some people object to market-based policies to reduce pollution, claiming that they place a dollar value on cleaning our air and water. Economists reply that society *implicitly* places a dollar value on environmental cleanup even under command-and-control policies. Discuss why this is true.

15. (This problem is challenging.) There are three industrial firms in Happy Valley.

Firm	Initial Pollution Level	Cost of Reducing Pollution by 1 Unit
A	70 units	$20
B	80	25
C	50	10

The government wants to reduce pollution to 120 units, so it gives each firm 40 tradable pollution permits.

a. Who sells permits and how many do they sell? Who buys permits and how many do they buy? Briefly explain why the sellers and buyers are each willing to do so. What is the total cost of pollution reduction in this situation?

b. How much higher would the costs of pollution reduction be if the permits could not be traded?

INTERNET RESOURCES

- Environment Canada's website is at http://www.ec.gc.ca.

- The Intergovernmental Panel on Climate Change (IPCC) was established in 1988 by the World Meteorological Organization and the United Nations to assess the scientific and socioeconomic information relevant to human-induced climate change. The IPCC web site is at http://www.ipcc.ch.

- David R. Boyd, Eco-Research Chair of Environmental Law and Policy, University of Victoria, provides useful data on how Canada stacks up according to various environmental indicators in *Canada vs. the OECD: An Environmental Comparison*, at http://www.environmentalindicators.com.

http://

For more study tools, please visit http://www.mankiw3e.nelson.com.

11

Learning Objectives

In this chapter, you will …

- Learn the defining characteristics of public goods and common resources
- Examine why private markets fail to provide public goods
- Consider some of the important public goods in our economy
- See why the cost–benefit analysis of public goods is both necessary and difficult
- Examine why people tend to use common resources too much
- Consider some of the important common resources in our economy

PUBLIC GOODS AND COMMON RESOURCES

An old song lyric maintains that "the best things in life are free." A moment's thought reveals a long list of goods that the songwriter could have had in mind. Nature provides some of them, such as rivers, mountains, beaches, lakes, and oceans. The government provides others, such as playgrounds, parks, and parades. In each case, people do not pay a fee when they choose to enjoy the benefit of the good.

Free goods provide a special challenge for economic analysis. Most goods in our economy are allocated in markets, where buyers pay for what they receive and sellers are paid for what they provide. For these goods, prices are the signals that guide the decisions of buyers and sellers. When goods are available free of charge, however, the market forces that normally allocate resources in our economy are absent.

In this chapter we examine the problems that arise for goods without market prices. Our analysis will shed light on one of the ten principles of economics in Chapter 1: Governments can sometimes improve market outcomes. When a good does not have a price attached to it, private markets cannot ensure that the good is produced and consumed in the proper amounts. In such cases, government policy can potentially remedy the market failure and raise economic well-being.

THE DIFFERENT KINDS OF GOODS

How well do markets work in providing the goods that people want? The answer to this question depends on the good being considered. As we discussed in Chapter 7, we can rely on the market to provide the efficient number of ice-cream cones: The price of ice-cream cones adjusts to balance supply and demand, and this equilibrium maximizes the sum of producer and consumer surplus. Yet, as we discussed in Chapter 10, we cannot rely on the market to prevent aluminum manufacturers from polluting the air we breathe: Buyers and sellers in a market typically do not take account of the external effects of their decisions. Thus, markets work well when the good is ice cream, but they work badly when the good is clean air.

In thinking about the various goods in the economy, it is useful to group them according to two characteristics:

1. Is the good **excludable?** Can people be prevented from using the good?
2. Is the good **rival?** Does one person's use of the good diminish another person's ability to use it?

Using these two characteristics, Figure 11.1 divides goods into four categories:

1. **Private goods** are both excludable and rival. Consider an ice-cream cone, for example. An ice-cream cone is excludable because it is possible to prevent someone from eating an ice-cream cone—you just don't give it to him. An ice-cream cone is rival because if one person eats an ice-cream cone, another

excludability
the property of a good whereby a person can be prevented from using it

rivalry
the property of a good whereby one person's use diminishes other people's use

private goods
goods that are both excludable and rival

FIGURE 11.1

Four Types of Goods

Goods can be grouped into four categories according to two questions: (1) Is the good excludable? That is, can people be prevented from using it? (2) Is the good rival? That is, does one person's use of the good diminish other people's use of it? This diagram gives examples of goods in each of the four categories.

	Rival? Yes	Rival? No
Excludable? Yes	**Private Goods** • Ice-cream cones • Clothing • Congested toll roads	**Natural Monopolies** • Fire protection • Cable TV • Uncongested toll roads
Excludable? No	**Common Resources** • Fish in the ocean • The environment • Congested nontoll roads	**Public Goods** • Tornado siren • National defence • Uncongested nontoll roads

person cannot eat the same cone. Most goods in the economy are private goods like ice-cream cones. When we analyzed supply and demand in Chapters 4, 5, and 6 and the efficiency of markets in Chapters 7, 8, and 9, we implicitly assumed that goods were both excludable and rival.

2. **Public goods** are neither excludable nor rival. That is, people cannot be prevented from using a public good, and one person's use of a public good does not reduce another person's ability to use it. For example, national defence is a public good. Once the country is defended from foreign aggressors, it is impossible to prevent any single person from enjoying the benefit of this defence. Moreover, when one person enjoys the benefit of national defence, he or she does not reduce the benefit to anyone else.

3. **Common resources** are rival but not excludable. For example, fish in the ocean are a rival good: When one person catches fish, there are fewer fish for the next person to catch. Yet these fish are not an excludable good because, given the vast size of an ocean, it is difficult to stop fishermen from taking fish out of it.

4. When a good is excludable but not rival, it is an example of a *natural monopoly*. For instance, consider fire protection in a small town. It is easy to exclude people from using this good: The fire department can just let their house burn down. Yet fire protection is not rival. Firefighters spend much of their time waiting for a fire, so protecting an extra house is unlikely to reduce the protection available to others. In other words, once a town has paid for the fire department, the additional cost of protecting one more house is small. In Chapter 15 we give a more complete definition of natural monopolies and study them in some detail.

public goods
goods that are neither excludable nor rival

common resources
goods that are rival but not excludable

In this chapter we examine goods that are not excludable and, therefore, are available to everyone free of charge: public goods and common resources. As we will see, this topic is closely related to the study of externalities. For both public goods and common resources, externalities arise because something of value has no price attached to it. If one person were to provide a public good, such as a tornado siren, other people would be better off, and yet they could not be charged for this benefit. Similarly, when one person uses a common resource, such as the fish in the ocean, other people are worse off, and yet they are not compensated for this loss. Because of these external effects, private decisions about consumption and production can lead to an inefficient allocation of resources, and government intervention can potentially raise economic well-being.

QuickQuiz Define *public goods* and *common resources,* and give an example of each.

PUBLIC GOODS

To understand how public goods differ from other goods and what problems they present for society, let's consider an example: a fireworks display. This good is not excludable because it is impossible to prevent someone from seeing fireworks, and it is not rival because one person's enjoyment of fireworks does not reduce anyone else's enjoyment of them.

The Free-Rider Problem

The citizens of Smalltown, Canada, like seeing fireworks on Canada Day. Each of the town's 500 residents places a $10 value on the experience. The cost of putting on a fireworks display is $1000. Because the $5000 of benefits exceed the $1000 of costs, it is efficient for Smalltown residents to have a fireworks display on Canada Day.

Would the private market produce the efficient outcome? Probably not. Imagine that Ellen, a Smalltown entrepreneur, decided to put on a fireworks display. Ellen would surely have trouble selling tickets to the event because her potential customers would quickly figure out that they could see the fireworks even without a ticket. Because fireworks are not excludable, people have an incentive to be free riders. A **free rider** is a person who receives the benefit of a good but avoids paying for it.

free rider
a person who receives the benefit of a good but avoids paying for it

One way to view this market failure is that it arises because of an externality. If Ellen did put on the fireworks display, she would confer an external benefit on those who saw the display without paying for it. When deciding whether to put on the display, Ellen ignores these external benefits. Even though a fireworks display is socially desirable, it is not privately profitable. As a result, Ellen makes the socially inefficient decision not to put on the display.

Although the private market fails to supply the fireworks display demanded by Smalltown residents, the solution to Smalltown's problem is obvious: The local government can sponsor a Canada Day celebration. The town council can raise everyone's taxes by $2 and use the revenue to hire Ellen to produce the fireworks. Everyone in Smalltown is better off by $8—the $10 in value from the fireworks minus the $2 tax bill. Ellen can help Smalltown reach the efficient outcome as a public employee even though she could not do so as a private entrepreneur.

The story of Smalltown is simplified, but it is also realistic. In fact, many local governments in Canada do pay for fireworks on Canada Day. Moreover, the story shows a general lesson about public goods: Because public goods are not excludable, the free-rider problem prevents the private market from supplying them. The government, however, can potentially remedy the problem. If the government decides that the total benefits exceed the costs, it can provide the public good and pay for it with tax revenue, making everyone better off.

Some Important Public Goods

There are many examples of public goods. Here we consider three of the most important.

National Defence The defence of the country from foreign aggressors is a classic example of a public good. Once the country is defended, it is impossible to prevent any single person from enjoying the benefit of this defence, which makes it nonexcludable. Moreover, when one person enjoys the benefit of national defence, he does not reduce the benefit of anyone else, which makes it nonrival.

National defence in Canada falls under the control of the federal government. In 2002 the federal government spent about $10.6 billion on national defence, or around $340 per person. While this is a lot of money, other countries spend even more. In 2002 the U.S. federal government spent a total of US$348 billion, or about US$1200 per person, on national defence. Even economists who advocate small government spending agree that national defence is a public good the government should provide, although there is some disagreement on precisely how much it should be.

Basic Research   The creation of knowledge is a public good. If a mathematician proves a new theorem, the theorem enters the general pool of knowledge that anyone can use without charge. Because knowledge is a public good, profit-seeking firms tend to free-ride on the knowledge created by others and, as a result, devote too few resources to creating new knowledge.

In evaluating the appropriate policy toward knowledge creation, it is important to distinguish general knowledge from specific, technological knowledge. Specific, technological knowledge, such as the invention of a better battery, can be patented. The inventor thus obtains much of the benefit of the invention, although certainly not all of it. By contrast, a mathematician cannot patent a theorem; such general knowledge is freely available to everyone. In other words, the patent system makes specific, technological knowledge excludable, whereas general knowledge is not excludable.

The government tries to provide the public good of general knowledge in various ways. Federal government agencies, such as the Natural Sciences and Engineering Research Council of Canada and the Social Sciences and Humanities Research Council of Canada, subsidize basic research in medicine, mathematics, physics, chemistry, biology, and even economics. Determining the appropriate level of governmental support for basic research is difficult because the benefits are hard to measure. Morover, members of Parliament who determine the funding for these sorts of programs have little expertise in science and, therefore, are not in the best position to judge what lines of research will produce the largest benefits.

Fighting Poverty   Many government programs are aimed at helping poor people. The welfare programs administered by the provinces provide some income for low-income individuals. Many municipalities provide subsidized housing for low-income families. Other benefits to low-income individuals are delivered through the tax system by means of refundable tax credits, the value of which declines as a person's income increases.

Economists disagree among themselves about what role the government should play in fighting poverty. Here we note one important argument: Advocates of antipoverty programs claim that fighting poverty is a public good.

Suppose that everyone prefers to live in a society without poverty. Even if this preference is strong and widespread, fighting poverty is not a "good" that the private market can provide. No single individual can eliminate poverty, because the problem is so large. Moreover, private charity is hard-pressed to solve the problem: People who do not donate to charity can free-ride on the generosity of others. In this case, taxing the wealthy to raise the living standards of the poor can make everyone better off. The poor are better off because they now enjoy a higher standard of living, and those paying the taxes are better off because they enjoy living in a society with less poverty.

Case Study

ARE LIGHTHOUSES PUBLIC GOODS?

What kind of good?

Some goods can switch between being public goods and being private goods depending on the circumstances. For example, a fireworks display is a public good if performed in a town with many residents. Yet if performed at a private amusement park such as Canada's Wonderland, a fireworks display is more like a private good because visitors to the park pay for admission.

Another example is a lighthouse. Economists have long used lighthouses as an example of a public good. Lighthouses are used to mark specific locations so that passing ships can avoid treacherous waters. The benefit that the lighthouse provides to the ship captain is neither excludable nor rival, so each captain has an incentive to free-ride by using the lighthouse to navigate without paying for the service. Because of this free-rider problem, private markets usually fail to provide the lighthouses that ship captains need. As a result, most lighthouses today are operated by the government.

In some cases, however, lighthouses may be closer to private goods. On the coast of England in the nineteenth century, some lighthouses were privately owned and operated. Instead of trying to charge ship captains for the service, however, the owner of the lighthouse charged the owner of the nearby port. If the port owner did not pay, the lighthouse owner turned off the light, and ships avoided that port.

In deciding whether something is a public good, one must determine the number of beneficiaries and whether these beneficiaries can be excluded from using the good. A free-rider problem arises when the number of beneficiaries is large and exclusion of any one of them is impossible. If a lighthouse benefits many ship captains, it is a public good. Yet if it primarily benefits a single port owner, it is more like a private good. ●

The government provision of *public* goods should not be confused with government provision of *private* goods. As we have seen, there may be good reason for governments to provide public goods that are not excludable and not rival. However, governments sometimes provide goods and services that display neither of these characteristics, and are closer to being private than public goods.

In some cases this can be justified as a response to some other type of market failure. For example, governments are sometimes involved in the provision of electricity, water, and other utilities. While these goods are both excludable and rival, government provision may nonetheless be justified because of other characteristics associated with these goods that make them natural monopolies. As will be discussed in Chapter 15, public ownership is one possible response to market failure due to natural monopoly.

Governments also provide some goods that are closer to private goods than public goods for other reasons not associated with efficiency. For example, public swimming pools and hockey rinks are often provided by local governments. While these goods are both excludable and rival, government provision is sometimes justified on the grounds that low-income people may not be able to afford these goods if they were left to private provision. Government provision of these goods may thus be justified on redistributive grounds, in this case redistribution in kind. While economists are virtually unanimous in their agreement that government provision of public goods is justifiable on efficiency grounds, not surprisingly there is less agreement on the desirability of government provision of private goods on redistributive grounds.

The Difficult Job of Cost–Benefit Analysis

So far we have seen that the government provides public goods because the private market on its own will not produce an efficient quantity. Yet deciding that the government must play a role is only the first step. The government must then determine what kinds of public goods to provide and in what quantities.

Suppose that the government is considering a public project, such as building a new highway. To judge whether to build the highway, it must compare the total benefits of all those who would use it to the costs of building and maintaining it. To make this decision, the government might hire a team of economists and engineers to conduct a study, called a **cost–benefit analysis,** the goal of which is to estimate the total costs and benefits of the project to society as a whole.

Cost–benefit analysts have a tough job. Because the highway will be available to everyone free of charge, there is no price with which to judge the value of the highway. Simply asking people how much they would value the highway is not reliable: Quantifying benefits is difficult using the results from a questionnaire, and respondents have little incentive to tell the truth. Those who would use the highway have an incentive to exaggerate the benefit they receive to get the highway built. Those who would be harmed by the highway have an incentive to exaggerate the costs to them to prevent the highway from being built.

The efficient provision of public goods is, therefore, intrinsically more difficult than the efficient provision of private goods. Private goods are provided in the market. Buyers of a private good reveal the value they place on it by the prices they are willing to pay. Sellers reveal their costs by the prices they are willing to accept. By contrast, cost–benefit analysts do not observe any price signals when evaluating whether the government should provide a public good. Their findings on the costs and benefits of public projects are, therefore, rough approximations at best.

cost–benefit analysis
a study that compares the costs and benefits to society of providing a public good

Case Study

HOW MUCH IS A LIFE WORTH?

Imagine that you have been elected to serve as a member of your local town council. The town engineer comes to you with a proposal: The town can spend

$10 000 to build and operate a traffic light at a town intersection that now has only a stop sign. The benefit of the traffic light is increased safety. The engineer estimates, based on data from similar intersections, that the traffic light would reduce the risk of a fatal traffic accident over the lifetime of the traffic light from 1.6 to 1.1 percent. Should you spend the money for the new light?

To answer this question, you turn to cost–benefit analysis. But you quickly run into an obstacle: The costs and benefits must be measured in the same units if you are to compare them meaningfully. The cost is measured in dollars, but the benefit—the possibility of saving a person's life—is not directly monetary. To make your decision, you have to put a dollar value on a human life.

At first, you may be tempted to conclude that a human life is priceless. After all, there is probably no amount of money that you could be paid to voluntarily give up your life or that of a loved one. This suggests that a human life has an infinite dollar value.

For the purposes of cost–benefit analysis, however, this answer leads to nonsensical results. If we truly placed an infinite value on human life, we should be placing traffic lights on every street corner. Similarly, we should all be driving large cars with all the latest safety features, instead of smaller ones with fewer safety features. Yet traffic lights are not at every corner, and people sometimes choose to buy small cars without side-impact air bags or antilock brakes. In both our public and private decisions, we are at times willing to risk our lives to save some money.

Once we have accepted the idea that a person's life does have an implicit dollar value, how can we determine what that value is? One approach, sometimes used by courts to award damages in wrongful-death suits, is to look at the total amount of money a person would have earned if he or she had lived. Economists are often critical of this approach. It has the bizarre implication that the life of a retired or disabled person has no value.

A better way to value human life is to look at the risks that people are voluntarily willing to take and how much they must be paid for taking them. Mortality risk varies across jobs, for example. Construction workers in high-rise buildings face greater risk of death on the job than office workers do. By comparing wages in risky and less risky occupations, controlling for education, experience, and other determinants of wages, economists can get some sense about what value people put on their own lives. Studies using this approach conclude that the value of a human life is about $10 million.

We can now return to our original example and respond to the town engineer. The traffic light reduces the risk of fatality by 0.5 percentage points. Thus, the expected benefit from having the traffic light is 0.005 × $10 million, or $50 000. This estimate of the benefit well exceeds the cost of $10 000, so you should approve the project. ●

QuickQuiz What is the *free-rider problem?* • Why does the free-rider problem induce the government to provide public goods? • How should the government decide whether to provide a public good?

COMMON RESOURCES

Common resources, like public goods, are not excludable: They are available free of charge to anyone who wants to use them. Common resources are, however, rival: One person's use of the common resource reduces other people's ability to use it. Thus, common resources give rise to a new problem. Once the good is provided, policymakers need to be concerned about how much it is used. This problem is best understood from the classic parable called the **Tragedy of the Commons.**

Tragedy of the Commons
a parable that illustrates why common resources get used more than is desirable from the standpoint of society as a whole

The Tragedy of the Commons

Consider life in a small medieval town. Of the many economic activities that take place in the town, one of the most important is raising sheep. Many of the town's families own flocks of sheep and support themselves by selling the sheep's wool, which is used to make clothing.

As our story begins, the sheep spend much of their time grazing on the land surrounding the town, called the Town Common. No family owns the land. Instead, the town residents own the land collectively, and all the residents are allowed to graze their sheep on it. Collective ownership works well because land is plentiful. As long as everyone can get all the good grazing land they want, the Town Common is not a rival good, and allowing residents' sheep to graze for free causes no problems. Everyone in town is happy.

As the years pass, the population of the town grows, and so does the number of sheep grazing on the Town Common. With a growing number of sheep and a fixed amount of land, the land starts to lose its ability to replenish itself. Eventually, the land is grazed so heavily that it becomes barren. With no grass left on the Town Common, raising sheep is impossible, and the town's once prosperous wool industry disappears. Many families lose their source of livelihood.

What causes the tragedy? Why do the shepherds allow the sheep population to grow so large that it destroys the Town Common? The reason is that social and private incentives differ. Avoiding the destruction of the grazing land depends on the collective action of the shepherds. If the shepherds acted together, they could reduce the sheep population to a size that the Town Common can support. Yet no single family has an incentive to reduce the size of its own flock because each flock represents only a small part of the problem.

In essence, the Tragedy of the Commons arises because of an externality. When one family's flock grazes on the common land, it reduces the quality of the land available for other families. Because people neglect this negative externality when deciding how many sheep to own, the result is an excessive number of sheep.

If the tragedy had been foreseen, the town could have solved the problem in various ways. It could have regulated the number of sheep in each family's flock, internalized the externality by taxing sheep, or auctioned off a limited number of sheep-grazing permits. That is, the medieval town could have dealt with the problem of overgrazing in the way that modern society deals with the problem of pollution.

In the case of land, however, there is a simpler solution. The town can divide up the land among town families. Each family can enclose its parcel of land with a fence and then protect it from excessive grazing. In this way, the land becomes a private good rather than a common resource. This outcome in fact occurred during the enclosure movement in England in the seventeenth century.

The Tragedy of the Commons is a story with a general lesson: When one person uses a common resource, that person diminishes other people's enjoyment of it. Because of this negative externality, common resources tend to be used excessively. The government can solve the problem by reducing use of the common resource through regulation or taxes. Alternatively, the government can sometimes turn the common resource into a private good.

This lesson has been known for thousands of years. The ancient Greek philosopher Aristotle pointed out the problem with common resources: "What is common to many is taken least care of, for all men have greater regard for what is their own than for what they possess in common with others."

Some Important Common Resources

There are many examples of common resources. In almost all cases, the same problem arises as in the Tragedy of the Commons: Private decision makers use the

IN THE NEWS

THE SINGAPORE SOLUTION

Tolls are a simple way to solve the problem of road congestion and, according to some economists, are not used as much as they should be. In this opinion column, economist Lester Thurow describes Singapore's success in dealing with congestion.

Economics of Road Pricing

By Lester C. Thurow

Start with a simple observational truth. No city has ever been able to solve its congestion and pollution problems by building more roads.

Some of the world's cities have built a lot of roads (Los Angeles) and some have very few (Shanghai only recently has had a lot of autos) but the degrees of congestion and pollution don't differ very much. More roads simply encourage more people to use their cars, to live farther away from work, and thus use more road space. . . . A recent analysis of congestion problems in London came to the conclusion that London could tear the entire central city down to make room for roads and would still have something approaching gridlock.

Economists have always had a theoretical answer for auto congestion and pollution problems—road pricing. Charge people for using roads based on what roads they use, what time of day and year they use those roads, and the degree to which pollution problems exist at the time they are using those roads. Set prices at the levels that yield the optimal amounts of usage.

Until Singapore decided to try, no city had ever had the nerve to use road pricing. Many ideas seem good theoretically but have some hidden unexpected flaws. Singapore now has more than a decade of experience. The system works! There are no unexpected flaws. Singapore is the only city on the face of the common resource too much. Governments often regulate behaviour or impose fees to mitigate the problem of overuse.

Clean Air and Water

As we discussed in Chapter 10, markets do not adequately protect the environment. Pollution is a negative externality that can be remedied with regulations or with Pigovian taxes on polluting activities. One can view this market failure as an example of a common-resource problem. Clean air and clean water are common resources like open grazing land, and excessive pollution is like excessive grazing. Environmental degradation is a modern Tragedy of the Commons.

Congested Roads

Roads can be either public goods or common resources. If a road is not congested, then one person's use does not affect anyone else. In this case, use is not rival, and the road is a public good. Yet if a road is congested, then use of that road yields a negative externality. When one additional person drives on the road, it becomes more crowded, and other people must drive more slowly. In this case, the road is a common resource.

earth without congestion and auto-induced pollution problems.

In Singapore a series of toll booths surrounds the central core of the city. To drive into the city, each car must pay a toll based on the roads being used, the time of day when the driving will occur, and that day's pollution problem. Prices are raised and lowered to get optimal usage.

In addition, Singapore calculates the maximum number of cars that can be supported without pollution outside of the central city and auctions off the rights to license new cars each month. Different types of plates allow different degrees of usage. A plate that allows one to use their car at any time is much more expensive than a plate that only allows one to use their car on weekends—a time when congestion problems are much less intense. Prices depend on supply and demand.

With this system Singapore ends up not wasting resources on infrastructure projects that won't cure congestion and

pollution problems. The revenue collected from the system is used to lower other taxes.

If that is so, why then did London reject road pricing in its recent report on its auto congestion and pollution problems? They feared that such a system would be seen as too much interference from the heavy hand of government and that the public would not put up with a system that allows the rich to drive more than the poor.

Both arguments ignore the fact that we already have toll roads, but new technologies now also make it possible to avoid both problems.

Using bar codes and debit cards, a city can install bar code readers at different points around the city. As any car goes by each point a certain amount is deducted from the driver's debit card account depending upon weather, time of day, and location.

Inside the car, the driver has a meter that tells him how much he has been

charged and how much remains in his debit card account. . . .

If one is an egalitarian and thinks that driving privileges should be distributed equally (i.e., not based upon income) then each auto can be given a specified debit card balance every year and those who are willing to drive less can sell their unused balances to those that want to drive more.

Instead of giving the city extra tax revenue, this system gives those who are willing to live near work or to use public transit an income supplement. Since poor people drive less than rich people, the system ends up being an egalitarian redistribution of income from the rich to the poor.

One way for the government to address the problem of road congestion is to charge drivers a toll. A toll is, in essence, a Pigovian tax on the externality of congestion. Often, as in the case of local roads, tolls are not a practical solution because the cost of collecting them is too high.

Sometimes congestion is a problem only at certain times of day. If a bridge is heavily travelled only during rush hour, for instance, the congestion externality is larger during this time than during other times of day. The efficient way to deal with these externalities is to charge higher tolls during rush hour. This toll would provide an incentive for drivers to alter their schedules and would reduce traffic when congestion is greatest.

Another policy that responds to the problem of road congestion, discussed in a case study in the previous chapter, is the tax on gasoline. Gasoline is a complementary good to driving: An increase in the price of gasoline tends to reduce the quantity of driving demanded. Therefore, a gasoline tax reduces road congestion. A gasoline tax, however, is an imperfect solution to road congestion. The problem is that the gasoline tax affects other decisions besides the amount of driving on congested roads. For example, the gasoline tax discourages driving on noncongested roads, even though there is no congestion externality for these roads.

Fish, Whales, and Other Wildlife   Many species of animals are common resources. Fish and whales, for instance, have commercial value, and anyone can go to the ocean and catch whatever is available. Each person has little incentive to maintain the species for the next year. Just as excessive grazing can destroy the Town Common, excessive fishing and whaling can destroy commercially valuable marine populations.

The ocean remains one of the least regulated common resources. Two problems prevent an easy solution. First, many countries have access to the oceans, so any solution would require international cooperation among countries that hold different values. Second, because the oceans are so vast, enforcing any agreement is difficult. As a result, fishing rights have been a frequent source of international tension among normally friendly countries.

In Canada, various laws aim to protect fish and other wildlife. For example, the government charges for fishing and hunting licences, and it restricts the lengths of the fishing and hunting seasons. Fishermen are often required to throw back small fish, and hunters can kill only a limited number of animals. All these laws reduce the use of a common resource and help maintain animal populations.

Case Study

WHY THE COW IS NOT EXTINCT

Throughout history, many species of animals have been threatened with extinction. When Europeans first arrived in North America, more than 60 million buffalo roamed the continent. Yet hunting the buffalo was so popular during the nineteenth century that by 1900 the animal's population fell to only several hundred before the government stepped in to protect the species. In some African countries today, the elephant faces a similar challenge, as poachers kill the animals for the ivory in their tusks.

Yet not all animals with commercial value face this threat. The cow, for example, is a valuable source of food, but no one worries that the cow will soon be extinct. Indeed, the great demand for beef seems to ensure that the species will continue to thrive.

Why is the commercial value of ivory a threat to the elephant, while the commercial value of beef is a guardian of the cow? The reason is that elephants are a common resource, whereas cows are a private good. Elephants roam freely without any owners. Each poacher has a strong incentive to kill as many elephants as he can find. Because poachers are numerous, each poacher has only a slight incentive to preserve the elephant population. By contrast, cows live on ranches that are privately owned. Each rancher works hard to maintain the cow population on his ranch because he reaps the benefit of these efforts.

Governments have tried to solve the elephant's problem in two ways. Some countries, such as Kenya, Tanzania, and Uganda, have made it illegal to kill elephants and sell their ivory. Yet these laws have been hard to enforce, and elephant populations have continued to dwindle. By contrast, other countries, such as Botswana, Malawi, Namibia, and Zimbabwe, have made elephants a private good by allowing people to kill elephants, but only those on their own property. Landowners now have an incentive to preserve the species on their own land, and as a result, elephant populations have started to rise. With private ownership and the profit motive now on its side, the African elephant might someday be as safe from extinction as the cow. ●

"Will the market protect me?"

QuickQuiz Why do governments try to limit the use of common resources?

CONCLUSION: THE IMPORTANCE OF PROPERTY RIGHTS

In this chapter and the previous one, we have seen there are some "goods" that the market does not provide adequately. Markets do not ensure that the air we breathe is clean or that our country is defended from foreign aggressors. Instead, societies rely on the government to protect the environment and to provide for national defence.

Although the problems we considered in these chapters arise in many different markets, they share a common theme. In all cases, the market fails to allocate resources efficiently because *property rights* are not well established. That is, some item of value does not have an owner with the legal authority to control it. For example, although no one doubts that the "good" of clean air or national defence is valuable, no one has the right to attach a price to it and profit from its use. A factory pollutes too much because no one charges the factory for the pollution it emits. The market does not provide for national defence because no one can charge those who are defended for the benefit they receive.

When the absence of property rights causes a market failure, the government can potentially solve the problem. Sometimes, as in the sale of pollution permits, the solution is for the government to help define property rights and thereby unleash market forces. Other times, as in the restriction on hunting seasons, the solution is for the government to regulate private behaviour. Still other times, as in the provision of national defence, the solution is for the government to supply a good that the market fails to supply. In all cases, if the policy is well planned and well run, it can make the allocation of resources more efficient and thus raise economic well-being.

SUMMARY

- Goods differ in whether they are excludable and whether they are rival. A good is excludable if it is possible to prevent someone from using it. A good is rival if one person's use of the good reduces other people's ability to use the same unit of the good. Markets work best for private goods, which are both excludable and rival. Markets do not work as well for other types of goods.

- Public goods are neither rival nor excludable. Examples of public goods include fireworks displays, national defence, and the creation of fundamental knowledge. Because people are not

charged for their use of the public good, they have an incentive to free-ride when the good is provided privately. Therefore, governments provide public goods, making their decision about the quantity based on cost–benefit analysis.

- Common resources are rival but not excludable. Examples include common grazing land, clean air, and congested roads. Because people are not charged for their use of common resources, they tend to use them excessively. Therefore, governments try to limit the use of common resources.

KEY CONCEPTS

excludability, p. 228
rivalry, p. 228
private goods, p. 228

public goods, p. 229
common resources, p. 229
free rider, p. 230

cost–benefit analysis, p. 233
Tragedy of the Commons, p. 235

QUESTIONS FOR REVIEW

1. Explain what is meant by a good being "excludable." Explain what is meant by a good being "rival." Is a pizza excludable? Is it rival?

2. Define and give an example of a public good. Can the private market provide this good on its own? Explain.

3. What is cost–benefit analysis of public goods? Why is it important? Why is it hard?

4. Define and give an example of a common resource. Without government intervention, will people use this good too much or too little? Why?

PROBLEMS AND APPLICATIONS

1. The text says that both public goods and common resources involve externalities.

   a. Are the externalities associated with public goods generally positive or negative? Use examples in your answer. Is the free-market quantity of public goods generally greater or less than the efficient quantity?

b. Are the externalities associated with common resources generally positive or negative? Use examples in your answer. Is the free-market use of common resources generally greater or less than the efficient use?

2. Think about the goods and services provided by your local government.

a. Using the classification in Figure 11.1, explain into which category each of the following goods falls:
   - police protection
   - snowplowing
   - education
   - rural roads
   - city streets

b. Why do you think the government provides items that are not public goods?

3. Charlie loves watching *Teletubbies* on his local public TV station, but he never sends any money to support the station during its fundraising drives.

a. What name do economists have for Charlie?

b. How can the government solve the problem caused by people like Charlie?

c. Can you think of ways the private market can solve this problem? How does the existence of cable TV alter the situation?

4. The text states that private firms will not undertake the efficient amount of basic scientific research.

a. Explain why this is so. In your answer, classify basic research in one of the categories shown in Figure 11.1.

b. What sort of policy has Canada adopted in response to this problem?

c. It is often argued that this policy increases the technological capability of Canadian producers relative to that of foreign firms. Is this argument consistent with your classification of basic research in part (a)? (Hint: Can excludability apply to some potential beneficiaries of a public good and not others?)

5. Why is there litter along most highways but rarely in people's yards?

6. Highway 407 in Toronto has one of the most modern toll systems in the world. Tolls are determined electronically, and vary both by the time of day and by the type of vehicle. Why is this a good idea?

7. Timber companies in Canada cut down many trees on publicly owned land and many trees on privately owned land. Discuss the likely efficiency of logging on each type of land in the absence of government regulation. How do you think the government should regulate logging on publicly owned lands? Should similar regulations apply to privately owned land?

8. An *Economist* article (March 19, 1994) states: "In the past decade, most of the rich world's fisheries have been exploited to the point of near-exhaustion." The article continues with an analysis of the problem and a discussion of possible private and government solutions.

a. "Do not blame fishermen for overfishing. They are behaving rationally, as they have always done." In what sense is "overfishing" rational for fishermen?

b. "A community, held together by ties of obligation and mutual self-interest, can manage a common resource on its own." Explain how such management can work in principle, and what obstacles it faces in the real world.

c. "Until 1976 most world fish stocks were open to all comers, making conservation almost impossible. Then an international agreement extended some aspects of [national] jurisdiction from 12 to 200 miles offshore." Using the concept of property rights, discuss how this agreement reduces the scope of the problem.

d. The article notes that many governments come to the aid of suffering fishermen in ways that encourage increased fishing. How do such policies encourage a vicious cycle of overfishing?

e. "Only when fishermen believe they are assured a long-term and exclusive right to a fishery are they likely to manage it in the same far-sighted way as good farmers manage their land." Defend this statement.

f. What other policies to reduce overfishing might be considered?

9. In a market economy, information about the quality or function of goods and services is a valuable good in its own right. How does the private market provide this information? Can you think of any way in which the government plays a role in providing this information?

10. Do you think the Internet is a public good? Why or why not?

11. High-income people are willing to pay more than lower-income people to avoid the risk of death. For example, they are more likely to pay for safety features on cars. Do you think cost–benefit analysts should take this fact into account when evaluating public projects? Consider, for instance, a rich town and a poor town, both of which are considering the installation of a traffic light. Should the rich town use a higher dollar value for a human life in making this decision? Why or why not?

INTERNET RESOURCES

Go to http://www.speciesatrisk.gc.ca/default_e.cfm to find a list of endangered species in Canada. Can the market be relied on to protect these species?

http://   For more study tools, please visit http://www.mankiw3e.nelson.com.

© GEOFFREY CLIFFORD/IMAGE BANK

THE DESIGN OF THE TAX SYSTEM

Learning Objectives

In this chapter, you will …

- Gain an overview of how the Canadian government raises and spends money
- Examine the efficiency costs of taxes
- Learn alternative ways to judge the equity of a tax system
- See why studying tax incidence is crucial for evaluating tax equity
- Consider the tradeoff between efficiency and equity in the design of a tax system

As Benjamin Franklin said, "In this world nothing is certain but death and taxes." Taxes are inevitable because we as citizens expect the government to provide us with various goods and services. The previous two chapters have started to shed light on one of the ten principles of economics from Chapter 1: The government can sometimes improve market outcomes. When the government remedies an externality (such as air pollution), provides a public good (such as national defence), or regulates the use of a common resource (such as fish in a public lake), it can raise economic well-being. Yet the benefits of government come with costs. For the government to perform these and its many other functions, it needs to raise revenue through taxation.

We began our study of taxation in earlier chapters, where we saw how a tax on a good affects supply and demand for that good. In Chapter 6 we saw that a tax reduces the quantity sold in a market, and we examined how the burden of a tax is shared by buyers and sellers, depending on the elasticities of supply and demand. In Chapter 8 we examined how taxes affect economic well-being. We learned that taxes cause *deadweight losses:* The reduction in consumer and producer surplus resulting from a tax exceeds the revenue raised by the government.

In this chapter we build on these lessons to discuss the design of a tax system. We begin with a financial overview of the Canadian government. When thinking about the tax system, it is useful to know some basic facts about how the Canadian government raises and spends money. We then consider the fundamental principles of taxation. Most people agree that taxes should impose as small a cost on society as possible and that the burden of taxes should be distributed fairly. That is, the tax system should be both *efficient* and *equitable*. As we will see, however, stating these goals is easier than achieving them.

A FINANCIAL OVERVIEW OF THE CANADIAN GOVERNMENT

How much of the nation's income does the government take as taxes? Figure 12.1 shows government revenue, including federal, provincial, and local governments, as a percentage of total income for the Canadian economy. It shows that, over time, the government has taken a larger and larger share of total income. In 1961, the government collected 28 percent of total income; in 2002, it collected 41 percent. In other words, as the economy's income has grown, the government has grown even more.

The overall size of government tells only part of the story. Behind the total dollar figures lie thousands of individual decisions about taxes and spending. To understand the government's finances more fully, let's look at how the total breaks down into some broad categories.

Table 12.1 compares the tax burden for several major Organization of Economic Cooperation and Development (OECD) countries, as measured by the federal and provincial/state government's tax revenue as a percentage of the nation's total income (the figures do not include local government revenue). Canada's tax burden is slightly lower than the OECD average, but is quite a bit higher than that of the United States. Poorer countries, such as Mexico, tend to have relatively low tax burdens. This fact is consistent with the evidence in Figure 12.1 of a growing tax burden over time: As a nation becomes richer, the government typically takes a larger share of income in taxes. Before examining this breakdown, it is useful to know a few things about the structure of the government sector in Canada.

Canada has a *federalist* structure, which means political power is divided between the federal government and the provincial governments, with greater power going to the federal government. The third level of government, local or municipal, is granted powers by the provincial government. The British North America (BNA) Act of 1867, Canada's Constitution, sets out the responsibilities of the federal and provincial governments. The BNA Act has been amended several times, most recently in 1982; however, the federalist structure has remained intact. In fact, it is one of the defining features of our country.

The federal government is responsible for matters of national interest, including national defence and foreign policy, international trade, competition policy, criminal law, and money and banking. The federal government is also responsible for delivering some of Canada's national social programs, such as Employment Insurance and the Canada Pension Plan. This level of government has essentially unlimited taxing powers.

FIGURE 12.1

Government Revenue as a Percentage of GDP

This figure shows revenue of the federal government and of provincial and local governments as a percentage of gross domestic product (GDP), which measures total income in the economy. It shows that the government plays a large role in the Canadian economy and that its role has grown over time.

Source: Adapted from Statistics Canada, CANSIM database, Series D22641, D22683, and D22411, and author's calculations.

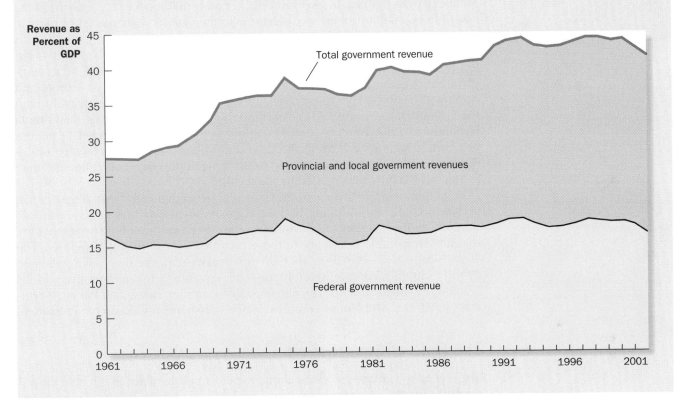

TABLE 12.1

Federal and Provincial/State Government Tax Revenue as a Percent of GDP

Source: *World Development Report 2002: Building Institutions for Markets* (New York: World Bank and Oxford University Press, 2001).

Country	Tax Revenue as % of GDP
Sweden	50.6%
France	44.2
Italy	41.4
Germany	36.2
United Kingdom	35.9
Canada	**33.5**
United States	28.9
Japan	27.3
Mexico	18.0
OECD Average	36.9%

The provinces are responsible for the areas of health care, education, welfare, natural resources within their boundaries, and civil law. The provinces have extensive taxing powers, although they are less extensive than the federal government's. Compared with provincial and state governments in most other federations, including the United States, Canadian provinces have a great deal of power. The provinces account for more than half of the activities undertaken by the public sector in Canada. Local governments—cities, towns, and municipalities—are creatures of the provinces, and receive their spending and taxing authority from the provinces. Figure 12.1 reveals that most of the growth in the size of the Canadian government sector over the past 40 years has taken place at the provincial and local levels.

An important aspect of our federalist government structure is the role of *transfers* from the federal government to the provinces. Although the federal government is not directly responsible for programs related to health, education, and welfare, it has been able to exercise substantial influence in these areas through the "power of the purse." The most important transfer program is the Canada Health and Social Transfer (CHST). Although the CHST is intended to finance provincial programs in health, education, and welfare, it is in fact a largely unconditional per capita grant that simply enters general provincial revenues and may be used as the provincial governments see fit.

Another important feature of the Canadian federation is the role of *equalization payments*. Under this system, the federal government provides general-purpose transfers to the "have-not" provinces so that they can provide services that are roughly comparable in quality to those provided by the "have" provinces. The "have" provinces—the ones that do not receive equalization payments—are British Columbia, Alberta, and Ontario. The remaining provinces receive various amounts of equalization payments, depending on their need. The Yukon, Northwest Territories, and Nunavut receive similar payments under a separate system.

The Federal Government

The federal government collects about 45 percent of the taxes in our economy. It raises this money in a number of ways, and it finds even more ways to spend it.

Receipts   Table 12.2 shows total federal government revenue in the 2002–2003 fiscal year ended March 31. Total revenue in this year was $1786 billion. To bring this huge number down to earth, we can divide it by the Canadian population, which was about 31.4 million in 2002. We then find that the average Canadian paid about $5670 to the federal government in 2002.

The biggest source of revenue for the federal government is the personal income tax, which accounts for almost half of total federal revenue. In 2002, over 14 million Canadian taxpayers filled out tax returns to determine how much income tax they owed. Taxpayers are required to report their income from all sources: employment income, interest on savings, dividends from corporations in which they own shares, and so on. An individual's *tax liability* (how much the person owes in taxes) is then based on that person's total income.

A person's tax liability is not simply proportional to the person's income. Instead, the law requires a more complicated calculation. Taxable income is computed by subtracting from total income various deductions for things such as con-

TABLE 12.2

Federal Government Revenue, 2002–2003

Source: Finance Canada, *Fiscal Reference Tables, 2003*. Numbers may not add up due to rounding.

Revenue Source	Amount (in billions)	Amount per Person	% of Revenue
Personal income taxes	$82	$2600	46%
Corporate income taxes	22	700	12
Goods and Services Tax	28	890	16
Excise taxes and duties	13	415	7
Employment Insurance payroll taxes	18	575	10
Other	15	480	9
Total	$178	$5670	100%

tributions to registered pension plans and registered retirement savings plans—both of which will be discussed later—child-care expenses, and so on. The person's basic tax liability is then calculated from taxable income using the schedule shown in Table 12.3.

Table 12.3 presents the *marginal tax rate*—the rate of tax applied to each additional dollar of income. There are four *tax brackets* in Canada (five if you count people who don't pay taxes at all because they don't earn enough income). Because the marginal tax rate rises as people enter higher tax brackets, higher-income individuals pay a larger percentage of their income in taxes than do lower-income individuals. (We will discuss the concept of the marginal tax rate more fully later in this chapter.) It bears emphasizing that the tax rates in Table 12.3 are federal tax rates only; provinces also levy personal income taxes, as will be discussed later in the chapter. From this basic tax liability are deducted various tax credits in order to determine the individual's final tax liability. There are many credits, including a basic individual credit that everyone receives, a spousal credit, a child tax credit for dependent children, a credit for charitable donations, and other credits for low-income individuals.

The next-largest source of federal revenue is the Goods and Services Tax (GST), which accounts for about 16 percent of federal government revenue. The GST is

TABLE 12.3

Federal Personal Income Tax Rates, 2003

On Taxable Income . . .	The Tax Rate Is
Up to $32 183	16%
$32 184 to $64 368	22
$64 369 to $104 648	26
Over $104 648	29

levied at a 7 percent rate on the sales of most goods in Canada, with some notable exceptions such as most food. The average Canadian paid $890 in GST in 2003. Excise and customs duties brought in an additional $415 per person, or 7 percent of federal revenue. Excise taxes are sales taxes on specific goods, such as gasoline, cigarettes, and alcohol. Customs duties are taxes applied to goods imported into the country. Total taxes on the sale of goods and services, consisting of the GST plus excise taxes and customs duties, account for 23 percent of federal revenue, or $1305 per person.

The corporate income tax accounts for 12 percent of federal revenue, or about $700 per person. A corporation is a business that is set up as a separate legal entity. The government taxes each corporation on the basis of its profits—the amount the corporation receives for its goods or services minus the cost of producing them.

Another important revenue source for the federal government is payroll taxes used to finance the Employment Insurance (EI) program. A *payroll tax* is a tax on the wages that a firm pays its workers. In Canada, EI payroll taxes are paid by both employees and employers. Employees pay a rate of 2.10 percent of wages when their income is under a *ceiling* of $39 000. Earnings in excess of this ceiling are not subject to the tax. Employers pay 1.4 times what employees pay, or a rate of 2.94 percent. The combined employee–employer EI payroll tax rate is thus 5.04 percent on earnings up to $39 000. Table 12.2 shows that the average Canadian paid about $575 in EI payroll taxes in 2003. Another program that is financed by payroll taxes is the Canada Pension Plan (CPP), which provides pensions to all retired Canadians. CPP payroll taxes are not included in Table 12.2 because the program operates under a separate budget.

Spending Table 12.4 shows federal government spending in 2003. Total spending was $171 billion, or about $5445 per person. Approximately 22 percent of this went to pay the interest on the federal government's debt. The remaining 78 percent, or $4265 per person, was devoted to *program spending*—that is, all government expenditures that are not debt payments.

TABLE 12.4

Federal Government Spending, 2002–2003

Source: Finance Canada, *Fiscal Reference Tables, 2003.* Numbers may not add up due to rounding.

Category	Amount (in billions)	Amount per Person	% of Spending
Old Age Security	$26	$830	15%
Canada Health and Social Transfer	21	670	12
Equalization	11	350	6
Employment Insurance	14	445	8
National defence	11	350	6
Other	51	1625	30
Total program spending	134	4265	78
Debt service	37	1180	22
Total spending	$171	$5445	100%

The single largest category of federal government expenditures, aside from debt payments, is payments to elderly people under the Old Age Security program, which in 2003 accounted for 15 percent of total spending. Payments to senior citizens are likely to grow in importance as increases in life expectancy and decreases in birthrates cause this population to grow more rapidly than the total population. Another important source of government-provided income for seniors is the CPP. As mentioned above, payments made under the CPP are accounted for separately.

Transfers to the provinces under the CHST account for 12 percent of program expenditures; equalization payments account for an additional 6 percent. Total transfers to the provinces thus make up 18 percent of federal government expenditures.

Payments under the EI program in 2003 amounted to $14 billion, or about 8 percent of total federal spending. It is interesting to note that the federal government collected $18 billion in EI payroll taxes in the same year (see Table 12.2). That is, EI revenue exceeded EI spending by $4 billion—a considerable surplus. In fact, the EI program has run a sizable surplus over the past several years, prompting many people to call for a reduction in EI payroll taxes.

In 2003, spending on national defence accounted for 6 percent of total federal expenditures. Canada spends substantially less in this area than the United States, which devotes roughly 17 percent of federal government expenditures to national defence.

You may have noticed that total federal government revenue shown in Table 12.2 exceeds its total spending shown in Table 12.4. Such an excess of revenue over spending is called a **budget surplus** (if spending exceeds revenue, a **budget deficit** results). In 2003, the budget surplus was $7 billion. The government may use the excess of revenue over spending to reduce its outstanding debts (resulting from past deficits), increase program funding, or reduce taxes.

budget surplus
an excess of government receipts over government spending

budget deficit
an excess of government spending over government receipts

Provincial and Local Governments

Provincial and local governments collect more than 50 percent of taxes in the economy. Let's look at how they obtain tax revenue and how they spend it.

Receipts   Table 12.5 (p. 250) shows the total revenue of provincial governments in 2003: $215 billion, or $6845 per person. However, $36 billion of total provincial revenue (17 percent) came from transfers from the federal government. Provincial own-source revenues therefore amounted to $179 billion, or $5700 per person.

The single most important source of revenue for the provinces, as for the federal government, is personal income taxes. In 2003, personal income taxes accounted for 25 percent of total provincial revenue, or about $1690 per person. The provinces levy personal taxes on the same taxable income base as the federal government but determine their own tax rates and brackets. Table 12.6 shows the basic personal income tax rates for the various tax brackets in each province. The combined federal–provincial tax rates are the sum of the federal rates in Table 12.3 and the provincial rates in Table 12.6 (p. 250).

The next-largest revenue source for the provinces is general sales taxes, which in 2003 accounted for 14 percent of total provincial revenue. All of the provinces except Alberta levy sales taxes collected at the retail level. The rates range from

TABLE 12.5

Provincial Government Revenue, 2003

Source: Adapted from Statistics Canada, CANSIM database, Series V206417-V206448.

Category	Amount (in billions)	Amount per Person	% of Revenue
Personal income taxes	$53	$1690	25%
Corporate income taxes	12	380	6
General sales taxes	30	955	14
Excise taxes	22	700	10
Property taxes	9	285	4
Payroll taxes	8	255	4
Health premiums	3	95	1
Transfers	36	1145	17
Other	42	1335	19
Total	$215	$6845	100%

TABLE 12.6

Provincial Personal Income Tax Rates, 2003

Province	Tax Rates	Tax Brackets
British Columbia	8.4%	$0–30 484
	11.9	30 485–60 969
	16.7	60 970–70 000
	18.7	70 001–85 000
	19.7	85 001 and over
Alberta	10.0%	All income
Saskatchewan	11.5%	$0–30 000
	13.5	30 001–60 000
	18.7	60 001 and over
Manitoba	10.9%	$0–30 554
	16.2	30 555–61 089
	17.5	61 090 and over
Ontario	6.2%	$0–30 814
	16.2	30 815–61 629
	17.5	61 630 and over
Quebec	18.0%	$0–26 000
	22.5	26 001–52 000
	27.5	52 001 and over
New Brunswick	9.86%	$0–29 590
	14.82	29 591–59 180
	16.52	59 181 and over
Nova Scotia	9.77%	$0–29 590
	14.95	29 591–59 180
	16.67	59 181 and over
Prince Edward Island	9.8%	$0–30 754
	13.80	30 755–61 509
	16.70	61 510 and over
Newfoundland and Labrador	10.57%	$0–29 590
	16.16	29 591–59 180
	18.02	59 181 and over

6.5 percent to 10.0 percent. Excise taxes on goods such as gasoline, cigarettes, and alcohol comprise another 10 percent of total provincial revenue. Thus, total taxes on consumption (general sales taxes plus excise taxes) account for 24 percent of provincial revenue, about the same as personal income taxes.

The provinces also levy their own taxes on corporations. The most important of these is the corporate income tax, which accounts for 6 percent of provincial revenues.

Provincial health premiums and payroll taxes together make up 5 percent of provincial revenues. Most provinces levy a payroll tax, paid by employers, to help fund health programs. Saskatchewan levies no such tax, and Alberta and British Columbia impose lump-sum health care premiums on a yearly basis that are paid by employees.

Spending   Table 12.7 shows total provincial government spending in 2003 and how it breaks down. Spending on health, education, and social services ("the big three") account for the lion's share of provincial spending—68 percent of total spending in 2003, or $4675 per person. Health is the biggest single component, followed by education and social services. Education includes spending on primary, secondary, and postsecondary schools. Health includes expenditures on hospital care, medical care, and preventive care. Social services primarily consist of welfare programs for low-income people.

Provincial government spending on police and protection together with transportation and communication accounted for 9 percent of provincial spending. Debt service charges accounted for 13 percent.

Notice that total provincial government spending exceeds total provincial government revenue in Table 12.5—the aggregate provincial budget in 2003 was in a slight deficit situation.

QuickQuiz What are the two most important sources of tax revenue for the federal government? • What are the two most important sources of tax revenue for provincial and local governments?

TABLE 12.7

Provincial Government Spending, 2003

Source: Adapted from Statistics Canada, CANSIM database, Series V206449-V206481.

Category	Amount (in billions)	Amount per Person	% of Spending
Health	$71	$2260	32%
Education	44	1400	20
Social services	35	1015	16
Transportation and communication	10	320	5
Police and protection	9	285	4
Debt service	27	860	13
Other	24	765	10
Total	$220	$7005	100%

TAXES AND EFFICIENCY

Now that we have seen how the Canadian government at various levels raises and spends money, let's consider how one might evaluate its tax policy. Obviously, the aim of a tax system is to raise revenue for the government. But there are many ways to raise any given amount of money. In designing a tax system, policymakers have two objectives: efficiency and equity.

One tax system is more efficient than another if it raises the same amount of revenue at a smaller cost to taxpayers. What are the costs of taxes to taxpayers? The most obvious cost is the tax payment itself. This transfer of money from the taxpayer to the government is an inevitable feature of any tax system. Yet taxes also impose two other costs, which well-designed tax policy tries to avoid or, at least, minimize:

1. The deadweight losses that result when taxes distort the decisions that people make
2. The administrative burdens that taxpayers bear as they comply with the tax laws

An efficient tax system is one that imposes small deadweight losses and small administrative burdens.

Deadweight Losses

One of the ten principles of economics is that people respond to incentives, and this includes incentives provided by the tax system. If the government taxes ice cream, people eat less ice cream and more frozen yogurt. If the government taxes housing, people live in smaller houses and spend more of their income on other things. If the government taxes labour earnings, people work less and enjoy more leisure.

Because taxes distort incentives, they entail deadweight losses. As we first discussed in Chapter 8, the deadweight loss of a tax is the reduction in economic well-being of taxpayers in excess of the amount of revenue raised by the government. The deadweight loss is the inefficiency that a tax creates as people allocate resources according to the tax incentive rather than the true costs and benefits of the goods and services that they buy and sell.

To recall how taxes cause deadweight losses, consider an example. Suppose that Joe places an $8 value on a pizza, and Jane places a $6 value on it. If there is no tax on pizza, the price of pizza will reflect the cost of making it. Let's suppose that the price of pizza is $5, so both Joe and Jane choose to buy one. Both consumers get some surplus of value over the amount paid. Joe gets consumer surplus of $3, and Jane gets consumer surplus of $1. Total surplus is $4.

Now suppose that the government levies a $2 tax on pizza and the price of pizza rises to $7. Joe still buys a pizza, but now he has consumer surplus of only $1. Jane now decides not to buy a pizza because its price is higher than its value to her. The government collects tax revenue of $2 on Joe's pizza. Total consumer surplus has fallen by $3 (from $4 to $1). Because total surplus has fallen by more than the tax revenue, the tax has a deadweight loss. In this case, the deadweight loss is $1.

Notice that the deadweight loss comes not from Joe, the person who pays the tax, but from Jane, the person who doesn't. The reduction of $2 in Joe's surplus exactly offsets the amount of revenue the government collects. The deadweight loss arises because the tax causes Jane to alter her behaviour. When the tax raises the price of pizza, Jane is worse off, and yet there is no offsetting revenue to the government. This reduction in Jane's welfare is the deadweight loss of the tax.

Case Study

SHOULD INCOME OR CONSUMPTION BE TAXED?

When taxes induce people to change their behaviour—such as inducing Jane to buy less pizza—the taxes cause deadweight losses and make the allocation of resources less efficient. As we have already seen, much government revenue comes from the individual income tax. In a case study in Chapter 8, we discussed how this tax discourages people from working as hard as they otherwise might. Another inefficiency caused by this tax is that it discourages people from saving.

Consider a person 25 years old who is considering saving $100. If he puts this money in a savings account that earns 8 percent and leaves it there, he would have $2172 when he retires at age 65. Yet if the government taxes one-fourth of his interest income each year, the effective interest rate is only 6 percent. After 40 years of earning 6 percent, the $100 grows to only $1029, less than half of what it would have been without taxation. Thus, because interest income is taxed, saving is much less attractive.

Some economists advocate eliminating the current tax system's disincentive toward saving by changing the basis of taxation. Rather than taxing the amount of income that people *earn*, the government could tax the amount that people *spend*. Under this proposal, all income that is saved would not be taxed until the saving is later spent. This alternative system, called a *consumption tax*, would not distort people's saving decisions.

A tax on consumption can be implemented in several ways. The approach that most people are familiar with is a sales tax on goods and services purchased by consumers. Examples include provincial sales taxes and the federal government's GST.

Some economists have suggested another approach to taxing consumption. People can do two basic things with their income: They can spend (consume) it, or they can save it. This gives rise to the model: Income = Consumption + Savings (or $I = C + S$). Rearranging this model, an individual's consumption can be defined simply as income minus savings (or $C = I - S$). This suggests that the tax system could be used to tax consumption in the following way. The individual's total income (I) could be determined and savings (S) could be allowed as a deduction. The interest (or dividends or capital gains) earned on the amount saved would then accumulate tax-free. When, some time later, the individual withdraws the savings in order to consume, the amount withdrawn would be fully taxable.

In fact, Canada's personal income tax system works in a very similar way. All contributions to Registered Retirement Savings Plans (RRSPs) and Registered Pension Plans (RPPs), up to a maximum of $13 500 per year, are fully deductible from income. Moreover, interest earned in these plans accumulates tax-free, and withdrawals may be made at any time, at which point they are fully taxable. RRSPs and RPPs are vehicles intended to encourage people to save for their retirement. For people who do most of their saving through RRSPs and RPPs—and figures show that very few Canadians contribute up to the allowed limits—Canada's personal income tax functions like a tax on consumption.

Combined with provincial sales taxes and the GST, the tax treatment of RPPs and RRSPs suggests that Canada's tax system as a whole raises most of its revenue by taxing consumption rather than income. ●

Administrative Burden

If you ask the typical person on April 30 for an opinion about the tax system, you might hear about the headache of filling out tax forms. The administrative burden of any tax system is part of the inefficiency it creates. This burden includes not only the time spent in April filling out forms but also the time spent throughout the year keeping records for tax purposes and the resources the government has to use to enforce the tax laws.

Many taxpayers—especially those in higher tax brackets—hire tax lawyers and accountants to help them with their taxes. These experts in the complex tax laws fill out the tax forms for their clients and help clients arrange their affairs in a way that reduces the amount of taxes owed. This behaviour is legal tax avoidance, which is different from illegal tax evasion.

Critics of our tax system say that these advisers help their clients avoid taxes by abusing some of the detailed provisions of the tax code, often dubbed "loopholes." In some cases, loopholes are government mistakes: They arise from ambiguities or omissions in the tax laws. More often, they arise because the government has chosen to give special treatment to specific types of behaviour. An example of this are the special provisions for contributions to RRSPs and RPPs discussed earlier.

The resources devoted to complying with the tax laws are a type of deadweight loss. The government gets only the amount of taxes paid. By contrast, the taxpayer loses not only this amount but also the time and money spent documenting, computing, and avoiding taxes.

The administrative burden of the tax system could be reduced by simplifying the tax laws. Yet simplification is often politically difficult. Most people are ready to simplify the tax code by eliminating the loopholes that benefit others, yet few are eager to give up the loopholes that they use. In the end, the complexity of the tax law results from the political process as various taxpayers with their own special interests lobby for their causes.

Marginal Tax Rates versus Average Tax Rates

average tax rate
total taxes paid divided by total income

marginal tax rate
the extra taxes paid on an additional dollar of income

When discussing the efficiency and equity of income taxes, economists distinguish between two notions of the tax rate: the average and the marginal. The **average tax rate** is total taxes paid divided by total income. The **marginal tax rate** is the extra taxes paid on an additional dollar of income.

For example, suppose that the government taxes 20 percent of the first $50 000 of income and 50 percent of all income above $50 000. Under this tax, a person who makes $60 000 pays a tax of $15 000: 20 percent of the first $50 000 (0.20 × $50 000 = $10 000) plus 50 percent of the next $10 000 (0.50 × $10 000 = $5000). For this person, the average tax rate is $15 000/$60 000, or 25 percent. But the marginal tax rate is 50 percent. If the taxpayer earned an additional dollar of income, that dollar would be subject to the 50 percent tax rate, so the amount the taxpayer would owe to the government would rise by $0.50.

The marginal and average tax rates each contain a useful piece of information. If we are trying to gauge the sacrifice made by a taxpayer, the average tax rate is more appropriate because it measures the fraction of income paid in taxes. By contrast, if we are trying to gauge how much the tax system distorts incentives, the marginal tax rate is more meaningful. One of the ten principles of economics in Chapter 1 is that rational people think at the margin. A corollary to this principle is that the marginal tax rate measures how much the tax system discourages people from working. If you are thinking of working an extra few hours, the marginal tax rate determines how much the government takes of your additional earnings. It is the marginal tax rate, therefore, that determines the deadweight loss of an income tax.

Case Study

ICELAND'S NATURAL EXPERIMENT

In the 1980s, Iceland changed its tax system in a way that, as a side effect, provided a natural experiment to show how taxes affect an economy. Before the reform, people paid taxes based on their *previous* year's income. After the reform, people paid taxes based on their *current* income. Thus, taxes in 1987 were based on 1986 income, but taxes in 1988 were based on 1988 income. Income earned in 1987 was never taxed. For this one year of transition, the marginal income tax rate fell to zero.

As reported in a December 2001 article in the *American Economic Review*, the citizens of Iceland took advantage of this tax holiday. Total hours worked rose by about 3 percent in 1987 and then fell back to its normal level in 1988. The production of goods and services in 1987 (as measured by real GDP) was 4 percent higher than the average of the year before and the year after. This episode confirms one of the ten principles of economics: People respond to incentives.

The fall in the Icelandic marginal tax rate was for one year only, and this fact surely influenced the response. On the one hand, some people may have put off vacations and worked overtime to take advantage of the temporary incentive. On the other hand, no one would alter career plans, and no business would restructure its work environment, in response to an incentive that would soon disappear. A permanent change in a marginal tax rate could have either a smaller or a larger incentive effect than a temporary change. ●

Lump-Sum Taxes

Suppose the government imposes a tax of $4000 on everyone. That is, everyone owes the same amount, regardless of earnings or any actions that a person might take. Such a tax is called a **lump-sum tax.**

lump-sum tax
a tax that is the same amount for every person

A lump-sum tax shows clearly the difference between average and marginal tax rates. For a taxpayer with income of $20 000, the average tax rate of a $4000 lump-sum tax is 20 percent; for a taxpayer with income of $40 000, the average tax rate is 10 percent. For both taxpayers, the marginal tax rate is zero because no tax is owed on an additional dollar of income.

A lump-sum tax is the most efficient tax possible. Because a person's decisions do not alter the amount owed, the tax does not distort incentives and, therefore, does not cause deadweight losses. Because everyone can easily compute the amount owed and because there is no benefit to hiring tax lawyers and accountants, the lump-sum tax imposes a minimal administrative burden on taxpayers.

If lump-sum taxes are so efficient, why do we rarely observe them in the real world? The reason is that efficiency is only one goal of the tax system. A lump-sum tax would take the same amount from the poor and the rich, an outcome most people would view as unfair. To understand the tax systems that we observe, in the next section, we consider the other major goal of tax policy: equity.

QuickQuiz What is meant by the *efficiency* of a tax system? • What can make a tax system inefficient?

TAXES AND EQUITY

Although economists tend to focus on the efficiency aspects of the tax system, Canadian policy debates about taxes tend to be dominated by discussions about the fairness of the tax system—in particular, whether its burden is distributed fairly. Of course, if we are to rely on the government to provide some of the goods and services we want, taxes must fall on someone. In this section we consider the equity of a tax system. How should the burden of taxes be divided among the population? How do we evaluate whether a tax system is fair? Everyone agrees that the tax system should be equitable, but there is much disagreement about what equity means and how the equity of a tax system can be judged.

The Benefits Principle

benefits principle
the idea that people should pay taxes based on the benefits they receive from government services

One principle of taxation, called the **benefits principle,** states that people should pay taxes based on the benefits they receive from government services. This principle tries to make public goods similar to private goods. It seems fair that a person who often goes to the movies pays more in total for movie tickets than a person who rarely goes. Similarly, a person who gets great benefit from a public good should pay more for it than a person who gets little benefit.

The gasoline tax, for instance, is sometimes justified using the benefits principle. In some provinces, revenues from the gasoline tax are used to build and maintain roads. Because those who buy gasoline are the same people who use the roads, the gasoline tax might be viewed as a fair way to pay for this government service.

The benefits principle can also be used to argue that wealthy citizens should pay higher taxes than poorer ones. Why? Simply because the wealthy benefit more from public services. Consider, for example, the benefits of police protection from theft. Citizens with much to protect get greater benefit from police services than do those with less to protect. Therefore, according to the benefits principle, the wealthy should contribute more than the poor to the cost of maintaining the police force. The same argument can be used for many other public services, such as fire protection, national defence, and the court system.

It is even possible to use the benefits principle to argue for antipoverty programs funded by taxes on the wealthy. As we discussed in Chapter 11, people prefer living in a society without poverty, suggesting that antipoverty programs are a public good. If the wealthy place a greater dollar value on this public good than members of the middle class do, perhaps just because the wealthy have more to spend, then, according to the benefits principle, they should be taxed more heavily to pay for these programs.

The Ability-to-Pay Principle

Another way to evaluate the equity of a tax system is called the **ability-to-pay principle,** which states that taxes should be levied on a person according to how well that person can shoulder the burden. This principle is sometimes justified by the claim that all citizens should make an "equal sacrifice" to support the government. The magnitude of a person's sacrifice, however, depends not only on the size of the person's tax payment but also on that person's income and other circumstances. A $1000 tax paid by a poor person may require a larger sacrifice than a $10 000 tax paid by a rich one.

The ability-to-pay principle leads to two corollary notions of equity: vertical equity and horizontal equity. **Vertical equity** states that taxpayers with a greater ability to pay taxes should contribute a larger amount. **Horizontal equity** states that taxpayers with similar abilities to pay should contribute the same amount. Although these notions of equity are widely accepted, applying them to evaluate a tax system is rarely straightforward.

Vertical Equity   If taxes are based on ability to pay, then richer taxpayers should pay more than poorer taxpayers. But how much more should the rich pay? Much of the debate over tax policy concerns this question.

Consider the three tax systems in Table 12.8. In each case, taxpayers with higher incomes pay more. Yet the systems differ in how quickly taxes rise with income. The first system is called **proportional** because all taxpayers pay the same fraction

ability-to-pay principle
the idea that taxes should be levied on a person according to how well that person can shoulder the burden

vertical equity
the idea that taxpayers with a greater ability to pay taxes should pay larger amounts

horizontal equity
the idea that taxpayers with similar abilities to pay taxes should pay the same amount

proportional tax
a tax for which high-income and low-income taxpayers pay the same fraction of income

TABLE 12.8

Three Tax Systems

Income	Proportional Tax		Regressive Tax		Progressive Tax	
	Amount of Tax	Percent of Income	Amount of Tax	Percent of Income	Amount of Tax	Percent of Income
$ 50 000	$12 500	25%	$15 000	30%	$10 000	20%
100 000	25 000	25	25 000	25	25 000	25
200 000	50 000	25	40 000	20	60 000	30

regressive tax
a tax for which high-income taxpayers pay a smaller fraction of their income than do low-income taxpayers

progressive tax
a tax for which high-income taxpayers pay a larger fraction of their income than do low-income taxpayers

of income. The second system is called **regressive** because high-income taxpayers pay a smaller fraction of their income, even though they pay a larger amount. The third system is called **progressive** because high-income taxpayers pay a larger fraction of their income.

Which of these three tax systems is most fair? There is no obvious answer, and economic theory does not offer any help in trying to find one. Equity, like beauty, is in the eye of the beholder.

Case Study

HOW THE TAX BURDEN IS DISTRIBUTED

Much of the debate over tax policy relates to whether the wealthy pay their fair share of taxes. There is no objective way to make this judgment. However, when evaluating this issue for yourself, it is useful to know how the burden of the current tax system is distributed among families with different incomes. To do this properly, we must take account of the fact that those who bear the burden of a tax may not be those who actually pay the tax.

A study published in the *Canadian Tax Journal* in 1994 used the theory of tax incidence to estimate the distribution of the burden of the major taxes in Canada. After making various assumptions about the incidence of various taxes and using data from 1988, the authors calculated the average effective tax rate for various income groups in Canada. The average effective tax rate is the total tax paid by families in a group divided by their total income, which includes various transfers from the federal government. The taxes included in the study were personal income taxes, corporate income taxes, sales and excise taxes, payroll taxes, and property taxes.

The results from the study are shown in Figures 12.2 and 12.3. The striking feature of Figure 12.2 is that the Canadian tax system, when viewed in its totality, appears to be only slightly progressive and, indeed, roughly proportional. That is, the fraction of total income that goes to pay taxes is about the same regardless of a family's income level. Figure 12.2 shows that all income groups in Canada pay between 30 and 38 percent of their income in taxes.

Although the tax system overall is roughly proportional, Figure 12.3 (p. 260) shows that individual aspects of the tax system are not. In particular, the personal income tax is quite progressive, with the average effective tax rate increasing with income; sales taxes and property taxes are regressive, with the effective tax rate declining with income; payroll taxes are progressive up to income levels of about $50 000 and then are regressive; and corporate taxes are roughly proportional (at very low rates) for income levels less than $100 000 and then markedly progressive. When the tax system is considered in its totality, all of these differences tend to "come out in the wash," yielding a system that is roughly proportional.

Some economists have criticized this approach to measuring the distribution of the burden of the tax system because it uses annual family incomes and taxes. They argue that consumption decisions are more closely related to a notion of lifetime income than to the value of income in any particular year. Family income may be temporarily high or low in any particular year, which means that an annual measure of income and taxes may make the family tax burden appear

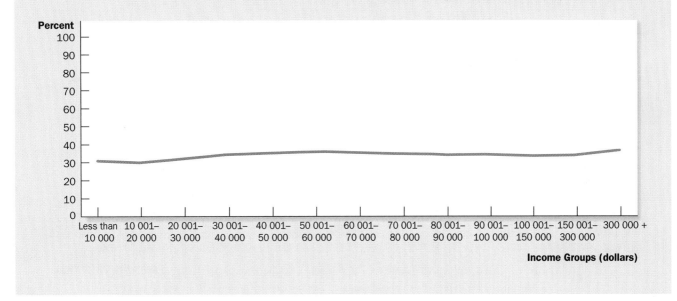

FIGURE 12.2

Effective Tax Rate, Total Taxes, Canada, 1988

This figure shows the total tax burden of various income groups as a percentage of family income. It shows that the tax system in Canada is essentially proportional, with low-income families bearing roughly the same percentage tax burden as high-income families.

Source: Frank Vermaeten, W. Irvin Gillespie, and Arndt Vermaeten, "Tax Incidence in Canada" (1994), *Canadian Tax Journal*, 42, 348–416, at p. 372, Figure 2. Reprinted with the permission of the Canadian Tax Foundation.

particularly low or high in those years. Moreover, families tend to move in and out of income groups over the course of their lifetimes. In light of these considerations, a more reasonable approach to measuring the distribution of the tax burden is to use a lifetime measure of income.

A study (based on Canadian data) that measured the distribution of the tax burden using lifetime income appeared in the *American Economic Review* in 1984. Some of the results are shown in Table 12.9 (p. 260). Families are ranked according to income and placed into ten groups of equal size, called *deciles*. The first decile represents the poorest 10 percent of the population, the second decile the next-poorest 10 percent, and so on, up to the tenth decile, which is the richest 10 percent. Lifetime income and tax burden are measured in present-value terms. Calculations are shown using both the annual-income and the lifetime-income approaches to measuring the distribution of the tax burden. Both approaches suggest a fairly proportional distribution of the burden of all taxes. Recall that the annual-income approach suggests that sales taxes are regressive, with taxes as a percentage of annual income declining steadily from the lowest to the highest decile. When lifetime income is used to measure the tax burden, however, the regressivity of sales taxes is drastically reduced. This has important implications for tax policy. Annual-incidence studies suggest that moving toward greater reliance on sales taxes would be regressive, which may be of concern to

FIGURE 12.3

Effective Tax Rate, by Revenue Source, Canada, 1988

This figure shows the tax burden of various types of taxes on different income groups as a percentage of family income. Personal and corporate income taxes are progressive. Sales taxes and property taxes are regressive. Payroll taxes are progressive for low-income groups, and then regressive for high-income groups.

Source: Frank Vermaeten, W. Irvin Gillespie, and Arndt Vermaeten, "Tax Incidence in Canada" (1994), *Canadian Tax Journal,* 42, 348–416, at p. 374, Figure 4. Reprinted with the permission of the Canadian Tax Foundation.

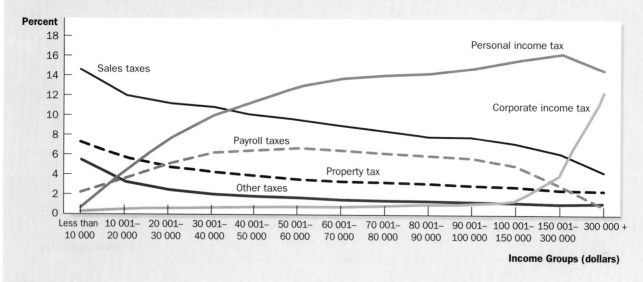

TABLE 12.9

Average Tax Rates of Canadian Households by Decile

Source: J. Davies, F. St-Hillaire, and J. Whalley, "Some Calculations of Lifetime Tax Incidence," *American Economic Review,* 74 (September 1984), p. 643.

Income Decile	Taxes as a Percentage of Lifetime Income		Taxes as a Percentage of Annual Income	
	Sales and Excise Taxes	All Taxes	Sales and Excise Taxes	All Taxes
1	15.0%	30.9%	27.2%	35.4%
2	14.3	35.5	20.3	28.4
3	14.1	35.9	15.8	30.1
4	13.9	37.7	14.6	31.9
5	13.8	38.1	14.0	32.6
6	13.5	39.3	13.4	33.6
7	13.6	39.8	13.5	33.7
8	13.3	42.2	13.2	35.0
9	13.2	41.3	12.8	36.8
10	12.4	46.5	8.5	46.0

policymakers. Lifetime studies, on the other hand, suggest that this is not necessarily the case. ●

Horizontal Equity   If taxes are based on ability to pay, then similar taxpayers should pay similar amounts of taxes. But what determines if two taxpayers are similar? Families differ in many ways. To evaluate whether a tax code is horizontally equitable, one must determine which differences are relevant for a family's ability to pay and which differences are not.

Suppose the Smith and Jones families each have income of $50 000. The Smiths have no children, but Mr. Smith has an illness that causes medical expenses of $20 000. The Joneses are in good health, but they have four children. Two of the Jones children are in university, generating tuition bills of $30 000. Would it be fair for these two families to pay the same tax because they have the same income? Would it be more fair to give the Smiths a tax break to help them offset their high medical expenses? Would it be more fair to give the Joneses a tax break to help them with their tuition expenses?

There are no easy answers to these questions. In practice, the Canadian income tax is filled with special provisions that alter a family's tax based on its specific circumstances.

Tax Incidence and Tax Equity

Tax incidence—the study of who bears the burden of taxes—is central to evaluating tax equity. As we first saw in Chapter 6, the person who bears the burden of a tax is not always the person who gets the tax bill from the government. Because taxes alter supply and demand, they alter equilibrium prices. As a result, they affect people beyond those who, according to statute, actually pay the tax. When evaluating the vertical and horizontal equity of any tax, it is important to take account of these indirect effects.

Many discussions of tax equity ignore the indirect effects of taxes and are based on what economists mockingly call the *flypaper theory* of tax incidence. According to this theory, the burden of a tax, like a fly on flypaper, sticks wherever it first lands. This assumption, however, is rarely valid.

For example, a person not trained in economics might argue that a tax on expensive fur coats is vertically equitable because most buyers of furs are wealthy. Yet if these buyers can easily substitute other luxuries for furs, then a tax on furs might only reduce the sale of furs. In the end, the burden of the tax will fall more on those who make and sell furs than on those who buy them. Because most workers who make furs are not wealthy, the equity of a fur tax could be quite different from what the flypaper theory indicates.

Case Study

WHO PAYS THE CORPORATE INCOME TAX?

The corporate income tax provides a good example of the importance of tax incidence for tax policy. The corporate tax is popular among voters. After all,

IN THE NEWS

INTERNATIONAL CORPORATE TAX COMPETITIVENESS IMPORTANT

In this opinion column, an economist identifies several issues faced by Canadian—in this case, Ontario—policymakers when choosing corporate income tax rates. Particularly important for a small open economy like Canada is the international competitiveness of our tax system, especially in relation to the United States.

Ontario Losing Tax Competitiveness
By Jack M. Mintz

The Ontario Liberals believe—quite erroneously—that their plan to hike corporate tax rates to 2001 levels would keep Ontario tax competitive. This belief is further undermined by recent events south of the border: The Republican-dominated House of Representatives and the Senate are looking at a proposed tax package that would cut corporate tax rates and put another nail in Ontario's coffin as an attractive location to do business.

The package's most important proposal would cut the U.S. federal corporate tax rate from 35% to 32% while removing some tax incentives. If the Ontario Liberals raise the corporate income tax rate from 12.5% to 14% in 2004, largely offsetting the final federal cut in the corporate rate in 2004 from 24.12% to 22.12%, the combined federal and provincial corporate income tax rate for Ontario companies in 2004 will be 36.12%. Since U.S. state corporate taxes—deductible from U.S. federal tax—average only 7%, the average U.S. corporate tax rate will virtually match the Ontario rate. States with little or no corporate taxes will have a corporate rate well below Ontario's.

Even when the statutory tax rates are about the same, the effective tax rate on capital in the United States will be substantially below Ontario's. The effective tax rate on capital not only takes into account statutory corporate income tax rates but also the effect of depreciation, inventory and other cost deductions as well as other taxes paid when investing in capital: capital taxes and sales taxes on business inputs.

Ontario companies are disadvantaged relative to U.S. companies since capital cost deductions, including bonus depreciation, are more generous in the United States, which also does not impose capital taxes, by and large. The effective tax rate on capital in Ontario currently averages about 50% more than that in the United States. Ontario's is also the third-highest in Canada, only surpassed by NDP-led Saskatchewan and Manitoba.

corporations are not people. Voters are always eager to have their taxes reduced and have some impersonal corporation pick up the tab.

But before deciding that the corporate income tax is a good way for the government to raise revenue, we should consider who bears the burden of the corporate tax. This is a difficult question on which economists disagree, but one thing is certain: *People pay all taxes.* When the government levies a tax on a corporation, the corporation is more like a tax collector than a taxpayer. The burden of the tax ultimately falls on people—the owners, customers, or workers of the corporation.

Other countries that have sharply lower effective tax rates on capital than Ontario include the Scandinavian countries, the United Kingdom, Ireland and Australia. Raising Ontario's corporate income tax rate when other jurisdictions have more attractive tax policies and just as equally attractive public services will surely hurt Ontario workers the most, as capital projects go elsewhere. Businesses remaining in Ontario faced with high taxes will invest in less capital and adopt fewer technologies. Labour productivity will suffer as a result and workers will get paid less. In the long run, high business taxes kill the golden goose that lays the egg.

As well, Ontario should not expect much revenue from a tax rate increase. Many businesses will shift their interest-deductible debt finance to Ontario-based subsidiaries, thereby undermining the revenue objective of increasing the rates.

With Wednesday's announcement of a significant deficit in Ontario, Greg Sorbara, the minister of finance, is caught between a rock and a hard place. By raising corporate taxes to try to fund public services at the present time, Ontario will lose investment activity, compromising its ability to fund the desirable public services the province will need in the future.

Another approach is available to the Ontario government. Instead of raising the statutory corporate tax rate that harms productive businesses, Ontario could follow Quebec's example and dismantle Ontario Inc., which Ernie Eves introduced when he was minister of finance. By eliminating ineffective tax incentives, business productivity would be improved and the tax system made much less complex for taxpayers to comply with and governments to administer.

A bewildering list of special tax incentives have been introduced in the past seven years, including tax credits for flow-through shares, co-operative education, graduate transitions, workplace child care, and educational technology, plus interest-exempt Ontario opportunity bonds and a host of others. Certainly, the Northern Ontario tax holiday should be cancelled and certainly small business tax rates should not be cut further below the general corporate tax rate, since that would only encourage people to incorporate business activities to avoid personal income tax and discourage businesses to grow. Whether any of these special tax incentives are effective is dubious at best; that they have added great complexity to the tax system is certain. Cancelling these ineffective tax incentives could help pay for lower corporate tax rates.

Further, it would not take long for any finance department to find some subsidies that have propped up businesses that would otherwise go into receivership.

The new Ontario government has a serious choice to make as it tackles its fiscal problem. It could follow through with an ill-advised policy to raise corporate tax rates, thereby using the worst economic policy to undermine productivity and competitiveness. Or it could do the right thing and eliminate ineffective corporate tax incentives and business subsidies. No smart minister of finance would have difficulty figuring this out.

Jack M. Mintz is president and CEO of the C.D. Howe Institute (http://www.cdhowe.org) *and Deloitte & Touche Professor of Taxation at the J.L. Rotman School of Management, University of Toronto.*

Source: *Financial Post*, October 31, 2003. Material reprinted with the express permission of "The National Post Company," a CanWest Partnership.

Many economists believe that workers and customers bear much of the burden of the corporate income tax. To see why, consider an example. Suppose that the government decides to raise the tax on the income earned by car companies. At first, this tax hurts the owners of the car companies, who receive less profit. But, over time, these owners will respond to the tax. Because producing cars is less profitable, they invest less in building new car factories. Instead, they invest their wealth in other ways—for example, by buying larger houses or by building factories in other industries or other countries. With fewer car factories, the supply of cars declines, as does the demand for autoworkers. Thus, a tax on

This worker pays part of the corporate income tax.

corporations making cars causes the price of cars to rise and the wages of autoworkers to fall.

The corporate income tax shows how dangerous the flypaper theory of tax incidence can be. The corporate income tax is popular in part because it appears to be paid by rich corporations. Yet those who bear the ultimate burden of the tax—the customers and workers of corporations—are often not rich. If the true incidence of the corporate tax were more widely known, this tax might be less popular among voters. ●

QuickQuiz Explain the *benefits principle* and the *ability-to-pay principle*. ● What are *vertical equity* and *horizontal equity*? ● Why is studying tax incidence important for determining the equity of a tax system?

CONCLUSION: THE TRADEOFF BETWEEN EQUITY AND EFFICIENCY

Almost everyone agrees that equity and efficiency are the two most important goals of the tax system. But often these two goals conflict. Many proposed changes in the tax laws increase efficiency while reducing equity, or increase equity while reducing efficiency. People disagree about tax policy often because they attach different weights to these two goals. As a result, tax policy is often the subject of heated political debate. Indeed, elections may be won and lost on the basis of the weights the political parties attach to the conflicting goals of efficiency and equity.

Economics alone cannot determine the best way to balance the goals of efficiency and equity. This issue involves political philosophy as well as economics. But economists do have an important role in the political debate over tax policy: They can shed light on the tradeoffs that society faces and can help us avoid policies that sacrifice efficiency without any benefit in terms of equity.

SUMMARY

- The Canadian government raises revenue using various taxes. The most important tax for the federal and the provincial governments is the personal income tax.

- The efficiency of a tax system refers to the costs it imposes on taxpayers. There are two costs of taxes beyond the transfer of resources from the taxpayer to the government. The first is the distortion in the allocation of resources that arises as taxes alter incentives and behaviour. The second is the administrative burden of complying with the tax laws.

- The equity of a tax system concerns whether the tax burden is distributed fairly among the population. According to the benefits principle, it is fair for people to pay taxes based on the benefits they receive from the government. According to the ability-to-pay principle, it is fair for people to pay taxes based on their capability to handle the financial burden. When evaluating the equity of a tax system, it is important to remember a lesson from the study of tax incidence: The distribution of tax burdens is not the same as the distribution of tax bills.

- When considering changes in the tax laws, policymakers often face a tradeoff between efficiency and equity. Much of the debate over tax policy arises because people give different weights to these two goals.

KEY CONCEPTS

budget surplus, p. 249
budget deficit, p. 249
average tax rate, p. 254
marginal tax rate, p. 254

lump-sum tax, p. 255
benefits principle, p. 256
ability-to-pay principle, p. 257
vertical equity, p. 257

horizontal equity, p. 257
proportional tax, p. 257
regressive tax, p. 258
progressive tax, p. 258

QUESTIONS FOR REVIEW

1. Over the past century, has government grown more or less slowly than the rest of the economy?

2. What are the two most important sources of revenue for the federal government?

3. Why is the burden of a tax to taxpayers greater than the revenue received by the government?

4. Why do some economists advocate taxing consumption rather than income?

5. Give two arguments why wealthy taxpayers should pay more taxes than poor taxpayers.

6. What is the concept of horizontal equity, and why is it hard to apply?

PROBLEMS AND APPLICATIONS

1. Government spending in Canada has grown as a share of national income over time. What changes in our economy and our society might explain this trend? Do you expect the trend to continue?

2. In a published source or on the Internet, find out whether the Canadian federal government had a budget deficit or surplus last year. What do policymakers expect to happen over the next few years?

3. Many of the tables in this chapter use data from Statistics Canada. To answer the following questions, use any Statistics Canada data source that is available to you, such as CANSIM (Statistics Canada's online database: http://www.statcan.ca/english/CANSIM) or Statistics Canada catalogues. Provide some numbers to support your answers.
   a. Figure 12.1 shows that government revenue as a percentage of total income has increased over time. Is this increase primarily attributable to changes in federal government revenue or in provincial and local government revenue?
   b. Looking at the combined revenue of the federal government and provincial and local governments, how has the composition of total revenue changed over time? Are personal income taxes more or less important? Sales taxes? Corporate profits taxes?
   c. Looking at federal government transfers to the provinces, have these transfers increased or decreased over time as a share of total provincial revenue?

4. Explain how individuals' behaviour is affected by the following features of the federal tax code.
   a. Contributions to charity are tax-deductible.
   b. Sales of beer are taxed.
   c. Realized capital gains are taxed, but accrued gains are not. (When someone owns a

share of stock that rises in value, she has an "accrued" capital gain. If she sells the share, she has a "realized" gain.)

5. Suppose that your province raises its sales tax from 5 percent to 6 percent. The government forecasts a 20 percent increase in sales tax revenue. Is this plausible? Explain.

6. Categorize each of the following funding schemes as examples of the benefits principle or the ability-to-pay principle.
   a. Visitors to many national parks pay an entrance fee.
   b. Local property taxes support elementary and secondary schools.
   c. An airport trust fund collects a tax on each plane ticket sold and uses the money to improve airports and the air traffic control system.

7. Any income tax schedule embodies two types of tax rates—average tax rates and marginal tax rates.
   a. The average tax rate is defined as total taxes paid divided by income. For the proportional tax system presented in Table 12.8, what are the average tax rates for people earning $50 000, $100 000, and $200 000? What are the corresponding average tax rates in the regressive and progressive tax systems?
   b. The marginal tax rate is defined as the extra taxes paid on additional income divided by the increase in income. Calculate the marginal tax rate for the proportional tax system as income rises from $50 000 to $100 000. Calculate the marginal tax rate as income rises from $100 000 to $200 000. Calculate the corresponding marginal tax rates for the regressive and progressive tax systems.
   c. Describe the relationship between average tax rates and marginal tax rates for each of these three systems. In general, which rate is relevant for someone deciding whether to accept a job that pays slightly more than her current job? Which rate is relevant for judging the vertical equity of a tax system?

8. If a salesman takes a client to lunch, part of the cost of the lunch is a deductible business expense for his company. Some MPs have argued that this feature of the tax code benefits relatively wealthy businesspeople and should be eliminated. Yet their arguments have been met with greater opposition from eating and drinking establishments than from companies themselves. Explain.

9. Provincial welfare programs have very high "clawback" rates. For example, when a person receiving welfare earns money from employment, that person's welfare benefits decline by as much as 75 cents for each dollar earned. What do you think is the effect of this feature of welfare programs on the labour supply of low-income individuals? Explain.

10. Federal payroll taxes to fund the EI program are levied at a combined rate of 5.04 percent up to a ceiling of about $39 000.
   a. If there were no limit on the income level at which these taxes apply, would they be proportional, progressive, or regressive? With the limit, are the taxes proportional, progressive, or regressive?
   b. The amount of EI benefits that people receive depends on the amount of payroll taxes they paid. Relative to people who had low earnings, people who had higher earnings and paid more in taxes receive more benefits, but not proportionally more. Does this feature of the EI system make EI a progressive or a regressive payroll tax?

11. What is the efficiency justification for taxing consumption rather than income? Suppose that Ottawa reduced personal tax rates and, to raise the same amount of revenue, increased the GST rate. Would this make the Canadian tax system more or less progressive? Explain.

12. Payroll taxes to fund the EI system are paid by both employees and employers. Does this legal division of responsibility indicate the true incidence of these taxes? Explain.

INTERNET RESOURCES

- Finance Canada's website (http://www.fin.gc.ca) contains a lot of information on tax and expenditure policy in Canada.

- The Canadian Tax Foundation website contains several links pertaining to taxation and other policy issues: http://www.ctf.ca/aboutctf/aim.asp.

- The C.D. Howe Institute (http://www.cdhowe.org) is an independent, nonprofit, economic and social policy research institution. Several publications dealing with tax policy are posted annually on its site.

http://   For more study tools, please visit http://www.mankiw3e.nelson.com.

5

FIRM BEHAVIOUR AND
THE ORGANIZATION OF INDUSTRY

13

THE COSTS OF PRODUCTION

Learning Objectives

In this chapter, you will …

- Examine what items are included in a firm's costs of production
- Analyze the link between a firm's production process and its total costs
- Learn the meaning of average total cost and marginal cost and how they are related
- Consider the shape of a typical firm's cost curves
- Examine the relationship between short-run and long-run costs

The economy is made up of thousands of firms that produce the goods and services you enjoy every day: General Motors produces automobiles, General Electric produces lightbulbs, and General Mills produces breakfast cereals. Some firms, such as these three, are large; they employ thousands of workers and have thousands of shareholders who share in the firms' profits. Other firms, such as the local barbershop or candy store, are small; they employ only a few workers and are owned by a single person or family.

In previous chapters we used the supply curve to summarize firms' production decisions. According to the law of supply, firms are willing to produce and sell a greater quantity of a good when the price of the good is higher, and this response leads to a supply curve that slopes upward. For analyzing many questions, the law of supply is all you need to know about firm behaviour.

In this chapter and the ones that follow, we examine firm behaviour in more detail. This topic will give you a better understanding of what decisions lie behind the supply curve in a market. In addition, it will introduce you to a part of economics called *industrial organization*—the study of how firms' decisions regarding prices and quantities depend on the market conditions they face. The town in which you live, for instance, may have several pizzerias but only one cable television company. How does this difference in the number of firms affect the prices in these markets and the efficiency of the market outcomes? The field of industrial organization addresses exactly this question.

Before we turn to these issues, however, we need to discuss the costs of production. All firms, from Bell Canada Enterprises to your local deli, incur costs as they make the goods and services that they sell. As we will see in the coming chapters, a firm's costs are a key determinant of its production and pricing decisions. In this chapter, we define some of the variables that economists use to measure a firm's costs, and we consider the relationships among them. A word of warning: This topic can seem dry and technical, but it provides a crucial foundation for the fascinating topics that follow.

WHAT ARE COSTS?

We begin our discussion of costs at Hungry Helen's Cookie Factory. Helen, the owner of the firm, buys flour, sugar, chocolate chips, and other cookie ingredients. She also buys the mixers and ovens, and hires workers to run this equipment. She then sells the resulting cookies to consumers. By examining some of the issues that Helen faces in her business, we can learn some lessons about costs that apply to all firms in the economy.

Total Revenue, Total Cost, and Profit

We begin with the firm's objective. To understand what decisions a firm makes, we must understand what it is trying to do. It is conceivable that Helen started her firm because of an altruistic desire to provide the world with cookies or, perhaps, out of love for the cookie business. More likely, Helen started her business to make money. Economists normally assume that the goal of a firm is to maximize profit, and they find that this assumption works well in most cases.

What is a firm's profit? The amount that the firm receives for the sale of its output (cookies) is called its **total revenue.** The amount that the firm pays to buy inputs (flour, sugar, workers, ovens, etc.) is called its **total cost.** Helen gets to keep any revenue that is not needed to cover costs. **Profit** is a firm's total revenue minus its total cost. That is,

$$\text{Profit} = \text{Total revenue} - \text{Total cost}$$

Helen's objective is to make her firm's profit as large as possible.

To see how a firm goes about maximizing profit, we must consider fully how to measure its total revenue and its total cost. Total revenue is the easy part: It equals the quantity of output the firm produces times the price at which it sells its output. If Helen produces 10 000 cookies and sells them at $2 a cookie, her total revenue is $20 000. By contrast, the measurement of a firm's total cost is more subtle.

Costs as Opportunity Costs

When measuring costs at Hungry Helen's Cookie Factory or any other firm, it is important to keep in mind one of the ten principles of economics from Chapter 1:

total revenue
the amount a firm receives for the sale of its output

total cost
the market value of the inputs a firm uses in production

profit
total revenue minus total cost

The cost of something is what you give up to get it. Recall that the *opportunity cost* of an item refers to all those things that must be forgone to acquire that item. When economists speak of a firm's cost of production, they include all the opportunity costs of making its output of goods and services.

A firm's opportunity costs of production are sometimes obvious and sometimes less so. When Helen pays $1000 for flour, that $1000 is an opportunity cost because Helen can no longer use that $1000 to buy something else. Similarly, when Helen hires workers to make the cookies, the wages she pays are part of the firm's costs. Because these costs require the firm to pay out some money, they are called **explicit costs.** By contrast, some of a firm's opportunity costs, called **implicit costs,** do not require a cash outlay. Imagine that Helen is skilled with computers and could earn $100 per hour working as a programmer. For every hour that Helen works at her cookie factory, she gives up $100 in income, and this forgone income is also part of her costs.

This distinction between explicit and implicit costs highlights an important difference between how economists and accountants analyze a business. Economists are interested in studying how firms make production and pricing decisions. Because these decisions are based on both explicit and implicit costs, economists include both when measuring a firm's costs. By contrast, accountants have the job of keeping track of the money that flows into and out of firms. As a result, they measure the explicit costs but often ignore the implicit costs.

The difference between economists and accountants is easy to see in the case of Hungry Helen's Cookie Factory. When Helen gives up the opportunity to earn money as a computer programmer, her accountant will not count this as a cost of her cookie business. Because no money flows out of the business to pay for this cost, it never shows up on the accountant's financial statements. An economist, however, will count the forgone income as a cost because it will affect the decisions that Helen makes in her cookie business. For example, if Helen's wage as a computer programmer rises from $100 to $500 per hour, she might decide that running her cookie business is too costly and choose to shut down the factory to become a full-time computer programmer.

explicit costs
input costs that require an outlay of money by the firm

implicit costs
input costs that do not require an outlay of money by the firm

The Cost of Capital as an Opportunity Cost

An important implicit cost of almost every business is the opportunity cost of the financial capital that has been invested in the business. Suppose, for instance, that Helen used $300 000 of her savings to buy her cookie factory from the previous owner. If Helen had instead left this money deposited in a savings account that pays an interest rate of 5 percent, she would have earned $15 000 per year. To own her cookie factory, therefore, Helen has given up $15 000 per year in interest income. This forgone $15 000 is one of the implicit opportunity costs of Helen's business.

As we have already noted, economists and accountants treat costs differently, and this is especially true in their treatment of the cost of capital. An economist views the $15 000 in interest income that Helen gives up every year as a cost of her business, even though it is an implicit cost. Helen's accountant, however, will not show this $15 000 as a cost because no money flows out of the business to pay for it.

To further explore the difference between economists and accountants, let's change the example slightly. Suppose now that Helen did not have the entire $300 000 to buy the factory but, instead, used $100 000 of her own savings and borrowed $200 000 from a bank at an interest rate of 5 percent. Helen's accountant, who measures only explicit costs, will now count the $10 000 interest paid on the bank loan every year as a cost because this amount of money now flows out of the firm. By contrast, according to an economist, the opportunity cost of owning the business is still $15 000. The opportunity cost equals the interest on the bank loan (an explicit cost of $10 000) plus the forgone interest on savings (an implicit cost of $5000).

Economic Profit versus Accounting Profit

economic profit
total revenue minus total cost, including both explicit and implicit costs

accounting profit
total revenue minus total explicit cost

Now let's return to the firm's objective—profit. Because economists and accountants measure costs differently, they also measure profit differently. An economist measures a firm's **economic profit** as the firm's total revenue minus all the opportunity costs (explicit and implicit) of producing the goods and services sold. An accountant measures the firm's **accounting profit** as the firm's total revenue minus only the firm's explicit costs.

Figure 13.1 summarizes this difference. Notice that because the accountant ignores the implicit costs, accounting profit is usually larger than economic profit. For a business to be profitable from an economist's standpoint, total revenue must cover all the opportunity costs, both explicit and implicit.

QuickQuiz Farmer McDonald gives banjo lessons for $20 an hour. One day, he spends 10 hours planting $100 worth of seeds on his farm. What opportunity cost

FIGURE 13.1

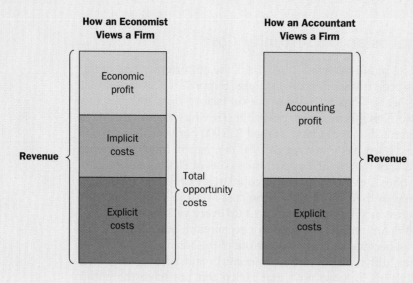

Economists versus Accountants

Economists include all opportunity costs when analyzing a firm, whereas accountants measure only explicit costs. Therefore, economic profit is smaller than accounting profit.

has he incurred? What cost would his accountant measure? If these seeds will yield $200 worth of crops, does McDonald earn an accounting profit? Does he earn an economic profit?

PRODUCTION AND COSTS

Firms incur costs when they buy inputs to produce the goods and services that they plan to sell. In this section we examine the link between a firm's production process and its total cost. Once again, we consider Hungry Helen's Cookie Factory.

In the analysis that follows, we make an important simplifying assumption: We assume that the size of Helen's factory is fixed and that Helen can vary the quantity of cookies produced only by changing the number of workers. This assumption is realistic in the short run, but not in the long run. That is, Helen cannot build a larger factory overnight, but she can do so within a year or so. This analysis, therefore, should be viewed as describing the production decisions that Helen faces in the short run. We examine the relationship between costs and time horizon more fully later in the chapter.

The Production Function

Table 13.3 (p. 278) shows how the quantity of cookies Helen's factory produces per hour depends on the number of workers. As you see in the first two columns, if there are no workers in the factory, Helen produces no cookies. When there is 1 worker, she produces 50 cookies. When there are 2 workers, she produces 90 cookies, and so on. Figure 13.2 (p. 278) presents a graph of these two columns of numbers. The number of workers is on the horizontal axis, and the number of cookies produced is on the vertical axis. This relationship between the quantity of inputs (workers) and quantity of output (cookies) is called the **production function.**

It is again important to emphasize that at this point we are dealing with a *short-run* production function, which allows the number of workers to vary but holds the size of Helen's factory fixed. In the long run, both the number of workers and the size of the factory may be varied. In this case, the relationship between the number of workers, the size of the factory, and the number of cookies produced will be captured by a *long-run* production function. We will return to this distinction later in the chapter. For now we will focus on the short-run production function.

One of the ten principles of economics introduced in Chapter 1 is that rational people think at the margin. As we will see in future chapters, this idea is the key to understanding the decision a firm makes about how many workers to hire and how much output to produce. To take a step toward understanding these decisions, the third column in the table gives the marginal product of a worker. The **marginal product** of any input in the production process is the increase in the quantity of output obtained from one additional unit of that input, holding all other inputs constant. When the number of workers goes from 1 to 2, cookie production increases from 50 to 90, so the marginal product of the second worker is 40 cookies. And when the number of workers goes from 2 to 3, cookie production increases from 90 to 120, so the marginal product of the third worker is 30 cookies.

Notice that as the number of workers increases, the marginal product declines. The second worker has a marginal product of 40 cookies, the third worker has a

production function
the relationship between quantity of inputs used to make a good and the quantity of output of that good

marginal product
the increase in output that arises from an additional unit of input

ECONOMISTS KNEW IT ALL ALONG

The concept of economic profits has been familiar to economists for over a hundred years. It took a management consulting company, however, to popularize the idea. Stern Stewart & Co., a U.S.-based consulting firm, has marketed the concept as a leading edge management tool under the copyrighted name Economic Value Added (EVA®).

The concept of economic profits (sorry, EVA®) is closely related to another important management tool: net present value (NPV).

To illustrate their relationship, understand that companies have two basic sources of money to finance their activities: debt and equity. Money from business operations is not a third source because, after paying for debt, any cash left over that is not returned to shareholders in the form of dividends is kept in the company on behalf of shareholders, and is therefore another source of equity.

When debtholders lend money to a company, they do so with the expectation that the company will repay the principal, with interest. The interest a company pays depends on the debtholders' expectations of other opportunities, of inflation, and of risk. The greater the risk, the greater the expectation of inflation, and the greater the opportunity to earn money elsewhere, the greater the interest rate charged the borrower.

Shareholders also consider other opportunities, inflation, and risk in determining whether to invest in a company. While there is no reason to believe debtholders and shareholders have different opportunities for investment or different expectations of inflation, returns on equity are more risky than returns on debt.

To make our analysis more concrete, let's say that half of the money used by corporations comes from debtholders and half from shareholders. If debtholders require a 10 percent return on their investment and shareholders require a 20 percent return, then on average, projects undertaken by a company will have to return 15 percent to satisfy debt and equity holders. The 15 percent is called the weighted average cost of capital, or WACC. The following is the WACC calculation for a $50 project:

Shareholder: 20% expected return from $50 investment
Debtholder: 10% expected from $50 investment
$$\text{WACC} = 0.5 \times 20\% + 0.5 \times 10\% = 15\%$$

The 15 percent WACC can serve as a hurdle rate of return. In order to be approved, projects must generate a rate of return that exceeds the hurdle. To check if a project's rate of return exceeds the hurdle, management can use a 15 percent discount rate to discount the cash flows of any proposed project. If a project has a positive expected NPV, that indicates the project has a return greater than the hurdle rate. If a project has a negative expected NPV, that indicates the project has a return less than the hurdle rate.

Table 13.1 shows a timeline for three alternative investments. Project A requires an initial outlay of $1000 and generates a net cash flow of $100 per year for five years. At the end of five years, the company receives back the $1000 investment. Table 13.1 also shows the NPV of each of the three projects. The present value factor for each year is calculated as 1 divided by $1.15n$, where n is the number of years in the future. For example, the present value factor of .658 for year 3 is calculated by dividing 1 by ($1.15 \times 1.15 \times 1.15$).

The present value of each year's cash flow is calculated by multiplying the cash flow by the appropriate present value factor. The present value of the $100 received for Project A in year 3 is $65.80.

When all the cash flows in Project A are multiplied by their respective present value factors and then added up, the NPV is shown to be negative $168. Project A has a return of less than 15 percent. Project B's NPV is zero, indicating that the return for Pro-

---

diminishing marginal product
the property whereby the marginal product of an input declines as the quantity of the input increases

marginal product of 30 cookies, and the fourth worker has a marginal product of 20 cookies. This property is called **diminishing marginal product.** At first, when only a few workers are hired, they have easy access to Helen's kitchen equipment. As the number of workers increases, additional workers have to share equipment and work in more crowded conditions. Hence, as more and more workers are hired, each additional worker contributes less to the production of cookies.

Diminishing marginal product is also apparent in Figure 13.2. The production function's slope (rise over run) tells us the change in Helen's output of cookies (rise) for each additional input of labour (run). That is, the slope of the production

TABLE 13.1 NPV AND INVESTMENT TIMELINE

Project A

Now	Year 1	Year 2	Year 3	Year 4	Year 5	NPV
-$1000	$100	$100	$100	$100	$1000	-$168

Project B

Now	Year 1	Year 2	Year 3	Year 4	Year 5	NPV
-$1000	$150	$150	$150	$150	$1150	0

Project C

Now	Year 1	Year 2	Year 3	Year 4	Year 5	NPV
-$1000	$200	$200	$200	$200	$1200	$168

ject B is exactly 15 percent. Project C has a positive NPV of $168, indicating that its return is greater than 15 percent.

Assuming no other considerations, a company with financial discipline would not invest in Project A because it does not meet shareholder and debtholder expectations. The company might invest in Project B, because it meets the minimum requirements for a return. Only Project C, which has a positive NPV, adds to shareholder value.

After shareholders and debtholders receive their expected return, the remaining $168 can either be returned to shareholders or invested in new projects on behalf of shareholders. If managers invest in Project C and Project C meets its expected return, the bag will grow by $168 in present value terms. Shareholders will be $168 richer, and the project will have added $168 to shareholder value.

To understand economic value added, consider Company A and Company B in Table 13.2. Company A is more profitable than Company B, but after taking into consideration the amount of capital used in each company and the cost of that capital, Company A is actually destroying shareholder value during the period in which economic value added was calculated and Company B is creating shareholder value. The key to the economic value added calculation and what distinguishes it from accounting income is the charge for capital, which, via the WACC, takes into account the required rate of return to both debt and equity. The connection between NPV analysis and economic value added is the WACC used in both calculations.

NPV analysis may be used to decide whether or not to invest in a project, while economic value added may be used to calculate the market, or shareholder, value of the firm and to manage operations.

TABLE 13.2 EVA

	Company A	Company B
Revenue	$1000	$500
Expenses	500	300
Profits	500	200
Capital	3000	1000

function measures the marginal product of a worker. As the number of workers increases, the marginal product declines, and the production function becomes flatter.

From the Production Function to the Total-Cost Curve

The last three columns of Table 13.3 show Helen's cost of producing cookies. In this example, the cost of Helen's factory is $30 per hour, and the cost of a worker

TABLE 13.3

A Production Function and Total Cost: Hungry Helen's Cookie Factory

Number of Workers	Output (quantity of cookies produced per hour)	Marginal Product of Labour	Cost of Factory	Cost of Workers	Total Cost of Inputs (cost of factory + cost of workers)
0	0		$30	$ 0	$30
		50			
1	50		30	10	40
		40			
2	90		30	20	50
		30			
3	120		30	30	60
		20			
4	140		30	40	70
		10			
5	150		30	50	80

FIGURE 13.2

Hungry Helen's Production Function

A production function shows the relationship between the number of workers hired and the quantity of output produced. Here the number of workers hired (on the horizontal axis) is from the first column in Table 13.3, and the quantity of output produced (on the vertical axis) is from the second column. The production function gets flatter as the number of workers increases, which reflects diminishing marginal product.

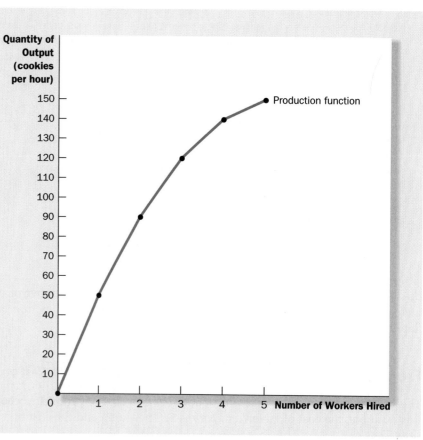

is $10 per hour. If she hires 1 worker, her total cost is $40. If she hires 2 workers, her total cost is $50, and so on. With this information, the table now shows how the number of workers Helen hires is related to the quantity of cookies she produces and to her total cost of production.

Our goal in the next several chapters is to study firms' production and pricing decisions. For this purpose, the most important relationship in Table 13.3 is between quantity produced (in the second column) and total costs (in the sixth column). Figure 13.3 graphs these two columns of data with the quantity produced on the horizontal axis and total cost on the vertical axis. This graph is called the *total-cost curve.*

Now compare the total-cost curve in Figure 13.3 with the production function in Figure 13.2. These two curves are opposite sides of the same coin. The total-cost curve gets steeper as the amount produced rises, whereas the production function gets flatter as production rises. These changes in slope occur for the same reason. High production of cookies means that Helen's kitchen is crowded with many workers. Because the kitchen is crowded, each additional worker adds less to production, reflecting diminishing marginal product. Therefore, the production function is relatively flat. But now turn this logic around: When the kitchen is crowded, producing an additional cookie requires a lot of additional labour and

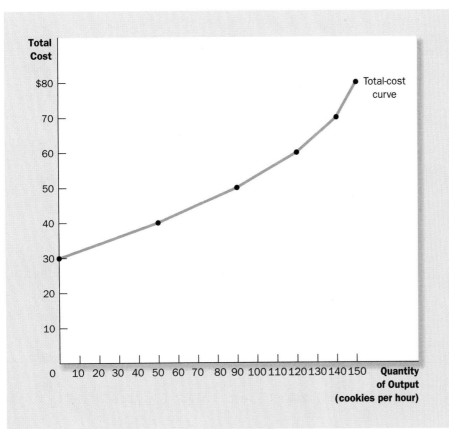

FIGURE 13.3

Hungry Helen's Total-Cost Curve

A total-cost curve shows the relationship between the quantity of output produced and total cost of production. Here the quantity of output produced (on the horizontal axis) is from the second column in Table 13.3, and the total cost (on the vertical axis) is from the sixth column. The total-cost curve gets steeper as the quantity of output increases because of diminishing marginal product.

is thus very costly. Therefore, when the quantity produced is large, the total-cost curve is relatively steep.

QuickQuiz If Farmer Jones plants no seeds on his farm, he gets no harvest. If he plants 1 bag of seeds, he gets 3 bushels of wheat. If he plants 2 bags, he gets 5 bushels. If he plants 3 bags, he gets 6 bushels. A bag of seeds costs $100, and seeds are his only cost. Use these data to graph the farmer's production function and total-cost curve. Explain their shapes.

THE VARIOUS MEASURES OF COST

Our analysis of Hungry Helen's Cookie Factory demonstrated how a firm's total cost reflects its production function. From data on a firm's total cost, we can derive several related measures of cost, which will turn out to be useful when we analyze production and pricing decisions in future chapters. To see how these related measures are derived, we consider the example in Table 13.4. This table presents cost data on Helen's neighbour: Thirsty Thelma's Lemonade Stand. Once again we are dealing with the short run, where the size of Thelma's stand is fixed.

TABLE 13.4

The Various Measures of Cost: Thirsty Thelma's Lemonade Stand

Quantity of Lemonade (glasses per hour)	Total Cost	Fixed Cost	Variable Cost	Average Fixed Cost	Average Variable Cost	Average Total Cost	Marginal Cost
0	$3.00	$3.00	$0.00	—	—	—	
							$0.30
1	3.30	3.00	0.30	$3.00	$0.30	$3.30	
							0.50
2	3.80	3.00	0.80	1.50	0.40	1.90	
							0.70
3	4.50	3.00	1.50	1.00	0.50	1.50	
							0.90
4	5.40	3.00	2.40	0.75	0.60	1.35	
							1.10
5	6.50	3.00	3.50	0.60	0.70	1.30	
							1.30
6	7.80	3.00	4.80	0.50	0.80	1.30	
							1.50
7	9.30	3.00	6.30	0.43	0.90	1.33	
							1.70
8	11.00	3.00	8.00	0.38	1.00	1.38	
							1.90
9	12.90	3.00	9.90	0.33	1.10	1.43	
							2.10
10	15.00	3.00	12.00	0.30	1.20	1.50	

The first column of the table shows the number of glasses of lemonade that Thelma might produce, ranging from 0 to 10 glasses per hour. The second column shows Thelma's total cost of producing lemonade. Figure 13.4 plots Thelma's total-cost curve. The quantity of lemonade (from the first column) is on the horizontal axis, and total cost (from the second column) is on the vertical axis. Thirsty Thelma's total-cost curve has a shape similar to Hungry Helen's. In particular, it becomes steeper as the quantity produced rises, which (as we have discussed) reflects diminishing marginal product.

Fixed and Variable Costs

Thelma's total cost can be divided into two types. Some costs, called **fixed costs,** do not vary with the quantity of output produced. They are incurred even if the firm produces nothing at all. Thelma's fixed costs include any rent she pays because this cost is the same regardless of how much lemonade Thelma produces. Similarly, if Thelma needs to hire a full-time bookkeeper to pay bills, regardless of the quantity of lemonade produced, the bookkeeper's salary is a fixed cost. The third column in Table 13.4 shows Thelma's fixed cost, which in this example is $3.00.

Some of the firm's costs, called **variable costs,** change as the firm alters the quantity of output produced. Thelma's variable costs include the cost of lemons,

fixed costs
costs that do not vary with the quantity of output produced

variable costs
costs that do vary with the quantity of output produced

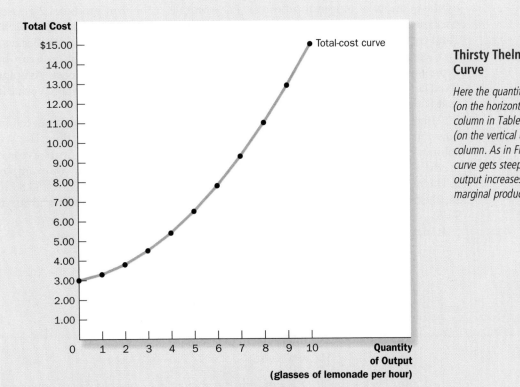

FIGURE 13.4

Thirsty Thelma's Total-Cost Curve

Here the quantity of output produced (on the horizontal axis) is from the first column in Table 13.4, and the total cost (on the vertical axis) is from the second column. As in Figure 13.3, the total-cost curve gets steeper as the quantity of output increases because of diminishing marginal product.

sugar, paper cups, and straws: The more lemonade Thelma makes, the more of these items she needs to buy. Similarly, if Thelma has to hire more workers to make more lemonade, the salaries of these workers are variable costs. The fourth column of the table shows Thelma's variable cost. The variable cost is 0 if she produces nothing, $0.30 if she produces 1 glass of lemonade, $0.80 if she produces 2 glasses, and so on.

A firm's total cost is the sum of fixed and variable costs. In Table 13.4, total cost in the second column equals fixed cost in the third column plus variable cost in the fourth column.

Average and Marginal Costs

As the owner of her firm, Thelma has to decide how much to produce. A key part of this decision is how her costs will vary as she changes the level of production. In making this decision, Thelma might ask her production supervisor the following two questions about the cost of producing lemonade:

- How much does it cost to make the typical glass of lemonade?
- How much does it cost to increase production of lemonade by 1 glass?

Although at first these two questions might seem to have the same answer, they do not. Both answers will turn out to be important for understanding how firms make production decisions.

To find the cost of the typical unit produced, we would divide the firm's costs by the quantity of output it produces. For example, if the firm produces 2 glasses per hour, its total cost is $3.80, and the cost of the typical glass is $3.80/2, or $1.90. Total cost divided by the quantity of output is called **average total cost.** Because total cost is just the sum of fixed and variable costs, average total cost can be expressed as the sum of average fixed cost and average variable cost. **Average fixed cost** is the fixed cost divided by the quantity of output, and **average variable cost** is the variable cost divided by the quantity of output.

Although average total cost tells us the cost of the typical unit, it does not tell us how much total cost will change as the firm alters its level of production. The last column in Table 13.4 shows the amount that total cost rises when the firm increases production by 1 unit of output. This number is called **marginal cost.** For example, if Thelma increases production from 2 to 3 glasses, total cost rises from $3.80 to $4.50, so the marginal cost of the third glass of lemonade is $4.50 minus $3.80, or $0.70.

It may be helpful to express these definitions mathematically:

$$\text{Average total cost} = \text{Total cost/Quantity}$$
$$ATC = TC/Q$$

and

$$\text{Marginal cost} = \text{Change in total cost/Change in quantity}$$
$$MC = \Delta TC/\Delta Q$$

Here Δ, the Greek letter *delta*, represents the change in a variable. These equations show how average total cost and marginal cost are derived from total cost. *Average*

average total cost
total cost divided by the quantity of output

average fixed cost
fixed costs divided by the quantity of output

average variable cost
variable costs divided by the quantity of output

marginal cost
the increase in total cost that arises from an extra unit of production

total cost tells us the cost of a typical unit of output if total cost is divided evenly over all the units produced. Marginal cost tells us the increase in total cost that arises from producing an additional unit of output. As we will see more fully in the next chapter, Thelma, our lemonade entrepreneur, will find the concepts of average total cost and marginal cost useful when deciding how much lemonade to produce.

Cost Curves and Their Shapes

Just as in previous chapters we found graphs of supply and demand useful when analyzing the behaviour of markets, we will find graphs of average and marginal cost useful when analyzing the behaviour of firms. Figure 13.5 graphs Thelma's costs using the data from Table 13.4. The horizontal axis measures the quantity the firm produces, and the vertical axis measures marginal and average costs. The graph shows four curves: average total cost (*ATC*), average fixed cost (*AFC*), average variable cost (*AVC*), and marginal cost (*MC*).

The cost curves shown here for Thirsty Thelma's Lemonade Stand have some features that are common to the cost curves of many firms in the economy. Let's examine three features in particular: the shape of marginal cost, the shape of average total cost, and the relationship between marginal and average total cost.

c

FIGURE 13.5

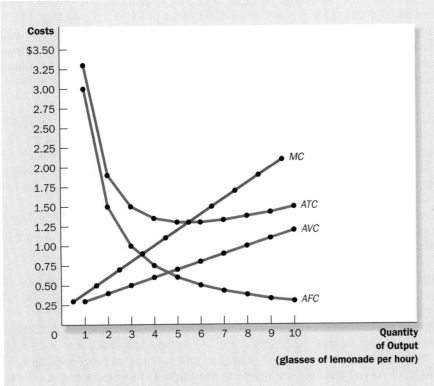

Thirsty Thelma's Average-Cost and Marginal-Cost Curves

This figure shows the average total cost (ATC), average fixed cost (AFC), average variable cost (AVC), and marginal cost (MC) for Thirsty Thelma's Lemonade Stand. All of these curves are obtained by graphing the data in Table 13.4. These cost curves show three features that are typical of many firms: (1) Marginal cost rises with the quantity of output. (2) The average-total-cost curve is U-shaped. (3) The marginal-cost curve crosses the average-total-cost curve at the minimum of average total cost.

Rising Marginal Cost   Thirsty Thelma's marginal cost rises with the quantity of output produced. This reflects the property of diminishing marginal product. When Thelma is producing a small quantity of lemonade, she has few workers and much of her equipment is not being used. Because she can easily put these idle resources to use, the marginal product of an extra worker is large, and the marginal cost of an extra glass of lemonade is small. By contrast, when Thelma is producing a large quantity of lemonade, her stand is crowded with workers and most of her equipment is fully utilized. Thelma can produce more lemonade by adding workers, but these new workers have to work in crowded conditions and may have to wait to use the equipment. Therefore, when the quantity of lemonade being produced is already high, the marginal product of an extra worker is low, and the marginal cost of an extra glass of lemonade is large.

U-Shaped Average Total Cost   Thirsty Thelma's average-total-cost curve is U-shaped. To understand why this is so, remember that average total cost is the sum of average fixed cost and average variable cost. Average fixed cost always declines as output rises because the fixed cost is spread over a larger number of units. Average variable cost typically rises as output increases because of diminishing marginal product. Average total cost reflects the shapes of both average fixed cost and average variable cost. As shown in Figure 13.5, at very low levels of output, such as 1 or 2 glasses per hour, average total cost is high because the fixed cost is spread over only a few units. Average total cost then declines as output increases until the firm's output reaches 5 glasses of lemonade per hour, when average total cost falls to $1.30 per glass. When the firm produces more than 6 glasses, average total cost starts rising again because average variable cost rises substantially.

The bottom of the U-shape occurs at the quantity that minimizes average total cost. This quantity is sometimes called the **efficient scale** of the firm. For Thirsty Thelma, the efficient scale is 5 or 6 glasses of lemonade. If she produces more or less than this amount, her average total cost rises above the minimum of $1.30.

efficient scale
the quantity of output that minimizes average total cost

The Relationship between Marginal Cost and Average Total Cost   If you look at Figure 13.5 (or back at Table 13.4), you will see something that may be surprising at first. *Whenever marginal cost is less than average total cost, average total cost is falling. Whenever marginal cost is greater than average total cost, average total cost is rising.* This feature of Thirsty Thelma's cost curves is not a coincidence from the particular numbers used in the example: It is true for all firms.

To see why, consider an analogy. Average total cost is like your cumulative grade point average. Marginal cost is like the grade in the next course you will take. If your grade in your next course is less than your grade point average, your grade point average will fall. If your grade in your next course is higher than your grade point average, your grade point average will rise. The mathematics of average and marginal costs is exactly the same as the mathematics of average and marginal grades.

This relationship between average total cost and marginal cost has an important corollary: *The marginal-cost curve crosses the average-total-cost curve at its minimum.* Why? At low levels of output, marginal cost is below average total cost, so average total cost is falling. But after the two curves cross, marginal cost rises above average total cost. For the reason we have just discussed, average total cost must start to rise at this level of output. Hence, this point of intersection is the minimum of average total cost. As you will see in the next chapter, this point of minimum average total cost plays a key role in the analysis of competitive firms.

Typical Cost Curves

In the examples we have studied so far, the firms exhibit diminishing marginal product and, therefore, rising marginal cost at all levels of output. Yet actual firms are often a bit more complicated than this. In many firms, diminishing marginal product does not start to occur immediately after the first worker is hired. Depending on the production process, the second or third worker might have higher marginal product than the first because a team of workers can divide tasks and work more productively than a single worker. Such firms would first experience increasing marginal product for a while before diminishing marginal product sets in.

The table in Figure 13.6 (p. 286) shows the cost data for such a firm, called Big Bob's Bagel Bin. These data are used in the graphs. Panel (a) shows how total cost (TC) depends on the quantity produced, and panel (b) shows average total cost (ATC), average fixed cost (AFC), average variable cost (AVC), and marginal cost (MC). In the range of output from 0 to 4 bagels per hour, the firm experiences increasing marginal product, and the marginal-cost curve falls. After 5 bagels per hour, the firm starts to experience diminishing marginal product, and the marginal-cost curve starts to rise. This combination of increasing then diminishing marginal product also makes the average-variable-cost curve U-shaped.

Despite these differences from our previous example, Big Bob's cost curves share the three properties that are most important to remember:

1. Marginal cost eventually rises with the quantity of output.
2. The average-total-cost curve is U-shaped.
3. The marginal-cost curve crosses the average-total-cost curve at the minimum of average total cost.

QuickQuiz Suppose Honda's total cost of producing 4 cars is $225 000 and its total cost of producing 5 cars is $250 000. What is the average total cost of producing 5 cars? What is the marginal cost of the fifth car? • Draw the marginal-cost curve and the average-total-cost curve for a typical firm, and explain why these curves cross where they do.

COSTS IN THE SHORT RUN AND IN THE LONG RUN

We noted at the beginning of this chapter that a firm's costs might depend on the time horizon being examined. Let's examine more precisely why this might be the case.

FIGURE 13.6

Big Bob's Cost Curves

Many firms, like Big Bob's Bagel Bin, experience increasing marginal product before diminishing marginal product and, therefore, have cost curves shaped like those in this figure. Panel (a) shows how total cost (TC) depends on the quantity produced. Panel (b) shows how average total cost (ATC), average fixed cost (AFC), average variable cost (AVC), and marginal cost (MC) depend on the quantity produced. These curves are derived by graphing the data from the table. Notice that marginal cost and average variable cost fall for a while before starting to rise.

Quantity of Bagels (per hour)	Total Cost	Fixed Cost	Variable Cost	Average Fixed Cost	Average Variable Cost	Average Total Cost	Marginal Cost
Q	TC = FC + VC	FC	VC	AFC = FC/Q	AVC = VC/Q	ATC = TC/Q	MC = ΔTC/ΔQ
0	$ 2.00	$2.00	$ 0.00	—	—	—	
							$1.00
1	3.00	2.00	1.00	$2.00	$1.00	$3.00	
							0.80
2	3.80	2.00	1.80	1.00	0.90	1.90	
							0.60
3	4.40	2.00	2.40	0.67	0.80	1.47	
							0.40
4	4.80	2.00	2.80	0.50	0.70	1.20	
							0.40
5	5.20	2.00	3.20	0.40	0.64	1.04	
							0.60
6	5.80	2.00	3.80	0.33	0.63	0.96	
							0.80
7	6.60	2.00	4.60	0.29	0.66	0.95	
							1.00
8	7.60	2.00	5.60	0.25	0.70	0.95	
							1.20
9	8.80	2.00	6.80	0.22	0.76	0.98	
							1.40
10	10.20	2.00	8.20	0.20	0.82	1.02	
							1.60
11	11.80	2.00	9.80	0.18	0.89	1.07	
							1.80
12	13.60	2.00	11.60	0.17	0.97	1.14	
							2.00
13	15.60	2.00	13.60	0.15	1.05	1.20	
							2.20
14	17.80	2.00	15.80	0.14	1.13	1.27	

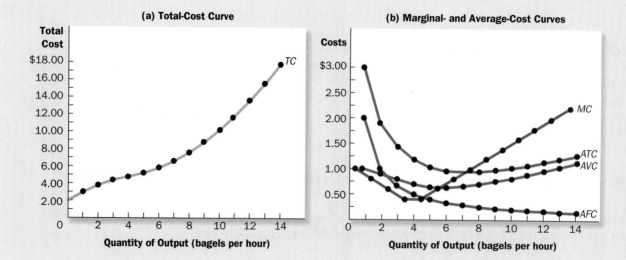

(a) Total-Cost Curve

(b) Marginal- and Average-Cost Curves

The Relationship between Short-Run and Long-Run Average Total Cost

For many firms, the division of total costs between fixed and variable costs depends on the time horizon. Consider, for instance, a car manufacturer, such as Ford Motor Company. Over a period of only a few months, Ford cannot adjust the number or sizes of its car factories. The only way it can produce additional cars is to hire more workers at the factories it already has. The cost of these factories is, therefore, a fixed cost in the short run. By contrast, over a period of several years, Ford can expand the size of its factories, build new factories, or close old ones. Thus, the cost of its factories is a variable cost in the long run.

Because many decisions are fixed in the short run but variable in the long run, a firm's long-run cost curves differ from its short-run cost curves. Figure 13.7 shows an example. The figure presents three short-run average-total-cost curves—for a small, medium, and large factory. It also presents the long-run average-total-cost curve. As the firm moves along the long-run curve, it is adjusting the size of the factory to the quantity of production.

This graph shows how short-run and long-run costs are related. The long-run average-total-cost curve is a much flatter U-shape than the short-run average-total-cost curve. In addition, all the short-run curves lie on or above the long-run curve. These properties arise because firms have greater flexibility in the long run. In essence, in the long run, the firm gets to choose which short-run curve it wants to use. But in the short run, it has to use whatever short-run curve it chose in the past.

The figure shows an example of how a change in production alters costs over different time horizons. When Ford wants to increase production from 1000 to 1200 cars per day, it has no choice in the short run but to hire more workers at its

FIGURE 13.7

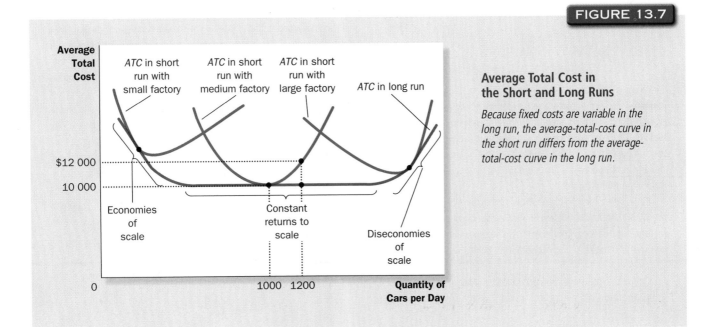

Average Total Cost in the Short and Long Runs

Because fixed costs are variable in the long run, the average-total-cost curve in the short run differs from the average-total-cost curve in the long run.

economies of scale
the property whereby long-run average total cost falls as the quantity of output increases

diseconomies of scale
the property whereby long-run average total cost rises as the quantity of output increases

constant returns to scale
the property whereby long-run average total cost stays the same as the quantity of output changes

existing medium-sized factory. Because of diminishing marginal product, average total cost rises from $10 000 to $12 000 per car. In the long run, however, Ford can expand both the size of the factory and its work force, and average total cost returns to $10 000.

How long does it take for a firm to get to the long run? The answer depends on the firm. It can take a year or longer for a major manufacturing firm, such as a car company, to build a larger factory. By contrast, a person running a lemonade stand can go and buy a larger pitcher within an hour or less. There is, therefore, no single answer about how long it takes a firm to adjust its production facilities.

Economies and Diseconomies of Scale

The shape of the long-run average-total-cost curve conveys important information about the technology for producing a good. When long-run average total cost declines as output increases, there are said to be **economies of scale.** When long-run average total cost rises as output increases, there are said to be **diseconomies of scale.** When long-run average total cost does not vary with the level of output, there are said to be **constant returns to scale.** In this example, Ford has economies of scale at low levels of output, constant returns to scale at intermediate levels of output, and diseconomies of scale at high levels of output.

LESSONS FROM A PIN FACTORY

"Jack of all trades, master of none." This well-known adage helps explain why firms sometimes experience economies of scale. A person who tries to do everything usually ends up doing nothing very well. If a firm wants its workers to be as productive as they can be, it is often best to give each a limited task that he or she can master. But this is possible only if a firm employs many workers and produces a large quantity of output.

In his celebrated book *An Inquiry into the Nature and Causes of the Wealth of Nations*, Adam Smith described a visit he made to a pin factory. Smith was impressed by the specialization among the workers and the resulting economies of scale. He wrote:

One man draws out the wire, another straightens it, a third cuts it, a fourth points it, a fifth grinds it at the top for receiving the

head; to make the head requires two or three distinct operations; to put it on is a peculiar business; to whiten it is another; it is even a trade by itself to put them into paper.

Smith reported that because of this specialization, the pin factory produced thousands of pins per worker every day. He conjectured that if the workers had chosen to work separately, rather than as a team of specialists, "they certainly could not each of them make twenty, perhaps not one pin a day." In other words, because of specialization, a large pin factory could achieve higher output per worker and lower average cost per pin than a small pin factory.

The specialization that Smith observed in the pin factory is prevalent in the modern economy. If you want to build a house, for instance, you could try to do all the work yourself. But most people turn to a builder, who in turn hires carpenters, plumbers, electricians, painters, and many other types of workers. These workers specialize in particular jobs, and this allows them to become better at their jobs than if they were generalists. Indeed, the use of specialization to achieve economies of scale is one reason modern societies are as prosperous as they are.

What might cause economies or diseconomies of scale? Economies of scale often arise because higher production levels allow *specialization* among workers, which permits each worker to become better at his or her assigned tasks. For instance, modern assembly-line production requires a large number of workers. If Ford were producing only a small quantity of cars, it could not take advantage of this approach and would have higher average total cost. Diseconomies of scale can arise because of *coordination problems* that are inherent in any large organization. The more cars Ford produces, the more stretched the management team becomes, and the less effective the managers become at keeping costs down.

This analysis shows why long-run average-total-cost curves are often U-shaped. At low levels of production, the firm benefits from increased size because it can take advantage of greater specialization. Coordination problems, meanwhile, are not yet acute. By contrast, at high levels of production, the benefits of specialization have already been realized, and coordination problems become more severe as the firm grows larger. Thus, long-run average total cost is falling at low levels of production because of increasing specialization and rising at high levels of production because of increasing coordination problems.

QuickQuiz If Bombardier produces 9 jets per month, its long-run total cost is $9.0 million per month. If it produces 10 jets per month, its long-run total cost is $9.5 million per month. Does Bombardier exhibit economies or diseconomies of scale?

CONCLUSION

The purpose of this chapter has been to develop some tools that we can use to study how firms make production and pricing decisions. You should now understand what economists mean by the term *costs* and how costs vary with the quantity of output a firm produces. To refresh your memory, Table 13.5 (p. 290) summarizes some of the definitions we have encountered.

By themselves, of course, a firm's cost curves do not tell us what decisions the firm will make. But they are an important component of that decision, as we will begin to see in the next chapter.

SUMMARY

- The goal of firms is to maximize profit, which equals total revenue minus total cost.

- When analyzing a firm's behaviour, it is important to include all the opportunity costs of production. Some of the opportunity costs, such as the wages a firm pays its workers, are explicit. Other opportunity costs, such as the wages the firm owner gives up by working in the firm rather than taking another job, are implicit.

- A firm's costs reflect its production process. A typical firm's production function becomes flatter as the quantity of an input increases, displaying the property of diminishing marginal product. As a result, a firm's total-cost curve becomes steeper as the quantity produced rises.

- A firm's total costs can be divided between fixed costs and variable costs. Fixed costs are costs that do not change when the firm alters the

TABLE 13.5

The Many Types of Cost: A Summary

Term	Definition	Mathematical Description
Explicit costs	Costs that require an outlay of money by the firm	—
Implicit costs	Costs that do not require an outlay of money by the firm	—
Fixed costs	Costs that do not vary with the quantity of output produced	FC
Variable costs	Costs that do vary with the quantity of output produced	VC
Total cost	The market value of all the inputs that a firm uses in production	$TC = FC + VC$
Average fixed cost	Fixed costs divided by the quantity of output	$AFC = FC/Q$
Average variable cost	Variable costs divided by the quantity of output	$AVC = VC/Q$
Average total cost	Total cost divided by the quantity of output	$ATC = TC/Q$
Marginal cost	The increase in total cost that arises from an extra unit of production	$MC = \Delta TC/\Delta Q$

quantity of output produced. Variable costs are costs that do change when the firm alters the quantity of output produced.

- From a firm's total cost, two related measures of cost are derived. Average total cost is total cost divided by the quantity of output. Marginal cost is the amount by which total cost rises if output increases by 1 unit.

- When analyzing firm behaviour, it is often useful to graph average total cost and marginal cost. For a typical firm, marginal cost rises with the quantity of output. Average total cost first falls as output increases and then rises as output increases further. The marginal-cost curve always crosses the average-total-cost curve at the minimum of average total cost.

- A firm's costs often depend on the time horizon being considered. In particular, many costs are fixed in the short run but variable in the long run. As a result, when the firm changes its level of production, average total cost may rise more in the short run than in the long run.

KEY CONCEPTS

total revenue, p. 272
total cost, p. 272
profit, p. 272
explicit costs, p. 273
implicit costs, p. 273
economic profit, p. 274
accounting profit, p. 274

production function, p. 275
marginal product, p. 275
diminishing marginal
    product, p. 276
fixed costs, p. 281
variable costs, p. 281
average total cost, p. 282

average fixed cost, p. 282
average variable cost, p. 282
marginal cost, p. 282
efficient scale, p. 284
economies of scale, p. 288
diseconomies of scale, p. 288
constant returns to scale, p. 288

QUESTIONS FOR REVIEW

1. What is the relationship between a firm's total revenue, profit, and total cost?

2. Give an example of an opportunity cost that an accountant might not count as a cost. Why would the accountant ignore this cost?

3. What is marginal product, and what does it mean if it is diminishing?

4. Draw a production function that exhibits diminishing marginal product of labour. Draw the associated total-cost curve. (In both cases, be sure to label the axes.) Explain the shapes of the two curves you have drawn.

5. Define total cost, average total cost, and marginal cost. How are they related?

6. Draw the marginal-cost and average-total-cost curves for a typical firm. Explain why the curves have the shapes that they do and why they cross where they do.

7. How and why does a firm's average-total-cost curve differ in the short run and in the long run?

8. Define *economies of scale* and explain why they might arise. Define *diseconomies of scale* and explain why they might arise.

PROBLEMS AND APPLICATIONS

1. This chapter discusses many types of costs: opportunity cost, total cost, fixed cost, variable cost, average total cost, and marginal cost. Fill in the type of cost that best completes each phrase below:
   a. The true cost of taking some action is its _____.
   b. _____ is falling when marginal cost is below it, and rising when marginal cost is above it.
   c. A cost that does not depend on the quantity produced is a(n) _____.
   d. In the ice-cream industry in the short run, _____ includes the cost of cream and sugar, but not the cost of the factory.
   e. Profits equal total revenue less _____.
   f. The cost of producing an extra unit of output is the _____.

2. Your aunt is thinking about opening a hardware store. She estimates that it would cost $500 000 per year to rent the location and buy the stock. In addition, she would have to quit her $50 000 per year job as an accountant.
   a. Define *opportunity cost*.
   b. What is your aunt's opportunity cost of running a hardware store for a year? If your aunt thought she could sell $510 000 worth of merchandise in a year, should she open the store? Explain.

3. Suppose that your school charges you separately for tuition and for room and board.
   a. What is a cost of attending school that is not an opportunity cost?
   b. What is an explicit opportunity cost of attending school?
   c. What is an implicit opportunity cost of attending school?

4. A commercial fisherman notices the following relationship between hours spent fishing and the quantity of fish caught:

Hours	Quantity of Fish (in kilograms)
0	0
1	10
2	18
3	24
4	28
5	30

   a. What is the marginal product of each hour spent fishing?
   b. Use these data to graph the fisherman's production function. Explain its shape.
   c. The fisherman has a fixed cost of $10 (his pole). The opportunity cost of his time is $5 per hour. Graph the fisherman's total-cost curve. Explain its shape.

5. Nimbus, Inc., makes brooms and then sells them door to door. Here is the relationship between the number of workers and Nimbus's output in a given day:

Workers	Output	Marginal Product	Total Cost	Average Total Cost	Marginal Cost
0	0		_____	_____	
		_____			_____
1	20		_____	_____	
		_____			_____
2	50		_____	_____	
		_____			_____
3	90		_____	_____	
		_____			_____
4	120		_____	_____	
		_____			_____
5	140		_____	_____	
		_____			_____
6	150		_____	_____	
		_____			_____
7	155		_____	_____	

a. Fill in the column of marginal products. What pattern do you see? How might you explain it?
b. A worker costs $100 a day, and the firm has fixed costs of $200. Use this information to fill in the column for total cost.
c. Fill in the column for average total cost. (Recall that $ATC = TC/Q$.) What pattern do you see?
d. Now fill in the column for marginal cost. (Recall that $MC = \Delta TC/\Delta Q$.) What pattern do you see?
e. Compare the column for marginal product and the column for marginal cost. Explain the relationship.
f. Compare the column for average total cost and the column for marginal cost. Explain the relationship.

6. Suppose that you and your roommate have started a bagel delivery service on campus. List some of your fixed costs and describe why they are fixed. List some of your variable costs and describe why they are variable.

7. Consider the following cost information for a pizzeria:

Q (dozens)	Total Cost	Variable Cost
0	$300	$ 0
1	350	50
2	390	90
3	420	120
4	450	150
5	490	190
6	540	240

a. What is the pizzeria's fixed cost?
b. Construct a table in which you calculate the marginal cost per dozen pizzas using the information on total cost. Also calculate the marginal cost per dozen pizzas using the information on variable cost. What is the relationship between these sets of numbers? Comment.

8. You are thinking about setting up a lemonade stand. The stand itself costs $200. The ingredients for each cup of lemonade cost $0.50.
a. What is your fixed cost of doing business? What is your variable cost per cup?
b. Construct a table showing your total cost, average total cost, and marginal cost for output levels varying from 0 to 45 L. (Hint: There are 4 cups in a litre.) Draw the three cost curves.

9. Your cousin Vinnie owns a painting company with fixed costs of $200 and the following schedule for variable costs:

Quantity of Houses Painted per Month	1	2	3	4	5	6	7
Variable Costs	$10	$20	$40	$80	$160	$320	$640

Calculate average fixed cost, average variable cost, and average total cost for each quantity. What is the efficient scale of the painting company?

10. Healthy Harry's Juice Bar has the following cost schedules:

Q (vats)	Variable Cost	Total Cost
0	$ 0	$ 30
1	10	40
2	25	55
3	45	75
4	70	100
5	100	130
6	135	165

a. Calculate average variable cost, average total cost, and marginal cost for each quantity.

b. Graph all three curves. What is the relationship between the marginal-cost curve and the average-total-cost curve? Between the marginal-cost curve and the average-variable-cost curve? Explain.

11. Consider the following table of long-run total cost for three different firms:

Quantity	1	2	3	4	5	6	7
Firm A	$60	$70	$80	$90	$100	$110	$120
Firm B	11	24	39	56	75	96	119
Firm C	21	34	49	66	85	106	129

Does each of these firms experience economies of scale or diseconomies of scale?

INTERNET RESOURCES

Although the idea of economic profits has been understood by economists for over a hundred years, in the 1990s the management consulting company Stern Stewart & Co. marketed the concept under the name Economic Value Added (EVA®). Stern Stewart & Co.'s website has several useful EVA® links: http://www.sternstewart.com.

http://   For more study tools, please visit http://www.mankiw3e.nelson.com.

FIRMS IN COMPETITIVE MARKETS

14

© COMSTOCK IMAGES/GETTY IMAGES

Learning Objectives

In this chapter, you will …

- Learn what characteristics make a market competitive
- Examine how competitive firms decide how much output to produce
- Examine how competitive firms decide when to shut down production temporarily
- Examine how competitive firms decide whether to exit or enter a market
- See how firm behaviour determines a market's short-run and long-run supply curves

If your local gas station raised the price it charges for gasoline by 20 percent, it would see a large drop in the amount of gasoline it sold. Its customers would quickly switch to buying their gasoline at other gas stations. By contrast, if your local water company raised the price of water by 20 percent, it would see only a small decrease in the amount of water it sold. People might water their lawns less often and buy more water-efficient showerheads, but they would be hard-pressed to reduce water consumption greatly and would be unlikely to find another supplier. The difference between the gasoline market and the water market is obvious: There are many firms pumping gasoline, but there is only one firm pumping water. As you might expect, this difference in market structure shapes the pricing and production decisions of the firms that operate in these markets.

In this chapter we examine the behaviour of competitive firms, such as your local gas station. You may recall that a market is competitive if each buyer and seller is small compared to the size of the market and, therefore, has little ability to influence market prices. By contrast, if a firm can influence the market price of the good it sells, it is said to have *market power*. Later in the book, we examine the behaviour of firms with market power, such as your local water company.

Our analysis of competitive firms in this chapter will shed light on the decisions that lie behind the supply curve in a competitive market. Not surprisingly, we will find that a market supply curve is tightly linked to firms' costs of production. (Indeed, this general insight should be familiar to you from our analysis in Chapter 7.) But among a firm's various costs—fixed, variable, average, and marginal—which ones are most relevant for its decision about the quantity to supply at any given price? We will see that all these measures of cost play important and interrelated roles.

WHAT IS A COMPETITIVE MARKET?

Our goal in this chapter is to examine how firms make production decisions in competitive markets. As a background for this analysis, we begin by considering what a competitive market is.

The Meaning of Competition

competitive market
a market with many buyers and sellers trading identical products so that each buyer and seller is a price taker

Although we have already discussed the meaning of competition in Chapter 4, let's review the lesson briefly. A **competitive market,** sometimes called a *perfectly competitive market,* has three characteristics:

1. There are many buyers and many sellers in the market.
2. The goods offered by the various sellers are largely the same.
3. There is perfect knowledge of prices and technology.

As a result of these conditions, the actions of any single buyer or seller in the market have a negligible impact on the market price. Each buyer and seller takes the market price as given.

An example is the market for milk. No single buyer of milk can influence the price of milk because each buyer purchases a small amount relative to the size of the market. Similarly, each seller of milk has limited control over the price because many other sellers are offering milk that is essentially identical. Because each seller can sell all he wants to at the going price, he has little reason to charge less, and if he charges more, buyers will go elsewhere. Buyers and sellers in competitive markets must accept the price the market determines and, therefore, are said to be *price takers.*

In addition to the foregoing three conditions for competition, there is a fourth condition sometimes thought to characterize perfectly competitive markets:

4. Firms can freely enter or exit the market in the long run.

If, for instance, anyone can decide to start a dairy farm, and if any existing dairy farmer can decide to leave the dairy business, then the dairy industry would satisfy this condition. It should be noted that much of the analysis of competitive firms does not rely on the assumption of free entry and exit, because this condition is not necessary for firms to be price takers. But as we will see later in this chapter, entry and exit are often powerful forces in shaping the long-run outcome in competitive markets.

The Revenue of a Competitive Firm

A firm in a competitive market, like most other firms in the economy, tries to maximize profit, which equals total revenue minus total cost. To see how it does this, we first consider the revenue of a competitive firm. To keep matters concrete, let's consider a specific firm: the Smith Family Dairy Farm.

The Smith farm produces a quantity of milk, Q, and sells each unit at the market price, P. The farm's total revenue is $P \times Q$. For example, if a 4-L jug of milk sells for $6 and the farm sells 1000 jugs, its total revenue is $6000.

Because the Smith farm is small compared to the country's market for milk, it takes the price as given by market conditions. This means, in particular, that the price of milk does not depend on the quantity of output that the Smith farm produces and sells. If the Smiths double the amount of milk they produce, the price of milk remains the same, and their total revenue doubles. As a result, total revenue is proportional to the amount of output.

Table 14.1 shows the revenue for the Smith Family Dairy Farm. The first two columns show the amount of output the farm produces and the price at which it sells its output. The third column is the farm's total revenue. The table assumes that the price of milk is $6 per jug, so total revenue is simply $6 times the number of jugs.

TABLE 14.1

Total, Average, and Marginal Revenue for a Competitive Firm

Quantity	Price	Total Revenue	Average Revenue	Marginal Revenue
(Q)	(P)	$(TR = P \times Q)$	$(AR = TR/Q)$	$(MR = \Delta TR/\Delta Q)$
1 jug	$6	$ 6 6	$6	
				$6
2	6	12	6	
				6
3	6	18	6	
				6
4	6	24	6	
				6
5	6	30	6	
				6
6	6	36	6	
				6
7	6	42	6	
				6
8	6	48	6	

Just as the concepts of average and marginal were useful in the preceding chapter when analyzing costs, they are also useful when analyzing revenue. To see what these concepts tell us, consider these two questions:

1. How much revenue does the farm receive for the typical jug of milk?
2. How much additional revenue does the farm receive if it increases production of milk by 1 jug?

The last two columns in Table 14.1 answer these questions.

average revenue
total revenue divided by the quantity sold

The fourth column in the table shows **average revenue,** which is total revenue (from the third column) divided by the amount of output (from the first column). Average revenue tells us how much revenue a firm receives for the typical unit sold. In Table 14.1, you can see that average revenue equals $6, the price of a jug of milk. This illustrates a general lesson that applies not only to competitive firms but to other firms as well. Total revenue is the price times the quantity ($P \times Q$), and average revenue is total revenue ($P \times Q$) divided by the quantity (Q). Therefore, *for all firms, average revenue equals the price of the good.*

marginal revenue
the change in total revenue from an additional unit sold

The fifth column shows **marginal revenue,** which is the change in total revenue from the sale of each additional unit of output. In Table 14.1, marginal revenue equals $6, the price of a jug of milk. This result illustrates a lesson that applies only to competitive firms. Total revenue is $P \times Q$, and P is fixed for a competitive firm. Therefore, when Q rises by 1 unit, total revenue rises by P dollars. *For competitive firms, marginal revenue equals the price of the good.*

QuickQuiz When a competitive firm doubles the amount it sells, what happens to the price of its output and its total revenue?

PROFIT MAXIMIZATION AND THE COMPETITIVE FIRM'S SUPPLY CURVE

The goal of a competitive firm is to maximize profit, which equals total revenue minus total cost. We have just discussed the firm's revenue, and in the last chapter we discussed the firm's costs. We are now ready to examine how the firm maximizes profit and how that decision leads to its supply curve.

A Simple Example of Profit Maximization

Let's begin our analysis of the firm's supply decision with the example in Table 14.2. In the first column of the table is the number of 4-L jugs of milk the Smith Family Dairy Farm produces. The second column shows the farm's total revenue, which is $6 times the number of jugs. The third column shows the farm's total cost. Total cost includes fixed costs, which are $3 in this example, and variable costs, which depend on the quantity produced.

The fourth column shows the farm's profit, which is computed by subtracting total cost from total revenue. If the farm produces nothing, it has a loss of $3. If it produces 1 jug, it has a profit of $1. If it produces 2 jugs, it has a profit of $4, and

TABLE 14.2

Profit Maximization: A Numerical Example

Quantity	Total Revenue	Total Cost	Profit	Marginal Revenue	Marginal Cost	Change in Profit
(Q)	(TR)	(TC)	(TR − TC)	(MR = $\Delta TR/\Delta Q$)	(MC = $\Delta TC/\Delta Q$)	(MR − MC)
0 jugs	$ 0	$ 3	−$3			
				$6	$2	$4
1	6	5	1			
				6	3	3
2	12	8	4			
				6	4	2
3	18	12	6			
				6	5	1
4	24	17	7			
				6	6	0
5	30	23	7			
				6	7	−1
6	36	30	6			
				6	8	−2
7	42	38	4			
				6	9	−3
8	48	47	1			

so on. To maximize profit, the Smith farm chooses the quantity that makes profit as large as possible. In this example, profit is maximized when the farm produces 4 or 5 jugs of milk, when the profit is $7.

There is another way to look at the Smith farm's decision: The Smiths can find the profit-maximizing quantity by comparing the marginal revenue and marginal cost from each unit produced. The fifth and sixth columns in Table 14.2 compute marginal revenue and marginal cost from the changes in total revenue and total cost, and the last column shows the change in profit for each additional 4-L jug of milk produced. The first jug of milk the farm produces has a marginal revenue of $6 and a marginal cost of $2; hence, producing that jug increases profit by $4 (from −$3 to $1). The second jug produced has a marginal revenue of $6 and a marginal cost of $3, so that jug increases profit by $3 (from $1 to $4). As long as marginal revenue exceeds marginal cost, increasing the quantity produced raises profit.

Once the Smith farm has reached 5 4-L jugs of milk, however, the situation is very different. The sixth jug would have marginal revenue of $6 and marginal cost of $7, so producing it would reduce profit by $1 (from $7 to $6). As a result, the Smiths would not produce beyond 5 jugs of milk.

One of the ten principles of economics in Chapter 1 is that rational people think at the margin. We now see how the Smith Family Dairy Farm can apply this principle. If marginal revenue is greater than marginal cost—as it is at 1, 2, or 3 jugs—the Smiths should increase the production of milk. If marginal revenue is less than marginal cost—as it is at 6, 7, or 8 jugs—the Smiths should decrease production. If the Smiths think at the margin and make incremental adjustments to the level of production, they are naturally led to produce the profit-maximizing quantity.

The Marginal-Cost Curve and the Firm's Supply Decision

To extend this analysis of profit maximization, consider the cost curves in Figure 14.1. These cost curves have the three features that, as we discussed in the previous chapter, are thought to describe most firms: The marginal-cost curve (MC) is upward sloping. The average-total-cost curve (ATC) is U-shaped. And the marginal-cost curve crosses the average-total-cost curve at the minimum of average total cost. The figure also shows a horizontal line at the market price (P). The price line is horizontal because the firm is a price taker: The price of the firm's output is the same regardless of the quantity that the firm decides to produce. Keep in mind that, for a competitive firm, the firm's price equals both its average revenue (AR) and its marginal revenue (MR).

We can use Figure 14.1 to find the quantity of output that maximizes profit. Imagine that the firm is producing at Q_1. At this level of output, marginal revenue is greater than marginal cost. That is, if the firm raised its level of production and sales by 1 unit, the additional revenue (MR_1) would exceed the additional costs (MC_1). Profit, which equals total revenue minus total cost, would increase. Hence, if marginal revenue is greater than marginal cost, as it is at Q_1, the firm can increase profit by increasing production.

A similar argument applies when output is at Q_2. In this case, marginal cost is greater than marginal revenue. If the firm reduced production by 1 unit, the costs saved (MC_2) would exceed the revenue lost (MR_2). Therefore, if marginal revenue is less than marginal cost, as it is at Q_2, the firm can increase profit by reducing production.

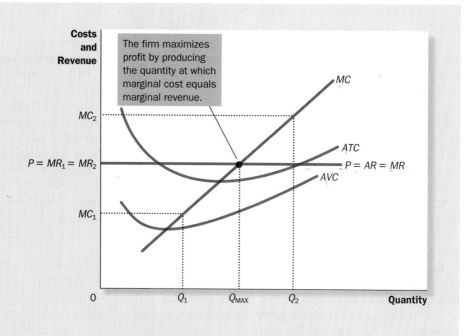

FIGURE 14.1

Profit Maximization for a Competitive Firm

This figure shows the marginal-cost curve (MC), the average-total-cost curve (ATC), and the average-variable-cost curve (AVC). It also shows the market price (P), which equals marginal revenue (MR) and average revenue (AR). At the quantity Q_1, marginal revenue MR_1 exceeds marginal cost MC_1, so raising production increases profit. At the quantity Q_2, marginal cost MC_2 is above marginal revenue MR_2, so reducing production increases profit. The profit-maximizing quantity Q_{MAX} is found where the horizontal price line intersects the marginal-cost curve.

The firm maximizes profit by producing the quantity at which marginal cost equals marginal revenue.

Where do these marginal adjustments to level of production end? Regardless of whether the firm begins with production at a low level (such as Q_1) or at a high level (such as Q_2), the firm will eventually adjust production until the quantity produced reaches Q_{MAX}. This analysis shows a general rule for profit maximization: *At the profit-maximizing level of output, marginal revenue and marginal cost are exactly equal.*

We can now see how the competitive firm decides the quantity of its good to supply to the market. Because a competitive firm is a price taker, its marginal revenue equals the market price. For any given price, the competitive firm's profit-maximizing quantity of output is found by looking at the intersection of the price with the marginal-cost curve. In Figure 14.1, that quantity of output is Q_{MAX}.

Figure 14.2 shows how a competitive firm responds to an increase in the price. When the price is P_1, the firm produces quantity Q_1, the quantity that equates marginal cost to the price. When the price rises to P_2, the firm finds that marginal revenue is now higher than marginal cost at the previous level of output, so the firm increases production. The new profit-maximizing quantity is Q_2, at which marginal cost equals the new higher price. *In essence, because the firm's marginal-cost curve determines the quantity of the good the firm is willing to supply at any price, it is the competitive firm's supply curve.*

The Firm's Short-Run Decision to Shut Down

So far we have been analyzing the question of how much a competitive firm will produce. In some circumstances, however, the firm will decide to shut down and not produce anything at all.

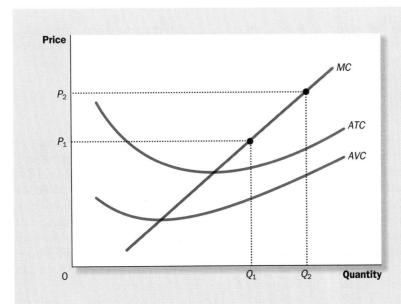

FIGURE 14.2

Marginal Cost as the Competitive Firm's Supply Curve

An increase in the price from P_1 to P_2 leads to an increase in the firm's profit-maximizing quantity from Q_1 to Q_2. Because the marginal-cost curve shows the quantity supplied by the firm at any given price, it is the firm's supply curve.

Here we should distinguish between a temporary shutdown of a firm and the permanent exit of a firm from the market. A *shutdown* refers to a short-run decision not to produce anything during a specific period of time because of current market conditions. *Exit* refers to a long-run decision to leave the market. The short-run and long-run decisions differ because most firms cannot avoid their fixed costs in the short run but can do so in the long run. That is, a firm that shuts down temporarily still has to pay its fixed costs, whereas a firm that exits the market saves both its fixed and its variable costs.

For example, consider the production decision that a farmer faces. The cost of the land is one of the farmer's fixed costs. If the farmer decides not to produce any crops one season, the land lies fallow and he cannot recover this cost. When making the short-run decision whether to shut down for a season, the fixed cost of land is said to be a *sunk cost*. By contrast, if the farmer decides to leave farming altogether, he can sell the land. When making the long-run decision whether to exit the market, the cost of land is not sunk. (We return to the issue of sunk costs shortly.)

Now let's consider what determines a firm's shutdown decision. If the firm shuts down, it loses all revenue from the sale of its product. At the same time, it saves the variable costs of making its product (but must still pay the fixed costs). Thus, *the firm shuts down if the revenue that it would get from producing is less than its variable costs of production.*

A small bit of mathematics can make this shutdown criterion more useful. If *TR* stands for total revenue, and *VC* stands for variable costs, then the firm's decision can be written as

$$\text{Shut down if } TR < VC$$

The firm shuts down if total revenue is less than variable cost. By dividing both sides of this inequality by the quantity *Q*, we can write it as

$$\text{Shut down if } TR/Q < VC/Q$$

Notice that this can be further simplified. *TR/Q* is total revenue divided by quantity, which is average revenue. As we discussed previously, average revenue for any firm is simply the good's price, *P*. Similarly, *VC/Q* is average variable cost *AVC*. Therefore, the firm's shutdown criterion is

$$\text{Shut down if } P < AVC$$

That is, a firm chooses to shut down if the price of the good is less than the average variable cost of production. This criterion is intuitive: When choosing to produce, the firm compares the price it receives for the typical unit to the average variable cost that it must incur to produce the typical unit. If the price doesn't cover the average variable cost, the firm is better off stopping production altogether. Thus, the price that coincides with the minimum point on the average-*variable*-cost curve is sometimes referred to as the *shutdown price*. If the market price is less than the shutdown price, the firm shuts down and ceases production. If conditions change in the future so that the price exceeds the shutdown price, the firm can reopen. Of course we could just as easily refer to it as the *start-up price*.

We now have a full description of a competitive firm's profit-maximizing strategy. If the firm produces anything, it produces the quantity at which marginal cost equals the price of the good. Yet if the price is less than average variable cost at that quantity, the firm is better off shutting down and not producing anything. These results are illustrated in Figure 14.3.

There are two parts to the competitive firm's short-run supply curve, with a discontinuity at the short-run shutdown price. For prices from zero up to the shutdown price, the firm supplies zero output and the short-run supply curve lies along the vertical axis. For prices above the short-run shutdown price, the competitive firm's *short-run* supply curve is the portion of its marginal-cost curve that lies above average *variable* cost.

Spilt Milk and Other Sunk Costs

Sometime in your life you have probably been told, "Don't cry over spilt milk," or "Let bygones be bygones." These adages hold a deep truth about rational decision making. Economists say that a cost is a **sunk cost** when it has already been committed and cannot be recovered. In a sense, a sunk cost is the opposite of an opportunity cost: An opportunity cost is what you have to give up if you choose to do one thing instead of another, whereas a sunk cost cannot be avoided, regardless of the choices you make. Because nothing can be done about sunk costs, you can ignore them when making decisions about various aspects of life, including business strategy.

Our analysis of the firm's shutdown decision is one example of the irrelevance of sunk costs. We assume that the firm cannot recover its fixed costs by temporarily stopping production. As a result, the firm's fixed costs are sunk in the short run, and the firm can safely ignore these costs when deciding how much to produce. The firm's short-run supply curve is the part of the marginal-cost curve that lies above average variable cost, and the size of the fixed cost does not matter for this supply decision.

sunk cost
a cost that has already been committed and cannot be recovered

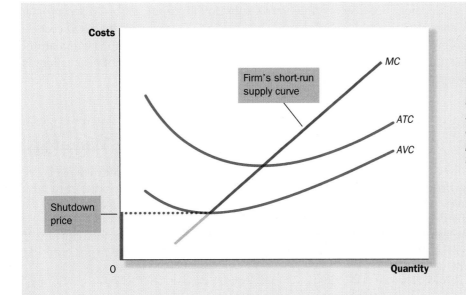

FIGURE 14.3

The Competitive Firm's Short-Run Supply Curve

In the short run, the competitive firm's supply curve is its marginal-cost curve (MC) above average variable cost (AVC). If the price falls below average variable cost, the firm is better off shutting down.

The irrelevance of sunk costs is also important for personal decisions. Imagine, for instance, that you place a $10 value on seeing a newly released movie. You buy a ticket for $7, but before entering the theatre, you lose the ticket. Should you buy another ticket? Or should you now go home and refuse to pay a total of $14 to see the movie? The answer is that you should buy another ticket. The benefit of seeing the movie ($10) still exceeds the opportunity cost (the $7 for the second ticket). The $7 you paid for the lost ticket is a sunk cost. As with spilt milk, there is no point in crying about it.

Case Study

NEAR-EMPTY RESTAURANTS AND OFF-SEASON MINIATURE GOLF

Have you ever walked into a restaurant for lunch and found it almost empty? Why, you might have asked, does the restaurant even bother to stay open? It might seem that the revenue from the few customers could not possibly cover the cost of running the restaurant.

In making the decision whether to open for lunch, a restaurant owner must keep in mind the distinction between fixed and variable costs. Many of a restaurant's costs—the rent, kitchen equipment, tables, plates, silverware, and so on—are fixed. Shutting down during lunch would not reduce these costs. In other words, these costs are sunk in the short run. When the owner is deciding whether to serve lunch, only the variable costs—the price of the additional food and the wages of the extra staff—are relevant. The owner shuts down the restaurant at lunchtime only if the revenue from the few lunchtime customers fails to cover the restaurant's variable costs.

An operator of a miniature-golf course in a summer resort community faces a similar decision. Because revenue varies substantially from season to season, the firm must decide when to open and when to close. Once again, the fixed costs—the costs of buying the land and building the course—are irrelevant. The miniature-golf course should be open for business only during those times of year when its revenue exceeds its variable costs. ●

Staying open can be profitable, even with many tables empty.

The Firm's Long-Run Decision to Exit or Enter a Market

The firm's long-run decision to exit the market is similar to its shutdown decision. If the firm exits, it again will lose all revenue from the sale of its product, but now it saves on both fixed and variable costs of production. Thus, *the firm exits the market if the revenue it would get from producing is less than its total costs.*

We can again make this criterion more useful by writing it mathematically. If *TR* stands for total revenue, and *TC* stands for total cost, then the firm's criterion can be written as

$$\text{Exit if } TR < TC$$

The firm exits if total revenue is less than total cost. By dividing both sides of this inequality by quantity Q, we can write it as

$$\text{Exit if } TR/Q < TC/Q$$

We can simplify this further by noting that TR/Q is average revenue, which equals the price P, and that TC/Q is average total cost ATC. Therefore, the firm's exit criterion is

$$\text{Exit if } P < ATC$$

That is, a firm chooses to exit if the price of the good is less than the average total cost of production. Thus, the price that coincides with the minimum point on the average-*total*-cost curve is sometimes referred to as the *exit price*. The exit price is related to the firm's efficient scale, as discussed in Chapter 13. If the market price is less than the exit price, the firm exits the industry.

It is useful to point out the difference between the exit price, a long-run concept, and the shutdown price, a short-run concept. The exit price coincides with the minimum point on the average-total-cost curve, while the shutdown price coincides with the minimum point on the average-variable-cost curve.

A parallel analysis applies to an entrepreneur who is considering starting a firm. The firm will enter the market if such an action would be profitable, which occurs if the price of the good exceeds the average total cost of production. The entry criterion is

$$\text{Enter if } P > ATC$$

The criterion for entry is exactly the opposite of the criterion for exit.

We can now describe a competitive firm's long-run profit-maximizing strategy. If the firm is in the market, it produces the quantity at which marginal cost equals the price of the good. Yet if the price is less than average total cost at that quantity, the firm chooses to exit (or not enter) the market. These results are illustrated in Figure 14.4 (p. 306).

In this diagram, for simplicity, ATC is drawn as U-shaped, without an extended horizontal portion coinciding with a range of production under constant returns to scale. There are two parts to the competitive firm's long-run supply curve, with a discontinuity at the exit price. For prices from zero up to the exit price, the firm exits (or chooses not to enter) the market, and the long-run supply curve lies along the vertical axis. For prices above the exit price, the competitive firm's *long-run* supply curve is the portion of its marginal-cost curve that lies above average *total* cost.

Measuring Profit in Our Graph for the Competitive Firm

As we analyze exit and entry, it is useful to be able to analyze the firm's profit in more detail. Recall that profit equals total revenue (TR) minus total cost (TC):

$$\text{Profit} = TR - TC$$

FIGURE 14.4

The Competitive Firm's Long-Run Supply Curve

In the long run, the competitive firm's supply curve is its marginal-cost curve (MC) above average total cost (ATC). If the price falls below average total cost, the firm is better off exiting the market.

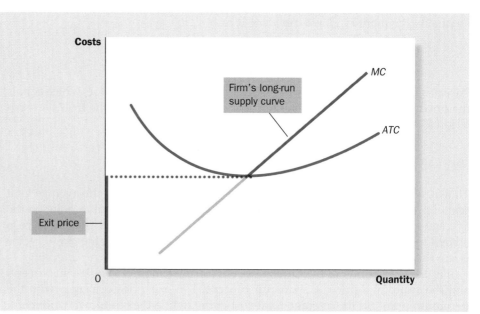

We can rewrite this definition by multiplying and dividing the right-hand side by Q:

$$\text{Profit} = (TR/Q - TC/Q) \times Q$$

But note that TR/Q is average revenue, which is the price P, and TC/Q is average total cost ATC. Therefore,

$$\text{Profit} = (P - ATC) \times Q$$

This way of expressing the firm's profit allows us to measure profit in our graphs.

Panel (a) of Figure 14.5 shows a firm earning positive profit. As we have already discussed, the firm maximizes profit by producing the quantity at which price equals marginal cost. Now look at the shaded rectangle. The height of the rectangle is $P - ATC$, the difference between price and average total cost. The width of the rectangle is Q, the quantity produced. Therefore, the area of the rectangle is $(P - ATC) \times Q$, which is the firm's profit.

Similarly, panel (b) of this figure shows a firm with losses (negative profit). In this case, maximizing profit means minimizing losses, a task accomplished once again by producing the quantity at which price equals marginal cost. Now consider the shaded rectangle. The height of the rectangle is $ATC - P$, and the width is Q. The area is $(ATC - P) \times Q$, which is the firm's loss. Because a firm in this situation is not making enough revenue to cover its average total cost, the firm would choose to exit the market.

QuickQuiz   How does the price faced by a profit-maximizing competitive firm compare to its marginal cost? Explain. • When does a profit-maximizing competitive firm decide to shut down? When does a profit-maximizing competitive firm decide to exit a market?

FIGURE 14.5

Profit as the Area between Price and Average Total Cost

The area of the shaded box between price and average total cost represents the firm's profit. The height of this box is price minus average total cost (P – ATC), and the width of the box is the quantity of output (Q). In panel (a), price is above average total cost, so the firm has positive profit. In panel (b), price is less than average total cost, so the firm has losses.

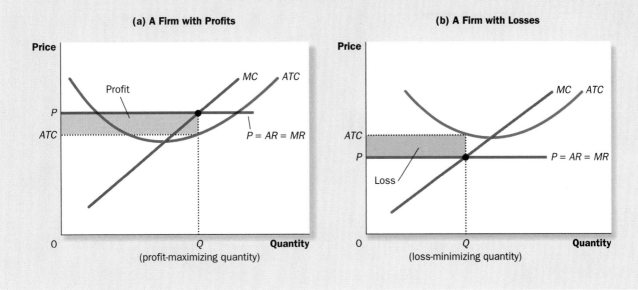

(a) A Firm with Profits

(b) A Firm with Losses

THE SUPPLY CURVE IN A COMPETITIVE MARKET

Now that we have examined the supply decision of a single firm, we can discuss the supply curve for a market. There are two cases to consider. First, we examine a market with a fixed number of firms. Second, we examine a market in which the number of firms can change as old firms exit the market and new firms enter. Both cases are important, for each applies over a specific time horizon. Over short periods of time, it is often difficult for firms to enter and exit, so the assumption of a fixed number of firms is appropriate. But over long periods of time, the number of firms can adjust to changing market conditions.

The Short Run: Market Supply with a Fixed Number of Firms

Consider first a market with 1000 identical firms. For any given price, each firm supplies a quantity of output so that its marginal cost equals the price, as shown in panel (a) of Figure 14.6 (p. 308). That is, as long as price is above average variable cost, each firm's marginal-cost curve is its supply curve. The quantity of output supplied to the market equals the sum of the quantities supplied by each of the 1000 individual firms. Thus, to derive the market supply curve, we add the quantity supplied by each firm in the market. As panel (b) of Figure 14.6 shows,

FIGURE 14.6

Market Supply with a Fixed Number of Firms

When the number of firms in the market is fixed, the market supply curve, shown in panel (b), reflects the individual firms' marginal-cost curves, shown in panel (a). Here, in a market of 1000 firms, the quantity of output supplied to the market is 1000 times the quantity supplied by each firm.

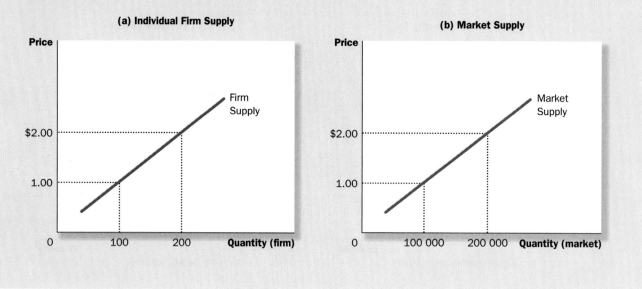

because the firms are identical, the quantity supplied to the market is 1000 times the quantity supplied by each firm.

The Long Run: Market Supply with Entry and Exit

Now consider what happens if firms are able to enter or exit the market. Let's suppose that everyone has access to the same technology for producing the good and access to the same markets to buy the inputs into production. Therefore, all firms and all potential firms have the same cost curves.

Decisions about entry and exit in a market of this type depend on the incentives facing the owners of existing firms and the entrepreneurs who could start new firms. If firms already in the market are profitable, then new firms will have an incentive to enter the market. This entry will expand the number of firms, increase the quantity of the good supplied, and drive down prices and profits. Conversely, if firms in the market are making losses, then some existing firms will exit the market. Their exit will reduce the number of firms, decrease the quantity of the good supplied, and drive up prices and profits. *At the end of this process of entry and exit, firms that remain in the market must be making zero economic profit.* Recall that we can write a firm's profits as

$$\text{Profit} = (P - ATC) \times Q$$

This equation shows that an operating firm has zero profit if and only if the price of the good equals the average total cost of producing that good. If price is above average total cost, profit is positive, which encourages new firms to enter. If price is less than average total cost, profit is negative, which encourages some firms to exit. *The process of entry and exit ends only when price and average total cost are driven to equality.*

This analysis has a surprising implication. We noted earlier in the chapter that competitive firms produce so that price equals marginal cost. We just noted that free entry and exit forces price to equal average total cost. But if price is to equal both marginal cost and average total cost, these two measures of cost must equal each other. Marginal cost and average total cost are equal, however, only when the firm is operating at the minimum of average total cost. Recall from the preceding chapter that the level of production with lowest average total cost is called the firm's *efficient scale*. Therefore, *the long-run equilibrium of a competitive market with free entry and exit must have firms operating at their efficient scale.*

Panel (a) of Figure 14.7 shows a firm in such a long-run equilibrium. In this figure, price P equals marginal cost MC, so the firm is profit-maximizing. Price also equals average total cost ATC, so profits are zero. New firms have no incentive to enter the market, and existing firms have no incentive to leave the market.

From this analysis of firm behaviour, we can determine the long-run supply curve for the market. In a market with free entry and exit, there is only one price consistent with zero profit—the minimum of average total cost. As a result, the long-run market supply curve must be horizontal at this price, as in panel (b) of

FIGURE 14.7

Market Supply with Entry and Exit

Firms will enter or exit the market until profit is driven to zero. Thus, in the long run, price equals the minimum of average total cost, as shown in panel (a). The number of firms adjusts to ensure that all demand is satisfied at this price. The long-run market supply curve is horizontal at this price, as shown in panel (b).

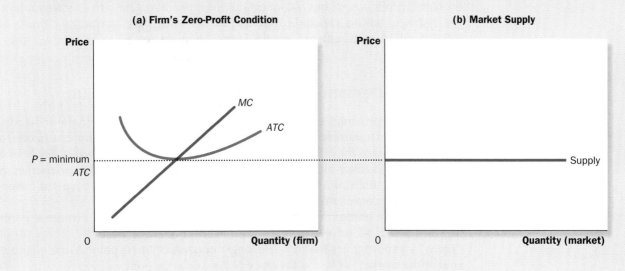

(a) Firm's Zero-Profit Condition

(b) Market Supply

Figure 14.7. Any price above this level would generate profit, leading to entry and an increase in the total quantity supplied. Any price below this level would generate losses, leading to exit and a decrease in the total quantity supplied. Eventually, the number of firms in the market adjusts so that price equals the minimum of average total cost, and there are enough firms to satisfy all the demand at this price.

Why Do Competitive Firms Stay in Business If They Make Zero Profit?

At first, it might seem odd that competitive firms earn zero profit in the long run. After all, people start businesses to make a profit. If entry eventually drives profit to zero, there might seem to be little reason to stay in business.

To understand the zero-profit condition more fully, recall that profit equals total revenue minus total cost, and that total cost includes all the opportunity costs of the firm. In particular, total cost includes the opportunity cost of the time and money that the firm owners devote to the business. In the zero-profit equilibrium, the firm's revenue must compensate the owners for the time and money that they expend to keep their business going.

Consider an example. Suppose that a farmer had to invest $1 million to establish his farm, which otherwise he could have deposited in a bank to earn $50 000 a year in interest. In addition, he had to give up another job that would have paid him $30 000 a year. Then the farmer's opportunity cost of farming includes both the interest he could have earned and the forgone wages—a total of $80 000. Even if his profit is driven to zero, his revenue from farming compensates him for these opportunity costs.

Keep in mind that accountants and economists measure costs differently. As we discussed in the previous chapter, accountants keep track of explicit costs but usually miss implicit costs. That is, they measure costs that require an outflow of money from the firm, but they fail to include opportunity costs of production that do not involve an outflow of money. As a result, in the zero-profit equilibrium, economic profit is zero, but accounting profit is positive. Our farmer's accountant, for instance, would conclude that the farmer earned an accounting profit of $80 000, which is enough to keep the farmer in business.

A Shift in Demand in the Short Run and Long Run

Because firms can enter and exit a market in the long run but not in the short run, the response of a market to a change in demand depends on the time horizon. To see this, let's trace the effects of a shift in demand. This analysis will show how a market responds over time, and it will show how entry and exit drive a market to its long-run equilibrium. This is an example of the type of comparative static exercise we first encountered back in Chapter 4.

Suppose the market for milk begins in long-run equilibrium. Firms are earning zero profit, so price equals the minimum of average total cost. Panel (a) of Figure 14.8 shows the situation. The long-run equilibrium is point A, the quantity sold in the market is Q_1, and the price is P_1.

FIGURE 14.8

An Increase in Demand in the Short Run and Long Run

The market starts in a long-run equilibrium, shown as point A in panel (a). In this equilibrium, each firm makes zero profit, and the price equals the minimum average total cost. Panel (b) shows what happens in the short run when demand rises from D_1 to D_2. The equilibrium goes from point A to point B, price rises from P_1 to P_2, and the quantity sold in the market rises from Q_1 to Q_2. Because price now exceeds average total cost, firms make profits, which over time encourage new firms to enter the market. This entry shifts the short-run supply curve to the right from S_1 to S_2, as shown in panel (c). In the new long-run equilibrium, point C, price has returned to P_1 but the quantity sold has increased to Q_3. Profits are again zero, price is back to the minimum of average total cost, but the market has more firms to satisfy the greater demand.

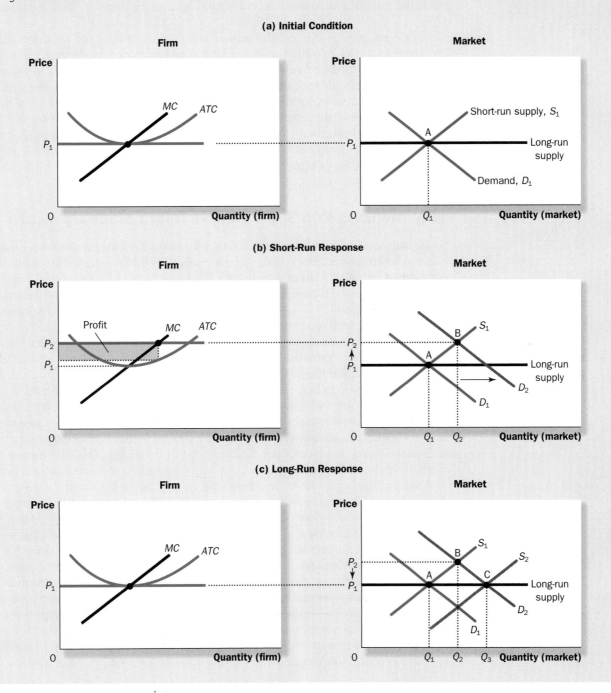

Now suppose scientists discover that milk has miraculous health benefits. As a result, the demand curve for milk shifts outward from D_1 to D_2, as in panel (b). The short-run equilibrium moves from point A to point B; as a result, the quantity rises from Q_1 to Q_2, and the price rises from P_1 to P_2. All of the existing firms respond to the higher price by raising the amount produced. Because each firm's supply curve reflects its marginal-cost curve, how much they each increase production is determined by the marginal-cost curve. In the new short-run equilibrium, the price of milk exceeds average total cost, so the firms are making positive profit.

Over time, the profit in this market encourages new firms to enter. Some farmers may switch to milk from other farm products, for example. As the number of firms grows, the short-run supply curve shifts to the right from S_1 to S_2, as in panel (c), and this shift causes the price of milk to fall. Eventually, the price is driven back down to the minimum of average total cost, profits are zero, and firms stop entering. Thus, the market reaches a new long-run equilibrium, point C. The price of milk has returned to P_1, but the quantity produced has risen to Q_3. Each firm is again producing at its efficient scale, but because more firms are in the dairy business, the quantity of milk produced and sold is higher.

Why the Long-Run Supply Curve Might Slope Upward

So far we have seen that entry and exit can cause the long-run market supply curve to be horizontal. The essence of our analysis is that there are a large number of potential entrants, each of which faces the same costs. As a result, the long-run market supply curve is horizontal at the minimum of average total cost. When the demand for the good increases, the long-run result is an increase in the number of firms and in the total quantity supplied, without any change in the price.

There are, however, two reasons that the long-run market supply curve might slope upward. The first is that some resource used in production may be available only in limited quantities. For example, consider the market for farm products. Anyone can choose to buy land and start a farm, but the quantity of land is limited. As more people become farmers, the price of farmland is bid up, which raises the costs of all farmers in the market. Thus, an increase in demand for farm products cannot induce an increase in quantity supplied without also inducing a rise in farmers' costs, which in turn means a rise in price. The result is a long-run market supply curve that is upward sloping, even with free entry into farming.

A second reason for an upward-sloping supply curve is that firms may have different costs. For example, consider the market for painters. Anyone can enter the market for painting services, but not everyone has the same costs. Costs vary in part because some people work faster than others and in part because some people have better alternative uses of their time than others. For any given price, those with lower costs are more likely to enter than those with higher costs. To increase the quantity of painting services supplied, additional entrants must be encouraged to enter the market. Because these new entrants have higher costs, the price must rise to make entry profitable for them. Thus, the market supply curve for painting services slopes upward even with free entry into the market.

Notice that if firms have different costs, some firms earn profit even in the long run. In this case, the price in the market reflects the average total cost of the *marginal firm*—the firm that would exit the market if the price were any lower. This firm earns zero profit, but firms with lower costs earn positive profit. Entry does not eliminate this profit because would-be entrants have higher costs than firms already in the market. Higher-cost firms will enter only if the price rises, making the market profitable for them.

Thus, for these two reasons, the long-run supply curve in a market may be upward sloping rather than horizontal, indicating that a higher price is necessary to induce a larger quantity supplied. Nonetheless, the basic lesson about entry and exit remains true. *Because firms can enter and exit more easily in the long run than in the short run, the long-run supply curve is typically more elastic than the short-run supply curve.*

QuickQuiz In the long run with free entry and exit, is the price in a market equal to marginal cost, average total cost, both, or neither? Explain with a diagram.

CONCLUSION: BEHIND THE SUPPLY CURVE

We have been discussing the behaviour of competitive profit-maximizing firms. You may recall from Chapter 1 that one of the ten principles of economics is that rational people think at the margin. This chapter has applied this idea to the competitive firm. Marginal analysis has given us a theory of the supply curve in a competitive market and, as a result, a deeper understanding of market outcomes.

We have learned that when you buy a good from a firm in a competitive market, you can be assured that the price you pay is close to the cost of producing that good. In particular, if firms are competitive and profit-maximizing, the price of a good equals the marginal cost of making that good. In addition, if firms can freely enter and exit the market, the price also equals the lowest possible average total cost of production.

Although we have assumed throughout this chapter that firms are price takers, many of the tools developed here are also useful for studying firms in less competitive markets. In the next chapter we will examine the behaviour of firms with market power. Marginal analysis will again be useful in analyzing these firms, but it will have quite different implications.

SUMMARY

- Because a competitive firm is a price taker, its revenue is proportional to the amount of output it produces. The price of the good equals both the firm's average revenue and its marginal revenue.

- To maximize profit, a firm chooses a quantity of output such that marginal revenue equals marginal cost. Because marginal revenue for a

competitive firm equals the market price, the firm chooses quantity so that price equals marginal cost. Thus, the firm's marginal cost curve is its supply curve.

- In the short run when a firm cannot recover its fixed costs, the firm will choose to shut down temporarily if the price of the good is less than average variable cost. In the long run when the firm can recover both fixed and variable costs, it will choose to exit if the price is less than average total cost.

- In a market with free entry and exit, profits are driven to zero in the long run. In this long-run equilibrium, all firms produce at the efficient scale, price equals the minimum of average total cost, and the number of firms adjusts to satisfy the quantity demanded at this price.

- Changes in demand have different effects over different time horizons. In the short run, an increase in demand raises prices and leads to profits, and a decrease in demand lowers prices and leads to losses. But if firms can freely enter and exit the market, then in the long run the number of firms adjusts to drive the market back to the zero-profit equilibrium.

KEY CONCEPTS

competitive market, p. 296
average revenue, p. 298

marginal revenue, p. 298

sunk cost, p. 303

QUESTIONS FOR REVIEW

1. What is meant by a competitive firm?

2. Draw the cost curves for a typical firm. For a given price, explain how the firm chooses the level of output that maximizes profit.

3. Under what conditions will a firm shut down temporarily? Explain.

4. Under what conditions will a firm exit a market? Explain.

5. Does a firm's price equal marginal cost in the short run, in the long run, or both? Explain.

6. Does a firm's price equal the minimum of average total cost in the short run, in the long run, or both? Explain.

7. Are market supply curves typically more elastic in the short run or in the long run? Explain.

PROBLEMS AND APPLICATIONS

1. What are the characteristics of a competitive market? Which of the following drinks do you think is best described by these characteristics? Why aren't the others?
   a. tap water
   b. bottled water
   c. cola
   d. beer

2. Your roommate's long hours in Chem lab finally paid off—she discovered a secret formula that lets people do an hour's worth of studying in 5 minutes. So far, she's sold 200 doses, and faces the following average-total-cost schedule:

Q	Average Total Cost
199	$199
200	200
201	201

If a new customer offers to pay your roommate $300 for one dose, should she make one more? Explain.

3. The licorice industry is competitive. Each firm produces 2 million strings of licorice per year. The strings have an average total cost of $0.20 each, and they sell for $0.30.
   a. What is the marginal cost of a string?
   b. Is this industry in long-run equilibrium? Why or why not?

4. You go out to the best restaurant in town and order a lobster dinner for $40. After eating half of the lobster, you realize that you are quite full. Your date wants you to finish your dinner, because you can't take it home and because "you've already paid for it." What should you do? Relate your answer to the material in this chapter.

5. Bob's lawn-mowing service is a profit-maximizing, competitive firm. Bob mows lawns for $27 each. His total cost each day is $280, of which $30 is a fixed cost. He mows 10 lawns a day. What can you say about Bob's short-run decision regarding shutdown and his long-run decision regarding exit?

6. Consider total cost and total revenue given in the table below:

Quantity	0	1	2	3	4	5	6	7
Total Cost	$8	$9	$10	$11	$13	$19	$27	$37
Total Revenue	0	8	16	24	32	40	48	56

   a. Calculate profit for each quantity. How much should the firm produce to maximize profit?
   b. Calculate marginal revenue and marginal cost for each quantity. Graph them. (Hint: Put the points between whole numbers. For example, the marginal cost between 2 and 3 should be graphed at 2.5.) At what quantity do these curves cross? How does this relate to your answer to part (a)?
   c. Can you tell whether this firm is in a competitive industry? If so, can you tell whether the industry is in a long-run equilibrium?

7. In 2003 a single case in Alberta of bovine spongiform encephalopathy, also known as mad cow disease, temporarily shut down export markets for Canadian beef.
   a. Using firm and industry diagrams, show the short-run effect of declining demand for Canadian beef due to the shutdown of its export markets. Label the diagram carefully and write out in words all of the changes that you can identify.

   b. Although export markets eventually began to open up later that same year, the demand for Canadian beef remained low. On a new diagram, show the long-run effect of the declining demand. Explain in words.

8. "High prices traditionally cause expansion in an industry, eventually bringing an end to high prices and manufacturers' prosperity." Explain, using appropriate diagrams.

9. Suppose the book-printing industry is competitive and begins in a long-run equilibrium.
   a. Draw a diagram describing the typical firm in the industry.
   b. Hi-Tech Printing Company invents a new process that sharply reduces the cost of printing books. What happens to Hi-Tech's profits and the price of books in the short run when Hi-Tech's patent prevents other firms from using the new technology?
   c. What happens in the long run when the patent expires and other firms are free to use the technology?

10. Many small boats are made of fibreglass, which is derived from crude oil. Suppose that the price of oil rises.
   a. Using diagrams, show what happens to the cost curves of an individual boat-making firm and to the market supply curve.
   b. What happens to the profits of boat makers in the short run? What happens to the number of boat makers in the long run?

11. Suppose that the Canadian textile industry is competitive, and there is no international trade in textiles. In long-run equilibrium, the price per unit of cloth is $30.
   a. Describe the equilibrium using graphs for the entire market and for an individual producer.

   Now suppose that textile producers in other countries are willing to sell large quantities of cloth in Canada for only $25 per unit.
   b. Assuming that Canadian textile producers have large fixed costs, what is the short-run effect of these imports on the quantity produced by an individual producer? What

is the short-run effect on profits? Illustrate your answer with a graph.

c. What is the long-run effect on the number of Canadian firms in the industry?

12. Suppose there are 1000 hot-pretzel stands operating in Toronto. Each stand has the usual U-shaped average-total-cost curve. The market demand curve for pretzels slopes downward, and the market for pretzels is in long-run competitive equilibrium.

a. Draw the current equilibrium, using graphs for the entire market and for an individual pretzel stand.

b. Now the city decides to restrict the number of pretzel-stand licences, reducing the number of stands to only 800. What effect will this action have on the market and on an individual stand that is still operating? Use graphs to illustrate your answer.

c. Suppose that the city decides to charge a licence fee for the 800 licences. How will this affect the number of pretzels sold by an individual stand, and the stand's profit?

The city wants to raise as much revenue as possible and also wants to ensure that 800 pretzel stands remain in the city. By how much should the city increase the licence fee? Show the answer on your graph.

13. Assume that the gold-mining industry is competitive.

a. Illustrate a long-run equilibrium using diagrams for the gold market and for a representative gold mine.

b. Suppose that an increase in jewellery demand induces a surge in the demand for gold. Using your diagrams from part (a), show what happens in the short run to the gold market and to each existing gold mine.

c. If the demand for gold remains high, what would happen to the price over time? Specifically, would the new long-run equilibrium price be above, below, or equal to the short-run equilibrium price in part (b)? Is it possible for the new long-run equilibrium price to be above the original long-run equilibrium price? Explain.

INTERNET RESOURCES

Supporters of school vouchers argue that the lack of competition between public schools causes problems. Go to http://www.schoolchoices.org/roo/vouchers.htm for a discussion. Think about how the theory of competitive markets discussed in this chapter applies to this debate.

http://

For more study tools, please visit http://www.mankiw3e.nelson.com.

15

Learning Objectives

In this chapter, you will …

- Learn why some markets have only one seller
- Analyze how a monopoly determines the quantity to produce and the price to charge
- See how the monopoly's decisions affect economic well-being
- Consider the various public policies aimed at solving the problem of monopoly
- See why monopolies try to charge different prices to different customers

MONOPOLY

If you own a personal computer, it probably uses some version of Windows, the operating system sold by the Microsoft Corporation. When Microsoft first designed Windows many years ago, it applied for and received a copyright from the government. The copyright gives Microsoft the exclusive right to make and sell copies of the Windows operating system. So if a person wants to buy a copy of Windows, he or she has little choice but to give Microsoft the approximately $150 that the firm has decided to charge for its product. Microsoft is said to have a *monopoly* in the market for Windows.

Microsoft's business decisions are not well described by the model of firm behaviour we developed in the previous chapter. In that chapter we analyzed competitive markets, in which there are many firms offering essentially identical products, so each firm has little influence over the price it receives. By contrast, a monopoly such as Microsoft has no close competitors and, therefore, can influence the market price of its product. While a competitive firm is a *price taker*, a monopoly firm is a *price maker*.

In this chapter we examine the implications of this market power. We will see that market power alters the relationship between a firm's costs and the price at which it sells its product to the market. A competitive firm takes the price of its output as given by the market and then chooses the quantity it will supply so that price equals marginal cost. By contrast, the price charged by a monopoly exceeds marginal cost. This result is clearly true in the case of Microsoft's Windows. The marginal cost of Windows—the extra cost that Microsoft would incur by printing one more copy of the program onto a CD—is only a few dollars. The market price of Windows is many times marginal cost.

It is perhaps not surprising that monopolies charge high prices for their products. Customers of monopolies might seem to have little choice but to pay whatever the monopoly charges. But, if so, why does a copy of Windows not cost $500? Or $5000? The reason, of course, is that if Microsoft set the price that high, fewer people would buy the product. People would buy fewer computers, switch to other operating systems, or make illegal copies. Monopolies cannot achieve any level of profit they want, because high prices reduce the amount that their customers buy. Although monopolies can control the prices of their goods, their profits are not unlimited.

As we examine the production and pricing decisions of monopolies, we also consider the implications of monopoly for society as a whole. Monopoly firms, like competitive firms, aim to maximize profit. But this goal has very different ramifications for competitive and monopoly firms. As we first saw in Chapter 7, self-interested buyers and sellers in competitive markets are unwittingly led by an invisible hand to promote general economic well-being. By contrast, because monopoly firms are unchecked by competition, the outcome in a market with a monopoly is often not in the best interest of society.

One of the ten principles of economics in Chapter 1 is that governments can sometimes improve market outcomes. The analysis in this chapter will shed more light on this principle. As we examine the problems that monopolies raise for society, we will also discuss the various ways in which government policymakers might respond to these problems. The U.S. government, for example, keeps a close eye on Microsoft's business decisions. In 1994, it prevented Microsoft from buying Intuit, a software firm that sells the leading program for personal finance, on the grounds that the combination of Microsoft and Intuit would concentrate too much market power in one firm. Similarly, in 1998 the U.S. Justice Department objected when Microsoft started integrating its Internet browser into its Windows operating system, claiming that this would impede competition from other companies, such as Netscape. This concern led the Justice Department to file suit against Microsoft. When the suit was finally settled in 2002, Microsoft agreed to some restrictions on its business practices, but it was allowed to keep the browser as part of Windows.

WHY MONOPOLIES ARISE

monopoly
a firm that is the sole seller of a product without close substitutes

A firm is a **monopoly** if it is the sole seller of its product and if its product does not have close substitutes. The fundamental cause of monopoly is *barriers to entry:* A monopoly remains the only seller in its market because other firms cannot enter the market and compete with it. Barriers to entry, in turn, have three main sources:

1. A key resource is owned by a single firm.
2. The government gives a single firm the exclusive right to produce some good or service.

3. The costs of production make a single producer more efficient than a large number of producers, creating a natural monopoly.

Let's briefly discuss each of these.

Monopoly Resources

The simplest way for a monopoly to arise is for a single firm to own a key resource. For example, consider the market for water in a small town in the Old West. If dozens of town residents have working wells, the competitive model discussed in the preceding chapter describes the behaviour of sellers. As a result, the price of a litre of water is driven to equal the marginal cost of pumping an extra litre. But if there is only one well in town and it is impossible to get water from anywhere else, then the owner of the well has a monopoly on water. Not surprisingly, the monopolist has much greater market power than any single firm in a competitive market. In the case of a necessity like water, the monopolist could command quite a high price, even if the marginal cost is low.

Although exclusive ownership of a key resource is a potential cause of monopoly, in practice, monopolies rarely arise for this reason. Actual economies are large, and resources are owned by many people. Indeed, because many goods are traded internationally, the natural scope of their markets is often worldwide. There are, therefore, few examples of firms that own a resource for which there are no close substitutes.

Case Study

THE DE BEERS DIAMOND MONOPOLY

A classic example of a monopoly that arises from the ownership of a key resource is De Beers, the South African diamond company. De Beers controls about 80 percent of the world's production of diamonds. Although the firm's share of the market is not 100 percent, it is large enough to exert substantial influence over the market price of diamonds.

How much market power does De Beers have? The answer depends in part on whether there are close substitutes for its product. If people view emeralds, rubies, and sapphires as good substitutes for diamonds, then De Beers has relatively little market power. In this case, any attempt by De Beers to raise the price of diamonds would cause people to switch to other gemstones. But if people view these other stones as very different from diamonds, then De Beers can exert substantial influence over the price of its product.

De Beers pays for large amounts of advertising. At first, this decision might seem surprising. If a monopoly is the sole seller of its product, why does it need to advertise? One goal of the De Beers ads is to differentiate diamonds from other gems in the minds of consumers. When its slogan tells you that "a diamond is forever," you are meant to think that the same is not true of emeralds, rubies, and sapphires. (And notice that the slogan is applied to all diamonds, not just De Beers diamonds—a sign of De Beers's monopoly position.) If the ads are successful, consumers will view diamonds as unique, rather than as one among many gemstones, and this perception will give De Beers greater market power. With the discovery of the Ekati diamond mine in the Northwest Territories, which began production in 1998, Canada has become an important player in the international diamond market. De Beers has responded by opening a Canadian office in the hope of marketing Canadian diamonds. ●

Government-Created Monopolies

In many cases, monopolies arise because the government has given one person or firm the exclusive right to sell some good or service. Sometimes the monopoly arises from the sheer political clout of the would-be monopolist. Kings, for example, once granted exclusive business licences to their friends and allies. At other times, the government grants a monopoly because doing so is viewed to be in the public interest. For instance, in 1996 the Canadian government created NAV CANADA as a private, nonprofit monopoly provider of air traffic control in Canada on the grounds that a centralized, integrated system of air traffic control is required for safety reasons. Another example is Canada Post, which has a government-granted monopoly on the delivery of first-class mail (see the In the News feature, "A Government Monopoly in Letters," later in this chapter).

The patent and copyright laws are two important examples of how the government creates a monopoly to serve the public interest. When a pharmaceutical company discovers a new drug, it can apply to the government for a patent. If the government deems the drug to be truly original, it approves the patent, which gives the company the exclusive right to manufacture and sell the drug for 20 years. Similarly, when a novelist finishes a book, she can copyright it. The copyright is a government guarantee that no one can print and sell the work without the author's permission. The copyright makes the novelist a monopolist in the sale of her novel.

The effects of patent and copyright laws are easy to see. Because these laws give one producer a monopoly, they lead to higher prices than would occur under competition. But by allowing these monopoly producers to charge higher prices and earn higher profits, the laws also encourage some desirable behaviour. Drug companies are allowed to be monopolists in the drugs they discover in order to encourage research. Authors are allowed to be monopolists in the sale of their books to encourage them to write more and better books.

Thus, the laws governing patents and copyrights have a benefit and costs. The benefit of the patent and copyright laws is the increased incentive for creative activity. This benefit is offset, to some extent, by the costs of monopoly pricing, which we examine fully later in this chapter.

natural monopoly
a monopoly that arises because a single firm can supply a good or service to an entire market at a smaller cost than could two or more firms

Natural Monopolies

An industry is a **natural monopoly** when a single firm can supply a good or service to an entire market at a lower cost than could two or more firms. A natural monopoly arises when there are economies of scale over the relevant range of output. Figure 15.1 shows the average total costs of a firm with economies of scale. In this case, a single firm can produce any amount of output at least cost. That is, for any given amount of output, a larger number of firms leads to less output per firm and higher average total cost.

An example of a natural monopoly is the distribution of water. To provide water to residents of a town, a firm must build a network of pipes throughout the town. If two or more firms were to compete in the provision of this service, each firm would have to pay the fixed cost of building a network. Thus, the average total cost of water is lowest if a single firm serves the entire market.

We saw other examples of natural monopolies when we discussed public goods and common resources in Chapter 11. We noted in passing that some goods in the economy are excludable but not rival. An example is a bridge used so infrequently that it is never congested. The bridge is excludable because a toll collector can prevent someone from using it. The bridge is not rival because use of the bridge by one person does not diminish the ability of others to use it. Because there is a fixed cost of building the bridge and a negligible marginal cost of additional users, the average total cost of a trip across the bridge (the total cost divided by the number of trips) falls as the number of trips rises. Hence, the bridge is a natural monopoly.

When a firm is a natural monopoly, it is less concerned about new entrants eroding its monopoly power. Normally, a firm has trouble maintaining a monopoly position without ownership of a key resource or government protection. The monopolist's profit attracts entrants into the market, and these entrants make the market more competitive. By contrast, entering a market in which

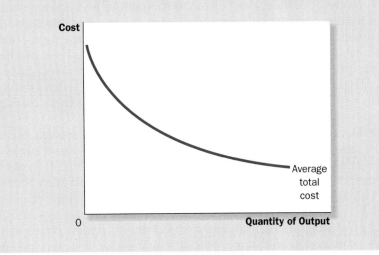

FIGURE 15.1

Economies of Scale as a Cause of Monopoly

When a firm's average-total-cost curve continually declines, the firm has what is called a natural monopoly. In this case, when production is divided among more firms, each firm produces less, and average total cost rises. As a result, a single firm can produce any given amount at the smallest cost.

another firm has a natural monopoly is unattractive. Would-be entrants know that they cannot achieve the same low costs that the monopolist enjoys because, after entry, each firm would have a smaller piece of the market.

In some cases, the size of the market is one determinant of whether an industry is a natural monopoly. Again, consider a bridge across a river. When the population is small, the bridge may be a natural monopoly. A single bridge can satisfy the entire demand for trips across the river at lowest cost. Yet as the population grows and the bridge becomes congested, satisfying the entire demand may require two or more bridges across the same river. Thus, as a market expands, a natural monopoly can evolve into a competitive market.

QuickQuiz What are the three reasons that a market might have a monopoly? •
Give two examples of monopolies, and explain the reason for each.

HOW MONOPOLIES MAKE PRODUCTION AND PRICING DECISIONS

Now that we know how monopolies arise, we can consider how a monopoly firm decides how much of its product to make and what price to charge for it. The analysis of monopoly behaviour in this section is the starting point for evaluating whether monopolies are desirable and what policies the government might pursue in monopoly markets.

Monopoly versus Competition

The key difference between a competitive firm and a monopoly is the monopoly's ability to influence the price of its output. A competitive firm is small relative to the market in which it operates and, therefore, takes the price of its output as given by market conditions. By contrast, because a monopoly is the sole producer in its market, it can alter the price of its good by adjusting the quantity it supplies to the market.

One way to view this difference between a competitive firm and a monopoly is to consider the demand curve that each firm faces. When we analyzed profit maximization by competitive firms in the preceding chapter, we drew the market price as a horizontal line. Because a competitive firm can sell as much or as little as it wants at this price, the competitive firm faces a horizontal demand curve, as in panel (a) of Figure 15.2. In effect, because the competitive firm sells a product with many perfect substitutes (the products of all the other firms in its market), the demand curve that any one firm faces is perfectly elastic.

By contrast, because a monopoly is the sole producer in its market, its demand curve is the market demand curve. Thus, the monopolist's demand curve slopes downward for all the usual reasons, as in panel (b) of Figure 15.2. If the monopolist raises the price of its good, consumers buy less of it. Looked at another way, if the monopolist reduces the quantity of output it sells, the price of its output increases.

The market demand curve provides a constraint on a monopoly's ability to profit from its market power. A monopolist would prefer, if it were possible, to

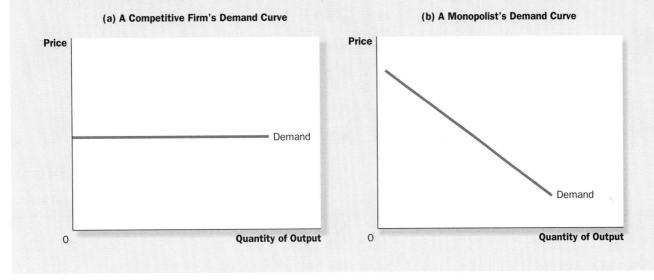

FIGURE 15.2

Demand Curves for Competitive and Monopoly Firms

Because competitive firms are price takers, they in effect face horizontal demand curves, as in panel (a). Because a monopoly firm is the sole producer in its market, it faces the downward-sloping market demand curve, as in panel (b). As a result, the monopoly has to accept a lower price if it wants to sell more output.

(a) A Competitive Firm's Demand Curve

Price

Demand

0   Quantity of Output

(b) A Monopolist's Demand Curve

Price

Demand

0   Quantity of Output

charge a high price and sell a large quantity at that high price. The market demand curve makes that outcome impossible. In particular, the market demand curve describes the combinations of price and quantity that are available to a monopoly firm. By adjusting the quantity produced (or, equivalently, the price charged), the monopolist can choose any point on the demand curve, but it cannot choose a point off the demand curve.

What point on the demand curve will the monopolist choose? As with competitive firms, we assume that the monopolist's goal is to maximize profit. Because the firm's profit is total revenue minus total costs, our next task in explaining monopoly behaviour is to examine a monopolist's revenue.

A Monopoly's Revenue

Consider a town with a single producer of water. Table 15.1 (p. 324) shows how the monopoly's revenue might depend on the amount of water produced.

The first two columns show the monopolist's demand schedule. If the monopolist produces 1 L of water, it can sell that litre for $10. If it produces 2 L, it must lower the price to $9 in order to sell both litres. And if it produces 3 L, it must lower the price to $8. And so on. If you graphed these two columns of numbers, you would get a typical downward-sloping demand curve.

The third column of the table presents the monopolist's *total revenue*. It equals the quantity sold (from the first column) times the price (from the second column). The

TABLE 15.1

A Monopoly's Total, Average, and Marginal Revenue

Quantity of Water (Q)	Price (P)	Total Revenue (TR = P × Q)	Average Revenue (AR = TR/Q)	Marginal Revenue (MR = ΔTR/ΔQ)
0 litres	$11	$ 0	—	
				$10
1	10	10	$10	
				8
2	9	18	9	
				6
3	8	24	8	
				4
4	7	28	7	
				2
5	6	30	6	
				0
6	5	30	5	
				−2
7	4	28	4	
				−4
8	3	24	3	

fourth column computes the firm's *average revenue,* the amount of revenue the firm receives per unit sold. We compute average revenue by taking the number for total revenue in the third column and dividing it by the quantity of output in the first column. As we discussed in the previous chapter, average revenue always equals the price of the good. This is true for monopolists as well as for competitive firms.

The last column of Table 15.1 computes the firm's *marginal revenue,* the amount of revenue that the firm receives for each additional unit of output. We compute marginal revenue by taking the change in total revenue when output increases by 1 unit. For example, when the firm is producing 3 L of water, it receives total revenue of $24. Raising production to 4 L increases total revenue to $28. Thus, marginal revenue is $28 minus $24, or $4.

Table 15.1 shows a result that is important for understanding monopoly behaviour: *A monopolist's marginal revenue is always less than the price of its good.* For example, if the firm raises production of water from 3 to 4 L, it will increase total revenue by only $4, even though it will be able to sell each litre for $7. For a monopoly, marginal revenue is lower than price because a monopoly faces a downward-sloping demand curve. To increase the amount sold, a monopoly firm must lower the price of its good. Hence, to sell the fourth litre of water, the monopolist must get less revenue for each of the first three litres.

Marginal revenue for monopolies is very different from marginal revenue for competitive firms. When a monopoly increases the amount it sells, it has two effects on total revenue ($P \times Q$):

1. *The output effect:* More output is sold, so Q is higher.
2. *The price effect:* The price falls, so P is lower.

Because a competitive firm can sell all it wants at the market price, there is no price effect. When it increases production by 1 unit, it receives the market price for that unit, and it does not receive any less for the units it was already selling. That is, because the competitive firm is a price taker, its marginal revenue equals the price of its good. By contrast, when a monopoly increases production by 1 unit, it must reduce the price it charges for every unit it sells, and this cut in price reduces revenue on the units it was already selling. As a result, a monopoly's marginal revenue is less than its price.

Figure 15.3 graphs the demand curve and the marginal-revenue curve for a monopoly firm. The demand curve is also the firm's average-revenue curve, because average revenue is equal to total revenue divided by the quantity of the output. But total revenue is equal to the quantity of the output times its price. Dividing total revenue by the quantity to get average revenue results in the firm's price equalling its average revenue; thus, the demand curve is also the average-revenue curve. Notice that the marginal-revenue curve and the demand (average-revenue) curve always start at the same point on the vertical axis. This is because the marginal revenue of the first unit sold equals the price of the good. But thereafter, for the reason we just discussed, the monopolist's marginal revenue is less than the price of the good. Thus, a monopoly's marginal-revenue curve lies below its demand curve.

You can see in the figure (as well as in Table 15.1) that marginal revenue can even become negative. Marginal revenue is negative when the price effect on revenue is greater than the output effect. In this case, when the firm produces an extra unit of output, the price falls by enough to cause the firm's total revenue to decline, even though the firm is selling more units.

Profit Maximization

Now that we have considered the revenue of a monopoly firm, we are ready to examine how such a firm maximizes profit. Recall from Chapter 1 that one of the

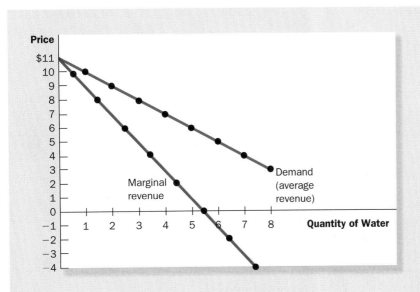

FIGURE 15.3

Demand and Marginal-Revenue Curves for a Monopoly

The demand curve shows how the quantity affects the price of the good. The marginal-revenue curve shows how the firm's revenue changes when the quantity increases by 1 unit. Because the price on all units sold must fall if the monopoly increases production, marginal revenue is always less than the price.

ten principles of economics is that rational people think at the margin. This lesson is as true for monopolists as it is for competitive firms. Here we apply the logic of marginal analysis to the monopolist's decision about how much to produce.

Figure 15.4 graphs the demand curve, the marginal-revenue curve, and the cost curves for a monopoly firm. All these curves should seem familiar: The demand and marginal-revenue curves are like those in Figure 15.3, and the cost curves are like those we encountered in the last two chapters. These curves contain all the information we need to determine the level of output that a profit-maximizing monopolist will choose.

Suppose, first, that the firm is producing at a low level of output, such as Q_1. In this case, marginal cost is less than marginal revenue. If the firm increased production by 1 unit, the additional revenue would exceed the additional costs, and profit would rise. Thus, when marginal cost is less than marginal revenue, the firm can increase profit by producing more units.

A similar argument applies at high levels of output, such as Q_2. In this case, marginal cost is greater than marginal revenue. If the firm reduced production by 1 unit, the costs saved would exceed the revenue lost. Thus, if marginal cost is greater than marginal revenue, the firm can raise profit by reducing production.

In the end, the firm adjusts its level of production until the quantity reaches Q_{MAX}, at which marginal revenue equals marginal cost. *Thus, the monopolist's profit-maximizing quantity of output is determined by the intersection of the marginal-revenue curve and the marginal-cost curve.* In Figure 15.4, this intersection occurs at point A.

You might recall from the last chapter that competitive firms also choose the quantity of output at which marginal revenue equals marginal cost. In following this rule for profit maximization, competitive firms and monopolies are alike. But there is also an important difference between these types of firm: The marginal

FIGURE 15.4

Profit Maximization for a Monopoly

A monopoly maximizes profit by choosing the quantity at which marginal revenue equals marginal cost (point A). It then uses the demand curve to find the price that will induce consumers to buy that quantity (point B).

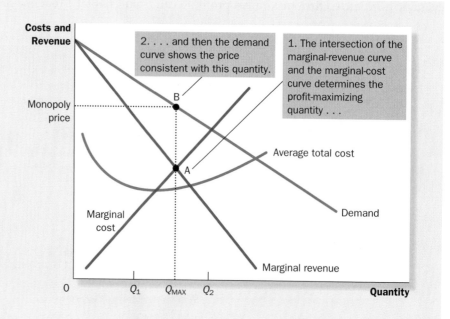

FYI

WHY A MONOPOLY DOES NOT HAVE A SUPPLY CURVE

You may have noticed that we have analyzed the price in a monopoly market using the market demand curve and the firm's cost curves. We have not made any mention of the market supply curve. By contrast, when we analyzed prices in competitive markets beginning in Chapter 4, the two most important words were always *supply* and *demand*.

What happened to the supply curve? Although monopoly firms make decisions about what quantity to supply (in the way described in this chapter), a monopoly does not have a supply curve. A supply curve tells us the quantity that firms choose to supply at any given price. This concept makes sense when we are analyzing competitive firms, which are price takers. But a monopoly firm is a price maker, not a price taker. It is not meaningful to ask what such a firm would produce at any price because the firm sets the price at the same time it chooses the quantity to supply.

Indeed, the monopolist's decision about how much to supply is impossible to separate from the demand curve it faces. The shape of the demand curve determines the shape of the marginal-revenue curve, which in turn determines the monopolist's profit-maximizing quantity. In a competitive market, supply decisions can be analyzed without knowing the demand curve, but that is not true in a monopoly market. Therefore, we never talk about a monopoly's supply curve.

revenue of a competitive firm equals its price, whereas the marginal revenue of a monopoly is less than its price. That is,

$$\text{For a competitive firm:} \quad P = MR = MC$$
$$\text{For a monopoly firm:} \quad P > MR = MC$$

The equality of marginal revenue and marginal cost at the profit-maximizing quantity is the same for both types of firm. What differs is the relationship of the price to marginal revenue and marginal cost.

How does the monopoly find the profit-maximizing price for its product? The demand curve answers this question because the demand curve relates the amount that customers are willing to pay to the quantity sold. Thus, after the monopoly firm chooses the quantity of output that equates marginal revenue and marginal cost, it uses the demand curve to find the price consistent with that quantity. In Figure 15.4, the profit-maximizing price is found at point B.

We can now see a key difference between markets with competitive firms and markets with a monopoly firm: *In competitive markets, price equals marginal cost. In monopolized markets, price exceeds marginal cost.* As we will see in a moment, this finding is crucial to understanding the social cost of monopoly.

A Monopoly's Profit

How much profit does the monopoly make? To see the monopoly's profit, recall that profit equals total revenue (*TR*) minus total costs (*TC*):

$$\text{Profit} = TR - TC$$

We can rewrite this as

$$\text{Profit} = (TR/Q - TC/Q) \times Q$$

TR/Q is average revenue, which equals the price P, and TC/Q is average total cost ATC. Therefore,

$$\text{Profit} = (P - ATC) \times Q$$

This equation for profit (which is the same as the profit equation for competitive firms) allows us to measure the monopolist's profit in our graph.

Consider the shaded box in Figure 15.5. The height of the box (the segment BC) is price minus average total cost, $P - ATC$, which is the profit on the typical unit sold. The width of the box (the segment DC) is the quantity sold, Q_{MAX}. Therefore, the area of this box is the monopoly firm's total profit.

Case Study

MONOPOLY DRUGS VERSUS GENERIC DRUGS

According to our analysis, prices are determined quite differently in monopolized markets from the way they are in competitive markets. A natural place to test this theory is the market for pharmaceutical drugs, because this market takes on both market structures. When a firm discovers a new drug, patent laws give the firm a

FIGURE 15.5

The Monopolist's Profit

The area of the box BCDE equals the profit of the monopoly firm. The height of the box (BC) is price minus average total cost, which equals profit per unit sold. The width of the box (DC) is the number of units sold.

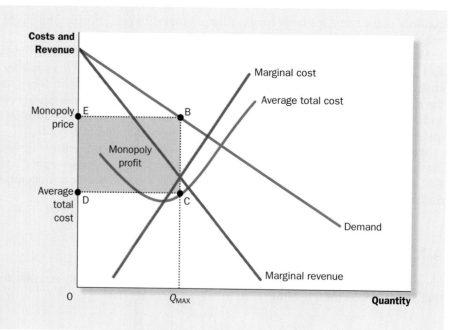

monopoly on the sale of that drug. But eventually the firm's patent runs out, and any company can make and sell the drug. At that time, the market switches from being monopolistic to being competitive.

What should happen to the price of a drug when the patent runs out? Figure 15.6 shows the market for a typical drug. In this figure, the marginal-cost curve is drawn as a horizontal, rather than upward-sloping, line. This is because the drug industry is characterized by large fixed costs (primarily associated with research and development) and constant marginal production costs. This is somewhat true in other industries with large fixed costs, such as airlines.

During the life of the patent, the monopoly firm maximizes profit by producing the quantity at which marginal revenue equals marginal cost and charging a price well above marginal cost. But when the patent runs out, the profit from making the drug should encourage new firms to enter the market. As the market becomes more competitive, the price should fall to equal marginal cost.

Experience is, in fact, consistent with our theory. When the patent on a drug expires, other companies quickly enter and begin selling so-called generic products that are chemically identical to the former monopolist's brand-name product. And just as our analysis predicts, the price of the competitively produced generic drug is well below the price that the monopolist was charging.

The expiration of a patent, however, does not cause the monopolist to lose all its market power. Some consumers remain loyal to the brand-name drug, perhaps out of fear that the new generic drugs are not actually the same as the drug they have been using for years. As a result, the former monopolist can continue to charge a price at least somewhat above the price charged by its new competitors. ●

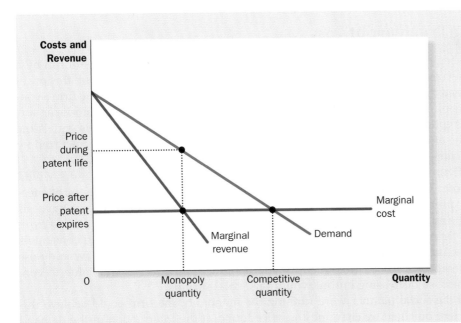

FIGURE 15.6

The Market for Drugs

When a patent gives a firm a monopoly over the sale of a drug, the firm charges the monopoly price, which is well above the marginal cost of making the drug. When the patent on a drug runs out, new firms enter the market, making it more competitive. As a result, the price falls from the monopoly price to marginal cost.

QuickQuiz Explain how a monopolist chooses the quantity of output to produce and the price to charge.

THE WELFARE COST OF MONOPOLY

Is monopoly a good way to organize a market? We have seen that a monopoly, in contrast to a competitive firm, charges a price above marginal cost. From the standpoint of consumers, this high price makes monopoly undesirable. At the same time, however, the monopoly is earning profit from charging this high price. From the standpoint of the owners of the firm, the high price makes monopoly very desirable. Is it possible that the benefits to the firm's owners exceed the costs imposed on consumers, making monopoly desirable from the standpoint of society as a whole?

We can answer this question using the type of analysis we first discussed in Chapter 7. As in that chapter, we use total surplus as our measure of economic well-being. Recall that total surplus is the sum of consumer surplus and producer surplus. Consumer surplus is consumers' willingness to pay for a good minus the amount they actually pay for it. Producer surplus is the amount producers receive for a good minus their costs of producing it. In this case, there is a single producer—the monopolist.

You might already be able to guess the result of this analysis. In Chapter 7 we concluded that the equilibrium of supply and demand in a competitive market is not only a natural outcome but a desirable one. In particular, the invisible hand of the market leads to an allocation of resources that makes total surplus as large as it can be. Because a monopoly leads to an allocation of resources different from that in a competitive market, the outcome must, in some way, fail to maximize total economic well-being.

The Deadweight Loss

We begin by considering what the monopoly firm would do if it were run by a benevolent social planner. The social planner cares not only about the profit earned by the firm's owners but also about the benefits received by the firm's consumers. The planner tries to maximize total surplus, which equals producer surplus (profit) plus consumer surplus. Keep in mind that total surplus equals the value of the good to consumers minus the costs of making the good incurred by the monopoly producer.

Figure 15.7 analyzes what level of output a benevolent social planner would choose. The demand curve reflects the value of the good to consumers, as measured by their willingness to pay for it. The marginal-cost curve reflects the costs of the monopolist. *Thus, the socially efficient quantity is found where the demand curve and the marginal-cost curve intersect.* Below this quantity, the value to consumers exceeds the marginal cost of providing the good, so increasing output would raise total surplus. Above this quantity, the marginal cost exceeds the value to consumers, so decreasing output would raise total surplus.

If the social planner were running the monopoly, the firm could achieve this efficient outcome by charging the price found at the intersection of the demand

FIGURE 15.7

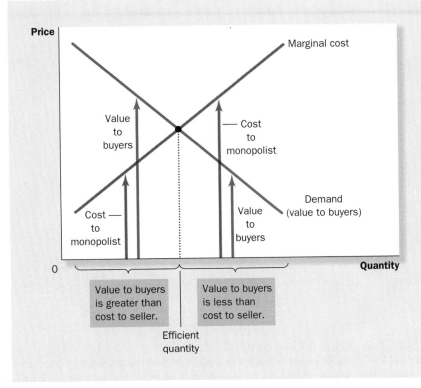

The Efficient Level of Output

A benevolent social planner who wanted to maximize total surplus in the market would choose the level of output where the demand curve and marginal-cost curve intersect. Below this level, the value of the good to the marginal buyer (as reflected in the demand curve) exceeds the marginal cost of making the good. Above this level, the value to the marginal buyer is less than marginal cost.

and marginal-cost curves. Thus, like a competitive firm and unlike a profit-maximizing monopoly, a social planner would charge a price equal to marginal cost. Because this price would give consumers an accurate signal about the cost of producing the good, consumers would buy the efficient quantity.

We can evaluate the welfare effects of monopoly by comparing the level of output that the monopolist chooses to the level of output that a social planner would choose. As we have seen, the monopolist chooses to produce and sell the quantity of output at which the marginal-revenue and marginal-cost curves intersect; the social planner would choose the quantity at which the demand and marginal-cost curves intersect. Figure 15.8 (p. 332) shows the comparison. *The monopolist produces less than the socially efficient quantity of output.*

We can also view the inefficiency of monopoly in terms of the monopolist's price. Because the market demand curve describes a negative relationship between the price and quantity of the good, a quantity that is inefficiently low is equivalent to a price that is inefficiently high. When a monopolist charges a price above marginal cost, some potential consumers value the good at more than its marginal cost but less than the monopolist's price. These consumers do not end up buying the good. Because the value these consumers place on the good is greater than the cost of providing it to them, this result is inefficient. Thus, monopoly pricing prevents some mutually beneficial trades from taking place.

Just as we measured the inefficiency of taxes with the deadweight loss triangle in Chapter 8, we can similarly measure the inefficiency of monopoly. Figure 15.8 shows the deadweight loss. Recall that the demand curve reflects the value to

FIGURE 15.8

The Inefficiency of Monopoly

Because a monopoly charges a price above marginal cost, not all consumers who value the good at more than its cost buy it. Thus, the quantity produced and sold by a monopoly is below the socially efficient level. The deadweight loss is represented by the area of the triangle between the demand curve (which reflects the value of the good to consumers) and the marginal-cost curve (which reflects the costs of the monopoly producer).

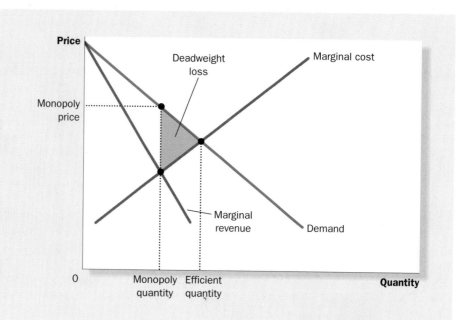

consumers and the marginal-cost curve reflects the costs to the monopoly producer. Thus, the area of the deadweight loss triangle between the demand curve and the marginal-cost curve equals the total surplus lost because of monopoly pricing.

The deadweight loss caused by monopoly is similar to the deadweight loss caused by a tax. Indeed, a monopolist is like a private tax collector. As we saw in Chapter 8, a tax on a good places a wedge between consumers' willingness to pay (as reflected in the demand curve) and producers' costs (as reflected in the supply curve). Because a monopoly exerts its market power by charging a price above marginal cost, it places a similar wedge. In both cases, the wedge causes the quantity sold to fall short of the social optimum. The difference between the two cases is that the government gets the revenue from a tax, whereas a private firm gets the monopoly profit.

The Monopoly's Profit: A Social Cost?

It is tempting to decry monopolies for "profiteering" at the expense of the public. And, indeed, a monopoly firm does earn a higher profit by virtue of its market power. According to the economic analysis of monopoly, however, the firm's profit is not in itself necessarily a problem for society.

Welfare in a monopolized market, like all markets, includes the welfare of both consumers and producers. Whenever a consumer pays an extra dollar to a producer because of a monopoly price, the consumer is worse off by a dollar, and the producer is better off by the same amount. This transfer from the consumers of the good to the owners of the monopoly does not affect the market's total surplus—the sum of consumer and producer surplus. In other words, the monopoly profit itself does not represent a shrinkage in the size of the economic pie; it merely represents a bigger slice for producers and a smaller slice for consumers. Unless consumers are for some reason more deserving than producers—a judgment that goes beyond the realm of economic efficiency—the monopoly profit is not a social problem.

The problem in a monopolized market arises because the firm produces and sells a quantity of output below the level that maximizes total surplus. The deadweight loss measures how much the economic pie shrinks as a result. This inefficiency is connected to the monopoly's high price: Consumers buy fewer units when the firm raises its price above marginal cost. But keep in mind that the profit earned on the units that continue to be sold is not the problem. The problem stems from the inefficiently low quantity of output. Put differently, if the high monopoly price did not discourage some consumers from buying the good, it would raise producer surplus by exactly the amount it reduced consumer surplus, leaving total surplus the same as could be achieved by a benevolent social planner.

There is, however, a possible exception to this conclusion. Suppose that a monopoly firm has to incur additional costs to maintain its monopoly position. For example, a firm with a government-created monopoly might need to hire lobbyists to convince lawmakers to continue its monopoly. In this case, the monopoly may use up some of its monopoly profits paying for these additional costs. If so, the social loss from monopoly includes both these costs and the deadweight loss resulting from a price above marginal cost.

QuickQuiz How does a monopolist's quantity of output compare to the quantity of output that maximizes total surplus?

PUBLIC POLICY TOWARD MONOPOLIES

We have seen that monopolies, in contrast to competitive markets, fail to allocate resources efficiently. Monopolies produce less than the socially desirable quantity of output and, as a result, charge prices above marginal cost. Policymakers in the government can respond to the problem of monopoly in one of four ways:

1. By trying to make monopolized industries more competitive
2. By regulating the behaviour of the monopolies
3. By turning some private monopolies into public enterprises
4. By doing nothing at all

Competition Law

One way that the government can respond to the inefficiencies resulting from market power in general, and monopoly in particular, is through legislation designed to encourage competition and discourage the use of monopoly practices. For example, if a merger between two companies would make the industry less competitive and, as a result, reduce the economic well-being of the country as a whole, the government could pass laws that prevent such mergers. Competition law has a long history in Canada; the first competition statute, the Act for the Prevention and Suppression of Combinations Formed in Restraint of Trade, was passed in 1889. The act was introduced in response to public concern over the pricing practices of large and powerful organized groups of companies. (These groups were known as "combines" or "trusts," so competition policy is sometimes referred to as "anticombines" or "antitrust" policy.)

In its early form, competition law in Canada was narrow in scope and ineffective in its application. In 1910, the original act was replaced with the Combines Investigation Act, which substantially expanded the types of activities subject to review; the most important of these were mergers and monopolization activities. Over the years, the act was revised and amended to give it broader coverage and more effective means of enforcement. In 1986, competition law in Canada changed dramatically when the old act was replaced by two new statutes, the Competition Act and the Competition Tribunal Act.

The Competition Act recognizes that competition is a means to an end (or several ends) and firmly places competition policy in Canada in a global context. In its preamble, the act states that its purpose

is to maintain and encourage competition in Canada in order to promote the efficiency and adaptability of the Canadian economy, in order to expand opportunities for Canadian participation in world markets while at the same time recognizing the role of foreign competition in Canada, in order to ensure that small and medium-sized enterprises have an equitable opportunity to participate in the Canadian economy, and in order to provide consumers with competitive prices and product choices.

Competition law in Canada is enforced by the Commissioner of Competition of the Competition Bureau, a unit within the federal government's Industry Canada. Lawyers and economists in the bureau investigate anticompetitive practices that fall within the scope of the act. When appropriate, the director may refer cases for criminal prosecution to the attorney general of Canada. In other cases, the director may apply to the Competition Tribunal for review and adjudication.

The tribunal is a quasi-judicial body that is similar in many ways to a court. It consists of judges and lay members who are experts from the business, academic, and civil service communities. In most of the cases it deals with, the tribunal must determine whether a particular practice or action has an adverse effect on competition. If it concludes that there is an anticompetitive effect, the tribunal can issue an order to prohibit the practice or action. For example, the tribunal can block a merger or require that a firm divest itself of assets. In 1990 the tribunal ruled that the merger of two of Canada's largest integrated petroleum companies, Imperial Oil and Texaco Canada, would have substantial anticompetitive effects. Although the merger was allowed to proceed, the tribunal ordered that many of the merged entity's assets be given up. This divestiture ultimately involved 414 service stations, 13 terminals, and 1 refinery.

Competition law in Canada prevents other kinds of anticompetitive practices, some of which we will discuss in Chapter 16.

Competition laws have costs as well as benefits. Sometimes companies merge not to reduce competition but to lower costs through more efficient joint production. The benefits of greater efficiency as a result of mergers are called *synergies*. These considerations are particularly important in a global context because some Canadian companies are large and dominant in the domestic market but small in the international market. For example, although the banking market in Canada is dominated by the "Big Five," these banks are small players on the international banking scene. Some bankers have argued that Canadian banks can compete in international markets only by realizing the synergies that would result when operations are combined. Using this argument, four of Canada's largest banks sought permission to merge in 1998: the Royal Bank with the Bank of Montreal, and the Canadian Imperial Bank of Commerce with the Toronto-Dominion Bank. Both merger deals were rejected by the federal government. As a result, the Canadian banks are now seeking merger partners in the United States, which would be less likely to run afoul of Canada's competition laws.

If competition laws are to raise social welfare, the government must be able to determine which mergers are desirable and which are not. That is, it must be able to measure and compare the social benefit from synergies with the social cost of reduced competition. However, critics of competition laws are skeptical that the government can perform the necessary cost–benefit analysis with sufficient accuracy.

Regulation

Another way in which the government deals with the problem of monopoly is by regulating the behaviour of monopolists. This solution is common in the case of natural monopolies, such as water and electric companies. These companies are not allowed to charge any price they want. Instead, government agencies regulate their prices.

What price should the government set for a natural monopoly? This question is not as easy as it might at first appear. One might conclude that the price should equal the monopolist's marginal cost. If price equals marginal cost, customers will buy the quantity of the monopolist's output that maximizes total surplus, and the allocation of resources will be efficient.

There are, however, two practical problems with marginal-cost pricing as a regulatory system. The first is illustrated in Figure 15.9 (p. 336). Natural monopolies, by definition, have declining average total cost. As we discussed in Chapter 13, when average total cost is declining, marginal cost is less than average total cost. If regulators are to set price equal to marginal cost, that price will be less than the firm's average total cost, and the firm will lose money. Instead of charging such a low price, the monopoly firm would just exit the industry.

Regulators can respond to this problem in various ways, none of which is perfect. One way is to subsidize the monopolist. In essence, the government picks up the losses inherent in marginal-cost pricing. Yet to pay for the subsidy, the government needs to raise money through taxation, which involves its own deadweight losses. Alternatively, the regulators can allow the monopolist to charge a price higher than marginal cost. If the regulated price equals average total cost, the monopolist earns exactly zero economic profit. Yet average-cost pricing leads to deadweight losses, because the monopolist's price no longer reflects the marginal cost of producing the good. In essence, average-cost pricing is like a tax on the good the monopolist is selling.

The second problem with marginal-cost pricing as a regulatory system (and with average-cost pricing as well) is that it gives the monopolist no incentive to reduce costs. Each firm in a competitive market tries to reduce its costs because lower costs mean higher profits. But if a regulated monopolist knows that regulators will reduce prices whenever costs fall, the monopolist will not benefit from

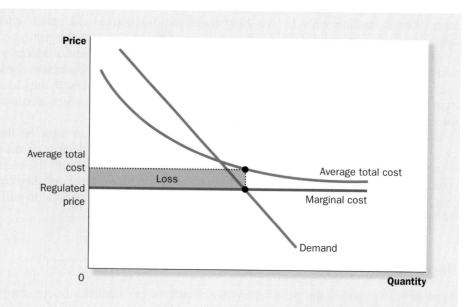

FIGURE 15.9

Marginal-Cost Pricing for a Natural Monopoly

Because a natural monopoly has declining average total cost, marginal cost is less than average total cost. Therefore, if regulators require a natural monopoly to charge a price equal to marginal cost, price will be below average total cost, and the monopoly will lose money.

lower costs. In practice, regulators deal with this problem by allowing monopolists to keep some of the benefits from lower costs in the form of higher profit, a practice that requires some departure from marginal-cost pricing.

Public Ownership

The third policy used by the government to deal with monopoly is public ownership. That is, rather than regulating a natural monopoly that is run by a private firm, the government can run the monopoly itself. In contrast to the United States, where there is very little public ownership, this solution is common in many European countries. It is also relatively common in Canada, although somewhat less so in recent years.

In Canada, government ownership occurs at both the federal and the provincial levels. Government-owned firms are known as Crown corporations. Federal Crown corporations include Canada Post, the Canadian Broadcasting Corporation, and Atomic Energy of Canada Limited. In the past decade, the federal government has privatized some of its Crown corporations, including Petro-Canada, Air Canada, and Canadian National Railway.

At the provincial level, Crown corporations exist in insurance (Saskatchewan Government Insurance), hydroelectricity (Manitoba Hydro and Hydro-Québec), and telecommunications (Saskatchewan Tel and BC Telephone). Gas and water utilities are also publicly owned in most provinces.

Economists usually prefer private to public ownership of natural monopolies. The key issue is how the ownership of the firm affects the costs of production. Private owners have an incentive to minimize costs as long as they reap part of the benefit in the form of higher profit. If the firm's managers are doing a bad job of keeping costs down, the firm's owners will fire them. By contrast, if the government bureaucrats who run a monopoly do a bad job, the losers are the customers and taxpayers, whose only recourse is the political system. The bureaucrats may become a special-interest group and attempt to block cost-reducing reforms. Put simply, as a way of ensuring that firms are well run, the voting booth is less reliable than the profit motive.

Doing Nothing

Each of the foregoing policies aimed at reducing the problem of monopoly has drawbacks. As a result, some economists argue that it is often best for the government not to try to remedy the inefficiencies of monopoly pricing. Here is the assessment of economist George Stigler, who won the Nobel Prize for his work in industrial organization, writing in the *Fortune Encyclopedia of Economics:*

> A famous theorem in economics states that a competitive enterprise economy will produce the largest possible income from a given stock of resources. No real economy meets the exact conditions of the theorem, and all real economies will fall short of the ideal economy—a difference called "market failure." In my view, however, the degree of "market failure" for the American economy is much smaller than the "political failure" arising from the imperfections of economic policies found in real political systems.

As this quotation makes clear, determining the proper role of the government in the economy requires judgments about politics as well as economics.

QuickQuiz Describe the ways policymakers can respond to the inefficiencies caused by monopolies. List a potential problem with each of these policy responses.

PRICE DISCRIMINATION

So far we have been assuming that the monopoly firm charges the same price to all customers. Yet in many cases firms try to sell the same good to different customers for different prices, even though the costs of producing for the two customers are the same. This practice is called **price discrimination.**

Before discussing the behaviour of a price-discriminating monopolist, we should note that price discrimination is not possible when a good is sold in a competitive market. In a competitive market, many firms are selling the same good at the market price. No firm is willing to charge a lower price to any customer because the firm can sell all it wants at the market price. And if any firm tried to charge a higher price to a customer, that customer would buy from another firm. For a firm to price-discriminate, it must have some market power.

price discrimination
the business practice of selling the same good at different prices to different customers

A Parable about Pricing

To understand why a monopolist would want to price-discriminate, let's consider a simple example. Imagine that you are the president of Readalot Publishing

IN THE NEWS

A GOVERNMENT MONOPOLY IN LETTERS

Canada Post has a government-granted monopoly for the delivery of first-class mail. But this Crown corporation provides other services as well, and the U.S.-based courier company UPS thinks that Canada Post uses its monopoly position in first-class mail to cross-subsidize its other activities.

As the following article shows, competition policy is becoming an increasingly international issue. Canada's Competition Act is not the only relevant statute governing monopolies—the North American Free Trade Agreement (NAFTA) also contains a competition provision.

UPS Suing Ottawa for $230M: Canada Post Case—Corporation Accused under NAFTA of Unfair Practices

By Ian Jack

OTTAWA — The federal government is being sued for $230 million in a groundbreaking NAFTA case that for the first time uses the trade deal's competition provision to attack a government monopoly.

United Parcel Service of America Inc. alleges in documents filed with federal officials that Ottawa has failed to regulate Canada Post Corp. properly. UPS is accusing Canada Post of subsidizing its courier services, including XpressPost, Priority Courier and Purolator with revenue from its regular letter delivery service.

If UPS wins, Canada Post may be forced to divest its 96% holding in Purolator, set up its courier services as a completely separate company, or get out of the business entirely. And the reach of NAFTA into domestic regulation and policy, already feared by nationalists, will be lengthened.

The competition section of the North American Free Trade Agreement, known as chapter 15, says governments must ensure, "through regulatory control," that government monopolies do not engage, "in anticompetitive practices in a non-monopolized market," including "cross-subsidization or predatory conduct."

This is the first time anyone has used the chapter to pursue a case against a government monopoly.

"We're not asking them to get out of the courier business. But they can't run them from under the same roof," Tad Segal, spokesman for UPS, said.

UPS makes extensive use in its case of a government-commissioned report

Company. Readalot's best-selling author has just written her latest novel. To keep things simple, let's imagine that you pay the author a flat $2 million for the exclusive rights to publish the book. Let's also assume that the cost of printing the book is zero. Readalot's profit, therefore, is the revenue it gets from selling the book minus the $2 million it has paid to the author. Given these assumptions, how would you, as Readalot's president, decide what price to charge for the book?

Your first step in setting the price is to estimate what the demand for the book is likely to be. Readalot's marketing department tells you that the book will attract two types of readers. The book will appeal to the author's 100 000 die-hard fans. These fans will be willing to pay as much as $30 for the book. In addition, the book into Canada Post in 1996, which found the Crown corporation was using its publicly funded service to help its competitive courier business.

"Canada Post openly admits that it does and will continue to leverage its existing network to achieve cost savings in the provision of all its product lines. It argues that this is merely efficient use of resources and sound business practice," wrote George Radwanski in the 1996 study.

"It is a finding of the review that Canada Post is an unfair and inappropriately aggressive competitor in the courier industry," the Radwanski report said, in urging the Crown corporation to get out of the courier business.

Canada Post has insisted it is not an unfair competitor.

Its offices were closed yesterday for the holiday. A government spokesman said Ottawa will fight the case vigorously, but declined further comment.

The UPS filing also attacks the Canada Customs and Revenue Service, formerly Revenue Canada, for allegedly not making sure Canada Post collects all the tax due on transborder packages. Its competitors face hefty penalties if they fail to collect tax, while Canada Post is exempt from retribution, giving it another unfair advantage, UPS alleges.

Canada Post shares trucks and planes between its various services, and does not allow competing courier products to be sold from its retail outlets. The private courier business has long accused the Crown corporation of undercharging for its competitive products, using letter-mail profits to maintain market share. UPS says Canada Post's market share is just under 50%.

Consumers could see some benefits if UPS wins, a company spokesman argued yesterday.

"It's our belief that the price of stamps is far higher than it need be," Mr. Segal said.

He said attempts to get the government to change its policy, or to get more information out of Canada Post, which is not subject to Access to Information Laws, have not worked.

"This is really a measure of last resort for us," Mr. Segal said. "Nobody can get into this Pandora's box, except through NAFTA."

The federal government appoints Canada Post's board of directors. Alfonso Gagliano, the minister of Public Works and Government Services, is also minister responsible for Canada Post, but that does not provide enough independent oversight, UPS argues.

"Other monopolies in the postal area have a regulatory body," said Mr. Segal,

citing the United States and Britain. "This monopoly in Canada is totally unregulated."

UPS also cites a consultant's report, by BDO Dunwoody LLP, that argues Purolator doesn't even turn much of a profit for Canada Post.

"The contribution of Purolator in total to CPC [Canada Post Corporation] after taking into consideration the amortization of goodwill is minimal," said the report, which suggests investing in government bonds would have returned a greater profit.

"The competition in 1999 outperformed Purolator by five times in profit return and two and one half times in 1998."

UPS argues its loss of market share and goodwill since 1997 totals at least $230 million, and it is also using NAFTA's chapter 11 to claim it has not received equitable treatment as an investor in Canada. Chapter 11, the investor-state provision of NAFTA, allows companies to sue if they feel one of the three governments is not treating them the same as a domestic corporation.

Source: *Financial Post,* April 22, 2000, pp. D1, D8. Material reprinted with the express permission of "The National Post Company," a CanWest Partnership.

will appeal to about 400 000 less enthusiastic readers who will be willing to pay up to $5 for the book.

What price maximizes Readalot's profit? There are two natural prices to consider: $30 is the highest price Readalot can charge and still get the 100 000 die-hard fans, and $5 is the highest price it can charge and still get the entire market of 500 000 potential readers. It is a matter of simple arithmetic to solve Readalot's problem. At a price of $30, Readalot sells 100 000 copies, has revenue of $3 million, and makes profit of $1 million. At a price of $5, it sells 500 000 copies, has revenue of $2.5 million, and makes a profit of $500 000. Thus, Readalot maximizes profit by charging $30 and forgoing the opportunity to sell to the 400 000 less enthusiastic readers.

Notice that Readalot's decision causes a deadweight loss. There are 400 000 readers willing to pay $5 for the book, and the marginal cost of providing it to them is zero. Thus, $2 million of total surplus is lost when Readalot charges the higher price. This deadweight loss is the usual inefficiency that arises whenever a monopolist charges a price above marginal cost.

Now suppose that Readalot's marketing department makes an important discovery: These two groups of readers are in separate markets. All the die-hard fans live in Australia, and all the other readers live in Canada. Moreover, it is difficult for readers in one country to buy books in the other. How does this discovery affect Readalot's marketing strategy?

In this case, the company can make even more profit. To the 100 000 Australian readers, it can charge $30 for the book. To the 400 000 Canadian readers, it can charge $5 for the book. In this case, revenue is $3 million in Australia and $2 million in Canada, for a total of $5 million. Profit is then $3 million, which is substantially greater than the $1 million the company could earn charging the same $30 price to all customers. Not surprisingly, Readalot chooses to follow this strategy of price discrimination.

Although the story of Readalot Publishing is hypothetical, it describes accurately the business practice of many publishing companies. Textbooks, for example, are often sold at a lower price in Europe than in Canada. Even more important is the price differential between hardcover books and paperbacks. When a publisher has a new novel, it initially releases an expensive hardcover edition and later releases a cheaper paperback edition. The difference in price between these two editions far exceeds the difference in printing costs. The publisher's goal is just as in our example. By selling the hardcover to die-hard fans and the paperback to less enthusiastic readers, the publisher price-discriminates and raises its profit.

The Moral of the Story

Like any parable, the story of Readalot Publishing is stylized. Yet, also like any parable, it teaches some important and general lessons. In this case, there are three lessons to be learned about price discrimination.

The first and most obvious lesson is that price discrimination is a rational strategy for a profit-maximizing monopolist. In other words, by charging different prices to different customers, a monopolist can increase its profit. In essence, a price-discriminating monopolist charges each customer a price closer to that customer's willingness to pay than is possible with a single price.

The second lesson is that price discrimination requires the ability to separate customers according to their willingness to pay. In our example, customers were separated geographically. But sometimes monopolists choose other differences, such as age or income, to distinguish among customers.

A corollary to this second lesson is that certain market forces can prevent firms from price-discriminating. In particular, one such force is *arbitrage*, the process of buying a good in one market at a low price and selling it in another market at a higher price in order to profit from the price difference. In our example, suppose that Australian bookstores could buy the book in Canada and resell it to Australian readers. This arbitrage would prevent Readalot from price-discriminating because no Australian would buy the book at the higher price.

The third lesson from our parable is perhaps the most surprising: Price discrimination can raise economic welfare. Recall that a deadweight loss arises when Readalot charges a single $30 price, because the 400 000 less enthusiastic readers do not end up with the book, even though they value it at more than its marginal cost of production. By contrast, when Readalot price-discriminates, all readers end up with the book, and the outcome is efficient. Thus, price discrimination can eliminate the inefficiency inherent in monopoly pricing.

Note that the increase in welfare from price discrimination shows up as higher producer surplus rather than higher consumer surplus. In our example, consumers are no better off for having bought the book: The price they pay exactly equals the value they place on the book, so they receive no consumer surplus. The entire increase in total surplus from price discrimination accrues to Readalot Publishing in the form of higher profit.

The Analytics of Price Discrimination

Let's consider a bit more formally how price discrimination affects economic welfare. We begin by assuming that the monopolist can price-discriminate perfectly. *Perfect price discrimination* describes a situation in which the monopolist knows exactly the willingness to pay of each customer and can charge each customer a different price. In this case, the monopolist charges each customer exactly his willingness to pay, and the monopolist gets the entire surplus in every transaction.

Figure 15.10 (p. 342) shows producer and consumer surplus with and without price discrimination. Without price discrimination, the firm charges a single price above marginal cost, as shown in panel (a). Because some potential customers who value the good at more than marginal cost do not buy it at this high price, the monopoly causes a deadweight loss. Yet when a firm can perfectly price-discriminate, as shown in panel (b), each customer who values the good at more than marginal cost buys the good and is charged his willingness to pay. All mutually beneficial trades take place, there is no deadweight loss, and the entire surplus derived from the market goes to the monopoly producer in the form of profit.

In reality, of course, price discrimination is not perfect. Customers do not walk into stores with signs displaying their willingness to pay. Instead, firms price-discriminate by dividing customers into groups: young versus old, weekday versus weekend shoppers, Canadians versus Australians, and so on. Unlike those in our parable of Readalot Publishing, customers within each group differ in their willingness to pay for the product, making perfect price discrimination impossible.

How does this imperfect price discrimination affect welfare? The analysis of these pricing schemes is quite complicated, and it turns out that there is no general answer to this question. Compared to the monopoly outcome with a single price, imperfect price discrimination can raise, lower, or leave unchanged total surplus in a market. The only certain conclusion is that price discrimination raises the monopoly's profit—otherwise the firm would choose to charge all customers the same price.

FIGURE 15.10

Welfare with and without Price Discrimination

Panel (a) shows a monopolist that charges the same price to all customers. Total surplus in this market equals the sum of profit (producer surplus) and consumer surplus. Panel (b) shows a monopolist that can perfectly price-discriminate. Because consumer surplus equals zero, total surplus now equals the firm's profit. Comparing these two panels, you can see that perfect price discrimination raises profit, raises total surplus, and lowers consumer surplus.

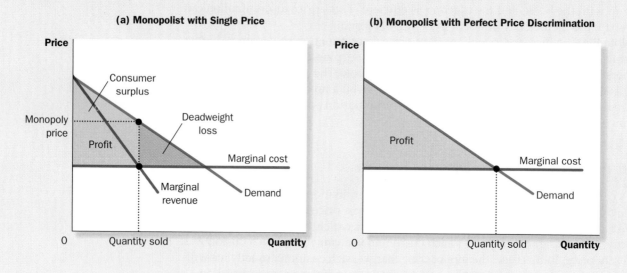

Examples of Price Discrimination

Firms in our economy use various business strategies aimed at charging different prices to different customers. Now that we understand the economics of price discrimination, let's consider some examples.

Movie Tickets Many movie theatres charge a lower price for children and senior citizens than for other patrons. This fact is hard to explain in a competitive market. In a competitive market, price equals marginal cost, and the marginal cost of providing a seat for a child or senior citizen is the same as the marginal cost of providing a seat for anyone else. Yet this fact is easily explained if movie theatres have some local monopoly power and if children and senior citizens have a lower willingness to pay for a ticket. In this case, movie theatres raise their profit by price-discriminating.

Airline Prices Seats on airplanes are sold at many different prices. Most airlines charge a lower price for a round-trip ticket between two cities if the traveller stays over a Saturday night. At first this seems odd. Why should it matter to the airline whether a passenger stays over a Saturday night? The reason is that this rule provides a way to separate business travellers and personal travellers. A passenger on a business trip has a high willingness to pay and, most likely, does not want to stay over a Saturday night. By contrast, a passenger travelling for personal reasons has a lower willingness to pay and is more likely to be willing to stay over a Saturday night. Thus, the airlines can successfully price-discriminate by charging a lower price for passengers who stay over a Saturday night.

Discount Coupons   Many companies offer discount coupons to the public in newspapers and magazines. A buyer simply has to clip out the coupon in order to get $0.50 off his next purchase. Why do companies offer these coupons? Why don't they just cut the price of the product by $0.50?

The answer is that coupons allow companies to price-discriminate. Companies know that not all customers are willing to spend the time to clip out coupons. Moreover, the willingness to clip coupons is related to the customer's willingness to pay for the good. A rich and busy executive is unlikely to spend her time clipping discount coupons out of the newspaper, and she is probably willing to pay a higher price for many goods. A person who is unemployed is more likely to clip coupons and has a lower willingness to pay. Thus, by charging a lower price only to those customers who clip coupons, firms can successfully price-discriminate.

Financial Aid   Many colleges and universities give financial aid to needy students. One can view this policy as a type of price discrimination. Wealthy students have greater financial resources and, therefore, a higher willingness to pay than needy students. By charging high tuition and selectively offering financial aid, schools charge prices to customers based on the value they place on going to that school. This behaviour is like that of any price-discriminating monopolist.

Quantity Discounts   So far in our examples of price discrimination, the monopolist charges different prices to different customers. Sometimes, however, monopolists price-discriminate by charging different prices to the same customer for different units that the customer buys. For example, many firms offer lower prices to customers who buy large quantities. A bakery might charge $0.50 for each donut, but $5 for a dozen. This is a form of price discrimination because the customer pays a higher price for the first unit bought than for the twelfth. Quantity discounts are often a successful way of price-discriminating because a customer's willingness to pay for an additional unit declines as the customer buys more units.

QuickQuiz Give two examples of price discrimination. • How does perfect price discrimination affect consumer surplus, producer surplus, and total surplus?

CONCLUSION: THE PREVALENCE OF MONOPOLY

This chapter has discussed the behaviour of firms that have control over the prices they charge. We have seen that these firms behave very differently from the competitive firms studied in the previous chapter. Table 15.2 (p. 345) summarizes some of the key similarities and differences between competitive and monopoly markets.

IN THE NEWS

PRICE DISCRIMINATION: OPPORTUNITIES FOR ARBITRAGE

In order for a firm to price-discriminate it must be difficult, or costly, for buyers to resell the good at a higher price. If this was not the case, an opportunity for arbitrage arises. Arbitrage occurs when an individual purchases a good at a low price and then immediately (or shortly thereafter) sells it for a higher price.

One common form of price discrimination is for firms to sell the same good for different prices in different countries, with demand conditions dictating the price in each country. Businesses hope that arbitrage will be too costly in this case. As the following article shows, if they are determined enough arbitragers can take advantage of this.

A Different Kind of Package Holiday

The same Louis Vuitton handbag costs about 40% more in Japan than in France. To economists, this is a market imperfection begging for arbitrage. And Hong Kong, that bastion of entrepreneurship, is obliging. Here is how.

Nine Hong Kong Chinese recently spent a fortnight travelling through Europe. They started in Frankfurt and ended in Rome, passing through one city a day. Early every morning, a van picked them up from their hotel and drove them to the first Louis Vuitton store on the day's agenda. It parked around the corner, and the Chinese entered the store in pairs. They each bought as many Louis Vuitton handbags as they could carry and then returned to the van, in order to be transferred to the next store.

It was gruelling work, complains a girl from the van. She, like the rest in the group, went on the trip because it was an all-expenses-paid way to see Europe. (In fact, those who bought more than their quota of handbags even earned a bonus.) But the itinerary did not allow for any sightseeing at all, and for meals the group are given Chinese takeaway in the van.

The sales staff in the stores tended to be rude; the tour's "boss," says the girl, had expressly asked for bags "with a certain monogram pattern" that is all the rage in Japan, and one shop simply refused to sell her the nine bags she brought to the counter.

The boss never introduced himself to the group, but when his troops returned he stood near the arrivals hall at Hong Kong's airport, watching them claim their luggage. His business seems to be going well—another tour group is apparently already on the way. Savvy Hong Kong tourists claim to know of several competing organisers—an industry, in other words. Nor is Louis Vuitton the only target: Gucci tours have also taken place.

Should companies whose prices are being arbitraged in this way mind? Louis Vuitton's sales benefit from such tourism, after all. "We definitely do not think that a sale is a sale," complains an irate spokeswoman in Paris. "It took 150 years to build this brand," she says, and losing part of the retail network to a netherworld of shady Asians damages it.

So Louis Vuitton, along with other owners of luxury brands, is working with the authorities to crack down on such tourism. This is tricky, not only because of arbitrageurs tending to pay cash, but also because Louis Vuitton would hate to confuse them with its genuine customers from Asia, who have also been known to binge on bags.

Source: *The Economist*, July 14, 2001, p. 57.

From the standpoint of public policy, a crucial result is that monopolists produce less than the socially efficient quantity and charge prices above marginal cost. As a result, they cause deadweight losses. In some cases, these inefficiencies can be mitigated through price discrimination by the monopolist, but other times they call for policymakers to take an active role.

How prevalent are the problems of monopoly? There are two answers to this question.

In one sense, monopolies are common. Most firms have some control over the prices they charge. They are not forced to charge the market price for their goods, because their goods are not exactly the same as those offered by other firms. A Ford Taurus is not the same as a Toyota Camry. Ben & Jerry's ice cream is not the same as Breyers'. Each of these goods has a downward-sloping demand curve, which gives each producer some degree of monopoly power.

Yet firms with substantial monopoly power are quite rare. Few goods are truly unique. Most have substitutes that, even if not exactly the same, are very similar. Ben & Jerry can raise the price of its ice cream a little without losing all its sales; but if the company raises it very much, sales will fall substantially.

In the end, monopoly power is a matter of degree. It is true that many firms have some monopoly power. It is also true that their monopoly power is usually limited. In these cases, we will not go far wrong assuming that firms operate in competitive markets, even if that is not precisely the case.

TABLE 15.2

Competition versus Monopoly: A Summary Comparison

	Competition	Monopoly
Similarities		
Goal of firms	Maximize profits	Maximize profits
Rule for maximizing	$MR = MC$	$MR = MC$
Can earn economic profits in the short run?	Yes	Yes
Differences		
Number of firms	Many	One
Marginal revenue	$MR = P$	$MR < P$
Price	$P = MC$	$P > MC$
Produces welfare-maximizing level of output?	Yes	No
Entry in long run?	Yes	No
Can earn economic profits in long run?	No	Yes
Price discrimination possible?	No	Yes

SUMMARY

- A monopoly is a firm that is the sole seller in its market. A monopoly arises when a single firm owns a key resource, when the government gives a firm the exclusive right to produce a good, or when a single firm can supply the entire market at a smaller cost than many firms could.

- Because a monopoly is the sole producer in its market, it faces a downward-sloping demand curve for its product. When a monopoly increases production by 1 unit, it causes the price of its good to fall, which reduces the amount of revenue earned on all units produced. As a result, a monopoly's marginal revenue is always below the price of its good.

- Like a competitive firm, a monopoly firm maximizes profit by producing the quantity at which marginal revenue equals marginal cost. The monopoly then chooses the price at which that quantity is demanded. Unlike a competitive firm, a monopoly firm's price exceeds its marginal revenue, so its price exceeds marginal cost.

- A monopolist's profit-maximizing level of output is below the level that maximizes the sum of consumer and producer surplus. That is, when the monopoly charges a price above marginal cost, some consumers who value the good more than its cost of production do not buy it. As a result, monopoly causes deadweight losses similar to the deadweight losses caused by taxes.

- Policymakers can respond to the inefficiency of monopoly behaviour in four ways. (1) They can use the antitrust laws to try to make the industry more competitive. (2) They can regulate the prices that the monopoly charges. (3) They can turn the monopolist into a government-run enterprise. (4) Or, if the market failure is deemed small compared to the inevitable imperfections of policies, they can do nothing at all.

- Monopolists often can raise their profits by charging different prices for the same good based on a buyer's willingness to pay. This practice of price discrimination can raise economic welfare by getting the good to some consumers who otherwise would not buy it. In the extreme case of perfect price discrimination, the deadweight losses of monopoly are completely eliminated. More generally, when price discrimination is imperfect, it can either raise or lower welfare compared to the outcome with a single monopoly price.

KEY CONCEPTS

monopoly, p. 318   natural monopoly, p. 320   price discrimination, p. 337

QUESTIONS FOR REVIEW

1. Give an example of a government-created monopoly. Is creating this monopoly necessarily bad public policy? Explain.

2. Define *natural monopoly*. What does the size of a market have to do with whether an industry is a natural monopoly?

3. Why is a monopolist's marginal revenue less than the price of its good? Can marginal revenue ever be negative? Explain.

4. Draw the demand, marginal-revenue, and marginal-cost curves for a monopolist. Show the profit-maximizing level of output. Show the profit-maximizing price.

5. In your diagram from the previous question, show the level of output that maximizes total surplus. Show the deadweight loss from the monopoly. Explain your answer.

6. What gives the government the power to regulate mergers between firms? From the standpoint of the welfare of society, give a good reason and a bad reason that two firms might want to merge.

7. Describe the two problems that arise when regulators tell a natural monopoly that it must set a price equal to marginal cost.

8. Give two examples of price discrimination. In each case, explain why the monopolist chooses to follow this business strategy.

PROBLEMS AND APPLICATIONS

1. A publisher faces the following demand schedule for the next novel of one of its popular authors:

Price	Quantity Demanded
$100	0
90	100 000
80	200 000
70	300 000
60	400 000
50	500 000
40	600 000
30	700 000
20	800 000
10	900 000
0	1 000 000

The author is paid $2 million to write the book, and the marginal cost of publishing the book is a constant $10 per book.

a. Compute total revenue, total cost, and profit at each quantity. What quantity would a profit-maximizing publisher choose? What price would it charge?

b. Compute marginal revenue. (Recall that $MR = \Delta TR/\Delta Q$.) How does marginal revenue compare to the price? Explain.

c. Graph the marginal-revenue, marginal-cost, and demand curves. At what quantity do the marginal-revenue and marginal-cost curves cross? What does this signify?

d. In your graph, shade in the deadweight loss. Explain in words what this means.

e. If the author were paid $3 million instead of $2 million to write the book, how would this affect the publisher's decision regarding the price to charge? Explain.

f. Suppose the publisher was not profit-maximizing but was concerned with maximizing economic efficiency. What price would it charge for the book? How much profit would it make at this price?

2. Suppose that a natural monopolist was required by law to charge average total cost. On a diagram, label the price charged and the deadweight loss to society relative to marginal-cost pricing.

3. Consider the delivery of mail. In general, what is the shape of the average-total-cost curve? How might the shape differ between isolated rural areas and densely populated urban areas? How might the shape have changed over time? Explain.

4. Suppose the Clean Springs Water Company has a monopoly on bottled water sales in British Columbia. If the price of tap water increases, what is the change in Clean Springs' profit-maximizing levels of output, price, and profit? Explain in words and with a graph.

5. A small town is served by many competing supermarkets, which have constant marginal cost.

a. Using a diagram of the market for groceries, show the consumer surplus, producer surplus, and total surplus.

b. Now suppose that the independent supermarkets combine into one chain. Using a new diagram, show the new consumer surplus, producer surplus, and total surplus. Relative to the competitive market, what is the transfer from consumers to producers? What is the deadweight loss?

6. Johnny Rockabilly has just finished recording his latest CD. His record company's marketing department determines that the demand for the CD is as follows:

Price	Number of CDs
$24	10 000
22	20 000
20	30 000
18	40 000
16	50 000
14	60 000

The company can produce the CD with no fixed cost and a variable cost of $5 per CD.

a. Find total revenue for quantity equal to 10 000, 20 000, and so on. What is the marginal revenue for each 10 000 increase in the quantity sold?

b. What quantity of CDs would maximize profit? What would be the price? What would be the profit?

c. If you were Johnny's agent, what recording fee would you advise Johnny to demand from the record company? Why?

7. A company is considering building a bridge across a river. The bridge would cost $2 million to build and nothing to maintain. The following table shows the company's anticipated demand over the lifetime of the bridge.

Price per Crossing	Number of Crossings (in thousands)
$8	0
7	100
6	200
5	300
4	400
3	500
2	600
1	700
0	800

a. If the company were to build the bridge, what would be its profit-maximizing price? Would that be the efficient level of output? Why or why not?

b. If the company is interested in maximizing profit, should it build the bridge? What would be its profit or loss?

c. If the government were to build the bridge, what price should it charge?

d. Should the government build the bridge? Explain.

8. The Placebo Drug Company holds a patent on one of its discoveries.

a. Assuming that the production of the drug involves rising marginal cost, draw a diagram to illustrate Placebo's profit-maximizing price and quantity. Also show Placebo's profits.

b. Now suppose that the government imposes a tax on each bottle of the drug produced. On a new diagram, illustrate Placebo's new price and quantity. How does each compare to your answer in part (a)?

c. Although it is not easy to see in your diagrams, the tax reduces Placebo's profit. Explain why this must be true.

d. Instead of the tax per bottle, suppose that the government imposes a tax on Placebo of $10 000 regardless of how many bottles are produced. How does this tax affect Placebo's price, quantity, and profits? Explain.

9. Larry, Curly, and Moe run the only saloon in town. Larry wants to sell as many drinks as possible without losing money. Curly wants the saloon to bring in as much revenue as possible. Moe wants to make the largest possible profits. Using a single diagram of the saloon's demand curve and its cost curves, show the price and quantity combinations favoured by each of the three partners. Explain.

10. For many years, both local and long-distance phone services have been provided by provincially owned or regulated monopolies.

a. Explain why long-distance phone service was originally a natural monopoly.

b. Over the past two decades, technological developments have allowed companies to launch communication satellites that can transmit a limited number of calls. How did the growing role of satellites change the cost structure of long-distance phone service?

c. In response to these technological developments, some provinces have deregulated the long-distance market in Canada. Local phone service has remained regulated. Why might it be efficient to have competition in long-distance phone service and regulated monopolies in local phone service?

11. The Best Computer Company just developed a new computer chip, on which it immediately acquired a patent.
    a. Draw a diagram that shows the consumer surplus, producer surplus, and total surplus in the market for this new chip.
    b. What happens to these three measures of surplus if the firm can perfectly price-discriminate? What is the change in deadweight loss? What transfers occur?

12. Explain why a monopolist will always produce a quantity at which the demand curve is elastic. (Hint: If demand is inelastic and the firm raises its price, what happens to total revenue and total costs?)

13. Singer Avril Lavigne has a monopoly over a scarce resource: herself. She is the only person who can produce an Avril Lavigne concert. Does this fact imply that the government should regulate the prices of her concerts? Why or why not?

14. Napster once operated an online file-swapping service that allowed people to use the Internet to download copies of their favourite songs from other people's computers without cost. In what sense did Napster enhance economic efficiency in the short run? In what sense might Napster have reduced economic efficiency in the long run? Why do you think the courts eventually shut down this Napster operation? Do you think this was the right policy?

15. Many schemes for price-discriminating involve some cost. For example, discount coupons take up the time and resources of both the buyer and the seller. This question considers the implications of costly price discrimination. To keep things simple, let's assume that our monopolist's production costs are simply proportional to output, so that average total cost and marginal cost are constant and equal to each other.
    a. Draw the cost, demand, and marginal-revenue curves for the monopolist. Show the price the monopolist would charge without price discrimination.
    b. In your diagram, mark the area equal to the monopolist's profit and call it X. Mark the area equal to consumer surplus and call it Y. Mark the area equal to the deadweight loss and call it Z.
    c. Now suppose that the monopolist can perfectly price-discriminate. What is the monopolist's profit? (Give your answer in terms of X, Y, and Z.)
    d. What is the change in the monopolist's profit from price discrimination? What is the change in total surplus from price discrimination? Which change is larger? Explain. (Give your answer in terms of X, Y, and Z.)
    e. Now suppose that there is some cost of price discrimination. To model this cost, let's assume that the monopolist has to pay a fixed cost C in order to price-discriminate. How would a monopolist make the decision whether to pay this fixed cost? (Give your answer in terms of X, Y, Z, and C.)
    f. How would a benevolent social planner, who cares about total surplus, decide whether the monopolist should price-discriminate? (Give your answer in terms of X, Y, Z, and C.)
    g. Compare your answers to parts (e) and (f). How does the monopolist's incentive to price-discriminate differ from the social planner's? Is it possible that the monopolist will price-discriminate even though it is not socially desirable?

INTERNET RESOURCES

- What is the most famous monopoly in the world? Monopoly the board game, of course, now owned by the Hasbro toy company. You can visit the Monopoly website at http://www.hasbro.com/monopoly.

- Many monopolies are formed by patenting a proprietary technology. Learn more about patents in Canada by visiting the Canadian Intellectual Property Office website at http://cipo.gc.ca.

http://   For more study tools, please visit http://www.mankiw3e.nelson.com.

© COMSTOCK IMAGES/GETTY IMAGES

OLIGOPOLY

16

Learning Objectives

In this chapter, you will …

- See what market structures lie between monopoly and competition
- Examine what outcomes are possible when a market is an oligopoly
- Learn about the prisoners' dilemma and how it applies to oligopoly and other issues
- Consider how competition laws try to foster competition in oligopolistic markets

If you go to a store to buy hockey skates, it is likely that you will come home with one of two brands: Bauer or CCM. These two companies make almost all of the skates sold in Canada. Together these firms determine the quantity of skates produced and, given the market demand curve, the price at which skates are sold.

How can we describe the market for skates? The previous two chapters discussed two types of market structure. In a competitive market, each firm is so small compared to the market that it cannot influence the price of its product and, therefore, takes the price as given by market conditions. In a monopolized market, a single firm supplies the entire market for a good, and that firm can choose any price and quantity on the market demand curve.

The market for skates fits neither the competitive nor the monopoly model. Competition and monopoly are extreme forms of market structure. Competition occurs when there are many firms in a market offering essentially identical products; monopoly occurs when there is only one firm in a market. It is natural to start the study of industrial organization with these polar cases, because they are the easiest cases to understand. Yet many industries, including the skate industry, fall somewhere between these two extremes. Firms in these industries have competitors but, at the same time, do not face so much competition that they are price takers. Economists call this situation *imperfect competition.*

In this chapter we discuss the types of imperfect competition and examine a particular type called *oligopoly.* The essence of an oligopolistic market is that there are only a few sellers. As a result, the actions of any one seller in the market can have a large impact on the profits of all the other sellers. That is, oligopolistic firms are interdependent in a way that competitive firms are not. Our goal in this chapter is to see how this interdependence shapes the firms' behaviour and what problems it raises for public policy.

BETWEEN MONOPOLY AND PERFECT COMPETITION

The previous two chapters analyzed markets with many competitive firms and markets with a single monopoly firm. In Chapter 14, we saw that the price in a perfectly competitive market always equals the marginal cost of production. We also saw that, in the long run, entry and exit drive economic profit to zero, so the price also equals the minimum of long-run average total cost. In Chapter 15, we saw how firms with market power can use that power to keep prices above marginal cost, leading to a positive economic profit for the firm and a deadweight loss for society.

The cases of perfect competition and monopoly illustrate some important ideas about how markets work. Most markets in the economy, however, include elements of both these cases and, therefore, are not completely described by either of them. The typical firm in the economy faces competition, but the competition is not so rigorous as to make the firm exactly described by the price-taking firm analyzed in Chapter 14. The typical firm also has some degree of market power, but its market power is not so great that the firm can be exactly described by the monopoly firm analyzed in Chapter 15. In other words, the typical firm in our economy is imperfectly competitive.

oligopoly
a market structure in which only a few sellers offer similar or identical products

monopolistic competition
a market structure in which many firms sell products that are similar but not identical

There are two types of imperfectly competitive markets. An **oligopoly** is a market with only a few sellers, each offering a product similar or identical to the others. One example is the market for hockey skates. Another is the world market for crude oil: A few countries in the Middle East control much of the world's oil reserves. **Monopolistic competition** describes a market structure in which there are many firms selling products that are similar but not identical. Examples include the markets for novels, movies, CDs, DVDs, and computer games. In a monopolistically competitive market, each firm has a monopoly over the product it makes, but many other firms make similar products that compete for the same customers.

Figure 16.1 summarizes the four types of market structure. The first question to ask about any market is how many firms are in it. If there is only one firm, the market is a monopoly. If there are only a few firms, the market is an oligopoly. If there are many firms, we need to ask another question: Do the firms sell identical or differentiated products? If the many firms sell differentiated products, the market is monopolistically competitive. If the many firms sell identical products, the market is perfectly competitive.

Reality, of course, is never as clear-cut as theory. In some cases, you may find it hard to decide what structure best describes a market. There is, for instance,

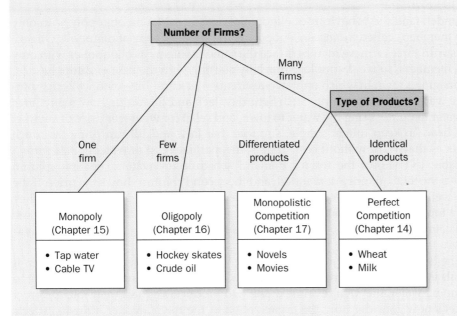

FIGURE 16.1

The Four Types of Market Structure

Economists who study industrial organization divide markets into four types—monopoly, oligopoly, monopolistic competition, and perfect competition.

no magic number that separates "few" from "many" when counting the number of firms. (Do the approximately dozen companies that now sell cars in Canada make this market an oligopoly or more competitive? The answer is open to debate.) Similarly, there is no sure way to determine when products are differentiated and when they are identical. (Are different brands of milk really the same? Again, the answer is debatable.) When analyzing actual markets, economists have to keep in mind the lessons learned from studying all types of market structure and then apply each lesson as it seems appropriate.

Now that we understand how economists define the various types of market structure, we can continue our analysis of them. In the next chapter we analyze monopolistic competition. In this chapter we examine oligopoly.

QuickQuiz Define *oligopoly* and *monopolistic competition* and give an example of each.

MARKETS WITH ONLY A FEW SELLERS

Because an oligopolistic market has only a small group of sellers, a key feature of oligopoly is the tension between cooperation and self-interest. The group of oligopolists is best off cooperating and acting like a monopolist—producing a small quantity of output and charging a price above marginal cost. Yet because each oligopolist cares about only its own profit, there are powerful incentives at work that hinder a group of firms from maintaining the monopoly outcome.

A Duopoly Example

To understand the behaviour of oligopolies, let's consider an oligopoly with only two members, called a *duopoly*. Duopoly is the simplest type of oligopoly. Oligopolies with three or more members face the same problems as oligopolies with only two members, so we do not lose much by starting with the case of duopoly.

Imagine a town in which only two residents—Jack and Jill—own wells that produce water safe for drinking. Each Saturday, Jack and Jill decide how many litres of water to pump, bring the water to town, and sell it for whatever price the market will bear. To keep things simple, suppose that Jack and Jill can pump as much water as they want without cost. That is, the marginal cost of water equals zero.

Table 16.1 shows the town's demand schedule for water. The first column shows the total quantity demanded, and the second column shows the price. If the two well owners sell a total of 10 L of water, water goes for $110 per litre. If they sell a total of 20 L, the price falls to $100 per litre. And so on. If you graphed these two columns of numbers, you would get a standard downward-sloping demand curve.

The last column in Table 16.1 shows the total revenue from the sale of water. It equals the quantity sold times the price. Because there is assumed to be no cost to pumping water, the total revenue of the two producers equals their total profit.

Let's now consider how the organization of the town's water industry affects the price of water and the quantity of water sold.

Competition, Monopolies, and Cartels

Before considering the price and quantity of water that would result from the duopoly of Jack and Jill, let's discuss briefly the two market structures we already understand: competition and monopoly.

Consider first what would happen if the market for water were perfectly competitive. In a competitive market, the production decisions of each firm drive price equal to marginal cost. In the market for water, marginal cost is zero. Thus, under competition, the equilibrium price of water would be zero, and the equilibrium quantity would be 120 L. The price of water would reflect the cost of producing it, and the efficient quantity of water would be produced and consumed.

Now consider how a monopoly would behave. Table 16.1 shows that total profit is maximized at a quantity of 60 L and a price of $60 per litre. A profit-maximizing monopolist, therefore, would produce this quantity and charge this price. As is standard for monopolies, price would exceed marginal cost. The result would be inefficient, because the quantity of water produced and consumed would fall short of the socially efficient level of 120 L.

What outcome should we expect from our duopolists? One possibility is that Jack and Jill get together and agree on the quantity of water to produce and the price to charge for it. Such an agreement among firms over production and price is called **collusion**, and the group of firms acting in unison is called a **cartel**. Once a cartel is formed, the market is in effect served by a monopoly, and we can apply our analysis from Chapter 15. That is, if Jack and Jill were to collude, they would agree on the monopoly outcome because that outcome maximizes the total profit that the producers can get from the market. Our two producers would produce a

collusion
an agreement among firms in a market about quantities to produce or prices to charge

cartel
a group of firms acting in unison

TABLE 16.1

The Demand Schedule for Water

Quantity (in litres)	Price	Total Revenue (and total profit)
0	$120	$ 0
10	110	1100
20	100	2000
30	90	2700
40	80	3200
50	70	3500
60	60	3600
70	50	3500
80	40	3200
90	30	2700
100	20	2000
110	10	1100
120	0	0

total of 60 L, which would be sold at a price of $60 per litre. Once again, price exceeds marginal cost, and the outcome is socially inefficient.

A cartel must agree not only on the total level of production but also on the amount produced by each member. In our case, Jack and Jill must agree how to split between themselves the monopoly production of 60 L. Each member of the cartel will want a larger share of the market because a larger market share means larger profit. If Jack and Jill agreed to split the market equally, each would produce 30 L, the price would be $60 per litre, and each would get a profit of $1800.

The Equilibrium for an Oligopoly

Although oligopolists would like to form cartels and earn monopoly profits, often that is not possible. As we discuss later in this chapter, competition laws prohibit explicit agreements among oligopolists as a matter of public policy. In addition, squabbling among cartel members over how to divide the profit in the market sometimes makes agreement among them impossible. Let's therefore consider what happens if Jack and Jill decide separately how much water to produce.

At first, one might expect Jack and Jill to reach the monopoly outcome on their own, because this outcome maximizes their joint profit. In the absence of a binding agreement, however, the monopoly outcome is unlikely. To see why, imagine that Jack expects Jill to produce only 30 L (half of the monopoly quantity). Jack would reason as follows:

"I could produce 30 L as well. In this case, a total of 60 L of water would be sold at a price of $60 per litre. My profit would be $1800 (30 L × $60 per litre). Alternatively, I could produce 40 L. In this case, a total of 70 L of water would be sold at a price of $50 per litre. My profit would be $2000 (40 L × $50 per litre). Even though total profit in the market would fall, my profit would be higher, because I would have a larger share of the market."

Of course, Jill might reason the same way. If so, Jack and Jill would each bring 40 L to town. Total sales would be 80 L, and the price would fall to $40. Thus, if the duopolists individually pursue their own self-interest when deciding how much to produce, they produce a total quantity greater than the monopoly quantity, charge a price lower than the monopoly price, and earn total profit less than the monopoly profit.

Although the logic of self-interest increases the duopoly's output above the monopoly level, it does not push the duopolists to reach the competitive allocation. Consider what happens when each duopolist is producing 40 L. The price is $40, and each duopolist makes a profit of $1600. In this case, Jack's self-interested logic leads to a different conclusion:

"Right now, my profit is $1600. Suppose I increase my production to 50 L. In this case, a total of 90 L of water would be sold, and the price would be $30 per litre. Then my profit would be only $1500. Rather than increasing production and driving down the price, I am better off keeping my production at 40 L."

The outcome in which Jack and Jill each produce 40 L looks like some sort of equilibrium. In fact, this outcome is called a *Nash equilibrium*. (It is named after economic theorist John Nash, whose life was portrayed in the book and movie *A Beautiful Mind*). A **Nash equilibrium** is a situation in which economic actors interacting with one another each choose their best strategy given the strategies the others have chosen. In this case, given that Jill is producing 40 L, the best strategy for Jack is to produce 40 L. Similarly, given that Jack is producing 40 L, the best strategy for Jill is to produce 40 L. Once they reach this Nash equilibrium, neither Jack nor Jill has an incentive to make a different decision.

This example illustrates the tension between cooperation and self-interest. Oligopolists would be better off cooperating and reaching the monopoly outcome. Yet because they pursue their own self-interest, they do not end up reaching the monopoly outcome and maximizing their joint profit. Each oligopolist is tempted to raise production and capture a larger share of the market. As each of them tries to do this, total production rises, and the price falls.

At the same time, self-interest does not drive the market all the way to the competitive outcome. Like monopolists, oligopolists are aware that increases in the amount they produce reduce the price of their product. Therefore, they stop short of following the competitive firm's rule of producing up to the point where price equals marginal cost.

In summary, *when firms in an oligopoly individually choose production to maximize profit, they produce a quantity of output greater than the level produced by monopoly and less than the level produced by competition. The oligopoly price is less than the monopoly price but greater than the competitive price (which equals marginal cost).*

Nash equilibrium
a situation in which economic actors interacting with one another each choose their best strategy given the strategies that all the other actors have chosen

How the Size of an Oligopoly Affects the Market Outcome

We can use the insights from this analysis of duopoly to discuss how the size of an oligopoly is likely to affect the outcome in a market. Suppose, for instance, that John and Joan suddenly discover water sources on their property and join Jack and Jill in the water oligopoly. The demand schedule in Table 16.1 remains the same, but now more producers are available to satisfy this demand. How would an increase in the number of sellers from two to four affect the price and quantity of water in the town?

If the sellers of water could form a cartel, they would once again try to maximize total profit by producing the monopoly quantity and charging the monopoly price. Just as when there were only two sellers, the members of the cartel would need to agree on production levels for each member and find some way to enforce the agreement. As the cartel grows larger, however, this outcome is less likely. Reaching and enforcing an agreement becomes more difficult as the size of the group increases.

If the oligopolists do not form a cartel—perhaps because the competition laws prohibit it—they must each decide on their own how much water to produce. To see how the increase in the number of sellers affects the outcome, consider the decision facing each seller. At any time, each well owner has the option to raise production by 1 litre. In making this decision, the well owner weighs two effects:

1. *The output effect:* Because price is above marginal cost, selling 1 more litre of water at the going price will raise profit.
2. *The price effect:* Raising production will increase the total amount sold, which will lower the price of water and lower the profit on all the other litres sold.

If the output effect is larger than the price effect, the well owner will increase production. If the price effect is larger than the output effect, the owner will not raise production. (In fact, in this case, it is profitable to reduce production.) Each oligopolist continues to increase production until these two marginal effects exactly balance, taking the other firms' production as given.

Now consider how the number of firms in the industry affects the marginal analysis of each oligopolist. The larger the number of sellers, the less concerned each seller is about its own impact on the market price. That is, as the oligopoly grows in size, the magnitude of the price effect falls. When the oligopoly grows very large, the price effect disappears altogether, leaving only the output effect. In this extreme case, each firm in the oligopoly increases production as long as the price is above marginal cost.

We can now see that a large oligopoly is essentially a group of competitive firms. A competitive firm considers only the output effect when deciding how much to produce: Because a competitive firm is a price taker, the price effect is absent. Thus, *as the number of sellers in an oligopoly grows larger, an oligopolistic market looks more and more like a competitive market. The price approaches marginal cost, and the quantity produced approaches the socially efficient level.*

This analysis of oligopoly offers a new perspective on the effects of international trade. Imagine that Toyota and Honda are the only automakers in Japan, Volkswagen and BMW are the only automakers in Germany, and Ford and General Motors are the only automakers in Canada. If these nations prohibited international trade in autos, each would have an auto oligopoly with only two members, and the market outcome would likely depart substantially from the competitive ideal. With international trade, however, the car market is a world market, and the oligopoly in this example has six members. Allowing free trade increases the number of producers from which each consumer can choose, and this increased competition keeps prices closer to marginal cost. Thus, the theory of oligopoly provides another reason, in addition to the theory of comparative advantage discussed in Chapter 3, why all countries can benefit from free trade.

Case Study

OPEC AND THE WORLD OIL MARKET

Our story about the town's market for water is fictional, but if we change water to crude oil, and Jack and Jill to Iran and Iraq, the story is quite close to being true. Much of the world's oil is produced by a few countries, mostly in the Middle East. These countries together make up an oligopoly. Their decisions about how much oil to pump are much the same as Jack and Jill's decisions about how much water to pump.

The countries that produce most of the world's oil have formed a cartel, called the Organization of Petroleum Exporting Countries (OPEC). As originally formed in 1960, OPEC included Iran, Iraq, Kuwait, Saudi Arabia, and Venezuela. In 2004, Qatar, Indonesia, Libya, the United Arab Emirates, Algeria, and Nigeria were also members. These countries control about three-fourths of the world's oil reserves. Like any cartel, OPEC tries to raise the price of its product through a coordinated reduction in quantity produced. OPEC tries to set production levels for each of the member countries.

The problem that OPEC faces is much the same as the problem that Jack and Jill faced in our scenario. The OPEC countries would like to maintain a high price of oil, but each member of the cartel is tempted to increase its production in order to get a larger share of the total profit. OPEC members frequently agree to reduce production but then cheat on their agreements.

OPEC was most successful at maintaining cooperation and high prices in the period from 1973 to 1985. The price of crude oil rose from US$2.64 per barrel in 1972 to US$11.17 in 1974 and then to US$35.10 in 1981. But in the early 1980s member countries began arguing about production levels, and OPEC became ineffective at maintaining cooperation. By 1986 the price of crude oil had fallen back to US$12.52 per barrel.

In recent years, the members of OPEC have continued to meet regularly, but the cartel has been far less successful at reaching and enforcing agreements. The price of crude oil, adjusted for overall inflation, has remained far below the level OPEC achieved in 1981. While this lack of cooperation has hurt the profits of the oil-producing nations, it has benefited consumers around the world.

We will explore the difficulties that cartels have in cooperating with each other later in this chapter. Aside from these difficulties, one of the factors that has made it more difficult for OPEC to reach agreement on quotas is the increased production of oil by non-OPEC countries. Particularly important in this regard has been the impact of new exports from Russia, which have helped keep prices low. A related issue concerns the vast supply of oil in Alberta's oil sands. As technology drives the cost of extracting these reserves lower, production from the oil sands has the potential to reach that of Saudi Arabia. This will make it even more difficult for OPEC to keep prices high by restricting output. ●

QuickQuiz If the members of an oligopoly could agree on a total quantity to produce, what quantity would they choose? • If the oligopolists do not act together but instead make production decisions individually, do they produce a total quantity more or less than in your answer to the previous question? Why?

GAME THEORY AND THE ECONOMICS OF COOPERATION

As we have seen, oligopolies would like to reach the monopoly outcome, but doing so requires cooperation, which at times is difficult to maintain. In this section we look more closely at the problems people face when cooperation is desirable but difficult. To analyze the economics of cooperation, we need to learn a little about game theory.

Game theory is the study of how people behave in strategic situations. By "strategic" we mean a situation in which each person, when deciding what action to take, must consider how others might respond to that action. Because the number of firms in an oligopolistic market is small, each firm must act strategically. Each firm knows that its profit depends not only on how much it produces but also on how much the other firms produce. In making its production decision, each firm in an oligopoly should consider how its decision might affect the production decisions of all the other firms.

Game theory is not necessary for understanding competitive or monopoly markets. In a competitive market, each firm is so small compared to the market that strategic interactions with other firms are not important. In a monopolized market, strategic interactions are absent because the market has only one firm. But, as we will see, game theory is quite useful for understanding the behaviour of oligopolies.

A particularly important "game" is called the **prisoners' dilemma.** This game provides insight into the difficulty of maintaining cooperation. Many times in life, people fail to cooperate with one another even when cooperation would make them all better off. An oligopoly is just one example. The story of the prisoners' dilemma contains a general lesson that applies to any group trying to maintain cooperation among its members.

game theory
the study of how people behave in strategic situations

prisoners' dilemma
a particular "game" between two captured prisoners that illustrates why cooperation is difficult to maintain even when it is mutually beneficial

The Prisoners' Dilemma

The prisoners' dilemma is a story about two criminals who have been captured by the police. Let's call them Bonnie and Clyde. The police have enough evidence to convict Bonnie and Clyde of the minor crime of carrying an unregistered gun, so that each would spend a year in jail. The police also suspect that the two criminals have committed a bank robbery together, but they lack hard evidence to convict them of this major crime. The police question Bonnie and Clyde in separate rooms, and they offer each of them the following deal:

"Right now, we can lock you up for one year. If you confess to the bank robbery and implicate your partner, however, we'll give you immunity and you can go free. Your partner will get 20 years in jail. But if you both confess to the crime, we won't need your testimony and we can avoid the cost of a trial, so you will each get an intermediate sentence of eight years."

If Bonnie and Clyde, heartless bank robbers that they are, care only about their own sentences, what would you expect them to do? Would they confess or remain silent? Figure 16.2 shows their choices. Each prisoner has two strategies: confess or remain silent. The sentence each prisoner gets depends on the strategy he or she chooses and the strategy chosen by his or her partner in crime.

Consider first Bonnie's decision. She reasons as follows: "I don't know what Clyde is going to do. If he remains silent, my best strategy is to confess, since then I'll go free rather than spending a year in jail. If he confesses, my best strategy is still to confess, since then I'll spend 8 years in jail rather than 20. So, regardless of what Clyde does, I am better off confessing."

dominant strategy
a strategy that is best for a player in a game regardless of the strategies chosen by the other players

In the language of game theory, a strategy is called a **dominant strategy** if it is the best strategy for a player to follow regardless of the strategies pursued by other players. In this case, confessing is a dominant strategy for Bonnie. She spends less time in jail if she confesses, regardless of whether Clyde confesses or remains silent.

Now consider Clyde's decision. He faces exactly the same choices as Bonnie, and he reasons in much the same way. Regardless of what Bonnie does, Clyde can reduce his time in jail by confessing. In other words, confessing is also a dominant strategy for Clyde.

In the end, both Bonnie and Clyde confess, and both spend eight years in jail. Yet, from their standpoint, this is a terrible outcome. If they had *both* remained silent, both of them would have been better off, spending only one year in jail on the gun charge. By each pursuing his or her own interests, the two prisoners together reach an outcome that is worse for each of them.

FIGURE 16.2

The Prisoners' Dilemma

In this game between two criminals suspected of committing a crime, the sentence that each receives depends both on his or her decision whether to confess or remain silent and on the decision made by the other.

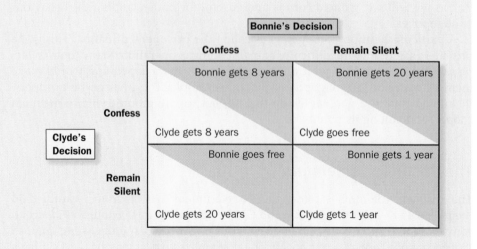

To see how difficult it is to maintain cooperation, imagine that, before the police captured Bonnie and Clyde, the two criminals had made a pact not to confess. Clearly, this agreement would make them both better off *if* they both live up to it, because they would each spend only one year in jail. But would the two criminals in fact remain silent, simply because they had agreed to? Once they are being questioned separately, the logic of self-interest takes over and leads them to confess. Cooperation between the two prisoners is difficult to maintain, because cooperation is individually irrational.

Oligopolies as a Prisoners' Dilemma

What does the prisoners' dilemma have to do with markets and imperfect competition? It turns out that the game oligopolists play in trying to reach the monopoly outcome is similar to the game that the two prisoners play in the prisoners' dilemma.

Consider an oligopoly with two members, called Oilopia and Enertia. Both countries sell crude oil. After prolonged negotiation, the countries agree to keep oil production low in order to keep the world price of oil high. After they agree on production levels, each country must decide whether to cooperate and live up to this agreement or to ignore it and produce at a higher level. Figure 16.3 shows how the profits of the two countries depend on the strategies they choose.

Suppose you are the president of Enertia. You might reason as follows: "I could keep production low as we agreed, or I could raise my production and sell more oil on world markets. If Oilopia lives up to the agreement and keeps its production low, then my country earns profit of $60 billion with high production and $50 billion with low production. In this case, Enertia is better off with high production. If Oilopia fails to live up to the agreement and produces at a high level, then my country earns $40 billion with high production and $30 billion with low production. Once again, Enertia is better off with high production. So, regardless of what Oilopia chooses to do, my country is better off reneging on our agreement and producing at a high level."

FIGURE 16.3

	Enertia's Decision	
	High Production	**Low Production**
Oilopia's Decision — **High Production**	Enertia gets $40 billion / Oilopia gets $40 billion	Enertia gets $30 billion / Oilopia gets $60 billion
Low Production	Enertia gets $60 billion / Oilopia gets $30 billion	Enertia gets $50 billion / Oilopia gets $50 billion

An Oligopoly Game

In this game between members of an oligopoly, the profit that each earns depends on both its production decision and the production decision of the other oligopolist.

Producing at a high level is a dominant strategy for Enertia. Of course, Oilopia reasons in exactly the same way, and so both countries produce at a high level. The result is the inferior outcome (from Oilopia and Enertia's standpoint) with low profits for each country.

This example illustrates why oligopolies have trouble maintaining monopoly profits. The monopoly outcome is jointly rational for the oligopoly, but each oligopolist has an incentive to cheat. Just as self-interest drives the prisoners in the prisoners' dilemma to confess, self-interest makes it difficult for the oligopoly to maintain the cooperative outcome with low production, high prices, and monopoly profits. It also sheds some light on why cartels such as OPEC find it difficult to restrict output and keep prices high.

Other Examples of the Prisoners' Dilemma

We have seen how the prisoners' dilemma can be used to understand the problem facing oligopolies. The same logic applies to many other situations as well. Here we consider three examples in which self-interest prevents cooperation and leads to an inferior outcome for the parties involved: arms races, advertising, and common resources.

Arms Races   An arms race is much like the prisoners' dilemma. To see this, consider the decisions of two countries—the United States and the Soviet Union—about whether to build new weapons or to disarm. Each country prefers to have more arms than the other because a larger arsenal would give it more influence in world affairs. But each country also prefers to live in a world safe from the other country's weapons.

Figure 16.4 shows the deadly game. If the Soviet Union chooses to arm, the United States is better off doing the same to prevent the loss of power. If the Soviet Union chooses to disarm, the United States is better off arming because doing so

---

FIGURE 16.4

An Arms-Race Game

In this game between two countries, the safety and power of each country depends on both its decision whether to arm and the decision made by the other country.

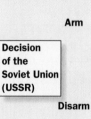

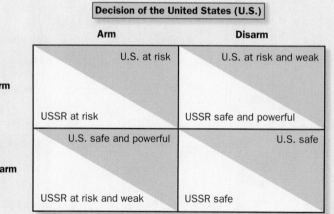

Decision of the United States (U.S.)

	Arm	**Disarm**
Arm	U.S. at risk / USSR at risk	U.S. at risk and weak / USSR safe and powerful
Disarm	U.S. safe and powerful / USSR at risk and weak	U.S. safe / USSR safe

Decision of the Soviet Union (USSR)

would make it more powerful. For each country, arming is a dominant strategy. Thus, each country chooses to continue the arms race, resulting in the inferior outcome in which both countries are at risk.

Throughout the era of the Cold War, the United States and the Soviet Union attempted to solve this problem through negotiation and agreements over arms control. The problems that the two countries faced were similar to those that oligopolists encounter in trying to maintain a cartel. Just as oligopolists argue over production levels, the United States and the Soviet Union argued over the amount of arms that each country would be allowed. And just as cartels have trouble enforcing production levels, the United States and the Soviet Union each feared that the other country would cheat on any agreement. In both arms races and oligopolies, the relentless logic of self-interest drives the participants toward a non-cooperative outcome that is worse for each party.

Advertising   When two firms advertise to attract the same customers, they face a problem similar to the prisoners' dilemma. For example, consider the decisions facing two beer companies, Molson and Labatt. If neither company advertises, the two companies split the market. If both advertise, they again split the market, but profits are lower, since each company must bear the cost of advertising. Yet if one company advertises while the other does not, the one that advertises attracts customers from the other.

Figure 16.5 shows how the profits of the two companies depend on their actions. You can see that advertising is a dominant strategy for each firm. Thus, both firms choose to advertise, even though both firms would be better off if neither firm advertised.

Common Resources   In Chapter 11 we saw that people tend to overuse common resources. One can view this problem as an example of the prisoners' dilemma.

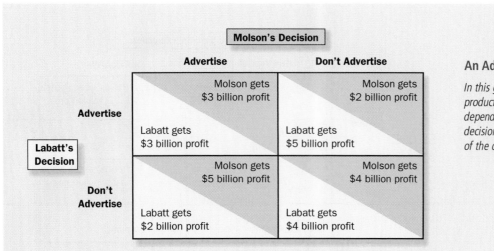

FIGURE 16.5

An Advertising Game

In this game between firms selling similar products, the profit that each earns depends on both its own advertising decision and the advertising decision of the other firm.

Imagine that two oil companies—Petro-Canada and Esso (Imperial Oil)—own adjacent oil fields. Under the fields is a common pool of oil worth $12 million. Drilling a well to recover the oil costs $1 million. If each company drills one well, each will get half of the oil and earn a $5 million profit ($6 million in revenue minus $1 million in costs).

Because the pool of oil is a common resource, the companies will not use it efficiently. Suppose that either company could drill a second well. If one company has two of the three wells, that company gets two-thirds of the oil, which yields a profit of $6 million. The other company gets one-third of the oil, for a profit of $3 million. Yet if each company drills a second well, the two companies again split the oil. In this case, each bears the cost of a second well, so profit is only $4 million for each company.

Figure 16.6 shows the game. Drilling two wells is a dominant strategy for each company. Once again, the self-interest of the two players leads them to an inferior outcome.

The Prisoners' Dilemma and the Welfare of Society

The prisoners' dilemma describes many of life's situations, and it shows that cooperation can be difficult to maintain, even when cooperation would make both players in the game better off. Clearly, this lack of cooperation is a problem for those involved in these situations. But is lack of cooperation a problem from the standpoint of society as a whole? The answer depends on the circumstances.

In some cases, the noncooperative equilibrium is bad for society as well as the players. In the arms-race game in Figure 16.4, both the United States and the Soviet Union end up at risk. In the common-resources game in Figure 16.6, the extra wells dug by Petro-Canada and Esso are pure waste. In both cases, society would be better off if the two players could reach the cooperative outcome.

FIGURE 16.6

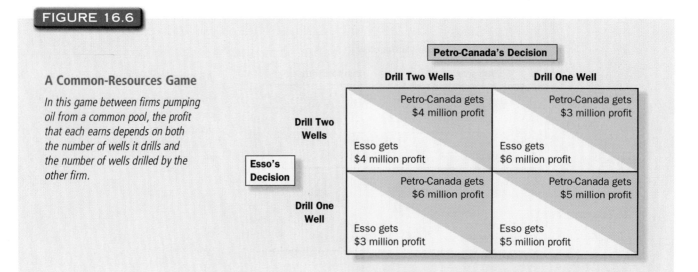

A Common-Resources Game

In this game between firms pumping oil from a common pool, the profit that each earns depends on both the number of wells it drills and the number of wells drilled by the other firm.

Petro-Canada's Decision

	Drill Two Wells	Drill One Well
Drill Two Wells	Petro-Canada gets $4 million profit / Esso gets $4 million profit	Petro-Canada gets $3 million profit / Esso gets $6 million profit
Drill One Well	Petro-Canada gets $6 million profit / Esso gets $3 million profit	Petro-Canada gets $5 million profit / Esso gets $5 million profit

Esso's Decision

By contrast, in the case of oligopolists trying to maintain monopoly profits, lack of cooperation is desirable from the standpoint of society as a whole. The monopoly outcome is good for the oligopolists, but it is bad for the consumers of the product. As we first saw in Chapter 7, the competitive outcome is best for society because it maximizes total surplus. When oligopolists fail to cooperate, the quantity they produce is closer to this optimal level. Put differently, the invisible hand guides markets to allocate resources efficiently only when markets are competitive, and markets are competitive only when firms in the market fail to cooperate with one another.

Similarly, consider the case of the police questioning two suspects. Lack of cooperation between the suspects is desirable, because it allows the police to convict more criminals. The prisoners' dilemma is a dilemma for the prisoners, but it can be a boon to everyone else.

Why People Sometimes Cooperate

The prisoners' dilemma shows that cooperation is difficult. But is it impossible? Not all prisoners, when questioned by the police, decide to turn in their partners in crime. Cartels sometimes do manage to maintain collusive arrangements, despite the incentive for individual members to defect. Very often, the reason that players can solve the prisoners' dilemma is that they play the game not once but many times.

To see why cooperation is easier to enforce in repeated games, let's return to our duopolists, Jack and Jill. Recall that Jack and Jill would like to maintain the monopoly outcome in which each produces 30 L, but self-interest drives them to an equilibrium in which each produces 40 L. Figure 16.7 shows the game they play. Producing 40 L is a dominant strategy for each player in this game.

Imagine that Jack and Jill try to form a cartel. To maximize total profit, they would agree to the cooperative outcome in which each produces 30 L. Yet, if Jack

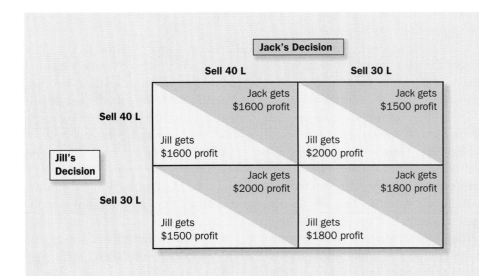

FIGURE 16.7

Jack and Jill's Oligopoly Game

In this game between Jack and Jill, the profit that each earns from selling water depends on both the quantity he or she chooses to sell and the quantity the other chooses to sell.

and Jill are to play this game only once, neither has any incentive to live up to this agreement. Self-interest drives each of them to renege and produce 40 L.

Now suppose that Jack and Jill know that they will play the same game every week. When they make their initial agreement to keep production low, they can also specify what happens if one party reneges. They might agree, for instance, that once one of them reneges and produces 40 L, both of them will produce 40 L forever after. This penalty is easy to enforce, because if one party is producing at a high level, the other has every reason to do the same.

The threat of this penalty may be all that is needed to maintain cooperation. Each person knows that defecting would raise his or her profit from $1800 to $2000. But this benefit would last for only one week. Thereafter, profit would fall to $1600 and stay there. As long as the players care enough about future profits, they will choose to forgo the one-time gain from defection. Thus, in a game of repeated prisoners' dilemma, the two players may well be able to reach the cooperative outcome.

Case Study

THE PRISONERS' DILEMMA TOURNAMENT

Imagine that you are playing a game of prisoners' dilemma with a person being "questioned" in a separate room. Moreover, imagine that you are going to play not once but many times. Your score at the end of the game is the total number of years in jail. You would like to make this score as small as possible. What strategy would you play? Would you begin by confessing or remaining silent? How would the other player's actions affect your subsequent decisions about confessing?

Repeated prisoners' dilemma is quite a complicated game. To encourage cooperation, players must penalize each other for not cooperating. Yet the strategy described earlier for Jack and Jill's water cartel—defect forever as soon as the other player defects—is not very forgiving. In a game repeated many times, a strategy that allows players to return to the cooperative outcome after a period of noncooperation may be preferable.

To see what strategies work best, political scientist Robert Axelrod held a tournament. People entered by sending computer programs designed to play repeated prisoners' dilemma. Each program then played the game against all the other programs. The "winner" was the program that received the fewest total years in jail.

The winner turned out to be a simple strategy called *tit-for-tat*. According to tit-for-tat, a player should start by cooperating and then do whatever the other player did last time. Thus, a tit-for-tat player cooperates until the other player defects; he then defects until the other player cooperates again. In other words, this strategy starts out friendly, penalizes unfriendly players, and forgives them if warranted. To Axelrod's surprise, this simple strategy did better than all the more complicated strategies that people had sent in.

The tit-for-tat strategy has a long history. It is essentially the biblical strategy of "an eye for an eye, a tooth for a tooth." The prisoners' dilemma tournament suggests that this may be a good rule of thumb for playing some of the games of life. ●

QuickQuiz Tell the story of the prisoners' dilemma. Prepare a table showing the prisoners' choices and explain what outcome is likely. • What does the prisoners' dilemma teach us about oligopolies?

PUBLIC POLICY TOWARD OLIGOPOLIES

One of the ten principles of economics in Chapter 1 is that governments can sometimes improve market outcomes. The application of this principle to oligopolistic markets is, as a general matter, straightforward. As we have seen, cooperation among oligopolists is undesirable from the standpoint of society as a whole, because it leads to production that is too low and prices that are too high. To move the allocation of resources closer to the social optimum, policymakers should try to induce firms in an oligopoly to compete rather than cooperate. Let's consider how policymakers do this and then examine the controversies that arise in this area of public policy.

Restraint of Trade and the Competition Act

Freedom to make contracts is an essential part of a market economy. Businesses and households use contracts to arrange mutually advantageous trades, relying on the court system to enforce those contracts. Yet for many years, Canadian judges have refused to enforce agreements that restrain trade among competitors (reducing quantities and raising prices, or price-fixing) as being against the public interest.

Canada's Competition Act codifies and reinforces this policy. Section 45(1) of the act states,

> Every one who conspires, combines, agrees or arranges with another person
> (a) to limit unduly the facilities for transporting, producing, manufacturing, supplying, storing or dealing in any product,
> (b) to prevent, limit or lessen, unduly, the manufacture or production of a product or to enhance unreasonably the price thereof,
> (c) to prevent or lessen, unduly, competition in the production, manufacture, purchase, barter, sale, storage, rental, transportation or supply of a product, or in the price of insurance on persons or property, or
> (d) to otherwise restrain or injure competition unduly,
> is guilty of an indictable offence and liable to imprisonment for a term not exceeding five years or to a fine not exceeding ten million dollars or both.

The Competition Act contains both civil and criminal provisions. As we discussed in Chapter 15, the Commissioner of Competition, as the head of the Competition Bureau, is responsible for enforcing the act. The commissioner refers criminal cases to the attorney general of Canada, while civil cases are heard by the Competition Tribunal. Mergers, also discussed in Chapter 15, are governed by the civil provisions of the act. Conspiracies in restraint of trade, such as those described in section 45(1), above, fall under the criminal provisions of the act.

IN THE NEWS

GAME THEORY AND *SURVIVOR*

Game theory is a very useful tool to help us understand strategic interaction of all kinds. It is therefore not surprising that the popular reality TV show Survivor, *which made its debut in 2000, has captured the attention of economists who specialize in game theory. Unfortunately, the authors of this book still suspect that an economist would be the first contestant voted off the island.*

Survivorology Evolves

By Patchen Barss

"Outwit, outplay, outlast." Contestants on the television show *Survivor* would do well to consider the word order in the game's motto. . . .

The winner of the inaugural version of the show in 2000 illustrated the importance of focusing first on outwitting his opponents as he cut a path to the finish line with a few sharp strokes of brilliant strategy.

The basic rules of the game are simple: each episode, contestants vote to determine which one of them must leave the remote wilderness location

where the show is filmed (*Survivor I* took place on an island). Contestants can temporarily protect themselves from being voted off the island by winning periodic "immunity challenges." The last one wins the prize of US$1 million.

The basics of strategy for *Survivor* tribe members—coalitions, cooperating and defecting, second-guessing other players—also happen to be the building blocks of game theory. Game theory, used in economics, sociology, and other disciplines that attempt to understand group dynamics, involves analyzing a conflict-of-interest situation mathematically, and trying to identify optimal choices that lead to a desired outcome.

Many aspects of *Survivor* can be better understood through game theory.

"I don't think there's a grand system. The game is far too complex for an optimal strategy," said Avinash Dixit, an economics professor who teaches game theory at Princeton University. "But the way I would think of this is, instead of trying to get a huge game model that would explain it all, I would use the conceptual insights of game theory to cast light on individual acts.". . .

Insights from game theory become increasingly important as the contest approaches the end game. An example of this occurred in *Survivor I* when only three contestants remained.

Other activities that are subject to criminal prosecution include bid-rigging, price discrimination, resale price maintenance, and predatory pricing. Bid-rigging occurs when potential bidders agree with other bidders to refrain from bidding on contracts, or rig bids in advance. Price discrimination occurs when a supplier charges different prices for similar quantities of goods sold to firms that compete with one another. Resale price maintenance occurs when a supplier "requires" retailers to sell its product at a specified (or minimum or maximum) price. Predatory pricing involves selling products at unreasonably low prices for the purpose of eliminating or substantially reducing competition. Criminal proceedings must be initiated by the commissioner, but individuals who have been harmed by criminal offences can sue for civil damages. These and other provisions of the Competition Act are used to prevent firms in oligopolistic industries from acting either individually or together in ways that make markets less competitive.

The best forward-looking strategic move was made by Richard Hatch in *Survivor I* when he gave up in the immunity contest involving him, Rudy, and Kelly. The challenge, an endurance test, required the players to stand in the sun and keep their hands on an idol raised high on a pedestal. Rich walked away long before he got tired.

Many people thought he dropped out because it made no difference whether or not he won immunity, but it would actually have been disadvantageous for him to outlast the others.

The winner of the last immunity challenge, plus whichever other player does not get voted out, moves to the final round, where they face a jury of the seven most recently eliminated players. These seven vote on who wins the million and who takes second prize. This final vote is essentially a popularity contest.

Rich could have tried to win immunity, thus guaranteeing himself one of the two spots in the final jury. But it happens that the final immunity challenge winner also determines which other player makes the cut: The two who lose the challenge can't vote for the person with immunity, and must, therefore, vote against each other. That leaves the person with immunity with the deciding vote over who stays.

Rich didn't want to make that decision, even though he knew whom he wanted to be up against in the final two.

Rudy, a retired Navy SEAL, was very popular with the other players. If Rich and Rudy made it to the last stage, Rudy would win. Rich wanted Rudy gone, but the two men had a pact, known to the other players, not to vote against one another. If Rich betrayed that agreement, not only would Rudy turn against him at the final vote, but other players would follow suit in solidarity. As unpopular as Kelly was, Rich would have a hard time beating her under those circumstances.

Rich correctly guessed that Kelly would beat Rudy at the idol challenge, and that she would cast out Rudy for the same reason Rich wanted him gone: He was too popular. By throwing the challenge, Rich got what he wanted—facing off against Kelly in the final two—without losing Rudy's support. Rich won the game.

Other players also managed to impress Dixit with their strategy. One was Sean, who voted alphabetically so as not to alienate the other players. Although Dixit admired Sean's strategy, he thinks it could have been refined. "I would actually have done something different. I would have explicitly randomized," he said. "If there were six people I would have thrown a die or something like that."

Not only would his vote not have been known to others, but it would have defused the ire of people whose names came low in the alphabet. "I would more explicitly be able to explain to the other guys, 'Hey, I'm picking randomly, I've got to pick somebody but I don't particularly want to be nasty to anybody," Dixit said.

Furthermore, he confided, "If you've thrown a die, you're going to be seen to be randomizing. But if you go off on your own, you don't actually have to follow what the die tells you, whereas with the alphabetical scheme, you're more or less compelled to follow the pattern. [Randomizing] kind of leaves you a little more Machiavellian freedom."

Such deceit might seem outright outrageous, but after all, it's only a game. At least, that's the theory.

Source: *National Post,* March 14, 2001, p. A12. Material reprinted with the express permission of "The National Post Company," a CanWest Partnership.

Case Study

COLLUSION IN QUEBEC DRIVING SCHOOLS

Firms in oligopolistic markets have a strong incentive both to collude with one another and to drive one another out of business. The goal of each of these actions is to reduce competition, raise prices, and increase profits. The great eighteenth-century economist Adam Smith was well aware of this potential market failure. With regard to collusion, in his book *The Wealth of Nations* he wrote, "People of the same trade seldom meet together, but the conversation ends in a conspiracy against the public, or in some diversion to raise prices."

A Canadian example of Smith's observation involved driving schools in the province of Quebec. Jacques Perreault was a director in a company that operated driving schools in the Sherbrooke area and the adjoining area of Magog. In 1987 Perreault entered into a conspiracy with several of his competitors to raise and fix the price of driving-school services in the Sherbrooke market. The co-conspirators held approximately 94 percent of the Sherbrooke driving-school market.

Shortly after the conspiracy was implemented, it broke down because several smaller competitors refused to follow the agreed-upon pricing scheme. Perreault made several threats against these renegade competitors in an attempt to restore the conspiracy. He also engaged in selective predatory pricing and drove several noncomplying competitors out of the Sherbrooke and Magog markets, using revenues earned from other regional markets to finance these activities. In 1996 a jury found Perreault and his co-conspirators guilty on numerous counts of price fixing and predatory pricing. Perreault was sentenced to a prison term of one year, while the other conspirators had to pay fines or carry out community service.

The Perreault case illustrates how firms in an oligopolistic industry can use both collusion and predatory pricing to reduce competition and raise prices. Also of interest is the nature of some of the arguments made by the Crown in its prosecution of the case. In Quebec, everyone who wants to get a driver's licence must pass an accredited driving-school course. As a result of the province's strict guidelines on the standards of training, driving schools offer a relatively homogeneous product. Moreover, Quebec restricts the number of accredited schools within each region of the province. A moratorium on new schools was imposed in 1987; schools leaving the market could sell their licences only to other accredited schools. The Crown argued that the large market share held by Perreault and his co-conspirators, the almost impassable barriers to entry, the virtual nonexistence of substitutes, and the high level of product homogeneity were all evidence of significant market power. The jury's guilty verdict suggests that the Crown's arguments were persuasive. Perhaps if the Quebec government had not restricted entry in the first place, collusion might not have been a problem. ●

Controversies over Competition Policy

Over time, much controversy has centred on the question of what kinds of behaviour the antitrust laws should prohibit. Most commentators agree that price-fixing agreements among competing firms should be illegal. Yet the competition laws have been used to condemn some business practices whose effects are not obvious. Here we consider three examples.

Resale Price Maintenance   One example of a controversial business practice is *resale price maintenance,* also called *fair trade.* Imagine that Superduper Electronics sells DVD players to retail stores for $300. If Superduper requires the retailers to charge customers $350, it is said to engage in resale price maintenance. Any retailer that charged less than $350 would have violated its contract with Superduper.

At first, resale price maintenance might seem anticompetitive and, therefore, detrimental to society. Like an agreement among members of a cartel, it prevents the retailers from competing on price. For this reason, the courts have often viewed resale price maintenance as a violation of the competition laws.

Yet some economists defend resale price maintenance on two grounds. First, they deny that it is aimed at reducing competition. To the extent that Superduper Electronics has any market power, it can exert that power through the wholesale price, rather than through resale price maintenance. Moreover, Superduper has no incentive to discourage competition among its retailers. Indeed, because a cartel of retailers sells less than a group of competitive retailers, Superduper would be worse off if its retailers were a cartel.

Second, economists believe that resale price maintenance has a legitimate goal. Superduper may want its retailers to provide customers with a pleasant show-room and a knowledgeable sales force. Yet, without resale price maintenance, some customers would take advantage of one store's service to learn about the DVD player's special features and then buy the item at a discount retailer that does not provide this service. To some extent, good service is a public good among the retailers that sell Superduper products. As we discussed in Chapter 11, when one person provides a public good, others are able to enjoy it without paying for it. In this case, discount retailers would free-ride on the service provided by other retailers, leading to less service than is desirable. Resale price maintenance is one way for Superduper to solve this free-rider problem.

The example of resale price maintenance illustrates an important principle: *Business practices that appear to reduce competition may in fact have legitimate purposes.* This principle makes the application of the competition laws all the more difficult. The economists, lawyers, and judges in charge of enforcing these laws must determine what kinds of behaviour public policy should prohibit as impeding competition and reducing economic well-being. Often that job is not easy.

Predatory Pricing   Firms with market power normally use that power to raise prices above the competitive level. But should policymakers ever be concerned that firms with market power might charge prices that are too low? This question is at the heart of a second debate over competition policy.

Imagine that a large airline, call it Coyote Air, has a monopoly on some route. Then Roadrunner Express enters and takes 20 percent of the market, leaving Coyote with 80 percent. In response to this competition, Coyote starts slashing its fares. Some competition analysts argue that Coyote's move could be anticompetitive: The price cuts may be intended to drive Roadrunner out of the market so Coyote can recapture its monopoly and raise prices again. Such behaviour is called *predatory pricing*.

Although predatory pricing is a common claim in competition suits, some economists are skeptical of this argument and believe that predatory pricing is rarely, and perhaps never, a profitable business strategy. Why? For a price war to drive out a rival, prices have to be driven below cost. Yet if Coyote starts selling cheap tickets at a loss, it had better be ready to fly more planes, because low fares will attract more customers. Roadrunner, meanwhile, can respond to Coyote's predatory move by cutting back on flights. As a result, Coyote ends up bearing more than 80 percent of the losses, putting Roadrunner in a good position to survive the price war. As in the old Roadrunner–Coyote cartoons, the predator suffers more than the prey.

Economists continue to debate whether predatory pricing should be a concern for antitrust policymakers. Various questions remain unresolved. Is predatory pricing ever a profitable business strategy? If so, when? Are the courts capable of telling which price cuts are competitive and thus good for consumers and which are predatory? There are no simple answers.

Tying   A third example of a controversial business practice is *tying*. Suppose that Makemoney Movies produces two new films—*Spiderman* and *Hamlet*. If Makemoney offers theatres the two films together at a single price, rather than separately, the studio is said to be tying its two products.

The practice of tying is banned under the civil provisions of the Competition Act. The commonly used justification for the ban goes as follows: Imagine that *Spiderman* is a blockbuster, whereas *Hamlet* is an unprofitable art film. By tying, the studio could use the high demand for *Spiderman* to force theatres to buy *Hamlet*. It seems that the studio could use tying as a mechanism for expanding its market power.

Many economists are skeptical of this argument. Imagine that theatres are willing to pay $20 000 for *Spiderman* and nothing for *Hamlet*. Then the most that a theatre would pay for the two movies together is $20 000—the same as it would pay for *Spiderman* by itself. Forcing the theatre to accept a worthless movie as part of the deal does not increase the theatre's willingness to pay. Makemoney cannot increase its market power simply by bundling the two movies together.

Why, then, does tying exist? One possibility is that it is a form of price discrimination. Suppose there are two theatres. City Theatre is willing to pay $15 000 for *Spiderman* and $5000 for *Hamlet*. Country Theater is just the opposite: It is willing to pay $5000 for *Spiderman* and $15 000 for *Hamlet*. If Makemoney charges separate prices for the two films, its best strategy is to charge $15 000 for each film, and each theatre chooses to show only one film. Yet if Makemoney offers the two movies as a bundle, it can charge each theatre $20 000 for the movies. Thus, if different theatres value the films differently, tying may allow the studio to increase profit by charging a combined price closer to the buyers' total willingness to pay.

The economic theory of tying is even more subtle and complex when considered in the context of vertical integration. This issue arose recently in a case involving Tele-Direct, a publisher of Yellow Pages directories in Canada. Tele-Direct required that any advertisements placed in its Yellow Pages be designed by its in-house staff. This requirement led to a vertically integrated service, starting with designing the ads, moving to providing advertising space, and ending with producing and distributing the directory. Ads designed by outside agencies were not allowed to appear in Tele-Direct's Yellow Pages. In this case, the provision of advertising space was tied to the design of the ads.

In 1995 the Competition Tribunal ruled that this practice violated the tying provisions of the Competition Act. The Tribunal ordered Tele-Direct to either unbundle its advertising space and design activities and quote separate prices for them, or pay an appropriate commission to outside designers. Yet the efficiency effects of tying in this case are ambiguous. On the one hand, tying in a vertically integrated firm may reduce costs and generate production efficiencies. On the other hand, it excludes competing providers of advertising services from entering the Yellow Pages market. The net effect is uncertain.

Tying remains a controversial business practice. The commonly heard argument that tying allows a firm to extend its market power to other goods is not well founded, at least in its simplest form. Yet economists have proposed more elaborate theories for how tying can impede competition. Given our current economic knowledge, it is unclear whether tying has adverse effects for society as a whole.

Case Study

THE MICROSOFT CASE

The most important and controversial antitrust case in recent years has been the U.S. government's suit against the Microsoft Corporation, filed in 1998. Certainly, the case did not lack drama. It pitted one of the world's richest men (Bill Gates) against one of the world's most powerful regulatory agencies (the U.S. Justice Department). Testifying for the government was a prominent economist (MIT professor Franklin Fisher). Testifying for Microsoft was an equally prominent economist (MIT professor Richard Schmalensee). At stake was the future of one of the world's most valuable companies (Microsoft) in one of the economy's fastest growing industries (computer software).

A central issue in the Microsoft case involved tying—in particular, whether Microsoft should be allowed to integrate its Internet browser into its Windows operating system. The government claimed that Microsoft was bundling these two products together to expand the power it had in the market for computer operating systems into an unrelated market (for Internet browsers). Allowing Microsoft to incorporate such products into its operating system, the government argued, would deter other software companies such as Netscape from entering the market and offering new products.

"Me? A monopolist? Now just wait a minute . . ."

Microsoft responded by pointing out that putting new features into old products is a natural part of technological progress. Cars today include stereos and air conditioners, which were once sold separately, and cameras come with built-in flashes. The same is true with operating systems. Over time, Microsoft has added many features to Windows that were previously stand-alone products. This has made computers more reliable and easier to use because consumers can be confident that the pieces work together. The integration of Internet technology, Microsoft argued, was the natural next step.

One point of disagreement concerned the extent of Microsoft's market power. Noting that more than 80 percent of new personal computers use a Microsoft operating system, the government argued that the company had substantial monopoly power, which it was trying to expand. Microsoft replied that the software market is always changing and that Microsoft's Windows was constantly being challenged by competitors, such as the Apple Mac and Linux operating systems. It also argued that the low price it charged for Windows—about $50 at that

IN THE NEWS

PREDATORY PRICING IN THE AIRLINE INDUSTRY

Canada's airline industry has undergone major changes and is now dominated by a single carrier, Air Canada, which accounts for over 80 percent of the domestic market. This poses some challenges and generates some controversy for Canada's competition policy, as the following article illustrates.

Airline Bill Could Boost Airfares, Not Competition

By Roger Ware and Andy Baziliauskas

Bill C-26, the new legislation governing Canada's monopoly airline, increases the commissioner of competition's powers to police allegedly anticompetitive behaviour in the airline industry.

This is bad news for all Canadians who now enjoy low airfares and high-quality service, because it is more likely to lead to higher airfares, less frequent service, and the entry and protection of inefficient airlines.

Once C-26 becomes law, the commissioner won't need to go to the courts or the Competition Tribunal to take action: He could instead immediately prohibit, for up to 80 days, behaviour that could injure competition or cause a competitor irreparable harm.

Predatory pricing is notoriously difficult to distinguish from low pricing that legitimately responds to market rivals. Thus, lawmakers and courts in Canada have been wary of overly stringent anti-predation laws, recognizing that a fear of fines or even imprisonment for their executives would discourage companies from adopting aggressive but legitimate competitive tactics that could benefit consumers.

Until recently, predatory pricing was thought to be rarely observed in practice. New economic research has

time, or only 3 percent of the price of a typical computer—was evidence that its market power was severely limited.

Like many large antitrust suits, the Microsoft case became a legal morass. In November 1999, after a long trial, Judge Penfield Jackson ruled that Microsoft had great monopoly power and that it had illegally abused that power. In June 2000, after hearings about possible remedies, he ordered that Microsoft be broken up into two companies—one that sold the operating system and one that sold applications software. A year later, an appeals court overturned Jackson's breakup order and handed the case to a new judge. In September 2001, the Justice Department announced that it no longer sought a breakup of the company and wanted to settle the case quickly.

A settlement was finally reached in November 2002. Microsoft accepted some restrictions on its business practices. The government accepted that a browser would remain part of the Windows operating system. •

indicated that predation may be greater than previously thought, but changes in Canadian enforcement policy may not yet have adjusted to these findings.

Canada's existing Competition Act provides a double layer of protection against predatory pricing. First, section 50, a criminal provision, prohibits a firm from charging "unreasonably low prices." In addition, section 79 prohibits practices considered an "abuse of dominant position." The list of such abuses can include predatory practices or, indeed, anything found by the Competition Tribunal to be anticompetitive.

Unfortunately for Canadian consumers, Bill C-26 would turn back the clock by permitting a government official to prohibit fares he believes would result in "irreparable harm" to a competitor, even if they would result in substantial savings for air travellers.

Because airline fares frequently change in response to economic, seasonal, and competitive factors, the authority to prevent low fares could

eliminate many of the discounts Canadian travellers now enjoy.

Equally troublesome, Bill C-26 prohibits not only behaviour that harms competition, but also behaviour that harms a competitor. This would represent a fundamental change in Canada's competition policy and law, which up until now has sought to encourage competitive activities aimed at besting market rivals—even if such activities harm some competitors—because they almost always benefit consumers. Where competition law does—and should— draw the line is where a dominant firm takes unfair actions that harm competition—that is, when its behaviour is likely to result in harm to consumers.

Bill C-26's broad power could be used to preclude almost any response to a new rival, including those normally regarded as being strongly pro-consumer—such as dropping prices and increasing flight frequency—whether or not Air Canada's response would ultimately make consumers worse off. Even

worse, Air Canada can never know, without consulting the commissioner, when its actions go too far in his opinion. It cannot look at a speedometer to see if its response to a new entrant has crossed the line. Since any response to entry may harm a competitor, this bill effectively gives the commissioner the power to regulate Air Canada's prices and capacities.

History makes it unmistakably clear that, sooner or later, the authority the government seeks will be exercised to protect inefficient producers and the illusion of "competition" while, in reality, depriving consumers of the benefits of real competition.

Source: *National Post,* National Edition, May 17, 2000, p. C19. Material reprinted with the express permission of "The National Post Company," a CanWest Partnership.

QuickQuiz   What kind of agreement is illegal for businesses to make? • Why are the competition laws controversial?

CONCLUSION

Oligopolies would like to act like monopolies, but self-interest drives them closer to competition. Thus, oligopolies can end up looking either more like monopolies or more like competitive markets, depending on the number of firms in the oligopoly and how cooperative the firms are. The story of the prisoners' dilemma shows why oligopolies can fail to maintain cooperation, even when cooperation is in their best interest.

Policymakers regulate the behaviour of oligopolists through the anticompetition laws. The proper scope of these laws is the subject of ongoing controversy.

Although price-fixing among competing firms clearly reduces economic welfare and should be illegal, some business practices that appear to reduce competition may have legitimate if subtle purposes. As a result, policymakers need to be careful when they use the substantial powers of the anticompetition laws to place limits on firms' behaviour.

SUMMARY

- Oligopolists maximize their total profits by forming a cartel and acting like a monopolist. Yet, if oligopolists make decisions about production levels individually, the result is a greater quantity and a lower price than under the monopoly outcome. The larger the number of firms in the oligopoly, the closer the quantity and price will be to the levels that would prevail under competition.

- The prisoners' dilemma shows that self-interest can prevent people from maintaining cooperation, even when cooperation is in their mutual interest. The logic of the prisoners' dilemma applies in many situations, including arms races, advertising, common-resource problems, and oligopolies.

- Policymakers use the anticompetition laws to prevent oligopolies from engaging in behaviour that reduces competition. The application of these laws can be controversial, because some behaviour that may seem to reduce competition may in fact have legitimate business purposes.

KEY CONCEPTS

oligopoly, p. 352
monopolistic competition, p. 352
collusion, p. 354

cartel, p. 354
Nash equilibrium, p. 356
game theory, p. 359

prisoners' dilemma, p. 359
dominant strategy, p. 360

QUESTIONS FOR REVIEW

1. If a group of sellers could form a cartel, what quantity and price would they try to set?

2. Compare the quantity and price of an oligopoly to those of a monopoly.

3. Compare the quantity and price of an oligopoly to those of a competitive market.

4. How does the number of firms in an oligopoly affect the outcome in its market?

5. What is the prisoners' dilemma, and what does it have to do with oligopoly?

6. Give two examples other than oligopoly to show how the prisoners' dilemma helps to explain behaviour.

7. What kinds of behaviour do the anticompetition laws prohibit?

8. What is resale price maintenance, and why is it controversial?

PROBLEMS AND APPLICATIONS

1. *The New York Times* (Nov. 30, 1993) reported that "the inability of OPEC to agree last week to cut production has sent the oil market into turmoil . . . [leading to] the lowest price for

domestic crude oil since June 1990."

a. Why were the members of OPEC trying to agree to cut production?

b. Why do you suppose OPEC was unable to agree on cutting production? Why did the oil market go into "turmoil" as a result?

c. The newspaper also noted OPEC's view "that producing nations outside the organization, like Norway and Britain, should do their share and cut production." What does the phrase "do their share" suggest about OPEC's desired relationship with Norway and Britain?

2. A large share of the world supply of diamonds comes from Russia and South Africa. Suppose that the marginal cost of mining diamonds is constant at $1000 per diamond, and the demand for diamonds is described by the following schedule:

Price	Quantity
$8000	5 000
7000	6 000
6000	7 000
5000	8 000
4000	9 000
3000	10 000
2000	11 000
1000	12 000

a. If there were many suppliers of diamonds, what would be the price and quantity?

b. If there were only one supplier of diamonds, what would be the price and quantity?

c. If Russia and South Africa formed a cartel, what would be the price and quantity? If the countries split the market evenly, what would be South Africa's production and profit? What would happen to South Africa's profit if it increased its production by 1000 while Russia stuck to the cartel agreement?

d. Use your answer to part (c) to explain why cartel agreements are often not successful.

3. This chapter discusses companies that are oligopolists in the market for the goods they sell. Many of the same ideas apply to companies that are oligopolists in the market for the inputs they buy.

a. If sellers who are oligopolists try to increase the price of goods they sell, what is the goal of buyers who are oligopolists?

b. Major League Baseball team owners have an oligopoly in the market for baseball players. What is the owners' goal regarding players' salaries? Why is this goal difficult to achieve?

c. Baseball players went on strike in 1994 because they would not accept the salary cap that the owners wanted to impose. If the owners were already colluding over salaries, why did the owners feel the need for a salary cap?

4. Describe several activities in your life in which game theory could be useful. What is the common link among these activities?

5. Consider trade relations between Canada and Mexico. Assume that the leaders of the two countries believe the payoffs to alternative trade policies are as follows:

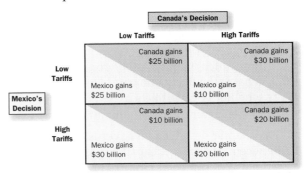

a. What is the dominant strategy for Canada? For Mexico? Explain.

b. Define *Nash equilibrium*. What is the Nash equilibrium for trade policy?

c. In 1993 Parliament ratified the North American Free Trade Agreement (NAFTA), in which Canada, the United States, and Mexico agreed to reduce trade barriers simultaneously. Do the perceived payoffs shown here justify this approach to trade policy?

d. Based on your understanding of the gains from trade (discussed in Chapters 3 and 9), do you think that these payoffs actually reflect a nation's welfare under the four possible outcomes?

6. Suppose that you and a classmate are assigned a project on which you will receive one combined grade. You each want to receive a good grade, but you also want to do as little work as possible. The decision box and payoffs are as follows:

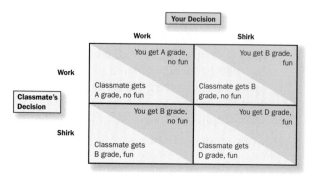

Assume that having fun is your normal state, but having no fun is as unpleasant as receiving a grade that is two letters lower.

a. Write out the decision box that combines the letter grade and the amount of fun you have into a single payoff for each outcome.

b. If neither you nor your classmate knows how much work the other person is doing, what is the likely outcome? Does it matter whether you are likely to work with this person again? Explain your answer.

7. The chapter described an advertising game between Molson and Labatt. Suppose the federal government is considering a law prohibiting beer commercials on television.

a. Would you expect the beer companies to oppose this law? Why?

b. Would you expect beer company profits to rise or fall? Why?

8. Farmer Singh and Farmer Vu graze their cattle on the same field. If there are 20 cows grazing in the field, each cow produces $4000 of milk over its lifetime. If there are more cows in the field, then each cow can eat less grass, and its milk production falls. With 30 cows on the field, each produces $3000 of milk; with 40 cows, each produces $2000 of milk. Cows cost $1000 apiece.

a. Assume that Farmer Singh and Farmer Vu can each purchase either 10 or 20 cows,

but that neither knows how many the other is buying when she makes her purchase. Calculate the payoffs of each outcome.

b. What is the likely outcome of this game? What would be the best outcome? Explain.

c. There used to be more common fields than there are today. Why? (For more discussion of this topic, reread Chapter 11.)

9. Little Kona is a small coffee company that is considering entering a market dominated by Big Brew. Each company's profit depends on whether Little Kona enters and whether Big Brew sets a high price or a low price:

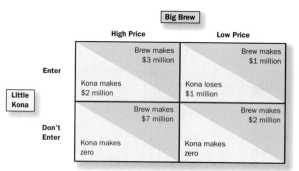

Big Brew threatens Little Kona by saying, "If you enter, we're going to set a low price, so you had better stay out." Do you think Little Kona should believe the threat? Why or why not? What do you think Little Kona should do?

10. Jeff and Steve are playing tennis. Every point comes down to whether Steve guesses correctly whether Jeff will hit the ball to Steve's left or right. The outcomes are:

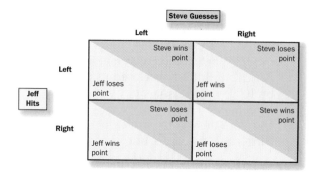

Does either player have a dominant strategy? If Jeff chooses a particular strategy (Left or Right)

and sticks with it, what will Steve do? Can you think of a better strategy for Jeff to follow?

11. Let's analyze a game between two airlines. Suppose that each airline can charge either a high price for tickets or a low price. If SpeedyJet charges $100, it earns low profits if Friendly Skies also charges $100, and high profits if Friendly Skies charges $200. On the other hand, if SpeedyJet charges $200, it earns very low profits if Friendly Skies charges $100, and medium profits if Friendly Skies also charges $200.

a. Draw the decision box for this game.
b. What is the Nash equilibrium in this game? Explain.
c. Is there an outcome that would be better than the Nash equilibrium for both airlines? How could it be achieved? Who would lose if it were achieved?

INTERNET RESOURCES

Competition law in Canada is enforced by the Competition Bureau: http://cb-bc.gc.ca. The Competition Tribunal's website is at http://www.ct-tc.gc.ca.

http://   For more study tools, please visit http://www.mankiw3e.nelson.com.

© COMSTOCK IMAGES/GETTY IMAGES

17

MONOPOLISTIC COMPETITION

Learning Objectives

In this chapter, you will ...

- Analyze competition among firms that sell differentiated products
- Compare the outcome under monopolistic competition and under perfect competition
- Consider the desirability of outcomes in monopolistically competitive markets
- Examine the debate over the effects of advertising
- Review the debate over the role of brand names

You walk into a bookstore to buy a book to read during your vacation. On the store's shelves you find novels by Canadian authors Carol Shields, Margaret Atwood, Rohinton Mistry, and many others. When you pick out a book and buy it, what kind of market are you participating in?

On the one hand, the market for books seems competitive. As you look over the shelves at your bookstore, you find many authors and many publishers vying for your attention. A buyer in this market has thousands of competing products from which to choose. And because anyone can enter the industry by writing and publishing a book, the book business is not very profitable. For every highly paid novelist, there are hundreds of struggling ones.

On the other hand, the market for books seems monopolistic. Because each book is unique, publishers have some latitude in choosing what price to charge. The sellers in this market are price makers rather than price takers. And, indeed, the price of books greatly exceeds marginal cost. The price of a typical hardcover novel, for instance, is about $35, whereas the cost of printing one additional copy of the novel is less than $5.

monopolistic competition
a market structure in which many firms sell products that are similar but not identical

In this chapter we examine markets that have some features of competition and some features of monopoly. This market structure is called **monopolistic competition.** Monopolistic competition describes a market with the following attributes:

- *Many sellers:* Many firms are competing for the same group of customers.
- *Product differentiation:* Each firm produces a product that is at least slightly different from those of other firms. Thus, rather than being a price taker, each firm faces a downward-sloping demand curve.
- *Free entry:* Firms can enter (or exit) the market without restriction. Thus, the number of firms in the market adjusts until economic profits are driven to zero.

A moment's thought reveals a long list of markets with these attributes: books, CDs, DVDs, movies, computer games, restaurants, piano lessons, cookies, furniture, and so on.

Monopolistic competition, like oligopoly, is a market structure that lies between the extreme cases of competition and monopoly. But oligopoly and monopolistic competition are quite different. Oligopoly departs from the perfectly competitive ideal of Chapter 14 because there are only a few sellers in the market. The small number of sellers makes rigorous competition less likely, and it makes strategic interactions among them vitally important. By contrast, under monopolistic competition, there are many sellers, each of which is small compared to the market. A monopolistically competitive market departs from the perfectly competitive ideal because each of the sellers offers a somewhat different product.

COMPETITION WITH DIFFERENTIATED PRODUCTS

To understand monopolistically competitive markets, we first consider the decisions facing an individual firm. We then examine what happens in the long run as firms enter and exit the industry. Next, we compare the equilibrium under monopolistic competition to the equilibrium under perfect competition that we examined in Chapter 14. Finally, we consider whether the outcome in a monopolistically competitive market is desirable from the standpoint of society as a whole.

The Monopolistically Competitive Firm in the Short Run

Each firm in a monopolistically competitive market is, in many ways, like a monopoly. Because its product is different from those offered by other firms, it faces a downward-sloping demand curve. (By contrast, a perfectly competitive firm faces a horizontal demand curve at the market price.) Thus, the monopolistically competitive firm follows a monopolist's rule for profit maximization: It chooses the quantity at which marginal revenue equals marginal cost and then uses its demand curve to find the price consistent with that quantity.

Figure 17.1 shows the cost, demand, and marginal-revenue curves for two typical firms, each in a different monopolistically competitive industry. In both panels of this figure, the profit-maximizing quantity is found at the intersection of the marginal-revenue and marginal-cost curves. The two panels in this figure show different outcomes for the firm's profit. In panel (a), price exceeds average total cost, so the firm makes a profit. In panel (b), price is below average total cost. In

FIGURE 17.1

Monopolistic Competitors in the Short Run

Monopolistic competitors, like monopolists, maximize profit by producing the quantity at which marginal revenue equals marginal cost. The firm in panel (a) makes a profit because, at this quantity, price is above average total cost. The firm in panel (b) makes losses because, at this quantity, price is less than average total cost.

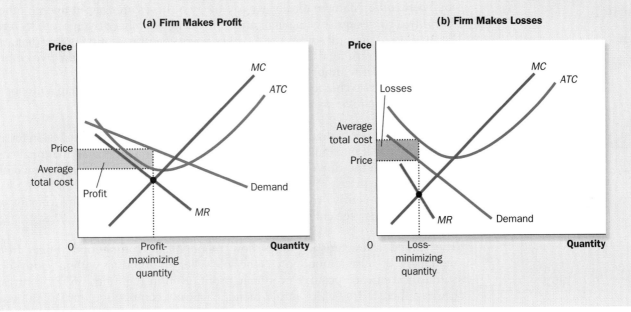

this case, the firm is unable to make a positive profit, so the best the firm can do is to minimize its losses.

All this should seem familiar. A monopolistically competitive firm chooses its quantity and price just as a monopoly does. In the short run, these two types of market structure are similar.

The Long-Run Equilibrium

The situations depicted in Figure 17.1 do not last long. When firms are making profits, as in panel (a), new firms have an incentive to enter the market. This entry increases the number of products from which customers can choose and, therefore, reduces the demand faced by each firm already in the market. In other words, profit encourages entry, and entry shifts the demand curves faced by the incumbent firms to the left. As the demand for incumbent firms' products fall, these firms experience declining profit.

Conversely, when firms are making losses, as in panel (b), firms in the market have an incentive to exit. As firms exit, customers have fewer products from which to choose. This decrease in the number of firms expands the demand faced by those firms that stay in the market. In other words, losses encourage exit, and exit shifts the demand curves of the remaining firms to the right. As the demand for the remaining firms' products rises, these firms experience rising profit (that is, declining losses).

This process of entry and exit continues until the firms in the market are making exactly zero economic profit. Figure 17.2 depicts the long-run equilibrium. Once the market reaches this equilibrium, new firms have no incentive to enter, and existing firms have no incentive to exit.

Notice that the demand curve in this figure just barely touches the average-total-cost curve. Mathematically, we say the two curves are *tangent* to each other. These two curves must be tangent once entry and exit have driven profit to zero. Because profit per unit sold is the difference between price (found on the demand curve) and average total cost, the maximum profit is zero only if these two curves touch each other without crossing.

To sum up, two characteristics describe the long-run equilibrium in a monopolistically competitive market:

1. As in a monopoly market, price exceeds marginal cost. This conclusion arises because profit maximization requires marginal revenue to equal marginal cost and because the downward-sloping demand curve makes marginal revenue less than the price.
2. As in a competitive market, price equals average total cost. This conclusion arises because free entry and exit drive economic profit to zero.

The second characteristic shows how monopolistic competition differs from monopoly. Because a monopoly is the sole seller of a product without close substitutes, it can earn positive economic profit, even in the long run. By contrast, because there is free entry into a monopolistically competitive market, the economic profit of a firm in this type of market is driven to zero.

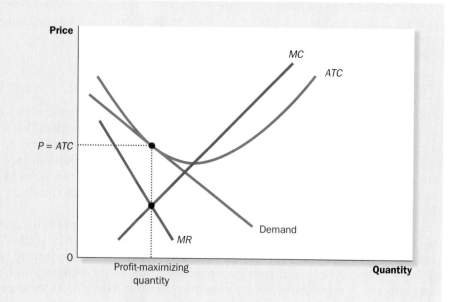

FIGURE 17.2

A Monopolistic Competitor in the Long Run

In a monopolistically competitive market, if firms are making profit, new firms enter, and the demand curves for the incumbent firms shift to the left. Similarly, if firms are making losses, old firms exit, and the demand curves of the remaining firms shift to the right. Because of these shifts in demand, a monopolistically competitive firm eventually finds itself in the long-run equilibrium shown here. In this long-run equilibrium, price equals average total cost, and the firm earns zero profit.

Monopolistic versus Perfect Competition

Figure 17.3 compares the long-run equilibrium under monopolistic competition to the long-run equilibrium under perfect competition. (Chapter 14 discussed the equilibrium with perfect competition.) There are two noteworthy differences between monopolistic and perfect competition—excess capacity and the markup.

Excess Capacity As we have just seen, entry and exit drive each firm in a monopolistically competitive market to a point of tangency between its demand and average-total-cost curves. Panel (a) of Figure 17.3 shows that the quantity of output at this point is smaller than the quantity that minimizes average total cost. Thus, under monopolistic competition, firms produce on the downward-sloping portion of their average-total-cost curves. In this way, monopolistic competition contrasts starkly with perfect competition. As panel (b) of Figure 17.3 shows, free entry in competitive markets drives firms to produce at the minimum of average total cost.

The quantity that minimizes average total cost is called the *efficient scale* of the firm. In the long run, perfectly competitive firms produce at the efficient scale,

FIGURE 17.3

Monopolistic versus Perfect Competition

Panel (a) shows the long-run equilibrium in a monopolistically competitive market, and panel (b) shows the long-run equilibrium in a perfectly competitive market. Two differences are notable: (1) The perfectly competitive firm produces at the efficient scale, where average total cost is minimized. By contrast, the monopolistically competitive firm produces at less than the efficient scale. (2) Price equals marginal cost under perfect competition, but price is above marginal cost under monopolistic competition.

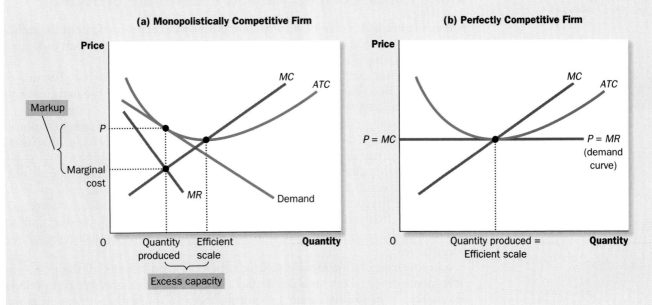

whereas monopolistically competitive firms produce below this level. Firms are said to have *excess capacity* under monopolistic competition. In other words, a monopolistically competitive firm, unlike a perfectly competitive firm, could increase the quantity it produces and lower the average total cost of production.

Markup over Marginal Cost   A second difference between perfect competition and monopolistic competition is the relationship between price and marginal cost. For a competitive firm, such as that shown in panel (b) of Figure 17.3, price equals marginal cost. For a monopolistically competitive firm, such as that shown in panel (a), price exceeds marginal cost, because the firm always has some market power.

How is this markup over marginal cost consistent with free entry and zero profit? The zero-profit condition ensures only that price equals average total cost. It does *not* ensure that price equals marginal cost. Indeed, in the long-run equilibrium, monopolistically competitive firms operate on the declining portion of their average-total-cost curves, so marginal cost is below average total cost. Thus, for price to equal average total cost, price must be above marginal cost.

In this relationship between price and marginal cost, we see a key behavioural difference between perfect competitors and monopolistic competitors. Imagine that you were to ask a firm the following question: "Would you like to see another customer come through your door ready to buy from you at your current price?" A perfectly competitive firm would answer that it didn't care. Because price exactly equals marginal cost, the profit from an extra unit sold is zero. By contrast, a monopolistically competitive firm is always eager to get another customer. Because its price exceeds marginal cost, an extra unit sold at the posted price means more profit. According to an old quip, monopolistically competitive markets are those in which sellers send holiday greeting cards to the buyers.

Monopolistic Competition and the Welfare of Society

Is the outcome in a monopolistically competitive market desirable from the standpoint of society as a whole? Can policymakers improve on the market outcome? There are no simple answers to these questions.

One source of inefficiency is the markup of price over marginal cost. Because of the markup, some consumers who value the good at more than the marginal cost of production (but less than the price) will be deterred from buying it. Thus, a monopolistically competitive market has the normal deadweight loss of monopoly pricing. We first saw this type of inefficiency when we discussed monopoly in Chapter 15.

Although this outcome is clearly undesirable compared to the first-best outcome of price equal to marginal cost, there is no easy way for policymakers to fix the problem. To enforce marginal-cost pricing, policymakers would need to regulate all firms that produce differentiated products. Because such products are so common in the economy, the administrative burden of such regulation would be overwhelming.

Moreover, regulating monopolistic competitors would entail all the problems of regulating natural monopolies. In particular, because monopolistic competitors are making zero profits already, requiring them to lower their prices to equal marginal cost would cause them to make losses. To keep these firms in business, the government would need to help them cover these losses. Rather than raising taxes to pay for these subsidies, policymakers may decide it is better to live with the inefficiency of monopolistic pricing.

Another way in which monopolistic competition may be socially inefficient is that the number of firms in the market may not be the "ideal" one. That is, there may be too much or too little entry. One way to think about this problem is in terms of the externalities associated with entry. Whenever a new firm considers entering the market with a new product, it considers only the profit it would make. Yet its entry would also have two external effects:

1. *The product-variety externality:* Because consumers get some consumer surplus from the introduction of a new product, entry of a new firm conveys a positive externality on consumers.
2. *The business-stealing externality:* Because other firms lose customers and profits from the entry of a new competitor, entry of a new firm imposes a negative externality on existing firms.

Thus, in a monopolistically competitive market, there are both positive and negative externalities associated with the entry of new firms. Depending on which externality is larger, a monopolistically competitive market could have either too few or too many products.

Both of these externalities are closely related to the conditions for monopolistic competition. The product-variety externality arises because a new firm would offer a product different from those of the existing firms. The business-stealing externality arises because firms post a price above marginal cost and, therefore, are always eager to sell additional units. Conversely, because perfectly competitive firms produce identical goods and charge a price equal to marginal cost, neither of these externalities exists under perfect competition.

In the end, we can conclude only that monopolistically competitive markets do not have all the desirable welfare properties of perfectly competitive markets. That is, the invisible hand does not ensure that total surplus is maximized under monopolistic competition. Yet because the inefficiencies are subtle, hard to measure, and hard to fix, there is no easy way for public policy to improve the market outcome.

QuickQuiz List the three key attributes of monopolistic competition. • Draw and explain a diagram to show the long-run equilibrium in a monopolistically competitive market. How does this equilibrium differ from that in a perfectly competitive market?

ADVERTISING

It is nearly impossible to go through a typical day in a modern economy without being bombarded with advertising. Whether you are reading a newspaper, watching television, or driving down the highway, some firm will try to convince you to buy its product. Such behaviour is a natural feature of monopolistic

IS EXCESS CAPACITY A SOCIAL PROBLEM?

As we have seen, monopolistically competitive firms produce a quantity of output below the level that minimizes average total cost. By contrast, firms in perfectly competitive markets are driven to produce at the quantity that minimizes average total cost. This comparison between perfect and monopolistic competition led some economists in the past to argue that the excess capacity of monopolistic competitors was a source of inefficiency.

Today economists understand that the excess capacity of monopolistic competitors is not directly relevant for evaluating economic welfare. There is no reason that society should want all firms to produce at the minimum of average total cost. For example, consider a publishing firm. Producing a novel might take a fixed cost of $50 000 (the author's time) and variable costs of $5 per book (the cost of printing). In this case, the average total cost of a book declines as the number of books increases because the fixed cost is spread over more and more units. The average total cost is minimized by printing an infinite number of books. But in no sense is infinity the right number of books for society to produce.

In short, monopolistic competitors do have excess capacity, but this fact tells us little about the desirability of the market outcome.

competition. When firms sell differentiated products and charge prices above marginal cost, each firm has an incentive to advertise in order to attract more buyers to its particular product.

The amount of advertising varies substantially across products. Firms that sell highly differentiated consumer goods, such as over-the-counter drugs, perfumes, soft drinks, razor blades, breakfast cereals, and dog food, typically spend between 10 and 20 percent of revenue for advertising. Firms that sell industrial products, such as drill presses and communications satellites, typically spend very little on advertising. And firms that sell homogeneous products, such as wheat, peanuts, or crude oil, spend nothing at all. For the economy as a whole, spending on advertising comprises about 2 percent of total firm revenue, or about $20 billion per year.

Advertising takes many forms. Most advertising spending is for commercials on television and radio (31 percent of total spending in 2001), space in newspapers and magazines (24 percent), direct mail (19 percent), the Yellow Pages (6 percent), and the Internet (3 percent). The remainder (17 percent) is for miscellaneous other ways of reaching customers, such as billboards and the Goodyear blimp.

The Debate over Advertising

Is society wasting the resources it devotes to advertising? Or does advertising serve a valuable purpose? Assessing the social value of advertising is difficult and often generates heated argument among economists. Let's consider both sides of the debate.

The Critique of Advertising
Critics of advertising argue that firms advertise in order to manipulate people's tastes. Much advertising is psychological rather than informational. Consider, for example, the typical television commercial for some brand of soft drink. The commercial most likely does not tell the viewer

about the product's price or quality. Instead, it might show a group of happy people at a party on a beach on a beautiful sunny day. In their hands are cans of the soft drink. The goal of the commercial is to convey a subconscious (if not subtle) message: "You too can have many friends and be happy, if only you drink our product." Critics of advertising argue that such a commercial creates a desire that otherwise might not exist.

Critics also argue that advertising impedes competition. Advertising often tries to convince consumers that products are more different than they truly are. By increasing the perception of product differentiation and fostering brand loyalty, advertising makes buyers less concerned with price differences among similar goods. With a less elastic demand curve, each firm charges a larger markup over marginal cost.

The Defence of Advertising Defenders of advertising argue that firms use advertising to provide information to customers. Advertising conveys the prices of the goods being offered for sale, the existence of new products, and the locations of retail outlets. This information allows customers to make better choices about what to buy and, thus, enhances the ability of markets to allocate resources efficiently.

Defenders also argue that advertising fosters competition. Because advertising allows customers to be more fully informed about all the firms in the market, customers can more easily take advantage of price differences. Thus, each firm has less market power. In addition, advertising allows new firms to enter more easily, because it gives entrants a means to attract customers from existing firms.

Over time, policymakers have come to accept the view that advertising can make markets more competitive. One important example is the regulation of advertising for certain professions, such as lawyers, doctors, and pharmacists. In the past, these groups succeeded in getting state governments to prohibit advertising in their fields on the grounds that advertising was "unprofessional." In recent years, however, the courts have concluded that the primary effect of these restrictions on advertising was to curtail competition. They have, therefore, overturned many of the laws that prohibit advertising by members of these professions.

Case Study

ADVERTISING AND THE PRICE OF EYEGLASSES

What effect does advertising have on the price of a good? On the one hand, advertising might make consumers view products as being more different than they otherwise would. If so, it would make markets less competitive and firms' demand curves less elastic, and this would lead firms to charge higher prices. On the other hand, advertising might make it easier for consumers to find the firms offering the best prices. In this case, it would make markets more competitive and firms' demand curves more elastic, and this would lead to lower prices.

In an article published in *The Journal of Law and Economics* in 1972, economist Lee Benham tested these two views of advertising. In the United States during the

1960s, the various state governments had vastly different rules about advertising by optometrists. Some states allowed advertising for eyeglasses and eye examinations. Many states, however, prohibited it. For example, the Florida law read as follows:

> It is unlawful for any person, firm, or corporation to . . . advertise either directly or indirectly by any means whatsoever any definite or indefinite price or credit terms on prescriptive or corrective lens, frames, complete prescriptive or corrective glasses, or any optometric service. . . . This section is passed in the interest of public health, safety, and welfare, and its provisions shall be liberally construed to carry out its objects and purposes.

Professional optometrists enthusiastically endorsed these restrictions on advertising.

Benham used the differences in state law as a natural experiment to test the two views of advertising. The results were striking. In those states that prohibited advertising, the average price paid for a pair of eyeglasses was $33. (This number is not as low as it seems, because this price is from 1963, when all prices were much lower than they are today. To convert 1963 prices into today's dollars, you can multiply them by 5.) In those states that did not restrict advertising, the average price was $26. Thus, advertising reduced average prices by more than 20 percent. In the market for eyeglasses, and probably in many other markets as well, advertising fosters competition and leads to lower prices for consumers. ●

Advertising as a Signal of Quality

Many types of advertising contain little apparent information about the product being advertised. Consider a firm introducing a new breakfast cereal. A typical advertisement might have some highly paid actor eating the cereal and exclaiming how wonderful it tastes. How much information does the advertisement really provide?

The answer is: more than you might think. Defenders of advertising argue that even advertising that appears to contain little hard information may in fact tell consumers something about product quality. The willingness of the firm to spend a large amount of money on advertising can itself be a *signal* to consumers about the quality of the product being offered.

Consider the problem facing two firms—Post and Kellogg. Each company has just come up with a recipe for a new cereal, which it would sell for $3 a box. To keep things simple, let's assume that the marginal cost of making cereal is zero, so the $3 is all profit. Each company knows that if it spends $10 million on advertising, it will convince 1 million consumers to try its new cereal. And each company knows that if consumers like the cereal, they will buy it not once but many times.

First consider Post's decision. Based on market research, Post knows that its cereal is only mediocre. Although advertising would sell one box to each of 1 million consumers, the consumers would quickly learn that the cereal is not very good and stop buying it. Post decides it is not worth paying $10 million in advertising to get only $3 million in sales. So it does not bother to advertise. It sends its cooks back to the drawing board to find another recipe.

Kellogg, on the other hand, knows that its cereal is great. Each person who tries it will buy a box a month for the next year. Thus, the $10 million in advertising will bring in $36 million in sales. Advertising is profitable here because Kellogg has a good product that consumers will buy repeatedly. Thus, Kellogg chooses to advertise.

Now that we have considered the behaviour of the two firms, let's consider the behaviour of consumers. We began by asserting that consumers are inclined to try a new cereal that they see advertised. But is this behaviour rational? Should a consumer try a new cereal just because the seller has chosen to advertise it?

In fact, it may be completely rational for consumers to try new products that they see advertised. In our story, consumers decide to try Kellogg's new cereal because Kellogg advertises. Kellogg chooses to advertise because it knows that its cereal is quite good, while Post chooses not to advertise because it knows that its cereal is only mediocre. By its willingness to spend money on advertising, Kellogg signals to consumers the quality of its cereal. Each consumer thinks, quite sensibly, "Boy, if the Kellogg Company is willing to spend so much money advertising this new cereal, it must be really good."

What is most surprising about this theory of advertising is that the content of the advertisement is irrelevant. Kellogg signals the quality of its product by its willingness to spend money on advertising. What the advertisements say is not as important as the fact that consumers know ads are expensive. By contrast, cheap advertising cannot be effective at signalling quality to consumers. In our example, if an advertising campaign cost less than $3 million, both Post and Kellogg would use it to market their new cereals. Because both good and mediocre cereals would be advertised, consumers could not infer the quality of a new cereal from the fact that it is advertised. Over time, consumers would learn to ignore such cheap advertising.

This theory can explain why firms pay famous actors large amounts of money to make advertisements that, on the surface, appear to convey no information at all. The information is not in the advertisement's content, but simply in its existence and expense.

Brand Names

Advertising is closely related to the existence of brand names. In many markets, there are two types of firms. Some firms sell products with widely recognized brand names, while other firms sell generic substitutes. For example, in a typical drugstore, you can find Bayer aspirin on the shelf next to a generic aspirin. In a typical grocery store, you can find Pepsi next to less familiar colas. Most often, the firm with the brand name spends more on advertising and charges a higher price for its product.

Just as there is disagreement about the economics of advertising, there is disagreement about the economics of brand names. Let's consider both sides of the debate.

Critics of brand names argue that brand names cause consumers to perceive differences that do not really exist. In many cases, the generic good is almost

IN THE NEWS

BRAND NAMES IN THE FAST-FOOD INDUSTRY

Brand names convey information to consumers about the goods that firms are offering. Establishing a brand name is thought to be an important strategy for many businesses. As the following article shows, branding has deeply changed the food-service industry in Canada.

It's the Brand, Stupid

By Ross Laver

The kids are in the backseat, fidgeting and demanding to be fed. You and your spouse could use a bite, too. The only question is where to stop: up ahead there's a Pizza Hut, across the road is Taco Bell, and just beyond that is the familiar red roof of KFC. Will it be pizza, Mexican, or fried chicken?

You can take your pick as far as John Bitove Jr. is concerned. Thanks to some clever deal-making over the past few months, he now controls the largest collection of franchise restaurants in Canada, with 639 KFC, Pizza Hut, and

Taco Bell outlets in 400 communities. This year, the company expects to serve 60 million customers. That's 25 million chickens, 6.2 million pizzas, 3.5 million L of gravy, and 11.3 million kg of fries, all washed down with 35 million soft drinks—enough to fill 17 Olympic-sized swimming pools.

Food connoisseurs may sneer, but Bitove, 39, is certain he's on to a good thing. Drive through any major city or town in Canada and it would be easy to conclude that the fast-food business—the industry prefers the term QSR, short for quick-service restaurants—is saturated. Far from it, says Bitove. Canadians eat only about two-thirds as much fast

food as Americans. And in both countries, consumption—particularly of takeout and home-delivered food—is growing rapidly. "The home-meal-replacement market is becoming a larger and larger part of the North American lifestyle," Bitove says. "People's attitude has become, 'What am I hungry for—what's fast and easy?'"

Bitove is well qualified to respond. His grandfather, who emigrated from Macedonia in 1919, used to run a small butcher shop on Toronto's Queen Street East. A generation later, John Jr.'s father opened the first of a string of restaurants. Later, he expanded beyond Toronto as holder of the Canadian

indistinguishable from the brand-name good. Consumers' willingness to pay more for the brand-name good, these critics assert, is a form of irrationality fostered by advertising. Economist Edward Chamberlin, one of the early developers of the theory of monopolistic competition, concluded from this argument that brand names were bad for the economy. He proposed that the government discourage their use by refusing to enforce the exclusive trademarks that companies use to identify their products.

More recently, economists have defended brand names as a useful way for consumers to ensure that the goods they buy are of high quality. There are two related arguments. First, brand names provide consumers with *information* about quality when quality cannot be easily judged in advance of purchase. Second, brand names give firms an *incentive* to maintain high quality, because firms have a financial stake in maintaining the reputation of their brand names.

franchise rights to the Big Boy chain of family restaurants, with 32 locations in Ontario, Quebec, and Alberta. Today, the family-owned catering and hospitality business, Bitove Corp., controls food and beverage concessions in airports, hospitals, and sports facilities across Canada, as well as Wayne Gretzky's Restaurant in downtown Toronto.

John Jr. began his career working for the family business, then went off and spearheaded the group that started the Toronto Raptors NBA franchise. A diehard basketball fan, Bitove was the team's first president but sold his 39.5 percent share of the team after a dispute with the other owners.

Despite the bad blood, Bitove has fond memories of his time with the Raptors. "It's the Raptors experience that woke me up to the importance of branding—I mean, wow. Our goal was to create momentum by going after younger adults and kids, because we knew the Blue Jays and the Maple Leafs had the older set. So coming up with the name and logo was radical in itself. Then we tested it and came out with it and—boom!—the merchandise started flying off the shelves. So holy cow, there's method to this madness. You do the

research and target where you want to go, and you can fundamentally create more value than you had before."

In his own lifetime, Bitove has seen the same phenomenon in the food-service industry. When his father got into the business, most restaurants were independently owned. Now, brands pull in the big money. "Our generation is a lot more brand-specific than our parents were, and we'll pay to make things easier because often we don't have time for a traditional restaurant where you sit down and wait," he says. "We can say brands are a horrible thing, but that's the way the world is going. And I'd rather be on the bandwagon as opposed to trying to educate the world on what I think is a better way."

In practical terms that means more locations, more advertising, and more of an effort to implant the KFC, Pizza Hut, and Taco Bell names in Canadians' daily lives. Already, the three chains combined have one of the largest ad budgets in the country and the largest food home-delivery operation, worth $100 million a year in sales. Bitove intends to consolidate the company's five call centres—in Montreal, Toronto, Calgary, Edmonton, and Vancouver—perhaps replacing

them with a single toll-free call centre in New Brunswick.

Also on the horizon are hundreds of tiny, kiosk-style outlets that can be dropped into office buildings and other locations that wouldn't support a conventional outlet. "It would blow you away how small a kitchen we need to get the job done." Think Fotomat, he says. Now think Pizza Hut in the lobby of a large apartment building. Think three-in-one outlets, combining KFC, Pizza Hut, and Taco Bell under a single roof. Kids can't agree where to eat? No problem. It's like a gas pump: regular, mid-grade, and super from one nozzle. Drive in and fuel up.

Bitove knows something the food snobs don't. It isn't about the food. It's about the brand. It's about mass-marketed carbohydrate and deep-fried protein, fuel to get you through the day. Come and get it. Or phone and they'll deliver.

Source: *Maclean's*, January 31, 2000. Retrieved July 27, 2001, from http://www.macleans.ca. Reprinted with permission from Maclean's Magazine, Rogers Publishing Limited 2004.

To see how these arguments work in practice, consider a famous brand name: McDonald's. Imagine that you are driving through an unfamiliar town and want to stop for lunch. You see a McDonald's and a local restaurant next to it. Which do you choose? The local restaurant may in fact offer better food at lower prices, but you have no way of knowing that. By contrast, McDonald's offers a consistent product across many cities. Its brand name is useful to you as a way of judging the quality of what you are about to buy.

The McDonald's brand name also ensures that the company has an incentive to maintain quality. For example, if some customers were to become ill from bad food sold at a McDonald's, the news would be disastrous for the company. McDonald's would lose much of the valuable reputation that it has built up with years of expensive advertising. As a result, it would lose sales and profit not just in the outlet that sold the bad food but in its many outlets throughout the country.

By contrast, if some customers were to become ill from bad food at a local restaurant, that restaurant might have to close down, but the lost profits would be much smaller. Hence, McDonald's has a greater incentive to ensure that its food is safe.

The debate over brand names thus centres on the question of whether consumers are rational in preferring brand names over generic substitutes. Critics of brand names argue that brand names are the result of an irrational consumer response to advertising. Defenders of brand names argue that consumers have good reason to pay more for brand-name products because they can be more confident about the quality of these products.

QuickQuiz How might advertising make markets less competitive? How might it make markets more competitive? • Give the arguments for and against brand names.

CONCLUSION

Monopolistic competition is true to its name: It is a hybrid of monopoly and competition. Like a monopoly, each monopolistic competitor faces a downward-sloping demand curve and, as a result, charges a price above marginal cost. As in a perfectly competitive market, there are many firms, and entry and exit drive the profit of each monopolistic competitor toward zero. Table 17.1 summarizes these lessons.

Because monopolistically competitive firms produce differentiated products, each firm advertises in order to attract customers to its own brand. To some extent, advertising manipulates consumers' tastes, promotes irrational brand loyalty, and impedes competition. To a larger extent, advertising provides information, establishes brand names of reliable quality, and fosters competition.

The theory of monopolistic competition seems to describe many markets in the economy. It is somewhat disappointing, therefore, that the theory does not yield simple and compelling advice for public policy. From the standpoint of the economic theorist, the allocation of resources in monopolistically competitive markets is not perfect. Yet, from the standpoint of a practical policymaker, there may be little that can be done to improve it.

SUMMARY

- A monopolistically competitive market is characterized by three attributes: many firms, differentiated products, and free entry.

- The equilibrium in a monopolistically competitive market differs from that in a perfectly competitive market in two related ways. First, each firm in a monopolistically competitive market has excess capacity. That is, it operates on the downward-sloping portion of the average-total-cost curve. Second, each firm charges a price above marginal cost.

TABLE 17.1

Monopolistic
Competition:
Between Perfect
Competition and
Monopoly

	Market Structure		
	Perfect Competition	Monopolistic Competition	Monopoly
Features that all three market structures share			
Goal of firms	Maximize profits	Maximize profits	Maximize profits
Rule for maximizing	$MR = MC$	$MR = MC$	$MR = MC$
Can earn economic profits in the short run?	Yes	Yes	Yes
Features that monopoly and monopolistic competition share			
Price taker?	Yes	No	No
Price	$P = MC$	$P > MC$	$P > MC$
Produces welfare-maximizing level of output?	Yes	No	No
Features that perfect competition and monopolistic competition share			
Number of firms	Many	Many	One
Entry in long run?	Yes	Yes	No
Can earn economic profits in long run?	No	No	Yes

- Monopolistic competition does not have all the desirable properties of perfect competition. There is the standard deadweight loss of monopoly caused by the markup of price over marginal cost. In addition, the number of firms (and thus the variety of products) can be too large or too small. In practice, the ability of policymakers to correct these inefficiencies is limited.

- The product differentiation inherent in monopolistic competition leads to the use of advertising and brand names. Critics of advertising and brand names argue that firms use them to take advantage of consumer irrationality and to reduce competition. Defenders of advertising and brand names argue that firms use them to inform consumers and to compete more vigorously on price and product quality.

KEY CONCEPTS

monopolistic competition, p. 382

QUESTIONS FOR REVIEW

1. Describe the three attributes of monopolistic competition. How is monopolistic competition like monopoly? How is it like perfect competition?

2. Draw a diagram depicting a firm in a monopolistically competitive market that is making profits. Now show what happens to this firm as new firms enter the industry.

3. Draw a diagram of the long-run equilibrium in a monopolistically competitive market. How is price related to average total cost? How is price related to marginal cost?

4. Does a monopolistic competitor produce too much or too little output compared to the most efficient level? What practical considerations make it difficult for policymakers to solve this problem?

5. How might advertising reduce economic well-being? How might advertising increase economic well-being?

6. How might advertising with no apparent informational content in fact convey information to consumers?

7. Explain two benefits that might arise from the existence of brand names.

PROBLEMS AND APPLICATIONS

1. Classify the following markets as perfectly competitive, monopolistic, or monopolistically competitive, and explain your answers.
   a. wooden #2 pencils
   b. bottled water
   c. copper
   d. local telephone service
   e. peanut butter
   f. lipstick

2. What feature of the product being sold distinguishes a monopolistically competitive firm from a monopolistic firm?

3. The chapter states that monopolistically competitive firms could increase the quantity they produce and lower the average total cost of production. Why don't they do so?

4. Sparkle is one firm of many in the market for toothpaste, which is in long-run equilibrium.
   a. Draw a diagram showing Sparkle's demand curve, marginal-revenue curve, average-total-cost curve, and marginal-cost curve. Label Sparkle's profit-maximizing output and price.
   b. What is Sparkle's profit? Explain.
   c. On your diagram, show the consumer surplus derived from the purchase of Sparkle toothpaste. Also show the deadweight loss relative to the efficient level of output.
   d. If the government forced Sparkle to produce the efficient level of output, what would happen to the firm? What would happen to Sparkle's customers?

5. Do monopolistically competitive markets typically have the optimal number of products? Explain.

6. The chapter says that monopolistically competitive firms may send holiday greeting cards to their customers. What do they accomplish by this? Explain in words and with a diagram.

7. If you were thinking of entering the ice-cream business, would you try to make ice cream that is just like one of the existing brands? Explain your decision using the ideas of this chapter.

8. Describe three commercials that you have seen on TV. In what ways, if any, were each of these commercials socially useful? In what ways were they socially wasteful? Did the commercials affect the likelihood of your buying the product? Why or why not?

© CHRIS BAKER/STONE

THE MARKETS FOR
THE FACTORS OF PRODUCTION

When you finish school, your income will be determined largely by the kind of job you take. If you become a computer programmer, you will earn more than if you become a gas station attendant. This fact is not surprising, but it is not obvious why it is true. No law requires that computer programmers be paid more than gas station attendants. No ethical principle says that programmers are more deserving. What then determines which job will pay you the higher wage?

Your income, of course, is a small piece of a larger economic picture. In 2002 the total income of all Canadian residents was about $1 trillion. People earned this income in various ways. Workers earned about three-fourths of it in the form of wages and fringe benefits. The rest went to landowners and to the owners of *capital*—the economy's stock of equipment and structures—in the form of rent, profit, and interest. What determines how much goes to workers? To landowners? To the owners of capital? Why do some workers earn higher wages than others, some landowners higher rental income than others, and some capital owners greater profit than others? Why, in particular, do computer programmers earn more than gas station attendants?

18

Learning Objectives

In this chapter, you will …

- Analyze the labour demand of competitive, profit-maximizing firms
- Consider the household decisions that lie behind labour supply
- Learn why equilibrium wages equal the value of the marginal product of labour
- Consider how the other factors of production— land and capital—are compensated
- Examine how a change in the supply of one factor alters the earnings of all the factors

The answers to these questions, like most in economics, hinge on supply and demand. The supply and demand for labour, land, and capital determine the prices paid to workers, landowners, and capital owners. To understand why some people have higher incomes than others, therefore, we need to look more deeply at the markets for the services they provide. That is our job in this and the next two chapters.

This chapter provides the basic theory for the analysis of factor markets. As you may recall from Chapter 2, the **factors of production** are the inputs used to produce goods and services. Labour, land, and capital are the three most important factors of production. When a computer firm produces a new software program, it uses programmers' time (labour), the physical space on which its offices sit (land), and an office building and computer equipment (capital). Similarly, when a gas station sells gas, it uses attendants' time (labour), the physical space (land), and the gas tanks and pumps (capital).

Although in many ways factor markets resemble the goods markets we have analyzed in previous chapters, they are different in one important way: The demand for a factor of production is a *derived demand*. That is, a firm's demand for a factor of production is derived from its decision to supply a good in another market. The demand for computer programmers is inextricably tied to the supply of computer software, and the demand for gas station attendants is inextricably tied to the supply of gasoline.

In this chapter we analyze factor demand by considering how a competitive, profit-maximizing firm decides how much of any factor to buy. We begin our analysis by examining the demand for labour. Labour is the most important factor of production, for workers receive most of the total income earned in the Canadian economy. Later in the chapter, we see that the lessons we learn about the labour market apply directly to the markets for the other factors of production.

The basic theory of factor markets developed in this chapter takes a large step toward explaining how the income of the Canadian economy is distributed among workers, landowners, and owners of capital. Chapter 19 will build on this analysis to examine in more detail why some workers earn more than others. Chapter 20 will examine how much inequality results from this process and then consider what role the government should and does play in altering the distribution of income.

factors of production
the inputs used to produce goods and services

THE DEMAND FOR LABOUR

Labour markets, like other markets in the economy, are governed by the forces of supply and demand. This is illustrated in Figure 18.1. In panel (a) the supply and demand for apples determine the price of apples. In panel (b) the supply and demand for apple pickers determine the price, or wage, of apple pickers.

As we have already noted, labour markets are different from most other markets because labour demand is a derived demand. Most labour services, rather than being final goods ready to be enjoyed by consumers, are inputs into the production of other goods. To understand labour demand, we need to focus on the firms that hire the labour and use it to produce goods for sale. By examining the link between the production of goods and the demand for labour, we gain insight into the determination of equilibrium wages.

FIGURE 18.1

The Versatility of Supply and Demand

The basic tools of supply and demand apply to goods and to labour services. Panel (a) shows how the supply and demand for apples determine the price of apples. Panel (b) shows how the supply and demand for apple pickers determine the wage of apple pickers.

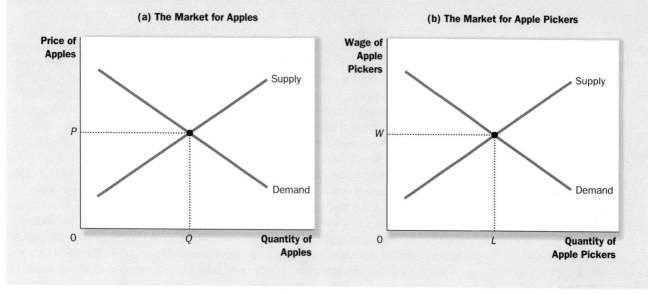

(a) The Market for Apples

(b) The Market for Apple Pickers

The Competitive, Profit-Maximizing Firm

Let's look at how a typical firm, such as an apple producer, decides the quantity of labour to demand. The firm owns an apple orchard and each week must decide how many apple pickers to hire to harvest its crop. After the firm makes its hiring decision, the workers pick as many apples as they can. The firm then sells the apples, pays the workers, and keeps what is left as profit.

We make two assumptions about our firm. First, we assume that our firm is *competitive* both in the market for apples (where the firm is a seller) and in the market for apple pickers (where the firm is a buyer). Recall from Chapter 14 that a competitive firm is a price taker. Because there are many other firms selling apples and hiring apple pickers, a single firm has little influence over the price it gets for apples or the wage it pays apple pickers. The firm takes the price and the wage as given by market conditions. It has to decide only how many workers to hire and how many apples to sell.

Second, we assume that the firm is *profit-maximizing*. Thus, the firm does not directly care about the number of workers it has or the number of apples it produces. It cares only about profit, which equals the total revenue from the sale of apples minus the total cost of producing them. The firm's supply of apples and its demand for workers are derived from its primary goal of maximizing profit.

The Production Function and the Marginal Product of Labour

To make its hiring decision, the firm must consider how the size of its work force affects the amount of output produced. In other words, it must consider how the number of apple pickers affects the quantity of apples it can harvest and sell. Table 18.1 gives a numerical example. In the first column is the number of workers. In the second column is the quantity of apples the workers harvest each week.

production function
the relationship between the quantity of inputs used to make a good and the quantity of output of that good

These two columns of numbers describe the firm's ability to produce. As we noted in Chapter 13, economists use the term **production function** to describe the relationship between the quantity of the inputs used in production and the quantity of output from production. Here the "input" is the apple pickers and the "output" is the apples. The other inputs—the trees themselves, the land, the firm's trucks and tractors, and so on—are held fixed for now. This firm's production function shows that if the firm hires 1 worker, that worker will pick 100 bushels of apples per week. If the firm hires 2 workers, the two workers together will pick 180 bushels per week, and so on.

Figure 18.2 graphs the data on labour and output presented in Table 18.1. The number of workers is on the horizontal axis, and the amount of output is on the vertical axis. This figure illustrates the production function.

marginal product of labour
the increase in the amount of output from an additional unit of labour

One of the ten principles of economics introduced in Chapter 1 is that rational people think at the margin. This idea is the key to understanding how firms decide what quantity of labour to hire. To take a step toward this decision, the third column in Table 18.1 gives the **marginal product of labour**, the increase in the amount of output from an additional unit of labour. When the firm increases the number of

---

TABLE 18.1

How the Competitive Firm Decides How Much Labour to Hire

Labour	Output	Marginal Product of Labour	Value of the Marginal Product of Labour	Wage	Marginal Profit
L (number of workers)	Q (bushels per week)	$MPL = \Delta Q/\Delta L$ (bushels per week)	$VMPL = P \times MPL$	W	$\Delta Profit = VMPL - W$
0	0				
		100	$1000	$500	$500
1	100				
		80	800	500	300
2	180				
		60	600	500	100
3	240				
		40	400	500	−100
4	280				
		20	200	500	−300
5	300				

FIGURE 18.2

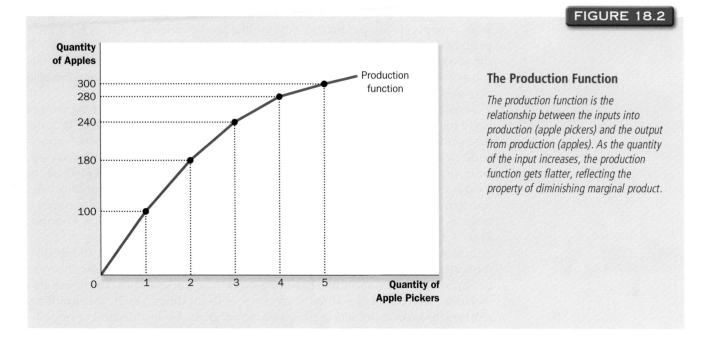

The Production Function

The production function is the relationship between the inputs into production (apple pickers) and the output from production (apples). As the quantity of the input increases, the production function gets flatter, reflecting the property of diminishing marginal product.

workers from 1 to 2, for example, the amount of apples produced rises from 100 to 180 bushels. Therefore, the marginal product of the second worker is 80 bushels.

Notice that as the number of workers increases, the marginal product of labour declines. As you may recall from Chapter 13, this property is called **diminishing marginal product.** At first, when only a few workers are hired, they pick apples from the best trees in the orchard. As the number of workers increases, additional workers have to pick from the trees with fewer apples. Hence, as more and more workers are hired, each additional worker contributes less to the production of apples. For this reason, the production function in Figure 18.2 becomes flatter as the number of workers rises.

diminishing marginal product
the property whereby the marginal product of an input declines as the quantity of the input increases

The Value of the Marginal Product and the Demand for Labour

Our profit-maximizing firm is concerned more with money than with apples. As a result, when deciding how many workers to hire, the firm considers how much profit each worker would bring in. Because profit is total revenue minus total cost, the profit from an additional worker is the worker's contribution to revenue minus the worker's wage.

To find the worker's contribution to revenue, we must convert the marginal product of labour (which is measured in bushels of apples) into the *value* of the marginal product (which is measured in dollars). We do this using the price of apples. To continue our example, if a bushel of apples sells for $10 and if an additional worker produces 80 bushels of apples, then the worker produces $800 of revenue.

The **value of the marginal product** of any input is the marginal product of that input multiplied by the market price of the output. The fourth column in Table 18.1

value of the marginal product
the marginal product of an input times the price of the output

shows the value of the marginal product of labour in our example, assuming the price of apples is $10 per bushel. Because the market price is constant for a competitive firm, the value of the marginal product (like the marginal product itself) diminishes as the number of workers rises. Economists sometimes call this column of numbers the firm's *marginal revenue product:* It is the extra revenue the firm gets from hiring an additional unit of a factor of production.

Now consider how many workers the firm will hire. Suppose that the market wage for apple pickers is $500 per week. In this case, as you see in Table 18.1, the first worker that the firm hires is profitable: The first worker yields $1000 in revenue, or $500 in profit. Similarly, the second worker yields $800 in additional revenue, or $300 in profit. The third worker produces $600 in additional revenue, or $100 in profit. After the third worker, however, hiring workers is unprofitable. The fourth worker would yield only $400 of additional revenue. Because the worker's wage is $500, hiring the fourth worker would mean a $100 reduction in profit. Thus, the firm hires only three workers.

It is instructive to consider the firm's decision graphically. Figure 18.3 graphs the value of the marginal product. This curve slopes downward because the marginal product of labour diminishes as the number of workers rises. The figure also includes a horizontal line at the market wage. To maximize profit, the firm hires workers up to the point where these two curves cross. Below this level of employment, the value of the marginal product exceeds the wage, so hiring another worker would increase profit. Above this level of employment, the value of the marginal product is less than the wage, so the marginal worker is unprofitable. Thus, *a competitive, profit-maximizing firm hires workers up to the point where the value of the marginal product of labour equals the wage.*

Having explained the profit-maximizing hiring strategy for a competitive firm, we can now offer a theory of labour demand. Recall that a firm's labour demand

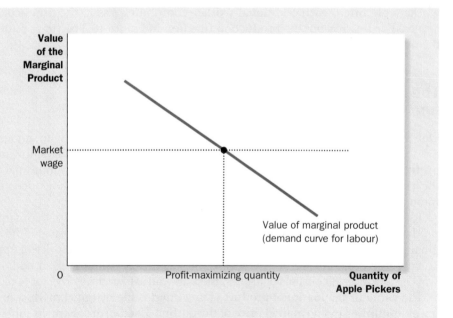

FIGURE 18.3

The Value of the Marginal Product of Labour

This figure shows how the value of the marginal product (the marginal product times the price of the output) depends on the number of workers. The curve slopes downward because of diminishing marginal product. For a competitive, profit-maximizing firm, this value-of-marginal-product curve is also the firm's labour demand curve.

FYI

INPUT DEMAND AND OUTPUT SUPPLY: TWO SIDES OF THE SAME COIN

In Chapter 14 we saw how a competitive, profit-maximizing firm decides how much of its output to sell: It chooses the quantity of output at which the price of the good equals the marginal cost of production. We have just seen how such a firm decides how much labour to hire: It chooses the quantity of labour at which the wage equals the value of the marginal product. Because the production function links the quantity of inputs to the quantity of output, you should not be surprised to learn that the firm's decision about input demand is closely linked to its decision about output supply. In fact, these two decisions are two sides of the same coin.

To see this relationship more fully, let's consider how the marginal product of labour (MPL) and marginal cost (MC) are related. Suppose an additional worker costs $500 and has a marginal product of 50 bushels of apples. In this case, producing 50 more bushels costs $500; the marginal cost of a bushel is $500/50, or $10. More generally, if W is the wage, and an extra unit of labour produces MPL units of output, then the marginal cost of a unit of output is $MC = W/MPL$.

This analysis shows that diminishing marginal product is closely related to increasing marginal cost. When our apple orchard grows crowded with workers, each additional worker adds less to the production of apples (MPL falls). Similarly, when the apple firm is producing a large quantity of apples, the orchard is already crowded with workers, so it is more costly to produce an additional bushel of apples (MC rises).

Now consider our criterion for profit maximization. We determined earlier that a profit-maximizing firm chooses the quantity of labour so that the value of the marginal product (P × MPL) equals the wage (W). We can write this mathematically as

$$P \times MPL = W$$

If we divide both sides of this equation by MPL, we obtain

$$P = W/MPL$$

We just noted that W/MPL equals marginal cost MC. Therefore, we can substitute to obtain

$$P = MC$$

This equation states that the price of the firm's output is equal to the marginal cost of producing a unit of output. *Thus, when a competitive firm hires labour up to the point at which the value of the marginal product equals the wage, it also produces up to the point at which the price equals marginal cost.* Our analysis of labour demand in this chapter is just another way of looking at the production decision we first saw in Chapter 14.

curve tells us the quantity of labour that a firm demands at any given wage. We have just seen in Figure 18.3 that the firm makes that decision by choosing the quantity of labour at which the value of the marginal product equals the wage. As a result, *the value-of-marginal-product curve is the labour demand curve for a competitive, profit-maximizing firm.*

What Causes the Labour Demand Curve to Shift?

We now understand the labour demand curve: It reflects the value of the marginal product of labour. With this insight in mind, let's consider a few of the things that might cause the labour demand curve to shift.

The Output Price   The value of the marginal product is marginal product times the price of the firm's output. Thus, when the output price changes, the value of the marginal product changes, and the labour demand curve shifts. An increase in the price of apples, for instance, raises the value of the marginal product of each worker who picks apples and, therefore, increases labour demand from the firms that supply apples. Conversely, a decrease in the price of apples reduces the value of the marginal product and decreases labour demand.

Technological Change   Between 1976 and 2000, the amount of output a typical Canadian worker produced in an hour rose by 27 percent. Why? The most important reason is technological progress: Scientists and engineers are constantly figuring out new and better ways of doing things. This has profound implications for the labour market. Technological advance raises the marginal product of labour, which in turn increases the demand for labour. Such technological advance explains persistently rising employment in the face of rising wages: Even though wages (adjusted for inflation) increased by 50 percent over the period from 1976 to 2000, firms nonetheless increased by 56 percent the amount of labour they employed.

The Supply of Other Factors   The quantity available of one factor of production can affect the marginal product of other factors. A fall in the supply of ladders, for instance, will reduce the marginal product of apple pickers and thus the demand for apple pickers. We consider this linkage among the factors of production more fully later in the chapter.

QuickQuiz   Define *marginal product of labour* and *value of the marginal product of labour.* • Describe how a competitive, profit-maximizing firm decides how many workers to hire.

THE SUPPLY OF LABOUR

Having analyzed labour demand in detail, let's turn to the other side of the market and consider labour supply. A formal model of labour supply is included in Chapter 21, where we develop the theory of household decision making. Here we discuss briefly and informally the decisions that lie behind the labour supply curve. The discussion is slightly stylized, assuming, for example, that workers are unconstrained in their choice of how many hours they work. While this is obviously not always true for everybody in the short run, individuals do have more flexibility over the hours that they work in the long run.

The Tradeoff between Work and Leisure

One of the ten principles of economics in Chapter 1 is that people face tradeoffs. Probably no tradeoff is more obvious or more important in a person's life than the tradeoff between work and leisure. The more hours you spend working, the fewer hours you have to watch TV, have dinner with friends, or pursue your favourite hobby. The tradeoff between labour and leisure lies behind the labour supply curve.

Another of the ten principles of economics is that the cost of something is what you give up to get it. What do you give up to get an hour of leisure? You give up an hour of work, which in turn means an hour of wages. Thus, if your wage is $15 per hour, the opportunity cost of an hour of leisure is $15. And when you get a raise to $20 per hour, the opportunity cost of enjoying leisure goes up.

The labour supply curve reflects how workers' decisions about the labour–leisure tradeoff respond to a change in that opportunity cost. An upward-sloping labour supply curve means that an increase in the wage induces workers to increase the quantity of labour they supply. Because time is limited, more hours of work means that workers are enjoying less leisure. That is, workers respond to the increase in the opportunity cost of leisure by taking less of it.

It is worth noting that the labour supply curve need not be upward sloping. Imagine you got that raise from $15 to $20 per hour. The opportunity cost of leisure is now greater, but you are also richer than you were before. You might decide that with your extra wealth you can now afford to enjoy more leisure. That is, at the higher wage, you might choose to work fewer hours. If so, your labour supply curve would slope backward. In Chapter 21, we discuss this possibility in terms of conflicting effects on your labour-supply decision (called the income and substitution effects). For now, we ignore the possibility of backward-sloping labour supply and assume that the labour supply curve is upward sloping.

What Causes the Labour Supply Curve to Shift?

The labour supply curve shifts whenever people change the amount they want to work at a given wage. Let's now consider some of the events that might cause such a shift.

Changes in Attitudes   In 1950, 34 percent of women were employed at paid jobs or looking for work. In 2000, the number had risen to 60 percent. There are, of course, many explanations for this development, but one of them is changing attitudes toward work. A generation or two ago, it was the norm for women to stay at home while raising children. Today, family sizes are smaller, and more mothers choose to work. The result is an increase in the supply of labour.

Changes in Alternative Opportunities   The supply of labour in any one labour market depends on the opportunities available in other labour markets. If the wage earned by pear pickers suddenly rises, some apple pickers may choose to switch occupations. The supply of labour in the market for apple pickers falls.

Immigration   Movement of workers from region to region, or country to country, is an obvious and often important source of shifts in labour supply. When immigrants come to Canada, for instance, the supply of labour in Canada increases and the supply of labour in the immigrants' home countries contracts. In fact, much of the policy debate about immigration centres on its effect on labour supply and, thereby, equilibrium in the labour market.

QuickQuiz Who has a greater opportunity cost of enjoying leisure—a janitor or a brain surgeon? Explain. Can this help explain why doctors work such long hours?

EQUILIBRIUM IN THE LABOUR MARKET

So far we have established two facts about how wages are determined in competitive labour markets:

1. The wage adjusts to balance the supply and demand for labour.
2. The wage equals the value of the marginal product of labour.

At first, it might seem surprising that the wage can do both these things at once. In fact, there is no real puzzle here, but understanding why there is no puzzle is an important step to understanding wage determination.

Figure 18.4 shows the labour market in equilibrium. The wage and the quantity of labour have adjusted to balance supply and demand. When the market is in this equilibrium, each firm has bought as much labour as it finds profitable at the equilibrium wage. That is, each firm has followed the rule for profit maximization: It has hired workers until the value of the marginal product equals the wage. Hence, the wage must equal the value of the marginal product of labour once it has brought supply and demand into equilibrium.

This brings us to an important lesson: *Any event that changes the supply or demand for labour must change the equilibrium wage and the value of the marginal product by the same amount, because these must always be equal.* To see how this works, let's consider some events that shift these curves.

FIGURE 18.4

Equilibrium in a Labour Market

Like all prices, the price of labour (the wage) depends on supply and demand. Because the demand curve reflects the value of the marginal product of labour, in equilibrium, workers receive the value of their marginal contribution to the production of goods and services.

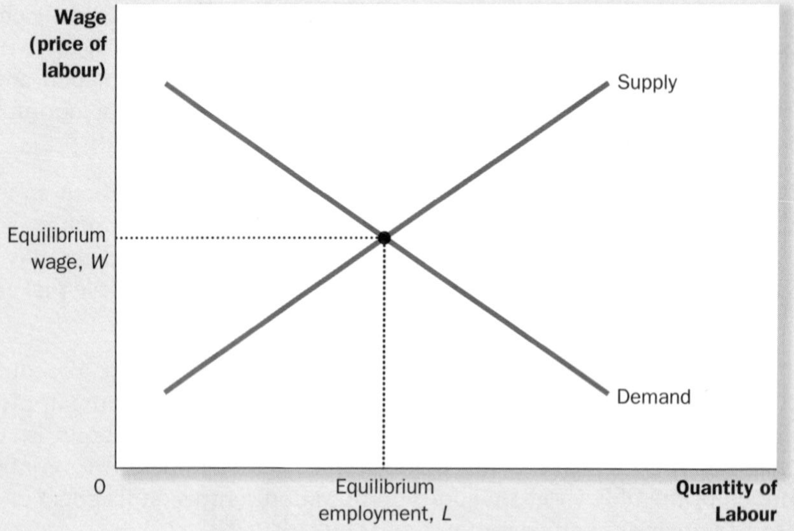

Shifts in Labour Supply

Suppose that immigration increases the number of workers willing to pick apples. As Figure 18.5 shows, the supply of labour shifts to the right from S_1 to S_2. At the initial wage W_1, the quantity of labour supplied now exceeds the quantity demanded. This surplus of labour puts downward pressure on the wage of apple pickers, and the fall in the wage from W_1 to W_2 in turn makes it profitable for firms to hire more workers. As the number of workers employed in each apple orchard rises, the marginal product of a worker falls, and so does the value of the marginal product. In the new equilibrium, both the wage and the value of the marginal product of labour are lower than they were before the influx of new workers.

An episode in Israel illustrates how a shift in labour supply can alter the equilibrium in a labour market. During most of the 1980s, many thousands of Palestinians regularly commuted from their homes in the Israeli-occupied West Bank and Gaza Strip to jobs in Israel, primarily in the construction and agriculture industries. In 1988, however, political unrest in these occupied areas induced the Israeli government to take steps that, as a byproduct, reduced this supply of workers. Curfews were imposed, work permits were checked more thoroughly, and a ban on overnight stays of Palestinians in Israel was enforced more rigorously. The economic impact of these steps was exactly as theory predicts: The number of Palestinians with jobs in Israel fell by half, while those who continued to work in Israel enjoyed wage increases of about 50 percent. With a reduced number of Palestinian workers in Israel, the value of the marginal product of the remaining workers was much higher.

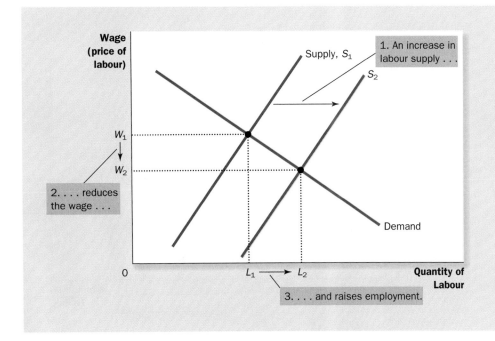

FIGURE 18.5

A Shift in Labour Supply

When labour supply increases from S_1 to S_2, perhaps because of an immigration of new workers, the equilibrium wage falls from W_1 to W_2. At this lower wage, firms hire more labour, so employment rises from L_1 to L_2. The change in the wage reflects a change in the value of the marginal product of labour: With more workers, the added output from an extra worker is smaller.

Shifts in Labour Demand

Now suppose that an increase in the popularity of apples causes their price to rise. This price increase does not change the marginal product of labour for any given number of workers, but it does raise the *value* of the marginal product. With a higher price of apples, hiring more apple pickers is now profitable. As Figure 18.6 shows, when the demand for labour shifts to the right from D_1 to D_2, the equilibrium wage rises from W_1 to W_2, and equilibrium employment rises from L_1 to L_2. Once again, the wage and the value of the marginal product of labour move together.

This analysis shows that prosperity for firms in an industry is often linked to prosperity for workers in that industry. When the price of apples rises, apple producers make greater profit, and apple pickers earn higher wages. When the price of apples falls, apple producers earn smaller profit, and apple pickers earn lower wages. This lesson is well known to workers in industries with highly volatile prices. Workers in oil fields, for instance, know from experience that their earnings are closely linked to the world price of crude oil.

From these examples, you should now have a good understanding of how wages are set in competitive labour markets. Labour supply and labour demand together determine the equilibrium wage, and shifts in the supply or demand curve for labour cause the equilibrium wage to change. At the same time, profit maximization by the firms that demand labour ensures that the equilibrium wage always equals the value of the marginal product of labour.

FIGURE 18.6

A Shift in Labour Demand

When labour demand increases from D_1 to D_2, perhaps because of an increase in the price of the firms' output, the equilibrium wage rises from W_1 to W_2, and employment rises from L_1 to L_2. Again, the change in the wage reflects a change in the value of the marginal product of labour: With a higher output price, the added output from an extra worker is more valuable.

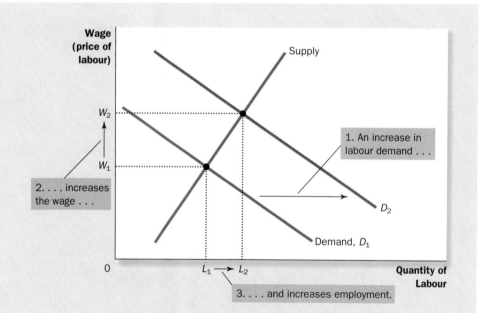

Case Study

PRODUCTIVITY AND WAGES

One of the ten principles of economics in Chapter 1 is that our standard of living depends on our ability to produce goods and services. We can now see how this principle works in the market for labour. In particular, our analysis of labour demand shows that wages equal productivity as measured by the value of the marginal product of labour. Put simply, highly productive workers are highly paid, and less productive workers are less highly paid.

This lesson is key to understanding why workers today are better off than workers in previous generations. Table 18.2 presents some data on growth in productivity and growth in wages (adjusted for inflation). From 1961 to 1999, productivity as measured by output per hour of work grew about 1.9 percent per year; at this rate, productivity doubles about every 40 years. Over this period, wages grew at a similar rate of 1.7 percent per year.

Table 18.2 also shows that, beginning around 1974, growth in productivity slowed from 3.2 to 1.2 percent per year. This 2.0-percentage-point slowdown in productivity coincided with a slowdown in wage growth of 2.8 percentage points. Because of this productivity slowdown, workers in the 1980s and 1990s did not experience the same rapid growth in living standards that their parents enjoyed. A slowdown of 2.0 percentage points might not seem large, but accumulated over many years, even a small change in a growth rate is significant. If productivity and wages had grown at the same rate since 1973 as they did previously, workers' earnings would now be about 90 percent higher than they are.

TABLE 18.2

Productivity and Wage Growth in Canada

Time Period	Growth Rate of Productivity	Growth Rate of Real Wages
1961–1999	1.9	1.7
1961–1973	3.2	3.6
1974–1999	1.2	0.8

Source: Productivity data from Statistics Canada, *Productivity Growth in Canada*, 2001, Catalogue No. 15-204 XIE, Table 2, Appendix 5. Compensation per hour calculated from the Statistics Canada CANSIM database. Growth in productivity is measured here as the annualized rate of change in value-added per hour in the business sector. Growth in real wages is measured as the annualized change in total compensation per hour in the business sector divided by the consumer price index. These productivity data measure average productivity—the quantity of output divided by the quantity of labour—rather than marginal productivity, but average and marginal productivity are thought to move closely together.

The link between productivity and wages also sheds light on international experience. Table 18.3 presents some data on productivity growth and wage growth for a representative group of countries, ranked in order of their productivity growth. Although these international data are far from precise, a close link between the two variables is apparent. In South Korea, Hong Kong, and Singapore, productivity has grown rapidly, and so have wages. In Mexico, Argentina, and Iran, productivity has fallen, and so have wages. Canada falls in the middle of the distribution. By international standards, Canadian productivity and wage growth have been neither exceptionally bad nor exceptionally good. Over the past decade, however, real wages have remained essentially unchanged.

What causes productivity and wages to vary so much over time and across countries? A complete answer to this question requires an analysis of long-run economic growth, a topic beyond the scope of this chapter. We can, however, briefly note three key determinants of productivity:

1. *Physical capital:* When workers work with a larger quantity of equipment and structures, they produce more.
2. *Human capital:* When workers are more educated, they produce more.
3. *Technological knowledge:* When workers have access to more sophisticated technologies, they produce more.

TABLE 18.3

Productivity and Wage Growth around the World, 1980–1992

Country	Growth Rate of Productivity	Growth Rate of Real Wages
South Korea	8.5	7.9
Hong Kong	5.5	4.9
Singapore	5.3	5.0
Indonesia	4.0	4.4
Japan	3.6	2.0
India	3.1	3.4
United Kingdom	2.4	2.4
Canada	1.8	0.0
United States	1.7	0.5
Brazil	0.4	−2.4
Mexico	−0.2	−3.0
Argentina	−0.9	−1.3
Iran	−1.4	−7.9

Source: World Bank, *World Development Report 1994: Infrastructure for Development* (New York: World Bank and Oxford University Press, 1994), Table 1, pp. 162–63, and Table 7, pp. 174–75. Growth in productivity is measured here as the annualized rate of change in gross national product per person from 1980 to 1992. Growth in wages is measured as the annualized change in earnings per employee in manufacturing from 1980 to 1991.

MONOPSONY

On the preceding pages, we built our analysis of the labour market with the tools of supply and demand. In doing so, we assumed that the labour market was competitive. That is, we assumed that there were many buyers of labour and many sellers of labour, so each buyer or seller had a negligible effect on the wage.

Yet imagine the labour market in a small town dominated by a single large employer. That employer can exert a large influence on the going wage, and it may well use that market power to alter the outcome. Such a market in which there is a single buyer is called a *monopsony*.

A monopsony is in many ways similar to a monopoly (a market with one seller). Recall from Chapter 15 that a monopoly firm produces less of the good than would a competitive firm; by reducing the quantity offered for sale, the monopoly firm moves along the product's demand curve, raising the price and also its profits. Similarly, a monopsony firm in a labour market hires fewer workers than would a competitive firm; by reducing the number of jobs available, the monopsony firm moves along the labour supply curve, reducing the wage it pays and raising its profits. Thus, both monopolists and monopsonists reduce economic activity in a market below the socially optimal level. In both cases, the existence of market power distorts the outcome and causes deadweight losses.

This book does not present the formal model of monopsony because, in the real world, monopsonies are rare. In most labour markets, workers have many possible employers, and firms compete with one another to attract workers. In this case, the model of supply and demand is the best one to use.

Physical capital, human capital, and technological knowledge are the ultimate sources of most of the differences in productivity, wages, and standards of living. ●

QuickQuiz   How does an immigration of workers affect labour supply, labour demand, the marginal product of labour, and the equilibrium wage?

THE OTHER FACTORS OF PRODUCTION: LAND AND CAPITAL

We have seen how firms decide how much labour to hire and how these decisions determine workers' wages. At the same time that firms are hiring workers, they are also deciding about other inputs to production. For example, our apple-producing firm might have to choose the size of its apple orchard and the number of ladders to make available to its apple pickers. We can think of the firm's factors of production as falling into three categories: labour, land, and capital.

The meaning of the terms *labour* and *land* is clear, but the definition of *capital* is somewhat tricky. Economists use the term **capital** to refer to the stock of equipment

capital
the equipment and structures used to produce goods and services

and structures used for production. That is, the economy's capital represents the accumulation of goods produced in the past that are being used in the present to produce new goods and services. For our apple firm, the capital stock includes the ladders used to climb the trees, the trucks used to transport the apples, the buildings used to store the apples, and even the trees themselves.

Equilibrium in the Markets for Land and Capital

What determines how much the owners of land and capital earn for their contribution to the production process? Before answering this question, we need to distinguish between two prices: the purchase price and the rental price. The *purchase price* of land or capital is the price a person pays to own that factor of production indefinitely. The *rental price* is the price a person pays to use that factor for a limited period of time. It is important to keep this distinction in mind because, as we will see, these prices are determined by somewhat different economic forces.

Having defined these terms, we can now apply the theory of factor demand that we developed for the labour market to the markets for land and capital. The wage is, after all, simply the rental price of labour. Therefore, much of what we have learned about wage determination applies also to the rental prices of land and capital. As Figure 18.7 illustrates, the rental price of land, shown in panel (a), and the rental price of capital, shown in panel (b), are determined by supply and

FIGURE 18.7

The Markets for Land and Capital

Supply and demand determine the compensation paid to the owners of land, as shown in panel (a), and the compensation paid to the owners of capital, as shown in panel (b). The demand for each factor, in turn, depends on the value of the marginal product of that factor.

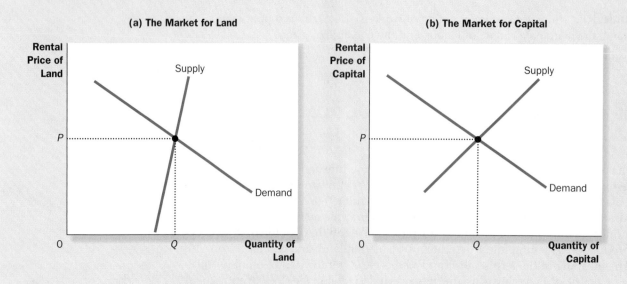

demand. Moreover, the demand for land and capital is determined just like the demand for labour. That is, when our apple-producing firm is deciding how much land and how many ladders to rent, it follows the same logic as when deciding how many workers to hire. For both land and capital, the firm increases the quantity hired until the value of the factor's marginal product equals the factor's price. Thus, the demand curve for each factor reflects the marginal productivity of that factor.

We can now explain how much income goes to labour, how much goes to landowners, and how much goes to the owners of capital. As long as the firms using the factors of production are competitive and profit-maximizing, each factor's rental price must equal the value of the marginal product for that factor. *Labour, land, and capital each earn the value of their marginal contribution to the production process.*

Now consider the purchase price of land and capital. The rental price and the purchase price are obviously related: Buyers are willing to pay more for a piece of land or capital if it produces a valuable stream of rental income. And, as we have just seen, the equilibrium rental income at any point in time equals the value of that factor's marginal product. Therefore, the equilibrium purchase price of a piece of land or capital depends on both the current value of the marginal product and the value of the marginal product expected to prevail in the future.

Linkages among the Factors of Production

We have seen that the price paid to any factor of production—labour, land, or capital—equals the value of the marginal product of that factor. The marginal product of any factor, in turn, depends on the quantity of that factor that is available. Because of diminishing marginal product, a factor in abundant supply has a low marginal product and thus a low price, and a factor in scarce supply has a high marginal product and a high price. As a result, when the supply of a factor falls, its equilibrium factor price rises.

When the supply of any factor changes, however, the effects are not limited to the market for that factor. In most situations, factors of production are used together in a way that makes the productivity of each factor dependent on the quantities of the other factors available to be used in the production process. As a result, a change in the supply of any one factor alters the earnings of all the factors.

For example, suppose a hurricane destroys many of the ladders that workers use to pick apples from the orchards. What happens to the earnings of the various factors of production? Most obviously, the supply of ladders falls and, therefore, the equilibrium rental price of ladders rises. Those owners who were lucky enough to avoid damage to their ladders now earn a higher return when they rent out their ladders to the firms that produce apples.

Yet the effects of this event do not stop at the ladder market. Because there are fewer ladders with which to work, the workers who pick apples have a smaller marginal product. Thus, the reduction in the supply of ladders reduces the demand for the labour of apple pickers, and this causes the equilibrium wage to fall.

This story shows a general lesson: An event that changes the supply of any factor of production can alter the earnings of all the factors. The change in earnings of any factor can be found by analyzing the impact of the event on the value of the marginal product of that factor.

WHAT IS CAPITAL INCOME?

Labour income is an easy concept to understand: It is the paycheque that workers receive from their employers. The income earned by capital, however, is less obvious.

In our analysis, we have been implicitly assuming that households own capital—ladders, drill presses, warehouses, and so on—and rent it to the firms that use it. This assumption has simplified our analysis of how capital owners are compensated, but it is not very realistic. In fact, most firms own the capital they use, and therefore they receive the earnings from this capital.

These earnings eventually are paid by firms to households in various ways. Some of the earnings are paid in the form of *interest* to households who have lent money to the firms, either directly by investing in company bonds, or indirectly by depositing their money in banks, which in turn lend it to businesses. Thus, when you receive interest on your bank account, that income is part of the economy's capital income.

Capital income may be distributed to households in two other ways. First, some of the earnings from capital are paid to households in the form of dividends. *Dividends* are payments by a firm to its shareholders. A shareholder is a person who has bought a share in the ownership of the firm and, therefore, is entitled to a share in the firm's profits.

Second, shareholders may receive income through the companies they own through capital gains. A *capital gain* occurs when the value of a company's stock increases. A firm does not have to pay out all of its earnings to shareholders in the form of dividends. Instead, it can retain some of those earnings and use them to buy additional capital. Although the earnings retained by the firm are not paid out to shareholders, shareholders benefit from them nonetheless. This is because retained earnings increase the amount of capital the firm owns, which increases future earnings, which increase the value of the firm's shares, which generate a capital gain.

So, in a sense, rather than renting capital to firms and receiving the capital income in the form of rental payments, households can be viewed as renting money to firms, which in turn use this money to purchase capital. The rental payments on this money take the form of interest, dividends, and capital gains.

What determines the interest rate required by debtholders and the rate of return required by shareholders? The answer to this question is beyond the scope of this chapter, but it is related to the concept of opportunity cost. Debtholders must earn interest and shareholders must earn dividends and capital gains to compensate them for the income they could have earned by investing their money elsewhere.

These institutional details are interesting and important, but they do not alter our conclusion about the income earned by the owners of capital. Capital is paid according to the value of its marginal product, regardless of whether this income is transmitted to the shareholders in the form of interest, dividends, or capital gains.

However, the fact that capital income is derived as a return on financial investments in businesses does have implications for the equilibrium determination of the rental price of capital. Canada's financial markets are very small compared with the world's financial markets, so the savings and investment decisions of Canadians have very little impact on world interest rates or rates of return. Canada's financial markets are also very open, in that Canadians can invest in companies anywhere in the world and residents of other countries are free to invest in Canadian companies.

These two market characteristics—small and open—mean that interest rates and rates of return on investments in Canadian companies are, to a large extent, independent of the amount of financial capital provided by Canadians. For a small open economy like Canada's, then, the supply curve for capital can be viewed as perfectly horizontal, or perfectly elastic, at the rental rate implied by the world interest rate, at least as a first approximation. As a result, changes in either the demand or the supply of capital in Canada have no impact on the rental price of capital.

Case Study

THE ECONOMICS OF THE BLACK DEATH

In fourteenth-century Europe, the bubonic plague wiped out about one-third of the population within a few years. This event, called the *Black Death*, provides a grisly natural experiment to test the theory of factor markets that we have just developed. Consider the effects of the Black Death on those who were lucky enough to survive. What do you think happened to the wages earned by workers and the rents earned by landowners?

To answer this question, let's examine the effects of a reduced population on the marginal product of labour and the marginal product of land. With a smaller supply of workers, the marginal product of labour rises. (This is simply diminishing marginal product working in reverse.) Thus, we would expect the Black Death to raise wages.

Because land and labour are used together in production, a smaller supply of workers also affects the market for land, the other major factor of production in medieval Europe. With fewer workers available to farm the land, an additional unit of land produced less additional output. In other words, the marginal product of land fell. Thus, we would expect the Black Death to lower rents.

In fact, both predictions are consistent with the historical evidence. Wages approximately doubled during this period, and rents declined 50 percent or more. The Black Death led to economic prosperity for the peasant classes and reduced incomes for the landed classes. ●

Workers who survived the plague were lucky in more ways than one.

QuickQuiz   What determines the income of the owners of land and capital? • How would an increase in the quantity of capital affect the incomes of those who already own capital? How would it affect the incomes of workers?

CONCLUSION

This chapter explained how labour, land, and capital are compensated for the roles they play in the production process. The theory developed here is called the *neoclassical theory of distribution.* According to the neoclassical theory, the amount paid to each factor of production depends on the supply and demand for that factor. The demand, in turn, depends on that particular factor's marginal productivity. In equilibrium, each factor of production earns the value of its marginal contribution to the production of goods and services.

The neoclassical theory of distribution is widely accepted. Most economists begin with the neoclassical theory when trying to explain how the Canadian economy's $1 trillion of income is distributed among the economy's various members. In the following two chapters, we consider the distribution of income in more detail. As you will see, the neoclassical theory provides the framework for this discussion.

Even at this point you can use the theory to answer the question that began this chapter: Why are computer programmers paid more than gas station attendants? It is because programmers can produce a good of greater market value than can a gas station attendant. People are willing to pay dearly for a good computer game, but they are willing to pay little to have their gas pumped and their windshield washed. The wages of these workers reflect the market prices of the goods they produce. If people suddenly got tired of using computers and decided to spend more time driving, the prices of these goods would change, and so would the equilibrium wages of these two groups of workers.

SUMMARY

- The economy's income is distributed in the markets for the factors of production. The three most important factors of production are labour, land, and capital.

- The demand for factors, such as labour, is a derived demand that comes from firms that use the factors to produce goods and services. Competitive, profit-maximizing firms hire each factor up to the point at which the value of the marginal product of the factor equals its price.

- The supply of labour arises from individuals' tradeoff between work and leisure. An upward-sloping labour supply curve means that people

respond to an increase in the wage by enjoying less leisure and working more hours.

- The price paid to each factor adjusts to balance the supply and demand for that factor. Because factor demand reflects the value of the marginal product of that factor, in equilibrium, each factor is compensated according to its marginal contribution to the production of goods and services.

- Because factors of production are used together, the marginal product of any one factor depends on the quantities of all factors that are available. As a result, a change in the supply of one factor alters the equilibrium earnings of all the factors.

KEY CONCEPTS

factors of production, p. 402
production function, p. 404
marginal product of
    labour, p. 404

diminishing marginal
    product, p. 405
value of the marginal
    product, p. 405

capital, p. 415

QUESTIONS FOR REVIEW

1. Explain how a firm's production function is related to its marginal product of labour, how a firm's marginal product of labour is related to the value of its marginal product, and how a firm's value of marginal product is related to its demand for labour.

2. Give two examples of events that could shift the demand for labour.

3. Give two examples of events that could shift the supply of labour.

4. Explain how the wage can adjust to balance the supply and demand for labour while simultaneously equalling the value of the marginal product of labour.

5. If the population of Canada suddenly grew because of a large immigration, what would happen to wages? What would happen to the rents earned by the owners of land and capital?

PROBLEMS AND APPLICATIONS

1. Suppose that the prime minister proposes a new law aimed at reducing heath care costs: All Canadians are to be required to eat one apple daily.
   a. How would this apple-a-day law affect the demand and equilibrium price of apples?
   b. How would the law affect the marginal product and the value of the marginal product of apple pickers?
   c. How would the law affect the demand and equilibrium wage for apple pickers?

2. Henry Ford once said: "It is not the employer who pays wages—he only handles the money. It is the product that pays wages." Explain.

3. Show the effect of each of the following events on the market for labour in the computer manufacturing industry.
   a. The government buys personal computers for all college and university students.
   b. More postsecondary students major in engineering and computer science.
   c. Computer firms build new manufacturing plants.

4. Your enterprising uncle opens a sandwich shop that employs 7 people. The employees are paid $6 per hour, and a sandwich sells for $3. If your uncle is maximizing his profit, what is the value of the marginal product of the last worker he hired? What is that worker's marginal product?

5. Imagine a firm that hires two types of workers—some with computer skills and some without. If technology advances so that computers become more useful to the firm, what happens to the marginal product of the two types? What happens to equilibrium wages? Explain, using appropriate diagrams.

6. Suppose a freeze in British Columbia destroys part of the apple crop.
   a. Explain what happens to the price of apples and the marginal product of apple pickers as a result of the freeze. Can you say what happens to the demand for apple pickers? Why or why not?

   b. Suppose the price of apples doubles and the marginal product falls by 30 percent. What happens to the equilibrium wage of apple pickers?
   c. Suppose the price of apples rises by 30 percent and the marginal product falls by 50 percent. What happens to the equilibrium wage of apple pickers?

7. During the 1980s and 1990s Canada experienced a significant inflow of capital from other countries.
   a. Using a diagram of the Canadian capital market, show the effect of this inflow on the rental price of capital in Canada and on the quantity of capital in use.
   b. Using a diagram of the Canadian labour market, show the effect of the capital inflow on the average wage paid to Canadian workers.

8. Suppose that labour is the only input used by a perfectly competitive firm that can hire workers for $50 per day. The firm's production function is as follows:

Days of Labour	Units of Output
0	0
1	7
2	13
3	19
4	25
5	28
6	29

Each unit of output sells for $10. Plot the firm's demand for labour. How many days of labour should the firm hire? Show this point on your graph.

9. (This question is challenging.) This chapter has assumed that labour is supplied by individual workers acting competitively. In some markets, however, the supply of labour is determined by a union of workers.
   a. Explain why the situation faced by a labour union may resemble the situation faced by a monopoly firm.

b. The goal of a monopoly firm is to maximize profits. Is there an analogous goal for labour unions?

c. Now extend the analogy between monopoly firms and unions. How do you suppose that the wage set by a union compares to the

wage in a competitive market? How do you suppose employment differs in the two cases?

d. What other goals might unions have that make unions different from monopoly firms?

INTERNET RESOURCES

The Centre for the Study of Living Standards is a nonprofit, national, independent organization that seeks to contribute, through research, to a better understanding of trends in and determinants of productivity, living standards, and economic and social well-being. Its website provides several links to research on productivity in Canada, including an annual assessment of personal income and productivity trends in Canada and the United States: http://www.csls.ca.

http://   For more study tools, please visit http://www.mankiw3e.nelson.com.

© CHRIS BAKER/STONE

19

EARNINGS AND DISCRIMINATION

In Canada today, the typical physician earns about $200 000 per year, the typical police officer about $50 000, and the typical farmworker about $20 000. These examples illustrate the large differences in earnings that are so common in our economy. They also explain why some people live in mansions, ride in limousines, and vacation on the French Riviera, while other people live in small apartments, ride the bus, and vacation in their own backyards.

Why do earnings vary so much from person to person? Chapter 18, which developed the basic neoclassical theory of the labour market, offers an answer to this question. There we saw that wages are governed by labour supply and labour demand. Labour demand, in turn, reflects the marginal productivity of labour. In equilibrium, each worker is paid the value of his or her marginal contribution to the economy's production of goods and services.

This theory of the labour market, though widely accepted by economists, is only the beginning of the story. To understand the wide variation in earnings that we observe, we must go beyond this general framework and examine more precisely what determines the supply and demand for different types of labour. That is our goal in this chapter.

Learning Objectives

In this chapter, you will …

- Examine how wages compensate for differences in job characteristics
- Learn and compare the human-capital and signalling theories of education
- Examine why in some occupations a few super-stars earn tremendous incomes
- Learn why wages rise above the level that balances supply and demand
- Consider why it is difficult to measure the impact of discrimination on wages
- See when market forces can and cannot provide a natural remedy for discrimination
- Consider the debate over comparable worth as a system for setting wages

SOME DETERMINANTS OF EQUILIBRIUM WAGES

Workers differ from one another in many ways. Jobs also have differing characteristics—both in terms of the wage they pay and in terms of their nonmonetary attributes. In this section we consider how the characteristics of workers and jobs affect labour supply, labour demand, and equilibrium wages.

Compensating Differentials

When a worker is deciding whether to take a job, the wage is only one of many job attributes that the worker takes into account. Some jobs are easy, fun, and safe; others are hard, dull, and dangerous. The better the job as gauged by these nonmonetary characteristics, the more people there are who are willing to do the job at any given wage. In other words, the supply of labour for easy, fun, and safe jobs is greater than the supply of labour for hard, dull, and dangerous jobs. As a result, "good" jobs will tend to have lower equilibrium wages than "bad" jobs.

For example, imagine you are looking for a summer job in a local beach community. Two kinds of jobs are available. You can take a job as a beach-badge checker, or you can take a job as a garbage collector. The beach-badge checkers take leisurely strolls along the beach during the day and check to make sure the tourists have bought the required beach permits. The garbage collectors wake up before dawn to drive dirty, noisy trucks around town to pick up garbage. Which job would you want? Most people would prefer the beach job if the wages were the same. To induce people to become garbage collectors, the town has to offer higher wages to garbage collectors than to beach-badge checkers.

Economists use the term **compensating differential** to refer to a difference in wages that arises from nonmonetary characteristics of different jobs. Compensating differentials are prevalent in the economy. Here are some examples:

compensating differential
a difference in wages that arises to offset the nonmonetary characteristics of different jobs

- Coal miners are paid more than other workers with similar levels of education. Their higher wage compensates them for the dirty and dangerous nature of coal mining, as well as the long-term health problems that coal miners experience.
- Workers who work the night shift at factories are paid more than similar workers who work the day shift. The higher wage compensates them for having to work at night and sleep during the day, a lifestyle that most people find undesirable.
- Professors are paid less than lawyers and doctors, who have similar amounts of education. Professors' lower wages compensate them for the great intellectual and personal satisfaction that their jobs offer.

Human Capital

As we discussed in the previous chapter, the word *capital* usually refers to the economy's stock of equipment and structures. The capital stock includes the farmer's tractor, the manufacturer's factory, and the teacher's chalkboard. The essence of capital is that it is a factor of production that itself has been produced.

There is another type of capital that, while less tangible than physical capital, is just as important to the economy's production. **Human capital** is the accumulation

human capital
the accumulation of investments in people, such as education and on-the-job training

of investments in people. The most important type of human capital is education. Like all forms of capital, education represents an expenditure of resources at one point in time to raise productivity in the future. But, unlike an investment in other forms of capital, an investment in education is tied to a specific person, and this linkage is what makes it human capital.

Not surprisingly, workers with more human capital on average earn more than those with less human capital. University graduates in Canada, for example, earn about 45 percent more than workers who end their education with a high-school diploma. This large difference has been documented in many countries around the world. It tends to be even larger in less developed countries, where educated workers are in scarce supply.

It is easy to see why education raises wages from the perspective of supply and demand. Firms—the demanders of labour—are willing to pay more for the highly educated because highly educated workers have higher marginal products. Workers—the suppliers of labour—are willing to pay the cost of becoming educated only if there is a reward for doing so. In essence, the difference in wages between highly educated workers and less educated workers may be considered a compensating differential for the cost of becoming educated.

Case Study

THE VALUE OF SKILLS

"The rich get richer and the poor get poorer." Like many adages, this one is not always true, but has it been true in Canada? We'll talk more about income distribution in the next chapter, but at this point we will address what many feel is an important determinant of the distribution of income in an economy: the wage gap between workers with high skills and workers with low skills. Numerous studies have documented and tried to explain movements in this wage gap, or "premium," over time.

Figure 19.1 (p. 426) shows the ratio of the median earnings of university graduates to the median earnings of high-school graduates without any additional education; the data are for males in Canada and the United States from 1981 to 1999. The figure shows that in the United States the ratio has grown steadily over time. In 1981, U.S. university graduates earned about 33 percent more than high-school graduates; in 1999 they earned about 77 percent more. The situation has been somewhat different in Canada. Although the relative wages of Canadian university graduates are clearly higher than the wages of high-school graduates, the wage premium has not grown over time. In 1981, Canadian university graduates earned about 40 percent more than high-school graduates; in 1999 they earned about 35 percent more.

What explains these different trends in the earnings gap between skilled and unskilled workers? No one knows the full explanation, but economists have proposed various hypotheses. One explanation relies on the supply and demand of skilled labour relative to the supply and demand of unskilled labour in the two countries to explain differences in relative wages.

FIGURE 19.1

Ratio of Earnings of University Graduates to High-School Graduates, 1981–1999

Source: Adapted from J. Burbidge, L. MaGee, and A. Robb, "The Education Premium in Canada and the United States," *Canadian Public Policy*, 28:2, 2002.

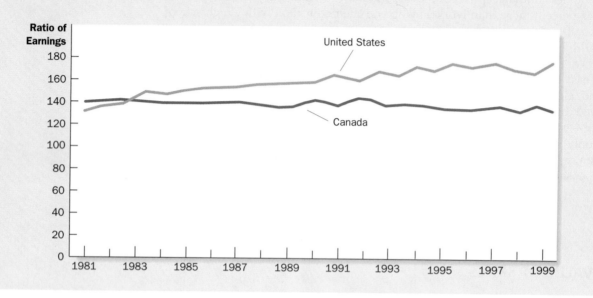

One explanation for the rising wage premium in the United States is that demand for skilled labour there increased more quickly than the relative supply. With the relative demand curve for skilled labour shifting outward faster than the relative supply curve, there has been a corresponding increase in relative wages, which in turn has contributed to greater wage inequality in the United States.

Economists have offered two hypotheses for the U.S. trend. The first explanation is that international trade has increased the relative demand for skilled labour. In recent years, the amount of trade between the United States and other countries has increased dramatically. Because unskilled labour is plentiful and cheap in many foreign countries, the United States tends to import goods produced with unskilled labour and to export goods produced with skilled labour. Thus, the expansion in international trade has increased the domestic (relative) demand for skilled labour.

The second hypothesis is that changes in technology have altered the relative demand for skilled and unskilled labour. Consider the growing use of computers. Computers raise the demand for skilled workers who can use the new machines and reduce the demand for unskilled workers whose jobs are replaced by computers. For example, many companies now rely more on computer databases and less on filing cabinets to keep business records. This change raises the demand for computer programmers and reduces the demand for filing clerks. Thus, with increased computerization, the demand for skilled labour rises and the demand for unskilled labour falls.

Economists have found it difficult to gauge the validity of these two hypotheses. It is possible, perhaps even likely, that both are true: Increasing international trade and technological change may both be responsible for the growing U.S. wage gap.

But why haven't we observed a similar increase in the relative earnings of Canadian skilled workers? Canada's trade with other countries has also grown significantly, and Canadian companies have access to the same technologies as U.S. companies. Yet the wage gap in Canada has remained relatively constant over time. Are Canadian labour markets not subject to similar influences?

This question was addressed by three economists (Kevin Murphy, Craig Riddell, and Paul Romer) in a paper published in the book *General Purpose Technologies and Economic Growth* (MIT Press, 1998). They find no evidence that the relative demand for skilled labour is shifting at a greater rate in the United States than it is in Canada. As it did in the United States, the relative demand for skilled labour in Canada increased at a steady rate over the period studied. The explanation for the different trends in the relative wages of skilled workers in the two countries, then, must lie on the supply side of the labour market.

Murphy, Riddell, and Romer find that the relative supply of skilled labour has increased faster in Canada than it has in the United States. Indeed, the relative supply of skilled labour has roughly kept pace with the relative demand for skilled labour over the period studied. As a result, the gap between the earnings of skilled workers and the earnings of unskilled workers has remained roughly constant. In short, change in the relative supply of skilled workers is an important determinant of variations in relative wages both over time and across the two countries.

This finding has important implications for government policy, particularly policy responses to the possibility of growing wage inequality brought about by international trade and technological change. It seems that the government can more readily influence the relative supply of skilled workers than the relative demand through policies related to things like education and training. For example, if the government introduces policies that raise the educational level of workers, it simultaneously increases the relative supply of skilled workers and lowers the relative supply of less skilled workers. As Murphy, Riddell, and Romer put it, "Educational subsidies can therefore have a doubly powerful effect on the relative supply." ●

Ability, Effort, and Chance

Why do NHL hockey players get paid more than those in the minor leagues? Certainly, the higher wage is not a compensating differential. Playing in the NHL is not a less pleasant task than playing in the minor leagues; in fact, the opposite is true. The NHL does not require more years of schooling or more experience. To a large extent, players in the NHL earn more just because they have greater natural ability.

Natural ability is important for workers in all occupations. Because of heredity and upbringing, people differ in their physical and mental attributes. Some people are strong, others weak. Some people are smart, others less so. Some people are outgoing, others awkward in social situations. These and many other personal characteristics determine how productive workers are and, therefore, play a role in determining the wages they earn.

Closely related to ability is effort. Some people work hard, others are lazy. We should not be surprised to find that those who work hard are more productive and earn higher wages. To some extent, firms reward workers directly by paying people on the basis of what they produce. Salespeople, for instance, are often paid as a percentage of the sales they make. At other times, hard work is rewarded less directly in the form of a higher annual salary or a bonus.

Chance also plays a role in determining wages. If a person attended a trade school to learn how to repair televisions with vacuum tubes and then found this skill was made obsolete by the invention of solid-state electronics, he or she would end up earning a low wage compared to others with similar years of training. The low wage of this worker is due to chance—a phenomenon that economists recognize but do not shed much light on.

How important are ability, effort, and chance in determining wages? It is hard to say, because ability, effort, and chance are hard to measure. But indirect evidence suggests that they are very important. When labour economists study wages, they relate a worker's wage to those variables that can be measured—years of schooling, years of experience, age, and job characteristics. Although all of these measured variables affect a worker's wage as theory predicts, they account for less than half of the variation in wages in our economy. Because so much of the variation in wages is left unexplained, omitted variables, including ability, effort, and chance, must play an important role.

Case Study

THE BENEFITS OF BEAUTY

People differ in many ways. One difference is in how attractive they are. The actor Brad Pitt, for instance, is a handsome man. In part for this reason, his movies attract large audiences. Not surprisingly, the large audiences mean a large income for Pitt.

How prevalent are the economic benefits of beauty? Labour economists Daniel Hamermesh and Jeff Biddle tried to answer this question in a study published in the December 1994 issue of *The American Economic Review*. Hamermesh and Biddle examined data from surveys of individuals in the United States and Canada. The interviewers who conducted the survey were asked to rate each respondent's physical appearance. Hamermesh and Biddle then examined how much the wages of the respondents depended on the standard determinants—education, experience, and so on—and how much they depended on physical appearance.

Hamermesh and Biddle found that beauty pays. People who are deemed to be more attractive than average earn 5 percent more than people of average looks.

Good looks pay.

People of average looks earn 5 to 10 percent more than people considered less attractive than average. Similar results were found for men and women.

What explains these differences in wages? There are several ways to interpret the "beauty premium."

One interpretation is that good looks are themselves a type of innate ability determining productivity and wages. Some people are born with the attributes of a movie star; other people are not. Good looks are useful in any job in which workers present themselves to the public—such as acting, sales, and waiting on tables. In this case, an attractive worker is more valuable to the firm than an unattractive worker. The firm's willingness to pay more to attractive workers reflects its customers' preferences.

A second interpretation is that reported beauty is an indirect measure of other types of ability. How attractive a person appears depends on more than just heredity. It also depends on dress, hairstyle, personal demeanour, and other attributes that a person can control. Perhaps a person who successfully projects an attractive image in a survey interview is more likely to be an intelligent person who succeeds at other tasks as well.

A third interpretation is that the beauty premium is a type of discrimination, a topic to which we return later. ●

An Alternative View of Education: Signalling

Earlier we discussed the human-capital view of education, according to which schooling raises workers' wages because it makes them more productive. Although this view is widely accepted, some economists have proposed an alternative theory, which emphasizes that firms use educational attainment as a way of sorting between high-ability and low-ability workers. According to this alternative view, when people earn a college or university degree, for instance, they do not become more productive, but they do *signal* their high ability to prospective employers. Because it is easier for high-ability people to earn a college or university degree than it is for low-ability people, more high-ability people get postsecondary degrees. As a result, it is rational for firms to interpret a postsecondary degree as a signal of ability.

The signalling theory of education is similar to the signalling theory of advertising discussed in Chapter 17. In the signalling theory of advertising, the advertisement itself contains no real information, but the firm signals the quality of its product to consumers by its willingness to spend money on advertising. In the signalling theory of education, schooling has no real productivity benefit, but the worker signals his innate productivity to employers by his willingness to spend years at school. In both cases, an action is being taken not for its intrinsic benefit but because the willingness to take that action conveys private information to someone observing it.

Thus, we now have two views of education: the human-capital theory and the signalling theory. Both views can explain why better-educated workers tend to earn more than less-educated workers. According to the human-capital view, education makes workers more productive; according to the signalling view, education is correlated with natural ability. But the two views have radically different

IN THE NEWS

ARE ELITE COLLEGES WORTH THE COST?

Economist Alan Krueger teaches at Princeton University, one of the most expensive schools in the United States. According to his research, however, his students would do just as well attending a less expensive school.

Children Smart Enough to Get into Elite Schools May Not Need to Bother
By Alan B. Krueger

Your son or daughter has just been accepted to both the University of Pennsylvania and to Penn State. The deadline for decision is May 1. Where should he or she go?

Many factors should be considered, of course, but lots of parents and stu-dents are particularly interested in the potential economic payoff from higher education. Until recently, there was a consensus among economists that stu-dents who attend more selective col-leges—ones with tougher admissions standards—land better paying jobs as a result. Having smart, motivated class-mates and a prestigious degree were thought to enhance learning and give students access to job networks.

But is it true?

A study that I conducted with Stacy Dale of the Andrew W. Mellon Founda-tion, "Estimating the Payoff to Attending a More Selective College" (available online at http://papers.nber.org), has unin-tentionally undermined this consensus.

It is easy to see how one could think that elite colleges enhance their gradu-ates' earnings. According to the College and Beyond Survey, data collected by the Mellon Foundation, the average student who entered a highly selective college

predictions for the effects of policies that aim to increase educational attainment. According to the human-capital view, increasing educational levels for all workers would raise all workers' productivity and thereby their wages. According to the signalling view, education does not enhance productivity, so raising all workers' educational levels would not affect wages.

Most likely, truth lies somewhere between these two extremes. The benefits to education are probably a combination of the productivity-enhancing effects of human capital and the productivity-revealing effects of signalling. The open ques-tion is the relative size of these two effects.

The Superstar Phenomenon

Although most singers earn very little and often have to take other jobs to support themselves, singer Sarah McLachlan has earned millions of dollars making music. Similarly, although most people who play hockey do it for free as a hobby, Mats Sundin earns millions as an NHL hockey player with the Toronto Maple Leafs. Sarah McLachlan and Mats Sundin are superstars in their fields, and their great public appeal is reflected in high incomes.

like Yale, Swarthmore or the University of Pennsylvania in 1976, earned $92,000 in 1995. The average student from a moderately selective college, like Penn State, Denison or Tulane, earned $22,000 less.

The problem with this comparison is that students who attend more selective colleges are likely to have higher earnings regardless of where they attend college for the very reasons that they were admitted to the more selective colleges in the first place.

Trying to address the problem, earlier studies compared students with similar standardized test scores and grade point averages who attended more and less selective schools. But this approach takes account of much less information than admissions committees see. There is no guarantee that all the relevant differences among students have been held constant.

This problem is known as selection bias. More selective schools accept students with greater earnings potential, and students with greater earnings potential are more likely to apply to more selective schools.

To overcome the problem, Ms. Dale and I restricted the comparison to students who applied to and were accepted by comparable colleges. Some students chose more selective schools; some less selective ones. . . .

Our research found that earnings were unrelated to the selectivity of the college that students had attended among those who had comparable options. For example, the average earnings for the 519 students who were accepted by both moderately selective (average College Board scores of 1,000 to 1,099) and highly selective schools (average scores greater than 1,275) varied little, no matter which type of college they attended.

One group of students, however, clearly benefited from attending a highly selective college: those from lower-income families—defined approximately as the bottom quarter of families who send children to college. For them, attending a more selective school increased earnings significantly. . . .

My advice to students: Don't believe that the only school worth attending is one that would not admit you. That you go to college is more important than *where* you go. Find a school whose academic strengths match your interests and which devotes resources to instruction in those fields. Recognize that your own motivation, ambition, and talents will determine your success more than the college name on your diploma.

My advice to elite colleges: Recognize that the most disadvantaged students benefit most from your instruction. Set financial aid and admission policies accordingly.

Source: *The New York Times*, April 27, 2000, p. C2. © 2000 by The New York Times Co. Reprinted by permission.

Why do Sarah McLachlan and Mats Sundin earn so much? It is not surprising that there are differences in incomes within occupations. Good carpenters earn more than mediocre carpenters, and good plumbers earn more than mediocre plumbers. People vary in ability and effort, and these differences lead to differences in income. Yet the best carpenters and plumbers do not earn the many millions that are common among the best performers and athletes. What explains the difference?

To understand the tremendous incomes of Sarah McLachlan and Mats Sundin, we must examine the special features of the markets in which they sell their services. Superstars arise in markets that have two characteristics:

1. Every customer in the market wants to enjoy the good supplied by the best producer.
2. The good is produced with a technology that makes it possible for the best producer to supply every customer at low cost.

If Sarah McLachlan is one of the best singers around, then everyone will want to buy her next CD; buying twice as many CDs by a singer half as good is not a good substitute. Moreover, it is *possible* for everyone to enjoy the singing of Sarah

McLachlan. Because it is easy to make multiple copies of a CD, Sarah McLachlan can provide her service to millions of people simultaneously. Similarly, because hockey games are broadcast on television, millions of fans can enjoy the extraordinary athletic skills of Mats Sundin.

We can now see why there are no superstar carpenters and plumbers. Other things equal, everyone prefers to employ the best carpenter, but a carpenter, unlike a musician, can provide his services to only a limited number of customers. Although the best carpenter will be able to command a somewhat higher wage than the average carpenter, the average carpenter will still be able to earn a good living.

Above-Equilibrium Wages: Minimum-Wage Laws, Unions, and Efficiency Wages

Most analyses of wage differences among workers are based on the equilibrium model of the labour market—that is, wages are assumed to adjust to balance labour supply and labour demand. But this assumption does not always apply. For some workers, wages are set above the level that brings supply and demand into equilibrium. Let's consider three reasons why this might be so.

One reason for above-equilibrium wages is minimum-wage laws, as we first saw in Chapter 6. Most workers in the economy are not affected by these laws because their equilibrium wages are well above the legal minimum. But for some workers, especially the least skilled and experienced, minimum-wage laws raise wages above the level they would earn in an unregulated labour market.

union
a worker association that bargains with employers over wages and working conditions

A second reason that wages might rise above their equilibrium level is the market power of labour unions. A **union** is a worker association that bargains with employers over wages and working conditions. Unions often raise wages above the level that would prevail without a union, perhaps because they can threaten to withhold labour from the firm by calling a **strike**. Studies suggest that union workers earn about 10 to 20 percent more than similar nonunion workers.

strike
the organized withdrawal of labour from a firm by a union

A third reason for above-equilibrium wages is suggested by the theory of **efficiency wages.** This theory holds that a firm can find it profitable to pay high wages because doing so increases the productivity of its workers. In particular, high wages may reduce worker turnover, increase worker effort, and raise the quality of workers who apply for jobs at the firm. If this theory is correct, then some firms may choose to pay their workers more than they would normally earn.

efficiency wages
above-equilibrium wages paid by firms in order to increase worker productivity

Above-equilibrium wages, whether caused by minimum-wage laws, unions, or efficiency wages, have similar effects on the labour market. In particular, pushing a wage above the equilibrium level raises the quantity of labour supplied and reduces the quantity of labour demanded. The result is a surplus of labour, or unemployment. The study of unemployment and the public policies aimed to deal with it is usually considered a topic within macroeconomics, so it goes beyond the scope of this chapter. But it would be a mistake to ignore these issues completely when analyzing earnings. Although most wage differences can be understood while maintaining the assumption of equilibrium in the labour market, above-equilibrium wages play a role in some cases.

QuickQuiz Define *compensating differential* and give an example. • Give two reasons why more-educated workers earn more than less-educated workers.

THE ECONOMICS OF DISCRIMINATION

Another source of differences in wages is discrimination. **Discrimination** occurs when the marketplace offers different opportunities to similar individuals who differ only by race, ethnic group, sex, age, or other personal characteristics. Discrimination reflects some people's prejudice against certain groups in society. Although discrimination is an emotionally charged topic that often generates heated debate, economists try to study the topic objectively in order to separate myth from reality.

discrimination
the offering of different opportunities to similar individuals who differ only by race, ethnic group, sex, age, or other personal characteristics

Measuring Labour-Market Discrimination

How much does discrimination in labour markets affect the earnings of different groups of people? This question is important, but answering it is not easy.

It might seem natural to gauge the amount of discrimination in labour markets by looking at the average wages of different groups. For example, Canadian studies show that women who are members of ethnic minorities receive lower wages than white women and that men who are members of ethnic minorities are paid less than white men. The average wage of female workers is about 80 percent of the average wage of male workers. Recent studies have found that Aboriginal people living off reserves earn about 10 percent less than non-Aboriginal people. There is also some evidence that earnings differences exist among workers of different language origins. In particular, some studies find a significant unilingual-francophone earnings disadvantage, although recent evidence suggests that the size of the disadvantage is decreasing. These wage differentials are sometimes presented in political debates as evidence that many employers discriminate against minority groups and women.

Yet there is an obvious problem with this approach. Even in a labour market that is free of discrimination, different people earn different wages. People differ in the amount of human capital they have and in the kinds of work they are able and willing to do. People also differ in the amount of experience they have and the extent to which that experience is continuous or uninterrupted. The wage differences we observe in the economy may be, to a large extent, attributable to the determinants of equilibrium wages we discussed in the previous section. Simply observing differences in wages among broad groups—minorities and nonminorities, women and men—tells us little about the prevalence of discrimination.

Human capital is particularly important. The proportion of individuals with high-school, college, and university degrees differs substantially across various groups. For example, the proportion of white males and females with high-school, college, and university degrees in Canada exceeds the proportion of Aboriginal people with these degrees. Moreover, a greater proportion of males than females have college and university degrees. With the sizable wage gap between skilled and unskilled labour discussed earlier in this chapter, no doubt some of the wage differences between groups can be attributed to differences in education levels.

Differences in human capital may themselves be a function of discrimination of a more subtle form. "Pre-market differences" in productive characteristics, such as schooling, may be influenced by various social factors, and these social influences may themselves be the result of systemic pre-market discrimination that affects people's choices and opportunities. For example, for many years schools directed girls away from science and math courses even though these subjects may have had greater value in the marketplace than some of the alternatives.

Human capital acquired in the form of job experience can also help explain wage differences. In particular, women tend to have less job experience on average than men. One reason is that female labour-force participation has increased over the past several decades. Because of this historic change, the average female worker today is younger than the average male worker. In addition, women are more likely to interrupt their careers to raise children. For both reasons, the experience of the average female worker is less than the experience of the average male worker. (Of course, this still doesn't explain the wage gap between women and men of the same age and with the same experience.)

Yet another source of wage differences is compensating differentials. Some analysts suggest that women choose jobs that are more compatible with the disproportionate child-care burden that they bear, the latter fact being well supported by survey data. Women may opt for jobs that have, for example, more flexible hours, less mandatory overtime, and less travel, all of which may add up to lower wages. For example, women are more likely to be administrative assistants, and men are more likely to be truck drivers. The relative wages for these jobs depend in part on the working conditions of each job. Because these nonmonetary aspects are hard to measure, it is difficult to gauge the practical importance of compensating differentials in explaining the wage differences that we observe. As such, it is difficult to say whether this "occupational segregation" is a matter of choice or is due to pre-market discrimination.

In the end, the study of wage differences among groups does not establish any clear conclusion about the prevalence of discrimination in Canadian labour markets. Most economists believe that some of the observed wage differentials are attributable to discrimination, but there is no consensus about how much. The only conclusion about which economists are in consensus is a negative one: *Because the differences in average wages among groups in part reflect differences in human capital and job characteristics, they do not by themselves say anything about how much discrimination there is in the labour market.*

Discrimination by Employers

Let's now turn from measurement to the economic forces that lie behind discrimination in labour markets. If one group in society receives a lower wage than another group, even after controlling for human capital and job characteristics, who is to blame for this differential?

The answer is not obvious. It might seem natural to blame employers for discriminatory wage differences. After all, employers make the hiring decisions that determine labour demand and wages. If some groups of workers earn lower wages than they should, then it seems that employers are responsible. Yet many economists are skeptical of this easy answer. They believe that competitive, market economies provide a natural antidote to employer discrimination. That antidote is called the profit motive.

Imagine an economy in which workers are differentiated by their hair colour. Blondes and brunettes have the same skills, experience, and work ethic. Yet, because of discrimination, employers prefer not to hire workers with blonde hair.

Thus, the demand for blondes is lower than it otherwise would be. As a result, blondes earn a lower wage than brunettes.

How long can this wage differential persist? In this economy, there is an easy way for a firm to beat out its competitors: It can hire blonde workers. By hiring blondes, a firm pays lower wages and thus has lower costs than firms that hire brunettes. Over time, more and more "blonde" firms enter the market to take advantage of this cost advantage. The existing "brunette" firms have higher costs and, therefore, begin to lose money when faced with the new competitors. These losses induce the brunette firms to go out of business. Eventually, the entry of blonde firms and the exit of brunette firms cause the demand for blonde workers to rise and the demand for brunette workers to fall. This process continues until the wage differential disappears.

Put simply, business owners who care only about making money are at an advantage when competing against those who also care about discriminating. As a result, firms that do not discriminate tend to replace those that do. In this way, competitive markets have a natural remedy for employer discrimination.

Case Study

EXPLAINING THE GENDER WAGE GAP

Tables 19.1 and 19.2 illustrate ratios of female to male earnings in Canada by education, industry, and occupation for 1997. Note some interesting details in these tables. Table 19.1 shows that although the overall ratio is 80.3 percent, the ratio tends to increase (the wage gap declines) with education. For example, for people with a high-school diploma, the ratio is 78.4 percent; for people with a university degree, the ratio is 84.5 percent. Table 19.2 (p. 436) shows that there is quite a bit of variation in the ratio across industries and occupations.

TABLE 19.1

Ratio of Female to Male Earnings by Education, 1997

Education	Female-to-Male Earnings Ratio
Less than high school	69.1%
High school	78.4
Incomplete postsecondary	80.5
Postsecondary diploma/certificate	79.4
Postsecondary degree	84.5
Overall	80.3

Source: Marie Drolet, "The Persistent Gap: New Evidence on the Canadian Gender Wage Gap," 2001, Analytical Studies Branch—Research Paper Series, Statistics Canada, Catalogue No. 11F0019MIE2001157, Table 5.

TABLE 19.2

Ratio of Female to Male Earnings by Industry and Occupation, 1997

Source: Marie Drolet, "The Persistent Gap: New Evidence on the Canadian Gender Wage Gap," 2001, Analytical Studies Branch—Research Paper Series, Statistics Canada, Catalogue No. 11F0019MIE2001157, Table 7.

Industry	Ratio	Occupation	Ratio
Agriculture/fishing	77.6	Professional/manager	78.9
Forestry/mining	93.9	Natural or social sciences	83.1
Construction	73.2	Clerical	86.7
Manufacturing	72.8	Sales	66.4
Business services	92.2	Services	68.0
Distribution services	71.3	Primary, processing, machinery	65.9
Consumer services	74.4	Construction	69.6
Public services	83.0	Other	86.7

As discussed previously, unadjusted (gross) data can be misleading. The size and variability of the earnings gap across age groups, educational levels, and occupations suggest that many factors are at work, and it is important to attempt to identify and control for those factors. Economists typically do this by using data on individual workers and accounting for individual characteristics that would be expected to influence earnings: education, experience, occupation or industry, hours of work, and so on. Statistical techniques are then used to divide the gross female–male earnings gap into two components: the part that is explained by differences in individual worker characteristics, and the part that is unexplained. The unexplained component is typically attributed to discrimination.

An example of this approach, based on a recent Statistics Canada study, is shown in Table 19.3. This table shows the percentage of the female–male wage gap that is explained by differences in various worker characteristics and the percentage that is then left unexplained. Fifty-one percent of the wage gap is unexplained and could therefore be attributed to discrimination of some kind. Of the factors that help to explain the wage gap, the most important are the industry that a person works in, the person's occupation, and his or her full-year, full-time equivalent (FYFTE) on-the-job experience. ●

Discrimination by Customers and Governments

Although the profit motive is a strong force acting to eliminate discriminatory wage differentials, there are limits to its corrective abilities. Here we consider two of the most important limits: *customer preferences* and *government policies.*

To see how customer preferences for discrimination can affect wages, consider again our imaginary economy with blondes and brunettes. Suppose that restaurant owners discriminate against blondes when hiring servers. As a result, blonde servers earn lower wages than brunette servers. In this case, a restaurant could open up with blonde servers and charge lower prices. If customers cared only about the quality and price of their meals, the discriminatory firms would be driven out of business, and the wage differential would disappear.

TABLE 19.3

Fraction of the Female-to-Male Wage Gap Explained by Various Factors

Source: Marie Drolet, "The Persistent Gap: New Evidence on the Canadian Gender Wage Gap," 2001, Analytical Studies Branch—Research Paper Series, Statistics Canada, Catalogue No. 11F0019MIE2001157, Tables 8 and 9.

Factors Explaining Gap	Fraction of Gap Explained
Education	4.5
FYFTE (see note)	10.1
Tenure	2.8
Age of youngest family member	0.7
Marital status	0.8
Part-time status	3.6
Region	0.0
Urban size	−0.6
Union status	0.8
Firm size	0.9
Duties	4.3
Influence on budget and staffing decisions	1.3
Industry	11.2
Occupation	8.6
Total explained	49.0
Total unexplained	51.0

FYFTE is full-year, full-time equivalent experience.

On the other hand, it is possible that customers prefer being served by brunettes. If this preference for discrimination is strong, the entry of blonde restaurants need not succeed in eliminating the wage differential between brunettes and blondes. That is, if customers have discriminatory preferences, a competitive market is consistent with a discriminatory wage differential. An economy with such discrimination would contain two types of restaurants: Blonde restaurants hire blondes, have lower costs, and charge lower prices. Brunette restaurants hire brunettes, have higher costs, and charge higher prices. Customers who did not care about the hair colour of their servers would be attracted to the lower prices at the blonde restaurants. Bigoted customers would go to the brunette restaurants. They would pay for their discriminatory preference in the form of higher prices.

Another way for discrimination to persist in competitive markets is for the government to mandate discriminatory practices. If, for instance, the government passed a law stating that blondes could wash dishes in restaurants but could not work as servers, then a wage differential could persist in a competitive market. For example, before South Africa abandoned its system of apartheid, blacks were prohibited from working in some jobs. Discriminatory governments pass such laws to suppress the normal equalizing force of free and competitive markets.

To sum up: *Competitive markets contain a natural remedy for employer discrimination. The entry into the market of firms that care only about profit tends to eliminate discriminatory wage differentials. These wage differentials persist in competitive markets only when customers are willing to pay to maintain the discriminatory practice or when the government mandates it.*

Case Study
DISCRIMINATION IN SPORTS

As we have seen, measuring discrimination is difficult. To determine whether one group of workers is discriminated against, a researcher must correct for differences in productivity between that group and other workers in the economy. Yet, in most firms, it is difficult to measure a particular worker's contribution to the production of goods and services.

One type of firm in which measurement is easier is the sports team. Professional teams have many objective measures of productivity. In baseball, for example, we can measure a player's batting average, home runs, stolen bases, and so on. In hockey, we can measure a player's goals, assists, and plus–minus statistics.

Economists focus on three main types of potential discrimination in sports: (1) salary discrimination; (2) position segregation, where certain positions are systematically assigned to certain groups; and (3) hiring, or entry, discrimination, where only the most productive elements of the discriminated group are hired.

U.S. studies have tended to focus on wage discrimination on racial grounds. These studies suggest that racial discrimination has indeed existed in sports teams, and that much of the blame may lie with customers. For example, a study published in the *Journal of Labor Economics* in 1988 (6:1) found that Black basketball players earned 20 percent less than white players of comparable ability. The study also found that attendance at basketball games was larger for teams with a greater proportion of white players. A similar situation also existed for baseball players, although more recent studies of salaries have found no evidence of discriminatory wage differentials. One interpretation of these findings is that customer discrimination makes Black players less profitable than white players for team owners. In the presence of such customer discrimination, a discriminatory wage gap can persist, even if team owners care only about profit.

A series of studies that appeared in *Canadian Public Policy* between 1987 and 1995 examined the existence of discrimination against francophone hockey players in the NHL. Early work focused on hiring discrimination. Using various performance measures for NHL players, it was determined that francophone players are underrepresented in the NHL and have tended to outperform their anglophone counterparts. One interpretation of this evidence is that francophones have been subjected to hiring discrimination. As a result of discrimination, francophones must outperform anglophones by a significant margin to get into the league in the first place.

Subsequent studies have questioned this interpretation. For example, an alternative interpretation is that the inability of marginal francophone players to communicate well in English impedes their ability to adapt to the needs of the team. Thus, for marginal players, selecting partially on the basis of language maximizes the success of the team both on and off the ice.

Other work has emphasized differences in playing styles between junior hockey teams in Quebec (the primary providers of francophone players to the NHL) and junior hockey teams in English-speaking provinces. In particular, the

Quebec-based teams tend to favour smaller players with offensive abilities, whereas NHL teams tend to favour bigger players with defensive abilities, especially for marginal or "role" players. This suggests that the underrepresentation of francophones in the NHL is not due to hiring discrimination but to different preferences in playing styles. Yet another study, using updated data, has found no evidence of either hiring or wage discrimination against francophones.

A recent salvo in the debate introduces the role of the location of NHL cities. The premise of this study is that the historic tensions between English Canadians and French Canadians suggests that francophones playing for teams based in English Canada may face salary discrimination, while francophones playing for teams based in the United States, where no such tensions exist, do not. Using this approach, the study finds evidence that francophones playing in English Canada do indeed suffer significant salary discrimination. ●

QuickQuiz Why is it hard to establish whether a group of workers is being discriminated against? • Explain how profit-maximizing firms tend to eliminate discriminatory wage differentials. • How might a discriminatory wage differential persist?

CONCLUSION

In competitive markets, workers earn a wage equal to the value of their marginal contribution to the production of goods and services. Many things, however, affect the value of the marginal product. Firms pay more for workers who are more talented, more diligent, more experienced, and more educated because these workers are more productive. Firms pay less to those workers against whom customers discriminate because these workers contribute less to revenue.

The theory of the labour market we have developed in the last two chapters explains why some workers earn higher wages than other workers. The theory does not say that the resulting distribution of income is equal, fair, or desirable in any way. That is the topic we take up in Chapter 20.

SUMMARY

- Workers earn different wages for many reasons. To some extent, wage differentials compensate workers for job attributes. Other things equal, workers in hard, unpleasant jobs get paid more than workers in easy, pleasant jobs.

- Workers with more human capital get paid more than workers with less human capital. The return to accumulating human capital is high and has increased over the past two decades.

- Although years of education, experience, and job characteristics affect earnings as theory predicts, there is much variation in earnings that cannot be explained by things that economists can measure. The unexplained variation in earnings is largely attributable to natural ability, effort, and chance.

- Some economists have suggested that more-educated workers earn higher wages not because education raises productivity but because workers with high natural ability use education as a way to signal their high ability to employers. If this signalling theory is correct, then increasing the educational attainment of all workers would not raise the overall level of wages.

- Wages are sometimes pushed above the level that brings supply and demand into balance. Three reasons for above-equilibrium wages are minimum-wage laws, unions, and efficiency wages.

- Some differences in earnings are attributable to discrimination on the basis of race, sex, or other factors. Measuring the amount of discrimination is difficult, however, because one must correct for differences in human capital and job characteristics.

- Competitive markets tend to limit the impact of discrimination on wages. If the wages of a group of workers are lower than those of another group for reasons not related to marginal productivity, then nondiscriminatory firms will be more profitable than discriminatory firms. Profit-maximizing behaviour, therefore, can reduce discriminatory wage differentials. Discrimination persists in competitive markets, however, if customers are willing to pay more to discriminatory firms or if the government passes laws requiring firms to discriminate.

KEY CONCEPTS

compensating differential, p. 424
human capital, p. 424

union, p. 432
strike, p. 432

efficiency wages, p. 432
discrimination, p. 433

QUESTIONS FOR REVIEW

1. Why are coal miners paid more than other workers with similar amounts of education?

2. In what sense is education a type of capital?

3. How might education raise a worker's wage without raising the worker's productivity?

4. What conditions lead to economic superstars? Would you expect to see superstars in dentistry? In music? Explain.

5. Give three reasons why a worker's wage might be above the level that balances supply and demand.

6. What difficulties arise in deciding whether a group of workers has a lower wage because of discrimination?

7. Do the forces of economic competition tend to exacerbate or ameliorate discrimination on the basis of race?

8. Give an example of how discrimination might persist in a competitive market.

PROBLEMS AND APPLICATIONS

1. University and college students sometimes work as summer interns for private firms or the government. Many of these positions pay little or nothing.
   a. What is the opportunity cost of taking such a job?
   b. Explain why students are willing to take these jobs.

   c. If you were to compare the earnings later in life of workers who had worked as interns and those who had taken summer jobs that paid more, what would you expect to find?

2. As explained in Chapter 6, a minimum-wage law distorts the market for low-wage labour. To reduce this distortion, some economists advocate a two-tiered minimum-wage system,

with a regular minimum wage for adult workers and a lower, "sub-minimum" wage for teenage workers. Give two reasons why a single minimum wage might distort the labour market for teenage workers more than it would the market for adult workers.

3. A basic finding of labour economics is that workers who have more experience in the labour force are paid more than workers who have less experience (holding constant the amount of formal education). Why might this be so? Some studies have also found that experience at the same job (called "job tenure") has an extra positive influence on wages. Explain.

4. At some colleges and universities, economics professors receive higher salaries than professors in some other fields.
    a. Why might this be true?
    b. Some other colleges and universities have a policy of paying equal salaries to professors in all fields. At some of these schools, economics professors have lighter teaching loads than professors in some other fields. What role do the differences in teaching loads play?

5. Sara works for Steve, whom she dislikes because of his snobbish attitude. Yet when she looks for other jobs, the best she can do is find a job paying $10 000 less than her current salary. Should she take the job? Analyze Sara's situation from an economic point of view.

6. Imagine that someone offers you a choice: You could spend four years studying at the world's best university, but you would have to keep your attendance there a secret. Or you could be awarded an official degree from the world's best university, but you couldn't actually attend. Which choice do you think would enhance your future earnings more? What does your answer say about the debate over signalling versus human capital in the role of education?

7. When recording devices were first invented almost 100 years ago, musicians could suddenly supply their music to large audiences at low cost. How do you suppose this development affected the income of the best musicians? How do you suppose it affected the income of average musicians?

8. A case study in this chapter described how customer discrimination in sports seems to have an important effect on players' earnings. Note that this is possible because sports fans know the players' characteristics, including their race. Why is this knowledge important for the existence of discrimination? Give some specific examples of industries where customer discrimination is and is not likely to influence wages.

9. Suppose that all young women were channelled into careers as secretaries, nurses, and teachers; at the same time, young men were encouraged to consider these three careers and many others as well.
    a. Draw a diagram showing the combined labour market for secretaries, nurses, and teachers. Draw a diagram showing the combined labour market for all other fields. In which market is the wage higher? Do men or women receive higher wages on average?
    b. Now suppose that society changed and encouraged both young women and young men to consider a wide range of careers. Over time, what effect would this change have on the wages in the two markets you illustrated in part (a)? What effect would the change have on the average wages of men and women?

10. Economist June O'Neill argues that "until family roles are more equal, women are not likely to have the same pattern of market work and earnings as men." What does she mean by the "pattern" of market work? How do these characteristics of jobs and careers affect earnings?

11. This chapter considers the economics of discrimination by employers, customers, and governments. Now consider discrimination by workers. Suppose that some brunette workers did not like working with blonde workers. Do you think this worker discrimination could explain lower wages for blonde workers? If such a wage differential existed, what would a profit-maximizing entrepreneur do? If there were many such entrepreneurs, what would happen over time?

INTERNET RESOURCES

- This chapter discussed some of the economics of discrimination. The Canadian Human Rights Commission (CHRC) administers the Canadian Human Rights Act, which legislates against discrimination on several grounds. The CHRC website is at http://www.chrc-ccdp.ca and the Canadian Human Rights Act can be found on the Justice Canada website at http://laws.justice.gc.ca/en/H-6/31077.html.

- In relation to the case study on discrimination in sports, the salary history of every NHL hockey player since 1989 can be found on the Hockey Zone Plus website: http://www.hockeyzoneplus.com.

http://   For more study tools, please visit http://www.mankiw3e.nelson.com.

© CHRIS BAKER/STONE

20

INCOME INEQUALITY AND POVERTY

Learning Objectives

In this chapter, you will …

- Examine the degree of economic inequality in our society
- Consider some problems that arise when measuring economic inequality
- See how political philosophers view the government's role in redistributing income
- Consider the various policies aimed at helping poor families escape poverty

"**T**he only difference between the rich and other people," Mary Colum once said to Ernest Hemingway, "is that the rich have more money." Maybe so. But this claim leaves many questions unanswered. The gap between rich and poor is a fascinating and important topic of study—for the comfortable rich, for the struggling poor, and for the aspiring and worried middle class.

From the previous two chapters you should have some understanding about why different people have different incomes. A person's earnings depend on the supply and demand for that person's labour, which in turn depend on natural ability, human capital, compensating differentials, discrimination, and so on. Because labour earnings make up about three-fourths of the total income in the Canadian economy, the factors that determine wages are also largely responsible for determining how the economy's total income is distributed among the various members of society. In other words, they determine who is rich and who is poor.

In this chapter we discuss the distribution of income—a topic that raises some fundamental questions about the role of economic policy. One of the ten principles of economics in Chapter 1 is that governments can sometimes improve market outcomes. This possibility is particularly important when considering the distribution of income. The invisible hand of the marketplace acts to allocate resources efficiently, but it does not necessarily ensure that resources are allocated fairly. As a result, many economists—though not all—believe that the government should redistribute income to achieve greater equality. In doing so, however, the government runs into another of the ten principles of economics: *People face tradeoffs.* When the government enacts policies to make the distribution of income more equitable, it distorts incentives, alters behaviour, and makes the allocation of resources less efficient.

Our discussion of the distribution of income proceeds in three steps. First, we assess how much inequality there is in our society. Second, we consider some different views about what role the government should play in altering the distribution of income. Third, we discuss various public policies aimed at helping society's poorest members.

THE MEASUREMENT OF INEQUALITY

We begin our study of the distribution of income by addressing four questions of measurement:

1. How much inequality is there in our society?
2. How many people live in poverty?
3. What problems arise in measuring the amount of inequality?
4. How often do people move among income classes?

These measurement questions are the natural starting point from which to discuss public policies aimed at changing the distribution of income.

Canadian Income Inequality

The distribution of income in the economy can be described in various ways. Table 20.1 presents a particularly simple way. Imagine that you lined up all of the families in the economy according to their annual family income. Then you divided the families into five equal groups: the bottom fifth, the second fifth, the middle fifth, the fourth fifth, and the top fifth. Table 20.1 shows the income ranges

TABLE 20.1

Distribution of Income in Canada, 2001

Source: Statistics Canada, *Income Trends in Canada*, Catalogue 13F0022, December 22, 2003.

Group	Annual Family Income	% of Income
Bottom fifth	Under $30 050	5.0%
Second fifth	$30 051–$43 642	11.0
Middle fifth	$43 643–$58 568	16.7
Fourth fifth	$58 569–$79 041	24.3
Top fifth	$79 042 and over	43.1

for each of these groups as well as the share of total income that each group of families received in Canada in 2001.

These numbers give us a way of gauging how the economy's total income is distributed. If income were equally distributed across all families, each one-fifth of families would receive one-fifth (20 percent) of income. If all income were concentrated among just a few families, the top fifth would receive 100 percent and the other fifths would receive 0 percent. The actual economy, of course, is between these two extremes.

Using family income after taxes and transfers as the income measure, Table 20.1 shows that in 2001, the bottom fifth of all families received 5.0 percent of all after-tax income and the top fifth of all families received 43.1 percent. In other words, even though the top and bottom fifths include the same number of families, the top fifth has about eight times as much income as the bottom fifth.

Case Study
THE WOMEN'S MOVEMENT AND INCOME DISTRIBUTION

Over the past several decades, there has been a dramatic change in women's role in the economy. The percentage of women who hold jobs rose from about 30 percent in the 1950s to over 50 percent in the 1990s. As full-time homemakers have become less common, a woman's earnings have become a more important determinant of the total income of a typical family.

While the women's movement has led to more equality between men and women in access to education and jobs, it has also led to less equality in family incomes. The reason is that the rise in women's labour-force participation has not been the same across all income groups. In particular, the women's movement has had its greatest impact on women from high-income households. Women from low-income households have long had high rates of participation in the labour force, even in the 1950s, and their behaviour has changed much less.

In essence, the women's movement has changed the behaviour of the wives of high-income men. In the 1950s, a male executive or physician was likely to marry a woman who would stay at home and raise their children. Today, the wife of a male executive or physician is more likely to be an executive or physician herself. The result is that rich households have become even richer, a pattern that increases the inequality in family incomes.

As this example shows, there are social as well as economic determinants of the distribution of income. Moreover, the simplistic view that "income inequality is bad" can be misleading. Increasing the opportunities available to women was surely a good change for society, even if one effect was greater inequality in family incomes. When evaluating any change in the distribution of income, policymakers must look at the reasons for that change before deciding whether it presents a problem for society. ●

Equality for women has meant less equality for family incomes.

Case Study

INCOME INEQUALITY AROUND THE WORLD

How does the amount of income inequality in Canada compare to that in other countries? This question is interesting, but answering it is problematic. For some countries, data are not available. Even when they are, not every country collects data in the same way; for example, some countries collect data on individual incomes, whereas other countries collect data on family incomes, and still others collect data on expenditure rather than income. As a result, whenever we find a difference between two countries, we can never be sure whether it reflects a true difference in the economies or merely a difference in the way data are collected.

With this warning in mind, consider Table 20.2, which compares inequality in 12 countries. The countries are ranked from the most equal to the most unequal. On the top of the list is Japan, where the richest tenth of the population has income only 4.5 times that of the poorest tenth. On the bottom of the list is Brazil, where the richest tenth has income of 46.7 times that of the poorest tenth. Although all countries have substantial inequality, the degree of inequality varies substantially around the world.

When countries are ranked by inequality as measured by the ratio of the share of income earned by the lowest and highest 10 percent of the population, Canada ends up near the top of the pack. In particular, Canada has substantially less inequality than the United States. Note that inequality is substantially higher in developing countries, such as Mexico, South Africa, and Brazil. ●

The Poverty Rate

In assessing income inequality in Canada, we may be interested not only in the distribution of income but also in the number of Canadians living in poverty.

TABLE 20.2

Income Inequality around the World

This table shows the percent of income or expenditure of the lowest and highest 10 percent of the population. The ratio of these two numbers measures the gap between rich and poor.

Source: *World Development Report: 2002,* pp. 234–35. © 2002 World Bank. Reproduced with permission of World Bank in the format Textbook via Copyright Clearance Center.

Country	Lowest 10%	Highest 10%	Ratio
Japan	4.8%	21.7%	4.5
Germany	3.3	23.7	7.2
Canada	2.8	23.8	8.5
India	3.5	33.5	9.6
United Kingdom	2.6	27.3	10.5
China	2.4	30.4	12.7
United States	1.8	30.5	16.9
Russia	1.7	38.7	22.8
Nigeria	1.6	40.8	25.5
Mexico	1.6	41.1	25.7
South Africa	1.1	45.9	41.7
Brazil	1.0	46.7	46.7

Being relatively worse off is different from living in poverty, and government policies regarding income distribution should recognize the distinction.

The **poverty rate** is the percentage of the population with family income below the poverty line. The **poverty line** is the level of family income below which a family is considered poor. Unfortunately, the poverty line is not a well-defined concept. Indeed, unlike the United States but like most other nations, Canada does not have an official measure of the poverty line.

Statistics Canada does, however, produce an annual estimate called the low-income cutoff (LICO), which has been widely used as a measure of the "official" poverty line in Canada. The LICO is calculated as the level of income at which a household of a given size in a community with a given population spends 20 percent more than average on food, shelter, and clothing. Canadian families spend an average of about 36 percent of their income on these three goods. Thus, families that spend more than 56 percent of their income on food, clothing, and shelter fall under the LICO. In 2001 the poverty rate in Canada using the LICO approach was 10.4 percent.

As Statistics Canada is always quick to point out, the problem with using the LICO as a measure of poverty is that it is a relative measure that is defined in relation to average income. Critics claim that relative measures such as the LICO provide a means of gauging the extent of income inequality, not the extent of poverty. Although the extent of income inequality in the country is an important consideration, it is not the same thing as poverty. It is possible for a country to have a great deal of income inequality but not to have any citizens living in poverty.

To overcome the limitations of relative measures such as the LICO, some people advocate the use of an absolute measure of the poverty line. An absolute measure involves measuring the cost of acquiring essential goods and services, or what are called basic needs. The problem with this approach is that it is difficult to come up with a list of basic needs, which is bound to be at least somewhat subjective and arbitrary (but no more so than any other measure of poverty).

A study by economist Christopher Sarlo presented a measure of the absolute poverty line in Canada based on the basic needs approach. This approach involves measuring the cost of basic necessities—such as a nutritious diet, shelter, clothing, health care, and transportation—for families of different sizes in different communities. The cost of these basic necessities then determines the poverty line. Using this approach, Sarlo determined that the poverty rate for Canadian households was about 9 percent in 1996, which is slightly lower than the poverty rate determined using the LICO.

Figure 20.1 (p. 448) shows the poverty rate for Canadian households using Sarlo's basic needs approach over the period from 1951 to 1996. What is remarkable is that the poverty rate fell drastically over the 30-year period—from over 40 percent in 1951 to about 9 percent in 1981. Over the 1980s and 1990s, the poverty rate remained stable at around 9 percent.

Poverty is an economic malady that affects all groups in society, but it does not affect all groups with equal frequency. For example, although the poverty rate based on the LICO measure was just over 10 percent in 2001, the rate for single-parent families with a female head was 36 percent.

poverty rate
the percentage of the population whose family income falls below an absolute level called the *poverty line*

poverty line
an absolute level of income set by the federal government for each family size, below which a family is deemed to be in poverty

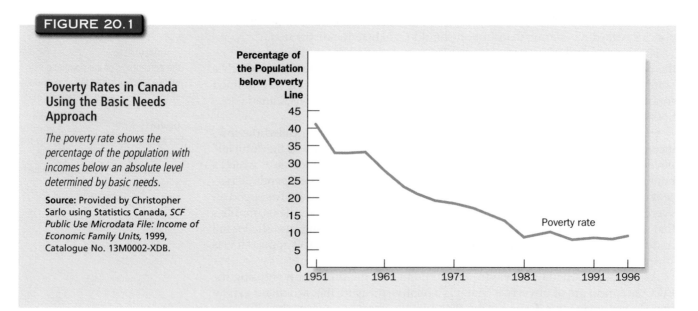

FIGURE 20.1

Poverty Rates in Canada Using the Basic Needs Approach

The poverty rate shows the percentage of the population with incomes below an absolute level determined by basic needs.

Source: Provided by Christopher Sarlo using Statistics Canada, *SCF Public Use Microdata File: Income of Economic Family Units*, 1999, Catalogue No. 13M0002-XDB.

Problems in Measuring Inequality

Although data on the income distribution and the poverty rate help to give us some idea about the degree of inequality in our society, interpreting these data is not as straightforward as it might first appear. The data are based on households' annual incomes. What people care about, however, is not their incomes but their ability to maintain a good standard of living. For various reasons, data on the income distribution and the poverty rate give an incomplete picture of inequality in living standards. We examine these reasons below.

In-Kind Transfers Measurements of the distribution of income and the poverty rate are based on families' *money* income. Through various government programs, however, the poor receive many nonmonetary items, including food stamps, housing vouchers, and medical services. Transfers to the poor given in the form of goods and services rather than cash are called **in-kind transfers.** Standard measurements of the degree of inequality do not take account of these in-kind transfers.

Because in-kind transfers are received mostly by the poorest members of society, the failure to include in-kind transfers as part of income greatly affects the measured poverty rate. Unfortunately, it is difficult to obtain data on the value of these in-kind transfers.

The important role of in-kind transfers makes evaluating changes in poverty more difficult. Over time, as public policies to help the poor evolve, the composition of assistance between cash and in-kind transfers changes. Some of the fluctuations in the measured poverty rate, therefore, reflect the form of government assistance rather than the true extent of economic deprivation.

The Economic Life Cycle Incomes vary predictably over people's lives. A young worker, especially one in school, has a low income. Income rises as the

in-kind transfers
transfers to the poor given in the form of goods and services rather than cash

worker gains maturity and experience, peaks at around age 50, and then falls sharply when the worker retires at around age 65. This regular pattern of income variation is called the **life cycle.**

Because people can borrow and save to smooth out life cycle changes in income, their standard of living in any year depends more on lifetime income than on that year's income. The young often borrow, perhaps to go to school or to buy a house, and then repay these loans later when their incomes rise. People have their highest saving rates when they are middle-aged. Because people can save in anticipation of retirement, the large declines in incomes at retirement need not lead to similar declines in the standard of living.

This normal life cycle pattern causes inequality in the distribution of annual income, but it does not represent true inequality in living standards. To gauge the inequality of living standards in our society, the distribution of lifetime incomes is more relevant than the distribution of annual incomes. Unfortunately, data on lifetime incomes are not readily available. When looking at any data on inequality, however, it is important to keep the life cycle in mind. Because a person's lifetime income smooths out the highs and lows of the life cycle, lifetime incomes are surely more equally distributed across the population than are annual incomes.

life cycle
the regular pattern of income variation over a person's life

Transitory versus Permanent Income   Incomes vary over people's lives not only because of predictable life cycle variation but also because of random and transitory forces. One year, freezing rain may damage maple trees in Quebec, causing the income of Quebec maple syrup producers to decline temporarily. Over time the damaged trees will recover, and the incomes of maple syrup producers will rise again.

Just as people can borrow and lend to smooth out life cycle variations in income, they can borrow and lend to smooth out transitory variation in income. When maple syrup producers have a good year, they would be foolish to spend all of their additional income. Instead, they will likely save some of it against a "rainy day." Similarly, they respond to temporarily low incomes by drawing on their savings or by borrowing.

To the extent that a family saves and borrows to buffer itself from transitory changes in income, these changes do not affect its standard of living. A family's ability to buy goods and services depends largely on its **permanent income,** which is its normal, or average, income.

permanent income
a person's normal income

To gauge inequality of living standards, the distribution of permanent income is more relevant than the distribution of annual income. Although permanent income is hard to measure, it is an important concept. Because it excludes transitory changes in income, permanent income is more equally distributed than is current income.

Economic Mobility

People sometimes speak of "the rich" and "the poor" as if these groups consisted of the same families year after year. In fact, this is not at all the case. Economic mobility, the movement of people among income classes, is substantial in the Canadian economy. Movements up the income ladder can be due to good luck or hard work, and movements down the ladder can be due to bad luck or laziness.

Some of this mobility reflects transitory variation in income, while some reflects more persistent changes in income.

Economic mobility suggests that many families may be poor only temporarily. An article by Garry Barrett and Michael Cragg in the February 1998 issue of *The Canadian Journal of Economics* using data from British Columbia provides evidence that continuous, long-term use of and dependence on welfare is not very common in Canada. Similarly, research by Statistics Canada shows that only about half of the individuals who fall under the LICO remain there from year to year.

This evidence suggests a fairly high degree of economic mobility at lower income levels in Canada. Nonetheless, Barrett and Cragg also found that a fairly high proportion of welfare recipients do revisit the welfare rolls periodically. The Statistics Canada research shows also that half of all individuals under the LICO remain under the cutoff from year to year—so the glass is either half empty or half full, depending on your perspective. These studies suggest that two types of groups are poor at any time: the temporarily poor and the persistently poor. Because the temporarily poor and the persistently poor are likely to face different problems, policies that aim to combat poverty need to distinguish between the two groups.

Another way to gauge economic mobility is the persistence of economic success from generation to generation. Economists who have studied this topic find substantial mobility. If a father earns 20 percent above his generation's average income, his son will most likely earn 8 percent above his generation's average income. There is almost no correlation between the income of a grandfather and the income of a grandson. There is much truth to the old saying, "From shirtsleeves to shirtsleeves in three generations."

QuickQuiz What does the poverty rate measure? • Describe three potential problems in interpreting the measured poverty rate.

THE POLITICAL PHILOSOPHY OF REDISTRIBUTING INCOME

We have just seen how the economy's income is distributed and have considered some of the problems in interpreting measured inequality. This discussion was *positive* in the sense that it merely described the world as it is. We now turn to the *normative* question facing policymakers: What should the government do about economic inequality?

This question is not just about economics. Economic analysis alone cannot tell us whether policymakers should try to make our society more egalitarian. Our views on this question are, to a large extent, a matter of political philosophy. Yet because the government's role in redistributing income is central to so many debates over economic policy, here we digress from economic science to consider a bit of political philosophy.

utilitarianism
the political philosophy according to which the government should choose policies to maximize the total utility of everyone in society

Utilitarianism

A prominent school of thought in political philosophy is **utilitarianism.** The founders of utilitarianism are the English philosophers Jeremy Bentham

(1748–1832) and John Stuart Mill (1806–1873). To a large extent, the goal of utilitarians is to apply the logic of individual decision making to questions concerning morality and public policy.

The starting point of utilitarianism is the notion of **utility**—the level of happiness or satisfaction that a person receives from his or her circumstances. Utility is a measure of well-being and, according to utilitarians, is the ultimate objective of all public and private actions. The proper goal of the government, they claim, is to maximize the sum of utility of everyone in society.

The utilitarian case for redistributing income is based on the assumption of *diminishing marginal utility*. It seems reasonable that an extra dollar of income to a poor person provides that person with more additional utility than does an extra dollar to a rich person. In other words, as a person's income rises, the extra well-being derived from an additional dollar of income falls. This plausible assumption, together with the utilitarian goal of maximizing total utility, implies that the government should try to achieve a more equal distribution of income.

The argument is simple. Imagine that Peter and Paul are the same, except that Peter earns $80 000 and Paul earns $20 000. In this case, taking a dollar from Peter to pay Paul will reduce Peter's utility and raise Paul's utility. But, because of diminishing marginal utility, Peter's utility falls by less than Paul's utility rises. Thus, this redistribution of income raises total utility, which is the utilitarian's objective.

At first, this utilitarian argument might seem to imply that the government should continue to redistribute income until everyone in society has exactly the same income. Indeed, that would be the case if the total amount of income— $100 000 in our example—were fixed. But, in fact, it is not. Utilitarians reject complete equalization of incomes because they accept one of the ten principles of economics presented in Chapter 1: People respond to incentives.

To take from Peter to pay Paul, the government must pursue policies that redistribute income, such as the Canadian income tax and welfare system. Under these policies, people with high incomes pay high taxes, and people with low incomes receive income transfers. Yet, as we saw in Chapters 8 and 12, taxes distort incentives and cause deadweight losses. If the government takes away additional income a person might earn through higher income taxes or reduced transfers, both Peter and Paul have less incentive to work hard. As they work less, society's income falls, and so does total utility. The utilitarian government has to balance the gains from greater equality against the losses from distorted incentives. To maximize total utility, therefore, the government stops short of making society fully egalitarian.

A famous parable sheds light on the utilitarian's logic. Imagine that Peter and Paul are thirsty travellers trapped at different places in the desert. Peter's oasis has much water; Paul's has little. If the government could transfer water from one oasis to the other without cost, it would maximize total utility from water by equalizing the amount in the two places. But suppose that the government has only a leaky bucket. As it tries to move water from one place to the other, some of the water is lost in transit. In this case, a utilitarian government might still try to move some water from Peter to Paul, depending on how thirsty Paul is and how leaky the bucket is. But, with only a leaky bucket at its disposal, a utilitarian government will not try to reach complete equality.

utility
a measure of happiness or satisfaction

Liberalism

liberalism
the political philosophy according to which the government should choose policies deemed to be just, as evaluated by an impartial observer behind a "veil of ignorance"

A second way of thinking about inequality might be called **liberalism.** Philosopher John Rawls develops this view in his book *A Theory of Justice.* This book was first published in 1971, and it quickly became a classic in political philosophy.

Rawls begins with the premise that a society's institutions, laws, and policies should be just. He then takes up the natural question: How can we, the members of society, ever agree on what justice means? It might seem that every person's point of view is inevitably based on that person's particular circumstances—whether he or she is talented or less talented, diligent or lazy, educated or less educated, born to a wealthy family or a poor one. Could we ever *objectively* determine what a just society would be?

To answer this question, Rawls proposes the following thought experiment. Imagine that before any of us is born, we all get together for a meeting to design the rules that govern society. At this point, we are all ignorant about the station in life each of us will end up filling. In Rawls's words, we are sitting in an "original position" behind a "veil of ignorance." In this original position, Rawls argues, we can choose a just set of rules for society because we must consider how those rules will affect every person. As Rawls puts it, "Since all are similarly situated and no one is able to design principles to favor his particular conditions, the principles of justice are the result of fair agreement or bargain." Designing public policies and institutions in this way allows us to be objective about what policies are just.

Rawls then considers what public policy designed behind this veil of ignorance would try to achieve. In particular, he considers what income distribution a person would consider fair if that person did not know whether he or she would end up at the top, bottom, or middle of the distribution. Rawls argues that a person in the original position would be especially concerned about the possibility of being at the *bottom* of the income distribution. In designing public policies, therefore, we should aim to raise the welfare of the worst-off person in society. That is, rather than maximizing the sum of everyone's utility, as a utilitarian would do, Rawls would maximize the minimum utility. Rawls's rule is called the **maximin criterion.**

maximin criterion
the claim that the government should aim to maximize the well-being of the worst-off person in society

Because the maximin criterion emphasizes the least fortunate person in society, it justifies public policies aimed at equalizing the distribution of income. By transferring income from the rich to the poor, society raises the well-being of the least fortunate. The maximin criterion would not, however, lead to a completely egalitarian society. If the government promised to equalize incomes completely, people would have no incentive to work hard, society's total income would fall substantially, and the least fortunate person would be worse off. Thus, the maximin criterion still allows disparities in income, because such disparities can improve incentives and thereby raise society's ability to help the poor. Nonetheless, because Rawls's philosophy puts weight on only the least fortunate members of society, it calls for more income redistribution than does utilitarianism.

Rawls's views are controversial, but the thought experiment he proposes has much appeal. In particular, this thought experiment allows us to consider the redistribution of income as a form of *social insurance.* That is, from the perspective of the original position behind the veil of ignorance, income redistribution is like an insurance policy. Homeowners buy fire insurance to protect themselves from the risk of their housing burning down. Similarly, when we as a society choose policies that tax the rich to supplement the incomes of the poor, we are all insuring ourselves against the possibility that we might have been a member of a poor family. Because people dislike risk, we should be happy to have been born into a society that provides us this insurance.

It is not at all clear, however, that rational people behind the veil of ignorance would truly be so averse to risk as to follow the maximin criterion. Indeed, because a person in the original position might end up anywhere in the distribution of outcomes, he or she might treat all possible outcomes equally when designing public policies. In this case, the best policy behind the veil of ignorance would be to maximize the average utility of members of society, and the resulting notion of justice would be more utilitarian than Rawlsian.

Libertarianism

A third view of inequality is called **libertarianism.** The two views we have considered so far—utilitarianism and liberalism—both view the total income of society as a shared resource that a social planner can freely redistribute to achieve some social goal. By contrast, libertarians argue that society itself earns no income—only individual members of society earn income. According to libertarians, the government should not take from some individuals and give to others in order to achieve any particular distribution of income.

For instance, philosopher Robert Nozick writes the following in his famous 1974 book *Anarchy, State, and Utopia:*

libertarianism
the political philosophy according to which the government should punish crimes and enforce voluntary agreements but not redistribute income

> We are not in the position of children who have been given portions of pie by someone who now makes last minute adjustments to rectify careless cutting. There is no *central* distribution, no person or group entitled to control all the resources, jointly deciding how they are to be doled out. What each person gets, he gets from others who give to him in exchange for something, or as a gift. In a free society, diverse persons control different resources, and new holdings arise out of the voluntary exchanges and actions of persons.

Whereas utilitarians and liberals try to judge what amount of inequality is desirable in a society, Nozick denies the validity of this very question.

The libertarian alternative to evaluating economic *outcomes* is to evaluate the *process* by which these outcomes arise. When the distribution of income is achieved unfairly—for instance, when one person steals from another—the government has the right and duty to remedy the problem. But, as long as the process determining the distribution of income is just, the resulting distribution is fair, no matter how unequal.

Nozick criticizes Rawls's liberalism by drawing an analogy between the distribution of income in society and the distribution of grades in a course. Suppose you were asked to judge the fairness of the grades in the economics course you are now taking. Would you imagine yourself behind a veil of ignorance and choose a grade distribution without knowing the talents and efforts of each student? Or would you ensure that the process of assigning grades to students is fair without regard for whether the resulting distribution is equal or unequal? For the case of grades at least, the libertarian emphasis on process over outcomes is compelling.

Libertarians conclude that equality of opportunities is more important than equality of incomes. They believe that the government should enforce individual rights to ensure that everyone has the same opportunity to use his or her talents and achieve success. Once these rules of the game are established, the government has no reason to alter the resulting distribution of income.

QuickQuiz Pam earns more than Pauline. Someone proposes taxing Pam in order to supplement Pauline's income. How would a utilitarian, a liberal, and a libertarian evaluate this proposal?

POLICIES TO REDUCE POVERTY

As we have just seen, political philosophers hold various views about what role the government should take in altering the distribution of income. Political debate among the larger population of voters reflects a similar disagreement. Despite these continuing debates, however, most people believe that, at the very least, the government should try to help those most in need. According to a popular metaphor, the government should provide a "safety net" to prevent any citizen from falling too far.

Poverty is one of the most difficult problems that policymakers face. Poor families are more likely than the overall population to experience homelessness, drug dependency, domestic violence, health problems, teenage pregnancy, illiteracy, unemployment, and low educational attainment. Members of poor families are both more likely to commit crimes and more likely to be victims of crimes. Although it is hard to separate the causes of poverty from the effects, there is no doubt that poverty is associated with various economic and social ills.

Suppose that you were a policymaker in the government, and your goal was to reduce the number of people living in poverty. How would you achieve this goal? Here we consider some of the policy options that you might consider. Although each of these options does help some people escape poverty, none of them is perfect, and deciding which is best is not easy.

Minimum-Wage Laws

Laws setting a minimum wage that employers can pay workers are a perennial source of debate. Advocates view the minimum wage as a way of helping the working poor without any cost to the government. Critics view it as hurting those it is intended to help.

The minimum wage is easily understood using the tools of supply and demand, as we first saw in Chapter 6. For workers with low levels of skill and experience, a high minimum wage forces the wage above the level that balances supply and demand. It therefore raises the cost of labour to firms and reduces the quantity of labour that those firms demand. The result is higher unemployment among those groups of workers affected by the minimum wage. Although those workers who remain employed benefit from a higher wage, those who might have been employed at a lower wage are worse off.

The magnitude of these effects depends crucially on the elasticity of demand. Advocates of a high minimum wage argue that the demand for unskilled labour is relatively inelastic, so that a high minimum wage depresses employment only slightly. Critics of the minimum wage argue that labour demand is more elastic, especially in the long run when firms can adjust employment and production more fully. They also note that many minimum-wage workers are teenagers from middle-class families, so that a high minimum wage is imperfectly targeted as a policy for helping the poor.

Welfare

One way to raise the living standards of the poor is for the government to supplement their incomes. The primary way in which the government does this is through the welfare system. **Welfare** is a broad term that encompasses various government programs. In Canada, welfare programs are the responsibility of provincial governments, which receive some help in funding the programs from the federal government.

welfare
government programs that
supplement the incomes of the needy

The features of welfare programs and the levels of benefits vary significantly from province to province. However, the programs share some common features. Most programs distinguish between people who are considered employable and those who are not. People who are considered employable typically receive lower benefits. Individuals who are not considered employable, families with dependent children, and individuals with disabilities receive higher benefits.

A common criticism of welfare programs is that they reduce the incentive to work. One way in which they do this is by reducing welfare benefits when an individual earns other income. In the past many provinces reduced welfare payments dollar for dollar when an individual earned other income. This resulted in a marginal tax rate on earned income of 100 percent. This reduces the incentive for welfare recipients to find work to supplement their welfare cheques, and results in what many refer to as a "welfare trap." In response to this criticism, many provinces have lowered the implicit tax-back rates on welfare benefits, but they are still very high—in excess of 70 percent in most provinces.

Negative Income Tax

Whenever the government chooses a system to collect taxes, it affects the distribution of income. This is clearly true in the case of a progressive income tax, whereby high-income families pay a larger percentage of their income in taxes than do low-income families. As we discussed in Chapter 12, equity across income groups is an important criterion in the design of a tax system.

Many economists have advocated supplementing the income of the poor using a **negative income tax.** According to this policy, every family would report its income to the government. High-income families would pay a tax based on their incomes. Low-income families would receive a subsidy. In other words, they would "pay" a "negative tax."

negative income tax
a tax system that collects revenue
from high-income households and
gives transfers to low-income
households

For example, suppose the government used the following formula to compute a family's tax liability:

$$\text{Taxes owed} = (1/3 \text{ of income}) - \$10\,000$$

In this case, a family that earned $60 000 would pay $10 000 in taxes, and a family that earned $90 000 would pay $20 000 in taxes. A family that earned $30 000 would owe nothing. And a family that earned $15 000 would "owe" −$5000. In other words, the government would send this family a cheque for $5000.

Under a negative income tax, poor families would receive financial assistance without having to demonstrate need. The only qualification required to receive assistance would be a low income. Depending on one's point of view, this feature can be either an advantage or a disadvantage. On the one hand, a negative income tax does not encourage illegitimate births and the breakup of families, as critics of the welfare system believe current policy does. On the other hand, a negative income tax would subsidize those who are simply lazy and, in some people's eyes, undeserving of government support.

In-Kind Transfers

Another way to help the poor is to provide them directly with some of the goods and services they need to raise their living standards. For example, charities provide the needy with food, shelter, and children's toys for special occasions. In Canada, in-kind transfers supplied by the government include subsidized housing and daycare. Publicly funded health care, financed by income taxes and payroll taxes, can also be thought of as an in-kind transfer to the poor.

Is it better to help the poor with these in-kind transfers or with direct cash payments? There is no clear answer.

Advocates of in-kind transfers argue that such transfers ensure that the poor get what they need most. Among the poorest members of society, alcohol and drug addiction is more common than it is in society as a whole. By providing the poor with food and shelter, society can be more confident that it is not helping to support such addictions. This is one reason why in-kind transfers are more politically popular than cash payments to the poor.

Advocates of cash payments, on the other hand, argue that in-kind transfers are inefficient and disrespectful. The government does not know what goods and services the poor need most. Many of the poor are ordinary people down on their luck. Despite their misfortune, they are in the best position to decide how to raise their own living standards. Rather than giving the poor in-kind transfers of goods and services that they may not want, it may be better to give them cash and allow them to buy what they think they need most.

Employment Insurance

Until recently, unemployment rates in Canada have hovered around 10 percent. In some parts of the country, and for some demographic groups (notably young people), unemployment rates remain higher than 13 percent. Employment

Insurance (EI) is one way the government provides some income support to people who find themselves temporarily out of work.

EI is available to workers who lose their jobs through no fault of their own; those who quit their jobs for no good reason or who are fired for cause receive no benefits. To qualify for EI, people must have worked a certain number of hours since their last spell of unemployment. Benefit levels are set at 55 percent of the individual's previous salary, up to a maximum equal to the average industrial wage. Unemployed workers can receive benefits for a maximum of 45 weeks.

There is ongoing debate in Canada on whether the EI system should be organized along the principles of an insurance program, or whether it should be operated as simply an income-transfer program. Those who argue that the EI system should embody insurance principles focus on various features of the current system. The EI system is funded from payroll taxes paid by both employees and employers. The payroll tax rates are the same for employees and employers in all industries, even though some industries and occupations have a much higher risk of unemployment than others. The construction industry, for example, tends to be both cyclical and seasonal. As a result, construction workers are more likely to be laid off than, say, university professors. Yet if a construction worker earns the same salary as a university professor, the construction worker and her employer will pay the same amount in EI payroll taxes as the university professor and his employer.

This equality in payroll tax payments contravenes one of the most important principles of insurance: High-risk individuals should pay higher insurance premiums than low-risk individuals. For example, young, single males pay much higher car insurance premiums than older, married males because they are more likely to have a car accident; similarly, people with poor driving records pay higher premiums than people with good driving records.

In effect, EI provides an implicit wage subsidy to industries that employ workers with a high risk of unemployment. In the absence of EI, construction workers would demand higher wages to compensate them for the higher risk of unemployment (recall our discussion of compensating differentials in Chapter 19). However, in the presence of EI, construction companies can pay their workers relatively lower wages because EI benefits provide a cushion if workers are laid off: Workers do not demand as much to compensate them for the risk of unemployment because their income will not fall by as much. For this reason, it is argued that EI payroll tax rates should be experience-rated. Under an experience-rated system, EI payroll tax rates would be higher in industries with a high risk of unemployment than in industries with a low risk of unemployment. Experience rating, it is claimed, would make the EI system more like true insurance and eliminate the implicit wage subsidies granted to some industries under the current system.

Not only is there currently no experience rating of EI in Canada, but some aspects of the EI system actually act as a sort of negative experience rating. For example, EI qualifying periods are shorter and benefit periods are longer in areas with persistently high unemployment rates; Atlantic Canada is one such area. Sound insurance principles would require that workers in areas with high unemployment rates pay higher payroll taxes or receive lower benefits than workers in areas with low unemployment rates. However, by reducing the qualifying period and lengthening the benefit period in regions with high unemployment, the EI

IN THE NEWS

EI AND WORK INCENTIVES

Government programs designed to address poverty may also reduce the incentive to work. The following article explains how this can happen.

EI Claimants Bough Out

By David Johnston

The economy is going from bad to worse on the Gaspé peninsula, but people aren't grasping at straws just yet. In fact, they're grasping at Christmas-tree branches, and it's putting money in people's pockets.

In recent weeks, 250 people have been out in the woods, snipping small branches off balsam fir trees and hauling them to a new company that makes Christmas wreaths and other festive products.

When the company, WreathsPlus, was founded last fall in the industrial park outside the town of Gaspé, people took notice. New businesses are rare in the region, and seasonal workers who hadn't worked enough during the summer to get Employment Insurance over the winter saw an opportunity to qualify.

And so WreathsPlus had no trouble finding workers when it opened for a two-month production run last fall. Even

Emploi-Québec got in the act, agreeing to pay half the wages of 40 of the 70 original workers, under a job-training scheme.

The provincial subsidy was good for WreathsPlus, good for the workers, and even good for the government, as it helped the 40 qualify for Employment Insurance and kept them from falling onto welfare rolls.

But then something remarkable happened: The wreaths the workers made sold like mad. Wholesalers loved them. This year, they put in orders for tens of thousands of them, as well as for other related balsam and cedar decorative products.

And so when three WreathsPlus facilities in Gaspé, Murdochville, and Rivière au Renard opened last month for another two-month run, there was work for 170 people, not just 70.

That's when the trouble started. Try as it did, the company could find only 150 people willing to work, even though the region's official unemployment rate is 19 percent, the highest in Quebec. The

problem, said WreathsPlus co-owner Bruce Jones, is that most of the people he tried to recruit said they'd already qualified for EI and didn't want to work. WreathsPlus had outgrown the local economy's demand for EI qualifying weeks. . . .

WreathsPlus's seasonal production employees earn a minimum wage of $6.90 per hour, plus a small bonus that sees the most productive earn $8.50 per hour. This compares with the $7.10 per hour for people on EI, when you consider that the average Quebec EI recipient received a weekly cheque of $284.

People on EI would be looking at a 20-cent-per-hour pay cut if they went out to work for WreathsPlus instead of staying at home.

And so it is that one of the fastest-growing companies in the Gaspé faces an unofficial labour shortage.

Source: *The Gazette* (Montreal), Final Edition, November 11, 2000, p. A19.

system does just the opposite. In this regard, the EI system acts as an income-transfer system to regions with high unemployment.

The debate over how closely the EI system in Canada should reflect insurance principles is a complicated and ongoing one.

QuickQuiz List three policies aimed at helping the poor, and discuss the pros and cons of each.

CONCLUSION

People have long reflected on the distribution of income in society. Plato, the ancient Greek philosopher, concluded that in an ideal society the income of the richest person would be no more than four times the income of the poorest person. Although the measurement of inequality is difficult, it is clear that our society has much more inequality than Plato recommended.

One of the ten principles of economics discussed in Chapter 1 is that governments can sometimes improve market outcomes. There is little consensus, however, about how this principle should be applied to the distribution of income. Philosophers and policymakers today do not agree on how much income inequality is desirable, or even whether public policy should aim to alter the distribution of income. Much of public debate reflects this disagreement. Whenever taxes are raised, for instance, lawmakers argue over how much of the tax hike should fall on the rich, the middle class, and the poor.

Another of the ten principles of economics is that people face tradeoffs. This principle is important to keep in mind when thinking about economic inequality. Policies that penalize the successful and reward the unsuccessful reduce the incentive to succeed. Thus, policymakers face a tradeoff between equality and efficiency. The more equally the pie is divided, the smaller the pie becomes. This is the one lesson concerning the distribution of income about which almost everyone agrees.

SUMMARY

- Data on the distribution of income show wide disparity in our society. The richest fifth of families earns about eight times as much income as the poorest fifth.

- Because in-kind transfers, the economic life cycle, transitory income, and economic mobility are so important for understanding variation in income, it is difficult to gauge the degree of inequality in our society using data on the distribution of income in a single year. When these other factors are taken into account, they tend to suggest that economic well-being is more equally distributed than is annual income.

- Political philosophers differ in their views about the role of government in altering the distribution of income. Utilitarians (such as John Stuart Mill) would choose the distribution

of income to maximize the sum of utility of everyone in society. Liberals (such as John Rawls) would determine the distribution of income as if we were behind a "veil of ignorance" that prevented us from knowing our own stations in life. Libertarians (such as Robert Nozick) would have the government enforce individual rights to ensure a fair process but then not be concerned about inequality in the resulting distribution of income.

- Various policies aim to help the poor— minimum-wage laws, welfare, negative income taxes, and in-kind transfers. Although each of these policies helps some families escape poverty, they also have unintended side effects. Because financial assistance declines as income rises, the poor often face effective marginal tax rates that are very high. Such high effective tax rates discourage poor families from escaping poverty on their own.

KEY CONCEPTS

poverty rate, p. 447
poverty line, p. 447
in-kind transfers, p. 448
life cycle, p. 449

permanent income, p. 449
utilitarianism, p. 450
utility, p. 451
liberalism, p. 452

maximin criterion, p. 452
libertarianism, p. 453
welfare, p. 455
negative income tax, p. 455

QUESTIONS FOR REVIEW

1. Does the richest fifth of the Canadian population earn two, four, or eight times the income of the poorest fifth?

2. How does the extent of income inequality in Canada compare to that of other nations around the world?

3. What groups in the population are most likely to live in poverty?

4. When gauging the amount of inequality, why do transitory and life cycle variations in income cause difficulties?

5. How would a utilitarian, a liberal, and a libertarian determine how much income inequality is permissible?

6. What are the pros and cons of in-kind (rather than cash) transfers to the poor?

7. Describe how antipoverty programs can discourage the poor from working. How might you reduce this disincentive? What are the disadvantages with your proposed policy?

PROBLEMS AND APPLICATIONS

1. By most measures, over the past 20 years, income inequality in the United States has increased relative to income inequality in Canada. Some factors that may explain this difference were discussed in Chapter 19. What are they?

2. What do you think would happen to wage rates in the construction industry if Canada introduced full experience rating to the EI system? Explain.

3. Economists often view life cycle variation in income as one form of transitory variation in income around people's lifetime, or permanent, income. In this sense, how does your current income compare to your permanent income? Do you think your current income accurately reflects your standard of living?

4. The chapter discusses the importance of economic mobility.
   a. What policies might the government pursue to increase economic mobility *within* a generation?
   b. What policies might the government pursue to increase economic mobility *across* generations?
   c. Do you think we should reduce spending on current welfare programs in order to increase spending on programs that enhance economic mobility? What are some of the advantages and disadvantages of doing so?

5. Consider two communities. In one community, ten families have incomes of $100 each and ten families have incomes of $20 each. In the other

community, ten families have incomes of $200 each and ten families have incomes of $22 each.

a. In which community is the distribution of income more unequal? In which community is the problem of poverty likely to be worse?

b. Which distribution of income would Rawls prefer? Explain.

c. Which distribution of income do you prefer? Explain.

6. The chapter uses the analogy of a "leaky bucket" to explain one constraint on the redistribution of income.

a. What elements of the Canadian system for redistributing income create the leaks in the bucket? Be specific.

b. Do you think that the NDP or Conservative political parties generally believe that the bucket used for redistributing income is more leaky? How does that belief affect their views about the amount of income redistribution that the government should undertake?

7. Suppose there are two possible income distributions in a society of ten people. In the first distribution, nine people would have incomes of $30 000 and one person would have an income of $10 000. In the second distribution, all ten people would have incomes of $25 000.

a. If the society had the first income distribution, what would be the utilitarian argument for redistributing income?

b. Which income distribution would Rawls consider more equitable? Explain.

c. Which income distribution would Nozick consider more equitable? Explain.

8. Most measures of the poverty rate do not include the value of in-kind transfers in family income. Yet the value of in-kind transfers can be substantial. An example of an in-kind transfer is a housing subsidy. Let's say that the value of the housing subsidy is $5000 for each recipient family.

a. If the government gave each recipient family an amount of cash equal to $5000 instead of the housing subsidy, do you think that most of these families would spend that much on additional housing? Why or why not?

b. How does your answer to part (a) affect your view about whether we should determine the poverty rate by valuing in-kind transfers at the price the government pays for them? Explain.

c. How does your answer to part (a) affect your view about whether we should provide assistance to the poor in the form of cash transfers or in-kind transfers? Explain.

9. Suppose that a family's tax liability equalled its income multiplied by one-half, minus $10 000. Under this system, some families would pay taxes to the government, and some families would receive money from the government through a "negative income tax."

a. Consider families with pre-tax incomes of $0, $10 000, $20 000, $30 000, and $40 000. Make a table showing pre-tax income, taxes paid to the government or money received from the government, and after-tax income for each family.

b. What is the marginal tax rate in this system? (See Chapter 12 if you need to review the definition of marginal tax rate.) What is the maximum amount of income at which a family *receives* money from the government?

c. Now suppose that the tax schedule is changed, so that a family's tax liability equals its income multiplied by one-quarter, minus $10 000. What is the marginal tax rate in this new system? What is the maximum amount of income at which a family receives money from the government?

d. What is the main advantage of each of the tax schedules discussed here?

10. John and Jeremy are utilitarians. John believes that labour supply is highly elastic, whereas Jeremy believes that labour supply is quite inelastic. How do you suppose their views about income redistribution differ?

11. Do you agree or disagree with each of the following statements? What do your views imply for public policies, such as taxes on inheritance?

a. "Every parent has the right to work hard and save in order to give his or her children a better life."

b. "No child should be disadvantaged by the sloth or bad luck of his or her parents."

INTERNET RESOURCES

The Canadian Council on Social Development is a non-profit social policy and research organization focusing on issues such as poverty, social inclusion, disability, cultural diversity, and child well-being. Its website is at http://www.ccsd.ca.

http://   For more study tools, please visit http://www.mankiw3e.nelson.com.

7

TOPICS FOR FURTHER STUDY

© JIM STEINHART

THE THEORY OF CONSUMER CHOICE

21

Learning Objectives

In this chapter, you will …

- See how a budget constraint represents the choices a consumer can afford
- Learn how indifference curves can be used to represent a consumer's preferences
- Analyze how a consumer's optimal choices are determined
- See how a consumer responds to changes in income and changes in prices
- Decompose the impact of a price change into an income effect and a substitution effect
- Apply the theory of consumer choice to three questions about household behaviour

When you walk into a store, you are confronted with thousands of goods that you might buy. Of course, because your financial resources are limited, you cannot buy everything that you want. You therefore consider the prices of the various goods being offered for sale and buy a bundle of goods that, given your resources, best suits your needs and desires.

In this chapter we develop the theory that describes how consumers make decisions about what to buy. So far throughout this book, we have summarized consumers' decisions with the demand curve. As we discussed in Chapters 4 through 7, the demand curve for a good reflects consumers' willingness to pay for it. When the price of a good rises, consumers are willing to pay for fewer units, so the quantity demanded falls. We now look more deeply at the decisions that lie behind the demand curve. The theory of consumer choice presented in this chapter provides a more complete understanding of demand, just as the theory of the competitive firm in Chapter 14 provides a more complete understanding of supply.

One of the ten principles of economics discussed in Chapter 1 is that people face tradeoffs. The theory of consumer choice examines the tradeoffs that people face in their role as consumers. When a consumer buys more of one good, he can afford less of other goods. When he spends more time enjoying leisure and less time working, he has lower income and can afford less consumption. When he spends more of his income in the present and saves less of it, he must accept a lower level of consumption in the future. The theory of consumer choice examines how consumers facing these tradeoffs make decisions and how they respond to changes in their environment.

After developing the basic theory of consumer choice, we apply it to three questions about household decisions. In particular, we ask:

1. Do all demand curves slope downward?
2. How do wages affect labour supply?
3. How do interest rates affect household saving?

At first, these questions might seem unrelated. But, as we will see, we can use the theory of consumer choice to address each of them.

THE BUDGET CONSTRAINT:
WHAT THE CONSUMER CAN AFFORD

Most people would like to increase the quantity or quality of the goods they consume—to take longer vacations, drive fancier cars, or eat at better restaurants. People consume less than they desire because their spending is *constrained*, or limited, by their income. We begin our study of consumer choice by examining this link between income and spending.

To keep things simple, we examine the decision facing a consumer who buys only two goods: Pepsi and pizza. Of course, real people buy thousands of different kinds of goods. Yet assuming there are only two goods greatly simplifies the problem without altering the basic insights about consumer choice.

We first consider how the consumer's income constrains the amount he spends on Pepsi and pizza. Suppose that the consumer has an income of $1000 per month and that he spends his entire income each month on Pepsi and pizza. The price of a litre of Pepsi is $2, and the price of a pizza is $10.

The table in Figure 21.1 shows some of the many combinations of Pepsi and pizza that the consumer can buy. The first line in the table shows that if the consumer spends all his income on pizza, he can eat 100 pizzas during the month, but he would not be able to buy any Pepsi at all. The second line shows another possible consumption bundle: 90 pizzas and 50 L of Pepsi. And so on. Each consumption bundle in the table costs exactly $1000.

The graph in Figure 21.1 illustrates the consumption bundles that the consumer can choose. The vertical axis measures the number of litres of Pepsi, and the horizontal axis measures the number of pizzas. Three points are marked on this figure. At point A, the consumer buys no Pepsi and consumes 100 pizzas. At point B, the consumer buys no pizza and consumes 500 L of Pepsi. At point C, the consumer buys 50 pizzas and 250 L of Pepsi. Point C, which is exactly at the middle of the line from A to B, is the point at which the consumer spends an equal amount ($500) on Pepsi and pizza. Of course, these are only three of the many combinations of Pepsi and pizza that the consumer can choose. All the points on the line

FIGURE 21.1

The Consumer's Budget Constraint

The budget constraint shows the various bundles of goods that the consumer can afford for a given income. Here the consumer buys bundles of Pepsi and pizza. The table and graph show what the consumer can afford if his income is $1000, the price of Pepsi is $2 per litre, and the price of a pizza is $10.

Litres of Pepsi	Number of Pizzas	Spending on Pepsi	Spending on Pizza	Total Spending
0	100	$ 0	$1000	$1000
50	90	100	900	1000
100	80	200	800	1000
150	70	300	700	1000
200	60	400	600	1000
250	50	500	500	1000
300	40	600	400	1000
350	30	700	300	1000
400	20	800	200	1000
450	10	900	100	1000
500	0	1000	0	1000

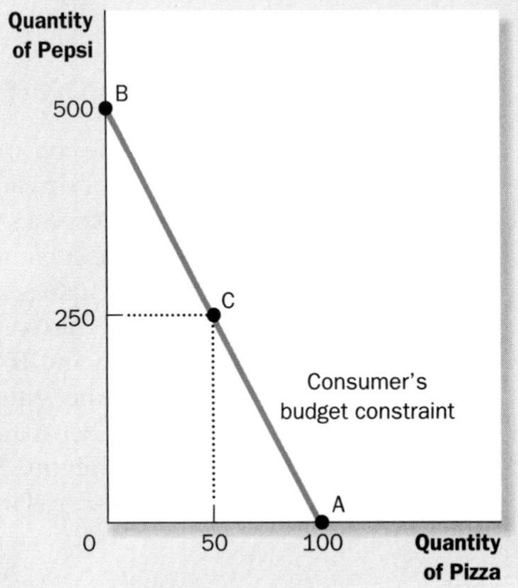

from A to B are possible. This line, called the **budget constraint,** shows the consumption bundles that the consumer can afford. In this case, it shows the tradeoff between Pepsi and pizza that the consumer faces.

The slope of the budget constraint measures the rate at which the consumer can trade one good for the other. Recall from the appendix to Chapter 2 that the slope between two points is calculated as the change in the vertical distance divided by the change in the horizontal distance ("rise over run"). From point A to point B, the vertical distance is 500 L, and the horizontal distance is 100 pizzas. Thus, the slope is 5 L per pizza. (Actually, because the budget constraint slopes downward, the slope is a negative number. But for our purposes we can ignore the minus sign.)

Notice that the slope of the budget constraint equals the *relative price* of the two goods—the price of one good compared to the price of the other. A pizza costs 5 times as much as a litre of Pepsi, so the opportunity cost of a pizza is 5 L of Pepsi. The budget constraint's slope of 5 reflects the tradeoff the market is offering the consumer: 1 pizza for 5 L of Pepsi.

budget constraint
the limit on the consumption bundles that a consumer can afford

QuickQuiz Draw the budget constraint for a person with income of $1000 if the price of Pepsi is $5 per litre and the price of a pizza is $10. What is the slope of this budget constraint?

PREFERENCES: WHAT THE CONSUMER WANTS

Our goal in this chapter is to see how consumers make choices. The budget constraint is one piece of the analysis: It shows what combination of goods the consumer can afford given his income and the prices of the goods. The consumer's choices, however, depend not only on his budget constraint but also on his preferences regarding the two goods. Therefore, the consumer's preferences are the next piece of our analysis.

Representing Preferences with Indifference Curves

indifference curve
a curve that shows consumption bundles that give the consumer the same level of satisfaction

The consumer's preferences allow him to choose among different bundles of Pepsi and pizza. If you offer the consumer two different bundles, he chooses the bundle that best suits his tastes. If the two bundles suit his tastes equally well, we say that the consumer is *indifferent* between the two bundles.

Just as we have represented the consumer's budget constraint graphically, we can also represent his preferences graphically. We do this with indifference curves. An **indifference curve** shows the bundles of consumption that make the consumer equally happy. In this case, the indifference curves show the combinations of Pepsi and pizza with which the consumer is equally satisfied.

Figure 21.2 shows two of the consumer's many indifference curves. The consumer is indifferent among combinations A, B, and C, because they are all on the

---

FIGURE 21.2

The Consumer's Preferences

The consumer's preferences are represented with indifference curves, which show the combinations of Pepsi and pizza that make the consumer equally satisfied. Because the consumer prefers more of a good, points on a higher indifference curve (I_2 here) are preferred to points on a lower indifference curve (I_1). The marginal rate of substitution (MRS) shows the rate at which the consumer is willing to trade Pepsi for pizza.

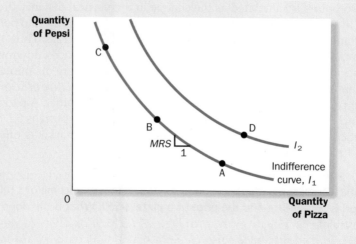

same curve. Not surprisingly, if the consumer's consumption of pizza is reduced, say from point A to point B, consumption of Pepsi must increase to keep him equally happy. If consumption of pizza is reduced again, from point B to point C, the amount of Pepsi consumed must increase yet again.

The slope at any point on an indifference curve equals the rate at which the consumer is willing to substitute one good for the other. This rate is called the **marginal rate of substitution** (*MRS*). In this case, the marginal rate of substitution measures how much Pepsi the consumer requires in order to be compensated for a one-unit reduction in pizza consumption (as indicated by the numeral "1" in Figure 21.2). Notice that because the indifference curves are not straight lines, the marginal rate of substitution is not the same at all points on a given indifference curve. The rate at which a consumer is willing to trade one good for the other depends on the amounts of the goods he is already consuming. That is, the rate at which a consumer is willing to trade pizza for Pepsi depends on whether he is more hungry or more thirsty, which in turn depends on how much pizza and Pepsi he has.

marginal rate of substitution
the rate at which a consumer is willing to trade one good for another

The consumer is equally happy at all points on any given indifference curve, but he prefers some indifference curves to others. Because he prefers more consumption to less, higher indifference curves are preferred to lower ones. In Figure 21.2, any point on curve I_2 is preferred to any point on curve I_1.

A consumer's set of indifference curves gives a complete ranking of the consumer's preferences. That is, we can use the indifference curves to rank any two bundles of goods. For example, the indifference curves tell us that point D is preferred to point A because point D is on a higher indifference curve than point A. (That conclusion may be obvious, however, because point D offers the consumer both more pizza and more Pepsi.) The indifference curves also tell us that point D is preferred to point C because point D is on a higher indifference curve. Even though point D has less Pepsi than point C, it has more than enough extra pizza to make the consumer prefer it. By seeing which point is on the higher indifference curve, we can use the set of indifference curves to rank any combinations of Pepsi and pizza.

Four Properties of Indifference Curves

Because indifference curves represent a consumer's preferences, they have certain properties that reflect those preferences. Here we consider four properties that describe most indifference curves:

- *Property 1: Higher indifference curves are preferred to lower ones.* Consumers usually prefer more of something to less of it. This preference for greater quantities is reflected in the indifference curves. As Figure 21.2 shows, higher indifference curves represent larger quantities of goods than lower indifference curves. Thus, the consumer prefers being on higher indifference curves.
- *Property 2: Indifference curves are downward sloping.* The slope of an indifference curve reflects the rate at which the consumer is willing to substitute one good for the other. In most cases, the consumer likes both goods. Therefore, if the quantity of one good is reduced, the quantity of the other good must increase in order for the consumer to be equally happy. For this reason, most indifference curves slope downward.
- *Property 3: Indifference curves do not cross.* To see why this is true, suppose that two indifference curves did cross, as in Figure 21.3 (p. 470). Then, because point A is on the same indifference curve as point B, the two points would make the

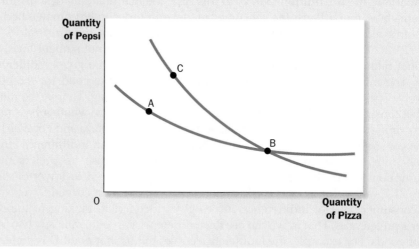

FIGURE 21.3

The Impossibility of Intersecting Indifference Curves

A situation like this can never happen. According to these indifference curves, the consumer would be equally satisfied at points A, B, and C, even though point C has more of both goods than point A.

consumer equally happy. In addition, because point B is on the same indifference curve as point C, these two points would make the consumer equally happy. But these conclusions imply that points A and C would also make the consumer equally happy, even though point C has more of both goods. This contradicts our assumption that the consumer always prefers more of both goods to less. Thus, indifference curves cannot cross.

- *Property 4: Indifference curves are bowed inward.* The slope of an indifference curve is the marginal rate of substitution—the rate at which the consumer is willing to trade off one good for the other. The marginal rate of substitution (*MRS*) usually depends on the amount of each good the consumer is currently consuming. In particular, because people are more willing to trade away goods that they have in abundance and less willing to trade away goods of which they have little, the indifference curves are bowed inward. As an example, consider Figure 21.4. At point A, because the consumer has a lot of Pepsi and only a little pizza, he is very hungry but not very thirsty. To induce the consumer to give up 1 pizza, the consumer has to be given 6 L of Pepsi: The marginal rate of substitution is 6 L per pizza. By contrast, at point B, the consumer has little Pepsi and a lot of pizza, so he is very thirsty but not very hungry. At this point, he would be willing to give up 1 pizza to get 1 L of Pepsi: The marginal rate of substitution is 1 L per pizza. Thus, the bowed shape of the indifference curve reflects the consumer's greater willingness to give up a good that he already has in large quantity.

Two Extreme Examples of Indifference Curves

The shape of an indifference curve tells us about the consumer's willingness to trade one good for the other. When the goods are easy to substitute for each other,

FIGURE 21.4

Bowed Indifference Curves

Indifference curves are usually bowed inward. This shape implies that the marginal rate of substitution (MRS) depends on the quantity of the two goods the consumer is consuming. At point A, the consumer has little pizza and much Pepsi, so he requires a lot of extra Pepsi to induce him to give up one of the pizzas: The marginal rate of substitution is 6 L of Pepsi per pizza. At point B, the consumer has much pizza and little Pepsi, so he requires only a little extra Pepsi to induce him to give up one of the pizzas: The marginal rate of substitution is 1 L of Pepsi per pizza.

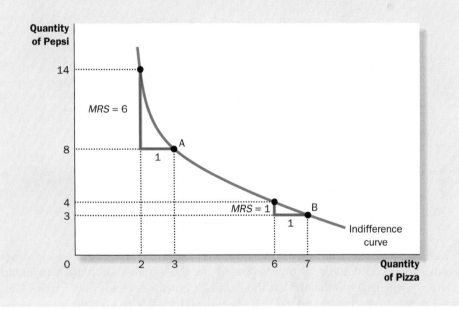

the indifference curves are less bowed; when the goods are hard to substitute, the indifference curves are very bowed. To see why this is true, let's consider the extreme cases.

Perfect Substitutes   Suppose that someone offered you bundles of nickels and dimes. How would you rank the different bundles?

Most likely, you would care only about the total monetary value of each bundle. If so, you would judge a bundle based on the number of nickels plus twice the number of dimes. In other words, you would always be willing to trade 1 dime for 2 nickels, regardless of the number of nickels and dimes in the bundle. Your marginal rate of substitution between nickels and dimes would be a fixed number: 2.

We can represent your preferences about nickels and dimes with the indifference curves in panel (a) of Figure 21.5 (p. 472). Because the marginal rate of substitution is constant, the indifference curves are straight lines. In this extreme case of straight indifference curves, we say that the two goods are **perfect substitutes.**

Perfect Complements   Suppose now that someone offered you bundles of shoes. Some of the shoes fit your left foot, others your right foot. How would you rank these different bundles?

perfect substitutes
two goods with straight-line indifference curves

FIGURE 21.5

Perfect Substitutes and Perfect Complements

When two goods are easily substitutable, such as nickels and dimes, the indifference curves are straight lines, as shown in panel (a). When two goods are strongly complementary, such as left shoes and right shoes, the indifference curves are right angles, as shown in panel (b).

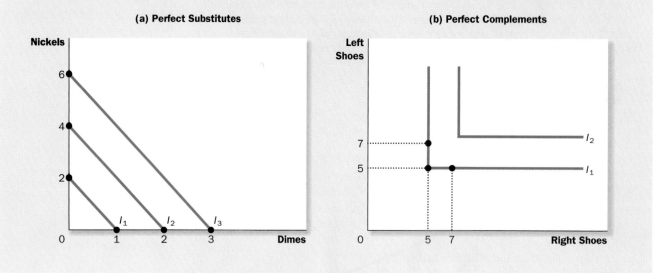

In this case, you might care only about the number of pairs of shoes. In other words, you would judge a bundle based on the number of pairs you could assemble from it. A bundle of 5 left shoes and 7 right shoes yields only 5 pairs. Getting 1 more right shoe has no value if there is no left shoe to go with it.

We can represent your preferences for right and left shoes with the indifference curves in panel (b) of Figure 21.5. In this case, a bundle with 5 left shoes and 5 right shoes is just as good as a bundle with 5 left shoes and 7 right shoes. It is also just as good as a bundle with 7 left shoes and 5 right shoes. The indifference curves, therefore, are right angles. In this extreme case of right-angle indifference curves, we say that the two goods are **perfect complements.**

In the real world, of course, most goods are neither perfect substitutes (like nickels and dimes) nor perfect complements (like right shoes and left shoes). More typically, the indifference curves are bowed inward, but not so bowed as to become right angles.

perfect complements
two goods with right-angle indifference curves

QuickQuiz Draw some indifference curves for Pepsi and pizza. Explain the four properties of these indifference curves.

OPTIMIZATION: WHAT THE CONSUMER CHOOSES

The goal of this chapter is to understand how a consumer makes choices. We have the two pieces necessary for this analysis: the consumer's budget constraint and the consumer's preferences. Now we put these two pieces together and consider the consumer's decision about what to buy.

The Consumer's Optimal Choices

Consider once again our Pepsi and pizza example. The consumer would like to end up with the best possible combination of Pepsi and pizza—that is, the combination on the highest possible indifference curve. But the consumer must also end up on or below his budget constraint, which measures the total resources available to him.

Figure 21.6 shows the consumer's budget constraint and three of his many indifference curves. The highest indifference curve that the consumer can reach (I_2 in the figure) is the one that just barely touches the budget constraint. The point at which this indifference curve and the budget constraint touch is called the *optimum*. The consumer would prefer point A, but he cannot afford that point because it lies above his budget constraint. The consumer can afford point B, but that point is on a lower indifference curve and, therefore, provides the consumer less satisfaction. The optimum represents the best combination of consumption of Pepsi and pizza available to the consumer.

Notice that, at the optimum, the slope of the indifference curve equals the slope of the budget constraint. We say that the indifference curve is *tangent* to the budget constraint. The slope of the indifference curve is the marginal rate of substitution between Pepsi and pizza, and the slope of the budget constraint is the relative price of Pepsi and pizza. Thus, *the consumer chooses consumption of the two goods so that the marginal rate of substitution equals the relative price.*

In Chapter 7 we saw how market prices reflect the marginal value that consumers place on goods. This analysis of consumer choice shows the same result in another way. In making his consumption choices, the consumer takes as given the relative price of the two goods and then chooses an optimum at which his marginal rate of substitution equals this relative price. The relative price is the rate at which the *market* is willing to trade one good for the other, whereas the marginal rate of substitution is the rate at which the *consumer* is willing to trade one good for the other. At the consumer's optimum, the consumer's valuation of the two goods (as measured by the marginal rate of substitution) equals the market's valuation (as

FIGURE 21.6

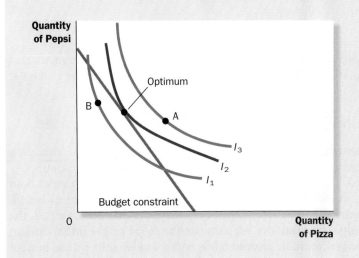

The Consumer's Optimum

The consumer chooses the point on his budget constraint that lies on the highest indifference curve. At this point, called the optimum, the marginal rate of substitution equals the relative price of the two goods. Here the highest indifference curve the consumer can reach is I_2. The consumer prefers point A, which lies on indifference curve I_3, but the consumer cannot afford this bundle of Pepsi and pizza. By contrast, point B is affordable, but because it lies on a lower indifference curve, the consumer does not prefer it.

UTILITY: AN ALTERNATIVE WAY TO DESCRIBE PREFERENCES AND OPTIMIZATION

We have used indifference curves to represent the consumer's preferences. Another common way to represent preferences is with the concept of *utility*. Utility is an abstract measure of the satisfaction or happiness that a consumer receives from a bundle of goods. Economists say that a consumer prefers one bundle of goods to another if the first provides more utility than the second.

Indifference curves and utility are closely related. Because the consumer prefers points on higher indifference curves, bundles of goods on higher indifference curves provide higher utility. Because the consumer is equally happy with all points on the same indifference curve, all these bundles provide the same utility. You can think of an indifference curve as an "equal-utility" curve.

The *marginal utility* of any good is the increase in utility that the consumer gets from an additional unit of that good. Most goods are assumed to exhibit *diminishing marginal utility:* The more of the good the consumer already has, the lower the marginal utility provided by an extra unit of that good.

The *marginal rate of substitution* between two goods depends on their marginal utilities. For example, if the marginal utility of good X is twice the marginal utility of good Y, then a person would need 2 units of good Y to compensate for losing 1 unit of good X, and the

marginal rate of substitution equals 2. More generally, the marginal rate of substitution (and thus the slope of the indifference curve) equals the marginal utility of one good divided by the marginal utility of the other good.

Utility analysis provides another way to describe consumer optimization. Recall that at the consumer's optimum, the marginal rate of substitution equals the ratio of prices. That is,

$$MRS = P_X/P_Y$$

Because the marginal rate of substitution equals the ratio of marginal utilities, we can write this condition for optimization as

$$MU_X/MU_Y = P_X/P_Y$$

Now rearrange this expression to become

$$MU_X/P_X = MU_Y/P_Y$$

This equation has a simple interpretation: At the optimum, the marginal utility per dollar spent on good X equals the marginal utility per dollar spent on good Y. (Why? If this equality did not hold, the consumer could increase utility by spending less on the good that provided lower marginal utility per dollar and more on the good that provided higher marginal utility per dollar.)

When economists discuss the theory of consumer choice, they might express the theory using different words. One economist might say that the goal of the consumer is to maximize utility. Another economist might say that the goal of the consumer is to end up on the highest possible indifference curve. The first economist would conclude that at the consumer's optimum, the marginal utility per dollar is the same for all goods, whereas the second would conclude that the indifference curve is tangent to the budget constraint. In essence, these are two ways of saying the same thing.

measured by the relative price). As a result of this consumer optimization, market prices of different goods reflect the value that consumers place on those goods.

How Changes in Income Affect the Consumer's Choices

Now that we have seen how the consumer makes the consumption decision, let's examine how consumption responds to changes in income. To be specific, suppose that income increases. With higher income, the consumer can afford more of both goods. The increase in income, therefore, shifts the budget constraint outward, as in Figure 21.7. Because the relative price of the two goods has not changed, the slope of the new budget constraint is the same as the slope of the initial budget constraint. That is, an increase in income leads to a parallel shift in the budget constraint.

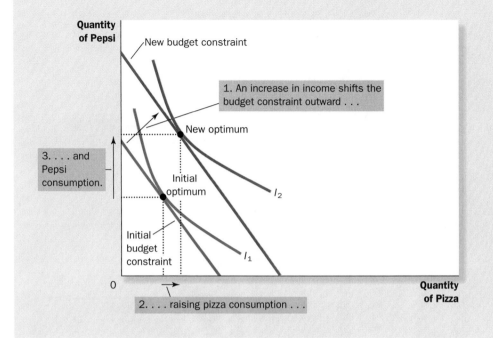

FIGURE 21.7

Quantity of Pepsi

New budget constraint

1. An increase in income shifts the budget constraint outward . . .

New optimum

3. . . . and Pepsi consumption.

Initial optimum

I_2

Initial budget constraint

I_1

0

2. . . . raising pizza consumption . . .

Quantity of Pizza

An Increase in Income

When the consumer's income rises, the budget constraint shifts out. If both goods are normal goods, the consumer responds to the increase in income by buying more of both of them. Here the consumer buys more pizza and more Pepsi.

The expanded budget constraint allows the consumer to choose a better combination of Pepsi and pizza. In other words, the consumer can now reach a higher indifference curve. Given the shift in the budget constraint and the consumer's preferences as represented by his indifference curves, the consumer's optimum moves from the point labelled "initial optimum" to the point labelled "new optimum."

Notice that, in Figure 21.7, the consumer chooses to consume more Pepsi and more pizza. Although the logic of the model does not require increased consumption of both goods in response to increased income, this situation is the most common one. As you may recall from Chapter 4, if a consumer wants more of a good when his income rises, economists call it a **normal good.** The indifference curves in Figure 21.7 are drawn under the assumption that both Pepsi and pizza are normal goods.

Figure 21.8 (p. 476) shows an example in which an increase in income induces the consumer to buy more pizza but less Pepsi. If a consumer buys less of a good when his income rises, economists call it an **inferior good.** Figure 21.8 is drawn under the assumption that pizza is a normal good and Pepsi is an inferior good.

Although most goods are normal goods, there are some inferior goods in the world. One example is bus rides. High-income consumers are more likely to own cars and less likely to ride the bus than low-income consumers. Bus rides, therefore, are an inferior good.

normal good
a good for which an increase in income raises the quantity demanded

inferior good
a good for which an increase in income reduces the quantity demanded

How Changes in Prices Affect the Consumer's Choices

Let's now use this model of consumer choice to consider how a change in the price of one of the goods alters the consumer's choices. Suppose, in particular, that the

FIGURE 21.8

An Inferior Good

A good is an inferior good if the consumer buys less of it when his income rises. Here Pepsi is an inferior good: When the consumer's income increases and the budget constraint shifts outward, the consumer buys more pizza but less Pepsi.

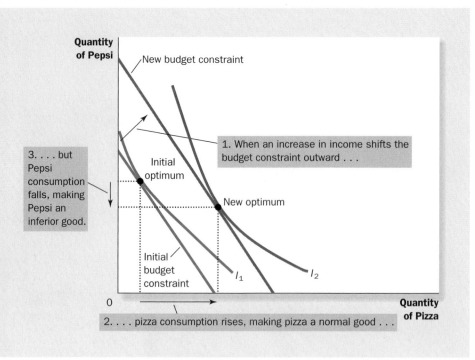

Quantity of Pepsi

New budget constraint

3. . . . but Pepsi consumption falls, making Pepsi an inferior good.

1. When an increase in income shifts the budget constraint outward . . .

Initial optimum

New optimum

Initial budget constraint

I_1

I_2

0

2. . . . pizza consumption rises, making pizza a normal good . . .

Quantity of Pizza

price of Pepsi falls from $2 to $1 per litre. It is no surprise that the lower price expands the consumer's set of buying opportunities. In other words, a fall in the price of any good shifts the budget constraint outward.

Figure 21.9 considers more specifically how the fall in price affects the budget constraint. If the consumer spends his entire $1000 income on pizza, then the price of Pepsi is irrelevant. Thus, point A in the figure stays the same. Yet if the consumer spends his entire income of $1000 on Pepsi, he can now buy 1000 rather than only 500 L. Thus, the end point of the budget constraint moves from point B to point D.

Notice that in this case the outward shift in the budget constraint changes its slope. (This differs from what happened previously when prices stayed the same but the consumer's income changed.) As we have discussed, the slope of the budget constraint reflects the relative price of Pepsi and pizza. Because the price of Pepsi has fallen to $1 from $2, while the price of pizza has remained at $10, the consumer can now trade a pizza for 10 rather than 5 L of Pepsi. As a result, the new budget constraint is more steeply sloped.

How such a change in the budget constraint alters the consumption of both goods depends on the consumer's preferences. For the indifference curves drawn in this figure, the consumer buys more Pepsi and less pizza.

Income and Substitution Effects

The impact of a change in the price of a good on consumption can be decomposed into two effects: an **income effect** and a **substitution effect.** To see what these two

income effect
the change in consumption that results when a price change moves the consumer to a higher or lower indifference curve

substitution effect
the change in consumption that results when a price change moves the consumer along a given indifference curve to a point with a new marginal rate of substitution

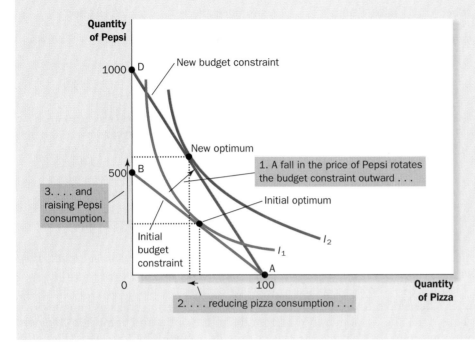

FIGURE 21.9

A Change in Price

When the price of Pepsi falls, the consumer's budget constraint shifts outward and changes slope. The consumer moves from the initial optimum to the new optimum, which changes his purchases of both Pepsi and pizza. In this case, the quantity of Pepsi consumed rises, and the quantity of pizza consumed falls.

effects are, consider how our consumer might respond when he learns that the price of Pepsi has fallen. He might reason in the following ways:

- "Great news! Now that Pepsi is cheaper, my income has greater purchasing power. I am, in effect, richer than I was. Because I am richer, I can buy both more Pepsi and more pizza." (This is the income effect.)
- "Now that the price of Pepsi has fallen, I get more litres of Pepsi for every pizza that I give up. Because pizza is now relatively more expensive, I should buy less pizza and more Pepsi." (This is the substitution effect.)

Which statement do you find more compelling?

In fact, both of these statements make sense. The decrease in the price of Pepsi makes the consumer better off. If Pepsi and pizza are both normal goods, the consumer will want to spread this improvement in his purchasing power over both goods. This income effect tends to make the consumer buy more pizza and more Pepsi. Yet, at the same time, consumption of Pepsi has become less expensive relative to consumption of pizza. This substitution effect tends to make the consumer choose more Pepsi and less pizza.

Now consider the end result of these two effects. The consumer certainly buys more Pepsi, because the income and substitution effects both act to raise purchases of Pepsi. But it is ambiguous whether the consumer buys more pizza, because the income and substitution effects work in opposite directions. This conclusion is summarized in Table 21.1 (p. 478).

We can interpret the income and substitution effects using indifference curves. *The income effect is the change in consumption that results from the movement to a higher*

TABLE 21.1				

	Good	Income Effect	Substitution Effect	Total Effect
Income and Substitution Effects When the Price of Pepsi Falls	Pepsi	Consumer is richer, so he buys more Pepsi.	Pepsi is relatively cheaper, so consumer buys more Pepsi.	Income and substitution effects act in same direction, so consumer buys more Pepsi.
	Pizza	Consumer is richer, so he buys more pizza.	Pizza is relatively more expensive, so consumer buys less pizza.	Income and substitution effects act in opposite directions, so the total effect on pizza consumption is ambiguous.

indifference curve. The substitution effect is the change in consumption that results from being at a point on an indifference curve with a different marginal rate of substitution.

Figure 21.10 shows graphically how to decompose the change in the consumer's decision into the income effect and the substitution effect. When the price of Pepsi falls, the consumer moves from the initial optimum, point A, to the new optimum, point C. We can view this change as occurring in two steps. First, the consumer moves *along* the initial indifference curve I_1 from point A to point B. The consumer is equally happy at these two points, but at point B, the marginal rate of substitution reflects the new relative price. (The dashed line through point B reflects the new relative price by being parallel to the new budget constraint.) Next, the consumer *shifts* to the higher indifference curve I_2 by moving from point B to point C. Even though point B and point C are on different indifference curves, they have the same marginal rate of substitution. That is, the slope of the indifference curve I_1 at point B equals the slope of the indifference curve I_2 at point C.

Although the consumer never actually chooses point B, this hypothetical point is useful to clarify the two effects that determine the consumer's decision. Notice that the change from point A to point B represents a pure change in the marginal rate of substitution without any change in the consumer's welfare. Similarly, the change from point B to point C represents a pure change in welfare without any change in the marginal rate of substitution. Thus, the movement from A to B shows the substitution effect, and the movement from B to C shows the income effect.

Deriving the Demand Curve

We have just seen how changes in the price of a good alter the consumer's budget constraint and, therefore, the quantities of the two goods that he chooses to buy. The demand curve for any good reflects these consumption decisions. Recall that a demand curve shows the quantity demanded of a good for any given price. We can view a consumer's demand curve as a summary of the optimal decisions that arise from his budget constraint and indifference curves.

For example, Figure 21.11 considers the demand for Pepsi. Panel (a) shows that when the price of a litre falls from $2 to $1, the consumer's budget constraint shifts outward. Because of both income and substitution effects, the consumer increases his purchases of Pepsi from 250 to 750 L. Panel (b) shows the demand curve that

FIGURE 21.10

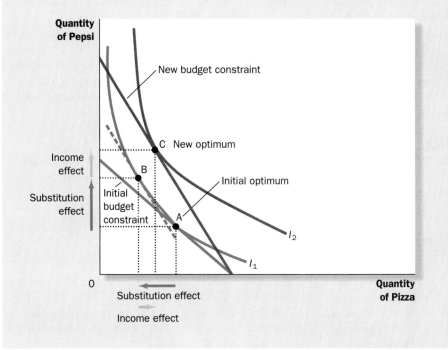

Income and Substitution Effects

The effect of a change in price can be broken down into an income effect and a substitution effect. The substitution effect—the movement along an indifference curve to a point with a different marginal rate of substitution—is shown here as the change from point A to point B along indifference curve I_1. The income effect—the shift to a higher indifference curve—is shown here as the change from point B on indifference curve I_1 to point C on indifference curve I_2.

FIGURE 21.11

Deriving the Demand Curve

Panel (a) shows that when the price of Pepsi falls from $2 to $1, the consumer's optimum moves from point A to point B, and the quantity of Pepsi consumed rises from 250 to 750 L. The demand curve in panel (b) reflects this relationship between the price and the quantity demanded.

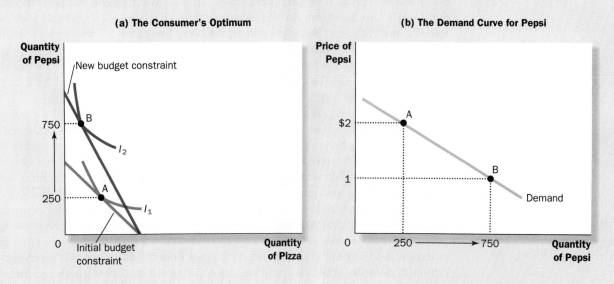

results from this consumer's decisions. In this way, the theory of consumer choice provides the theoretical foundation for the consumer's demand curve, which we first introduced in Chapter 4.

Although it is comforting to know that the demand curve arises naturally from the theory of consumer choice, this exercise by itself does not justify developing the theory. There is no need for a rigorous, analytic framework just to establish that people respond to changes in prices. The theory of consumer choice is, however, very useful. As we see in the next section, we can use the theory to delve more deeply into the determinants of household behaviour.

QuickQuiz Draw a budget constraint and indifference curves for Pepsi and pizza. Show what happens to the budget constraint and the consumer's optimum when the price of pizza rises. In your diagram, decompose the change into an income effect and a substitution effect.

THREE APPLICATIONS

Now that we have developed the basic theory of consumer choice, let's use it to shed light on three questions about how the economy works. These three questions might at first seem unrelated. But because each question involves household decision making, we can address it with the model of consumer behaviour we have just developed.

Do All Demand Curves Slope Downward?

Normally, when the price of a good rises, people buy less of it. Chapter 4 called this usual behaviour the *law of demand.* This law is reflected in the downward slope of the demand curve.

As a matter of economic theory, however, demand curves can sometimes slope upward. In other words, consumers can sometimes violate the law of demand and buy *more* of a good when the price rises. To see how this can happen, consider Figure 21.12. In this example, the consumer buys two goods—meat and potatoes. Initially, the consumer's budget constraint is the line from point A to point B. The optimum is point C. When the price of potatoes rises, the budget constraint shifts inward and is now the line from point A to point D. The optimum is now point E. Notice that a rise in the price of potatoes has led the consumer to buy a larger quantity of potatoes.

Why is the consumer responding in a seemingly perverse way? The reason is that potatoes here are a strongly inferior good. When the price of potatoes rises, the consumer is poorer. The income effect makes the consumer want to buy less meat and more potatoes. At the same time, because the potatoes have become more expensive relative to meat, the substitution effect makes the consumer want to buy more meat and less potatoes. In this particular case, however, the income effect is so strong that it exceeds the substitution effect. In the end, the consumer responds to the higher price of potatoes by buying less meat and more potatoes.

Economists use the term **Giffen good** to describe a good that violates the law of demand. (The term is named for economist Robert Giffen, who first noted this possibility.) In this example, potatoes are a Giffen good. Giffen goods are inferior

Giffen good
a good for which an increase in the price raises the quantity demanded

FIGURE 21.12

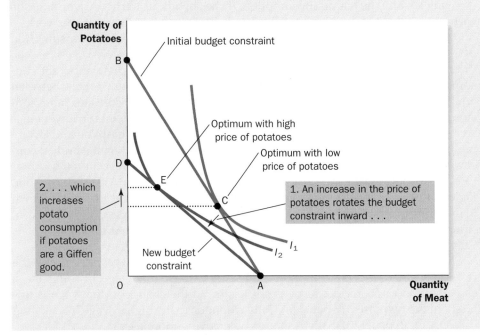

A Giffen Good

In this example, when the price of potatoes rises, the consumer's optimum shifts from point C to point E. In this case, the consumer responds to a higher price of potatoes by buying less meat and more potatoes.

goods for which the income effect dominates the substitution effect. Therefore, they have demand curves that slope upward.

Economists disagree about whether any Giffen good has ever been discovered. Some historians suggest that potatoes were in fact a Giffen good during the Irish potato famine of the nineteenth century. Potatoes were such a large part of people's diet that when the price of potatoes rose, it had a large income effect. People responded to their reduced living standard by cutting back on the luxury of meat and buying more of the staple food of potatoes. Thus, it is argued that a higher price of potatoes actually raised the quantity of potatoes demanded.

Whether or not this historical account is true, it is safe to say that Giffen goods are very rare. The theory of consumer choice does allow demand curves to slope upward. Yet such occurrences are so unusual that the law of demand is as reliable a law as any in economics.

How Do Wages Affect Labour Supply?

So far we have used the theory of consumer choice to analyze how a person decides how to allocate his income between two goods. We can use the same theory to analyze how a person decides to allocate his time between work and leisure.

Consider the decision facing Sally, a freelance software designer. Sally is awake for 100 hours per week. She spends some of this time enjoying leisure—riding her bike, watching television, studying economics, and so on. She spends the rest of this time developing software at her computer. For every hour she spends developing software, she earns $50, which she spends on consumption goods. Thus, her wage ($50) reflects the tradeoff Sally faces between leisure and consumption. For every hour of leisure she gives up, she works one more hour and gets $50 of consumption.

Figure 21.13 shows Sally's budget constraint. If she spends all 100 hours enjoying leisure, she has no consumption. If she spends all 100 hours working, she earns a weekly consumption of $5000 but has no time for leisure. If she works a normal 40-hour week, she enjoys 60 hours of leisure and has weekly consumption of $2000.

Figure 21.13 uses indifference curves to represent Sally's preferences for consumption and leisure. Here consumption and leisure are the two "goods" between which Sally is choosing. Because Sally always prefers more leisure and more consumption, she prefers points on higher indifference curves to points on lower ones. At a wage of $50 per hour, Sally chooses a combination of consumption and leisure represented by the point labelled "optimum." This is the point on the budget constraint that is on the highest possible indifference curve, which is curve I_2.

Now consider what happens when Sally's wage increases from $50 to $60 per hour. Figure 21.14 shows two possible outcomes. In each case, the budget constraint, shown in the left-hand graph, shifts outward from BC_1 to BC_2. In the process, the budget constraint becomes steeper, reflecting the change in relative price: At the higher wage, Sally gets more consumption for every hour of leisure that she gives up.

Sally's preferences, as represented by her indifference curves, determine the resulting responses of consumption and leisure to the higher wage. In both panels, consumption rises. Yet the response of leisure to the change in the wage is different in the two cases. In panel (a), Sally responds to the higher wage by enjoying less leisure. In panel (b), Sally responds by enjoying more leisure.

Sally's decision between leisure and consumption determines her supply of labour because the more leisure she enjoys, the less time she has left to work. In each panel, the right-hand graph in Figure 21.14 shows the labour supply curve implied by Sally's decision. In panel (a), a higher wage induces Sally to enjoy less leisure and work more, so the labour supply curve slopes upward. In panel (b), a higher wage induces Sally to enjoy more leisure and work less, so the labour supply curve slopes "backward."

FIGURE 21.13

The Work–Leisure Decision

This figure shows Sally's budget constraint for deciding how much to work, her indifference curves for consumption and leisure, and her optimum.

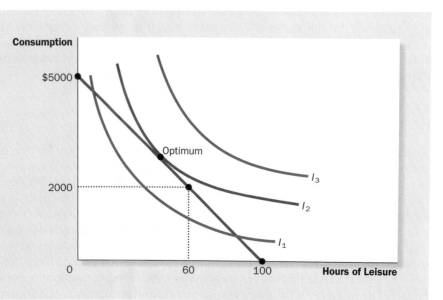

FIGURE 21.14

An Increase in the Wage

The two panels of this figure show how a person might respond to an increase in the wage. The graphs on the left show the consumer's initial budget constraint BC_1 and new budget constraint BC_2, as well as the consumer's optimal choices over consumption and leisure. The graphs on the right show the resulting labour supply curve. Because hours worked equal total hours available minus hours of leisure, any change in leisure implies an opposite change in the quantity of labour supplied. In panel (a), when the wage rises, consumption rises and leisure falls, resulting in a labour supply curve that slopes upward. In panel (b), when the wage rises, both consumption and leisure rise, resulting in a labour supply curve that slopes backward.

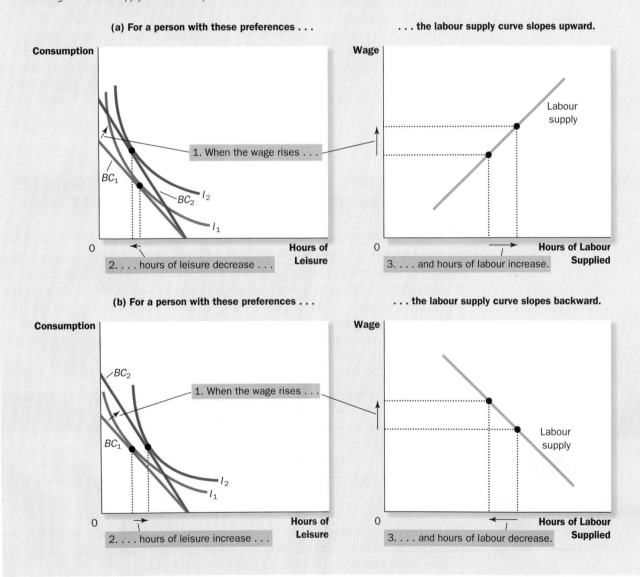

At first, the backward-sloping labour supply curve is puzzling. Why would a person respond to a higher wage by working less? The answer comes from considering the income and substitution effects of a higher wage.

Consider first the substitution effect. When Sally's wage rises, leisure becomes more costly relative to consumption, and this encourages Sally to substitute consumption for leisure. In other words, the substitution effect induces Sally to work harder in response to higher wages, which tends to make the labour supply curve slope upward.

Now consider the income effect. When Sally's wage rises, she moves to a higher indifference curve. She is now better off than she was. As long as consumption and leisure are both normal goods, she tends to want to use this increase in well-being to enjoy both higher consumption and greater leisure. In other words, the income effect induces her to work less, which tends to make the labour supply curve slope backward.

In the end, economic theory does not give a clear prediction about whether an increase in the wage induces Sally to work more or less. If the substitution effect is greater than the income effect for Sally, she works more. If the income effect is greater than the substitution effect, she works less. The labour supply curve, therefore, could be either upward or backward sloping.

Case Study

INCOME EFFECTS ON LABOUR SUPPLY: HISTORICAL TRENDS, LOTTERY WINNERS, AND THE CARNEGIE CONJECTURE

The idea of a backward-sloping labour supply curve might at first seem like a mere theoretical curiosity, but in fact it is not. Evidence indicates that the labour supply curve, considered over long periods of time, does in fact slope backward. A hundred years ago many people worked six days a week. Today five-day workweeks are the norm. At the same time that the length of the workweek has been falling, the wage of the typical worker (adjusted for inflation) has been rising.

Here is how economists explain this historical pattern: Over time, advances in technology raise workers' productivity and, thereby, the demand for labour. The increase in labour demand raises equilibrium wages. As wages rise, so does the reward for working. Yet rather than responding to this increased incentive by working more, most workers choose to take part of their greater prosperity in the form of more leisure. In other words, the income effect of higher wages dominates the substitution effect.

Further evidence that the income effect on labour supply is strong comes from a very different kind of data: winners of lotteries. Winners of large prizes in a lottery see large increases in their incomes and, as a result, large outward shifts in their budget constraints. Because the winners' wages have not changed, however, the *slopes* of their budget constraints remain the same. There is, therefore, no substitution effect. By examining the behaviour of lottery winners, we can isolate the income effect on labour supply.

The results from studies of lottery winners are striking. Of those winners who win more than $50 000, almost 25 percent quit working within a year, and another 9 percent reduce the number of hours they work. Of those winners who win more than $1 million, almost 40 percent stop working. The income effect on labour supply of winning such a large prize is substantial.

© CORBIS IMAGES

"No more 9-to-5 for me."

Similar results were found in a study, published in the May 1993 issue of *The Quarterly Journal of Economics*, of how receiving a bequest affects a person's labour supply. The study found that a single person who inherits more than $150 000 is four times as likely to stop working as a single person who inherits less than $25 000. This finding would not have surprised the nineteenth-century American industrialist Andrew Carnegie. Carnegie warned that "the parent who leaves his son enormous wealth generally deadens the talents and energies of the son, and tempts him to lead a less useful and less worthy life than he otherwise would." That is, Carnegie viewed the income effect on labour supply to be substantial and, from his paternalistic perspective, regrettable. During his life and at his death, Carnegie gave much of his vast fortune to charity. ●

How Do Interest Rates Affect Household Saving?

An important decision that every person faces is how much income to consume today and how much to save for the future. We can use the theory of consumer choice to analyze how people make this decision and how the amount they save depends on the interest rate their savings will earn.

Consider the decision facing Sam, a worker planning ahead for retirement. To keep things simple, let's divide Sam's life into two periods. In the first period, Sam is young and working. In the second period, he is old and retired. When young, Sam earns $100 000. He divides this income between current consumption and saving. When he is old, Sam will consume what he has saved, including the interest that his savings have earned.

Suppose that the interest rate is 10 percent. Then, for every dollar that Sam saves when young, he can consume $1.10 when old. We can view "consumption when young" and "consumption when old" as the two goods that Sam must choose between. The interest rate determines the relative price of these two goods.

Figure 21.15 (p. 486) shows Sam's budget constraint. If he saves nothing, he consumes $100 000 when young and nothing when old. If he saves everything, he consumes nothing when young and $110 000 when old. The budget constraint shows these and all the intermediate possibilities.

Figure 21.15 uses indifference curves to represent Sam's preferences for consumption in the two periods. Because Sam prefers more consumption in both periods, he prefers points on higher indifference curves to points on lower ones. Given his preferences, Sam chooses the optimal combination of consumption in both periods of life, which is the point on the budget constraint that is on the highest possible indifference curve. At this optimum, Sam consumes $50 000 when young and $55 000 when old.

Now consider what happens when the interest rate increases from 10 percent to 20 percent. Figure 21.16 (p. 486) shows two possible outcomes. In both cases, the budget constraint shifts outward and becomes steeper. At the new higher interest rate, Sam gets more consumption when old for every dollar of consumption that he gives up when young.

The two panels show different preferences for Sam and the resulting response to the higher interest rate. In both cases, consumption when old rises. Yet the response of consumption when young to the change in the interest rate is different in the two cases. In panel (a), Sam responds to the higher interest rate by consuming less when young. In panel (b), Sam responds by consuming more when young.

FIGURE 21.15

The Consumption–Saving Decision

This figure shows the budget constraint for a person deciding how much to consume in the two periods of his life, the indifference curves representing his preferences, and the optimum.

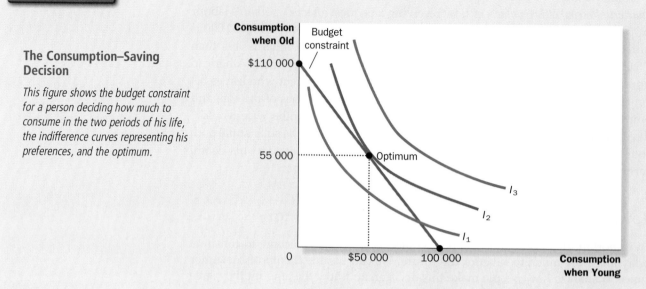

FIGURE 21.16

An Increase in the Interest Rate

In both panels, an increase in the interest rate shifts the budget constraint outward. In panel (a), consumption when young falls, and consumption when old rises. The result is an increase in saving when young. In panel (b), consumption in both periods rises. The result is a decrease in saving when young.

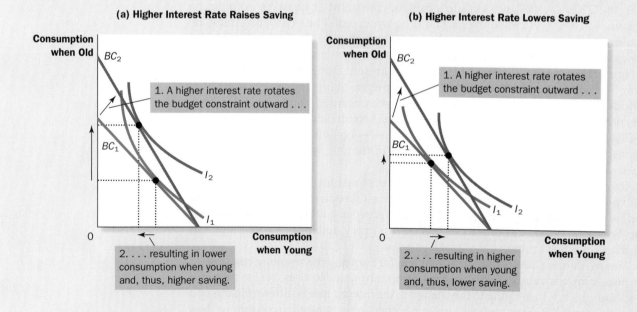

Sam's saving, of course, is his income when young minus the amount he consumes when young. In panel (a), consumption when young falls when the interest rate rises, so saving must rise. In panel (b), Sam consumes more when young, so saving must fall.

The case shown in panel (b) might at first seem odd: Sam responds to an increase in the return to saving by saving less. Yet this behaviour is not as peculiar as it might seem. We can understand it by considering the income and substitution effects of a higher interest rate.

Consider first the substitution effect. When the interest rate rises, consumption when old becomes less costly relative to consumption when young. Therefore, the substitution effect induces Sam to consume more when old and less when young. In other words, the substitution effect induces Sam to save more.

Now consider the income effect. When the interest rate rises, Sam moves to a higher indifference curve. He is now better off than he was. As long as consumption in both periods consists of normal goods, he tends to want to use this increase in well-being to enjoy higher consumption in both periods. In other words, the income effect induces him to save less.

The end result, of course, depends on both the income and substitution effects. If the substitution effect of a higher interest rate is greater than the income effect, Sam saves more. If the income effect is greater than the substitution effect, Sam saves less. Thus, the theory of consumer choice says that an increase in the interest rate could either encourage or discourage saving.

Although this ambiguous result is interesting from the standpoint of economic theory, it is disappointing from the standpoint of economic policy. It turns out that an important issue in tax policy hinges in part on how saving responds to interest rates. Some economists have advocated reducing the taxation of interest and other capital income, arguing that such a policy change would raise the after-tax interest rate that savers can earn and would thereby encourage people to save more. Other economists have argued that because of offsetting income and substitution effects, such a tax change might not increase saving and could even reduce it. Unfortunately, research has not led to a consensus about how interest rates affect saving. As a result, there remains disagreement among economists about whether changes in tax policy aimed to encourage saving would, in fact, have the intended effect.

QuickQuiz Explain how an increase in the wage can potentially decrease the amount that a person wants to work.

CONCLUSION: DO PEOPLE REALLY THINK THIS WAY?

The theory of consumer choice describes how people make decisions. As we have seen, it has broad applicability. It can explain how a person chooses between Pepsi and pizza, work and leisure, consumption and saving, and on and on.

At this point, however, you might be tempted to treat the theory of consumer choice with some skepticism. After all, you are a consumer. You decide what to buy every time you walk into a store. And you know that you do not decide by writing down budget constraints and indifference curves. Doesn't this knowledge about your own decision making provide evidence against the theory?

The answer is no. The theory of consumer choice does not try to present a literal account of how people make decisions. It is a model. And, as we first discussed in Chapter 2, models are not intended to be completely realistic.

The best way to view the theory of consumer choice is as a metaphor for how consumers make decisions. No consumer (except an occasional economist) goes through the explicit optimization envisioned in the theory. Yet consumers are aware that their choices are constrained by their financial resources. And, given those constraints, they do the best they can to achieve the highest level of satisfaction. The theory of consumer choice tries to describe this implicit, psychological process in a way that permits explicit, economic analysis.

The proof of the pudding is in the eating. And the test of a theory is in its applications. In the last section of this chapter we applied the theory of consumer choice to three practical issues about the economy. If you take more advanced courses in economics, you will see that this theory provides the framework for much additional analysis.

SUMMARY

- A consumer's budget constraint shows the possible combinations of different goods he can buy given his income and the prices of the goods. The slope of the budget constraint equals the relative price of the goods.

- The consumer's indifference curves represent his preferences. An indifference curve shows the various bundles of goods that make the consumer equally happy. Points on higher indifference curves are preferred to points on lower indifference curves. The slope of an indifference curve at any point is the consumer's marginal rate of substitution—the rate at which the consumer is willing to trade one good for the other.

- The consumer optimizes by choosing the point on his budget constraint that lies on the highest indifference curve. At this point, the slope of the indifference curve (the marginal rate of substitution between the goods) equals the slope of the budget constraint (the relative price of the goods).

- When the price of a good falls, the impact on the consumer's choices can be broken down into an income effect and a substitution effect. The income effect is the change in consumption that arises because a lower price makes the consumer better off. The substitution effect is the change in consumption that arises because a price change encourages greater consumption of the good that has become relatively cheaper. The income effect is reflected in the movement from a lower to a higher indifference curve, whereas the substitution effect is reflected by a movement along an indifference curve to a point with a different slope.

- The theory of consumer choice can be applied in many situations. It can explain why demand curves can potentially slope upward, why higher wages could either increase or decrease the quantity of labour supplied, and why higher interest rates could either increase or decrease saving.

KEY CONCEPTS

budget constraint, p. 467
indifference curve, p. 468
marginal rate of
   substitution, p. 469

perfect substitutes, p. 471
perfect complements, p. 472
normal good, p. 475
inferior good, p. 475

income effect, p. 476
substitution effect, p. 476
Giffen good, p. 480

QUESTIONS FOR REVIEW

1. A consumer has income of $3000. Wine costs $3 per glass, and cheese costs $6 per kilogram. Draw the consumer's budget constraint. What is the slope of this budget constraint?

2. Draw a consumer's indifference curves for wine and cheese. Describe and explain four properties of these indifference curves.

3. Pick a point on an indifference curve for wine and cheese and show the marginal rate of substitution. What does the marginal rate of substitution tell us?

4. Show a consumer's budget constraint and indifference curves for wine and cheese. Show the optimal consumption choice. If the price of wine is $3 per glass and the price of cheese is $6 per kilogram, what is the marginal rate of substitution at this optimum?

5. A person who consumes wine and cheese gets a raise, so his income increases from $3000 to $4000. Show what happens if both wine and cheese are normal goods. Now show what happens if cheese is an inferior good.

6. The price of cheese rises from $6 to $10 per kilogram, while the price of wine remains $3 per glass. For a consumer with a constant income of $3000, show what happens to consumption of wine and cheese. Decompose the change into income and substitution effects.

7. Can an increase in the price of cheese possibly induce a consumer to buy more cheese? Explain.

PROBLEMS AND APPLICATIONS

1. Jennifer divides her income between coffee and croissants (both of which are normal goods). An early frost in Brazil causes a large increase in the price of coffee in Canada.
   a. Show the effect of the frost on Jennifer's budget constraint.
   b. Show the effect of the frost on Jennifer's optimal consumption bundle, assuming that the substitution effect outweighs the income effect for croissants.
   c. Show the effect of the frost on Jennifer's optimal consumption bundle, assuming that the income effect outweighs the substitution effect for croissants.

2. Compare the following two pairs of goods:
   - Coke and Pepsi
   - Skis and ski bindings

   In which case do you expect the indifference curves to be fairly straight, and in which case do you expect the indifference curves to be very bowed? In which case will the consumer respond more to a change in the relative price of the two goods?

3. Mario consumes only cheese and crackers.

   a. Could cheese and crackers both be inferior goods for Mario? Explain.
   b. Suppose that cheese is a normal good for Mario while crackers are an inferior good. If the price of cheese falls, what happens to Mario's consumption of crackers? What happens to his consumption of cheese? Explain.

4. Jim buys only milk and cookies.
   a. In 2004, Jim earns $100, milk costs $2 per litre, and cookies cost $4 per dozen. Draw Jim's budget constraint.
   b. Now suppose that all prices increase by 10 percent in 2005 and that Jim's salary increases by 10 percent as well. Draw Jim's new budget constraint. How would Jim's optimal combination of milk and cookies in 2005 compare to his optimal combination in 2004?

5. Consider your decision about how many hours to work.
   a. Draw your budget constraint assuming that you pay no taxes on your income. On the same diagram, draw another budget constraint assuming that you pay a 15 percent tax.

b. Show how the tax might lead to more hours of work, fewer hours, or the same number of hours. Explain.

6. Sarah is awake for 100 hours per week. Using one diagram, show Sarah's budget constraints if she earns $6 per hour, $8 per hour, and $10 per hour. Now draw indifference curves such that Sarah's labour supply curve is upward sloping when the wage is between $6 and $8 per hour, and backward sloping when the wage is between $8 and $10 per hour.

7. Draw the indifference curve for someone deciding how much to work. Suppose the wage increases. Is it possible that the person's consumption would fall? Is this plausible? Discuss. (Hint: Think about income and substitution effects.)

8. Suppose you take a job that pays $30 000 and set some of this income aside in a savings account that pays an annual interest rate of 5 percent. Use a diagram with a budget constraint and indifference curves to show how your consumption changes in each of the following situations. To keep things simple, assume that you pay no taxes on your income.
   a. Your salary increases to $40 000.
   b. The interest rate on your bank account rises to 8 percent.

9. As discussed in the text, we can divide an individual's life into two hypothetical periods: "young" and "old." Suppose that the individual earns income only when young and saves some of that income to consume when old. If the interest rate on savings falls, can you tell what happens to consumption when young? Can you tell what happens to consumption when old? Explain.

10. (This problem is challenging.) The welfare system provides income to some needy families. Typically, the maximum payment goes to families that earn no income; then, as families begin to earn income, the welfare payment declines gradually and eventually disappears. Let's consider the possible effects of this program on a family's labour supply.
    a. Draw a budget constraint for a family assuming that the welfare system did not exist. On the same diagram, draw a budget constraint that reflects the existence of the welfare system.
    b. Adding indifference curves to your diagram, show how the welfare system could reduce the number of hours worked by the family. Explain, with reference to both the income and substitution effects.
    c. Using your diagram from part (b), show the effect of the welfare system on the well-being of the family.

11. (This problem is challenging.) Suppose that an individual owed no taxes on the first $10 000 she earned and 15 percent of any income she earned over $10 000. (This is a simplified version of the actual Canadian income tax.) Now suppose that Parliament is considering two ways to reduce the tax burden: a reduction in the tax rate and an increase in the amount on which no tax is owed.
    a. What effect would a reduction in the tax rate have on the individual's labour supply if she earned $30 000 to start? Explain in words using the income and substitution effects. You do not need to use a diagram.
    b. What effect would an increase in the amount on which no tax is owed have on the individual's labour supply? Again, explain in words using the income and substitution effects.

12. (This problem is challenging.) Consider a person deciding how much to consume and how much to save for retirement. This person has particular preferences: Her lifetime utility depends on the lowest level of consumption during the two periods of her life. That is,

Utility = Minimum {consumption when young, consumption when old}

   a. Draw this person's indifference curves. (Hint: Recall that indifference curves show the combinations of consumption in the two periods that yield the same level of utility.)
   b. Draw the budget constraint and the optimum.
   c. When the interest rate increases, does this person save more or less? Explain your answer using income and substitution effects.

13. Economist George Stigler once wrote that, according to consumer theory, "if consumers do not buy less of a commodity when their incomes rise, they will surely buy less when the price of the commodity rises." Explain this statement.

INTERNET RESOURCES

Indifference curves were introduced into economics by Francis Edgeworth in his 1881 work *Mathematical Psychics: An Essay on the Application of Mathematics to the Moral Sciences.* You can read about Edgeworth at http://cepa.newschool.edu/het/profiles/edgew.htm.

http://   For more study tools, please visit http://www.mankiw3e.nelson.com.

22

FRONTIERS OF MICROECONOMICS

Learning Objectives

In this chapter, you will …

- Learn how to examine problems caused by asymmetric information
- Examine the market solutions to asymmetric information
- Consider why democratic voting systems may not represent the preferences of society
- Realize why people may not always behave as rational maximizers

Economics is a study of the choices that people make and the resulting interactions they have with one another. This study has many facets, as we have seen in the preceding chapters. Yet it would be a mistake to think that all the facets we have seen make up a finished jewel, perfect and unchanging. Like all scientists, economists are always on the lookout for new areas to study and new phenomena to explain. This final chapter on microeconomics offers an assortment of three topics at the discipline's frontier to see how economists are trying to expand their understanding of human behaviour and society.

The first topic is the economics of *asymmetric information.* Many times in life, some people are better informed than others, and this difference in information can affect the choices they make and how they deal with one another. Thinking about this asymmetry can shed light on many aspects of the world, from the market for used cars to the custom of gift giving.

The second topic we examine in this chapter is *political economy.* Throughout this book we have seen many examples where markets fail and government policy can potentially improve matters. But "potentially" is a needed qualifier: Whether this potential is realized depends on how well our political institutions work. The field of political economy applies the tools of economics to understand the functioning of government.

The third topic in this chapter is *behavioural economics*. This field brings some of the insights from psychology into the study of economic issues. It offers a view of human behaviour that is more subtle and complex than that found in conventional economic theory, but this view may also be more realistic.

This chapter covers a lot of ground. To do so, it offers not a full helping of these three topics but, instead, a taste of each. One goal is to show a few of the directions economists are heading in their effort to expand knowledge of how the economy works. Another goal is to whet your appetite for more courses in economics.

ASYMMETRIC INFORMATION

"I know something you don't know." This statement is a common taunt among children, but it also conveys a deep truth about how people sometimes interact with one another. Many times in life, one person knows more about what is going on than another. A difference in access to relevant knowledge is called an *information asymmetry*.

Examples abound. A worker knows more than his employer about how much effort he puts into his job. A seller of a used car knows more than the buyer about the car's condition. The first is an example of a *hidden action*, whereas the second is an example of a *hidden characteristic*. In each case, the party in the dark (the employer, the car buyer) would like to know the relevant information, but the informed party (the worker, the car seller) may have an incentive to conceal it.

Because asymmetric information is so prevalent, economists have devoted much effort in recent decades to studying its effects. And, indeed, the 2001 Nobel Prize in economics was awarded to three economists (George Akerlof, Michael Spence, and Joseph Stiglitz) for their pioneering work on this topic. Let's discuss some of the insights that this study has revealed.

Hidden Actions: Principals, Agents, and Moral Hazard

moral hazard
the tendency of a person who is imperfectly monitored to engage in dishonest or otherwise undesirable behaviour

agent
a person who is performing an act for another person, called the principal

principal
a person for whom another person, called the agent, is performing some act

Moral hazard is a problem that arises when one person, called the **agent,** is performing some task on behalf of another person, called the **principal.** If the principal cannot perfectly monitor the agent's behaviour, the agent tends to undertake less effort than the principal considers desirable. The phrase *moral hazard* refers to the risk, or "hazard," of inappropriate or otherwise "immoral" behaviour by the agent. In such a situation, the principal tries various ways to encourage the agent to act more responsibly.

The employment relationship is the classic example. The employer is the principal, and the worker is the agent. The moral-hazard problem is the temptation of imperfectly monitored workers to shirk their responsibilities. Employers can respond to this problem in various ways:

- *Better monitoring:* Parents hiring nannies have been known to plant hidden video cameras in their homes to record the nanny's behaviour when the parents are away. The aim is to catch irresponsible behaviour.
- *High wages:* According to *efficiency-wage theories* (discussed in Chapter 19), some employers may choose to pay their workers a wage above the level that equilibrates supply and demand in the labour market. A worker who earns an above-

equilibrium wage is less likely to shirk, because if she is caught and fired, she might not be able to find another high-paying job.

- *Delayed payment:* Firms can delay part of a worker's compensation, so if the worker is caught shirking and is fired, he suffers a larger penalty. One example of delayed compensation is the year-end bonus. Similarly, a firm may choose to pay its workers more later in their lives. Thus, the wage increases that workers get as they age may reflect not just the benefits of experience but also a response to moral hazard.

These various mechanisms to reduce the problem of moral hazard need not be used alone. Employers can use a combination of them.

Beyond the workplace, there are many other examples of moral hazard. A homeowner with fire insurance will likely buy too few fire extinguishers because the homeowner bears the cost of the extinguisher while the insurance company receives much of the benefit. A family may live near a river with a high risk of flooding because the family enjoys the scenic views, while the government bears the cost of disaster relief after a flood. Many regulations are aimed at addressing the problem: An insurance company may require homeowners to buy extinguishers, and the government may prohibit building homes on land with high risk of flooding. But the insurance company does not have perfect information about how cautious homeowners are, and the government does not have perfect information about the risk that families undertake when choosing where to live. As a result, the problem of moral hazard persists.

Hidden Characteristics: Adverse Selection and the Lemons Problem

Adverse selection is a problem that arises in markets where the seller knows more about the attributes of the good being sold than the buyer does. As a result, the buyer runs the risk of being sold a good of low quality. That is, the "selection" of goods being sold may be "adverse" from the standpoint of the uninformed buyer.

adverse selection
the tendency for the mix of unobserved attributes to become undesirable from the standpoint of an uninformed party

The classic example of adverse selection is the market for used cars. Sellers of used cars know their vehicles' defects while buyers often do not. Because owners of the worst cars are more likely to sell them than are the owners of the best cars, buyers are apprehensive about getting a "lemon." As a result, many people avoid buying vehicles in the used car market. This lemons problem can explain why a used car only a few weeks old sells for thousands of dollars less than a new car of the same type. A buyer of the used car might surmise that the seller is getting rid of the car quickly because the seller knows something about it that the buyer does not.

A second example of adverse selection occurs in the labour market. According to another efficiency-wage theory, workers vary in their abilities, and they may know their own abilities better than do the firms that hire them. When a firm cuts the wage it pays, the more talented workers are more likely to quit, knowing they are better able to find other employment. Conversely, a firm may choose to pay an above-equilibrium wage to attract a better mix of workers.

A third example of adverse selection occurs in markets for insurance. For example, buyers of life insurance know more about their own health problems than do insurance companies. Because people with greater hidden health problems are more likely to buy life insurance than are other people, the price of life insurance reflects the costs of a sicker-than-average person. As a result, people in average health may be discouraged from buying life insurance by the high price.

When markets suffer from adverse selection, the invisible hand does not necessarily work its magic. In the used car market, owners of good cars may choose to keep them rather than sell them at the low price that skeptical buyers are willing to pay. In the labour market, wages may be stuck above the level that balances supply and demand, resulting in unemployment. In insurance markets, buyers with low risk may choose to remain uninsured, because the policies they are offered fail to reflect their true characteristics. Advocates of government-provided insurance sometimes point to the problem of adverse selection as one reason not to trust the private market to provide the right amount of insurance on its own.

Signalling to Convey Private Information

Although asymmetric information is sometimes a motivation for public policy, it also motivates some individual behaviour that otherwise might be hard to explain. Markets respond to problems of asymmetric information in many ways. One of them is **signalling,** which refers to actions taken by an informed party for the sole purpose of credibly revealing his private information.

signalling
an action taken by an informed party to reveal private information to an uninformed party

We have seen examples of signalling in previous chapters. As we saw in Chapter 17, firms may spend money on advertising to signal to potential customers that they have high-quality products. As we saw in Chapter 20, students may earn postsecondary and postgraduate degrees to signal to potential employers that they are high-ability individuals. Recall that the signalling theory of education contrasts with the human-capital theory, which asserts that education increases a person's productivity, rather than merely conveying information about innate talent. These two examples of signalling (advertising, education) may seem very different, but below the surface they are much the same: In both cases, the informed party (the firm, the student) is using the signal to convince the uninformed party (the customer, the employer) that the informed party is offering something of high quality.

What does it take for an action to be an effective signal? Obviously, it must be costly. If a signal were free, everyone would use it, and it would convey no information. For the same reason, there is another requirement: The signal must be less costly, or more beneficial, to the person with the higher-quality product. Otherwise, everyone would have the same incentive to use the signal, and the signal would reveal nothing.

Consider again our two examples. In the advertising case, a firm with a good product reaps a larger benefit from advertising because customers who try the product once are more likely to become repeat customers. Thus, it is rational for the firm with the good product to pay for the cost of the signal (advertising), and it is rational for the customer to use the signal as a piece of information about the product's quality. In the education case, a talented person can get through school more easily than a less talented one. Thus, it is rational for the talented person to pay for the cost of the signal (education), and it is rational for the employer to use the signal as a piece of information about the person's talent.

The world is replete with instances of signalling. Magazine ads sometimes include the phrase "as seen on TV." Why does a firm selling a product in a magazine choose to stress this fact? One possibility is that the firm is trying to convey its willingness to pay for an expensive signal (a spot on television) in the hope that you will infer that its product is of high quality. For the same reason, graduates of elite schools are always sure to put that fact on their résumés.

Case Study

GIFTS AS SIGNALS

A man is debating what to give his girlfriend for her birthday. "I know," he says to himself, "I'll give her cash. After all, I don't know her tastes as well as she does, and with cash, she can buy anything she wants." But when he hands her the money, she is offended. Convinced he doesn't really love her, she breaks off the relationship.

What's the economics behind this story?

In some ways, gift giving is a strange custom. As the man in our story suggests, people typically know their own preferences better than others do, so we might expect everyone to prefer cash to in-kind transfers. If your employer substituted merchandise for your paycheque, you would likely object to the means of payment. But your reaction is very different when someone who (you hope) loves you does the same thing.

One interpretation of gift giving is that it reflects asymmetric information and signalling. The man in our story has private information that the girlfriend would like to know: Does he really love her? Choosing a good gift for her is a signal of his love. Certainly, picking out a gift has the right characteristics to be a signal. It is costly (it takes time), and its cost depends on the private information (how much he loves her). If he really loves her, choosing a good gift is easy because he is thinking about her all the time. If he doesn't love her, finding the right gift is more difficult. Thus, giving a gift that suits the girlfriend is one way for him to convey the private information of his love for her. Giving cash shows that he isn't even bothering to try.

The signalling theory of gift giving is consistent with another observation: People care most about the custom when the strength of affection is most in question. Thus, giving cash to a girlfriend or boyfriend is usually a bad move. But when students receive a cheque from their parents, they are less often offended. The parents' love is less likely to be in doubt, so the recipient probably won't interpret the cash gift as a signal of lack of affection. ●

"Now we'll see how much he loves me."

Screening to Induce Information Revelation

When an informed party takes actions to reveal his private information, the phenomenon is called signalling. When an uninformed party takes actions to induce the informed party to reveal private information, the phenomenon is called **screening**.

Some screening is common sense. A person buying a used car may ask that it be checked by an auto mechanic before the sale. A seller who refuses this request reveals his private information that the car is a lemon. The buyer may decide to offer a lower price or to look for another car.

Other examples of screening are more subtle. For example, consider a firm that sells car insurance. The firm would like to charge a low premium to safe drivers and a high premium to risky drivers. But how can it tell them apart? Drivers know whether they are safe or risky, but the risky ones won't admit to it. A driver's history is one piece of information (which insurance companies in fact use), but

screening
an action taken by an uninformed party to induce an informed party to reveal information

because of the intrinsic randomness of car accidents, history is an imperfect indicator of future risks.

The insurance company might be able to sort out the two kinds of drivers by offering different insurance policies that would induce them to separate themselves. One policy would have a high premium and cover the full cost of any accidents that occur. Another policy would have low premiums but would have, say, a $1000 deductible. (That is, the driver would be responsible for the first $1000 of damage, and the insurance company would cover the remaining risk.) Notice that the deductible is more of a burden for risky drivers because they are more likely to have an accident. Thus, with a large enough deductible, the low-premium policy with a deductible would attract the safe drivers, while the high-premium policy without a deductible would attract the risky drivers. Faced with these two policies, the two kinds of drivers would reveal their private information by choosing different insurance policies.

Asymmetric Information and Public Policy

We have examined two kinds of asymmetric information—moral hazard and adverse selection. And we have seen how individuals may respond to the problem with signalling or screening. Now let's consider what the study of asymmetric information suggests about the proper scope of public policy.

The tension between market success and market failure is central in microeconomics. We learned in Chapter 7 that the equilibrium of supply and demand is efficient in the sense that it maximizes the total surplus that society can obtain in a market. Adam Smith's invisible hand seemed to reign supreme. This conclusion was then tempered with the study of externalities (Chapter 10), public goods (Chapter 11), imperfect competition (Chapters 15 through 17), and poverty (Chapter 20). These examples of market failure showed that government can sometimes improve market outcomes.

The study of asymmetric information gives us new reason to be wary of markets. When some people know more than others, the market may fail to put resources to their best use. People with high-quality used cars may have trouble selling them because buyers will be afraid of getting a lemon. People with few health problems may have trouble getting low-cost health insurance because insurance companies lump them together with those who have significant (but hidden) health problems.

Although asymmetric information may call for government action in some cases, three facts complicate the issue. First, as we have seen, the private market can sometimes deal with information asymmetries on its own, using a combination of signalling and screening. Second, the government rarely has more information than the private parties. Even if the market's allocation of resources is not first-best, it may be second-best. That is, when there are information asymmetries, policymakers may find it hard to improve upon the market's admittedly imperfect outcome. Third, the government is itself an imperfect institution—a topic we take up in the next section.

QuickQuiz A person who buys a life insurance policy pays a certain amount per year and receives for his family a much larger payment in the event of his death. Would you expect buyers of life insurance to have higher or lower death rates than the average person? How might this be an example of moral hazard? Of adverse selection? How might a life insurance company deal with these problems?

POLITICAL ECONOMY

As we have seen, markets left on their own do not always reach a desirable allocation of resources. When we judge the market's outcome to be either inefficient or inequitable, there may be a role for the government to step in and improve the situation. Yet before we embrace an activist government, we need to consider one more fact: The government is also an imperfect institution. The field of *political economy* (sometimes called the field of *public choice*) applies the methods of economics to study how government works.

The Condorcet Voting Paradox

Most advanced societies rely on democratic principles to set government policy. When a city is deciding between two locations to build a new park, for example, we have a simple way to choose: The majority gets its way. Yet, for most policy issues, the number of possible outcomes far exceeds two. A new park, for instance, could be placed in many possible locations. In this case, as the eighteenth-century French political theorist Marquis de Condorcet famously noted, democracy might run into some problems trying to choose one of the outcomes.

For example, suppose there are three possible outcomes, labelled A, B, and C, and there are three voter types with the preferences shown in Table 22.1. The mayor of our town wants to aggregate these individual preferences into preferences for society as a whole. How should she do it?

At first, she might try some pairwise votes. If she asks voters to choose first between B and C, voter types 1 and 2 will vote for B, giving B the majority. If she then asks voters to choose between A and B, voter types 1 and 3 will vote for A, giving A the majority. Observing that A beats B, and B beats C, the mayor might conclude that A is the voters' clear choice.

But wait: Suppose the mayor then asks voters to choose between A and C. In this case, voter types 2 and 3 vote for C, giving C the majority. That is, under pairwise majority voting, A beats B, B beats C, and C beats A. Normally, we expect preferences to exhibit a property called *transitivity*: If A is preferred to B, and B is preferred to C, then we would expect A to be preferred to C. The **Condorcet paradox** is that democratic outcomes do not always obey this property. Pairwise voting might

Condorcet paradox
the failure of majority rule to produce transitive preferences for society

TABLE 22.1

The Condorcet Paradox

If voters have these preferences over outcomes A, B, *and* C, *then in pairwise majority voting,* A *beats* B, B *beats* C, *and* C *beats* A.

	Voter Type		
	Type 1	Type 2	Type 3
Percent of electorate	35	45	20
First choice	A	B	C
Second choice	B	C	A
Third choice	C	A	B

produce transitive preferences for a society, depending on the pattern of individual preferences, but as our example in the table shows, it cannot be counted on to do so.

One implication of the Condorcet paradox is that the order on which things are voted can affect the result. If the mayor suggests choosing first between A and B and then comparing the winner to C, the town ends up choosing C. But if the voters choose first between B and C and then compare the winner to A, the town ends up with A. And if the voters choose first between A and C and then compare the winner to B, the town ends up with B.

There are two lessons to be learned from the Condorcet paradox. The narrow lesson is that when there are more than two options, setting the agenda (that is, deciding the order in which items are voted) can have a powerful impact on the outcome of a democratic election. The broad lesson is that majority voting by itself does not tell us what outcome a society really wants.

Arrow's Impossibility Theorem

Since political theorists first noticed Condorcet's paradox, they have spent much energy studying voting systems and proposing new ones. For example, as an alternative to pairwise majority voting, the mayor of our town could ask each voter to rank the possible outcomes. For each voter, we could give 1 point for last place, 2 points for second to last, 3 points for third to last, and so on. The outcome that receives the most total points wins. With the preferences in Table 22.1, outcome B is the winner. (You can do the arithmetic yourself.) This voting method is called a *Borda count,* for the eighteenth-century French mathematician and political scientist who devised it. It is often used in polls that rank sports teams.

Is there a perfect voting system? Economist Kenneth Arrow took up this question in his 1951 book *Social Choice and Individual Values.* Arrow started by defining what a perfect voting system would be. He assumes that individuals in society have preferences over the various possible outcomes: A, B, C, and so on. He then assumes that society wants a voting scheme to choose among these outcomes that satisfies several properties:

- *Unanimity:* If everyone prefers A to B, then A should beat B.
- *Transitivity:* If A beats B, and B beats C, then A should beat C.
- *Independence of irrelevant alternatives:* The ranking between any two outcomes A and B should not depend on whether some third outcome C is also available.
- *No dictators:* There is no person who always gets his or her way, regardless of everyone else's preferences.

These all seem like desirable properties for a voting system to have. Yet Arrow proved, mathematically and incontrovertibly, that *no voting system can satisfy all of these properties.* This amazing result is called **Arrow's impossibility theorem.**

Arrow's impossibility theorem
a mathematical result showing that, under certain assumed conditions, there is no scheme for aggregating individual preferences into a valid set of social preferences

The mathematics needed to prove Arrow's theorem is beyond the scope of this book, but we can get some sense of why the theorem is true from a couple of examples. We have already seen the problem with the method of majority rule. The Condorcet paradox shows that majority rule fails to produce a ranking among the outcomes that always satisfies transitivity.

As another example, the Borda count fails to satisfy the independence of irrelevant alternatives. Recall that, using the preferences in Table 22.1, outcome B wins with a Borda count. But suppose that suddenly C disappears as an alternative. If the Borda count method is applied only to outcomes A and B, then A wins. (Once again, you can do the arithmetic on your own.) Thus, eliminating alternative C changes the ranking between A and B. The reason for this change is that the result of the Borda count depends on the number of points that A and B receive, and the number of points depends on whether the irrelevant alternative, C, is also available.

Arrow's impossibility theorem is a deep and disturbing result. It doesn't say that we should abandon democracy as a form of government. But it does say that, no matter what voting scheme society adopts for aggregating the preferences of its members, in some way it will be flawed as a mechanism for social choice.

The Median Voter Is King

Despite Arrow's theorem, voting is how most societies choose their leaders and public policies, often by majority rule. The next step in studying government is to examine how governments run by majority rule work. That is, in a democratic society, who determines what policy is chosen? In some cases, the theory of democratic government yields a surprisingly simple answer.

Let's consider an example. Imagine that society is deciding on how much money to spend on some public good, such as the CBC. Each voter has his own most preferred budget, and he always prefers outcomes closer to his most preferred value to outcomes further away. Thus, we can line up voters from those who prefer the smallest budget to those who prefer the largest. Figure 22.1 is an example. Here there are 100 voters, and the budget size varies from zero to $20 billion. Given these preferences, what outcome would you expect democracy to produce?

According to a famous result called the **median voter theorem,** majority rule will produce the outcome most preferred by the median voter. The *median voter* is the voter exactly in the middle of the distribution. In this example, if you take the line of voters ordered by their preferred budgets and count 50 voters from either end of the line, you will find that the median voter wants a budget of $10 billion. By contrast, the average preferred outcome (calculated by adding the preferred

median voter theorem
a mathematical result showing that if voters are choosing a point along a line and each voter wants the point closest to his most preferred point, then majority rule will pick the most preferred point of the median voter

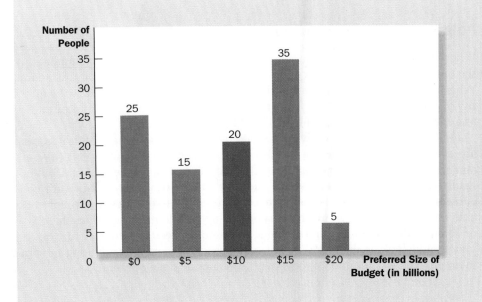

FIGURE 22.1

The Median Voter Theorem: An Example

This bar chart shows how 100 voters' most preferred budget is distributed over five options, ranging from zero to $20 billion. If society makes its choice by majority rule, the median voter (who here prefers $10 billion) determines the outcome.

outcomes and dividing by the number of voters) is $9 billion, and the modal outcome (the one preferred by the greatest number of voters) is $15 billion.

The median voter rules the day because his preferred outcome beats any other proposal in a two-way race. In our example, more than half the voters want $10 billion or more, and more than half want $10 billion or less. If someone proposes, say, $8 billion instead of $10 billion, everyone who prefers $10 billion or more will vote with the median voter. Similarly, if someone proposes $12 billion instead of $10 billion, everyone who wants $10 billion or less will vote with the median voter. In either case, the median voter has more than half the voters on his side.

What about the Condorcet voting paradox? It turns out that when the voters are picking a point along a line and each voter aims for his own most preferred point, the Condorcet paradox cannot arise. The median voter's most preferred outcome beats all comers.

One implication of the median voter theorem is that if each of two political parties is trying to maximize its chance of election, they will both move their positions toward the median voter. Suppose, for example, that the Liberal party advocates a budget of $15 billion, while the Conservative party advocates a budget of $10 billion. The Liberal position is more popular in the sense that $15 billion has more proponents than any other single choice. Nonetheless, the Conservative party gets more than 50 percent of the vote: It will attract the 20 voters who want $10 billion, the 15 voters who want $5 billion, and the 25 voters who want zero. If the Liberals want to win, they will move their platform toward the median voter. Thus, this theory can explain why the parties in a two-party system are similar to each other: They are both moving toward the median voter.

Another implication of the median voter theorem is that minority views are not given much weight. Imagine that 40 percent of the population want a lot of money spent on the national parks, and 60 percent want nothing spent. In this case, the median voter's preference is zero, regardless of the intensity of the minority's view. Such is the logic of democracy. Rather than reaching a compromise that takes into account everyone's preferences, majority rule looks only to the person in the exact middle of the distribution.

Politicians Are People Too

When economists study consumer behaviour, they assume that consumers buy the bundle of goods and services that gives them the greatest level of satisfaction. When economists study firm behaviour, they assume that firms produce the quantity of goods and services that yields the greatest level of profits. What should they assume when they study people involved in the practice of politics?

Politicians also have objectives. It would be nice to assume that political leaders are always looking out for the well-being of society as a whole, that they are aiming for an optimal combination of efficiency and equity. Nice, perhaps, but not realistic. Self-interest is as powerful a motive for political actors as it is for consumers and firm owners. Some politicians are motivated by desire for reelection and are willing to sacrifice the national interest when doing so solidifies their base of voters. Other politicians are motivated by simple greed. If you have any doubt, you should look at the world's poor nations, where corruption among government officials is a common impediment to economic development.

This book is not the place to develop a theory of political behaviour. That topic is best left to the political scientists. But when thinking about economic policy, remember that this policy is made not by a benevolent king, but by real people with their own all-too-human desires. Sometimes they are motivated to further the national interest, but sometimes they are motivated by their own political and financial ambitions. We shouldn't be surprised when economic policy fails to resemble the ideals derived in economics textbooks.

QuickQuiz A school district is voting on the school budget and the resulting student–teacher ratio. A poll finds that 35 percent of the voters want a ratio of 9:1, 25 percent want a ratio of 10:1, and 40 percent want a ratio of 12:1. What outcome would you expect the district to end up with?

BEHAVIOURAL ECONOMICS

Economics is a study of human behaviour, but it is not the only field that can make that claim. The social science of psychology also sheds light on the choices that people make in their lives. The fields of economics and psychology usually proceed independently, in part because they address a different range of questions. But recently a field called *behavioural economics* has emerged in which economists are making use of basic psychological insights. Let's consider some of these insights here.

People Aren't Always Rational

Economic theory is populated by a particular species of organism, sometimes called *homo economicus*. Members of this species are always rational. As firm managers, they maximize profits. As consumers, they maximize utility (or, equivalently, pick the point on the highest indifference curve). Given the constraints they face, they rationally weigh all the costs and benefits and always choose the best possible course of action.

Real people, however, are *homo sapiens*. Although in many ways they resemble the rational, calculating people assumed in economic theory, they are far more complex. They can be forgetful, impulsive, confused, emotional, and shortsighted. These imperfections of human reasoning are the bread-and-butter of psychologists, but until recently, economists have neglected them.

Herbert Simon, one of the first social scientists to work at the boundary of economics and psychology, suggested that humans should be viewed not as rational maximizers but as *satisficers*. Rather than always choosing the best course of action, they make decisions that are merely good enough. Similarly, other economists have suggested that humans are only "near rational" or that they exhibit "bounded rationality."

Studies of human decision making have tried to detect systematic mistakes that people make. Here are a few of the findings:

- *People are overconfident.* Imagine that you were asked some numerical questions, such as the number of African countries in the United Nations, the height of the tallest mountain in North America, and so on. Instead of being asked for a single estimate, however, you were asked to give a 90 percent confidence interval—a range such that you were 90 percent confident the true number falls within it. When psychologists run experiments like this, they find that most people give ranges that are too small: The true number falls within their intervals far less than 90 percent of the time. That is, most people are too sure of their own abilities.

- *People give too much weight to a small number of vivid observations.* Imagine that you are thinking about buying a car of brand X. To learn about its reliability, you read *Consumer Reports,* which has surveyed 1000 owners of car X. Then you run into a friend who owns car X, and she tells you that her car is a lemon. How do you treat your friend's observation? If you think rationally, you will realize that she has increased your sample size only from 1000 to 1001, which does not provide much new information. But because your friend's story is so vivid, you may be tempted to give it more weight in your decision making than you should.

- *People are reluctant to change their minds.* People tend to interpret evidence to confirm beliefs they already hold. In one study, subjects were asked to read and evaluate a research report on whether capital punishment deters crime. After reading the report, those who initially favoured the death penalty said they were more sure in their view, and those who initially opposed the death penalty also said they were more sure in their view. The two groups interpreted the same evidence in exactly opposite ways.

Think about decisions you have made in your own life. Do you exhibit some of these traits?

Why, you might ask, is economics built on the rationality assumption when psychology and common sense cast doubt on it? One answer is that the assumption, even if not exactly true, is still a good approximation. For example, when we studied the differences between competitive and monopoly firms, the assumption that firms rationally maximize profit yielded many important and valid insights. Recall from Chapter 2 that economic models are not meant to replicate reality but are supposed to show the essence of the problem at hand as an aid to understanding.

Another reason that economists so often assume rationality may be that economists are themselves not rational maximizers. Like most people, they are overconfident, and they are reluctant to change their minds. Their choice among alternative theories of human behaviour may exhibit excessive inertia. Moreover, economists may be content with a theory that is not perfect but is good enough. The model of rational man may be the theory of choice for a satisficing social scientist.

People Care About Fairness

Another insight about human behaviour is best illustrated with an experiment called the *ultimatum game.* The game works like this: Two volunteers (who are otherwise strangers to each other) are told that they are going to play a game and could win a total of $100. Before they play, they learn the rules. The game begins with a coin flip, which is used to assign the volunteers to the roles of player A and player B. Player A's job is to propose a division of the $100 prize between himself and the other player. After player A makes his proposal, player B decides whether to accept or reject it. If he accepts it, both players are paid according to the proposal. If player B rejects the proposal, both players walk away with nothing. In either case, the game then ends.

Before proceeding, stop and think about what you would do in this situation. If you were player A, what division of the $100 would you propose? If you were player B, what proposals would you accept?

Conventional economic theory assumes in this situation that people are rational wealth-maximizers. This assumption leads to a simple prediction: Player A should propose that he gets $99 and player B gets $1, and player B should accept the proposal. After all, once the proposal is made, player B is better off accepting it as long as he gets something out of it. Moreover, because player A knows that accepting the proposal is in player's B interest, player A has no reason to offer him more than $1. In the language of game theory (discussed in Chapter 16), the 99–1 split is the Nash equilibrium.

Yet when experimental economists ask real people to play the ultimatum game, the results are very different from this prediction. People in the role of player B usually reject proposals that give them only $1 or a similarly small amount. Knowing this, people in the role of player A usually propose giving player B much more than $1. Some people will offer a 50–50 split, but it is more common for player A to propose giving player B an amount such as $30 or $40, keeping the larger share for himself. In this case, player B usually accepts the proposal.

What's going on here? The natural interpretation is that people are driven in part by some innate sense of fairness. A 99–1 split seems so wildly unfair to many people that they reject it, even to their own detriment. By contrast, a 70–30 split is still unfair, but it is not so unfair that it induces people to abandon their normal self-interest.

Throughout our study of household and firm behaviour, the innate sense of fairness has not played any role. But the results of the ultimatum game suggest that perhaps it should. For example, in Chapters 18 and 19 we discussed how wages were determined by labour supply and labour demand. Some economists have suggested that the perceived fairness of what a firm pays its workers should also enter the picture. Thus, when a firm has an especially profitable year, workers (like player B) may expect to be paid a fair share of the prize, even if the standard equilibrium does not dictate it. The firm (like player A) might well decide to give workers more than the equilibrium wage for fear that the workers might otherwise try to punish the firm with reduced effort, strikes, or even vandalism.

People Are Inconsistent over Time

Imagine some dreary task, such as doing your laundry, shovelling snow off your driveway, or filling out your income tax forms. Now consider the following questions:

1. Would you prefer (A) to spend 50 minutes doing the task immediately or (B) to spend 60 minutes doing the task tomorrow?
2. Would you prefer (A) to spend 50 minutes doing the task in 90 days or (B) to spend 60 minutes doing the task in 91 days?

When asked questions like these, many people choose B to question 1 and A to question 2. When looking ahead to the future (as in question 2), they minimize the amount of time spent on the dreary task. But faced with the prospect of doing the task immediately (as in question 1), they choose to put it off.

In some ways, this behaviour is not surprising: Everyone procrastinates from time to time. But from the standpoint of the theory of rational man, it is puzzling. Suppose that, in response to question 2, a person chooses to spend 50 minutes in 90 days. Then, when the 90th day arrives, we allow him to change his mind. In effect, he then faces question 1, so he opts for doing the task the next day. But why should the mere passage of time affect the choices he makes?

Many times in life, people make plans for themselves, but then they fail to follow through. A smoker promises herself that she will quit, but within a few hours of smoking her last cigarette, she craves another and breaks her promise. A person trying to lose weight promises that he will stop eating dessert, but when the waiter brings the dessert cart, the promise is forgotten. In both cases, the desire for instant gratification induces the decision maker to abandon his own past plans.

Some economists believe that the consumption–saving decision is an important instance where people exhibit this inconsistency over time. For many people, spending provides a type of instant gratification. Saving, like passing up the cigarette or the dessert, requires a sacrifice in the present for a reward in the distant future. And just as many smokers wish they could quit and many overweight individuals wish they ate less, many consumers wish they saved more. According to one survey, 76 percent of Americans said they were not saving enough for retirement.

An implication of this inconsistency over time is that people should try to find ways to commit their future selves to following through on their plans. A smoker trying to quit may throw away her cigarettes, and a person on a diet may put a lock on the refrigerator. What can a person who saves too little do? He should find some way to lock up his money before he spends it. Some retirement accounts, such as retirement saving plans, do exactly that. A worker can agree to have some money taken out of his paycheque before he ever sees it. The money is deposited in an account that can be used before retirement only with a penalty. Perhaps that is one reason why these retirement accounts are so popular: They protect people from their own desires for instant gratification.

QuickQuiz Describe at least three ways in which human decision making differs from that of the rational individual of conventional economic theory.

CONCLUSION

This chapter has examined the frontier of microeconomics. You may have noticed that we have sketched out ideas rather than fully developing them. This is no accident. One reason is that you might study these topics in more detail in advanced courses. Another reason is that these topics remain active areas of research and, therefore, are still being fleshed out.

To see how these topics fit into the broader picture, recall the ten principles of economics from Chapter 1. One principle states that markets are usually a good way to organize economic activity. Another principle states that governments can sometimes improve market outcomes. As you study economics, you can more fully appreciate the truth of these principles as well as the caveats that go with them. The study of asymmetric information should make you more wary of market outcomes. The study of political economy should make you more wary of government solutions. And the study of behavioural economics should make you wary of any institution that relies on human decision making—including both the market and the government.

If there is a unifying theme to these topics, it is that life is messy. Information is imperfect, government is imperfect, and people are imperfect. Of course, you knew this long before you started studying economics, but economists need to understand these imperfections as precisely as they can if they are to explain, and perhaps even improve, the world around them.

SUMMARY

- In many economic transactions, information is asymmetric. When there are hidden actions, principals may be concerned that agents suffer from the problem of moral hazard. When there are hidden characteristics, buyers may be concerned about the problem of adverse selection among the sellers. Private markets sometimes deal with asymmetric information with signalling and screening.

- Although government policy can sometimes improve market outcomes, governments are themselves imperfect institutions. The Condorcet paradox shows that majority rule fails to produce transitive preferences for society, and Arrow's impossibility theorem shows that no

voting scheme will be perfect. In many situations, democratic institutions will produce the outcome desired by the median voter, regardless of the preferences of the rest of the electorate. Moreover, the individuals who set government policy may be motivated by self-interest rather than the national interest.

- The study of psychology and economics reveals that human decision making is more complex than is assumed in conventional economic theory. People are not always rational, they care about the fairness of economic outcomes (even to their own detriment), and they can be inconsistent over time.

KEY CONCEPTS

moral hazard, p. 494
agent, p. 494
principal, p. 494
adverse selection, p. 495

signalling, p. 496
screening, p. 497
Condorcet paradox, p. 499

Arrow's impossibility
   theorem, p. 500
median voter theorem, p. 501

QUESTIONS FOR REVIEW

1. What is moral hazard? List three things an employer might do to reduce the severity of this problem.

2. What is adverse selection? Give an example of a market in which adverse selection might be a problem.

3. Define *signalling* and *screening*, and give an example of each.

4. What unusual property of voting did Condorcet notice?

5. Explain why majority rule respects the preferences of the median voter rather than the average voter.

6. Describe the ultimatum game. What outcome from this game would conventional economic theory predict? Do experiments confirm this prediction? Explain.

PROBLEMS AND APPLICATIONS

1. Each of the following situations involves moral hazard. In each case, identify the principal and the agent, and explain why there is asymmetric information. How does the action described reduce the problem of moral hazard?
   a. Landlords require tenants to pay security deposits.
   b. Firms compensate top executives with options to buy company stock at a given price in the future.
   c. Car insurance companies offer discounts to customers who install antitheft devices in their cars.

2. Suppose that the Acme Life Insurance Company charges $5000 annually for an insurance policy. The company's president suggests that the company raise the annual price to $6000 in order to increase its profits. If the firm followed this suggestion, what economic problem might arise? Would the firm's pool of customers tend to become more or less healthy on average? Would the company's profits necessarily increase?

3. The case study in this chapter describes how a boyfriend can signal to a girlfriend that he loves her by giving an appropriate gift. Do you think saying "I love you" can also serve as a signal? Why or why not?

4. Some AIDS activists believe that life insurance companies should not be allowed to ask applicants if they are infected with the HIV virus that causes AIDS. Would this rule help or hurt those who are HIV-positive? Would it help or hurt those who are not HIV-positive? Would it exacerbate or mitigate the problem of adverse selection in the market for life insurance? Do you think it would increase or decrease the number of people without life insurance? In your opinion, would this be a good policy?

5. The government is considering two ways to help the needy: giving them cash, or giving them free meals at soup kitchens. Give an argument for giving cash. Give an argument, based on asymmetric information, for why the soup kitchen may be better than the cash handout.

6. Ken walks into an ice-cream parlour.

   WAITER: We have vanilla and chocolate today.
   KEN: I'll take vanilla.
   WAITER: I almost forgot. We also have strawberry.
   KEN: In that case, I'll take chocolate.

   What standard property of decision making is Ken violating? (Hint: Reread the section on Arrow's impossibility theorem.)

7. Why might a political party in a two-party system choose not to move toward the median voter? (Hint: Think about abstentions from voting and political contributions.)

8. Two ice-cream stands are deciding where to locate along a one-kilometre beach. Each person sitting on the beach buys exactly one ice-cream cone per day from the stand nearest to him. Each ice-cream seller wants the maximum number of customers. Where along the beach will the two stands locate?

9. After a widely reported earthquake in California, many people call their insurance company to apply for earthquake insurance. Might this reaction reflect some deviation from rationality? Discuss.

INTERNET RESOURCES

The 2001 Bank of Sweden Prize in Economic Sciences in Memory of Alfred Nobel (usually called the Nobel Prize in Economics) was awarded jointly to three economists (George Akerlof, Michael Spence, and Joseph Stiglitz) for their analyses of markets with asymmetric information. You can read about these economists and their work at http://www.nobel.se/economics/laureates/2001/public.html.

http:// For more study tools, please visit http://www.mankiw3e.nelson.com.

ability-to-pay principle the idea that taxes should be levied on a person according to how well that person can shoulder the burden

absolute advantage the comparison among producers of a good according to their productivity

accounting profit total revenue minus total explicit cost

adverse selection the tendency for the mix of unobserved attributes to become undesirable from the standpoint of an uninformed party

agent a person who is performing an act for another person, called the principal

Arrow's impossibility theorem a mathematical result showing that, under certain assumed conditions, there is no scheme for aggregating individual preferences into a valid set of social preferences

average fixed cost fixed costs divided by the quantity of output

average revenue total revenue divided by the quantity sold

average tax rate total taxes paid divided by total income

average total cost total cost divided by the quantity of output

average variable cost variable costs divided by the quantity of output

benefits principle the idea that people should pay taxes based on the benefits they receive from government services

budget constraint the limit on the consumption bundles that a consumer can afford

budget deficit an excess of government spending over government receipts

budget surplus an excess of government receipts over government spending

business cycle fluctuations in economic activity, such as employment and production

capital the equipment and structures used to produce goods and services

cartel a group of firms acting in unison

circular-flow diagram a visual model of the economy that shows how dollars flow through markets among households and firms

Coase theorem the proposition that if private parties can bargain without cost over the allocation of resources, they can solve the problem of externalities on their own

collusion an agreement among firms in a market about quantities to produce or prices to charge

common resources goods that are rival but not excludable

comparative advantage the comparison among producers of a good according to their opportunity cost

compensating differential a difference in wages that arises to offset the non-monetary characteristics of different jobs

competitive market a market with many buyers and sellers trading identical products so that each buyer and seller is a price taker

complements two goods for which an increase in the price of one leads to a decrease in the demand for the other

Condorcet paradox the failure of majority rule to produce transitive preferences for society

constant returns to scale the property whereby long-run average total cost stays the same as the quantity of output changes

consumer surplus a buyer's willingness to pay minus the amount the buyer actually pays

cost the value of everything a seller must give up to produce a good

cost–benefit analysis a study that compares the costs and benefits to society of providing a public good

cross-price elasticity of demand a measure of how much the quantity demanded of one good responds to a change in the price of another good, computed as the percentage change in quantity demanded of the first good divided by the percentage change in the price of the second good

deadweight loss the fall in total surplus that results from a market distortion, such as a tax

demand curve a graph of the relationship between the price of a good and the quantity demanded

demand schedule a table that shows the relationship between the price of a good and the quantity demanded

diminishing marginal product the property whereby the marginal product of an input declines as the quantity of the input increases

discrimination the offering of different opportunities to similar individuals who differ only by race, ethnic group, sex, age, or other personal characteristics

diseconomies of scale the property whereby long-run average total cost rises as the quantity of output increases

dominant strategy a strategy that is best for a player in a game regardless of the strategies chosen by the other players

economic profit total revenue minus total cost, including both explicit and implicit costs

economics the study of how society manages its scarce resources

economies of scale the property whereby long-run average total cost falls as the quantity of output increases

efficiency the property of society getting the most it can from its scarce resources

efficiency wages above-equilibrium wages paid by firms in order to increase worker productivity

efficient scale the quantity of output that minimizes average total cost

elasticity   a measure of the responsiveness of quantity demanded or quantity supplied to one of its determinants

equilibrium   a situation in which the price has reached the level where quantity supplied equals quantity demanded

equilibrium price   the price that balances quantity supplied and quantity demanded

equilibrium quantity   the quantity supplied and the quantity demanded at the equilibrium price

equity   the property of distributing economic prosperity fairly among the members of society

excludability   the property of a good whereby a person can be prevented from using it

explicit costs   input costs that require an outlay of money by the firm

exports   goods produced domestically and sold abroad

externality   the uncompensated impact of one person's actions on the well-being of a bystander

factors of production   the inputs used to produce goods and services

fixed costs   costs that do not vary with the quantity of output produced

free rider   a person who receives the benefit of a good but avoids paying for it

game theory   the study of how people behave in strategic situations

Giffen good   a good for which an increase in the price raises the quantity demanded

horizontal equity   the idea that taxpayers with similar abilities to pay taxes should pay the same amount

human capital   the accumulation of investments in people, such as education and on-the-job training

implicit costs   input costs that do not require an outlay of money by the firm

import quota   a limit on the quantity of a good that can be produced abroad and sold domestically

imports   goods produced abroad and sold domestically

income effect   the change in consumption that results when a price change moves the consumer to a higher or lower indifference curve

income elasticity of demand   a measure of how much the quantity demanded of a good responds to a change in consumers' income, computed as the percentage change in quantity demanded divided by the percentage change in income

indifference curve   a curve that shows consumption bundles that give the consumer the same level of satisfaction

inferior good   a good for which, other things equal, an increase in income leads to a decrease in demand

inflation   an increase in the overall level of prices in the economy

in-kind transfers   transfers to the poor given in the form of goods and services rather than cash

internalize the externality   alter incentives so that people take account of the external effects of their actions

law of demand   the claim that, other things equal, the quantity demanded of a good falls when the price of the good rises

law of supply   the claim that, other things equal, the quantity supplied of a good rises when the price of the good rises

law of supply and demand   the claim that the price of any good adjusts to bring the quantity supplied and the quantity demanded for that good into balance

liberalism   the political philosophy according to which the government should choose policies deemed to be just, as evaluated by an impartial observer behind a "veil of ignorance"

libertarianism   the political philosophy according to which the government should punish crimes and enforce voluntary agreements but not redistribute income

life cycle   the regular pattern of income variation over a person's life

lump-sum tax   a tax that is the same amount for every person

macroeconomics   the study of economy-wide phenomena, including inflation, unemployment, and economic growth

marginal changes   small incremental adjustments to a plan of action

marginal cost   the increase in total cost that arises from an extra unit of production

marginal product   the increase in output that arises from an additional unit of input

marginal product of labour   the increase in the amount of output from an additional unit of labour

marginal rate of substitution   the rate at which a consumer is willing to trade one good for another

marginal revenue   the change in total revenue from an additional unit sold

marginal tax rate   the extra taxes paid on an additional dollar of income

market   a group of buyers and sellers of a particular good or service

market economy   an economy that allocates resources through the decentralized decisions of many firms and households as they interact in markets for goods and services

market failure   a situation in which a market left on its own fails to allocate resources efficiently

market power   the ability of a single economic actor (or small group of actors) to have a substantial influence on market prices

maximin criterion the claim that the government should aim to maximize the well-being of the worst-off person in society

median voter theorem a mathematical result showing that if voters are choosing a point along a line and each voter wants the point closest to his most preferred point, then majority rule will pick the most preferred point of the median voter

microeconomics the study of how households and firms make decisions and how they interact in markets

monopolistic competition a market structure in which many firms sell products that are similar but not identical

monopoly a firm that is the sole seller of a product without close substitutes

moral hazard the tendency of a person who is imperfectly monitored to engage in dishonest or otherwise undesirable behaviour

Nash equilibrium a situation in which economic actors interacting with one another each choose their best strategy given the strategies that all the other actors have chosen

natural monopoly a monopoly that arises because a single firm can supply a good or service to an entire market at a smaller cost than could two or more firms

negative income tax a tax system that collects revenue from high-income households and gives transfers to low-income households

normal good a good for which, other things equal, an increase in income leads to an increase in demand

normative statements claims that attempt to prescribe how the world should be

oligopoly a market structure in which only a few sellers offer similar or identical products

opportunity cost whatever must be given up to obtain some item

perfect complements two goods with right-angle indifference curves

perfect substitutes two goods with straight-line indifference curves

permanent income a person's normal income

Phillips curve a curve that shows the short-run tradeoff between inflation and unemployment

Pigovian taxes taxes enacted to correct the effects of negative externalities

positive statements claims that attempt to describe the world as it is

poverty line an absolute level of income set by the federal government for each family size, below which a family is deemed to be in poverty

poverty rate the percentage of the population whose family income falls below an absolute level called the poverty line

price ceiling a legal maximum on the price at which a good can be sold

price discrimination the business practice of selling the same good at different prices to different customers

price elasticity of demand a measure of how much the quantity demanded of a good responds to a change in the price of that good, computed as the percentage change in quantity demanded divided by the percentage change in price

price elasticity of supply a measure of how much the quantity supplied of a good responds to a change in the price of that good, computed as the percentage change in quantity supplied divided by the percentage change in price

price floor a legal minimum on the price at which a good can be sold

principal a person for whom another person, called the agent, is performing some act

prisoners' dilemma a particular "game" between two captured prisoners that illustrates why cooperation is difficult to maintain even when it is mutually beneficial

private goods goods that are both excludable and rival

producer surplus the amount a seller is paid for a good minus the seller's cost

production function the relationship between the quantity of inputs used to make a good and the quantity of output of that good

production possibilities frontier a graph that shows the combinations of output that the economy can possibly produce given the available factors of production and the available production technology

productivity the quantity of goods and services produced from each hour of a worker's time

profit total revenue minus total cost

progressive tax a tax for which high-income taxpayers pay a larger fraction of their income than do low-income taxpayers

proportional tax a tax for which high-income and low-income taxpayers pay the same fraction of income

public goods goods that are neither excludable nor rival

quantity demanded the amount of a good that buyers are willing to purchase

quantity supplied the amount of a good that sellers are willing to sell

regressive tax a tax for which high-income taxpayers pay a smaller fraction of their income than do low-income taxpayers

rivalry the property of a good whereby one person's use diminishes other people's use

scarcity the limited nature of society's resources

screening an action taken by an uninformed party to induce an informed party to reveal information

shortage a situation in which quantity demanded is greater than quantity supplied

signalling an action taken by an informed party to reveal private information to an uninformed party

strike the organized withdrawal of labour from a firm by a union

substitutes two goods for which an increase in the price of one leads to an increase in the demand for the other

substitution effect the change in consumption that results when a price change moves the consumer along a given indifference curve to a point with a new marginal rate of substitution

sunk cost a cost that has already been committed and cannot be recovered

supply curve a graph of the relationship between the price of a good and the quantity supplied

supply schedule a table that shows the relationship between the price of a good and the quantity supplied

surplus a situation in which quantity supplied is greater than quantity demanded

tariff a tax on goods produced abroad and sold domestically

tax incidence the manner in which the burden of a tax is shared among participants in a market

total cost the market value of the inputs a firm uses in production

total revenue (for a firm) the amount a firm receives for the sale of its output

total revenue (in a market) the amount paid by buyers and received by sellers of a good, computed as the price of the good times the quantity sold

Tragedy of the Commons a parable that illustrates why common resources get used more than is desirable from the standpoint of society as a whole

transaction costs the costs that parties incur in the process of agreeing and following through on a bargain

union a worker association that bargains with employers over wages and working conditions

utilitarianism the political philosophy according to which the government should choose policies to maximize the total utility of everyone in society

utility a measure of happiness or satisfaction

value of the marginal product the marginal product of an input times the price of the output

variable costs costs that vary with the quantity of output produced

vertical equity the idea that taxpayers with a greater ability to pay taxes should pay larger amounts

welfare government programs that supplement the incomes of the needy

welfare economics the study of how the allocation of resources affects economic well-being

willingness to pay the maximum amount that a buyer will pay for a good

world price the price of a good that prevails in the world market for that good

INDEX